MODERN POLITICAL IDEOLOGIES

To students past and present who have argued and disagreed

MODERN POLITICAL IDEOLOGIES

THIRD EDITION

Andrew Vincent

⊛WILEY-BLACKWELL

A John Wiley & Sons, Ltd., Publication

Registered Office
John Wiley & Sons Ltd, The Atrium, Southern Gate, Chichester, West Sussex, PO19 8SQ, United Kingdom

Editorial Offices
350 Main Street, Malden, MA 02148-5020, USA
9600 Garsington Road, Oxford, OX4 2DQ, UK
The Atrium, Southern Gate, Chichester, West Sussex, PO19 8SQ, UK

For details of our global editorial offices, for customer services, and for information about how to apply for permission to reuse the copyright material in this book please see our website at www.wiley.com/wiley-blackwell.

Library of Congress Cataloging-in-Publication Data

Vincent, Andrew.
    Modern political ideologies : Andrew Vincent. – 3rd ed.
       p. cm.
    Includes bibliographical references and index.
    ISBN 978-1-4051-5495-6 (pbk. : alk. paper) 1. Political science. 2. Right and left (Political science) 3. Ideology. I. Title.
    JA71.V55 2009
    320.5–dc22

                                                    2008038546

A catalogue record for this book is available from the British Library.

Set in 10/13pt Sabon by SPi Publisher Services, Pondicherry, India
Printed in Singapore by Ho Printing Pte Ltd

01   2010

I have come to believe that the whole world is an enigma, a harmless enigma that is made terrible by our own mad attempt to interpret it as though it had an underlying truth. (Umberto Eco, *Foucault's Pendulum*)

Contents

Preface to Third Edition

It is strange to come back to text which was written, in terms of the first edition, almost twenty years ago. It is rather like revisiting old photographs of oneself or one's family. There is an odd mixture of discomfiture, delight and genuine historical curiosity. In returning to this text in 2008, it is remarkable just how many ideas, events, colleagues and even publishers and editors have come and gone in the intervening years. Some ideologies have quite markedly declined or changed; others have remained relatively static. Some components of particular ideologies which were quite central to political discussion in 1993 have subsequently dropped into the background. In the same period the study of ideology has expanded and developed in sophistication. There is now *The Journal of Political Ideologies*, which is an excellent academic supplement to both teaching and research work on ideologies. There has also been a great deal of scholarly work done on the concept of ideology itself and its role within political studies. In terms of the substantive chapters of this text, it is a somewhat poignant sign of the times that I have included, in this third edition, a new chapter on fundamentalism. This new chapter was difficult to write, not least because I had to enter, once again, into the spirit of the original text and the manner in which it was initially constructed. However, there are also many who would contend that fundamentalism is a deeply problematic concept for inclusion. However, contention and ideology are old bedfellows. I leave it to students of ideology to draw their own conclusions.

Overall, in terms of revision, I have retained the basic structure of the chapters. I have though worked carefully through the whole text and changed stylistic aspects. In some cases I have revised, added, excised or redrafted. In certain sections of the text I have left the basic prose as it was and only sharpened the language. In all the chapters I have updated the bibliography. Some ideologies have remained static; others show fairly wide ranging developments in the literature. Certain chapters made me pause much longer, particularly fascism, feminism and ecology. The key difficulty in dealing with change in the perception of an ideology is that one still has to say something about the way the ideas developed. One therefore cannot ignore prior ideological concerns. Thus it is important to try to gain some judgemental balance in discussing the origin and development of the ideology, as well as integrating more current intellectual concerns. It is not an easy process.

In working on this third edition I have drawn upon the goodwill, advice and expertise of many academic friends and colleagues. I would like to thank particularly Michael Freeden for many years of friendship, collegiality and immensely fruitful conversations and critical insights into ideology and political theory. Further, thanks go to Andy Dobson, Roger Eatwell, Ian Fraser, Liz Frazer, Vince Geoghegan, Roger Griffin, Mathew Humphrey, Mike Kenny, Moya Lloyd, Noel O'Sullivan, Chris Pierson, Matt Sleat, Judith Squires, Jules Townsend and Rachael Vincent, for their kind advice, and in some cases reading of material. Thanks also to the long-suffering readers and editors from Wiley-Blackwell. The usual proviso applies here: none bear any responsibility for this final text except myself.

Andrew Vincent
University of Sheffield

1

The Nature of Ideology

This first chapter deals with three issues: first, a brief historical sketch of the concept of ideology will be presented; second, my own particular use of the concept of ideology is outlined; finally, and briefly, a synopsis of the structure of the book will be given.

This is not a book about the concept of ideology in its own right. It is a book about ideologies. However, it is impossible simply to leap into this task without saying something about the concept of ideology. The history of the concept of ideology is comparatively short – approximately two hundred years old – but complex. Like most substantive 'ideologies', the word 'ideology' dates from the French Revolution era of the 1790s. For the sake of brevity, the history will be broken down into a number of stages which have given rise to different senses. The discussion will begin with the inception of the word by the French philosopher Antoine Destutt de Tracy in the 1790s. It will move to Marx's usage in the 1840s and the ambiguous Marxist legacy into the twentieth century, then turn to the uses of the term in the 'end of ideology' movement of the 1950s. Finally, some of the more recent debates will be summarized.

The term 'ideology' was first coined between 1796 and 1798 by Antoine Destutt de Tracy in papers read in instalments to the National Institute in Paris under the title *Mémoire sur la faculté de penser*. His book entitled *The Elements of Ideology* was published later (1800–15). To some extent it is true that Tracy would probably now be a fairly obscure figure but for his association with the word 'ideology'. Oddly, there is no one unequivocal sense of the concept deriving from Tracy. In fact, four uses of the term can be discerned. First, there was Tracy's original explicit use to designate a new empirical science of ideas; second, the term came to denote an affiliation to a form of secular liberal republicanism; third, it took on a pejorative connotation implying intellectual and practical sterility as well as dangerous radicalism; finally, and most tenuously, it came in a limited sphere to denote 'political doctrine' in general. All these four senses moved into political currency between 1800 and 1830.

The word 'ideology' was a neologism compounded from the Greek terms *eidos* and *logos*. It can be defined as a 'science of ideas'. Tracy wanted a new term for a new science. He rejected the terms *métaphysique* and *psychologie* as inadequate.

For Tracy, the discipline of 'metaphysics' was misleading and discredited; 'psychology' also implied a science or knowledge of the soul, which could give a false, almost religious, impression. Tracy was both deeply anti-clerical and a materialist. Through the 1790s and early 1800s he was involved in bitter infighting with the Catholic Church, particularly over the control of education. Thus any term to describe his science had to be distinct from any taint of religion. It is also worth noting that the term 'ideology' more or less coincides with the early use of the term 'social science' (*la science sociale*). The latter term assumed, like ideology, an Enlightenment optimism in grasping and controlling, by reason, the laws governing social life for the greater happiness and improvement of human life.

Like many of the French Enlightenment *philosophes* and Encyclopaedist thinkers, Tracy believed that all areas of human experience, many of which had previously been examined in terms of theology, should now be examined by reason. The science of ideas was to investigate the natural origin of ideas. It proposed a precise knowledge of the causes of the generation of ideas from sensations. Innate ideas were rejected: ideas were all modified sensations. Tracy described ideology as a branch of zoology, indicating that the human intellect had a physiological basis. In the same rigorous empiricist vein as Bacon, Descartes, Newton, Lavoisier and Condillac, he proposed that the contents of such analyses should be carefully tabulated and detailed in terms of scientific procedures. Newton was particularly esteemed by Tracy.[1] Tracy's examination of the way in which ideas were generated, conceived and related to each other (in sum the 'science of ideas') might now be described as empirical psychology. In fact, one Tracy scholar remarks that he was a 'methodological precursor of behaviouralist approaches to the human sciences' (Head 1985, 4; see also Kennedy 1979; Head 1980). For Tracy, ideology was *la théorie des théories*. It was the queen of the sciences since it necessarily preceded all other sciences, which of necessity utilized 'ideas'.

Tracy, and those who admired his work, believed that such a science of ideas could have an immense impact, on education particularly. If the origin of ideas was understood, then it could be used with great benefit in enlightened education. It could diagnose the roots of human ignorance. It was potentially the foundation for a rational progressive society. Tracy and others thus advocated vigorously the social, political and educative uses of ideology. Between 1799 and 1800, under the Directory, Tracy was appointed Councillor of Public Instruction and issued circulars to schools stressing the role of 'ideology' in the curriculum. There was also the attempt, as in Bentham, to establish a 'science of legislation'. In pursuing these objectives, Tracy and the other *idéologues* became associated with a secular republican liberalism, stressing representative government by an enlightened elite. In this sense, ideology became, in the public perception, not so much an 'empirical science' as the political doctrine of a group of propertied liberal intellectuals. Hence, subtly, a second sense of ideology became prevalent – ideology became associated with a political doctrine, although of a very specific form.

Another lasting sense of the term 'ideology' derived from the political associations of Tracy and his compatriots. One of the early and brief honorary members of the *idéologues* was Napoleon Bonaparte. He appears to have had a stormy and ultimately deeply hostile relation to the *idéologues*, later, when in power and pursuing his own autocratic ambitions, accusing them of fomenting political unrest. Bonaparte referred to them as individuals who wished to reform the world simply in their heads, armchair metaphysicians with little or no political acumen. He denounced them before the Council of State in February 1801 as 'windbags', who none the less were trying to undermine political authority. Once Bonaparte had re-established his credibility with the Catholic Church in a Concordat of 1802, he also predictably denounced the *idéologues* as a 'College of Atheists'. Madame de Staël remarked at this time that Bonaparte seemed to suffer from 'ideophobia'. This pejorative use of ideology – indicating intellectual sterility, practical ineptitude and, more particularly, dangerous political sentiments – tended to stick. The conservative, restoration and royalist circles in France focused critically on the *idéologues* in the latter use, denouncing the republication of Tracy's *Elements* in 1829 as part of the attempt to overthrow 'the ancient confraternity of throne and altar'. One final sense of the term began to glimmer through here. If ideology was partially divorced from the 'science of ideas' of Tracy, Condillac and the sensationalist school, and became associated, more importantly, with a political doctrine (secular liberal republicanism initially), it was but a short step to identifying the royalist critics as espousing another political doctrine, which could equally be described as an 'ideology'. Ideology thus became, in a limited sphere in France, equivalent to 'a political doctrine'. The other senses of ideology co-existed with this latter view.

It remains perennially puzzling as to why Marx chose to use the term 'ideology'. In his early writings he alluded to Tracy in two senses. First, he noted, as a simple historical observation, the existence of a group of thinkers, namely, the *idéologues*. Tracy, as a key member of this group, is mentioned as a minor vulgar bourgeois liberal political economist. In consequence, there are passing references to the fourth volume of Tracy's *Elements*, the *Traité d'économie politique*. Second, Marx employed the concept in the title of his early work, *The German Ideology* (1845) – unpublished during his lifetime – as a more pejorative label referring to those (particularly the Young Hegelian group) who 'interpret' the world philosophically, but do not appear to be able to change it. Marx might also have found some parallels between the Young Hegelians and Tracy, given the emphasis in both on 'ideas'. Put loosely, Tracy's thinking contained some suggestions of 'idealist' philosophy.

Marx was obviously aware of something of the initial use of the term 'ideology', indicating a science of ideas. However, he paid scant attention to this. The only sense he utilized, at first, was Bonaparte's pejorative use. Crudely, he too considered the Young Hegelians as 'windbags' and armchair metaphysicians. In addition, he regarded both the *idéologues* and Hegelians as vulgar bourgeois liberals. This idea moves quite definitely away from the initial French royalist sense where the liberalism of the *idéologues* was regarded as a dangerous reforming radicalism.

Marx adds, though, in an unsystematic way, further dimensions to the meaning of the term, which take it into a different realm (see Seliger 1979; Parekh 1983). In Marx's work, ideology denotes not only practical ineffectiveness but also illusion and loss of reality. More importantly, it becomes associated with the division of labour in society, with collective groups called classes, and most significantly with the domination and power of certain classes. Some aspects of this extension, specifically the illusory aspect, were implicit in Bonaparte's pejorative use of the term, but it was not made fully explicit until Marx. Paradoxically, something of the *idéologues*' use remains in Marx, namely, the belief that societies can be rationally and scientifically interpreted and that humanity is progressing towards some form of rational social, economic and political enlightenment. To grasp Marx's use it is necessary to unpack briefly the materialist theory in which it is couched.

Although it is an ambiguous truism, Marx is essentially a materialist thinker of a particular type. What is of primary importance to humans is their need to subsist. To do so they need to labour and produce. Thought is involved in this process, but it is practice-orientated and therefore of secondary import. The material human needs are primary: thought and consciousness in general enable them to be satisfied. When humans produce, they develop complex social and exchange relations with each other. Humans also produce more effectively in groups; tasks initially become separated to enable people to work more productively. Here we see the earliest forms of the division of labour.

Without outlining the whole theory, it is important to grasp that what is primary is our social and economic being. Marx has a materialist ontology. Our consciousness is by and large explained through that ontology. Thought can both reflect and misunderstand this process. Much of the problem of the earliest 'division of labour' is that mental labour, by priests and intellectuals, was distinguished from physical labour. Intellectuals and priests tended to serve their own interests by regarding their work as superior to physical labour. They also sought the protection and patronage of the major possessing classes, those who, at a particular stage in the development of society, dominate and control the means of production, distribution and exchange. Directly, or most often indirectly, in exchange for patronage, such mental labourers gave wide-ranging intellectual justifications of an existing order, placing their intellectual benediction (in the nineteenth century) upon capitalism and the bourgeois state. They also provided solace for those who suffered from the social and economic arrangements. Such mental labourers are in essence the ideologists of a political and economic order. Yet much of their production is illusion and a distortion of reality.

It is important to realize that the original philosophical source of this materialist ontology (and Marx's conception of ideology) was premised on a critique of religion. The German romantic and, particularly, Hegelian understanding is important to note here. The German tradition, from Kant, Fichte and Hegel, had placed considerable emphasis on the human capacity for self-constitution. In simple terms, the human mind is involved in the structuring of the world and circumstances. It is not merely receiving sensations passively, as Tracy would have argued. In Hegel especially, this self-moulding or self-constituting activity is viewed within an historical framework. Consciousness not only constitutes much of what we call reality, it does so in a slowly changing historical process. Consciousness changes and constitutes reality differently over historical time. The Young Hegelians, particularly Ludwig Feuerbach, accused Hegel of dwelling too much upon mind in general, on consciousness or on some notion of spirit in history. It is not 'general mind' or spirit which constitutes itself, but rather it is the individual sensuous human being with physical needs who constitutes reality.

As Feuerbach noted in a famous phrase, 'all theology is anthropology'. Humans create God, spirit or history in their own image. Marx adapted this argument to his own ends. It is labouring productive humans, in particular economic classes, at particular stages of history (determined by economic needs and modes of production), who constitute the world. However, this constitution can be a distorted image. Throughout history, intellectuals have produced a multitude of such distortions which obscure the basic domination and exploitation of one class by another. In one reading, given a particular stage of society, mode of production and configuration of classes, it might be the most accurate account that could be given, yet it is still a distortion. The centrality of economic activity to this process meant that Marx subtly combined Germanic philosophical concerns with both British political economy and French materialism.

Subsequently Marxism, almost before the end of the nineteenth century, came under certain pressures and diverse interpretations on the subject of ideology. A number of questions arose. In his early writings Marx appeared to be contrasting ideology (as an illusion) to reality as practice – a form of philosophical materialist ontology. Liberal capitalism was in an equivalent position to religion as a distortion of the human essence. Later this contrast became ideology (as distortion) as against science (as truth or knowledge). Alienation in Marx's early writings became, in the later writings, expropriation of surplus value and economic exploitation. However, it was not clear whether Marx was using science in the sense of 'natural science' or in the older German sense of *Wissenschaft* (a connected body of systematic knowledge). Some Marxists refer to the change that marked these two dimensions as the 'epistemological break' in Marx, differentiating the young philosophical from the mature scientific Marx. Even within these two dimensions it is not clear as to what comes under the rubric of ideology. In some writings, Marx suggested that 'consciousness in general', including every aspect of human endeavour, namely art and natural science, is ideology. In others, it appears as though he was thinking only of social, political and economic ideas which uphold and distort a political and economic structure. In addition, the early reference that Marx made in *The German Ideology* to the *camera obscura* image was not particularly helpful. Marx writes of ideology's view of human consciousness being like the *camera obscura*, where the world appears inverted. The image is deeply mechanistic, rigid, and presents a very misleading conception, which Marx himself did not really accept.

Marx also did not make clear the precise relation between ideas (often referred to as superstructure) and the economic base. At some points this appears as a case of a clear 'one-way' determinism, namely, the base determines the superstructure. Yet again, Marx never clarifies what he means by the word 'determine'. For example, it is not obvious whether 'determine' means that A causes B, affects B, or sets parameters to B. At other points, this relation changes into symbiotic or mutually affective relations between ideology and the economic base. Many qualifying letters from Engels are usually discussed at this point to justify this latter view.

The subsequent fate of the Marxist notion of ideology breaks down into a number of contradictory components. The Second International, dominated by the German SPD and under the tutelage of Engels, took up the crude distinction between Marxist science and bourgeois ideology. Engels in particular coined the now notorious term 'false consciousness' for ideology, something that Marx did not do. The idea of true and false consciousness appears as too stark for Marx, at least in his more sensitive moments.

Lenin introduced another confusing dimension into ideology in works like *What Is to Be Done?* (1902). The pejorative connotations are suddenly stripped away. Lenin speaks confidently of socialism *being* an ideology, combating, in the general class struggle, bourgeois ideology. Lenin saw socialist ideology as a weapon of class struggle. This use comes close to that in France in the 1830s, and also to some contemporary usage, namely, in seeing all political doctrines *per se* as ideology. It certainly bears little resemblance to Engels' notion of 'false consciousness' or the laboured distinction of Marxist science against ideology.

The problem of ideology in Marxism is further complicated when we move into the twentieth century. With writers like Georg Lukács, dialectical materialism was accepted as an ideology, though it was seen, casuistically, as more scientific than bourgeois ideology. Also, for Lukács, ideology was more deeply embedded in social, economic and political life than Lenin had appreciated. In Antonio Gramsci we see the most sophisticated, if equivocal, treatment of ideology. For Gramsci, domination under capitalism is not achieved simply by coercion, but subtly through the hegemony of ideas. The ideology of the ruling class becomes vulgarized into the common sense of the average citizen. Power is not just crude legal or physical coercion but domination of language, morality, culture and common sense. The masses are quelled and co-opted by their internalization of ideational domination. The hegemonic ideas become, in fact, the actual experiences of the subordinate classes. Traditional intellectuals construct this complex hegemonic apparatus. Bourgeois hegemony moulds the personal convictions, norms and aspirations of the proletariat. Gramsci thus called for a struggle at the level of ideology. Organic intellectuals situated within the proletariat should combat this by constructing a counter-hegemony to traditional intellectuals upholding bourgeois hegemony.

In Gramsci we find refinements and qualifications to the Marxist science and ideology thesis (a science which Gramsci dismissed with the curt term 'economism'), dialectical materialism, simple-minded determinism, the false-consciousness thesis and, finally, the idea of socialist ideology. In Gramsci, ideology appears to be more generally applicable to political doctrine, although it is deeply embedded in all language and culture. Despite the subtlety of Gramsci's approach, it still asserted, behind complex and elusive argumentation, the 'truth' of Marxism as against other approaches. In this sense, the old distinctions might be said to be reappearing, but in a transformed apparel. Subsequently these apparels have mutated. Some writers, such as Terry Eagleton, Stuart Hall or an early Edward Said, were more straightforward if imaginative expositors of Gramsci's ideas. Gramsci's arguments have, though, often been blended in unexpected and sometimes perplexing ways with discourse analysis, as in the writings of Ernesto Laclau and Chantal Mouffe (Laclau and Mouffe 1985; see also Laclau 2006). In Althusser, ideology also developed a quasi-autonomous life of its own as a symbolic controller and imaginary representation, which functioned semi-autonomously from the material base, although in the final analysis it was still a dimension of the mode of production and an organic aspect of class struggle. Knowledge about ideology was therefore still, for Althusser, knowledge about the 'condition of its necessity' (Althusser 1969, 230). One prevailing theme has remained, however, with all these later Marxist and post-Marxist theories, namely, the intricate connection between ideology, power and domination.

One of Lukács' students, who utilized the Marxian terminology from within, but completely transformed its intellectual status, was Karl Mannheim. Mannheim's *Ideology and Utopia* (1929) can be used to take the discussion on to later phases of the concept of ideology. Mannheim's theory will not be discussed here, but one important question in Mannheim needs consideration. Paul Ricoeur calls it 'Mannheim's paradox'. Ricoeur formulates this paradox in the following question: 'What is the epistemological status of discourse about ideology if all discourse is ideological?' (Ricoeur 1986, 8). The question is asking Marx to justify his own thought in relation to his suppositions concerning ideology. The effect of following through the logic of the question is devastating on one level.

In the course of attempting to extend Marx's insights, Mannheim tried to formulate a comprehensive theory of ideology. There are six main components to it. The first element need not detain us, despite its intrinsic interest. Mannheim examined both ideologies and utopias. Ideologies, in the main, act to defend a particular established order, although they can in some circumstances be made subversive. Utopias (which, unlike Marx, Mannheim suggests are equally as important for social life as ideologies) tend to be forward-looking and a challenge to existing social reality, suggesting wide-scale change (see Geoghegan 2004; Kumar 2006).

Mannheim's notion of ideology distinguished between *particular* and *total* conceptions. The particular conception approached an 'individual', examining their psychology and personal interests, often in a polemical manner, in order to show the weakness of an opponent's position. The total idea approached ideology in terms of the assumptions of a complete 'world-view' of a collective culture and, possibly, an historical epoch. In other words, it dealt with a total structure of thought. In Mannheim's view, Marx had, comparative to much previous social theory, fused these two elements and shown that the expressions of individuals needed unmasking in order to unpack the total ideology of a culture. It was precisely at this point that Mannheim asked Marx to justify his own ideas in Marxist terms, something that Marx would have found difficult to do. As Mannheim remarked:

> it is hardly possible to avoid this general formulation of the total conception of ideology, according to which the thought of all parties in all epochs is of an ideological character. There is scarcely a single intellectual position, and Marxism furnishes no exception to this rule, which has not changed through history. ... It should not be too difficult for a Marxist to recognize their social basis. (Mannheim 1960, 69)

This question led Mannheim on to the third element of his theory. If Marxism imploded in this inquiry, then we still should not abandon its insights into ideology. Rather, we should become self-conscious concerning our own ideological beliefs, life-expressions and their historical situation, so preserving Marx's insights within a disciplined academic frame. Mannheim called this new academic frame the 'sociology of knowledge' – examining knowledge and every 'knower' in a particular social and historical context. As he remarked on the Marxist notion of ideology: 'What was once the intellectual armament of a party is transformed into a method of research in social and intellectual history' (Mannheim 1960, 69).

Mannheim claimed, fourthly, that his theory was not relativistic. Relativism was drawn distinct from what he called relationism. Some commentators suggest that this distinction does not really work (Ricoeur 1986, 167; Williams 1988, 26–8). Mannheim suggested that whereas relativism was linked with a static, ahistorical notion of truth, relationism 'takes account of the relational as distinct from the merely relative character of all historical knowledge' (Mannheim 1960, 70ff). In relationism, knowledge and epistemology were not separated from an historical or social context (as appears to be the suppressed premise of relativism). Fifth, Mannheim makes further elaborate additions to the above theory, distinguishing, under the rubric of a 'relational total conception of ideology', non-evaluative and evaluative approaches. For Mannheim, the latter 'evaluative' approach took a full self-conscious account of the situation of both the object studied and the observer, and was thus the most appropriate method for the sociology of knowledge. Finally, and probably most controversially, Mannheim suggested that this new discipline could only properly be studied by relatively classless individuals, who were both intelligent and capable of such self-analysis. He calls these, following the terminology of Alfred Weber, the *freischwebende Intelligenz* (the socially unattached intelligentsia) (Mannheim 1960, 137ff).

Mannheim has met with a very mixed, usually very critical, response: some totally dismissive of him; others at least appreciating his courage in facing the problematic issues of historical thought. His separation of relativism and relationism is not really adequately explained. In addition, the role of the intelligentsia is presented in only a very sketchy format. Finally, there are unexplained elements in his theory: was he suggesting that all thought, including science and mathematics, was socially and historically relative? This remains unclear. Also, by using the highly academic title 'sociology of knowledge', was he trying, despite the general thrust of the theory, to smuggle in a more objectivist 'social scientific' account, with all its subtle implications of a neutral observation language? There is a sense in which this latter criticism is partially valid and appears to turn the circle fully on Mannheim. We find him paying court to the very paradigm of truth which he has gone out his way to reject.

In another, rather oblique sense, Mannheim paves the way for the next phase of the concept which appears in the post-1945 era, often titled the 'end of ideology' (see McClellan 1986, 49). The gradual assimilation of active political ideology into the sanitized academic discipline of sociology not only means the loss of earthy, emotive ideological debate, but also the potential loss of utopias or forward-looking values. Political life becomes absorbed into a closely reasoned social science, conducted by expert intellectuals.

The 'end of ideology' school was a product and phase largely of the Cold War era, although the basic premises of the movement would still be upheld by many who regard themselves as social and political scientists. Some scholars, such as Francis

Fukuyama, were hasty in anticipating liberal capitalism's triumphant vindication in the turbulent late 1980s with the collapse of Eastern European communism and the turn to liberal market economies (Fukuyama 1989). The 'end of ideology' debate appeared first in the American social science establishment, although it was not without relation to certain developments in European thought. It has parallels not only with the 'death of political theory' movement but also with the more sinister McCarthyite anti-communist purges in the USA.

It is worth noting that this argument coincided with a number of different but resonant intellectual positions of the time. Within movements such as ordinary language philosophy and logical positivism during the 1950s, both political philosophy and ideology were seen as lifeless. Ideology was equivalent, in some perceptions, to morality or aesthetics, premising itself on emotion, with little or no rational substance. In a different format the political theorist Michael Oakeshott, in books such as *Rationalism in Politics* (1962), drew a distinction between a traditionalist and ideological stance in politics. A similar idea appears in the contemporaneous writings of Leo Strauss, Eric Voegelin and Hannah Arendt. The philosophical roots to this distinction need not concern us here (see Vincent 2004, 65–73). The basic point was that ideology represented a simplification, abstraction and what Oakeshott calls an 'abridgement' of social reality. Ideologists selected, and consequently distorted, a much more complex reality. Unsurprisingly this approach, which is portrayed as non-ideological, philosophical and more academic, and which also appreciates the subtle complexity of the totality of social reality, is a form of conservatism. Oakeshott's basic distinction appeared, with some qualifications, in the work of a number of writers in the 1980s (see Manning ed. 1980; Graham 1986; Williams 1988, especially ch. 3; Adams 1989).

Another important argument which resonated with the 'end of ideology' was the assertion that 'politics' was distinct from ideology. Ideology denoted a totalitarian mentality which prevented all political discussion other than on its own content. Ideology is distinct from a pluralist, free, tolerant and rational society, where 'politics' takes place. Writers as diverse as Ralf Dahrendorf, J. L. Talmon, Bernard Crick, Karl Popper and Raymond Aron, in their different ways, all spoke of 'totalizing ideology' and closed societies (fascism and communism), as distinct from tolerant civil politics and open societies. Ideology, in this reading, becomes an intolerant, unfree and limited perspective in comparison to forms of non-ideological, open and tolerant politics.

The initial impetus to the mainly American form of the 'end of ideology' derived from three main sources. First, there was clear belief in the 1950s among a generation that had lived through the 1930s and 1940s – with the wars, Gulags, show trials, Nazism, Jewish pogroms, Stalinism – that ideological politics was a set of dangerous delusions. These apparent delusions focused on Marxism-Leninism in the Cold War period. It was thus accepted that ideological politics was at the root of much of the mass of pain, misery and warfare of the mid-twentieth century. Some of the writers of the 1950s were in fact Jewish intellectuals who reflected with deep uneasiness on the fate of the Jews under ideological dogmas in the 1930s and 1940s. Active ideology appeals to the Don Quixote of politics, tilting at imaginary evil giants.

Second, in spite of the fact that ideologies serve a function in developing immature societies, it was held that in industrialized democratic societies they no longer served anything more than a decorative role. Consensus on basic aims was agreed. Most of the major parties in industrialized societies had achieved, in the welfare, mixed economy structure, the majority of their reformist aims. The Left had accepted the dangers of excessive state power and the Right had accepted the necessity of the welfare state and the rights of working people. Consensus and convergence of political aims were seen in many industrialized countries. As Seymour Martin Lipset remarked, 'This very triumph of the democratic social revolution of the West ends domestic politics for those intellectuals who must have ideologies or utopias to motivate them to political action' (Lipset 1969, 406; see also Bell 1965; Shils 1955 and 1968; Waxman 1968). Basic agreement on political values had been achieved. Politics was about more peripheral pragmatic adjustment, gross national products, prices, wages, the public-sector borrowing requirement, and the like. All else was froth. As Lipset commented, 'The democratic struggle will continue, but it will be a fight without ideologies, without red flags, without May Day parades' (Lipset 1969, 408).

In addition to this, the 1950s saw sustained productivity and growth in the GNPs of many developed industrial economies. In one sense, the 'end of ideology' episode was a partial reflection of the improvements and growth of the Western economies during this period (Duncan 1987, 649). Living standards rose and greater affluence was experienced by a larger number of citizens in America, Britain and Europe. Economic and social divisions in society were no longer seen as so pivotal. Economic prosperity, combined with the growth of the welfare state, was diminishing social, economic and political differences (see Butler and Stokes 1974).

Third, the 'end of ideology' coincided with the heroic age of sociology. American sociology, in particular, 'offered the world the prospect of freedom from ideology, for it offered a "science" of society, in place of superstition' (see Goldie in Ball et al. eds 1989, 268). In some ways this was a partial return to Tracy, although the terminology had changed. In Tracy, ideology was the science to unravel superstitions. In the social sciences of the 1950s, ideology *was* the superstition which needed unravelling. Despite the altered terminology, the impetus to both was remarkably similar, namely, contrasting an Enlightenment-based rational scientific endeavour with superstition and intellectual flummery. The development of empirical social science demanded a value-free rigour, scepticism and empirical verification, unsullied by the emotional appeals of ideological and normative political philosophy. A neo-positivism rigidly separating facts and values lurked behind these judgements.

In this context it was argued that ideology had literally ended in advanced industrialized democratic societies. Ideology was contrasted with empirically based social science. The latter was the path to political knowledge; the former connoted illusion. As Edward Shils commented: 'Science is not and never has been part of an ideological culture. Indeed the spirit in which science works is alien to ideology' (Shils 1968, 74).

There were a number of problems with the 'end of ideology' perspective. In many ways it was a temporary phase in industrialized societies reacting against the extremes of the war years. Populations identified themselves with material affluence, consumption and economic growth after the austerity of the preceding period.

Ideology was linked in complex ways with the memories of austerity. However, on a more general theoretical level, as Alasdair MacIntyre commented, the 'end of ideology' theorists 'failed to entertain one crucial alternative possibility: namely, that the end-of-ideology, far from marking the end-of-ideology, was itself a key expression of the ideology of the time and place where it arose' (MacIntyre 1971, 5). The views propounded by the 'end of ideology' school contain certain evaluative assumptions about human nature, how rationality ought to function, the value of consensus, and details on the characteristics of a tolerant, pragmatic civil society which ought be cultivated. To try to claim that these views are premised simply on a social scientific perspective and that all else is ideology is intellectual chicanery. The 'end of ideology' was an ideological position committed to a form of pragmatic liberalism. There was a clear failure, which permeated the 'end of ideology' perspective, to analyse liberalism as ideology.

Despite the resurgence of interest in the thesis in the late 1980s, the 'end of ideology' movement is now regarded with more scepticism, as a phase in the development of the concept of ideology. Yet the assumptions behind the 'end of ideology' movement still, almost unconsciously, pervade discussion and writing in the social science establishment.

The present status of ideology is complex and reflects all the phases that have so far been discussed. The most pervasive theme is still the fierce contrast between 'truth and ideology'. Many who discuss ideology would claim for themselves a non-ideological neutrality. The usual claimants for such neutrality or impartiality are commonly the natural and social sciences, philosophy and political theory. The complexity is intensified when we realize that many liberals, conservatives, feminists, Marxists, and so on, would also claim to be on the side of truth as against ideology.

It has been particularly characteristic of the Anglo-American approach to try to maintain a distinction between science and ideology. This is the deeply entrenched attitude which came to full self-consciousness in the social sciences in the 'end of ideology' movement. As one commentator complains: if the notion of ideology is linked with 'belief systems' in general, then 'such a definition simply fails to discriminate between different kinds of ideas. … It fails to discriminate between science and ideology' (Hamilton 1987, 22). The basic position is that for social or natural science to work, there must be some ultimate, and persistent, and objective foundation to our knowledge. This foundation is the yardstick for truth. It can be confirmed and acts as a final court of appeal. It is unaffected by our values and beliefs. The truth of our beliefs – that which enables us to characterize them as knowledge – is that they correspond as nearly as possible to this objective foundation. Rationality is also usually seen as possessing agreed and consensual universal standards, enabling us to establish correspondences. In social science, particularly, this scientific foundationalism must be kept distinct from the more subjective, emotive values and beliefs characterizing ideology. There is no external foundation to which ideologies correspond. Ideologies remain tied to 'theories'; their logic is therefore circular and cannot be tested against the world. Science, on the other hand, has a specific direction since the theory can be falsified by external foundational facts.

The problem with this view of science is that it is outdated and contested. The complex debates within the philosophy of science cannot be dealt with here. However, the work of philosophers of science like Thomas Kuhn, Paul Feyerabend, Imre Lakatos and Alan Musgrave, and Mary Hesse, among many others, moved the whole discussion of the nature of science beyond the above views.[2] Science, for Kuhn, does not progress by accretion and empirical confirmation; rather, 'dominant paradigms' are seen to take over, via gestalt switches or quasi-religious conversions. Paradigms determine the nature of the puzzles to be solved and what is, or is not, regarded as good or normal science. Once a paradigm is established, the scientific community works within it for a time. One paradigm does not 'fit' better than another; instead, a different paradigm creates different criteria and a different sense of reality. The history of science is not, therefore, a slow, progressive growth but rather a series of periodic paradigm-changes which alter the whole nature of science and its perception of reality. Feyerabend, on the other hand, describes claims to the impartiality and independence of natural science as a 'fairy tale' promulgated by the scientific community, often for the social and economic benefits which accrue to such claims. He contends that every standard of scientific method, whether it be rationality, verification or falsification, has been violated in the course of major discoveries in science. There are therefore no necessary or sufficient conditions to authenticate scientific behaviour and theory choice. These arguments throw a critical light on the supposedly hard-and-fast distinctions still sometimes drawn between science and ideology, particularly in the social sciences.

The situation becomes more fraught in the relation between ideology and political philosophy. The question usually turns on the nature of philosophy itself. There is no space to deal with all of these philosophies, thus some selective examples will have to suffice.

It is hazardous to generalize on broad and intricate philosophical movements; however, early twentieth-century analytic philosophy traditionally associated the path of political philosophy with a second-order function of solving identifiable conceptual problems, usually arising out of the pre-eminent areas of first-order knowledge in the natural sciences (judged in more traditional sense). Philosophy works via ethically neutral, rigorous conceptual analysis. It analyses the nature of necessarily true propositions about the world. The key assumption here is that it is only in the pure natural sciences that we find such knowledge. Ideology, like morality, aesthetics or religion, is another non-scientific, value-orientated, often emotive mode of theorizing. It exhorts actions and persuades rather than critically analyses (see Adams 1989, xxiii, 3; also Corbett 1965; Plamenatz 1971).

This latter point is fortuitously connected to a pervasive view of political philosophy during the twentieth century, namely, to see it as a higher, more critical calling. The most characteristic conception of ideology (in this perspective) is that of a sullied product which lacks the merits of political philosophy. In this interpretation political philosophy is generally marked out by a reflective openness, critical distance, a focus on following the argument regardless, and an awareness of human experience which transcends political struggles. Ideology would be viewed as the opposite. It closes reflection, throws itself into partisan struggle; its ideas are designed instrumentally to manipulate actors, close argument and ultimately to achieve political power. It has no concern with truth. In this case ideology has to be separated from the real. It was this kind of distinction which formed the intellectual backdrop to the bulk of Anglo-American political philosophy from the mid to the late twentieth century.[3] This general conception of political philosophy remained a subtext in the arguments of late twentieth-century normative philosophical liberalism, that is, the work of, for example, John Rawls, Robert Nozick, Ronald Dworkin and Brian Barry.

This latter conception was subject to a number of counter-pressures. First, linguistic philosophy, stemming particularly from the later writings of Wittgenstein, altered our perspective on the nature of language, truth and knowledge, reminding us of their social dimension. To formulate a concept implies having a speaker who knows how to use a language in a particular context. Languages are not discovered, but are socially constituted. The words embodied in languages do not hook on to things in the world but are subject to a prodigious diversity of uses within 'language games' or 'forms of life'. Learning a concept is not grasping its essence or mastering a mental image, but understanding its various uses in a publicly available language. Concepts do not, therefore, correspond to precise things in the world. In fact, the character of most of the concepts we encounter is their essential contestability (see Vincent 2004, 95ff; also Newey 2001). Meaning becomes a matter of the rules governing use within particular language games. One effect of this is to bring ideologies back into circulation under the rubric of language games. Ideology is not necessarily a distorted image of the world, but is rather part of the world of language and action. This conception has hampered a clear distinction between ideology and philosophy.

Second, intellectual movements such as postmodernism and hermeneutics have also raised doubts concerning any clear distinction of philosophy from ideology. Thinkers such as Michel Foucault, Richard Rorty and Paul Ricoeur have all, in their different ways, cast doubts on the comfortable distinctions concerning ideology which have often pervaded the social sciences and mainstream analytical philosophy. Language is not viewed as a transparent conveyor of meaning. Ricoeur, for example, considered 'The interpretative code of an ideology as something in which men live and think, rather than a conception *that* they pose. In other words, an ideology is operative and not thematic. It operates behind our backs, rather than appearing as a theme before our eyes' (Ricoeur 1981, 227). Further, Foucault in developing his own unique poststructural critique, even suggested abandoning the concepts of ideology and political philosophy altogether. They would be replaced by painstaking genealogical explanation, which examines how certain discourses and regimes of truth (*epistemes*) come about. For Foucault, all knowledge relates to power. As he stated:

> what one seeks then is not to know what is true or false, justified or not justified, real or illusory. … One seeks to know what are the ties, what are the connections that can be marked between mechanisms of coercion and elements of knowledge, what games of dismissal and support are developed from the one to the others, what it is that enables some element of knowledge to take up effects of power assigned in a similar system to a true or probable or uncertain or false element, and what it is that

enables some process of coercion to acquire the form and the justification proper to a rational, calculated, technically efficient, and so forth, element. (Foucault in Schmidt ed. 1996, 393)

Knowledge always conforms to restraints and rules; power also needs something approximating to knowledge.[4] Thus neither political philosophy nor ideology represents any external objective reality. In a similar vein, Richard Rorty suggested the utter uselessness of 'the distinction between "ideology" and a form of thought ... which escapes being "ideology"' (Rorty 1989, 59). In this context, there are no clear criteria to differentiate them. If political philosophy still claims a special insight into reality, as distinct from ideology, then it is simply mistaken and abstracts itself further from the realities of politics.

The most sophisticated treatment of this issue can be found in the work of Michael Freeden. For Freeden, ideologies are not the poor relation of political philosophy. On the contrary, they provide equally valid insights. Ideologies are also far more subtle and pervasive than commonly understood. Freeden calls his approach to ideology 'conceptual morphology'. This is semantically based, focusing on the question, 'what are the implications and insights of a particular set of political views, in terms of the conceptual connections it forms?'[5] For Freeden, meaning is always dependent on frameworks of interpretation. An ideology is 'thought-behaviour', embodied in ordinary spoken and written language.[6] Ideologies, in effect, are conceptual maps for navigating the political realm; they contain core, adjacent and peripheral conceptual elements.[7] Core concepts are the non-negotiable aspects of all ideologies: for example, liberty for liberalism or equality for socialism. Other concepts are relegated to the periphery of an ideological scheme and will sometimes drop out of use or migrate to other ideologies. Adjacent concepts flesh out the core concepts and confine their ability for over-interpretation. All concepts are essentially contested, although the majority do embody internal logical constraints on how far meanings can be stretched. However, each ideology (to use Freeden's term) will try to 'decontest' the core and adjacent components. Meanings of core concepts will thus be *fixed* within each ideology.

Concepts are arranged in such as way as to form a unique ideology; this ideology is an historically contingent conceptual pattern, a pattern governed by the proximity and permeability of concepts. These patterns can be rearranged within alternative ideological schemes – almost like modular furniture. Concepts such as liberty or equality have manifold meanings; different aspects of these meanings will be fixed, then utilized and arranged within different ideological frameworks. We should not be surprised therefore to find what looks on the surface like the same concept functioning as either a core or adjacent term within dissimilar ideological structures. Liberty, for example, is not *owned* by liberalism; it can reappear legitimately within other ideologies. This gives rise, in turn, to protracted competition over concepts between ideologies. This last point underpins another aspect of ideologies for Freeden, namely, they will often be (due to the manifold meanings of concepts) subject to vagueness and ambiguity. This does not imply deception. On the contrary, ideologies are often masterful at integrating and accommodating ambiguity or vagueness. In fact, in ideological discussion, vagueness can be functional, allowing latitude for interpretation, which is often a crucial prerequisite for political activity.

For Freeden, ideology 'includes, but is not identical with, the reflections and conjectures of political philosophers' (Freeden 1996, 2). Political theory is seen as a capacious category containing political philosophy and ideology as sub-categories. Freeden thus separates out the history of political theory, political philosophy and ideology. The easiest way of looking at the relation of these terms is to articulate, briefly, Freeden's view of the advantages of morphological study of ideology. It combines a *diachronic* approach (which traces in effect the historical development of language and records the various changes) with a *synchronic* approach (which examines language as it is actually is at a point in time with no reference to historical argument). Morphology balances both dimensions (Freeden 1996, 5). This provides a handle for understanding both political philosophy and the history of political theory. Political philosophy has often tended to be overly focused on the synchronic dimension, whereas the history of political theory has been predominantly diachronic. Ideology, among other things, balances both dimensions. Ideologies also contain a mixture of emotion and reason and occasionally flawed logic and vagueness. They are focused on the need to attract the attention of larger groups, not to persuade a small group of intellectual colleagues. They stand in the midst of tense, often contingent political debates, both within and between groups. In addition, they are, strictly, neither true nor false. This conclusion obviously leads to a degree of relativism, which Freeden considers inevitable.[8]

One problem, though, for Freeden is that Anglo-American liberal political philosophy (Rawls, Dworkin, and so forth), since the mid-twentieth century, has often tried to open up a chasm between itself and political ideology (see Freeden 1998). Freeden takes the primary functions of political philosophy as justifying, clarifying the consistency, truth and logicality of political theories and evaluating ethical prescriptions. However, this role should not be performed to the exclusion of ideological study. Ideology is not imperfect political philosophy. Further, an overemphasis on synchronic abstracted reason and logic can lead to a virtually semi-private professional academic language, which bears little or no relation to politics. Overall, Freeden puts in a plea for theoretical ecumenism, mutual fertilization and tolerance between these realms. It is important, in all this welter of argument, to realize that studying ideologies, in this context, is not the same as producing them. We should not confuse these practices.

There is one issue in Freeden's position which remains problematic, but it brings us pretty much up to date with certain key current debates. Is there any way of ascertaining what is and what is not ideological? Further, is there any sense in which we can disaggregate a notion of a political reality independently of ideology? Earlier theories had their own way of resolving this issue, drawing a distinction between, for example, social science and ideology or political philosophy and ideology. Ideology, in these latter senses, is seen to blur or distort the real. Freeden's argument, like those in the postmodern and hermeneutic positions, does not have this facility. He stresses, in fact, that the notion of the political *cannot* be formed independently of the ideological. A related question is: can certain ideologies mislead us more than others? This question implies there is some notion of political reality (independent of ideology) which allows us make this judgement. Additionally, how could we criticize ideologies which appear, to all intents and purposes, as unpalatable or just appalling? Some critics would suggest we need some standard – external to ideology – to make any secure judgement. Therefore, is there some way of distinguishing between a sense of a political reality as against political ideology? Certain contemporary writers have their own specific (if quite different) answers to this question.

This chapter will not resolve this latter question; however, one example of such a critique has been Jürgen Habermas's arguments concerning the necessity for a *critique of ideology*. Basically ideology fails to do justice to the real communicative structure of social relations. Ideology, for Habermas, is implicitly in conflict with the comprehensive 'power of reflection': that is to say, genuine communicative reasoning in Habermas is distinct from ideology (Habermas 1996, 170). Without trying to unpack the detail of Habermas's theories, there are a series of arguments which suggest that there is a form of underlying consensual reality present in the way that we communicate with one another, which is embedded in ordinary human discourse and knowledge claims. This reality is essentially concerned with what we *presuppose* when we speak and try to genuinely rationally understand each other. Habermas argues that there are common normative consensual underpinning rules which function in any discourse and these in turn embody ethical and political implications. The gist of this perspective, for Habermas, is that any speech act raises 'universal validity claims … that can be vindicated'. The validity claims are notions such as comprehensibility or intelligibility, truthfulness, sincerity and rightness. Insofar as anyone wants to 'participate in a process of reaching an understanding, [the agent] cannot avoid raising … validity claims' (Habermas 1979, 2). The normative content is thus presupposed in all genuine communication. In point it is only by engaging in such intersubjective communicative practices that we can arrive at any conclusions about what constitutes a morally worthwhile or autonomous life. Distortion-free dialogue and reasonable communication are the heart of Habermas's enterprise.[9]

To turn immediately to ideology, it is clear for Habermas that not all speech acts are aimed at genuine communication; many are purely strategic, instrumental or manipulative, aiming to further an agent's or a group's interest. A truly *communicative* use of language is thus wholly different to a *manipulative* use of language. Unfettered rational reflection (the power of reflection) will usually in fact reveal the power and manipulation implicit within certain language use – this is the essence of what Habermas sees as ideology critique.[10] If we wish to grasp ideology, we have to see it in the field of power, manipulation and distorted communication. Ideology is pseudo communication. In essence, ideology is about the subjugation of the communicative structure of reality. Thus communicative reason is equivalent to the 'real' and is distinct from ideology, understood as something which is manipulative and instrumental.

Unexpectedly, there is also a subtle distinction between the Real and the ideological present in the writings of Slavoj Žižek, although it is a *very* different

'Real' to Habermas's.[11] Žižek's account is not being compared on the same level as Habermas, insofar as Žižek's ideas are mediated largely through his reading of Lacan's psychoanalytical work. The political is thus viewed via the psychoanalytical. The Real in this case is something which signifies an internal dimension of unstructured and unconscious desire. It is outside the realm of language and 'reality' – a reality which is characteristic of the linguistic phantasy of ideology. This 'Real' (as distinct from reality) is felt as a form of internal lack and anxiety in the individual. None the less, it can still for Žižek stand as a negative antagonism to the imaginary and symbolic character of ideology. The Real is not a knowable thing in itself – as an anxious lack – it is, if anything, something that we try to escape from in the complex imaginary fantasies of ideology. Ideology thus always represents phantasy, a complex set of symbolic meanings that we invest in the world – a world which in the end always surpasses the reach of our phantasies.[12] The reality of ideology, however, shapes this world. The phantasies constituting ideology also make up our ordinary desires. Desires are never, though, simply *our* desires; desire is largely constituted (or interpellated) via the phantasies of inter-subjective ideologies. Ideological phantasies are a kind of impossible and ultimately flawed gaze, which constitute our political world, sometimes in dangerous and very alarming ways.

The Real therefore signifies for Žižek an antagonism which bears witness to the fragility of our ideological phantasies. It disrupts the fixity of the meaning of ideologies. It embodies a *negative* gesture of withdrawal from ideologies which constitute the external realities of our political world. Given this gesture of withdrawal, the Real, for Žižek, represents a space which is distinct from ideology (see Žižek 1995).[13] Not that this 'space' represents anything, since the Real is unknowable. Further, we have nothing to replace the phantasies of ideology; we see reality though the language of ideology. However, the Real represents an inevitable and endless struggle with the realities of ideology.[14]

The present position of ideology still remains profoundly contested and open to broad interpretation. Most, though not all, of the meanings that we have considered are still canvassed. It is no longer used to indicate an empirical 'science of ideas'; not that the aspiration to have such a science is not still present, under different names, in some areas of psychology. In addition, the term would not be used in the French royalist sense, to denote atheistic republicanism. Ideology is, however, still used pejoratively or negatively, indicating a limited perspective, a subjective value bias, a linguistic distortion, a symbolic phantasy or, most commonly, an illusory view of the world. Furthermore, ideology can simply denote an individual's political perspective, a conceptual map which helps groups to navigate the political world, a specific set of hegemonic views which tries to legitimate power (as in the belief structures of a particularly social class), or indeed all political views. Ideology can also signify the generic ideas of a political party, a total world-view, or indeed human consciousness in general, encompassing all beliefs, including art and science. The latter might imply the politicization of all ideas or simply that interpretative concerns permeate all our claims to knowledge. The permutations here are extremely diverse (see Thompson 1984).

Cautionary Points

In my own understanding, ideologies are bodies of concepts, values and symbols which incorporate conceptions of human nature and thus indicate what is possible or impossible for humans to achieve; critical reflections on the nature of human interaction; the values which humans ought either to reject or aspire to; and the correct technical arrangements for social, economic and political life which will meet the needs and interests of human beings. Ideologies thus claim both to *describe* and to *prescribe* for humans. The two tendencies are intermingled in ideology. Ideologies are also intended not only to legitimate certain activities or arrangements, but also to integrate individuals, enabling them to cohere around certain core conceptual themes, and to enable groups to navigate the political realm. Each ideology undoubtedly has certain core formal themes; however, all such themes are mutable and often interpreted in very different ways by schools within each ideology. I therefore call these *formal themes*, insofar as they gain substance and force only in the context of the arguments of the differing schools within ideologies.[15]

There are a number of critical points on ideology which need to be unpacked. Primarily, one of the criticisms that is made of ideologies is that they are far more action-orientated, and far less self-critical and rigorous, than philosophy. Occasionally some ideology looks like crude phrasemongering or propaganda. This is only a half-truth. Many philosophical and scientific ideas have often been integrated within ideologies. Ideology can be found in phrasemongering as well as, occasionally, within the more abstract philosophical arguments. Some ideological writing can indeed be immensely sophisticated theorizing, yet the same basic ideas can be expressed in the crudest form of propaganda. Also, whereas some ideology remains at a sophisticated theoretical level, some practical philosophy can claim a strong action-orientated role. The theme of Plato's philosopher-kings has been echoed throughout the history of philosophy to the present. It is therefore difficult to make any hard-and-fast distinctions here. Ideological ideas can be vapid or profoundly urbane.

A related point is that we should not, in consequence of the above, always expect to approach ideologies as coherent clear constructs. Ideological themes can be found on a continuum from the most banal, vague, jumbled rhetoric up to the most astute theorizing. This is probably one of the more significant issues arising, for example, from Michael Freeden's work on ideology: namely, that ideology functions very broadly within politics; however, a great deal of its basic work functions at the level of politicians, policy-makers, political activists and indeed everyday speech. It is at the more philosophical end of the ideological continuum that we could expect to find a strong stress on theoretical coherence. However, we should not always expect such coherence in ideology; we should therefore not rule out the functional role of vagueness and ambiguity in political success. We search for coherence but we should not always expect to find it. Further, coherence and sophisticated argument are not necessarily always the safest guides to ideological accomplishment.

One issue for the student of ideology is that a great deal of the 'durable' ideological work from the nineteenth and twentieth centuries has been written down in pamphlets and treatises; that is to say, we tend to familiarize ourselves with the genealogy of ideologies at the more theoretical end of the ideological continuum. This writing is not necessary done by academics, but certainly by intellectuals of one stripe or another. It is this kind of intellectual production which then gets whittled down, in particular historical circumstances, into policy, party programmes, political activism, sloganeering and indeed ordinary speech. The problem for the student of ideology is to find a balance here. On the one hand, in discussing ideologies, one has to articulate ideas at a certain level of moderate coherence, which can none the less still be grasped by ideological activists as representing their core beliefs – although it may still be thought of, in some renditions, as lacking theoretical sophistication. On the other hand, if one believes that ideologies are primarily real-world products, symbolic structures which mobilize collectivities and are rooted in policy and ordinary political discourse, then one faces a different critical unease. That is to say, in trying to maintain a moderately lucid ideological construct and concentrating on certain coherent texts, one thereby risks not grasping the 'real-world' empirical character of ideological speech. There is, though, a different potential danger in stressing this 'real-world' empirical dimension of ideology, and that is of entering into a particularized, micro-world of everyday discourse analysis, where one can lose sight of what makes the ideology function intellectually.[16] This present book tries to forge a middle path; however, it none the less continuously strays into both the more philosophical discourse, on the one hand, and the more ordinary real-world discourse, on the other hand. Overall, though, it tries to hold some balance.[17]

Another related concern is the level at which ideology works. This issue throws more light on the problem of coherence within an ideology. Martin Seliger drew a distinction between the *fundamental* and *operative* levels of ideology. Although arguing that 'politics is inseparable from ideology', Seliger maintains that the distinctive mark of ideology, as compared with philosophy, *is* the action-orientation of ideology. This latter point has been disputed. However, for Seliger, the fundamental principles, beliefs and prescriptions of ideology are faced continually by the demand for action or operation in the world, which inevitably involves compromises.[18] The result of this is a constant tension between the fundamental and operative/ technical spheres of ideology. Fundamental principles are often changed or revised, not only through conflict with other fundamental principles, but also via technical and operative demands. On the other hand, the operative and technical questions are also examined, judged and modified before the stringent court of moral and ideological purity.

Some ideologies, such as liberalism, have been more concerned with and more adept and successful at operationalizing their concerns. Others, such as anarchism, have remained for various reasons more caught up in the area of fundamental principles. Comparatively, anarchism has had far less chance to face technical operational questions than has liberalism or socialism. This can give rise to the mistaken judgement that liberalism is basically a more truthful, pragmatic and non-ideological doctrine, whereas anarchism lives in a world of ideological fantasies, which cannot be put into practice. However, it is a question not of truth here, but of the level at which an ideology has tended to function, coupled with the interpretative judgement that liberalism enables one to cope better in the world. Yet even if an ideology has functioned more operationally, this still does not diminish the tension that exists with the fundamental theoretical level within that ideology. The history of liberal policy-making is continually punctuated with the question: is this really liberalism?

The above fundamental/operational distinction is also useful in discussing ideological change. Change can occur in both the operative and the fundamental dimensions, but most often in the latter, partly because it is most subject to strain from the contingencies of the world. Contingencies can both reinforce and undermine fundamental principles. The only point to add to this is that the perception of contingencies still relates to ideological views. There are no absolute unmediated contingencies to which ideologies must correspond. As the affiliates of conceptual history (*Begriffsgeschichte*) have argued, one must understand political change conceptually. We live in a world of words; words determine who and what we are. We are thus tied by words and all we do 'is deeply delimited by the conceptual, argumentative and rhetorical resource of our language. The limits of my moral and political language, we might say, mark the limits of my moral and political world' (Ball 1988, 4). All perceptions of the necessity of contingencies are thus conceptually mediated.

A further point to note is the interweaving and overlapping of ideological continuums at both fundamental and operational levels. Often, the same basic core or adjacent idea, argument or thinker will be used by apparently quite alien ideologies for different reasons and outcomes. This overlap and interweaving increases the problem of clear identification and often gives rise to compounds such as liberal socialism, liberal conservatism, Marxist feminism or communist anarchism. Ideologies are complex structures of discourse which carry immense amounts of inherited, interwoven baggage. Every ideology is therefore a conjunction of intellectual hybrids.

Such overlapping of themes must lead to scepticism concerning ideologists who claim to be the inheritors of *a* true doctrine. Such a mentality appears, though, in all the ideological positions.[19] One consequence of this is the desire to maintain the objective purity of an ideology. A related problem can be called the 'need for ancestors'. Most ideologies claim ancient lineage, indicating in some cases that they correspond to perennial ahistorical human needs, implicit in human nature. This gives their theories more *gravitas*. Thus it is contended that the liberal market economy best matches human interests; that we are all naturally anarchists or conservatives; that palaeolithic or tribal peoples were genuine ecologists; that national identity is intrinsic to the human condition; or that the 'woman question' has existed since the dawn of time. In my own reading, ideologies are *all* comparatively recent forms of thought, stemming from the immediate post-French revolutionary era. In addition, there are no pure doctrines. All ideologies are internally complex, intermixed and overlapping. Claims to purity, as claims to greater truth, are usually bogus.

We examine ideology as fellow sufferers, not as neutral observers, although we do none the less need to acknowledge a distinction between ideology and the study of ideology. However, it is a central contention of this book that there is no given world to which ideologies do, or do not, approximate. There is also no way of excluding our own presuppositions. Embodying our own assumptions, we encounter ideologies as conceptions of reality. We cannot step completely outside these conceptions and compare or validate them with some definite external thing, although we can critically compare worlds. Ideologies do not stand side by side with something objective or real; rather they subtly constitute this reality. However, even though we are sufferers, we are not complete sufferers. We can, in the study of ideology (rather than the promulgation of an ideology), distance ourselves in the very fact of theorizing self-consciously.[20] Studying ideologies is a process of encountering a number of such worlds, some of which are quite febrile and limiting, others of which are expansive. The study of ideology itself is an attempt to fuse self-consciously and dialogically our scheme of understanding with that of another, which can be an enriching experience. In this context it becomes more problematic to speak of the truth or falsity of ideologies. Rather, some ideologies enrich us, some diminish us. Some appear to enable us to cope and function in the world; others less so.

The Text

There are multiple dangers when walking into the field of ideology, not least that there are many who claim proprietorial rights to the ground and become enraged that others should ramble there. It is also a field filled with snares and hidden hollows. Yet I make no apologies for rambling. The rights of way remain unsettled. The book is designed primarily for courses on ideologies. In such a controversial area, one cannot help but interpret, and there is a series of arguments running through this work which mark out certain idiosyncratic views.

Each chapter is written in a structured manner. In this sense it is hoped that it can be read in discrete sections if necessary. There is an initial introduction and examination of the particular terminology (i.e. fascism, liberalism, etc.), followed by a brief review of the accounts of the origin and history of the ideology at issue. The next section deals with the nature of the ideology. Under this rubric one main issue is discussed which is crucial for grasping the sections that follow. The ideology at issue is broken down loosely into various internal 'schools of thought' which are unpacked and clarified. The etymological character of the particular ideology, the history and origins, and the analysis of the nature of the schools vary in complexity between ideologies, thus the length of this section will fluctuate from chapter to chapter. There then follows a series of sections which encapsulate the more general and formal themes characterizing the ideology. These themes are then fleshed out by the varying contributions of 'schools of thought' and individual thinkers. Some of the more complex issues of differing intellectual interpretation and overlap are dealt with in these sections. Each chapter concludes with some brief critical remarks.

An ideologies course can be both a deeply rewarding and a highly frustrating experience.[21] On the one hand, the student tries to articulate the coherence of a body of thought, assuming that it has some kind of identity. On the other hand, dealing with this body of thought requires examining both differing schools of thought 'within' each ideology *and* contributions by individual thinkers and the manner in which that is reflected in ordinary discourse. This task places multiple problems of interpretation before the student. Further, does one approach the ideology via thinkers or thinkers via the ideology? Both paths carry dangers. The danger of the former method is of becoming lost in a morass of interpretation and contextualist questions. The danger of the latter is of circumscribing the richness of the intellectual content. Finally, what are the ideological views of the interpreter? Do they impinge on the ideological study? An ideologies course often moves along with these internal tensions, which can both exacerbate as well as enliven and enrich debate.

2

Liberalism

Liberalism is the most complex and intricate of ideologies. It has permeated so deeply into the cultural life of the West that it is difficult to disentangle the partisan from the more objective commentary. Much academic study (in fact the notion of the liberal academic mind) is founded on the assumptions of individualism, tolerance, progress. A great deal of contemporary political theory, specifically in the writings of major figures such as John Rawls, Robert Nozick, Michael Walzer and Friedrich Hayek, deals with liberal themes.

The oldest apolitical use of the word 'liberal' denotes a type of education. From the Middle Ages it implied two things: first, a broad or wide-ranging education; second, the education of a gentleman and freeman (*liber*). We have not lost the first sense of the term, although it seems to come into periodic disfavour in educational and political circles. The notion of a 'liberal education' is now often strongly linked with the disciplines of the humanities. The liberal education is said to cultivate a certain disposition or habit of mind. Yet the term can be complimentary or pejorative. The complimentary sense implies broadmindedness, tolerance or generosity (the latter is more easily caught in the word *liberality*), seen as a virtue. From the late sixteenth century there was another sense of the term which was opprobrious, namely, where liberal implied licence. This is close to the word *libertine*, which from the sixteenth century implied not only sexual licence and lack of regard for moral laws, but also addiction to antinomian opinions in religion. In *Othello*, when Desdemona refers to Iago as 'a most profane and liberal counsellor', she was not, we can assume, complimenting him. This opprobrious, more abusive sense of liberal is still in use today.

A third sense identifies the *concept* 'liberal' with certain kinds of moral values. In other words, there are a series of values (tolerance, progress, liberty, individualism) which pre-date the *word* 'liberal' by centuries, but are none the less seen to be characteristic of the 'liberal mind' from the nineteenth century. It is this sense of the term 'liberal' which is used to describe thinkers such as John Locke or Montesquieu who pre-date the existence of the ideology and the word 'liberalism' in European thought. Additionally the term 'liberal', because of its connotations of breadth of mind, tolerance, openness and generosity of spirit, was often equated with a philosophical demeanour. The broadest and most liberal minds were philosophical in character. In this sense, philosophy was the queen of the liberal arts.

The final sense of the term 'liberal' settles on its political usage. It must be realized that it is a comparatively new political word in the European vocabulary. The first explicit use of the term to denote a political allegiance or faction was in Spain between 1810 and 1820. *Liberales* was used to describe a group who opposed the more traditional royalist factions (sometimes referred to as *serviles* – namely, the nobles, clergy and deputies of the estates) (see Collins 1957, 3). The *liberales*, under the influence of events in France, were in favour of the establishment of a secular constitution and freedom of the press. The term was partly abusive, coined by the royalist faction to imply dangerous reformism and licence. In fact, events soon over-took the Spanish *liberales* with the return of royalist absolutism. This pejorative sense of the term became common currency in Europe after 1820. The Tory Prime Minister of Britain, Castlereagh, scathingly referred to some of the then Whig Party as 'English *liberales*' or 'English *libéraux*', implying radicalism and republicanism – the sentiments of revolutionaries. Presumably because of the older, complimentary uses of the term 'liberal', this opprobrium was not long-lasting. By the late 1850s it was more generally used in England to denote a member of Gladstone's party.

It is worth noting here that not all European societies followed Britain on this particular political course and the term 'liberal' did not commonly denote member-ship of a particular party. Figures such as François Guizot, Adophe Thiers, Benjamin Constant and Giuseppe Mazzini believed in a broad, over-arching political atti-tude, which typified generalized optimistic beliefs about human nature, constitu-tional government, free institutions, limited democracy and social progress, and which could contribute towards the improvement of the human species, but which did not have to be associated with a party. This political attitude, an affirmation of certain values outside party allegiance, is still highly significant. Many claimed, quite reasonably, that they could not become members of a Liberal Party because they *were* liberal. The history of the British Liberal Party is strewn with cases of those who left the party, and sometimes joined other parties, because they felt lib-eralism was not being effectively represented and might be better found in the Conservative or Socialist factions. It can be confusing, but it is important to bear in mind that a non-Liberal is not necessarily illiberal and a Liberal party is not necessarily liberal.

A discussion of political liberalism, in the words of one commentator, 'provides an ideological map of many of the major developments which have occurred in Britain and elsewhere since the seventeenth century' (Eccleshall 1986, 4). There is an inevi-table overlap with other ideologies – no pure doctrine of liberalism exists. There are no central core texts or thinkers to liberalism. There are also no unequivocal liberal themes. But there are formal core ideas which are interpreted very differently in dis-tinct contexts and thinkers. The past two centuries are cluttered with examples of liberal experimentation. Such diversity is not necessarily incoherent. It implies that there is a continual process of reflection and adaptation within liberalism. It is this continuing reflection which makes it one of the most pervasive and stimulating ideologies in the contemporary world.

The Origins of Liberal Thought

There are a number of debates concerning the origins of liberalism. Some scholars identify liberalism in the context of the history of nation states. German, Italian, Spanish, French and British liberalisms developed in unique political and socio-cultural environments. The push for national unification in Italy and Germany in the nineteenth century, the effects of the 1789 revolution in France and the comparative isolation of Britain tempered the character of liberalism in these countries. There is thus no overall coherence in liberalism, only different national traditions. While there is some truth to this, it can be over-emphasized.

Another approach focuses on the character of particular liberal ideological traditions. The most usual path here is to argue for a distinction between Continental and British liberalisms (see Hayek 1978, 119; also Gray 1986a, x). British liberalism is usually seen to be of greater antiquity and more empirical in character. Continental liberalism is related more to the French Enlightenment and the overactive use of 'abstract reason' in human affairs. The coherence here lies in the two different ideological traditions. Each is located within distinct cultural histories. This distinction can become narrowed down to British liberalism being the 'true' liberalism and others being revisionary or misleading doctrines. These particular views are not very helpful in accounting for the origins of the liberal movement, which are very much more complex and inchoate.

A third approach to the origin of liberalism locates it in the development of a particular type of economy. In the words of one writer: 'So long as capitalism survives, so will liberalism in its various alternative forms' (Arblaster 1984, 7). The rise of industrial capitalism can be seen as coterminous with liberalism (although this argument neglects the fact that it is equally coterminous with most ideologies). Liberalism is thus seen as the ideology of capitalism. This is a view which expresses primarily, though not exclusively, the Marxist and more general socialist reading of liberalism, and it can be found in a number of commentators on liberalism (see Laski 1936; Macpherson 1962; Arblaster 1984). In this view, private property tends to figure prominently in the liberal pantheon of values. Liberalism therefore needs to be unmasked and exposed to show its acquisitive sins. For some commentators it has therefore had far too good a press over the last two centuries (Hall 1988, 1–3). Such an argument represents, though, a restrictive and limited perspective on liberalism.

My own preference in accounting for the origins of liberalism is to see it as a focus, in the nineteenth century, of the constitutionalist tradition in European thought. In the nineteenth century, constitutionalism became virtually identified with liberalism. The two doctrines have subsequently become virtually coterminous. It is prudent to note, however, that such an identification is historically a relatively recent phenomenon.

It is unnecessary to trace the highly complex European constitutionalist tradition, the roots of which lie in the late medieval revival of Roman law, conciliarist ideas, the elaborate theories of resistance in Reformation and Counter-Reformation writers and the immensely tangled debates of the French Wars of Religion and the English

Civil War (see Vincent 1987, ch. 3). Out of these movements and events ideas on individual rights, individual freedoms, consent, the separation of the private and public realms, contract, limited and balanced government, popular sovereignty, increasingly became common political currency throughout Europe. Paradoxically, such ideas often derived from profoundly illiberal but vociferous sects, such as Calvinists or Jesuits, who were fighting for their own liberty of conscience within opposed religious majorities. However, without two further developments, constitutionalist thought would have remained somewhat one-dimensional: first, the Enlightenment and its offspring in France, England and Scotland; and, second, the revolutions in America, culminating in the Declaration of Independence in 1776, and in France in 1789.

The Enlightenment signalled the unfettered and experimental use of reason in human affairs. Theology, economics, politics, law and philosophy were all profoundly affected. No longer was authority in religion or politics unquestioned. In philosophy, the methods of the Enlightenment were pre-figured in thinkers such as Descartes (1596–1650) and Hobbes (1588–1679). For Descartes, nothing was accepted unless it was judged defensible by individual reason. The effects of the Enlightenment are often seen to vary across different societies. Some theorists, such as Hayek, tried to make a fairly rigorous ideological distinction between the effects of the Enlightenment on the Continent and in Scotland. In Scotland the major offspring was the Scottish school of political economy, whose most notable representatives were Adam Smith and Adam Ferguson. The use of reason by the latter was seen to be balanced, sceptical, empirical and limited in scope. In German and French thought the claims for reason were far more ambitious and ominous.

The revolutions in America, and more particularly in France, brought many ideas on popular sovereignty, natural rights, consent and contractualism into sharp political focus. The idealism of those, such as Tom Paine, who had sketched out utopian schemes for contractual societies based on individual equality, rights and freedom seemed to be coming to fruition. The various constitutional documents and bills of rights began to spread throughout Europe. The impetus of this movement has not ended to this day. One must recall here that it was a mere twenty years after the French Revolution that we find the word 'liberal' being coined for a definite faction, the Spanish *liberales*, who had been much influenced by events in France. It was also the campaigns of the revolutionary armies of the French Republic in the 1790s and 1800s which helped to spread these ideas on the Continent.

The legacy of the French Revolution was extremely ambiguous. The more balanced constitutionalist view found itself at loggerheads with the even more radical ideas of the *sans culottes*, those who advocated direct participatory democracy and, on occasions, communistic theories of property. Benjamin Constant, a key representative of the more balanced liberal constitutionalist persuasion, blamed the more extreme *étatiste* aspects of the Revolution on Jean-Jacques Rousseau and his theory of the General Will (see Constant 1988). Constant's judgment was much later supported by post-1945 liberal writers such as J. L. Talmon (see Talmon 1952). In France, after the Revolution, liberal opinion thus divided between the radical *étatiste* and the more conventional constitutional liberals.[1] In Britain it also divided between the Whigs and the radicals.

Once we move into the 1830s we begin to encounter the fully self-conscious liberal ideology. Constitutionalism is focused at this point within liberalism. In British and European thought, the initial heyday of liberalism coincides with the growth of industrialization and the expansion of markets in goods, capital and labour. Some twentieth-century liberal thinkers, such as Hayek, still looked back nostalgically to a golden age of liberalism in the mid-nineteenth century, roughly dating in Britain from the Catholic Emancipation Act of 1829 to Cobden's Free Trade Treaty with France of 1860.

The 1870s are sometimes seen as marking the beginning of a decline or radical change in liberalism. Liberalism, in this reading, went too far down the road of collectivism, though not all agree with such an assessment, as we shall see in later sections. In Europe, liberal ideas waned in France from the 1850s and in Germany from the 1870s with the rise of Bismarck (see Sheehan 1978). Its longest period of effective political and economic activity was in Britain. In the shape of the Liberal Party it dates from the 1840s until 1922, when the last Prime Minister who could be described as liberal, David Lloyd George, fell from office. A form of Liberal (or Liberal Democrat) party has carried on in Britain up to the present day. Adherents of liberalism have, though, been found increasingly outside the ranks of the official party; in fact, liberalism now seems to have stronger support in other political factions such as Labour and Conservative groups.

This very cursory survey of the origins of liberalism in constitutionalist thought suggests that some of the impetus behind ideas on rights, liberties, limitations on authority and tolerance derives from profoundly illiberal sources. No one would immediately describe either Jesuits or Calvinists as advocates of tolerance or individual liberty. Yet it was often the intolerant minorities, ruthlessly maintaining their independence in hostile environments, and searching for arguments to justify their independence, who were paradoxically driven to express ideas which, in the words of one scholar, 'put forth a theory of political liberty, which was the direct parent of the doctrines triumphant in 1688, and through Locke the ancestor of those in 1789' (Figgis 1922, 118). Even the exponents of popular sovereignty were not democrats. Locke, although preparing the ground for discussion of majority rule, was clearly not in the least interested in extending this to suffrage or periodic elections. There is thus something profoundly fortuitous about the growth of both constitutionalism and liberalism.

The Nature of Liberalism

In this section, certain schools of liberal thought will be examined. There is some debate, though, as to the key representative thinkers of liberalism. For example, the late-nineteenth-century thinker Herbert Spencer is variously cited as both the great summation of nineteenth-century liberalism and a complete 'maverick' who stood outside the mainstream beliefs.[2] A similar contradictory fate has befallen figures such as John Locke, Adam Smith, Jeremy Bentham, Alexis de Tocqueville, Immanuel Kant, John Stuart Mill and, more recently, Friedrich Hayek, Robert Nozick and John Rawls. It is thus a hazardous task trying to isolate the key liberal thinkers.

Some theorists have seen a definite single clear doctrine of liberalism. However, the more common line of interpretation has been to delineate schools of liberalism. The contention of this study is that there are different schools of liberal thought, and it will proceed along these lines as a means of clarifying an immensely complex tradition of discourse. Each school is seen to interpret in its own unique way certain core themes. The two major schools that will be reviewed are classical liberalism and social, or new, liberalism.[3]

The background to classical liberalism is complex. One important strand, particularly in Britain, lies in Whiggism. Over the nineteenth century, Whiggism became increasingly associated with conservatism. Because classical liberalism itself was not a simple entity, it could also be actively promoted within conservative factions. Whiggism came to prominence in Britain after 1688. The major preoccupations of Whigs then became the defence of parliamentary supremacy, upholding the rule of law and the defence of their landed property. Many were deeply attached to the mythology of the ancient constitution and the fundamental rights embodied in it. Some supported notions of freedom of the press and speech as such fundamental rights.

The ancient constitution was an idea promulgated by Whig figures such as Viscount Molesworth, who contended that there was an ancient British constitution going back to the Anglo-Saxons and possibly to the Goths and even the Trojans (see Giesey and Salmon introduction to Hotman 1972, 124). The ancient constitution did not, it should be added, embody Locke's natural rights. It rather incorporated immemorial customary rights justified by long and ancient usage. Many Whigs believed that vigilance was needed to protect such rights against any return to the arbitrariness and absolutist tendencies of the Stuarts. Monarchical power had to be retained, but as a limited component within a balanced constitution which required that power be constrained by a judicious balance of elements. Whiggism represented a curious mixture of defence of privilege combined with resistance to arbitrary rule. Whigs believed in limited suffrage and, unlike many Tories, learnt some lessons from the French Revolution. Yet even in 1832 they still saw the vote as a limited privilege and not as a right.

By the time of the French Revolution, Whiggism had begun to mutate. Older Whig factions still identified with the ancient constitution ideas. Lockian Whigs never really gained much of a foothold between the 1680s and 1776.[4] Others began to identify with commercial wealth, enlightenment and progress. These newer Whigs included the more optimistic Whiggery of Adam Smith, as well as the much more sceptical Whiggery of David Hume: figures such as Edmund Burke who, despite applauding the 1688 Settlement, identified neither with the ancient constitution Whigs nor with Locke's, Hume's or Smith's positions. The French Revolution was a catalyst. The older Whig ideas still persisted but new forms of discourse developed: the commercial ideas of Adam Smith; Jeremy Bentham's systematic use of utilitarianism; and Price and Priestley's radical distillation of Lockian language.

Tom Paine was the first and most effective voice of radicalism who tried to link the events of 1688 and 1789. His *Rights of Man* (1791) was immensely popular in Britain. Other important writers to explore this theme were Joseph Priestley, Richard

Price, James Mackintosh, William Godwin, Mary Wollstonecraft and Percy Shelley. The core of such radicalism lay in an interpretation of Locke's *Two Treatises* (1689) and Rousseau's *Social Contract* (1762), although some of Paine's language seems to have strong echoes of the 1640s Levellers. The basic thesis was the familiar one, that sovereignty did not lie in either monarchy or some privileged aristocratic faction, but in the people. Governments should only govern on the basis of the consent of the whole people, a consent which, as Locke made plain in the final chapter of his *Second Treatise*, could be withdrawn. The natural rights of the people should be enshrined or codified in constitutional documents, as in America and France. It was this radicalism that paved the way for the great age of constitution-making and bills of rights.

Much of the British radicalism, from the 1790s up to the 1820s, concentrated on the theme of parliamentary and electoral reform. This increasingly centred on groups such as the London Corresponding Society (founded in 1792). The language of such groups was based, like Paine's, on natural rights and popular sovereignty theory. In 1794, the London Corresponding Society and its related groups planned a national constitutional convention, virtually on the French revolutionary model. This led to the arrest of the leaders, Horne Tooke, John Thelwell and Thomas Hardy, for high treason. The conflict between France and Britain at the time aroused the suspicions of the government, and despite the acquittal of the leaders of the Corresponding Society, they were subject to harassment and continual fear of re-arrest. Such government activity blunted the practical impact of the movement. In spite of this, the radicals established a vocabulary for speaking of the democratic and natural rights of the sovereign people which became assimilated, during the next century, into the growing labour and socialist movements, and also remained as a strand within liberal thought.[5]

Whiggery and radicalism both fed into nineteenth-century classical liberalism. Classical liberalism is a peculiar blend of ideas and strategies about how best to acquire or defend liberty. Some elements of Whiggery became far more closely identified with conservatism. Many of the older Whigs also felt increasingly uncomfortable with the new commercial industrial spirit expressed by many liberals. Liberal Party figures in Britain, such as Bright and Cobden in the 1840s, expressed utter contempt for landed aristocratic privilege, whether it appeared in Tory or Whig form. They traced many of the ills of Britain to this class and its ownership of large tracts of land which held back the development of a class of yeoman freeholders. This latter argument in fact goes back to the seventeenth century.

Unlike Whiggery, there is some formal unity to classical liberalism – although the core themes are open to broad interpretation. It was clearly committed to the doctrine of individualism. Individualism can be defined as a political and moral doctrine which extols the value of the individual human being. Secondly, such liberalism was pledged to uphold liberty and the equal right of all individuals to equal freedom. Conventionally this freedom was understood negatively, namely, as freedom from arbitrary coercion. One of the areas where freedom was most in demand was in the economy. A free economy was most conducive to the satisfaction of human beings and the fulfilment of their interests. A free economy, where all have relatively equal rights to produce and consume, implies that the government must retain only minimal functions, such as maintaining the rule of law, internal order, the defence of private property and security. Zealous government is thus to be mistrusted. The most vigorous support for these arguments can be found in Britain between 1830 and 1914. It came most notably from the classical political economy school, the utilitarians, the Manchester school of economics, plus many theorists such as J. S. Mill, Herbert Spencer and Henry Sidgwick. In Europe such ideas, though far less concerned with political economy, were associated with the views of thinkers such as Benjamin Constant, François Guizot, Charles de Rémusat, Giuseppe Mazzini, Alexis de Tocqueville and Wilhelm von Humboldt.

It has been argued that this latter form of liberalism died in 1914. George Dangerfield, in his book *The Strange Death of Liberal England*, spoke of Britain in 1910 as 'about to shrug from its shoulders ... a venerable burden, a kind of sack. It was about to get rid of its Liberalism' (Dangerfield 1966, 20). Yet the reports of classical liberalism's demise were greatly exaggerated. In the post-1945 era, specifically from the late 1970s, classical liberalism has been anything but dead.[6] Like the nineteenth-century variant, this modern form of classical liberalism embodies a number of diverse views (see Harvey 2005). Notable among these are the views of the Austrian school of economics, whose most famous offspring were Ludwig von Mises and Friedrich Hayek (see Mises 2005). The Chicago school found its most avid popularizer in Milton Friedman; the Virginia public-choice school was associated with the work of James Buchanan; and a number of individual thinkers such as Ayn Rand and Robert Nozick made major contributions. In Britain this modern variant of classical liberalism had support not only from academics, politicians and many political activists, but also from research and propagandist bodies such as the Institute of Economic Affairs. Part of the origins of this perspective lie, to a degree, in post-war groupings such as the Mont Pelerin Society, amongst other related ideological ginger groups (see Harvey 2005; Turner 2007 and 2008).

By the 1990s this renewed classical liberalism gained the popular epithet 'neo-liberalism', although it did still represent a constellation of movements with subtly different ideas. It is difficult, at the present moment, to estimate the real long-term global significance of this neo-liberal ideology. After its passionate promotion by conservatives during the 1980s and 1990s, it entered the mainstream of public policy on a global scale, infecting, in its course, the ideas of both social democratic and socialist ideological traditions, as well as dominating in such international institutions such as the World Bank and IMF.[7] In many ways neo-liberalism seems now to conform to the classic Gramscian account of hegemonic common sense, for many contemporary states. That is to say, the ideology has not only become intrinsic to the vernaculars of international economics and public policy, but has also permeated into the everyday vocabulary of domestic politics in many developed states. In Britain, for example, it has been allowed to run riot into areas such as health, education, public transport, public energy utilities and social services, to name but a few areas. Not many see it as a particular historically contingent ideology; rather, it is seen as the common sense or inevitable truth of policy-making – the hallmark of a flourishing ideology.[8]

From the late 1880s, liberalism did change direction for a significant period of time, certainly up to the late 1970s.[9] There is an immense amount of scholarly debate on this issue, particularly in Britain (see Freeden 1978; Vincent 1990b; Simhony and Weinstein eds 2001). Some wished to deny that the new liberalism really was liberal. Formally, the new liberalism was committed to a 'social individualism': the good of the individual was seen as tied to the good of the whole community. The atomism of the formal classical view came to be regarded as morally and sociologically naïve. The social consequences of industrialization had to be dealt with at a much broader level and should not be left to individual charity. Poverty, unemployment and illness were not just the concern of the single individual, but were communal or social issues, and dealing with them transcended individual capacities. Further, liberty was not just leaving people alone, but was actually identified with the fuller life of genuine citizenship. Citizens should possess the economic, cultural, political and social means to partake of worthwhile lives. Such ideas were taken up in the twentieth century by most European reformist socialist parties. This new liberalism is often identified with the writings of figures such as T. H. Green, L. T. Hobhouse and J. A. Hobson from the 1880s up to the 1920s. In fact it also tends, in different ways, to characterize the general social democratic trends of Britain and other West European states from the 1930s to the mid-1970s. It is important, though, to realize that there are wide variations within this new social democratic liberalism which have only comparatively recently begun to be explored by scholars (see Freeden 1986 and 2005).

There remains a complex and unresolved debate on the relation between the classical and new liberalism. One view is that classical liberalism was the pristine doctrine which was betrayed by the quasi-socialist new liberalism. There are other interpretations on the theme of decline and betrayal. J. H. Hallowell saw the demise of integral liberalism through its loss of moral content. Religious respect for the individual soul had collapsed into moral relativism (Hallowell 1946, 20). The most popular line among historians up to the 1970s was that liberalism had two faces – the individualist and the collectivist. The new collectivist liberals adapted liberalism to the needs of a new age and thus seismic shifts took place in the ideology. In the last two decades this idea has been subject to critical scrutiny (see Vincent 1990a, 143–4; Freeden 1996, 178ff). It has also been argued that there was really no division at all between the classical and new liberalism. They were all part of a broad-church doctrine and that we should acknowledge more the close relations between the two variants (Bernstein 1986; Biagini and Reid 1991).

Classical liberalism was not simply reconciled to the new liberalism. Such terminology obscures a profound and subtle movement at work within liberal thought. Formal ideas were given substance in differing historical contexts. They were worked and reworked. There were no seismic shifts but a fluid development of interpretations around certain ideas. Many of these formal ideas were explored by other political movements. The major point to keep in mind is that much of this change in the character of liberalism was internal to the ideology. It was not externally imposed. Many of the ideas that were associated with classical liberalism were flexible enough to be used by the new liberals. One conclusion from this is that liberals in government progressively found themselves enacting measures which they felt increasingly uneasy about at a level of fundamental principle. As we will see in the following sections, there were often reasons both to oppose and to support the legislation.

Although a distinction has been drawn between classical and new liberalism, this should not be taken as hard and fast, for two important reasons. First, the schools of liberalism are not wholly distinct. The arguments of classical liberalism seem to evolve at certain points into the new liberalism. There are thus no sudden transitions. The second, related point is that liberal thinkers do not fit together neatly into the same school. The intellectual and moral preoccupations of classical liberals quite often differ markedly. We ignore such differences at our cost. In fact, at times such thinkers seem to fit into different ideologies. David Hume, Alexis de Tocqueville, Edmund Burke and Friedrich Hayek can thus be classified both as liberals and as conservatives. L. T. Hobhouse, J. A. Hobson, John Dewey and John Rawls have been classified both as social liberals and as socialists. There should be nothing intrinsically disturbing in this assessment.

Individualism

It is difficult to generalize on the liberal view of human nature, partly because the accounts are so diverse and complex. There is, however, one concept which figures consistently in liberal discussion, which can act as an important leitmotif. This is the concept of individualism. Liberals have been, and are, *formally* committed to individualism. It is the ontological core of liberal thought and the basis of moral, political, economic and cultural existence. The individual is seen as both more real than, and prior to, society. This priority has been differently interpreted: it could be natural or moral.[10] Values are also tied to the individual. The individual is the touchstone of morality and truth. Individualism therefore tends, as such, towards a form of egalitarianism. Each person is seen to be of equal value.

Yet these ideas of equality and individualism do not tell us a great deal about the more substantive views of liberals. The briefest acquaintance with liberal literature will throw up distinctions between types of individualism. The American liberal philosopher John Dewey was not alone, in his book *Individualism: Old and New*, in distinguishing between the 'abstract individual' of early nineteenth-century liberalism, and a more communal understanding of the individual found in social liberalism (Dewey 1931). This distinction is used differently by Hayek in his essay 'Individualism: True and False', where he distinguishes a rationalistic individualism – in writers such as Wilhelm von Humboldt and J. S. Mill – from a true individualism, which is more in line with the traditions and conventions of a spontaneous market society (see Hayek 1978). Purely rational individualism, for Hayek, is unworkable. Such distinctions are fairly commonplace in most works on liberalism over the last thirty years. Similar ideas reappeared in the context of the liberal-communitarian debates of the late 1980s and early 1990s (see Mulhall and Swift 1996).

In the classical liberal format, the 'individual' is usually understood as a single, self-enclosed being 'shut up in his own subjectivity'.[11] The limits of the body are the limits of the individual. The individual owns his or her own body, in terms of a natural right. This notion is often linked with the 'possessive individualist' theory, in the sense that a person is the 'proprietor' of his or her own body and its capacities and owes nothing to society. The goods which that person produces are seen as extensions of the proprietorial rights to the body.

The desires and interests of the individual are seen to be sovereign. Reason is instrumental to the achievement of one's desires. Each person is driven from within by desires and passions and is, by definition, the best judge of his or her own interests. In this sense, institutions should avoid judging for individuals. There could not be any collective or institutional responsibility, since only individuals can be responsible for themselves. The only good is individual good.

There are, however, a number of possible variations on the above theme. The purest and most consistent form of individualism is 'unconstrained individualism'. There is no morality or doctrine which can constrain the individual. Nobody can dictate to it, since it, logically, *is* the source of all value. This implies total individuality and autonomy. There is absolutely no possibility here of formulating any theory of public goods. The ultimate fruition of such a doctrine can be found in individualistic anarchy, of which the best European example is Max Stirner, whose theories will be examined in chapter 5.

Such an argument cannot uphold property rights or even a market economy. Yet it must be stressed that it *is* the logical direction of individualist argument. Most liberals stop short well before these conclusions, but there are some who draw close to them, teetering on the brink of anarchism. Some recent libertarian thought, although linking itself with liberalism, is better discussed under the umbrella of anarchy. This is partially recognized in the popular denotation 'anarcho-capitalism' or 'minarchism' in the writings of figures such as Murray Rothbard (who will be discussed in chapter 5). In Britain, at the turn of the twentieth century, some of the more extreme disciples of Herbert Spencer, such as Auberon Herbert and Wordsworth Donisthorpe, also came very close to anarchism through their radical individualism.

Auberon Herbert, in the words of a contemporary, 'out-Herberts Mr Herbert Spencer' (Ritchie 1902, 57, n. 1). Herbert even criticized the deeply individualist and Spencerite Liberty and Property Defence League, which he claimed was 'a little more warmly attached to the fair sister Property than … to the fair sister Liberty' (Herbert 1978, 14). He became obsessed with the liberty of the individual, advocating a voluntary state and voluntary taxation, redolent of anarcho-capitalists. He also found Spencer's later views distinctly conservative, yearning for the idealism of his mentor's early work, *Social Statics* (1851). In America Ayn Rand argued for more total liberty for the individual from an entirely different philosophical standpoint. A rational life for Rand was the pursuit of pure egoism by each individual. The philosophical premises of this doctrine lie in Rand's odd use of Aristotelian and Thomist thought. As one writer noted, 'Man's purpose [for Rand] lies in his own self-realization and it would be a perversion of that purpose for him to sacrifice himself for others, least of all for some fictitious entity called "society"' (Barry 1986, 106). Rand enshrined this idea in a doctrine entitled 'the virtue of selfishness'.[12] The individual's own life and survival are the sole criteria of value. Egoism is thus the only basis to ethics.

A rational life is purely self-interested. Altruism is moral cannibalism. Capitalism is the only type of arrangement which maximizes the possibility of such a life. Thus Rand contends that liberals 'must fight for capitalism, not as a "practical" issue, not as an economic issue, but, with the most righteous pride, as a *moral* issue' (quoted in Tame in Turner ed. 1979, 17).

Despite appearances neither Auberon Herbert nor Ayn Rand was prepared to accept the full logic of this individualistic argument. Herbert was enough of a Lockian and Spencerian to believe in the constraint of natural rights, and thus argued for the necessity of mutual respect and consent, something of which a pure individualist such as Stirner was duly contemptuous. Rand, critical of anarchism, also believed in an objective, rational order and saw the necessity of some form of minimal state (which has parallels with the arguments of Robert Nozick).

In Herbert Spencer and the Liberty and Property Defence League we find a type of 'constrained individualism', although it is worth recalling that its members were regarded by many liberal contemporaries as extremists. Spencer's main political concern was that, in the past, liberalism habitually stood for individual freedom versus state coercion. His famous book, *The Man versus the State* (1884), was meant to recall liberals to their true origins and away from Gladstone's empirical socialism and the sins of the legislators. For Spencer, individuals owned themselves by way of natural rights. Each had an equal right to equal freedom. Natural rights originated in a biological process of mutual limitation and contractualism which was necessary for social aggregation. The important point to note about Spencer is that his argument for individuality is rooted in an ambitious naturalistic evolutionary metaphysics. It was designed to free the individual from coercion. Only an industrial society which maximized such individuality could be genuinely liberal.

In Germany, the much earlier liberalism of Humboldt is worth comparing briefly with that of Spencer. Like Spencer, Humboldt detested the idea of the state's interference with individuality. Spencer would have had little trouble agreeing with Humboldt's comment that 'the State is to abstain from all solicitude for the positive welfare of the citizens, and not to proceed a step further than is necessary for their mutual security and protection against foreign enemies' (Humboldt 1969, 37). However, Humboldt's definition of individualism is markedly different from Spencer's. Humboldt wanted freedom for the maximum aesthetic development of the individual (*Bildung*), an idea explored extensively in German literature in the *Bildungsroman* tradition. Each person develops his or her own sensibilities. This is essentially an organic process. For Humboldt, 'the richer a man's feelings become in ideas, and his ideas in feelings, the more transcendent his nobility' (Humboldt 1969, 18). The individual grows, develops and becomes more cultured through diverse experiences. Freedom is the possibility for this *Bildung*. The ultimate aim 'is the highest and most harmonious development ... to a complete and consistent whole', an idea which J. S. Mill was to employ in *On Liberty* (1859) (Humboldt 1969, 16).[13] State coercion stifles such aesthetic development.

The idea of society being based on mutual individual limitation and contract, which can be found in Spencer, struck a not dissimilar note with another nineteenth-century classical liberal, Henry Sidgwick, in his *Elements of Politics* (1897).

For Sidgwick, contract is of fundamental importance to the individualistic system. The contract is essential to unite the individual atoms of society. However, the comparison with Spencer ends here, for Sidgwick was at pains to distance his moderate utilitarian individualism from Spencer's 'extreme individualism'. Whereas Spencer had been obdurate in his opposition to the Poor Law and public provision of education, Sidgwick saw a *via media* between Spencer's extremism and the empirical socialism of Gladstone's 1880s liberal administration. The minimum of personal security, enforcement of contracts and rights to private property are not total guarantees of individual well-being. There is a form of individualistic interference which aims 'to secure [the individual] from pain and loss' (Sidgwick 1897, 58). The care of children, the prescription of weights and measures, precautionary legislation on sanitary matters, housing and medical training, are matters best supervised by the state. They are also clearly compatible with individualism. Sidgwick maintained that individuals do not in fact always know their own best interest, and that they should not be allowed to suffer from their ignorance or profit by the debilitation of others.

Despite being critical of the 1880s Liberal administration, which was, in his view, paternalist in the worst sense of the term, Sidgwick was far closer to this type of social liberalism than was Spencer. Spencer held that suffering, pain and squalor are equivalent to the biological warning system of the body. Adversity is the efficient school for the transgressor. The artificial support of a backward individual lowers the whole evolutionary genus. As Spencer put it: 'Fostering the good-for-nothings at the expense of the good-for-somethings is an extreme cruelty' (quoted in Wiltshire 1978, 154; also Taylor 1992). Most of the measures mentioned by Sidgwick are explicitly repudiated by Spencer as totally incompatible with true liberal individualism.

Spencer's opposition to Sidgwick's utilitarian individualism was an extension of his general opposition to Benthamism as a philosophy of expediency. Despite A. V. Dicey's judgement on Benthamism as 'nothing else than systematized individualism' totally congruent with *laissez-faire*, Spencer maintained that such a philosophy was wide open to authoritarian abuse (see Dicey 1905, xxx). The 'greatest happiness' principle, as deployed by Bentham and later by J. S. Mill, could never be the basis for sound liberal legislation. Spencer was not alone in this judgement. Despite the reputation of figures such as Bentham and J. S. Mill as founding figures of liberalism, some liberals, such as Spencer and more recently Robert Nozick, have doubted their credentials.[14] Nozick has argued that one of the fundamental errors of utilitarianism is that in trying to aggregate utility it destroys the separateness and value of individuals.

Hayek has comparable objections. He doubts the rationalist premise built into utilitarianism, namely, that anyone *could* calculate the general happiness of society. He argues that reason is a limited practical tool which guides individuals to the satisfaction of their interests. No one can stand above their interests (Hayek 1960, 38, 57 and 61).[15] Utilitarians commit the philosophical mistake of not identifying the limits to reason and, whereas J. S. Mill wanted to free the individual from conventions, Hayek believed that social and moral traditions constitute individuality.

Hayek's argument on the social constitution of the individual forms a convenient bridge to the conception of individuality employed by the new liberals, although he uses it in a very different way. One of the principal motifs of the new liberal grasp of individuality was that it could be reconciled with community, an idea taken up again by liberal communitarians in the 1980s. In the case of the idealist liberals, the argument was quite directly metaphysical. Individuality was seen as the product of an ethical state. The individual who determined his or her actions within rational social parameters was essentially the rational citizen of an ethical state.

T. H. Green argued, on idealist grounds, that society was a means for individual self-realization and character development. Politics exists to draw forth the potentialities of the individual. The possibility for such development depends upon the existence of social institutions. Each individual is a spiritual possibility which can be realized through society. For Green, human good cannot be simply a succession of pleasures. Rather the true good is found in practices which provide an enduring contribution to the common good of one's fellow citizens. It is this common good which provides satisfaction for a more permanent understanding of the human self.[16] The permanent self is thus at one with the common good. Civic institutions are the outward form or expression of moral ideals. The only justification for civic institutions is the contribution they make towards the moral development of individuals. The communal good cannot therefore be divorced from the individual. Individuals only have rights and duties as members of the civic community – a community which should enable individuals to develop.

A similar doctrine can be found in the new liberal L. T. Hobhouse. As Hobhouse argued in his seminal work, *Liberalism*, liberalism was founded on the self-directing individual, yet 'in realizing his capacities of feeling, of living, of mental and physical energy … in Green's phrase, he finds his own good in the common good' (see Hobhouse 1911, 128, also Allett 1981, 204). Communal life provides the setting and enabling conditions whereby humans can develop. A society is free 'where all minds have that fullness of scope, which can only be obtained if certain fundamental conditions of their mutual intercourse are maintained by organized effort' (Hobhouse 1918, 60; also Collini 1979, 10, 97).

Such an idea did not represent a reversal of any commitment to individualism. It rather argued that individuality develops in a community and that part of individuality is a recognition of common goals. Liberals, in this argument, have been interested primarily in civic individualism. As Michael Freeden comments: 'New Liberals … interpreted the assumption of communal responsibility for defined areas of human activity as itself conducive to the development and perfection of individuals' (Freeden 1986, 108). Individuality, especially for the idealist liberals, and J. S. Mill to some degree, was a process of development towards a fuller life. Our personal development involves interdependence. We cannot divorce our own good from the good of others.

Many of the more traditional popular nineteenth-century views on individualism, associated with figures such as Samuel Smiles or Harriet Martineau, which concentrated on character, self-help and self-reliance, were subtly transformed in new liberal arguments. Self-reliance and self-help became moulded into self-realization. It became easier in this context for social reformers to speak of material obstacles to self-realization (and thus obstacles to self-help and character formation). Increasingly,

British public policy measures of the 1890s and 1900s, such as National Insurance and old-age pensions, were justified as providing a firmer basis to self-help. Some even described National Insurance as the nationalization of thrift.

One point to note here is that individualism and human nature remain ambiguous in liberalism. There is certainly no clear, unequivocal distinction between 'individualism' and 'collectivism'. These terms conceal more than they reveal. Further, there are different forms and perceptions of individualism justified from differing and occasionally incommensurable philosophical standpoints. Finally, the various views on individualism hover between complete antipathy to, and clear acceptance of the necessity for, state intervention.

The Value of Liberty

Liberty is a crucial value for liberals. We should, however, take note of Michael Freeden's comment: 'To observe that a belief in liberty is a core element in liberal thought is a truism. To hold that liberals were ideologically united through a belief in liberty is an error. Like other concepts, liberty covers a wide range of positions' (Freeden 1986, 266). The conventional distinction made within the concept is between negative and positive liberty.[17] In addition, it is often argued that positive liberty is not really part of liberalism. Hayek, for example, sees the decline of British liberalism from the 1870s as 'closely connected with a reinterpretation of freedom' (Hayek 1978, 134; see also Hayek 1944). The present account rejects such an assessment.

If the classical liberal literature is scanned it is not hard to find a commitment to the negative idea. Writers such as Benjamin Constant, Alexis de Tocqueville, Humboldt, Spencer, Sidgwick and, more recently, Isaiah Berlin, Hayek, Milton Friedman and Robert Nozick adhere to such a definition. The individual is free when left uncoerced or unrestrained. Much state intervention, conventionally, is seen to undermine individual initiative and offend against basic liberty.

The important question here is the meaning of restraint. It is obviously profoundly significant for establishing whether or not liberty has been violated. There are fairly precise conditions for the identification of restraint. First, restraints are usually regarded as physical in character – prisons and pointed guns. Second, they are external to the individual: a restraint is something that X imposes on Y. Finally, restraint involves deliberate intentional action. One cannot, in this reading, unintentionally restrain someone. Hayek in fact prefers the word 'coercion' to the more slippery term 'restraint', unless it is evident that there is a 'restraining agent' (Hayek 1960, 16–17). It is not clear here why coercion or restraint *has* to be intentional, other than that it is stipulated that this must be the case.

Hayek is also insistent that we should not confuse liberty with some inner sense of feeling free. Furthermore, inability and lack of capacity or of power are not restraints. An ability or power might provide possibilities for the use of liberty, but they are not synonymous with liberty. Liberty should not therefore be confused with the conditions under which it is exercised. This argument implies that disease, illness, old age, physical disability, poverty, unemployment and lack of opportunities are nothing to do with liberty since they are not intentional restraints.

Such a notion of liberty is often connected with property. From John Locke onwards, the issue of property has been intimately linked with liberty. John Gray, following Hayek, commented that 'private property is the embodiment of individual liberty' (Gray 1986b, 62).[18] Property becomes an extension of bodily rights. Many of the arguments used by liberals on freedom can often be traced to claims about 'freedom from' coercion or restraint by the state in bodily and property rights. The state usually figures high in such coercion stakes. In the case of the constitutional tradition, this is understandable, since most constitutional writing developed in the context of highly arbitrary absolutist rule. This fear of arbitrary state action was as true for classical liberals, such as Benjamin Constant in France in the early 1800s, as for classical liberals in the twentieth century who have opposed state socialism (see Constant 1988).

The justifications for negative liberty are, though, broader than simply the defence of property. Most of its proponents would also tend to claim that it is necessary for both genius and creativity. Negative liberty does not propound any single monolithic moral structure for individuals. In fact, it is supposed to rest on recognition, tolerance and respect for diversity. Individualism thus implies a diversity of goods. It is usually contended that positive liberty does the precise opposite of this.

Liberal arguments on restraint are not so straightforward in practice. The main initial constitutionalist concern of Whigs, struggling with an absolutist legacy in government, was to uphold civil freedoms of speech, worship, and the like. The point was to try to extend constitutional guarantees. In some Whigs and radicals the onus of restraint switched to political freedoms from the 1790s. Interest moved towards the extension of the franchise. However, as early as the 1750s the Whig Josiah Tucker was also calling for a 'Glorious Revolution' in the economic sphere (see Eccleshall 1986, 21). The demand for economic freedom centred in the 1840s on the ark of free trade and the repeal of the Corn Laws. In a sense, such economic freedom was seen by liberals such as Bright and Cobden as an extension of political freedom. Economic freedom was freedom from another of the political privileges of the aristocratic land-owning class who were artificially inflating the price of basic foodstuffs through their monopolistic control. The demand for such freedom reached a peak in the Anti-Corn Law League (see Howe and Morgan eds 2006).

By the 1870s many liberals had become more and more concerned by the restraint on individuals involved in an industrial culture. The concern focused increasingly on social freedoms. Social freedom often involved (like political and civil freedom) an extension of state regulation. As one of Spencer's contemporaries argued, people needed the state guarantee of enough education to be able to understand Spencer's argument about the need for the exclusion of state involvement from education (Ritchie 1902, 11–12).

What can be observed in the above is the shifting ground of restraint. From Adam Smith onwards, there have been stipulations on the necessity for different forms of legal restraint. Classical liberals, though suspicious of the range of state action, certainly did not envisage doing without it. The same point holds true for many more recent liberals. Even the minimalist classical liberal Robert Nozick envisages a 'state equivalent' – the Dominant Protection Agency – emerging naturally and spontaneously to provide protective services.[19]

Thus there seem to be implicit distinctions, within liberal thought, between justifiable and unjustifiable restraint. There are three points to note here. First, there is little consistency between those practices which liberals see as restraints; second, there is little indication of the reach of the argument on justifiable restraint; and, third, how does one define justifiable restraint without actually indicating what is worthwhile in certain types of action?

It is clear that the concept of negative liberty as such does not provide any guidance on state activity. C. B. Macpherson, for example, used a redefined negative liberty argument to support a socialist-orientated transformation of social and economic relations in Western industrialized societies.[20] This can hardly inspire confidence in the classical liberal mind. In addition, no classical liberals accept the principle that restraint *qua* restraint is an evil. State action *qua* state action is not necessarily a restraint (see Taylor 1985). Much state action can be perfectly innocuous. In fact, restraint is a movable feast in liberal thought. The extension of its application, as argued earlier, continued unabated through to the new liberal theories in the early 1900s. The character of some restraints has required more state activity than others. Certain restraints are justifiable partly because they help to remove unjustifiable restraints. This is specifically the case where unemployment, poverty, illness and old age have been viewed in the latter category. Here we see a fluid movement into the new liberalism.

The second point concerns the degree to which the argument on restraint can be extended. Some liberals, such as Hayek or Berlin, would tend to argue that the notion of restraint cannot encompass items such as poverty or unemployment. There are only 'positive external restraints' which involve intentional restraining agents. Thus no one intends that poverty or unemployment should exist. This is the only sense in which Hayek will accept the equivalent use of 'restraint' and 'coercion'. Yet, are there overriding reasons why the concept of restraint or coercion should be limited in this way? Severe migraines, debilitating illness, ignorance, lack of skills, poverty and unemployment are restraints upon individuals which could be said to coerce them into patterns of activity. To claim exclusivity solely for 'positive external restraint' is both conceptually unwarranted and historically and semantically odd. It also appears that many classical liberals did not adhere to such a limited idea.

Liberals extended the restraint argument well into the twentieth century, although they have also added to it. This is where we touch upon the more positive conception of liberty. How does one ascertain what a justifiable restraint is, without indicating what is worthwhile in certain actions? Unless one takes an extreme view, arguing that all restraint *qua* restraint is evil, which is recognized by the majority of liberals as plainly absurd, one is committed to a formal distinction between unjustifiable and justifiable restraint. In so doing, one is qualitatively discriminating between actions and, therefore, moving beyond the immediate remit of negative liberty. Liberty thus comes to be identified with certain types of worthwhile action. This is the domain of a more positive understanding of liberty.

T. H. Green argued in the 1880s that freedom cannot be understood as the absence of restraint or compulsion. He contended that 'we do not mean merely freedom to do as we like. We do not mean freedom that can be enjoyed by one man … at the cost of a loss of freedom to others.' Freedom, he continues, is 'a positive power of doing or enjoying, and that, too, something that we do or enjoy in common with others' (Green 1888, 370–1; see also Dimova-Cookson 2003 and Wempe 2004). The important points to note here are that progress in society is measured by the advance of such freedom, which Green believed was perfectly in accord with the development of liberalism, and that civil society is the precondition to the exercise of such freedom – which cannot be premised on others' unfreedom. Freedom coincides with the common good. In this way the freedom of the individual is reconciled with society. Freedom is the maximum power of *all* members of society to make the best of themselves. Thus Green contended that it was justifiable, on grounds of freedom, to interfere in the sale and consumption of alcohol, housing, public health provisions, employment, land ownership and education. Such action, although coercive, none the less removed unjustifiable coercion and so provided conditions for the genuine exercise of freedom. Law could thus contribute to the lives of the overworked, underfed, ill-housed and undereducated.

These themes on positive freedom are echoed in many new liberal writings. As Herbert Samuel remarked: 'There could be no true liberty if a man was confined and oppressed by poverty, by excessive hours of labour, by insecurity of livelihood. … To be truly free he must be liberated from these things also. In many cases, it was only the power of law that could effect this. More law might often mean more liberty' (Samuel 1945, 25; see also Samuel 1902).[21] Similar points are put by new liberal figures such as Hobhouse, Winston Churchill and H. H. Asquith (see Vincent and Plant 1984, 73–6). It is this understanding of social freedom which lies behind the Liberal administrations of 1906–14 and their welfare legislation. It is also this line of thought which has carried on into many aspects of the social democratic tradition to the present day. It has also developed in recent years into international debates concerning poverty and human rights.[22]

Justice and Equality

The most significant renditions of justice to appear in liberal literature in the nineteenth and twentieth centuries were procedural and distributive (or social justice) notions. Classical liberalism focused largely on the procedural and social liberalism on the distributive conceptions.[23] Justice for classical liberalism involves the maintenance of a general body of formal rules and procedures. It provides the over-arching structure, the rule of law within which individuals are protected in the pursuit of their interests. Law does not exist to interfere in particular human activities and choices. It is rather concerned with the conditions in which individuals express their preferences. Justice is not concerned with the outcomes of preferences. Poverty, economic inequality andr unemployment are therefore not in themselves issues of justice. Hayek called this particular notion 'commutative justice' and he contended that it was the essence of what classical liberals had always meant by justice (Hayek 1960, 440, n. 10).[24] Justice is concerned with facilitating the maximum freedom and spontaneity of individuals to pursue their own personal interests or goods. It is therefore concerned with maintaining procedural rules to provide the conditions for individual freedom. It is not concerned with fair outcomes.

This led to direct antagonism between procedural and distributive theories. Injustice for classical liberals is focused on intentional acts of restraint, interference or coercion. The outcomes of a market order are neither just nor unjust, since they are not the result of intentional actions (Hayek 1982, 65). Alternatively, distributive justice attempts to ameliorate social suffering and distress. In response, classically liberal theorists such as Hayek argued that there are no recognizable principles for welfare distribution in society. Even if such central principles could be found, they would not be put into practice in a society 'whose productivity rests on individuals being free to use their knowledge and abilities for their own purposes' (Hayek 1978, 140). Distribution implies a plan, and planners who will attempt to impose their principles upon others. Such processes inevitably create injustices by their very arbitrariness. This was the major theme of Hayek's *The Road to Serfdom* (1944). It was also a key theme in Herbert Spencer's notion of the decline from industrial society into a militant society. In this argument distributive justice tends to shunt societies, under the mirage of social justice, towards militancy or totalitarianism. Conversely, a genuinely just society should allow individuals maximum freedom to pursue their own interests without interference. If individuals were to receive benefits or burdens on the basis of need, then this would also undermine the efficiency of the market order. Hayek does, though, acknowledge some role for the state to alleviate extreme hardship.

It is not surprising in the above context that some classical liberal writers interpreted the impetus behind distributive justice as envy (Hayek 1960, 93). Those who do not succeed as entrepreneurs find other ways to undermine the successful, namely, by extracting their property through taxation. For Spencer, one of the major problems that distributive justice tries to address is suffering and pain caused by inequality of resources; yet this very suffering is equivalent to the biological warning system of the body. The unfit, idle and feckless should be weeded out. To save such individuals by redistributing resources to them is a misplaced paternalism. It is also a reversal of the whole evolutionary process.

The above arguments tie in closely with those used in the sphere of equality. Classical liberalism promoted a formal understanding of equality. Inequality arose as a natural fact, or an outcome of impersonal processes. Equality before the law in terms of civil rights was essential. Economic equality meant equal access to the market. Everyone should have equal freedom to follow his or her interests, provided this does not infringe an equal right of others to do so. False egalitarianism, from this position, tries to achieve better distribution of wealth via state action. This again is Spencer's feared 'militant society'. Spencer argued in 1903 that his aim was 'not the equality of man, but the equality of their claims to make the best of themselves' (cited in Greenleaf 1983, 81). The pursuit of substantive economic and social equality inevitably undermines the market process and destroys freedom. Freedom is thus always at loggerheads with equality. Substantive equality leads to coercion and bullying by the state (see Acton 1971, 71).

Despite the fulminations of many classical liberals against the notions of distributive justice and substantive equality, it is clear that these latter ideas have had an honoured place in the liberal tradition, going back to early liberal-minded radicals such as Tom Paine.[25] If it is acknowledged that each person has an equal right to equal freedom, and freedom is understood as the *power* to do something worth doing, then the liberal argument inevitably begins to shift focus. To guarantee equal freedom is then likely to entail some substantive redistributive actions by the state.

New liberals, in the early twentieth century, were therefore quite clear that gross disparities of wealth were unjust and needed to be remedied by a limited form of redistribution. They did not aim to undermine the free-market system, but they felt that its effects could be moderated. As T. H. Green argued: 'Left to itself, or to the operation of casual benevolence, a degraded population perpetuates and increases itself' (Green 1888, 376). The new liberalism recognized the need for redistribution for the sake of genuine freedom, equality and justice. In the early part of the twentieth century century, new liberal ideas on the minimum wage, health and unemployment insurance, school meals, old-age pensions, and so on, were the direct result of such lines of thought. This was not a move towards socialism, but rather an extension of arguments about equal rights to equal freedoms. These particular ideas were pursued with great theoretical sophistication, from the 1970s, in the social liberal writings of John Rawls.[26]

The basic idea in Rawls's social liberal theory of justice is startlingly simple, namely, to identify a fair arrangement in society for all parties to agree to without knowing how it will affect them. The idea is to remove the possibility of arbitrariness in decisions about justice. Justice, for Rawls, should not reflect arbitrary chance or interests, but rather should aim to nullify them for the sake of fairness (Rawls 1971, 101–2). The device by which this nullification is achieved in *A Theory of Justice* (1971) is the 'original position'. This allows individuals to choose principles of justice for society behind a 'veil of ignorance' – a form of rational disinterestedness equivalent, in function, to the old idea of the social contract and state of nature.[27] Rawls had a strong belief in underlying rules or norms of rationality which could be teased out.[28]

The procedure to reveal these underlying rules must be impartial and neutral, namely an agreed procedure. The basic question underlying this agreed procedure is what principles of justice would rational individuals choose in a situation of agreed equality? A veil of ignorance allows this 'teasing out' process to take place. This 'veil' device conceals particular abilities and powers from choosers, but allows general information, provided by the social scientific disciplines.

In this original position the individual is assumed to be a self-interested rational chooser, with a definite plan of life, who will try to minimize losses and maximize benefits in any choice situation. Benevolence and altruism are ruled out. Further, each individual is assumed to desire certain primary goods, that is, social primary goods such as self-respect, rights, liberties, opportunities, powers, income, and natural primary goods such as health and intelligence. Parties would try, as far as possible, to maximize their primary goods as part of a rational plan. These 'thin' goods are assumed to be desired by everyone and are distinct from any 'thick' substantial goods, which every person has, but which are more or less incommensurable in a pluralistic society. Rawls suggests that agreement can, however, be attained, even in a pluralistic setting, on a thin conception of goods. The goods that all individuals require can be derived from a model which, despite being premised on self-interest, none the less, is supposed to model ideal moral choice. This initial position thus attempts to account for our basic deep underlying sense of justice.

Rawls suggests that there would be certain constraints on our choices in this original situation (see Rawls 1971, 122–6 and 131–6). Any principles chosen would have to be general (embodying no particular interests), universal in application (thus holding for all moral persons), and public (that is, known by all and embodying no private administrative rules). They must also have a standard of ordering for conflicting claims between individuals. They must also be the final court of appeal in any practical reasoning. The precise choice procedure that Rawls adopts is the 'maximin principle' or maximum minimorum, namely, 'we rank alternatives by their worst possible outcomes: we adopt the alternative the worst outcome of which is superior to the worst outcomes of the others' (Rawls 1971, 152–3). Individuals in Rawls's view would naturally tend to be risk averse.

Rawls suggests that a general sense of justice derives from the maximin principle, namely, that liberty, income and wealth and the bases of self-respect would be distributed equally unless an unequal distribution of any or all of these goods is to the advantage of the least favoured. This general notion can be broken down into two basic principles. The first affirms an equal right to equal basic liberties for all; the second, commonly referred to as the difference principle, affirms that social and economic inequalities will be to the greatest benefit of the least advantaged and attached to offices and positions open to all under conditions of fair equality of opportunity. Both principles of justice apparently match our intuitive sense of what justice is. There is also a lexical ordering of these principles (Rawls 1971, 243). The first principle is rationally and intuitively prior. Liberty can only be restricted for the sake of liberty. Liberal distribution, in this context, for Rawls, would be neutral with regard to the good. Individuals would contract to a society and principles of distributive justice via their own reason and judgement. The actual basic goods to be distributed would also be agreed by all.

Overall, Rawls presents the most sophisticated argument for a social liberal account of distributive justice during the late twentieth century. Oddly, though, it is worth noting, in passing, that it was constructed at a time when neo-liberalism had already begun to dominate public policy ideological discourse, ultimately, by the 2000s, on a global scale. Despite the fact that Rawls's (and similar philosophical thinkers') ideas have been received with enormous enthusiasm by a broad swathe of the academic community, as well as by some social democratic politicians and activists, their impact has been negligible in comparison to the runaway success of neo-liberal thinking, at both the theoretical and more everyday policy levels. This particular point should draw our attention to the harsh limits on a purely philosophical understanding of political ideas. Theoretical academic sophistication and philosophical acumen do not necessary provide any significant insights into the pervasive logic of either politics or ideology.

Rights and Democracy

The place of natural rights in liberal thought is often traced back to thinkers such as John Locke or Tom Paine. Behind the original natural rights ideas was the panoply of natural law ideas and an optimistic deism which saw the world as ruled by laws of God implanted in our reasoning. Such rights were seen to be asocial, universal, inalienable claims premised on human nature. The possession of and respect for such rights was the precondition to human flourishing.

In the hands of John Locke and, more specifically, the American colonists and French revolutionaries, natural rights became a radical and disturbing doctrine. It represented a standing protest to established government. It was a tendency which quickly moved from demands for life, property, free speech, political self-determination and religious freedom into claims for minorities, racial groups, women and the poor. Many radicals, such as Paine, wanted these rights to be codified in constitutional documents. It should be noted, though, that not all these rights were commensurate. The right to freedom and the right to property were at odds in North America, where slaves were initially seen as part of the natural right to property.

The pursuit of substantive equality derived from natural rights eventually mutated into the early socialist movements of the nineteenth century. The other dimension of natural rights arguments metamorphosed, and occasionally calcified, into a dogmatic defence of existing property rights, as Marx noted in his early essay 'On the Jewish Question' (see Marx 1972). In other words, natural rights became simply a defence of an existing economic order. D. G. Ritchie commented on this process as providing 'another illustration of the way in which the conservative of one generation may take up the ideas of a past generation of Radicals' (Ritchie 1903, 16).

The notion of natural rights, specifically the concentration on natural rights to property, was subtly transformed by the end of the nineteenth century by certain liberals. T. H. Green, for example, argued that the idea of the asocial 'state of nature' is false. Humans are social creatures by nature. There are no 'natural' rights antecedent to society. Rights always imply normative recognition within society. Thus, natural rights are seen by Green as shorthand for those rights which contribute to both the individual good of the person and the common good of society. For Green, they are the negative conditions for the realization of individual capacities and powers.

Such arguments are particularly pertinent to the question of property rights. As most classical liberals affirmed, property is the precondition to the development of the person. To interfere with property is a gross infringement of rights and liberties. However, this argument has another side. If property is an important precondition to human development, then surely a liberal society is duty-bound to guarantee everyone access to some property. A Spencerian or a Hayekian, on the other hand, would tend to say negatively that only equality of access or opportunity must be guaranteed. No one must stop the individual participating in the market, but the outcome, whether failure or success, is solely the concern of the individual. The reverse of this argument (which has been conventionally part of the social liberal stance) contends that a more substantive equality of property must be guaranteed. In other words, belief in the importance of property for individual development implies the wider redistribution of wealth and the diffusion of property to all citizens. Individuality is premised upon property.

The more negative classical liberal proponents might still claim that the above argument will entail intervention in others' property rights, which are supposed to be sacrosanct. Some new liberals had ways round this. First, natural rights are not asocial claims but claims congruent with the common good. They imply normative social recognition. If some people have massive property holdings giving them power over others, who consequently cannot realize their potential, such property is then not a genuine right, since rights are dependent on the common good and on social recognition. Genuine liberty cannot be gained by the loss of liberty to others. Second, if property is a precondition to liberty, then all members of society ought to recognize a duty, via the common good, to provide the means for liberty to their fellow citizens. Finally, property was sometimes distinguished between property for use, or that which was genuinely earned, and property for power, quite often derived from unearned income and profit. It was the former which was seen to be the fundamental right, not the latter. This argument located an area of wealth which could be used for redistribution. The unearned increment of property values was in fact the main target for pre-1914 new liberal proposals on progressive taxation.

Admittedly, not all classical liberals have been at home with natural rights doctrine. In the nineteenth century the Benthamites were the clearest earliest example of a rejection of this doctrine. For them, rights were institutional arrangements for the protection of interests, premised ultimately on the science of utility. There were no pre-institutional or pre-social natural rights; such rights Bentham described as 'nonsense upon stilts'. In the late twentieth century, liberals such as Hayek adopted a more Kantian legalistic and procedural stance on rights. As John Gray commented, in Hayek 'we specify the content of the Liberal rights by reflecting on the demands of justice ... rather than by pondering the scope of Lockian rights in an imaginary state of nature' (Gray 1986b, 77). This kind of argument is usually premised on a distinction between the 'right' and the 'good'. The function of rights is to provide a fair procedural framework within which individuals can pursue their *own* good. Such a notion of rights does not propound any particular conception of the good. However, the more Kantian 'right-based' approach came in for criticism in 1980s discussions by communitarian critics such as Michael Sandel (see Sandel 1982).[29] There is almost a return here to the themes of the idealist social liberals, such as T. H. Green, who insisted that we must take the communal dimension seriously and consider the common purposes and ends of social existence in discussing any conception of rights (see Sandel ed. 1984, 5–6).[30]

One other significant issue here concerns the relation of liberalism to democracy. It might be assumed that liberalism has some kind of deep tie to democracy. Such an idea is misleading. First, classical liberalism is conventionally distinguished from liberal democracy. A form of democracy – representative democracy – became identified as one of the constitutional devices of liberalism from the nineteenth century. After the excesses of participatory democracy in the 1789 revolution, liberals, particularly in France, had little trust in democracy. In Britain, Whiggery also had very little interest in democracy. Whigs were still deeply elitist about political rule, despite their occasional forays into consent and popular sovereignty. Such dislike of the extension of the franchise was in fact characteristic of liberal writers into the twentieth century.

There was, though, an aspect of the liberal tradition which demanded an extension of the franchise as the basic right of property-owning citizens. Benthamites saw the franchise extension as a useful device for attaining maximum happiness by restraining and balancing the various interests of society so that neither sinister aristocratic interests nor the unruly mob could dominate. Such a conception of democracy was not educative or character-building but protective of basic property interests.

J. S. Mill was probably the most optimistic theorist on democracy, believing that it could have a beneficial effect on the moral development of citizens. This more developmental view of democracy can be found in some of the new liberals such as Green, Hobhouse and Dewey. However, in the twentieth century the scepticism about the role and need for democracy within classical liberalism continued. The problem with democracy, for some liberals, is that it does not always produce liberal policies. Jefferson and Madison had noted this problem in the eighteenth century, arguing in favour of the need for 'auxiliary precautions' against democracy. Hayek also saw democracy and liberty as having different goals which may or may not coincide. Limited protective democracy may protect liberty. But there are dangers. Hayek, reflecting on the German electorate in 1933, remarked: 'Perhaps the fact that we have seen millions voting themselves into complete dependence on a tyrant has made our generation understand that to choose one's government is not necessarily to secure freedom.' (Hayek 1960, 14). In recent years, since the 1990s, some social liberals in particular have developed a much more sophisticated reading of democracy. The most favoured of these ideas has focused on the theme of deliberative democracy, which sees reasoned deliberation as a key way to organize the public exercise of power within a liberal polity.[31]

The Economy

All liberals are aware of the value of the free-market economy. There are, however, very different views on its nature. It is doubtful that its origins were perceived in terms of either its efficiency or its value in promoting freedom. As Albert Hirschman has argued, from the Renaissance onwards there has been a view of humans as creatures dominated by their passions. The question arises as to how one deals with these passions. Various ideas had been canvassed – namely, the suppression of the passions; the use of countervailing passions, where the love of pleasure is restrained by the love of gain; and, finally, the harnessing of the passions in some innocent or socially innocuous activity. Hirschman shows how the term 'passion' became subtly transformed into the term 'interests'. These interests finally became economic interests, moving slowly from the council chambers of state to the economy. Interest 'bestowed on money-making – a *positive* and *curative* connotation' (Hirschman 1977, 42). Money-making was increasingly viewed through the lens of both interest and innocence. Traders were regarded as peaceful and inoffensive. Many believed that the spirit of conquest would be replaced by the spirit of commerce. All, including Adam Smith, were at this stage generally optimistic as to the effects of unhindered commerce on human civilization.

Although Adam Smith was keen on the development of commercial values, he was also concerned about their effects on martial virtues and civil order. The value of the free economy was its capacity for harnessing wayward passions. In addition, many liberals, from Tom Paine onwards, have seen participation in the market and property ownership as giving rise to responsible civic virtues. The promotion of liberty and efficiency is not therefore necessarily the prime effect of the market. In fact, there are many reasons why free-market economies might be valued. They teach self-reliance and self-discipline. They produce peace and order. Some theorists value the market order in itself; others the valuable consequences it produces. The most extreme example of the former is the praxeology of Ludwig von Mises, which argues that markets are good a priori, regardless of their consequences. Not many liberals follow this particular line.

One of the slightly uncomfortable factors behind the idea of the natural harmony of the free economy is that there is often an unspecified or unarticulated metaphysics underpinning the discussion. In writers such as Smith, the 'invisible hand' is encapsulated within a thinned-down but optimistic deism. God was really controlling the apparently random events of the market. However, apart from Hayek's attempt at specifying this metaphysics, in his notion of a spontaneous catallactic order, this factor remains inert and unargued in most modern liberalism.

Certain liberals contend that there was a golden age of the liberal economy. Even certain critics tend to agree (see Arblaster 1984). Sometimes it is called an age of *laissez-faire*. Some maintain that no coherent philosophy of state intervention was developed until the second half of the nineteenth century. The prevailing principle was non-intervention or *laissez-faire* (see Greenleaf 1983, 25). It is important to remember that *laissez-faire* was never an exclusively liberal idea. After its inception, it was quickly appropriated by the conservatives and has been used periodically by them since the mid-nineteenth century. For liberals during the nineteenth century, it was seen as a useful device to employ, initially, against privilege and monopoly. Its most active use was by the Manchester school of economists, whose supporters perceived the aristocratic landed monopoly which controlled basic foodstuffs as one of the greatest of evils. This was more of an anti-feudal rhetoric. John Bright, like his admirer T. H. Green, traced many of the ills of Britain to the Norman land-owning families.

Although there are figures such as Herbert Spencer who appear to be closely identified with the doctrine of *laissez-faire*, it is most clearly seen in Britain in organizations such as the Liberty and Property Defence League, which was in fact peopled by many conservatives, like its president, Lord Wemyss. Even extreme individualist critics of the League, such as Auberon Herbert, started their political lives in the

Conservative Party. While *laissez-faire* figured in many popular liberal discussions from 1830 onwards, by the 1880s it was largely dropping out of the mainstream of liberal thought and has never really re-entered since. In fact, some writers have doubted whether it actually existed during the middle years of the nineteenth century (Gray 1986a, 27–8).

Certain proponents of classical liberalism, in their desire to compartmentalize their own version of liberalism, argue that other liberals, such as the Benthamites, progressively gave up their commitment to the free economy and became obsessed with state intervention. In fact, this is misleading. If one examines the arguments of liberals over the nineteenth and twentieth centuries, one finds a continual and slowly developing commitment to the role of the state.[32] The new liberalism is an extension of this general thesis, a recognition that every citizen has the equal right to enjoy basic economic, political and cultural resources. This process entails some intervention and control of economic life. As J. A. Hobson argued: 'Liberals … never committed themselves to the theory or policy of this narrow *laissez-faire* individualism.' (Hobson 1909, 92–3). Enlargement of the sphere of the state, for new liberals, usually entails an increase in individual liberty.

It should be noted that none of the new liberals wanted to abandon the market economy. Many pre-1914 new liberals wanted to moralize capitalism. In the case of liberal economists such as John Maynard Keynes in the 1930s the emphasis was different, shifting to more technical economic argument concerning the state supervision of the market system in order to increase its effectiveness in reducing unemployment and poverty and thus to release the full productive capacities of capitalism. This had become a major theme of new liberalism in the 1920s, culminating in 1928 with *Britain's Industrial Future*. Known as the Yellow Book, from its cover, this was an extensive programme of state-led action involving public works, diffusion of ownership, extension of progressive taxation and encouragement of saving. In sum, it was suggesting a form of planned or managed capitalism. Keynes himself did not seem unduly aware of the problem of poverty, except as an underused economic resource. Comprehensive social policies on poverty were developed by W. H. Beveridge in his 1942 *Report on Social Insurance and Allied Services*, which laid the foundations for the social security system in Britain. It is clear that most of the major policy changes in economic and social spheres in Britain during the twentieth century, certainly until the 1970s, were developed by new or social liberals. This social policy development is not necessarily at odds with classical liberalism. There was a gradual extension and mutation of ideas over the nineteenth and twentieth centuries, which gave rise to increasing state involvement in economic and social policy.

Politics and the State

The liberal notion of the state arose from the much older intellectual tradition of constitutionalism. Liberalism has focused on constitutional themes since its inception. Of course, many early constitutional writers had no perception of many of the themes that we might now associate with liberalism, yet liberalism fed upon, and eventually virtually identified itself with, the constitutional tradition. The principal concern of this constitutional tradition, as in liberalism, was to limit the scope of the state, to make it accountable and responsible for its actions and to ensure that it was committed to certain values.

It has been contended that liberalism is committed to a minimal state, one limited to the tasks of internal order and external defence and distinguishing between the private and public realms. Although some classical liberals are periodically thrown into paroxysms of anxiety over how to limit the state, they are hamstrung by the fact that liberal constitutionalism is a theory of the state and concerned with the public good. If there are limitations, they are constructed within a state. The *sine qua non* of the limitations is the state itself. The boundary that is supposed to exist between public and private is a continually shifting one. The liberal state is formally committed to respect the realm of the private, and yet, as we have seen in previous sections, there is no hard-and-fast rule to distinguish the private from the public. Manifestly, in times of war, liberal states do, as a matter of course, change the boundaries.

As in the section on the economy, we find a slow and growing commitment by liberals over the nineteenth and twentieth centuries to the positive role of the state. The arguments of liberals have varied, once again, between those who hover close to anarchy, disliking the state or seeing it as an unfortunate necessity, and those who see a positive and active role for it in promoting genuine individuality and civic virtue.

In the minimalist case of figures such as Auberon Herbert, a totally voluntary state was advocated. Late twentieth-century liberals, such as Robert Nozick, were concerned to argue for a more definite, compulsory minimal state, limited by the side-constraints of natural rights. Yet Nozick was criticized by some Hayekian liberals for being too minimalist in scope (see Gray 1986a). Herbert Spencer saw the state as an unfortunate but necessary 'committee of management'. Spencer had an extensive list of 'do nots' for the state. He viewed the statute-book of Britain as an unmitigated disaster: legislation piled on more legislation to cure the defects of previous legislation. Such state growth interfered with social evolution towards the industrial society by cultivating dependence in the population and undermining individual self-reliance. The state, for Spencer, should therefore have no concern with aiding the poor, factory legislation, public health, drainage, sewerage and vaccination. Spencer, unlike Humboldt, Adam Smith and Malthus, also disapproved of any form of state involvement in education on the same grounds. He objected to state-organized postal networks and lighthouses, and, oddly, he took exception to the British Nursing Association and National Society for the Prevention of Cruelty to Children as overly 'collective' groups undermining individualism. On the other hand, Spencer did suggest the state control of libel laws and the regulation of pollution, noise and smoke. He toyed with a scheme for land nationalization by the state, land ownership being regarded as an aggression against individual rights. Later in life he also conceded the need for state involvement in the upkeep of roads, pavements and sewerage. All this greatly disappointed some of his disciples.

A similar ambivalence towards the state can be seen in the utilitarian liberals. Bentham, Mill and Sidgwick, despite overt commitment to a limited state, allowed it to perform progressively more tasks, going well beyond Spencer's proposals.

The science of utility allowed utilitarians to assess the value of legislative activity. There were no intrinsic grounds to oppose state activity *per se*. None of the Continental liberals, such as Constant, rivalled Spencer's minimalism. Constant and Tocqueville were looking more for limitations through balance and separation of powers within the state structure. Their major fear was the growth of popular dictatorship and the consequent decline of individual freedom. More recent classical liberals, such as Hayek, are not in favour of any ultra-minimalist or even minimalist state in the Nozickian sense, although they are clearly at odds with the utilitarian tradition from Bentham onwards.

The more positive view of the state is therefore neither the result of a sudden transition nor a fundamental revision of liberal thought. It is the result of a slow movement within liberal ideas. It would be true to say that this movement was somewhat accelerated by prominent thinkers such as Green. The idealist notion of the state envisages it as having a positive ethical role in society. The state is not just an abstract institution, but an outgrowth of the wills and aspirations of the citizens comprising it. It is an organic entity designed for the realization of the common purposes of humanity, which are coincidental with true individuality and freedom. Institutions in the state represent objectified ethical purposes. The meaning and significance of the state are dependent on the improvement of its members, thus it is still in an important sense individualist and committed to individual liberty. Such liberty, though, requires the state to provide the necessary conditions for all citizens to develop.

These ideas, plus more radical uses of utilitarian and evolutionary thought, lay firmly behind the advent of the new liberalism in Britain. For thinkers such as Hobson and Hobhouse, and in America, Dewey and Rawls, the state was increasingly viewed as an integral part of the economic and social life of the community. It was not just concerned with freeing individuals from obstacles to their economic activity, but was actively involved in the promotion of a better life for its citizens. Liberals, up to the present day, have never been completely content with the state. The two major world wars of the twentieth century and the penetration of the state into many spheres have genuinely unsettled them. This unease was true of new liberals in Britain during and after the First World War, who felt deeply unhappy about issues such as military conscription. However, discontent with the state has never stopped liberals from using it to promote freedom, utilizing distributive justice, establishing a legal framework for economic relations, promoting a mixed economy and providing certain public goods. The state in this sense can be an enabling institution for the good life for all citizens.

Conclusion

The main criticisms that may be encountered by the student of liberal thought will now be reviewed. Some of these are more generally directed at the whole liberal mentality; others are aimed at specific forms of liberal ideology. For the sake of convenience such criticisms will be divided into three main topics: the critique of the individualist mentality; the critique of the reality and illusion of liberal ideology; finally, some ideas on the direction and culmination of liberal thought in the twenty-first century.

The critique of the individualist mentality encompasses a large body of arguments which can only be briefly mentioned here. First, it is contended that liberals find it immensely difficult to formulate any clear and realistic concept of social life. They have been accused of a sociological naïvety by both socialist and conservative critics. If liberalism conceives of the fundamental units of experience as being isolated atoms, how can any collective notions be formed?

If one tried to formulate any genuine theory of individual consent, would it not be impossibly impractical, since it would assume that every act by a government would have to have the consent of every individual? In practice, liberals never argue this and thus are regarded as inconsistent with the general direction of their arguments. It is clear that many liberals have been quite prepared to accept that individuals should be coerced, which again seems utterly inconsistent with an individualist premise. In the same vein, some critics would contend that liberals try surreptitiously to smuggle in a moral or social consensus by the back door. Hayek, after long disquisitions on the importance of individual responsibility and the inconsistency of collective responsibility, refuses to face up to the logic of his own argument and tries to hold society together by subliminal moral conventions which all individuals are supposed to accept without thinking. This can look like sleight of hand. In one sense, the best liberal, who judges the world according to purely individual self-interest, would be the free-rider, regardless of the cost to others. Free-riding would be the most rational path, as long as others were publicly responsible.

If it is difficult to aggregate individual interests, it is virtually impossible to formulate any satisfactory theory of public goods or to reconcile the individual with public authority. Individualism implies, so critics argue, that all goods are purely private. How can one aggregate these? Individual preferences simply cannot be aggregated to provide public provisions, which in the end usually have to be imposed. Overall, it appears that liberals, though valuing individuals, are not really prepared to take on board the full logic of individualism. Individualism in its most radical sense implies solipsism and relativism in all matters of morality and truth. There appears to be no way to distinguish between the individual's true and false interests. In fact, the very idea of real interests appears faulty from a purely individualist perspective. This is one reason why so many complex moral issues are generated by liberal thought. Thus, can we condemn abortion, euthanasia or surrogate motherhood? Have we any right to censor pornography? It is the importance and value of individuals and their liberty which lie behind such questions of public and social policy.

The fundamental weakness in this line of criticism is that it applies to only a limited number of liberals. There is a social individualism (or in fact a liberal communitarianism) which can be found in many liberal writers, from the nineteenth century to the present day, which already acknowledges certain societal values in the social constitution of the individual. In fact many social liberals developed highly sophisticated theories of public goods and social theories of justice. In consequence, the criticism tends to miss the mark in terms of the liberal tradition as a whole.

The second body of criticism focuses on the reality and illusion of liberal ideology. This criticism can be encapsulated in a number of contradictions. Liberals, it is argued, celebrate the freedom of those who cannot use it, proclaim equal citizenship for all and make it innocuous for a majority. Liberalism is far more interested, in this sense, in civil rights than in hungry people. Many liberals would contend that it is preferable to be starving in a liberal society than well-fed and unfree in an authoritarian or totalitarian society. How well-fed liberals can know this has often struck critics as puzzling. Liberals speak in glowing terms of the importance of property, but effectively, through their economic institutions and markets, deny it to millions. In fact liberals, especially over the nineteenth century, were noted for their harsh attitudes to poverty. One only has to recall the words and actions of the Liberal administrations during the great Irish famines, or the attitudes of figures such as Malthus to the labouring poor, for confirmation of this thesis. Liberalism proclaims the common human values of civilization and then praises selfish individualism – a position most neatly summed up in Ayn Rand's doctrine of the virtue of selfishness. Liberalism is interested in legal equality for all, but not in equality of property or power. It sees no conflict between property ownership and equality of opportunity. Liberals, in the eyes of certain critics, have had far too favourable a press. One must therefore consider the reality behind the illusion.

What use is freedom or equal legal citizenship to an individual who is starving and ill? Liberalism does not see that unequal ownership of property can lead to unequal powers, which can then distort the interrelation of human beings. In classical and neo-liberal thinking, poverty, for example, is seen frequently to be the fault of the individual. The poor must therefore be made to be responsible. Property ownership is said to be fundamental, but the capitalist system recognizes that many will not partake in it. To interfere with someone's property is then seen to be a gross infringement of rights. So the sick, homeless individual dying in a street is free and no injustices have been perpetrated, whereas a multi-millionaire subject to progressive taxation is the victim of severe injustice. Thus Robert Nozick described the taxation of the wealthy as a form of forced labour. Many have found such conclusions of neo-liberal thinking either deeply strange or unpalatable.

A number of these criticisms strike at certain classical and neo-liberal perspectives. Yet, as we have seen in this chapter, different notions of freedom, citizenship, rights and property have been promulgated within liberalism. The fact that social liberals often focused on freedom as, for example, 'leading a worthwhile life' or 'developing as an active citizen', as opposed to being simply 'left alone' or 'not interfered with', should alert us to the point that freedom remained a deeply contested concept, even within the liberal fold.

The final set of criticisms focuses on the destiny of liberalism as a political doctrine. In a sense it is a criticism with a more positive note appended. The contention is that the particular freedoms and rights that have been sought by liberals have been experienced only by limited groups in society. As Ruggiero commented: 'Beneath the veil of a universal liberalism, the bourgeoisie disguised a privilege similar to that once flaunted by the aristocracy; and thus the proletariat's efforts to overthrow the new privilege, though anti-liberal in appearance, were in reality to bring into existence a wider liberalism' (Ruggiero 1927, 48). Until the twentieth century, the broad working masses and women were frequently excluded from the benefits of liberal civilization, in terms of equal political, cultural, economic and social rights. The character of liberalism has changed, though, due to its extension to these groups. This change took place initially with working-class groups and then, in the twentieth century, extended to women. Thus, as Ruggiero argued, the growing cooperation of liberal and labour groups from the 1890s 'is not an accident or an expression of political opportunism, but is deeply rooted in the necessities of the new democracy' (Ruggiero 1927, 157). This process has continued in various forms of social and liberal democracy to the present day (see Vincent 1998a and Freeden 2005).[33]

There is a further twist to this argument. From the 1930s, a number of Marxist-inspired critics of liberalism argued that liberalism was unable to cope with this natural extension of its logic, because to do so would have had tremendous repercussions on capitalism, profit maximization and property ownership. Liberalism had not realized that 'the political democracy it brought into being was established on the unstated assumption that it would leave untouched the private ownership of the means of production' (Laski 1936, 243). It was so obsessed with political forms that it failed adequately to take into account the economic foundations they expressed. The only way out for liberals was to seek some means to stop the whole process. They found this, so it is argued, in fascism. Fascism protected capital accumulation and oppressed the rising proletariat. Thus fascism 'emerges as the institutional technique of capitalism in its phase of contradiction' (Laski 1936, 248). This argument, of course, envisages liberalism as a declining creed tied indissolubly to a particular mode of production. The end of capitalism means the end of liberalism. One major weakness of this argument is that it does not explain why, in the 1920s, fascism occurred in a country with, at the time, a very weak liberal tradition (Germany), and, compared with Britain, one with a very undeveloped capitalist industrial base (Italy).

Liberalism has in fact stayed on the political scene particularly in Anglo-European European thought, although two world wars did alter the liberal demeanour. Much of the optimistic perfectibilism of the nineteenth- and early-twentieth-century liberals was dashed on the fields of the Somme, Ypres, and by the later knowledge of Dachau and Buchenwald. It became difficult to feel optimistic about the human species in these contexts. This led, in some liberals, to a loss of hope and a more pessimistic stance. In the 1930s, for those not caught up with the appeal of fascism or Marxism, the siren call of scepticism, individual self-cultivation and self-examination was heeded by many, although one must not forget the vigorous thinking conducted in the 1920s and 1930s in the progressive wing of the British Liberal Party, specifically in the 'Liberal Summer Schools' movement, in which most major liberals of the time participated (see Freeden 1986, ch. 4).

In the post-1945 era, liberalism has reappeared in a number of political guises. In the 1950s it was typified in the Cold War 'end of ideology' group, discussed in chapter 1, which had a considerable impact in both America and Europe. Liberalism stood, paradoxically, against the ideological mind. The ideological mind always seemed to be either partially or totally totalitarian. Liberalism, at this time, appealed to a consensual politics, which it mistook for non-ideological politics. Politics was only seen to take place, for some, in the liberal domain. Outside of this anti-totalitarian demeanour another strand of liberal thought developed, which repudi-ated the 'end of ideology' mentality. This was probably best expressed in the writings of Hayek or Friedman. It was an attempt to return Western societies to the pristine clarity of a utopian vision of classical liberalism. This was probably the most sig-nificant component of what has subsequently been called the neo-liberal mentality, which came to the fore in the 1980s, and still dominates – in various formats – public discourse in many states (in fact in certain global institutions as well) to the present day (see Harvey 2005; Turner 2008). However, it is important to put this into perspective. There is nothing pure in such classical liberal or neo-liberal ideology. The Hayekian, Friedmanite and neo-liberal schemes are as narrow a vision of liber-alism as the 'end of ideology' mentality.[34]

A third manifestation of liberalism concerns the continuance of diverse streams of social liberal and social democratic thought.[35] The electoral decline of liberalism, in Britain and other countries, did not mean the demise of liberal influence – far from it. Most of the reformist and revisionist socialist parties in Europe (and certainly the British Labour Party) simply took on the ideological mantle of this social liberalism. In fact, liberal thinking (in more general terms) was manifest in many political move-ments. For example, substantive political and economic debates in Britain, to the present day, have largely been between variants of classical and social liberal ideology, rather than between conservatism and socialism.

One final complex manifestation of liberalism concerns the efflorescence of Anglo-American liberal political philosophy from the 1970s, which again represents diverse impulses within liberal ideology. This can be seen initially in the work of figures such as John Rawls, Robert Nozick, Ronald Dworkin, David Gauthier, Brian Barry, Michael Walzer, amongst many others. Nozick and Gauthier appealed to the more classical liberal and libertarian factions, whereas Rawls became virtually the patron saint of the social liberal faction. It is not only social liberals such as Keynes and Beveridge who influenced, for example, British Labour Party thought and policy. In the 1980s, at the same moment that Hayek was being cited approvingly by liberal conservatives, Rawls was also being regularly alluded to by the social liberal factions within British Labour and Fabian circles. In the case of Rawls, Nozick and Hayek the conception of the liberal tradition remained somewhat selective, thus impover-ishing our understanding of it.

In more recent years, since the late 1990s, this form of philosophical liberalism has fragmented even further. On one count there has been a continuance of the more comprehensive and universalizing strand of philosophical liberalism, in the tradition of J. S. Mill. This can be seen in the writings of Ronald Dworkin and in a more per-fectibilist format in the work of Joseph Raz. This conception of liberalism is still committed to a rational foundational good for all liberals. Such theories also tend to be teleological. Institutions are thus just insofar as they promote this good. Alternatively the early Rawls and Brian Barry's work still maintained universal lib-eralism, but with only a thin non-perfectionist conception of the good.

However, the later writings of Rawls moved towards a different perspective focused on 'political liberalism'. This perspective tried to avoid the question of universal foundational truth in order to accommodate pluralism (Rawls 1993). The problem for political liberalism was reasonable pluralism. Citizens would disagree about metaphysical, religious and moral issues. However, such citizens could still draw upon the 'conditions of possibility' of interaction within liberal democratic cultures. These conditions provided a minimal thin structure of principles of practical reason, which supplied, in turn, a purely regulative political groundwork for cooperation, in effect an *overlapping consensus*. Rawls's vision of political liberalism was thus minimalist, constrained, protective and negative.[36] A more extreme version of this political liberalism can be found in the later writings of John Gray. This is a realist-inspired *modus vivendi* liberalism which tries to secure the conditions of a peaceful existence between radically different and incommensurable conceptions of the good (Gray 2000).

One danger implicit in this latter tradition of philosophical liberalism is its ahistorical synchronic character. When these latter liberals address issues of justice, rights and freedom, it is almost as if we are to assume that liberal thought *is* quite literally the sum of their particular conception of political philosophy. Thus we are supposed to see their studies simply as analytical, philosophical arguments which, in effect, sum up the whole liberal perspective on politics. This is a sad misconception. The major problem here is again a lack of critical and historical awareness that this is only *one* form of philosophical and liberal thought which has deep historical roots.

In summary, liberal values and ideas developed very slowly from the seventeenth century. The ideology itself crystallized in the early 1800s as a way of thinking and seeing ourselves and our relation to others in politics. It subsequently penetrated deeply into Anglo-European thought and clearly represents a profoundly attractive vision of politics. However, we should none the less be careful about viewing it as the complete truth about both the political world and humankind.

3
Conservatism

Like liberalism, conservatism is often seen to have both an ordinary and a more technical usage. The ordinary usage generally focuses on the idea of conserving or 'keeping something intact'. This idea has been dated to the fourteenth century. Late twentieth-century writers on conservatism, such as Russell Kirk and Robert Nisbet, have placed a heavy emphasis on this medieval origin. Kirk, for example, traced back the conservative perspective to 'conservators' (the guardians of medieval cities), an unwitting Chaucer and English justices of the peace – 'custodes paces' (Kirk ed. 1982, xii).

The more overt political use is usually dated, like liberalism, after the French Revolution. Most scholars admit that the actual political origin dates, more precisely, from the early 1800s in America, as an epithet implying a low or moderate estimate of a state of affairs. Some early American National Republicans styled themselves conservative in this sense. In France, the term was first coined in Chateaubriand's journal, *Le Conservateur*, in the 1820s. The periodical was designed to propagate ideas on clerical and political restoration. In Britain, the term first occurred in the *Quarterly Review* journal in 1830. By 1835 it became the more official designation for the Tory Party. Blake remarks that its gradual adoption from 1832 onwards 'was a deliberate attempt to purge the party of its old associations and symbolize, if not a break with the past, at least a change of course' (Blake 1985, 7). The term spread throughout Europe from the 1840s. The political upheavals of 1829–30 and 1848 focused the attention of conservative thought on the dangers of revolution, although industrialization and democratization also played a significant role.

There is a perennial debate on the relation between the more ordinary and the technical political uses. Many proponents of political conservatism see certain advantages in rooting their political sentiments in the ordinary use. There is some truth to the proposition that we are all a little conservative immediately after a good dinner. Some political conservatives have wanted to exploit this 'disposition' and have argued that we are all, in fact, conservative 'by nature'. Conservatism, it is concluded, is not only a political doctrine, but is also embedded in the stuff of life itself.

Such an idea makes humanity, *en masse*, conservative. The difficulty of such a notion is in explaining allegiances to other ideologies and articulating the beliefs to which all conservatives would supposedly adhere. It also bypasses the point that conservatism is historically a specific ideology, arising at the same time as liberalism and socialism, and indeed sharing some of their sentiments. Some commentators have therefore concluded that the ordinary use of conservatism provides very little insight into the technical political sense (O'Sullivan 1976, 9). In the urge to provide a coherent ideology, the simple notion of 'conserving' is thus seen to be both crude and unhelpful (Scruton 1980, 21).

Before moving on to the debates about the origins and nature of conservative ideology, a definitional problem should be considered. We should not assume that there is a definite body of core ideas to which all conservatives adhere. In fact, there are many conservatives who would deny the attribution of ideology to their beliefs. This has been called conservatism's 'political anti-philosophy' (Allison 1984, 2; Honderich 1991, ch. 2; Vincent 1994). In some cases this denial of theory is less convincing; in others it is rather better thought out.

There are five broad interpretations of the character of conservatism, which have very different implications. These can be schematized as follows: the aristocratic ideology; the pragmatic ideological position; the situational or positional view; conservatism as a disposition of habit or mind; and, finally, the ideological interpretation.

In the first view, conservatism is perceived as the negative doctrine of reaction expressed by a semi-feudal agrarian aristocratic class, specifically after the challenge of the French Revolution. Conservatism thus functioned in a highly specific historical and economic context. It represented the negative defensive posture of a declining aristocratic class in European societies. In this sense, the time span of conservatism can be roughly dated from 1790 to 1914. In Britain, 1832 (rather than 1914) was a crucial watershed, with the advent of growing democratization. The development of enfranchisement, industrialization and the success of the Anti-Corn Law League in the 1840s were mortal blows to the Tory Party. This view is recognized by commentators who draw a distinction between the older Toryism and the post-1832 ideas. Once the political and economic significance of this aristocratic class had faded, then the ideology also withered and was subtly but decisively superseded by classical liberal practice. Hence conservatism can be seen as a temporary historical phenomenon, representing the views of a class which was in serious political and economic decline.

The second argument is the least satisfactory. Conservatism is seen primarily as a form of political pragmatism – a doctrine with no principled content. It simply absorbs the prevailing political, cultural and economic ethos. Other political credos always make the running. Thus, it is contended, with a grain of truth, that in the last two hundred years conservatism has taken its policies from other political ideologies and defended them all at one time or another. If something works and is accepted, then it is legitimate material for conservative policy. Conservatism, as a number of scholars have noted, can be found espousing both statist and extreme libertarian sentiments. This argument does, though, over-play the negativism of conservative thought.

The above pragmatic view can sometimes be confused with the two further interpretations. The first of these – the situational or positional perspective – is in fact more in tune with ordinary discourse (see Huntingdon 1957).[1] It is revealed in commentators and journalists who, quite unwittingly, speak of conservative factions within, say, a socialist party. Conservatism, in this reading, is not tied to any particular class, historical events, pragmatism or even to a specific disposition. Like the pragmatic view, the situational perspective does not possess any definite substance. It has no ideal or utopia to strive for. On the contrary, it reflects the self-conscious defensive posture of any *institutionalized* political doctrine. Political schemes which are not institutionalized, transcend any present political realities and offer to change the world in line with the transcendent ideas are the natural enemies of conservatism. Conservatives are those rooted in an institutionalized way of life, offering an immanent defence of a particular order. The defence usually only arises in a 'situation' of challenge to institutions confronted with transcendent ideas. Conservatives thus stand for the existing order, whatever its political complexion, against the chaos of change and reform. In this situational reading it becomes possible to speak of a 'Conservative Left'. There is therefore no content to conservative ideology. Any institutional order (communism or liberalism) can be conservative.[2]

The fourth interpretation focuses on the idea of a disposition. There are two arguments here. The first is premised on the earlier claim that conservatism is part of the stuff of life itself. Hugh Cecil called this 'natural conservatism', which he defined as 'a tendency of the human mind. It is a disposition averse to change and it springs partly from a distrust of the unknown and a corresponding reliance on experience rather than on theoretic reasoning' (Cecil 1912, 9). The important point to note is that conservatism is not being viewed as an ideology; rather it is the natural disposition of human beings, preferring the tried habits or tools to the new and unfamiliar. This idea carries over very easily into politics. Imperfect established practices or institutions are preferred to the novel.

The second argument embodied in the dispositional claim is a more sophisticated philosophical defence of natural conservatism (see Oakeshott 1962; Greenleaf 1966; Gilmour 1977; Allison 1984; Kekes 1998). It focuses on subtle distinctions between types of reasoning (namely, theoretical and practical reason) and also inquires into the origin of human motivation. There is an ingenious if misleading argument at work here. The philosophical defence of the disposition thesis maintains, on the one hand, that conservatism is a non-ideational and natural phenomenon, and, on the other hand, tries to persuade us of the truth of this idea in an argument full of subtle ideational elements. This is what was referred to earlier as the 'political anti-philosophy', although 'philosophical anti-philosophy' might be a more appropriate term. The more sophisticated argument on the conservative disposition straddles the fourth ideological interpretation.

In the final category, conservatism is an unequivocal ideology which cannot be compromised by any pragmatic or situational considerations. It is not defined by its historical situation and is not necessarily identified with any class. It is also far more than a natural disposition. It is a body of ideas with a prescriptive content. Edmund Burke is often taken to be the founder of this ideology, which is seen to be profoundly relevant today. Conservatives, in this view, have consistently tried to oppose certain ideas, which have often been generated and used in revolutionary situations:

namely, the perfectibility of the human species through social and political conditions; the progress and development of human nature towards some ultimate good society; equality and liberty as individual human goals and the economic and political implications which follow from such ideas; the belief in the triumph of human reason in the world; and the neglect or disparagement of authority, privilege, hierarchy and tradition. Initially, in France and Germany, conservative criticism was directed at the Enlightenment and *Philosophes* tradition and its extreme offshoot – revolutionary Jacobinism. In Britain, the early radical liberal tradition (Paine and Price) also came in for sustained assault and, later, the utilitarians and liberal economists. Finally, in the nineteenth and twentieth centuries, the various manifestations of socialism have caused the greatest consternation in conservative ranks.

The non-ideological perception of conservatism will arise again in this discussion and its pervasiveness and influence cannot be neglected. It is also worth noting that this argument will be re-visited in the discussion of other ideologies. Conservatism is not alone in trying to make itself appear non-ideological. Having noted the definitional problems with conservatism, it is the latter ideological account which will occupy the rest of this chapter.

The Origins of Conservative Thought

Most writers on conservatism observe that the real watershed of conservative thought was the French Revolution. It was the events in France which spawned the famous reflections of Burke and, of course, it is not until the early 1800s that we find the first use of the word 'conservative' in the political sense. However, some scholars see important themes prior to 1789 which, though not self-consciously conservative, none the less contribute towards the conservative perspective. This might be said to be an 'unconscious conservatism'. There is something worryingly anachronistic in such claims.

The earliest inception of conservatism is thus seen in Greek and Roman thought. The writers most often cited here are Plato and the Roman Stoics, though the dramatist Aristophanes is also mentioned in the writings of Russell Kirk (Kirk ed. 1982, xii). A selection of Conservative writings published in 1976 begins with excerpts from Plato's *Republic* (see Schuettinger ed. 1976). Another writer comments that 'It is essential that a work on Conservatism begins with Plato's *Republic*' (Auerbach 1959, 5; also Austern 1984, 22). The next most favoured beginning is the Middle Ages, but it is difficult to feel confident about Morton Auerbach's description of the twelfth-century book *Policraticus* by John of Salisbury as a work of 'pure conservatism' (Auerbach 1959, 26). Nisbet, even more extravagantly, places the whole nineteenth- and twentieth-century conservative movement firmly under the banner of a recovered medievalism. For Nisbet, it is a mistake to see Burke as a Whig. Burke was really trying to revivify the local communities and guilds structures of a feudal society. Much has also been made of Burke's medieval natural law sentiments, but this is a different and more subtle argument (Nisbet 1986; also Stanlis 1958). Neo-medievalism is also seen more self-consciously in groups such as the mid-nineteenth-century

Disraelian 'Young England' Group. Paul Smith describes the group as a 'revivified and spiritualized feudalism', although it is worth noting that he later depicts them as a form of *opéra bouffe* (Smith 1967, 8 and 16). Other scholars have found the medievalist reading of both Burke and conservatism far-fetched (Pocock 1985, 210; O'Gorman ed. 1986, 9). There is indeed a strong element of anachronism and wishful thinking in these medievalist views.

Such anachronism continues into later periods. Whereas Keith Feiling (in Hearnshaw ed. 1949) and Hugh Cecil (1912) focus on the Reformation period as the main source of conservative ideology, writers such as Anthony Quinton (1978) and Robert Eccleshall (1977 and 1990) begin with Richard Hooker and the Elizabethan Settlement. For Eccleshall, Hooker is thus the grandfather of conservatism. He remarks that 'There is a line of development running through Hooker and Filmer to the formation of the Tory party in the latter part of the seventeenth century.' He parallels Hooker's attack on the Puritans with Burke's later attack on the Jacobins (Eccleshall 1977, 71). However, O'Gorman has commented that the Elizabethan Settlement lacks 'the historical perspective on social and political institutions proper to modern conservatism' (O'Gorman ed. 1986, 9).

Other scholars see the roots of conservative ideology in the doctrines of divine right and patriarchalism. For Gordon Schochet, for example, Robert Filmer's *Patriarcha* was the backbone of Tory thinking (Schochet 1975). The doctrines of divine right – that government is ordained by God, non-resistance and passive obedience are religious duties, society is natural to humans and resembles a family with an inbuilt natural hierarchy – are still, it is contended, implicit in nineteenth-century conservative thought. Opinions may have changed within conservatism about the source but not about the nature and sacred quality of national sovereignty. Sovereignty had simply moved from monarchy to Parliament (see Dickinson 1977, 18ff).

O'Gorman favours the 1660s Restoration period, when the term 'Tory' came into active political usage. As he states: 'It is more rewarding to note the emergence of a specifically "Tory" attitude to politics in the second half of the seventeenth century than it is to wrangle over spurious pedigrees' (O'Gorman ed. 1986, 9). Others appear to prefer the 1688 Settlement as the decisive moment. Halifax is often seen as the key conservative figure at this point – particularly his essay 'The Character of a Trimmer' (see Halifax 1969). There are hazards, though, in all these ideas. The doctrines of the Whigs and Tories after 1688 were closely allied. Neither group was a party in the modern sense. They had no formal rules, discipline or strict criteria of membership. They might better be described as shifting alliances of interests. Trying to identify a consistent conservative position in these periods is thus erroneous for some scholars (Kirk 1967, 4). Also, it is worth recalling that Burke was a Whig, not a Tory. He was an enthusiastic supporter of both the 1688 revolution and the American colonists in the 1770s. Unlike Tom Paine, he wanted to keep these revolutions distinct from that of 1789.[3]

One other eighteenth-century philosopher who is often mentioned by conservative writers as a founding figure is David Hume, although he is as frequently claimed for the liberal perspective. Opinions are divided on Hume. Some hail him as the great inspiration to conservative thought (Wolin 1954; Allison 1984; Muller 1997).

Another conservative writer, Ian Gilmour, has remarked of Hume: 'How could a man whose scepticism demolished God, the soul, miracles, causation, natural law, matter, and induction, be a good conservative?' (Gilmour 1977, 53).[4] Hume's deeply secular scepticism is not always to the taste of conservatives. Dr Johnson was not alone when, in conversation with Boswell, he described Hume as a 'Tory by chance' (Johnson and Boswell 1978, 342).

Most scholars agree that the self-conscious ideology of conservatism was worked out in response to the French Revolution. The period 1789–1914 is often taken as the heyday of conservative thought and practice (O'Sullivan 1976, 29–30).[5] The 1789 revolution gave rise to Burke's famous *Reflections* and also to the word 'conservatism' itself. European writers associated with conservatism, such as Samuel Taylor Coleridge, Joseph de Maistre, Louis Vicomte de Bonald, Felicité Robert de Lammenais, François Auguste René Chateaubriand, Novalis and Adam Müller, all clarified their ideas in relation to the revolutionary events, often taking Burke as their exemplar. Burke's position in conservative thought has remained pre-eminent to the present day for both admirers and critics. For Burke, the French Revolution was dynamically new. It was not of the same character as the revolutions of 1688 and 1776. Its central ideas proposed that humans were both equal and perfectible. Such improvement could be advanced by the cultivation of human reason and the reform of social and political institutions. For Burke, such ideas had profound implications for politics. It was these implications which he and subsequent conservatives resisted. Such resistance formed the real catalyst to the ideology of conservatism.[6]

The subsequent history of conservative ideology over the nineteenth century was characterized by a number of negative themes. Conservatives, specifically in Britain, tried to acclimatize themselves to the growth of democracy, but it was not a smooth passage (Honderich 1991, 12ff; Green 1995). Conservatives have often been unwilling to accord popular sovereignty or manhood suffrage much credence – a point also made by Tocqueville. They have, though, gradually found various strategies to cope with mass suffrage. They have usually kept the 'people' distinct from the 'rabble'. The people with property had some right to be represented, but not the ignorant rabble or mob. Stability and an interest in the common good of the community related to property ownership. Writers such as Matthew Arnold, Thomas Carlyle, Sir Henry Maine and W. H. Lecky, and particularly politicians such as Lord Salisbury, were still, though, bewailing the enfranchisement of the masses at the close of the nineteenth century. Even the property owners were subdivided by Burke, who argued for 'virtual representation', namely, 'the notion that even without the franchise, individuals could be "virtually" represented through others in their community' (Hampsher-Monk ed. 1987, 19; see also O'Gorman 1973, 55 and Dickinson 1977, 283). Burke reckoned on a property-owning franchise of roughly four hundred thousand citizens. British conservatives, however, adapted more pragmatically to democracy than (at least initially) many of their European counterparts.

Conservatives in the nineteenth century also had a very ambivalent reaction to industrialization and the rise of liberal political economy. There has been a strong anti-industrial, anti-individualistic strain in conservatism, from Justus Möser and Samuel Taylor Coleridge in the early nineteenth century, through William Cobbett and Benjamin Disraeli at mid-century, to Charles Maurras, T. S. Eliot and Christopher Dawson in the early twentieth century. Industrialization and individualism often meant the decline of community, tradition, order and religion. There is therefore a recognizably anti-capitalist streak in conservative thought (see Dawson 1931; Eliot 1939; Maurras in McLelland ed. 1971). None the less, the political success of the Conservative Party in Britain into the twentieth century was based upon its ability to adapt to and find a *modus vivendi* (at times an immensely enthusiastic one) with the industrial and indeed the democratic ethos (Smith 1967, 2; Blake 1985, 24–5; Hoover and Plant 1989, ch. 1).

The Nature of Conservatism

There are three broad approaches to the study of conservatism: the historical nation state, chronological and conceptual approaches. These are not mutually exclusive. They often overlap quite considerably in some studies. None of these approaches, except one dimension of the conceptual view, identifies any distinctive or necessary ideological conservative position.

The historical nation state idea argues that conservatism can only really be classified in terms of the particular historical and cultural circumstances of the nation state in which it occurs. In other words, it is German, British and French conservatism which are of most interest, not some over-arching theory. O'Sullivan toys with this stance, but combines it with a formal conceptual emphasis on imperfection. Thus French conservatism was attached initially to a more religious and moralistic vision of the world, appealing to eternal religious verities and order. German conservatism, by contrast, tended towards a more metaphysical and historical vision which emphasized a strong philosophical theory of history. Karl Mannheim concurs with this view, commenting that in German conservatism we have 'a philosophical deepening of the points Burke had posed, which are then combined with genuinely German elements. ... Germany achieved for the ideology of conservatism what France did for progressive Enlightenment – she worked it out most fully to its logical conclusions' (Mannheim 1986, 47; also Epstein 1966; Wood 2007). Finally, in Britain we see a sceptical and empiricist vision, which is intellectually messy, compromising and less coherent, but none the less in the end more politically successful (O'Sullivan 1976, 28, 82–3).

There is some value to this approach. In the USA many apparent conservatives have in fact been defending classical liberalism. For Louis Hartz, the Right in America is exemplified in the tradition of big propertied liberalism (Hartz 1955). Those in the USA in the 1930s who defended traditional classical liberal doctrine against the New Deal were branded conservative, whereas Roosevelt and Woodrow Wilson were considered liberal (see Noble 1978, 635).[7] In Germany also the particular problems of political unification in the nineteenth century, a vociferous nationalist movement emphasizing *völkisch* ideas, the dominant position of the authoritarian Prussian Junkers and the heavily metaphysical approach of their leading thinkers inevitably coloured the arguments on conservatism. By the late 1920s most nationalist and conservative thought had been influenced by the impact of national socialism (see Puhle 1978; Wood 2007; Beck 2008). Indigenous historical, cultural and political issues thus affect the character of conservatism in most states.

The second approach classifies conservatisms in chronological terms. The classification follows the fracture-lines and fortunes of Conservative Parties. In the British context, Peelite conservatism was superseded by Disraeli, Salisbury, and so on, until the 'middle way' of Macmillan in the 1950s and 'Thatcherism' in the 1980s. Each phase of conservatism is stamped by the dominant personalities and exigencies of the period. Such a chronology, however, despite being more easily grasped, can obscure the potential ideological coherence.

The final interpretation of conservatism focuses on conceptual classification. There are two general positions taken on the conceptual view. The first argues that there is one pure doctrine of conservatism. There are no conservatisms, even if there are different philosophical roots. It is therefore useless to try to classify types of conservatism (see Quinton 1978; Allison 1984, 7; Graham 1986; Scruton 2007). The second view sees differing schools of conservatism. There may be some formal unity on values and ideas, but the manner in which these core ideas are interpreted can lead to radically different conclusions. The problem with this latter view is that there are a bewildering variety of classifications in the literature. Sometimes, for example, conservatives are drawn distinct from traditionalists and reactionaries. Within conservatism itself we can find twofold classifications – collectivist and libertarian conservatives or substantive and procedural conservatives (see Greenleaf 1983, chs 7 and 8). There are threefold classifications – reactionary, status quo and reformist conservatives or liberal empiricist, liberal rationalist and anti-liberal intuitive conservatives (see Epstein 1966; Schuettinger ed. 1976). There are even more extensive classifications in the literature.[8]

There is obviously little consensus here. To make sense of the diversity of conservative thought it is necessary to consider a fivefold classification: traditionalist, romantic, paternalistic, liberal and New Right conservatives. The latter is the most recent area, dating from the 1980s. Yet none of these provides a totally airtight category. There is continual overlap and much of the time it is a matter of interpretative emphasis.

Traditionalist conservatism places greatest emphasis on the notions of custom, convention and tradition. This is the conservatism that we are most familiar with in the usual image of Burke. Theoretical reason is disparaged over and against prejudice and practical reason. The state is a communal enterprise with spiritual and organic qualities. The constitution of the community is not a human artefact but the cumulative, unpredictable result of years of practice. Change is something which, if it does happen, is not the result of intentional reasoned thought. It flows naturally out of the traditions of the community. Leadership, authority and hierarchy are again natural products. We obey as easily as we breathe. Our liberties and rights are rooted in our communal norms.

Romantic conservatism is characteristic specifically of many of the German theorists, such as Justus Möser, Adam Müller, the Schlegels, Novalis, as well as English conservatives such as Samuel Taylor Coleridge, William Wordsworth, Sir Walter

Scott, William Cobbett, Christopher Dawson and T. S. Eliot. In many of these writers we find a strong nostalgia for an idealized pastoral, rural, frequently quasi-feudal past, often combined with an elaborated utopian vision of what that restored society could look like. The general tenor of thought amongst the romantic conservatives was anti-industrial. They disliked the alienation and dehumanization of mechanistic industrial culture and were deeply critical of the view of humanity and the values expressed through the commercial mentality. Liberal political economy was seen to be fundamentally wrong about human nature. Romantic conservatives favoured a form of life which was simpler, religious and saturated with communal sentiments. There would be a natural hierarchy, as in traditionalist conservatism, which would incorporate chivalrous, heroic values, as in many of the characters of Scott's novels or Carlyle's imaginary heroes. This form of conservatism tends to be far less concerned to disparage the role of reason. The rationalism of the Jacobin revolutionaries was not attacked from the basis of either instinct or practical reason, but from the dizzy heights of speculative reason (or Reason with a capital R – *Vernunft*). This can be identified clearly in Coleridge's approach.

Paternalist conservatism is implicit in some aspects of the traditionalist and romantic perspectives. It interprets the duties of rule to imply fairly wide-ranging state activity to foster a good life for all citizens – a form of responsible aristocratic *noblesse oblige*. This principle has led many conservatives down the more *dirigiste* road.[9] Government is envisaged as a benevolent paternal figure setting goals and ensuring fair play and equal opportunity. Paternalist conservatism has been seen regularly over the last two centuries, from the work of Lord Shaftesbury in the 1830s, through Benjamin Disraeli, up to the 'middle-way' and more corporatist conservatism of Harold Macmillan and Edward Heath (see Harris 1972; Buck ed. 1975; Eccleshall 1990). It is also present in aspects of European Christian Democracy in Germany and Italy in the post-1945 era (see Pombeni in Freeden ed. 2001).

Combined with the elitist responsibility was a strong humanitarian element. In Britain this can initially be seen in the thinking of men such as Richard Oastler, Michael Thomas Sadler and Lord Shaftesbury, and their work on the Factory Acts. They engaged in a sustained critique of individualism, Benthamism and classical political economy. They disliked the New Poor Law (1834) and believed fervently in the role of the state in guaranteeing decent housing, working conditions, wages and treatment of the poor. Later in twentieth-century Britain this concern to uphold decent conditions for all took on the title 'one-nation' conservatism. It is debatable as to how effective it was, certainly in the nineteenth century.

One other motivation entered this paternalist strand from the 1830s. This was an electoral realism: a realism concerning the changing character of the electorate. It was signalled by Sir Robert Peel in his Tamworth Manifesto (1834) (see Buck ed. 1975, 56–8). The Manifesto was not a detailed body of ideas; in fact it was constructed hastily for an election. Yet most scholars agree that it reflected a change of mood, attempting to reconcile the older Tory Party with the new electorate of the 1832 Representation of the People Act. Strong government, law and order, the traditional constitution and existing property interests had to be linked with a new middle-class electorate. If the Conservative Party was to survive electorally, it had to adapt. This message came home to sections of the party, particularly after the repeal of the Corn Laws in 1846.

Disraeli consolidated the Peelite movement. The 'Young England' group, with which he was associated, was a more rhetorical version of this paternalism and realism concerning the new electorate. Their aim, which was espoused in Disraeli's novel *Sybil or the Two Nations* (1845), was the founding of a national Conservative Party, repudiating wealth-making for its own sake, liberal individualism and class divisions. Disraelian conservatism looked for both political representation and improved industrial and social conditions. This was to be linked with a renewed reverence for the Crown and the ancient constitution. In sum, its aim was 'one nation'. Disraeli's admiration for the older constitution was expressed in his early work *Vindication of the English Constitution* (1835), which paid homage to both Burke and Coleridge. The improvement of social and economic conditions was fairly superficial. However, the achievement of Disraeli's vision, apart from internal party reorganization, lay in the extension of the franchise movement in the 1867 Representation of the People Act.

The paternalist tradition has played a significant role in the Conservative Party for over a century. The emphasis on the responsibility of property, the extension of political rights, a preparedness to use the state for the welfare of the nation, were self-consciously upheld by figures such as Lord Randolph Churchill, Joseph Chamberlain, and by his son Neville in the 1920s. This approach also characterized the 'middle-way' conservatism of Harold Macmillan in the 1950s and some aspects of Edward Heath's premiership in the 1970s. One of its advocates in the British Conservative Party in the 1980s was Sir Ian Gilmour. In *Britain Can Work* (1983) Gilmour argued against the rise in unemployment, under the Thatcher administrations, on the grounds of its undermining the one-nation doctrine. Gilmour linked this perspective with a strong conservative tradition: the critique of the New Poor Law, the lenient attitude of Disraeli to the Chartists, the concern for factory legislation, were all seen to be part of a vigorous conservative position. In consequence, Gilmour expressed deep disquiet concerning the classical liberal views taken by many of his fellow party members in the 1980s and 1990s. Although a free economy was desirable, it should not become the dominant value for conservatism. For Gilmour, politics should always be prior to economics (Gilmour 1983; see also Macmillan 1966).

The maxim of liberal conservatism is the reverse of Gilmour's. Economics is prior to politics. There is an identifiable continuity of liberal-minded conservatism dating back to the nineteenth century. Some would include here thinkers such as Alexis de Tocqueville and indeed Friedrich Hayek. Yet it would still be a matter of debate as to whether this is a correct categorization. The liberal conservative tends to accept most of the formal tenets of classical liberalism: the emphasis on individualism, negative liberty, personal rights and a minimal rule-of-law state. But this conception of the state, sometimes combined in the nineteenth and early twentieth centuries with an understanding of imperial destiny, is usually more extreme than would normally be accepted by classical liberals. The post-1945 revival of liberal conservatism, in many European societies, has focused its attack on public-sector ownership and welfare state policies.

This latter form of liberal conservatism has been traced to Burke's *Thoughts and Details on Scarcity* (1800). Others see the late 1880s as a safer starting-point. In Britain in that decade, it is identifiable among the conservative membership of the Spencerian Liberty and Property Defence League. Organizations with membership connections to the Conservative Party, such as the Personal Rights Association, the Political Evolution Society (later the State Resistance Union), the British Constitution Association, the Anti-Socialist Union and the Industrial Freedom League also mani- fested the general temper of liberal conservatism. The campaigns of such groups were usually devoted to attacks on state growth. Wholesale deregulation and priva- tization were the desired ends (see Bristow 1975; Taylor 1992).

This particular tradition has been carried on by a number of societies in the post- war period and had a growing impact throughout Europe and America, specifically in the last two decades of the twentieth century. Probably the most famous of these intellectual groups is the Mont Pelerin Society. In Britain the torch has been carried by the Institute of Economic Affairs, Aims of Industry, the Adam Smith Institute, the Freedom Association and the Centre for Policy Studies. Over the late 1970s and early 1980s, many of the leading figures in the British Conservative Party were com- pletely absorbed by liberal conservatism, almost to the exclusion of other themes in the conservative tradition. Sir Keith Joseph and a host of lesser figures had all the enthusiasm of Damascus road converts (not a common characteristic of conserva- tives) to a new faith, involving the doctrinaire reiteration of the virtues of the liberal free market (see Denham and Garnett 2002). Their statements appeared virtually indistinguishable at times from classical liberalism.

The final category of conservatism, the New Right, is the most problematic. It is not something which is easy to describe, partly because it incorporates such a diverse membership. It is clearly very different to the older traditionalist, romantic and paternalist traditions. Liberal conservatism, paradoxically, could be said to be one of the strands of the New Right. Its immediate origins lie first in the persistence and durability of the liberal conservative tradition; second, in the anti-totalitarian critiques of the 1950s, specifically in writers such as Leo Strauss, Friedrich Hayek and Michael Oakeshott, who engaged in a running battle with all forms of socialism and radical- ism (see Devigne 1994). Further, the electoral defeats of the paternalist conserva- tives, over the 1960s and early 1970s, convinced many that a change of direction was needed. Finally, such people believed that the policies and strategies of nation- alization, corporatism, Keynesian demand management and the welfare state had failed. This disillusion coincided with deep-rooted fears of inflation in Western econ- omies in the 1970s.

Whom to include under the rubric of the New Right remains puzzling. It is usually seen as an amalgam of traditional liberal conservatism, Austrian liberal economic theory (Ludwig von Mises and Hayek), extreme libertarianism (anarcho-capitalism) and crude populism.[10] David Green, in his apologia, widens the liberal dimension to include the Friedmanite Chicago school and the Virginia public-choice school (Green 1987). None of these elements are necessarily intellectually commensurable. Some texts, such as Green's, though widening the study of the neo-liberal aspect, are not prepared to countenance the inclusion of the neo-conservative or neo-authoritarian elements. Roger Scruton and other members of the Salisbury Group are thus ruled out from discussion. Although one can see why this should be – since it fragments even further the ideological coherence of the New Right – none the less it does little justice to the actual movement.

It is worth also underlining here that one of the central components of the New Right is one that we have already encountered within the liberal chapter, namely neo-liberalism, that is, the attempt to recover a pure form of classical liberalism. This is quite a precise example of the way ideologies will often overlap in very significant respects and indeed share core beliefs and arguments. Further, the *prima facie* ideological coherence of the New Right stands some chance if it is limited to the neo-liberal element. The neo-liberal policy emphasis was enthusiastically orientated to the free market. State intervention was perceived to have failed totally. The consensual post-war politics of planning, state welfare, high taxation, public spending, bureaucratic growth, wages unrelated to productivity, and corporatism were seen to be redundant. There was therefore no alternative to the neo-liberal vision of the free market, which had to be the final arbiter for virtually all social issues (including health and education). In many ways, in both Britain and many other developed states, aspects of this neo-liberal ideological legacy have carried on, even under the New Labour administrations, into the 2000s. In this case the ideological neo-liberal overlaps have moved from conservatism into the socialist tradition.

The policy objectives of the New Right were the emancipation of the individual from state regulation, cuts in taxation, reduction of state welfare, controlling budgetary deficits and the money supply, and privatizing state monopolies. The difference from the older liberal conservative tradition was that there was an even greater reliance, in the neo-liberal New Right, on market criteria. Anarcho-capitalist or extreme libertarian elements in the New Right called, for example, for the deregulation of hard drugs, pornography and, in some cases, criminal activity, such as blackmail. It was contended that these would no longer be social problems if they were subject to a free market. If individuals valued their reputation and could settle a contract with someone not to reveal information about them, then even blackmail was conceivable on market criteria as a legitimate mode of exchange. No liberal conservatives could accept these extreme ideas. In fact, a liberal conservative such as Enoch Powell in Britain was not prepared to countenance either health or education being subject to market principles. There was thus a far-reaching dispute on the reach of the market in the 1980s and 1990s, a debate which has not ended, even in the first decade of the twenty-first century (see Mendilow 1996).

Free market theorists do not feel comfortable with the agenda of the neo-conservative element of the New Right, namely, nationalistic fervour, patriotism, national culture, purity of race, natural inequality, the importance of disciplined family life and patriarchal authority, and compulsory Christian religious education. The neo-conservatism of Roger Scruton, Irving Kristol, Russell Kirk, Maurice Cowling, John Kekes or Andrew Sullivan has much more in common with traditionalist conservatism (see Cowling ed. 1978; Scruton 1980 and 2007; Kekes 1998; Stelzer 2004; Sullivan 2006). They repudiate both paternalist and liberal conservatism with equal fervour. Freedom and equality are of little or no direct interest.

For some, citizens have in fact had too much freedom and equality in the post-1945 era. For Cowling, for example, both Marxism and liberalism should be equally subject to conservative ridicule. Thus, one of the self-conscious aims of the Salisbury Group (and the journal *The Salisbury Review*) was in fact to correct the trend towards classical liberalism and neo-liberalism within conservative ideology. True conservatives, for Cowling, should be concerned with issues such as upholding private property, having freedom over one's earnings, and the restoration of national identity.

Human Nature

Conservatism has a relatively constant judgement on human nature, except for the schools of liberal conservatism and the New Right, which have absorbed much of the classical liberal perspective. For traditionalist, romantic and paternalist conservatisms, humanity has a limited capacity for altruism, usually extending to family, neighbours and friends. We are naturally but not exclusively selfish. Our acquisitive instincts make us potentially corruptible, yet our laziness and liking for the tried and tested tends to limit the reach of such corruption. We cannot, in this sense, be rational utility maximizers. Such a notion of rationality is inappropriate to the complexities of the human condition. Humans may at times value their freedom and the maximization of their interests, but not to the exclusion of their love of leisure, natural laziness and enjoyment of life. Humans are not rational machines; they are a complex mesh of emotions, thoughts and often contradictory motivations. There is nothing to be ashamed of here. To seek for complete consistency is a rationalist myth. It is a superficial view of humans to see their primary motivation as reason. This observation also gives rise to a sceptical attitude towards the aspirations for human rationality. The latter point is linked with one of the primary objections voiced by conservative critics of liberal conservatism, namely, that it simplifies and misunderstands human nature.

For many conservatives, neither the idea of mass society nor that of atomized individuals is meaningful. The critique of individuality has given rise to acerbic interchanges between liberal conservatives and the other conservative schools. Both notions (individuality and mass society) are often seen as two sides of the same bad coin; the mass being constituted by alienated and isolated individuals. For many conservatives, human beings grow up within a complex process of historical and social acculturation. Individual freedom is the result of years of social development within a particular national tradition. Language, customs and thought are acquired pre-reflectively in the family, peer groups, schools and social interaction. Abstract individuals and cosmopolitan humanity are figments of the imagination. As Joseph de Maistre argued:

> The Constitution of 1795, like its predecessors, was made for *man*. But there is no such thing as *man* in the world. In my lifetime I have seen Frenchmen, Italians, Russians, etc.; thanks to Montesquieu, I even know that *one can be Persian*. But as for *man*, I declare I have never in my life met him; if he exists, he is unknown to me. (Maistre 1974, 97)

Scruton makes the same point when he comments: 'Individuality ... is an artefact, an achievement which depends upon the social life of man' (Scruton 1980, 34).

Despite the acclaimed historical sensitivity of much conservative writing, its vision of human nature is both universal and ahistorical. This universality is something conservative thinkers share with liberalism. Historical awareness can lead to the relativization of human nature. In the conservative case, despite being children of our time and community, our basic nature and motivations remain unchanged. Nature still moulds us in certain universal ways. On the one hand, this historical awareness has led conservatives to repudiate the doctrines of natural rights, contract theory and the state of nature. These doctrines are seen to alienate humans from the particular national traditions and institutions which make sense of their lives. Human beings cannot be imagined outside society. On the other hand, conservatives still envisage humans remaining constant over time and circumstances. Although this argues a compatibility between historical change and our unchanging nature, it is not convincing. Conservative writers want the benefits but none of the relativistic costs of historical consciousness.

Because we are socially and historically determinate creatures, we necessarily reflect the natural patterns of inequality in abilities and status in society. Authority is always necessary in society and authority entails inequality. Someone in authority gives the orders and others obey them. Conservatives have faith in the natural leadership powers of certain groups or individuals – something Burke referred to as the 'natural aristocracy'. Inequality is rooted in both natural and political circumstances. Some people are naturally superior, both intellectually and morally. Such inequality is nothing to be ashamed of. It cannot be eradicated by social or political means. Some are born to lead and some to be led. However, it should be noted at this point that some twentieth-century conservatives, both those who have assimilated liberal ideas and those following a more paternalist line, have been far more influenced by arguments for equality of opportunity and equal citizenship.

Finally, conservatism is concerned with the ineradicable and universal *imperfection of human nature*. This notion implies that humans will always remain flawed creatures and cannot be perfected in any way (Sullivan 2006, 180). This is an idea which no doubt gave rise to Peter Viereck's comment that conservatism may be described as the 'political secularization of the doctrine of original sin' (Viereck 1950, 44–5). There are two main sources to this vision of imperfection in human nature: the theological and the practical. The theological is the oldest view. In Christian theology the idea relates primarily to the doctrine of original sin. We live in a fallen sinful world. Nothing can be done except a holding operation by individuals and societies against corruption. This is the human condition. In the city of man (to use the appropriate Augustinian term), all that political authority can do is to make the best of a bad job. As Maistre commented, 'In the works of man, everything is as wretched as their author' (Maistre 1974, 23). Maistre was far more concerned about the wretched and sinful character of humanity than was Edmund Burke (see Lebrun 1965).[11]

There were twentieth-century conservatives who still held to the idea of religious imperfection (see, for example, Hogg 1947). However, many others were unable to accept such a view. Some in fact directly repudiated the religious theme. There has been a strong tradition of secular conservatism, certainly since the late nineteenth century, which has retained an undoubted intellectual pre-eminence. Secular conservatives hold to what broadly may be called the practical doctrine of imperfection. This calls upon the resources of moral theory, epistemology and psychology. The basic contention is that humans are imperfect in terms of their capacities to understand the world. We all have a very small stock of information at our command. We are also historically and socially limited in our horizons. The reach of human reason and knowledge is very small and not to be relied upon. Custom and tradition are therefore far safer guides for conduct. This limited knowledge and inability to determine the good of others with any precision is not something that will change. It is again a universal fact about humans. As the total stock of human knowledge increases, even within our own culture, we are doomed to increasing ignorance of the whole. Practical imperfection is inevitable. Thus, apart from the liberal conservative persuasion, the more general assumption of conservatism is that human nature is flawed and imperfect and will remain so whatever the politics.[12] A politics involving human perfectibilism therefore remains anathema.

Reason and Action

Before proceeding to any discussion of the economic and political ideas of conservatism, it is important to grasp one of the central and most elusive arguments of conservative ideology. This argument concerns the explanation of the nature of human action and the role of reason. This has been touched upon briefly in the previous sections and must now be expanded.

Because the inception of conservatism was linked with the refutation of ultra-rationalist arguments from the French Revolution, there has always been an impression of an anti-rationalist element in conservative ideology. The conservative view is sceptical concerning the relevance of rationalism to politics; in the words of Russell Kirk, 'Any informed conservative is reluctant to condense profound and intricate intellectual systems to a few pretentious phrases; he prefers to leave that technique to the enthusiasm of the radicals' (Kirk 1967, 6). The dislike of systematic political philosophy, the belief in a more pragmatic, sceptical and expedient approach to politics, has led conservatives from Burke to Oakeshott to repudiate the exclusive role of reason in politics. Yet it would be a mistake to call the more traditionalist, romantic and paternalist conservatives irrationalist. As Scruton has observed: 'Because there is no universal conservative policy, the illusion has arisen that there *is* no conservative thought' (Scruton 1980, 11).

Essentially, many conservatives have noted a distinction between two types of reason, 'practical' and 'theoretical'. This distinction, which goes back to Aristotle, can be found deployed by certain of the early traditionalist conservatives at the time of the French Revolution. For some, the distinction is not so clear and appears between 'reason' and 'instinct', or 'reason' and 'intuition'. In Maistre, philosophy generally 'corroded the cement that united men'. Modern philosophy, he contended, 'is at the same time too materialistic and too presumptuous to perceive the real mainsprings of the political world'. It is not reason which differentiates us from animal creation, but our ability to intuit a spiritual world. True legislators 'act on instinct and impulse more than on reasoning' (Maistre 1974, 88, 95, 103). In Justus Möser this argument appears as a confrontation between *thought*, which is rigid and immobile, and *life*, which is active and growing but also rooted in time-honoured custom (see Aris 1965, 224; Mannheim 1986, 139–40).

Burke deployed a distinction between *abstraction* and *principle* (see Kirk ed. 1982, xv). Principles, which Burke used with great reluctance, were rooted in custom and tradition, as distinct from the dry abstractions of metaphysical reason. Burke's sentiments on the metaphysics of Enlightenment reason are clearly stated in the *Reflections*:

> Four hundred years have gone over us; but I believe we are not materially changed. …
> Thanks to our sullen resistance to innovation, thanks to the cold sluggishness of our
> national character, we still bear the stamp of our forefathers. We have not (as I con-
> ceive) lost the generosity and dignity of thinking of the fourteenth century; nor as yet
> have we subtilized ourselves into savages. We are not the converts of Rousseau; we are
> not the disciples of Voltaire; Helvetius has made no progress amongst us. … We know
> that *we* have made no discoveries, and we think that no discoveries are to be made, in
> morality; nor many in the great principles of government. (Burke in Hampsher-Monk
> ed. 1987, 188–9)

Burke's point was not to undermine all reason in politics, but to suggest that politics should not be determined by abstract theoretical notions such as natural rights. The fact of the existence over time of an institution or custom was evidence of an intrinsic practical rationality, something which might not always be obvious to the observer. Change might be needed, but it should not be premised on a priori abstract ideas, but rather on a close attention to the concrete problems and spirit of the institutions concerned (see Acton 1952–3). To wipe out institutions and to start again on rational premises was the primary error of the French revolutionaries. Such an idea was nicely encapsulated in Justus Möser's remark: 'Whenever I encounter an old custom or habit which does not square with our modern notions I tell myself there is no reason to believe that our ancestors were fools. I then explore the problem until I find a reasonable explanation … having found it I can return and ridicule those who have ignorantly attacked old customs' (quoted in Epstein 1966). Michael Oakeshott's terminology for this is the primacy of practical over technical knowledge. Practical knowledge works within a tradition, attending sensitively to its 'flow of sympathy'. Rational technical knowledge distorts and simplifies (see Oakeshott 1962, essay 1; also Sullivan 2006, 198ff).

Not all conservatives fit neatly into the above framework. Romantic conservatives, such as Coleridge, placed a heavy emphasis on the Germanic notion of 'philosophical reason' as against the 'understanding'. Philosophical reason grasped the sense of the *whole*, in contrast to the fragmentary nature of the understanding.[13] Reason became almost a symbol of the organic wholeness of society. Benthamism and liberal political economy became examples (in Coleridge's mind) of the more fragmentary false *understanding* of society. Indeed, liberal conservatives, who in fact rely on the more instrumentalist notion of reason present in liberal political economy, inhabit an Enlightenment rationalist world which is repudiated by most traditionalist and romantic conservatives.

The argument on two types of reason leads many conservatives to the notion of two types of truth. These are the truths of reason and logic, which exist in the realm of ideas. Such truths may have little or no relevance to the empirical world we inhabit on a day-by-day basis. Practical truth is found in customs and traditions. True legislators act by such practical impulses (Maistre 1974, 95). As Möser argued: 'Practice which adapts itself closely to every individual circumstance and knows how to make use of it is bound to be more competent than theory which in its high flights is bound to overlook many circumstances' (quoted in Mannheim 1986, 132). When the truths of theoretical reason are applied to the world, distortion ensues. This was the root of Maistre's fulmination against the building of the city of Washington, which he predicted would fail simply because it was the result of rational calculation and decision. It is also the basis to Michael Oakeshott's discussions of the fallacy of learning to cook or ride a bicycle by reading a book. Such practices cannot be learnt from technical rules (see Oakeshott 1962).

The distinction between types of reason also throws some light on the conservative reputation for scepticism. There are, to continue the above theme, two forms of scepticism. Pure scepticism is a radical critical doubt of every human belief, which uses the tools of reason to turn reason on its head. Conservatives do not hold this view. This line of scepticism is present potentially in David Hume with his experimental method of reasoning. Hume does not, though, take his scepticism very far in politics or political economy. He is more inclined to view the latter in terms of history, human nature and custom (Wolin 1954, 1001). Hume's real target is abstract Enlightenment reason in epistemology and morality. Many conservatives have sensed the general direction of Hume's arguments, especially in his writings on religion, and drawn back in horror.

The second form of scepticism, which is characteristic of traditionalist and paternalist conservatives, is a limited, tempering one, pessimistic about the reach of theoretical reason. It expresses a philosophic doubt as to whether rational ideals can be achieved or, in fact, whether they mean anything (Allison 1984, 36). The exceptions to the above arguments are, first, many of the romantic conservatives. As mentioned earlier, these tend to deploy confidently the notion of philosophic reason. There is little room here for scepticism. Secondly, liberal conservatives also have assured beliefs concerning human nature, instrumental reason and the nature of economic activity, which eschew any wavering doubts. In liberal conservatives and the market-orientated aspects of the New Right there is a breezy sense of abstract rational truth.

In traditionalist conservatism the basis of human action is not theoretical reason, but custom, prejudice and habit. Such practices embody practical reason. For Maistre, the cradle should be surrounded by prejudice in order to give secure content to the mind of the child. Such prejudices and habits are derived from the historical and social circumstances of the individual. Prejudice is not simply blind or irrational behaviour; on the contrary, it is 'pre-judgement', a distillation of experience over generations. It is a way of knowing *what* to do, which is innately superior to abstract reason. Prejudice allows the agent to know what to do, without reflections, in morality and politics. To act on prejudice is to act as one's forebears acted. It is, in essence, tradition. Scruton thus remarks that 'When a man acts from tradition he sees what he *now* does as belonging to a pattern that transcends the focus of his present interest, binding it to what has previously been done, and done successfully' (Scruton 1980, 42). Burke aptly called this 'wisdom without reflection'. As Iain Hampsher-Monk notes, Burke's view of prejudice 'is a defence of the unexamined assumptions which, as a result of associations formed in our society's past, make up its political and moral beliefs ... he [Burke] defends prejudice itself without regard to the content because it renders human behaviour within society more predictable and manageable' (Hampsher-Monk ed. 1987, 36). Prejudices, because of their durability, form the substance of traditions and human action. Jacobinism and other such political creeds represent the attempt to eradicate prejudice in the name of enlightenment. No wonder Burke could assert, with gusto, 'Thank God we are not enlightened.'

Paradoxically, one of the results of the concentration on prejudice, habit and custom, and thus tradition, is that history acquires a higher profile. Burke was led by his arguments on tradition towards a rich sense of history. Unwittingly, he was preparing the ground for the enormous burgeoning of nineteenth-century historical thought, specifically in Germany. This has led to some comparisons between Hegel and Burke. It is in this area that we find romantic and traditionalist conservatives in agreement. Both read history teleologically as the embodiment of a deeper and more spiritual purpose. The point at which most conservatives part company with such historical thought is where history becomes non-teleological, namely, where human thought and activity become simply the expression of a particular historical moment with no meaning or purpose above or beyond that moment. Conservatives, understandably, cannot abide such historical relativism.

Politics and the State

For most conservative schools, political life is viewed organically. Such conservatism also tends to be communitarian and suspicious of individualism. Finally, society is viewed hierarchically, namely, leadership and political judgement are skills limited to a few. Political judgement is for the connoisseur. The marked exception to this perspective is the liberal conservative and neo-liberal persuasion, specifically the more extreme, market-orientated theorists of the New Right.

The organic view of society conveys the idea that society is not an artifice or mechanism but is a mutually dependent interrelation of parts. Most conservatives, with rare exceptions, use organicism analogically. Each individual has a place in the organic whole. Change or reform has to be consonant with the pace of the whole organism. Theorists such as Lammenais, Maistre and Müller gave this organic idea a religious and mystical reading. Probably the most extreme example of this tendency was Novalis in *Christianity or Europe* (1802), who interpreted the state as a vast organic *makroanthropos* (large man).[14] More secular-minded conservatives have simply used the organic analogy to symbolize the importance of community or nationhood.

Political life is seen to be part of a much larger drama, whether religious or secular. There is an order implicit in the world. Political or moral order cannot be invented or imposed; rather it is internal to political and moral institutions. It is taken *from* the world at large. Thus James Cobban remarks that Burke 'spent his life on his knees before the great mystery of social life' (Cobban 1962, 88). Conservative writers have read the nature of this order in different ways. The more religiously minded, such as Maistre, saw God as the author of order. As he remarked, institutions are 'only strong and durable to the degree that they are, so to speak, *deified*' (Maistre 1974, 80). For Maistre (and Burke to a much lesser degree) the French Revolution was an evil act against a divine order. Such a religious reading of order is still to be found in some conservative interpretations.[15] Other writers identify the secular historical development of society and tradition as the meaningful order. In some case this involves a clear repudiation of the religious theme. In post-1945 Britain, Michael Oakeshott is probably the best example of such secular conservatism.[16]

The communitarian and anti-individualist tendencies of conservatism derive, to some extent, from the organic analogy. The individual is part of an organic whole and cannot be understood except through the whole organism. The notion of community remains somewhat inchoate, however. For Nisbet, it is 'a fusion of tradition and commitment, of membership and volition'. It was used as an oppositional theme against Enlightenment individualism. Nisbet contends that the family, kindred, parish, village, church or folk are 'all obviously the historically formed molecules of the greater reality of society. These, and not abstract, atomistic individuals of natural law fancy are the true subjects of a true science of man' (Nisbet 1970, 48). The idea of community suggests that a deeper identity and sense of belonging was the source of human contentment and sanity. Such a theme is present in Coleridge, Disraeli and later in T. S. Eliot's and Christopher Dawson's barely disguised contempt for the individualism of liberal society, as against the virtues of the more pastoral and semi-feudal community.

One of the implications of the organic community is a veneration for established customs. Piety to the established order is a necessary concomitant to realizing the importance of tradition. Tradition incorporates more wisdom than the individual, since it embodies a concrete manner of life over generations. Traditions can be trusted, unlike abstract theories. Change, in itself, within a tradition is not repudiated, but rather the 'selfish spirit of innovation' which changes on rational grounds for the sake of change.

Finally, such piety to the established order means that we respect the existing natural hierarchy and inequality of society. All the conservative schools, except liberal conservatism, adhere to this idea. Social order will always entail authority and a natural leadership group or elite. As Allison comments: 'Hierarchy, authority and coercion are necessary if there are to be "arts, letters and society"' (Allison 1984, 32). Burke referred to this leadership as a natural aristocracy. Whereas Burke, Maistre, Möser and Novalis thought in terms of a more fixed hereditary and landed aristocracy, Coleridge and Eliot included a broader elite – incorporating an intelligentsia – namely, Coleridge's 'national clerisy' and Eliot's 'Community of Christians' (see Coleridge 1976, 77ff; Eliot 1939, 42–3). Others, such as W. H. Mallock, in *Aristocracy and Evolution*, put forward the idea of an entrepreneurial meritocratic aristocracy, premised on its evolutionary fitness to rule (Mallock 1901).[17] Peter Viereck argued that the important point was not the content of the elite aristocracy, but the moral qualities of the leaders of 'dutiful public service, insistence on quality and standards, the decorum and inner ethical check of *noblesse oblige*' (Viereck 1950, 30).[18]

Government is needed because of the imperfection of human nature. For conservatives, government is a positive but not unmixed blessing. There is also some variation on the nature of government. Writers such as Maistre and Möser obviously felt more at ease with quasi-feudal and monarchical regimes. Even in nineteenth-century Britain Thomas Carlyle, hovering on the edges of conservative thought, showed deep impatience with the British parliamentary structure and longed for both hero-worship and a strong dictatorial leader such as Oliver Cromwell. However, Burke and the majority of the British conservative tradition have felt happier with the balanced constitution and parliamentary government.

Government should provide a strong framework of procedural rules and customs which maintain peace, justice, liberty and property. For the majority of conservatives, government is a necessity of life which can have positive or negative aspects. Apart from liberal and market-orientated aspects, conservatives have not been frightened to use the powers of the state. Romantic and paternalist conservatives have been fairly open in their intention to use the state to help provide a better life for citizens. The 'middle-way' conservatism of Macmillan and others utilized corporatist ideas, Keynesian demand management, and actively promoted state involvement in social security, education and health-care. The British Conservative Party was the first to begin the nationalization process in the inter-war years, as well as initiating the state broadcasting system. Furthermore, the concept of the welfare state in most European societies owes as much to conservatism as to other ideologies.

Although there are no very specific conservative ideals of government, there are general features worth noting. First, conservatives have tended to repudiate purely autocratic rule. They are not proponents of weak government, but favour something which is both strong enough to cope with internal or external order and yet is still constitutionally limited or balanced. They do not usually believe in liberal constitutionalism. A constitution understood as a body of created written rules and rights has no real meaning. Rules and rights are the result of years of social and political development (Scruton 1980, 48; Covell 1986, 63; Sullivan 2006, 244ff). Written laws are declarations of the pre-existing customs which make society cohere. As Maistre commented: 'Although written laws are merely declarations of anterior rights, it is far from true that everything can be written down; in fact there are always some things in every constitution that cannot be written and that must be allowed to remain dark ... on pain of upsetting the state' (Maistre 1974, 92). Constitutions, for Maistre, are not created by human deliberation but germinate unconsciously with God's help. Burke does not go as far as Maistre, but the same basic idea of the unconscious immemorial constitution is still present in his thinking. Even a late twentieth-century conservative writer such as Nisbet felt compelled to redeem the American constitution from the clutches of liberal constitutionalism, arguing, in effect, that apart from the Bill of Rights, much else in the constitution, such as the separation of powers, was intrinsically informed by unwritten immemorial customs (Nisbet 1986, 40).

Such a customary constitutional settlement involves a command structure, fixed inequalities of powers and a natural leadership or aristocracy. These were premised on a limitation on powers, a defence of certain rights to liberty and property, and some separation between state and civil society. This latter point did not involve a doctrinaire, fixed separation, as in the formal account of classical liberal thought. In fact, a fixed separation in an organic community was regarded as suspect. If the citizen was part of an interrelated whole, how could any firm separation occur? None the less, conservatives, and liberal conservatives in particular, have acknowledged the moral and political importance of the private realm.

Traditionalist, romantic and paternalist conservatives place considerable value on rights. Such rights are not those of liberal individualism. They are not private, natural or pre-social. Rights are legal concessions from the community. In other words, rights are problem-solving devices within political communities. As a conservative propagandist has argued: 'Just as you cannot have a private language, because words derive their meaning from use, and therefore it is inevitable that language inheres in community …, so you cannot have private rights which no one else acknowledges. When we talk about rights, we are talking about communal life' (Waldegrave 1978, 90).

Although the right to property is fundamental, it is not an absolute right which is located in the individual. On the contrary, it is a right which is acknowledged and conceded as such (for secular or religious reasons) by the political community. It may be accorded fundamental importance in terms of social stability, but it is still not a totally private entity. It also, for many conservatives, implies duties and responsibilities.[19]

Property is also linked with freedom – 'No man is fully free unless possessing some rights of property' (Hogg 1947, 99). Freedom is not regarded as an abstract liberal freedom – the right to engage in unconstrained or uncoerced action (Scruton 1980, 72–3). Freedom is usually viewed by traditionalist and paternalist conservatives as a legal right *within* the parameters of tradition and the rule of law. It is premised on established institutional life. This is an important theme in the conservative tradition (Dickinson 1977, 285). Freedom is concerned with the protection of the individual (usually in the context of the family) and his or her property. Freedom is not, however, an absolute value. It is relative to the ends of the community. Incessant liberation undermines the social order. Freedom is not attained by allowing everyone greater liberty to participate in the political process. This was the great error of the Jacobins and later socialists. Freedom is experienced by the citizen of a state with sound authority and the rule of law.

It is worth mentioning at this point that conservatives in general, even those of the more liberal persuasion, have not been overly sympathetic to the value of democracy. For a host of writers, including Burke, Maistre, Charles Maurras, Maurice

Barrès, Sir Henry Maine, William Lecky, W. H. Mallock, T. S. Eliot and Christopher Dawson, perfect democracy implied perfect despotism and the destruction of sane political life and liberty. Fear of the mass mediocrity of democracy was also present in the liberal writings of Benjamin Constant, Alexis de Tocqueville, J. S. Mill and Friedrich Hayek, as well as in a wide spectrum of European writers such as Jacob Burckhardt, Friedrich Nietzsche and probably most notably José Ortega y Gasset in his famous book, *The Revolt of the Masses* (1972). It was thus not a fear shared simply by conservatives.

Democracy, in its more unlimited participatory form, was seen to be implicit in most revolutionary movements. It was also linked with the worrying doctrine of popular sovereignty. For most schools of conservatism, humans cannot govern themselves; they need the wise guidance of prejudice and a natural governing elite. Freedom is not acquired through democracy. Charles Maurras in France and Christopher Dawson in Britain were led by the same logic to criticize even limited representative parliamentary democracy (see Maurras in McLelland ed. 1971; also O'Sullivan 1976, 135ff). In the 1920s and 1930s, this was also a tempting path for the conservative elements of Germany and Italy, but it had different consequences to those in France and Britain. Society needs authority and hierarchy, which are incompatible with popular rule. For conservatives, pure democracy implies rampant self-interest, a destruction of community into an alienated, atomized mass, and the end of authority and civilization.

Many conservatives have accepted a limited, controlled and representative democracy. There are qualifications within this idea, however. Burke, for example, put forward the idea of 'virtual representation', namely, that even without any franchise, individuals could still be represented by others. Burke had in mind a minuscule franchise. This notion has been influential in the British conservative tradition. Martin Pugh catches the spirit of the point well when he remarks that late nineteenth-century conservatives (and liberals)

> did not claim that their system was democratic, a term that smacked of continental abstraction and implied an excess of equality characteristic of American society; rather, it produced effective government, it guaranteed 'liberty', and it was representative. What it represented directly was those considered fit by reason of their independence, their material stake in society, their education and political knowledge to exercise the parliamentary franchise. (Pugh 1982, 3)

Non-electors could be spoken for: labourers by land-owners, wives and children by husbands, the illiterate and propertyless by the literate and property owner. One can thus sense a strong irritation with democracy in the Conservative Prime Minister Lord Salisbury (see Smith 1972). Roger Scruton, in the 1980s, still thought of democracy as a 'contagion' in British society. In remarking on the relation of the state to trade unions, he continued: 'The true nature of the relation between state and trade union will be understood only when the democratic principle has been put aside' (Scruton 1980, 59). It seemed logical for Scruton, in the 1980s, to help to found the Conservative propagandist journal, *The Salisbury Review*.

Genuine freedom therefore requires communal constraint. Even recent conservatives argue that post-war Britain has had (to use the title of an essay by Peregrine Worsthorne) too much freedom. Worsthorne, warning against the rise of liberal conservatism in the 1980s, argued that: 'The urgent need today is for the State to regain control over "the people", to re-exert its authority, and it is useless to imagine that this will be helped by some libertarian mish-mash drawn from the writings of Adam Smith, John Stuart Mill, and the warmed-up milk of nineteenth-century liberalism' (Worsthorne in Cowling ed. 1978, 149). Freedom is not about individual autonomy but, conversely, about upholding certain traditional rights in an established state.

This idea of liberty is clearly at odds with all but the most minimal or formal view of equality – as in equality before the law. Demands for substantive social, economic or political equality are associated, in the conservative mind, with the levelling demands of Jacobinism or socialism. People should know their place in society. For most traditionalist, romantic and paternalist conservatives, humans are naturally unequal. Some are cleverer and will receive greater benefits, some are luckier in terms of family, others are more adept at ruling. Society is necessarily and inevitably an unequal hierarchy.

The Economy

There are two basic positions taken on the economy within conservative ideology. The first, reflected in the traditionalist, romantic and paternalist schools, tends to adopt a more sceptical stance to the notion of a free-market economy. The other position is the pro-market view of liberal conservatism and aspects of the New Right.

The debate on the economic views of conservatism goes back to one of the founding fathers, Edmund Burke. Some commentators see him as a clear exponent of a free-market view, specifically in his essay *Thoughts and Details on Scarcity* (1795). It is argued that there is very little distinction between the thought of Burke and Adam Smith (see MacPherson 1980). Robert Eccleshall remarks that in Burke 'for the first time, bourgeois economics was fused with the older conception of society as a command structure' (Eccleshall in Eccleshall et al. eds 1984, 102; see also Auerbach 1959, 37; Nisbet 1986, 37). Others appear less impressed with this view. Ian Gilmour sees Burke's political economy writings as an aberration, incorporating some 'barbarous metaphysics' (Gilmour 1983, 65–6). On the other hand, Iain Hampsher-Monk observed that in Burke 'the real political argument for regulated free trade as against taxation was that free trade limited the Crown's access to the spoils of empire and consequently its resources for political management at home. Burke did not need Adam Smith's economic arguments for free trade' (Hampsher-Monk ed. 1987, 20). In this sense, there were political rather than directly economic factors at work in Burke's arguments.

Despite the significance of liberal conservatives over the last three decades, and the emphasis on the free market, most of their ideas reflect the formal themes of classical liberalism. There is therefore little point in rehearsing arguments for markets which have already been discussed in chapter 2. However, it should be noted that liberal conservatives tend to be slightly less optimistic about human capacities than do classical liberals. For them, the market needs a stronger, more secure framework of law and order than would normally be contemplated by classical liberals. In this sense, liberal conservatives are more willing to use the state to defend or promote market interests, although internal debates do arise over imperatives towards markets and social controls, particularly in relation to some of the New Right proposals.[20]

Despite the dominance of liberal conservatism and the New Right in Europe and America over the last few decades, it would be a truism to say that historically many conservatives have been committed to a statist view and sceptical of unregulated markets.[21] This does not mean that such traditionalist and paternalist conservatives have been in favour of anything like a command economy. They have usually adopted a more pragmatic and flexible approach containing markets within certain socially defined parameters. In fact, the European Christian Democratic idea of the 'social market economy' appears far more consonant with the conservative tradition (see Pombeni in Freeden ed. 2001).

The development of industrialization and the market economy entails the pursuit of private interest and accumulation of capital. There are subtle responses to this issue within conservatism. Some romantic conservatives obviously had very mixed feelings about industrialization and the market economy; others were tolerant as long as such processes did not impinge on prior values such as community. Writers as diverse as Coleridge, Southey, Lammenais, Maurras and Eliot expressed profound anxiety as to whether liberal market economies were conducive to genuine community. Eliot, in his *Idea of a Christian Society*, bewailed the fact that

> the dominant vice of our time ... will be proved to be Avarice. Surely there is something wrong in our attitude to money. The acquisitive, rather than the creative and spiritual instincts, are encouraged. ... I am by no means sure that it is right for me to improve my income by investing in the shares of a company, making I know not what, operating perhaps thousands of miles away. ... I am still less sure of the morality of my being a moneylender. (Eliot 1939, 97–8)

In encouraging private gain and cupidity over all else, market ideas atomized society, encouraged philistinism in tastes, and undermined education and culture (see Schuettinger ed. 1976, 17).

Furthermore, in creating poverty (Coleridge used to refer to liberal political economy as the 'poverty-making wealth machine'), the market economy only aggravated existing tensions in society (Calleo 1966, 3). Such tensions seemed, in fact, to be incipient in the market process. For Nisbet, Richard Southey's *Letters from England* (1807) reads like a late nineteenth-century socialist indictment of the factory system (Nisbet 1986, 65). The same could be said of some of Cobbett's outbursts. Cobbett, like Coleridge and Southey, detested liberal political economy, directing some marvellous sallies at Thomas Malthus in his *Rural Rides* (1830).[22]

One commentator on Coleridge compares favourably his views on taxation with twentieth-century under-consumptionist economic theories. Coleridge had called for a replacement of the 'spirit of commerce' with the 'spirit of the state'. For Coleridge, the business cycles of the market economy 'bring not only hardship to the poor, but moral decay to the rest of society' (Coleridge quoted in Calleo 1966, 13, 20). In addition, the whole conception of life and humanity present within classical liberal economics was regarded as false. It was a technical, arid and mechanistic view. Humans were not, for Coleridge, simply acquisitive machines. The health of a nation could not be measured by its economic prosperity. Such a narrow notion of life destroyed everything of value. The spirit of commerce was thus viewed as incarnate philistinism. Coleridge was echoing sentiments also found in German romantic conservatism. In the early twentieth century, Maurras and Action Française showed an equally intense dislike of liberal capitalism and its implicit materialism and found more in common with Sorelian syndicalism[23] (Griffiths 1978, 723 and 735). Maurras's disquiet was shared by Dawson and Eliot.

However, conservatives and classical liberal economists were mutually agreed on the importance of private property. Yet even here there were differences in their views. Acquiring property through liberal market processes could interfere with the traditional pattern of stable property rights. There was an implicit struggle here between what may broadly be called landed aristocratic property and financial property. For liberals, anyone, regardless of social status, could theoretically become a financial property owner and lose that property as quickly through the market. Such a notion appeared horrific to the more traditional conservative interests. How would people know their place in the hierarchy of society if such wealth could be gained by anyone, without proper status? This unstable pattern undermined landed property rights and corroded the traditional social structures and authority patterns of society. Society became a mass of competing, restless, anomic and self-interested individuals.

In British conservatism, from Coleridge and Disraeli onwards, 'one nation' concerns have often been seen as prior to the interests of the liberal market economy. Writers and practitioners of conservatism from the 1980s still reflected this sentiment in their own idiosyncratic ways (see Waldegrave 1978, 58; Scruton 1980, 94ff; Covell 1986, 56–7). One of the clearer expositions of this outlook was in Ian Gilmour. He argued that 'Economics is not a self-contained science. ... Economics and its objectives are the means to wider ends' (Gilmour 1983, 12). For Gilmour, liberal economists, like Marxists, do not appear to live in the real world. The Austrian liberal economist Ludwig von Mises is taken to be a precise dogmatic mirror-image of Marx. Both theorists subsist in 'mystical' realms. Gilmour maintained that their views of human nature and society were equally false. Conservatives should thus never have succumbed to liberal economic theories, partly because they 'habitually treated theory as subordinate to practice and ... traditionally had a far greater liking for facts than for doctrine' (Gilmour 1983, 101). Historically, conservatives have often favoured the careful use of the state to curb the market. As Herbert Spencer noted in *The Man versus the State* (1884), conservatives have a disposition towards a more controlled militant society. For Gilmour, a moderate Keynesianism and a mixed economy had much to be said for them. Keynesianism was not the cause of the decline of the post-war British economy, which Gilmour attributed to factors such as primitive trade union practices, poor management and too much 'stop–go' government policy. He looked somewhat mournfully, therefore, for a return of economic sanity within the Conservative Party.

Overall, it is clear that conservatism has had a very ambivalent attitude to economic policy, reflecting quite diverse positions. However, the dominant view has been that of a more flexible and pragmatic recognition that markets are useful within certain social and political parameters.

Conclusion

One of the most elusive arguments within conservatism, mentioned earlier, is that it is not an ideology in the ordinary sense of the term. The paradox here is that it is a theory which rejects theory. The anti-intellectualism is, in other words, apparent rather than actual. The most convincing account which lies behind some of the theoretical dismissals of theory is that a different kind of theory is at work. Practical reason is distinct from theoretical reason. Theoretical reason, based upon preconceived a priori ideas, is seen to be inappropriate to politics. In this sense conservatives cannot, by definition, have clearly worked-out *theoretical* answers to political questions. Some see this as a weakness; others argue that it is an implicit strength.

One problem is that the anti-intellectualism is not a consistent feature of all conservatism. Romantic and liberal conservatives are a case in point. Further, there is something quite misleading and self-contradictory in such denials of abstract theorizing. It is odd to construct a clearly reasoned attack *against* the use of reason in politics, especially when such an attack has strong implications for political life. The usual way out of this dilemma is to appeal to practical reason. Yet, is practical reason so clearly different from theoretical reason? Some conservatives argue that practical reason is based on tradition and practice, but this is often a very selective and partial reading of practice and tradition. Tradition is not a single unequivocal thing waiting to be read or discovered. There are multiple traditions of all types. There can, after all, be traditions of rationalism and radical political traditions. Moreover, some traditions might not be worth retaining, certainly not *just* because they are traditions. Traditions or prejudices such as cannibalism, anti-Semitism or slavery are profoundly objectionable and unquestionably worth abandoning. Why, therefore, should 'tradition' or 'prejudice' *per se* be regarded as valuable? Traditions have to be critically assessed by certain rational standards.

There is surely nothing intrinsically mistaken about theoretical change within traditions. Such a process is commonplace. Theoretical ideas are also often tried out in practice. From physics to morality, technical knowledge is applied to the world. Individuals read cookery books or computer manuals before they cook or compute, and they perform far better than if they had not read these books. Abstract theories and rational technical knowledge permeate practices in all spheres of human activity, including politics.

Like other ideologies, there are clearly theoretical differences between forms of conservatism. As we have seen, even more so than in liberalism, ideas that are canonized by some conservatives are utterly rejected by others. Some conservatives, specifically the romantics and the traditionalists, are haunted by a form of regret and nostalgia. Novalis's medieval Europe, Eliot's pastoral society, Maistre's *ancien régime*, are caught up with certain *idées fixes*, and seem incapable of looking forward. Other conservatives, who accept change, are trapped by a self-contradictory logic: having resisted certain ideas, once these become integrated they begin to praise the immemorial wisdom of ages which has incorporated such ideas. Tradition becomes whatever happens to be the case. Liberal conservatives, on the other hand, appeared to accept certain changes with open arms. In fact, it would be no exaggeration to say that much of the deeply disturbing social and economic change of the last two decades of the twentieth century, in many industrialized societies, was fomented by liberal conservatism and New Right neo-liberalism, particularly in Britain and America. Many have found this a strange contradiction. It will be curious to see if the older aspects of traditionalist or paternalist conservatism reassert themselves in the twenty-first century. Given the unerring ability of conservatives to survive politically, no doubt some change will take place.

4

Socialism

The word 'socialism' finds its root in the Latin *sociare*, which means to combine or to share. The related, more technical term in Roman and then medieval law was *societas*. This latter word could mean companionship and fellowship as well as the more legalistic idea of a consensual contract between freemen. We find two distinct senses of the term 'social' here which have implications for the much later use of the word 'socialism'. 'Social' could refer either to a more formal legalistic contractual relation between free citizens or to a more emotive relationship of fellowship and companionship.

For some commentators, the more legalistic and contractual use of the term 'social' implied something distinct from the state and therefore from politics in general. Individuals make contracts and confer obligations upon themselves, thus reinforcing the common distinction between a 'society' of free contracting individuals and a rule-of-law 'state'.[1] The contractual use is also connected to the contrast, which dates from the 1800s, between a political and social revolution. For example, some writers argued that the failure of the French Revolution, and its collapse into Napoleonic dictatorship, was due to the fact that it had only been a political revolution at the level of the state apparatus. It was not a social revolution (in the socialist sense) of the people and of their attitudes and mode of existence. This was basically Marx's interpretation of the revolution as an act of bourgeois politics.[2] This critique, with enormous amounts of supplementation, carried on into twentieth-century socialist and anarchist assessments of revolution.

The notion of 'civil society', which is also rooted in the contractual idea, entered into European political economy and particularly into ideologies like classical liberalism. Yet it was not without some impact on early socialism and anarchism. The anarchist Pierre-Joseph Proudhon's notion of society was firmly rooted in the contractual idea. Usually, though, civil society became part of the opposition to the alternative meaning of the word social, namely, the sense which implied fellowship and community. Society, in the fellowship sense, was contrasted to the negativity of individualism (as embodied in one meaning of civil society). We would recognize this distinction better now under the rubric of the opposition between socialism and individualism, or collectivism versus individualism, which became popular in European thought from the 1880s.

Another implication of the communal and fellowship understanding of the word 'social' was its connection with the idea of the *populus* (the sovereign people). If 'society' were identified with the whole community, it could legitimately be seen as equivalent to the entire people. Thus the 'social will' could imply the popular or general will. Social ownership was ownership by the people. Socialized property was owned by the whole. Social welfare or socialized medicine would be available for all the people. Social participation in government was popular participation. Social, in this sense, formed strong connections with the ideas of democracy and popular sovereignty. These ideas have a long conceptual pedigree in European thought, but they acquired their characteristic present form during the era of the French Revolution. Furthermore, because moral significance was often accorded to the popular democratic will, the term 'social' also took on a moral lustre.

In a similar manner, the other sense of 'social' (vis-à-vis civil society and contractualism) was often subtly linked with moral and political individualism and formed one of the elements of the later theory of representative liberal democracy. By the 1840s, the connection of 'social' and 'democracy' was firmly in place, as in the parallel link between 'liberal' and 'democracy'. Terms like social democracy, democratic socialist and socialist democrat were relatively well-known throughout Europe, although enormous ambiguities still remained (Claeys 1989, 323; also Wolfe 1975, Sassoon 1996 and Eley 2002).

Socialism, indicating a political stance and set of beliefs, has been fairly precisely dated by a number of scholars. Like conservatism and liberalism it is a child of the post-French Revolution era. There is some argument as to where exactly it first appeared. France and Britain are the main contenders (Lichtheim 1969, 219; also Beer 1984). However, no one disagrees that the 1820s and 1830s are the critical periods. The word *socialisme* appeared in February 1832 in the Saint-Simonian journal *La Globe* edited by Pierre Lerroux. Before this it had figured briefly in 1827 in the Owenite journal *The Cooperative Magazine* (see Newman 2005, 6ff). The Owenites in Britain and the Saint-Simonians and Fourierists[3] in France were the first to use the word self-consciously. Marx was later to tag these as the 'utopian socialists' in *The Communist Manifesto* (1848), a label which had unfortunate and misleading connotations.

The concept of socialism has had a chequered and tortuous relation to a number of other concepts, particularly collectivism, communism and social democracy. This relation will be examined briefly to clear up any potential misunderstandings. Collectivism is a late nineteenth-century concept originating in France. It denotes, with reasonable consistency up to the present day, the use of the state and governmental apparatus to control, command and regulate sectors of the economy and civil society. It is an instrumental device of public policy. It usually entails, in varying degrees, central state planning. Since the late nineteenth century the notion of collectivism has often been linked with socialism. There are a number of problems with such an identification, however. First, despite the fact that many socialists have used collectivism in practice, a significant number have either ignored it or repudiated it.

Second, many other ideologies like conservatism and liberalism, as we have already seen, have been prepared to use collectivist methods. Finally, it is worth emphasizing that collectivism refers to an instrumental device, *not* a thesis or set of beliefs about human nature and equality, as one would expect to find in socialism. Collectivism, in itself, is thus much narrower, more formal and procedural than socialism.

We will now briefly turn to certain other concepts which are closely linked with socialism. In Émile Durkheim's *Socialism and Saint-Simon* (1928), communism is seen as a much older and more primitive form of organization than socialism. Communism is concerned to regulate human consumption in an egalitarian manner. It had been practised in early monastic communities and some more primitive tribal units. Socialism, on the other hand, is viewed by Durkheim as a very modern device of industrialized societies, which regulates productive relations. Here we see a clear separation of the terms, though not all would accept such a distinction.

The term 'communism', denoting a self-conscious political adherence, predates socialism by only a few years. In France, Gracchus Babeuf and the Society of Equals, which appeared on the political scene between 1794 and 1797, were often called the Babouvists and occasionally 'communionists'. Babeuf was in fact guillotined in 1797 under the orders of the Directory. The Society of Equals was essentially a conspiratorial sect devoted to revolutionary overthrow, the establishment of a dictatorship and a community based upon perfect substantive equality. The communist element, oddly, did not appear in Babeuf's trial; it became more significant in the politics of his followers, Buonarroti and Blanqui. It has also been subsequently traced through to the Russian Populists and the young Lenin in the 1890s. Another French writer to explore this radical equality and communal ownership, but from a very imaginative utopian angle, was Étienne Cabet in the late 1830s. His elaborate imaginary world of Icaria is often described as utopian communism (see Johnson 1974; Newman 2005, 8).

Marx in his earliest writings saw communism as a primitive form of socialism, but by 1848, in *The Communist Manifesto*, a firm contrast appeared between 'revolutionary communism' and 'utopian socialism'; although, under the influence of the anthropologist Lewis Morgan, both Engels and Marx still accepted the notion of primitive communism.[4] Marx gradually formed an antipathy to the word 'socialism', which lasted right up to his last works in the late 1870s. Socialism appeared to denote a softer, classless, utopian, in sum, *bourgeois* doctrine. Despite this, Engels referred to *The Communist Manifesto* in a later preface of 1888 as 'socialist literature'.[5] Marx's antipathy reappears among some of the Bolsheviks in 1917, who saw communism as a more mature historical phase beyond socialism. In Britain, William Morris and H. M. Hyndman (the founder of the first British Marxist group) also preferred not to use the denotation 'socialist', associating it with reformist Fabian socialism. Despite these circumlocutions, it is hard to fix a definite barrier between the terms. Revolutionary fervour is certainly not the test or standard. If one compares the constitutional views of many Eurocommunists of the 1960s and 1970s with the multiple revolutionary splinter groups of the same period calling themselves 'socialist', then the term 'revolutionary' appears to attach itself more closely to socialism than to communism.

'Social democracy' is subject to a similar ambivalence. H. M. Hyndman referred to himself as a social democrat, indicating thereby his adherence to Marxism. He was following here the German example. The driving force of Marxism from the Second International, which dominated European Marxism up to 1914, was the German Sozialdemokratische Partei Deutschlands (SPD) – the formal title adopted in 1890 – deriving originally from the 1869 Social Democratic Workers' Party (see Joll 1974). Despite some ambivalence, social democracy became virtually equivalent to organized Marxism. Marxism, as social democracy, set its theoretical face firmly against the revisionist socialism of Eduard Bernstein (see Miller and Pothoff 1986; Tudor and Tudor 1988; Tilton 1991). After the break-up of the Second International, with the outbreak of the First World War, the Soviet Union began to take over as the central interpreter of Marxism. The Bolsheviks changed their name from the Social Democratic Labour Party to the Communist Party of the Soviet Union. Because of their dominance of the Third International it became essential that the term 'communist' replaced 'social democracy' for all groups who wished to be part of the International. Before the First World War, ambivalences were already creeping in, with the title 'social democracy' being taken over by some revisionists, ethical socialists and new or social liberals. After 1920, and up to the present, the term 'social democracy' has had its strongest links with the related reformist socialism and the social liberal tradition. In this sense, the founding of the Social Democratic Party in Britain in the 1980s was not that novel or significant.

In sum, we should be careful about attributing definite parameters to socialism, either to say that all socialists are collectivists, or that communism is wholly distinct from socialism, or that social democracy is a non-socialist tradition. All of these judgements are both historically and ideologically misleading. There is a complex overlap of discourses between these various elements.

The Origins of Socialist Thought

Although the roots of socialist thought are contested, they are less tangled than those of conservatism and liberalism (see also Cole 1953–60; Eley 2002; Boggs 1995; Sassoon 1996). There are two broad accounts of the origins of socialist thought. The first covers a lot of ground, usually tracing socialist themes back to movements of ideas in the early modern period. The second account focuses on the post-French Revolution period.

In terms of the first account the two figures most often discussed are Sir Thomas More, because of his book *Utopia* (1516), and the anabaptist Thomas Münster. The doyen of German Marxism, Karl Kautsky (often referred to as the 'Pope of Marxism'), wrote *Thomas More and His Utopia* (1888) to demonstrate this particular origin (see also Dennis and Halsey 1988).[6] The other main hunting ground of this same period is the English Civil War. Groups like the Levellers and Diggers are often given a high profile in such an interpretation (see Greenleaf 1983, 351). For example, Christopher Hill remarks on the Diggers' leader:

> Winstanley was working out a collectivist theory which looks forward to nineteenth- and twentieth-century socialism and communism. ... Winstanley had grasped a crucial

point in modern political thinking: that state power is related to the property system and to the body of ideas which supports that system. He is modern too in wanting a revolution which would replace competition by concern for the community, in insisting that political freedom is impossible without economic equality. (Hill introduction to Winstanley 1973, 9)[7]

There do seem to be worrying problems with this type of analysis, partly because at the time no body of beliefs existed equivalent to nineteenth- and twentieth-century socialism. It could be argued that the concept preceded the word. Yet the theological and cultural context within which the arguments of the Diggers appeared seems to be ignored in such accounts. There is a danger of reading our present concerns into the past, which, as argued in chapter 1, can be an anachronistic and misleading enterprise.

The second account focuses upon the immediate post-French Revolution period. The interplay with the Industrial Revolution is also explored by some scholars (see Hobsbawm 1977a). George Lichtheim comments on the 1790s: 'A history of socialism must begin with the French Revolution, for the simple reason that France was the cradle of "utopian socialism" and "utopian communism" alike ... both currents stemmed from the great upheaval of 1789–99' (Lichtheim 1969, viii). The revolution was the crucible from which socialism derived, both the word 'socialism' itself and the social movements which adhered self-consciously to the ideology. All these phenomena find their roots in the revolution and post-revolution period. The vigorous attempts to extend democracy, rights, justice and equality, through radical social and political action, although hardly beneficent in all their effects, sent immense shock waves through European thought which are still reverberating today.

In many ways the Industrial Revolution also acted as a further catalyst, not least because it facilitated the growth of capitalism and the maturation of the urban working class, who became the focus and vital membership of many socialist movements. This particular point becomes more problematic if we take into consideration some of the notions developed by Maoism or by Frantz Fanon, which relied heavily on the revolutionary potential of the agricultural peasantry (Schwartz 1951, 73ff; Fanon 1965). Industrial capitalism also created the tensions and conflicts which became the crucial target for socialist criticism. Capitalism was initially seen by most socialists as the *bête noire*, the source of all injustice and inequality.[8] In criticizing capitalism and trying to find alternative policies, socialists drew upon the language of the radical French Revolution tradition which incorporated demands for the extension of democratic suffrage, trade union rights, parliamentary reform and social justice for working people. As the French revolutionaries had demonstrated, such ideas could be pursued successfully through the use of mass movements.

The above account does not, however, negate the point that many of the ideas utilized by socialists were derived from previous intellectual traditions, in some cases pre-dating the revolution. Socialism, in fact, took on ideas from diverse sources: civic republicanism, Enlightenment rationalism, romanticism, forms of materialism, Christianity (both Catholic and Protestant), natural law and natural rights theory, utilitarianism and liberal political economy. All these and more form the backdrop for socialist theorizing. Various elements of the socialist movement coalesced around certain of these intellectual traditions, thus formulating their proponents' arguments in markedly different ways.

As already stated, the first self-conscious socialist movements developed in the 1820s and 1830s. The Owenites, Saint-Simonians and Fourierists provided a series of coherent analyses and interpretations of society (see Goodwin and Taylor 1982; Geoghegan 1987). They also, especially in the case of the Owenites, overlapped with a number of other working-class movements like the Chartists. The radical tradition, as expressed in groups like the Chartists, trade unions, and the like, often indirectly coincided with, rather than directly pursued, socialist aims. By the 1880s, however, socialist discourse was coming to be widely accepted as the most adequate account of working-class aspirations.

After a brief hiatus, from the late 1840s until the late 1860s, another surge of socialist development took place in Europe. Socialism through this period, up to the 1880s, was gradually maturing and becoming self-conscious of its ideological content. The crucial place of Marx in the socialist pantheon is in part due to the fact that he provided such an intellectually powerful synthesis of ideas and convincing explanations at such a pivotal moment. With the exception of Britain and possibly Sweden,[9] Marxist language set the tone of much subsequent European socialist discussion. The Marxist German SPD became the dominant force in European socialism up to 1914, imposing its ideological pattern on the French socialists under Jules Guesde. This dominance and consensus gave rise to the description 'the golden age of Marxism' during the period of the Second International (1889–1914; see Joll 1974).

However, the phenomenon of most of the major Marxist-orientated parties in France, Germany and Austria voting for war credits in 1914 rapidly undermined all sense of international unity or solidarity. The Third International, which emerged out of the furnace of the 1914–18 war, was this time premised on the Bolsheviks in the USSR. Lenin was now the leading figure and Marxist-Leninism became the key official doctrine. Yet from the 1930s further polarization of the movement took place. Marxist revisionism, which had been festering since the early 1900s, carried on unabated throughout Europe. The German SPD moved gradually towards a more revisionist democratic socialist stance, especially in the post-1945 era. British socialism continued to take its own unique and idiosyncratic reformist course. Further deep fissures developed within Marxism, which widened into chasms through the post-1945 era. Trotskyism, Stalinism, Leninism, revisionist Marxism, humanistic Marxism, Maoism, African Marxism, existential Marxism, Eurocommunism, structuralist Marxism, feminist Marxism and many other currents proliferated. A vast scholastic catalogue of often mutually hostile Marxisms developed, each claiming orthodox truth (see McLellan 1980 or Kolakowski 1981). The river had run into the multiple silted channels of the estuary. The surviving socialism of the 1990s and 2000s (apart from slowly mutating rarities such as Cuba) is by and large reformist, democratic, revisionist and more market-orientated in nature (see Pierson 1995; Giddens 1998 and 2001; on Cuba see Pérez-Stable 1999).

The Nature of Socialism

The first point which should already be obvious is that there is no such single thing as socialism. There are, rather, socialism*s*, which often overlap with other ideologies. No pristine doctrine exists. One has to be very careful at this juncture since the dominant position of Marxism in the history of the movement has often led to a reading of socialism through Marxist eyes. Marxism is not the true socialism; it is a species within the genus of socialism. Whether Marxist-inclined or not, it is easy, too easy, to adopt unthinkingly the terminology and categories of Marxism. A typical case is the distinction between utopian and scientific socialism or the assertion of the importance of class to socialism. There are, in fact, no such neat demarcations in the discussion of socialism. There are multiple definitions of the concept and numerous ways of actually conceptualizing it. Should socialisms be identified by beliefs, values or political strategies? Socialism is a rich body of formal arguments and values which are interpreted in different ways by the varying schools.

There are a number of possible ways of distinguishing forms of socialism. Marx and Engels (the latter particularly) started the process of categorizing types of social-ism. One of the early distinctions was between revolutionary scientific socialism as against utopian socialism. This distinction, apart from its essentialist reading of socialism, ignores many of the scientific pretensions of the utopians and the com-monality of beliefs within Marxism itself. Another mode of classification of social-isms is by strategies. The neatest division here would appear between revolutionary and reformist traditions, although this would not necessarily catch all the subtle and occasionally stark differences *within* each category. The differing views on rev-olution of Rosa Luxemburg and Lenin or Stalin and Trotsky would need to be accounted for within such a distinction. Furthermore, if another typology were adopted, distinguishing authoritarian and libertarian socialisms, then reformist socialists like Beatrice and Sidney Webb could be seen as 'reformist authoritarians', whereas Luxemburg or, in a different setting, Wilhelm Reich and Herbert Marcuse might be considered 'revolutionary libertarians'. W. H. Greenleaf adopts a slightly different categorization, namely, collectivist organizational socialism as against liber-tarian socialism (Greenleaf 1983, 350ff). Again, a number of cross-cutting issues arise. Some collectivists have been concerned with libertarian issues. Collectivists could also be authoritarian, revolutionary or reformist. Similar problems arise with libertarianism. In this sense, these more simple distinctions do not catch quite enough of the nuances.

One of the major problems here is that socialism inherits a number of intellectual traditions and values. It has accepted wholeheartedly *and* repudiated the role of Enlightenment rationalism. It has fulsomely praised the growth of industrialism *and* resisted it in a longing for pastoral communes. It has embraced modernity *and* opposed it. It has utilized the state *and* attacked it. Some theorists, in despair of finding a consistent pattern, have sought to delineate certain core themes. R. N. Berki is a good example of this tendency. He sees four values: egalitarianism, moralism, rationalism and libertarianism. These exist in harmony and disharmony in different socialist thinkers. When combined in various formats they inevitably yield very different views (see Berki 1975).

My own approach will be to try to distinguish certain schools of socialism according to a dominant pattern in their argument or approach. The particular schools outlined are not hard-and-fast categories. The thinkers within them often have very different perceptions on certain issues. The typology is an attempt to make sense of a diverse, complex and nuanced tradition without undue simplification. A number of arguments and beliefs within these schools overlap not only with other socialisms but also with other ideologies. The schools of socialism are: utopian socialism, revolutionary socialism (Marxism), reformist state socialism, ethical socialism, pluralist group-based socialism and market socialism.

Utopian socialism is not just a primitive phase leading to Marxism. Each of the early utopian socialists – Saint-Simon (1760–1825), Charles Fourier (1772–1837), Robert Owen (1771–1858) – is an interesting and significant person in his own right. The distinguishing feature of utopian socialism, which figures in socialist thought into the twentieth century, is its attempt to sketch out, sometimes in minute detail, the ordering of a possible form of social life which corresponds to the true nature of humanity, including even the reproduction pattern, family arrangements, diet or dress of community members (see Manuel 1956 and 1962; Manuel and Manuel 1979; Goodwin 1978; Kumar 1991). Such a well-structured society, in harmony with the natural springs of human nature, would provide the conditions for fully satisfied, happy and virtuous human beings. The utopians did not specify static social structures. Their societies were dynamic and creative entities allowing for (especially in the case of Fourier) the full flowering of humans (see Fourier 1996; Riasanovsky 1969). Such utopias – Fourier's *Phalansterie*, Owen's New Harmony, Saint-Simon's Administered Industrial society – were placed in the context of an historical development and required radical changes in the economies and property relations of existing societies (on Saint-Simon see Manuel 1956; Saint-Simon 1964; Ionescu 1976; and on Robert Owen see Morton 1962, Owen 1991).

Revolutionary socialism is best expressed through the medium of Marxism. Marxism provided the most powerful and masterful integrating theory of socialism, premised upon a critical combination of Enlightenment materialism, Hegelian idealism, liberal political economy and utopian socialism. The main distinguishing feature of Marxism is a powerful historical interpretation of societies. The material and economic conditions of life form the basis for all social and political structures, as well as for human consciousness. Relations of production are the real foundations upon which the legal and political superstructures arise. The state reflects the intrinsic class struggle which takes place at the economic base of society. As material conditions, productive relations and modes of exchange alter, so do class and political relations. Ultimately, societies will develop into the capitalist mode of production, where a particular configuration of classes occurs – confrontation between proletarians and bourgeois capitalists. The end to this conflict will be the revolutionary overthrow of capitalism.

The major philosophical division that has subsequently occurred within Marxism is between more humanistic and scientific claims. The former is often identified with the writings of Antonio Gramsci, Karl Korsch and Georg Lukács, and tries to incorporate a much stronger element of human autonomy into the social and economic theory. The other side of the debate is the more stultifying legacy of scientific socialism, which derives from the later writings of Engels and Karl Kautsky, and leads through in a more veiled form to the structuralist Marxism of the 1960s and the writings of Louis Althusser. This theory discerns certain objective determining structural laws of development. The autonomy or individuality of the human subject counts for very little in this brand of Marxism.

Reformist state socialism is being employed as a broad category here. The use of the notion of collectivism, as synonymous with socialism, reveals something of the conceptual ancestry of this idea. Reformist state socialism incorporates the revisionism of Eduard Bernstein, the Fabians (at least a number of the important Fabians), the post-1945 German SPD and British Croslandite[10] reformist socialism from the 1950s. It is also very close to the tradition of social liberalism. The characteristic features of this form of socialism are, first, that by and large it has always either repudiated or tried to revise Marxism. Second, it has always, from the 1880s, advocated democratic gradualism and constitutional reform as the path to socialism. Socialism has never wanted to dispense with parliaments, adversarial parties or representative democracy. Third, it has nearly always accepted a role for the free market, usually within the framework of a mixed economy. Fourth, its critique of capitalism is more often than not conducted in instrumental terms. Capitalism is seen to be primarily inefficient and wasteful rather than immoral. This is not to say that there are no ethical concerns within this category; these have taken a slightly different path and are dealt with under a separate category. Finally, and most significantly, it has advocated the use of the state to achieve its aims of greater efficiency, equality, social justice and rights. Reformist state socialism, which has been most prominent in political practice in the post-1945 era, has also been closely associated with the development of welfare states throughout Europe.

Ethical socialism is closely allied to reformist state socialism. In fact, in many aspects it overlaps directly with it, although its perception of the state is often distinct. Furthermore, reformist state socialism has often utilized ethical motifs, but it usually only accords them a secondary significance. The distinguishing characteristic of ethical socialism is its emphasis on the ethical dimension. Socialism is concerned with correct or true values. Capitalism is adjudged not economically inefficient, but ethically deficient. Political, social or economic reforms in themselves are not enough. The establishment of material entitlements to welfare, social security, free healthcare or unemployment benefit do not constitute genuine socialism. Rather, moral change in the citizens themselves precedes adequate political change. State action can facilitate this moral change through education, but it is not crucially necessary. Education cannot make humans moral. The Christian Socialists in Britain, France and Germany over the nineteenth and twentieth centuries, by and large, held to this position. This is an attitude which also seemed to inform the twentieth-century exponents of 'liberation theology', although their views were usually a unique amalgam of humanistic Marxism and Christian ethics. In Britain at the turn of the twentieth century, many of the early Independent Labour Party (ILP) leaders, such as Keir

Hardie, Robert Blatchford and J. Bruce Glasier, also had ethical views of socialism. These figures derived their ethical socialism from writers like Ruskin, Carlyle, Dickens and Thoreau. Such a view is also characteristic of many in the contemporaneous social liberal tradition, like L. T. Hobhouse. In twentieth-century Britain, R. H. Tawney is probably the best-known representative. He undoubtedly perceived the state as an institution having ethical functions (see Dennis and Halsey 1988).

Pluralist socialism is to be found in various formats (see Rustin 1985; Hirst 1988). In using the word 'pluralism' I am not suggesting any necessary connotation of moral or political pluralism. In other words, there is no allusion here to the tolerance or co-existence of moral, political or economic alternatives. Beliefs in 'moral pluralism' can also be found in forms of ethical and reformist state socialism. Conversely, many proponents of pluralist socialism present 'totalizing' perspectives, acknowledging no alternatives to their own. In my own use of 'pluralist', the basic distinguishing feature is that the state is not regarded as a device for introducing or furthering socialism. Socialism can *only* come about from a plurality of groups of self-organized workers: producer associations which would gradually take over all the functions of administration and welfare (previously performed by the state) for themselves. The category of pluralist socialism therefore covers those socialists who have had no truck with the state and prefer to rely on the plurality of workers' associations. There is a strong overlap here with some schools of anarchy.

Such a pluralist view is, paradoxically, present in the conciliar communism of Gramsci. It is half-heartedly present in Lenin's call for 'all power to the Soviets'. Marx partially and unwittingly supports it in his comments on the 1871 commune in France in 'The Civil Wars in France' (1871), and his advocacy of decentralized communes (see Marx and Engels 1968). It found a firm endorsement, moving into the border regions of anarchism, in the syndicalist and anarcho-syndicalist movement. Theorists such as Gustav Landauer or Pierre-Joseph Proudhon also subscribed to such a view; however, their general theories appear difficult to categorize, hanging precariously between pluralist socialism and anarchy (Landauer 1978).[11] Finally, and most representatively, the view found a clear expression in the guild socialist movement in Britain, which developed in the Edwardian era. There are also some loose parallels to be drawn with the cooperative and shop stewards' movement in the post-1945 era. The state, in the pluralist view, was seen to replace the coercion of the market with the coercion of bureaucracy or centralized administration. There are, though, undoubtedly broad differences between these pluralists. Conciliar communism and syndicalism were totalizing perspectives, believing in violent revolution and dismissive of constitutional and reformist procedures, whereas the guild socialists were, in the main, the precise opposite. Despite these marked differences, they shared an antipathy to the state as a vehicle for socialism and favoured instead group activity.

Market socialism is a fairly recent phenomenon of the 1980s, although some trace its ancestry further back, finding sources of the doctrine in Marx (see Nove 1983; Miller 1987 and 1990; Hsu 2007). It is premised, largely, on the perceived failure of reformist state socialism in the twentieth century. The most important distinguishing feature of market socialism is the notion that the market economy can be decoupled from capitalism. Many socialists in other schools would find such an idea immediately unacceptable. For market socialists, capitalism may be impossible without markets, but markets can function without capitalism; in fact they can be used to further socialist aims, bringing a concern for equality, welfare and ethics together with economic efficiency. Market socialists tend to be suspicious of the state, favouring more decentralized economic decision-making premised on market activity. Liberty is also seen to be a neglected value by market socialists. But liberty needs an effective ability to choose. Market socialism is thus concerned to maximize the possibility for choice. Because markets are accepted as an allocative device, this does not mean that some limited indicative planning cannot be used with care. Some market socialists are also, with certain qualifications, supportive of workers' cooperatives (see Forbes 1986; Le Grand and Estrin eds 1989; Miller 1990).

It is worth noting in passing that socialist thought and practice had one further brief 'flash in the pan' mutation in the later 1990s and early 2000s. This was so-called 'New Labour' or 'third way' socialism, although it might also be seen as an attempt to reformulate social democracy (see Giddens 1998 and 2001; Vincent 1998a; Freeden 1999; Pierson 2005). Some have completely overestimated the significance of this movement (Bevir 2005). Indeed, its purported project has now all but disappeared. It saw itself as a form of 'middle way' between the neo-liberal and New Right focus on the crucial role of the free market, as the most efficient allocator of resources, and the older, post-1945, ethical and reformist socialist concerns for fairness, social justice and ethical responsibility. In many ways this apparent third way of New Labour began and remained a faint and ill-worked-out blend of themes from reformist socialism, marketized neo-liberalism, market socialism and social liberalism.[12] Although it struggled with these ideas, it never reconciled the ideological overlaps. The dissolution of this third way in the later 2000s (even in Labour circles) was due largely to this lack of any ideological resolution. If there has been a lasting legacy of New Labour it has been the, partly unintentional, strengthening and deepening of the foundations of a hegemonic neo-liberal ideology in public policy, in part encouraged and facilitated by a broader global dominance of the same doctrine.

The themes of this third way were, first: the idea that markets could, in part, be partially decoupled from capitalism, in the manner of market socialism and social liberalism. Thus, the distributive and democratic aims of socialism could be linked with the efficiency-inducing properties of markets. Markets could also apparently help to dissolve power by dispersing it amongst consumers. Dispersed power in a market also increases participation of ordinary people. When citizens own property and can make decision about their own lives, they apparently act responsibly – a central theme of the New Right which underpinned a range of 1980s conservative policies, such as broadening share ownership, selling public housing, deregulation of state industries, and ultimately the idea of the 'poll tax' for financing local services. The same general idea was implied in the New Labour policy of 'stake-holding'. In sum, markets can be used to further socialist aims, bringing together a concern for freedom, equality, welfare, democracy and ethics with economic efficiency.

Third way socialism also expressed some unstructured misgivings about the role of the state, something again shared with market and pluralist socialism and the neo-liberal New Right. This unease was premised on the point that the state tended towards excessive bureaucracy and economic inertia. Thus, more favour was shown (in appearance) towards decentralized economic decision-making. Maximizing citizens' access to production was preferred to the state becoming involved in redistribution. This did not mean that public goods were abandoned; rather they had a more minimal indicative role in planning processes.

Finally, there was a moral agenda within some (but certainly not all) formulations of the third way, which links up with the older minority element of ethical socialism. Unlike the more 'mechanistic' and 'instrumental' policies of reformist state socialism, the third way variant tried to develop a moral stance. This thin morality usually focused on issues such as rights implying obligations – an idea implicit in the policy of workfare. Further, there was an assumption of the importance of non-market communal values, such as respecting other persons and communities. The area where this impacted most forcefully was social policy, namely, where the social rights of citizenship correlated with individual duties. The state thus had an enabling task, both to encourage a productive economy and to provide conditional opportunities for citizens. Rights not only correlated with obligations, but, in addition, obligations related to opportunities.[13]

How far the above points provide a clear difference from older forms of socialism remains indeterminate. The older forms of socialism embodied a cluster of ideas and movements which lacked overall coherence. The more dominant form of socialism during the period 1945–70 was reformist state socialism. The New Labour and market socialisms of the 1990s and early 2000s certainly took a more optimistic stance towards the market, they lowered expectations concerning the role of the state and public ownership, and adopted a more moralistic (in the case of New Labour), rather than mechanistic, stance to social and economic policy. However, as indicated above, this whole position was largely an unresolved eclectic blending of elements from earlier socialist positions.

Human Nature

It is always difficult to generalize in any area of ideology. However, socialists usually have a more optimistic developmental view of human beings than ideologies such as conservatism or liberalism. Many have embraced, to some degree, a perfectibility thesis. Human beings can grow and improve in moral stature.[14] Socialists also tend to see the roots of human nature in social life. We are not simply asocial impervious individuals. We are part of one another through a common social existence. The conditions under which humans develop explain a great deal about their character and nature. In other words, both the material and moral condition of human beings must be understood in the context of a society. Furthermore, for many socialists, humans are seen to be capable of reason and self-development. Like liberalism, and unlike much conservatism, socialism tends towards a more cosmopolitan doctrine. The belief is that *all* humans are capable of self-development, regardless of country, class, sex or race.

Despite these more common formal beliefs about human nature, there are subtly distinct and often contradictory ontologies at work in socialism. Such ontologies do not fall neatly into any of the types of socialism; instead they tend to cross-cut the various schools. In the writings of certain of the early utopian socialists such as Robert Owen and Saint-Simon, in the arguments of many early Fabians, and also in 'scientific Marxism', there is an Enlightenment rationalist stance on humanity. This is an ontology which rejects tradition and believes that human nature can be manipulated, controlled or built afresh through the use of reason and the right circumstances. Socialism becomes, in this context, a rational modernizing doctrine. If one can modernize and improve the conditions for human development, then the character of humans can be formed anew. Marx's historical materialism is one example of this tendency. It tells us how humans will act under certain conditions or material circumstances. If the material circumstances can be changed, then human nature will also be modified.

On the other hand, in the more romantic and humanistic ontology of socialist thought there is a powerful belief in the autonomy of individuals. Humans cannot simply be built anew from material circumstances. They have to be persuaded and educated to identify moral truths. Humans are also creatures of tradition. They do not reject the past or always seek radically to modernize social life. In addition, they do not necessarily associate progress with rapid industrial development; in fact, in some cases it is the precise opposite. There are socialisms which look on a slower pastoral existence as the ideal form of life (see Penty 1906; Landauer 1978). Human beings are creative creatures who can fulfil themselves through thoughtful labour. The ideas of Arthur Penty and William Morris concerning creative labour, of ethical socialists on the moral development of humans, and of Antonio Gramsci on humanistic Marxism reveal different aspects of this general ontology.

One debate which reveals much of the ambiguity of human nature under socialism focuses on the perennial issue of morality and science. The debate does not break down into a simple argument between a rigidly rationalist science inimical to free will and morality. There is an ethical passion present in the thinking of nearly all socialists, however deeply obscured in scientific jargon.

The grounds for scientifically orientated socialism lie, first, in the Enlightenment project to explain reality via the principles of reason and thus to repudiate all superstition and, often, tradition; the second premise is the late nineteenth-century admiration for the empirical sciences. Natural science during the nineteenth century was increasingly associated with 'truth'. Socialism, in order to appear more truthful, often utilized the language of natural science. The original grounding of scientific socialism can be found in the utopians. They were impressed with the project of finding the precise inner structure of human nature. If the structure could be identified and tabulated, then societies could be designed to fulfil all the aspirations of human nature. Food, sexual activity, clothing, architecture and even the most minute human desires could be catered for. Fourier's idea of the basic passions of each individual, precisely balanced and matched within the utopian *Phalansterie*, is typical of this process.[15] Equally, it is not accidental that Owenites were the first to popularize the idea of social science in Britain (Claeys 1989, 16; Owen 1991).

The real dynamism for scientific socialism came with Marx and Engels. Engels particularly embraced a crude positivism in popular works such as *Anti-Dühring* (1877), *Socialism Utopian and Scientific* (1880) and *Dialectics of Nature* (1883) (see McLellan 1977, 73). *Anti-Dühring* was particularly influential in developing the scientific perspective. It is questionable exactly how far down this road Marx was prepared to go. Marx's application of materialism was more tentative and finely balanced than that of Engels. As far as is known, Marx never anticipated the application of dialectics to nature. Engels set the tone of this particular strand of Marxist socialism, allying it with scientific development in general. As he stated in his 'Speech at the Graveside of Marx': 'Just as Darwin discovered the law of development of organic nature, so Marx discovered the law of development of human history' (Engels in Marx and Engels 1968, 435). This line of thought was closely followed not only by German Marxists, like Kautsky and Bebel, but also by the Russian Marxist Plekhanov in works like *In Defence of Materialism* (1895), by Lenin in *Materialism and Empirio-Criticism* (1909), and subsequently by Bukharin and Stalin.[16] Engels's work 'came to be accepted as the authoritative frame of reference through which Marx's work was to be viewed' (Wright 1987, 43). In this reading, humans were material creatures determined by certain objective 'dialectical laws' operating both in nature and in society. The individual was identified with a class which had a determinate role in the economic process. The material base of society determined the superstructure of human thought. It was this doctrine which became embodied in the official SPD programme, agreed in the city of Erfurt in 1891 – subsequently known as the Erfurt programme (Miller and Potthoff 1986, 240). However, the same doctrine was rejected at the time by the revisionist Eduard Bernstein (see Tudor and Tudor 1988), and in more recent times the claims of scientific socialism have been regarded with considerably greater scepticism.

The Marxists were not the only socialists to utilize the notion of science. Many of the early Fabians in Britain 'were inspired by a belief in the possibility, and indeed the necessity, of rational and scientific reform and administration' (Arblaster in Parekh ed. 1975, 148). For the Fabians Beatrice and Sidney Webb, good socialism was premised on sound social science. Social science was a process of strict systematic empirical investigation.[17] The Webbs showed very little overt patience with talk of socialist ethics. Their language was permeated with Social Darwinism (in the case of Beatrice Webb, most probably derived from Herbert Spencer), eugenics, Comtian positivism, neo-classical political economy and radical utilitarianism (Crosland 1980, 84).

One of the initial Fabian Tracts – *Facts for Socialists* (1887) – established a general trend of thinking for many socialists in Britain. It was confidently asserted that 'no reasonable person who knows the facts can fail to become a socialist' (Sidney Webb quoted in Cole 1961, 18). The case for the scientific inevitability of socialism was to be made on an empirical level. Progress through socialism was to be revealed by empirical social science. Doubters were to be overwhelmed with the sheer mass of empirical detail concerning the efficiency and cost-effectiveness of socialism and the inefficiency of capitalism. Socialism, in this case, was the politics of rational control and good filing systems. Such efficiency included not only an elite of trained social science experts controlling affairs by precise plans, but also, ultimately, controlled breeding and the establishment of labour camps for the work-shy. How much actual science existed in this perspective is open to severe doubt. None of the major Fabians were scientifically trained or even fully scientifically literate. The term 'science' (although having strong roots in economic science) was more of a term of approbation. As W. H. Greenleaf has remarked, 'constant repetition [of the word 'science'] was intended to inspire confidence' (Greenleaf 1983, 371).

The judgement of capitalism in these cases was premised on its inevitable collapse, a demise based either on its inherent class tensions or alternatively, for the Fabians, on its total inefficiency and waste. Where a clear difference exists between classical Marxism and the Fabians it is over the issue of distribution. The Fabians, in general, did not accept any notion of historical determinism, namely, that all depends on the historical stage of an economy and its production. They believed in governmental action and the distribution of resources, not necessarily on moral grounds but rather on grounds of national and economic efficiency (see McBriar 1962). Marxists, on the other hand, placed little theoretical value on distribution via the state. Influenced by Engels's perspective, up to 1914 the state in vulgar Marxist theory always reflected class interests and could never achieve social justice.

Yet, with regard to the above point, nothing could be farther from the judgement of other socialist schools. The case to be made against capitalism for many socialists *was* its immorality. This moralistic stance can be found, paradoxically, also in some of the early utopians like Owen and Saint-Simon, combined with their enlightened rationalism. Neither Saint-Simon nor Owen was Christian, but Saint-Simon's final work, *The New Christianity* (1825) (see Saint-Simon 1964), which was taken up vigorously by the Saint-Simonian school as a quasi-religious doctrine, and Owen's later oracular spiritualism had all the resonance of the prophecy of a future spiritual golden age. Fourier also saw his role in cosmic and prophetic terms. The utopians frequently commented on capitalism and liberal political economy in tones of high moral disapproval.[18] This theme can be found expressed strongly in the work of mid-nineteenth-century Christian socialists such as Charles Kingsley, who overtly linked Christianity and socialism. It can equally be found in the twentieth-century exponents of liberation theology.

This view is also reflected in another aspect of Marxism: Marx's early philosophical writings. The so-called *Economic and Philosophical Manuscripts* in particular, discovered in the 1920s, reveal another side to Marx, namely, one which is concerned with the autonomous human self and free will (see Marx 1972; see also Leopold 2007). Alienation, in these early writings, is a moral and philosophical dilemma, not just inherent in capitalism. History is concerned not with rigid objective laws, but with loose tendencies and the redemption of humans from spiritual alienation. Consciousness and moral beliefs are seen to have a definite role in human affairs. This general current of thought, carried on into the twentieth century, is associated with the work of writers such as Gramsci, Marcuse, Lukács, Korsch and the Frankfurt school (see Jay 1976; Kolakowski 1981, vol. 3, chs vi–xi; Simon 1991). In more recent years it has been revived by a number of social theorists like Agnes Heller and Ferenc Fehér. These writers, as intellectual disciples of Lukács (see Lukács

1968), try to accommodate the themes of autonomy and occasionally morality within the Marxist perspective. This more autonomy-based Marxism has in the 1990s and early 2000s blended with elements of poststructuralism and postmodern theory. This has given rise, in some cases, to either a postmodern conception of Marx or, alternatively a more eclectic post-Marxian vision (often linked to themes of new social movements and identity politics), where class and similar concepts become 'social imaginaries', rather than definite empirical realities (see Laclau and Mouffe 1985; Carver 1998; Carver in Freeden ed. 2001; Derrida 2006). This has in turn generated long-standing debates between Marxists and post-Marxists to the present day in journals such as *New Left Review*.

The issues of morality and autonomy also figure in the revisionist debates. Eduard Bernstein, one of the key figures in the German SPD until his expulsion, argued that the case for socialism should be made on moral grounds, citing Kant as his mentor (see Bernstein 1961; also Gay 1952). This theme is by no means absent from the Fabian ranks. Writers like Sydney Olivier and Sidney Ball, contrary to the Webbs, premised their whole case on the morality of socialism (see Olivier in Shaw ed. 1931, 96ff; also Ball 1896). Their position had strong affinities with many in the social liberal faction, like L. T. Hobhouse (Hobhouse 1911).

The ethical and religious tendency also figures prominently in British socialism. Some commentators trace it back as an important facet of British political culture (see Dennis and Halsey 1988, 125–6).[19] From the late nineteenth century both William Morris and Belfort Bax looked to socialism as a remoralized order in society. Similarly, most of the early ILP figures, including Keir Hardie, spoke of their socialism continually in religious language. As one commentator has put it, in the 1880s 'the conversion to socialism seems often to have involved all the intense emotion of religious experience' (Callaghan 1990, 55). R. H. Tawney, who in Tony Wright's words 'shaped and expressed the thinking of a whole generation of British socialists', provides the clearest example of this ethical and religious theme (Wright 1983, 2). His attack on capitalism and the acquisitive society was premised upon their immorality and anti-Christian nature. Capitalism both was sinful and encouraged immoral tendencies in citizens (see Tawney 1921; Dennis and Halsey 1988, 151; Greenleaf 1983, 414; also Terrill 1974; Wright 1983 and 1987). In fact, Tawney came close to saying that to be a genuine Christian was to be a socialist. A functional socialist society would be a correct ordering and instantiation of Christian values, which would automatically deny a role for capitalism. Material progress required, first of all, moral progress and social evolution of the human personality.

In this stance humans are seen to shape their own order, whether moral or immoral. They make history autonomously. The major criticism directed by such moralists at the more scientific socialism was not only its hollow scientific pretensions but also its denial of the prime motivation for socialist criticism – morality. The scientifically minded socialists allowed little room for moral choice and moral critique. Determinism cuts away the foundation of socialism itself. A socialist cannot, from the scientific perspective, pursue values such as rights, social justice or equality, since socialism, by definition, is not about values at all. From a scientific socialist standpoint, the subsequent discussion of this chapter might be considered relatively worthless.

Values and morality, as many Marxists have seen them, are bourgeois illusions (see Lukes 1985; Vincent in Chadwick ed. 1998).

A critique of this rigid determinism, in a veiled form, can even be found within Marxism, in Gramsci's condemnation of 'economism' and, most significantly, within the loose intellectual association of the Frankfurt school. The problem with the ethical position, apart from the danger of 'high-minded moral whistling', is the very diversity of moral beliefs which have characterized the socialist critiques. Christian, Kantian, utilitarian, Hegelian idealism, natural law and natural rights theory and many others have constituted the bases of socialist morality. Such a diversity of often mutually hostile beliefs weakens the claim of socialism to any objective moral stance.

Other related perspectives which link up with questions of human nature and morality in socialism are the values associated with cooperation, fellowship, fraternity and community.[20] There is a strong core of belief, from the utopians up to early twenty-first-century socialism, that humans are cooperative creatures.[21] Society is ontologically prior to the individual. Furthermore, cooperation and community are superior values to individualism and egoism. Individualism denotes isolation and competition. Socialists have often argued that we are part of one another. This idea can be found even within Marxism in a more muted form. One sense of the term 'social' definitely implies commonality, mutuality and sharing. It can be identified in the earliest trade unions, friendly societies and cooperative societies. Despite this commitment to mutuality, however, it is clear that socialism was more directly communitarian in its earlier phases, where community denoted a more stateless decentralized situation. Later in the nineteenth century, many reformist and Marxist socialists tended, conversely, to rely on the state apparatus to achieve common aims via social welfare policy. However, the communal tendency, as found in groups like the guild socialists, was certainly not absent in the twentieth century. It was still a strong value in the writings of New Left figures like Raymond Williams and Edward Thompson (see Williams 1961; Chun 1993; Kenny 1995 and 2000).

There are both strong and weak senses of community and cooperation in socialism. The stronger sense of community is usually premised on a belief in a more objective, identifiable moral or religious consensus. The belief in common reason, common religious or moral beliefs or, in more restrained terms, what George Orwell might have called a common belief in the decency of humans pervades much socialist writing (Crick 1982, 507). The kind of society envisaged is more directly homogeneous and consensual. Such a notion, although superficially attractive, is difficult to uphold in an industrial scenario with rapid social, political and economic mobility. Many twentieth-century socialists, in the face of industrialism, contemplated much weaker and more formal understandings of community, premised on the mutual respect of citizens (see Miller in Paul et al. eds 1989; also Plant 1984). This tendency can be seen most clearly in reformist state socialism and the arguments for market socialism. One factor which has contributed to this weaker sense of community is the perception that strong communitarianism can be either simply foolishly nostalgic or reactionary. It must be recalled that over the nineteenth and twentieth centuries a number of conservative and fascist writers appealed with immense enthusiasm to the value of traditional communities (see Plant 1974; Vincent 2002, 139–40).

Equality and Liberty

Many commentators on socialism have taken equality as the key socialist value (Newman 2005, 141–2; see also Jackson 2003). All socialists, it is argued, must be first and foremost egalitarian. Conversely, liberty is not so often cited. The division between equality and liberty is frequently stressed by critics of socialism at this point. It is argued that to uphold equality (as is pointed out *ad nauseam* by Hayek and his disciples) is to deny the possibility of liberty. To uphold liberty is therefore to deny the possibility of equality. Thus it is contended that socialists cannot uphold liberty (see Sumption and Joseph 1979).

Equality is undoubtedly a crucial socialist value, but a number of questions remain to be answered. Have all socialists believed in equality? Further, have all socialists adhered to the same concept of equality? Finally, is equality automatically in contradiction with liberty? In other words, can there be a socialist conception of liberty which does not conflict with equality?

It is a common misapprehension to believe that all socialists have adhered to the core value of equality. Primarily a lot depends on what sense of equality is being discussed. Furthermore, it is not a value which figures prominently with all the utopian socialists. Fourier regarded egalitarian ideas as a poison. He accepted that there would be, in the socialist utopia, hierarchical orders, and wide inequalities in abilities, wealth and position. The rich were assured by Fourier that they could retain and indeed gain in wealth in a *Phalansterie*. Saint-Simon had similar beliefs to Fourier, although not quite so stark. Saint-Simon held that various hierarchical orders of society should be maintained. Given that both thinkers relied on the prospect of bankers and entrepreneurs financing their projects, they could hardly have wished to attack such privileges too vigorously.

Marx also, from a different perspective, was critical of egalitarian beliefs, seeing such normative claims and arguments as liberal bourgeois theorizing. As Allen Wood comments, Marx was 'no friend to the idea that "equality" is something good in itself' (Wood 1979, 281; also Vincent in Jessop and Wheatley eds 1999). The end result of communism might be egalitarian, but it would be pointless utopianism to speculate about such things. We could not *know* what society would look like until the consequences which flowed from given economic conditions gave shape to particular forms of life. In this latter argument we see an aspect of Marx's scientific legacy. Regardless of this, Marx did occasionally lapse into some speculation on equality and justice, although this tells us very little systematically about any egalitarian beliefs that he may or may not have had.

One common theme on equality within socialism, including Marx, is the wholesale rejection of the notion of literal factual equality, which is one of the most overexploited and hackneyed myths concerning socialism (Crick in Pimlott ed. 1984, 157). The nearest we come to such literal equality is in some of the more extreme communist views of Gracchus Babeuf or Étienne Cabet. The greater part of the socialist tradition has regarded such notions as absurd. Literal factual equality is nothing but a straw man set up by rival ideologies. The only mild exception to this is the claim advanced by some socialists, particularly in welfare state theories, that 'need' can be an empirical egalitarian principle for distribution in society. The concept of need is difficult to articulate and has a number of intrinsic problems.[22] Despite these problems, 'need' still falls far short of any sense of literal factual equality, as exemplified in some critiques of socialism. The response to need also does not imply universally equal treatment, as is often insinuated in the idea of literal equality.

A related question concerns whether socialists hold the same concept of equality. The answer to this must be somewhat negative. We must disentangle a number of points here to illustrate the complexity of this question. First, equality as a value is distinct from any literal or factual assertions about human equality. Second, the various justifications for the value of equality should be analysed. Third, 'equality as a goal' must be kept distinct from 'equality as a condition'. Finally, the means to achieve equality should not be confused with the goals of equality.

Firstly, contrary to the claims of some critics, socialists, with some exceptions, adhere to the belief that equality is something that 'ought' to be pursued. It is not an empirical or factual notion (apart from some of the claims made for need). Socialists do not assert that humans are, or can be, literally equal in physical or mental abilities. Conversely, they argue that regardless of natural differences in race, sex, abilities or class, there are valuable morally relevant qualities which should direct us to treat individuals equally. However, to move on to the second point, the moral justifications for such equality have varied considerably. The most mundane has been the Fabian belief that greater equality would lead to greater efficiency. Equality, according to this definition, is an instrumental value, although not all Fabians were so impressed with equality, even in this minimal sense.[23] Most justifications of equality involve either, somewhat negatively, a questioning of the acceptance of inequality, or a more positive advancement of reasons for equal treatment.

On the positive side, that is, justifying substantive equality, the Christian socialists, Tawney, and the like, have focused on the Judaeo-Christian idea of the equality of souls before God (see Tawney 1964). Many ethical and state socialists have utilized variations of idealist, natural rights, Kantian and utilitarian arguments, particularly the latter two. The equality in the last two arguments is premised, first, on each individual being considered equal in terms of possessing a rational will, which is of equal worth and deserving of equal respect; and, second, on each individual being capable of satisfying his or her interests and of achieving happiness and thus meriting equal consideration in both respects.[24]

The third theme is that equality as a goal or outcome should be kept distinct from equality as a condition. Socialism has been predominantly associated with achieving the goal of equality in society. The outcomes of human endeavours should not give rise to inequality. Socialism has also advocated the idea that equality can be a condition or opportunity for the development of human beings, what is now sometimes referred to as a 'starting-gate' equality. Without a basic minimum of educational, health and welfare conditions as a point of departure, individuals cannot develop their potentialities and powers. Social and economic outcomes, from this original starting-point, could reflect moderate levels of inequality. Such a notion of equality is more compatible with liberty than 'equality as a goal' (see Plant in Le Grand and Estrin eds 1989).

Finally, the *means* to achieve equality should not be confused with either the justifications, goals or conditions of equality. Because nationalization (in Britain) or a command economy (in the old USSR) has been associated with socialism, it is occasionally assumed that all egalitarian socialists are seeking to justify these particular means, and that all socialists therefore believe in command economies or nationalization. This is plainly wrong. The means for achieving equality have been reflected in a wide spectrum of proposals. Certainly, command economies and nationalization have been adopted as means. Socialists (including Marxists in France, Italy and Britain) have also advocated equality within both mixed and market economies. There are many shades of grey within these arguments. In the attempt to achieve economic equality, at one extreme, equality of income has been suggested by such diverse figures as the Fabian George Bernard Shaw and the Bolshevik Lenin. However, the redistribution of wealth through progressive taxation, welfare benefits and established national minimums has probably been the most popular option adopted by revisionist, state and ethical socialism since the twentieth century (see White 2003 and 2006). There are, in sum, a bewildering range of methods utilized in this domain.

Socialists have not limited themselves to economic equality. They have also shared with some liberals the demands for political equality of suffrage for all citizens. The call for full legal equality of civil rights has thus been another characteristic theme. Social equality, in terms of equal rights to a modicum of civilized existence, implying equality in health and education, has been another important facet of the idea. In recent years there has been a strong tendency to extend all these dimensions of equality towards gender issues, the argument being that women have often been subtly excluded from such developments in the past (see Squires 2007). This question will be taken up within the chapter on feminism. Admittedly all these entitlement rights and justice-based proposals have been more characteristic of the reformist traditions within socialism. Classical Marxism tended to repudiate rights-based theories, although in last decades of the twentieth century European Communist Parties, for example, in Britain and the Italy, moved substantially towards the constitutional socialist position.

It should be recalled, though, that pluralist socialists have not accepted statist methods, but have favoured distributing power and authority to groups and associations (see Hirst 1988). Guild socialists and syndicalists, particularly, favoured a very minimal or non-state situation (see Cole 1917 and 1980). Equality, in this case, would be attained within groups of workers. Thus, overall, equality within socialism has many means available to it and should not be irrevocably tied to any particular one policy.

Finally, the rigid separation between equality and liberty should be regarded with scepticism. The separation is premised upon an equally rigid definition of negative liberty as 'non-restraint', 'restraint' being understood also in very limited stipulative terms, as examined in chapter 2 (see Dimova-Cookson 2003). If it is argued that liberty is concerned with maximizing choices and the development of the individual (which many socialists have believed), then creating the equal conditions for making informed choices (implying adequate education, health and income), and thus developing human potential, denotes the compatibility of the values of liberty and equality. A socialist conception of liberty is thus a perfectly feasible idea and does not necessarily conflict with equality as a conditional notion.

State and Democracy

It is sometimes presumed that all socialists are statists. It is also assumed that all state socialists hold to the same concept of the state and that all are equally self-conscious about the state. These assumptions are inaccurate. It is undeniable that from the 1880s onwards a dominant strain of reformist socialism, and also Marxism in institutional practice rather than theory, has been overtly statist. It should not, however, be assumed that such statism characterizes the whole movement, or that such statist practice implies some form of coherent theory. Both points are questionable. There are a number of profoundly difficult questions on the issue of the state in relation to socialism which need to be unpacked. A relatively convenient heuristic distinction can be made initially between, on the one hand, the more state-organizational socialism and, on the other hand, the pluralist and libertarian socialisms.

The notion of state-organizational socialism is often regarded as synonymous with collectivism. This synonymity has already been questioned. Collectivism is not only a method which transcends socialism, but it also implies a number of different potential strategies, and has been repudiated by many socialists. Furthermore, despite the fact that Marxism is often regarded as a deeply statist doctrine and is conventionally taken as the archetype of the centralized socialist state, one looks in vain within the corpus of Marx and Engels's writings for any positive theory of the state. What one finds instead is an overwhelmingly negative analysis of the state (see Vincent 1987, ch. 5; Bobbio 1987; Bartelson 2001, 116ff).

A basic summary of Marx's position would be that the material conditions of life are primary. These form the base for social and political structures as well as for human consciousness. Humans must produce in order to survive before they can think in any systematic way. Classes form or condense around economic interests within a mode of production, at any particular epoch in history. Individuals are defined by their class position. They relate to each other as members of classes. Because classes receive differential rewards of power and property and such differences are a consequence of exploitative relations, the state structure is premised upon certain property, class and, thus, exploitative interests. The state is not a product of human thought or intention. On the contrary, it is determined by class and the struggle between classes. The state is usually, therefore, regarded as an oppressive agent for a particular class.

There are a number of difficulties with this more conventional view. First, Marx never offers a precise account as to what the state embraces. Does it include all administration – educational institutions, police, local government – as well as the executive, judiciary and legislature? No clear guidance on this is offered in any of the writings of Marx and Engels. In addition, no systematic account is given of the alternatives to the state, only vague hints on federalized communes which bear a closer relationship to anarchy. Furthermore, no clear description is given of the nature of class, its precise relation to property ownership and the state.

Occasionally Marx and Engels see the state as simply emerging from the material base. *The Communist Manifesto*, and other popular writings, often identify the state as simply an expression or instrument of class rule – the executive committee of the bourgeoisie, which had to be smashed by revolution. This was a doctrine which not only dominated the official views of the German SPD, but later became enshrined in the Russian-dominated Comintern. At other points, in writings such as *The Eighteenth Brumaire of Louis Bonaparte* (1852), the state appears as a more complex structure, possessing some autonomy and also independent of any particular class. Marx even suggested that countries like Britain might not require a revolution for the transformation to socialism. Later writers in the Marxist tradition, particularly those influenced by the work of Gramsci, see the state as having considerable autonomy and have consequently criticized the crude deterministic 'economism' and positivism which are particularly characteristic of Engels's views.

Marxism is not alone in this ambivalence on the state. Reformist state socialists, such as the Fabians, have also been notoriously vague on the question. As one writer has put it, 'Early Fabian writings contain scant examination or description of what the state might actually be' (see Barker in Pimlott ed. 1984, 28). Much the same could be said of most Fabian writings into the 2000s. There are some doubts raised about the state in Fabian circles, even, oddly, by the Webbs, but overall the tendency of the Fabians has been to see the state as a neutral instrumental device or apparatus, won over by representative democracy and utilized for the purpose of greater social and economic efficiency. Salvation would come about through a trained expert bureaucracy. In spite of the fact that the name Fabianism earlier the twentieth century was associated with local or municipal government and even industrial democracy, the Webbs and their acolytes none the less favoured centralized elite control and a benevolent paternal state apparatus.

The above view of many of the Fabians, particularly the Webbs, also links up with their idea of democracy. Some still see democracy as crucial to the whole socialist position (see Hirst in Hindess ed. 1990). Yet, if one looks more closely at the socialist tradition, not all Fabians share this view. At least, they share different visions of democracy. For the Webbs or G. B. Shaw, extending suffrage or even women's rights had limited appeal. They had little faith in the average citizen. Government was generally *for* the people, not *by* the people. In the case of the early utopian writers there was also little interest *per se* in democracy, certainly that associated with representation. Robert Owen was extremely doubtful of parliamentary democracy as being anything but a loose veil over corruption and injustice. Neither did Marx show much interest in the topic. The nearest he came to this was in his unsystematic speculations about direct democracy in the Paris Commune. This vision of direct participatory democracy lurks in the wings of both anarchy and some later Marxist socialists. However, for Marx and Engels, democracy looked more like another capitalist and bourgeois illusion obscuring real class interests. Such a view would not represent the ideas of more recent Communist Parties in Europe, where there has been a great deal of rethinking and name-changing over the last few decades.

Reformist state socialists since the twentieth century, as in the British Labour and French socialist parties and the German SPD, market socialists and some ethical socialists, have fully accepted the notion of representative parliamentary democracy. Reformist state socialism has acquired some relative electoral success, although if one looks now at the periods of the Labour Party or German SPD in political office, the results are not terribly impressive, with the key exception of the New Labour administration at the turn of the twenty-first century. There has also been some tentative interest in industrial democracy and cooperatives, usually muted by scepticism about their true efficacy or efficiency. Direct participatory democracy has had little interest for the mainstream of reformist state socialism.

The above tendency has not reflected the totality of the socialist response on either the state or democracy. Within the Marxist tradition, as indicated, there has been a strong anti-statist tendency which derives from Marx and Engels's own views. In the case of Lenin's *The State and Revolution* (1917) there was a vision of a non-state, commune-based society, run by local soviets of workers. This 'odd' line of thought in Lenin (associated as he later was with totalitarian views of the state) was taken very seriously in Gramsci's council communism premised on his experiences in Turin. Such a conciliar communism was closely tied to Gramsci's theoretical position, which emphasized the proletariats' self-organization. Organic working-class intellectuals could formulate and express this new proletarian consciousness (see Gramsci 1986; also Femia 1981 and Simon 1991).

Within guild socialism in Britain there was also a strong anti-state and pluralist line of thought at work, although it should be noted that there was no one clear position on this. Without trying to complicate matters unduly, there were a number of tendencies within the movement, particularly the medieval as against the national guildists (see Penty 1906; Hobson 1920; Cole 1980). The guild socialists not only suggested that authority, welfare, and the like, should be devolved to producer groups; they also subscribed, even in the national guild scheme, to very minimal functions for the state. In the case of G. D. H. Cole and S. G. Hobson, geographical representative democracy was to be supplemented by both direct participatory democracy, within producer groups, and functional democracy premised upon producer associations, forming more or less an industrial parliament. Tawney's dislike of the policy of nationalization and his discussions of a functional society owe much to the guild perspective (see Tawney 1921). The guild or pluralist perspective has had a perennial appeal for generations of socialists up to the present (Rustin 1985; Hirst 1988). It has even reappeared on the peripheries of the very recent discussions of market socialism. Its support still raises the temperature and diversity of contemporary political debate within socialism (Plant 1984, 5).

The prevailing problem of the state in socialism is that in Britain – a political culture which has not been historically receptive to state theory – the socialist tradition has not formulated a clear or consistent theory of the state (Vincent 1992). In many other European countries, like Germany and France, which do have self-conscious state traditions, the socialist discussion has historically been more dominated by Marxian vocabulary and has incorporated three tendencies: a deeply negative critique of the state; an ambivalence about what happens to the state under communism;

and, in Eastern Europe, an institutional record which was depressingly authoritarian and distant from all socialist aspirations. The question of democracy has cross-cut all these issues. There is therefore no consistent socialist picture on either democracy or the state within socialism.

In the same manner, there is very little consistency on socialist proposals for social and political change. The extremities of socialist strategy lie in revolution and constitutional reform. In between these extremes lies a bewildering range of proposals. Originally utopians sought the help of wealthy bankers to set up experimental socialist communities, which would generate further communities by example. They assumed, too, common resources of reason. This notion of creating an example for others to admire and follow was also suggested by guild socialists in the twentieth century.

By the later nineteenth century a number of dominant strategies had developed. Reformist state socialists advocated setting up constitutional socialist parties committed to the existing representational democratic arrangements. Socialism would gradually evolve through the electoral process. This method was often called socialist gradualism. In the case of the Fabians it was sometimes coupled with the strategy of placing trained experts in key political and administrative positions, thereby gradually permeating government and administration with socialism.

On the more revolutionary side, some guild socialists toyed with the syndicalist notion of direct action, namely, the latter's crucial concept of the 'general strike' of all workers which would bring about a capitalist collapse. Those influenced by Lenin favoured a more direct insurrectionary tactic through a vanguard party of trained and disciplined revolutionaries. This was attacked by other Marxists as employing the means of Jacobin revolutionaries and not working with the proletariat. Within the mainstream of Marxism, strategy was an immensely sore issue. Marx and Engels had formulated no single consistent view, thus support could be found in their writings for most methods: a long-term proletarian struggle; short-term insurrection; waiting for industrial capitalism to come to fruition with all its attendant contradictions, when revolution would happen inevitably; a proletarian revolutionary party committed to educating the proletariat; a self-organized conciliar structure within the proletariat, committed to intellectual and political struggle against bourgeois hegemony; revolution in one country; world revolution, and so on. All these strategies, and more, have found support within the Marxist tradition.

This uncertainty over strategy is reflected in the ambiguities as to who should carry it through. Who are the actors of socialism? The most popular contender is that elusive entity 'the working class'. Many socialists have had doubts about the existence of the working class (see Gorz 1982; Kitching 1983, 62–3). There are even ambiguities in Marx's accounts as to who, or what, constitutes their ranks. However, while the working class have constituted an electoral majority since the twentieth century in all European states, they have been equally active in support of deeply conservative, liberal, national socialist and fascist groups. There is nothing intrinsically socialist here.

It is also clear that many socialists have not believed in the working class as the chief actor of socialism. The utopians had virtually no conceptions of class;

socialism was to be brought about by prophetic figures like themselves, with the support of wealthy patrons. Lenin, in a different context, in his famous *What Is to Be Done?* (1902), suggested that socialist consciousness had to be injected into the working class from outside by the true socialist actors, an elite of vanguardist revolutionaries. Others, like Rosa Luxemburg, advocated a much wider proletarian party taking the lead with an intrinsically revolutionary proletariat. Gramsci added organic intellectuals to a self-organized proletariat. Mao Tse-tung identified the agricultural peasantry as the revolutionary actors. The more syndicalist-inspired cooperative socialists and guild socialists have seen producer groups, like cooperatives and trade unions, as the true actors of socialism. Yet for the Fabians, like Shaw and the Webbs, both trade unionists and the working class in general were viewed as ignorant and stupid.[25] The true socialist actors were an expert bureaucracy trained in the social sciences. In the broad reformist tradition, socialists have veered away from classes and elites and seen socialism as pursued by all men and women of good sense and goodwill. Thus, again, one looks in vain for a consistent account of the true actors of socialism.

Markets and the Economy

If there is one view which purports to be socialist, it is that socialism is always critical of free markets and capitalism and proposes a planned economy as the alternative. This is an essential part of the popular myth about socialism. It is, however, an odd and mistaken view. There are varieties of both public ownership and state action in the economy, as there are also varieties of market activity.

On a very simple level, public ownership could imply total collective control and ownership of an industry by the state. This is usually the archetype of ownership. It could also mean ownership of the commanding industries, banks and insurance companies of an economy. This alone would allow a vast private sector. Alternatively, it could imply the ownership of what are sometimes regarded as natural monopolies, as in communications and water supplies. Furthermore, ownership could be decentralized to a company; in the latter case, the state could keep a weather eye on industry, with the option of some indirect influence on major policy or strategic investment decisions, or possibly allowing grants or financial incentives to certain enterprises. This is perfectly consistent with privatization initiatives. The nature of state involvement in the economy, in whatever format, could also vary considerably. Apart from outright ownership, managers could be state-appointed, with responsibility to a minister. They could be expected to set financial targets. The state could take a majority shareholding, a significant shareholding, or simply lay down broad policy parameters. It could also provide a financial environment, training or preferential finance to benefit certain industries. It is, in fact, difficult to see any economy where some of these conditions do not exist.[26]

Such diversity in the understanding of state action in the economy needs to be extended to the understanding of markets and capitalism. Capitalism has varied considerably according to the societies in which it has appeared. Also, although markets are necessary to the existence of capitalism – which itself has an obscure and odd history often linked closely to the development of the state – it is questionable as to whether markets *per se* necessarily require capitalism. Even in the heyday of the lumbering command economy of what was the USSR, markets existed and in some cases flourished both in the black economy and in the state sector. The notion of a market cannot therefore be restricted to capitalism – an argument which is central to market socialism.

It is true that socialism has been overtly critical of capitalism. Yet the substance of that criticism has been discordant. Generally capitalism has been linked, since the mid-nineteenth century, with poverty, unemployment and social distress. This has been a perennial reproach.[27] Further, capitalism is seen both to generate and to exacerbate inequalities, creating deep social tension. It fosters harmful, anti-social and competitive attitudes. Private consumption and want satisfaction are encouraged, whereas public goods and the satisfaction of genuine human needs are neglected. Consequently capitalism undermines fellowship, solidarity and cooperation. The patterns of distribution in capitalist societies are uncontrolled and arbitrary. Profit is always prioritized over the creative production of goods. Capitalism therefore destroys the enjoyment and aesthetic pleasure of production. It ignores the costs to people, unless they can be measured as tangible profits or losses. People themselves are viewed as commodities which can be bought or sold.

Many socialists have tended to see the above amalgam of criticisms through moral lenses. Capitalism, for Tawney and the ethical socialists, was basically immoral. It adhered to the wrong value order. While such capitalist values remained, society could never be redeemed, reformed or improved. Yet the classical Marxist tradition, even within the humanist perspective, tended to take a more historical view of capitalism. As a mode of production, capitalism would be historically superseded, whether by the inevitabilities of materialist dialectics, direct revolutionary overthrow or the subtle strategies of intellectual and political manoeuvre. Ethics was not significant in this reading. The upshot of Fabian criticism, on the other hand, was that capitalism was both inefficient and wasteful. There was no interest in either historical inevitability or morality. Capitalism had to be superseded or managed by a socialist-controlled state apparatus to bring about efficiency in the economy. Inequality was not so much ethically suspect as wasteful of human resources.

It should also be noted that within this same argument the sources of socialist economic theory have been as varied as their criticisms of capitalism. Marxian economic theory, Ricardian and classical economic theory, the neo-classical writings of Philip Wicksteed and Francis Edgeworth, Keynesianism, have all been utilized by the diverse schools of socialism in their analyses of capitalism. In fact, in terms of reformist state socialism in Britain, from 1945 up to the late 1970s, the social liberal John Maynard Keynes was undoubtedly the most influential economist.

Equally, if we look for socialist alternatives to capitalism we find many different and often contradictory projects. The initial ideas developed by some utopians were anti-political in nature. In the case of writers as diverse as William Morris and Charles Fourier we are presented with a future that is non-industrial, non-statist, communal and pastoral. In this form of society, work would become an aesthetic and sensual pleasure. No roles or tasks would be fixed. Production would be for basic well-made goods to satisfy human needs. Marxism, as it developed, however, despite its often vague decentralist communist suggestions for a future society, became associated in practice with highly industrialized 'total' societies, organized and commanded by a state apparatus. The future abundance would be determined by state direction of industries. As the anarchist Mikhail Bakunin had predicted during the early years of classical Marxism, a new state despotism would result from such Marxian doctrine.

Reformist state socialists since the twentieth century have accepted industrial development with open arms, but usually with a mix of private and public owner-ship, a developed nationalization programme with a vigorous free-market sector. Pluralist socialists have varied in their response. Some, such as A. J. Penty, called for a return to an anti-industrial, pastoral and medieval guild-based society. Others, like G. D. H. Cole, argued for the abandonment of capitalism (but not industrialism) and the wage system, and the adoption of an economy premised upon industrial guilds (see Penty 1906; Wright 1979; Cole 1980). These would control prices, wages and the welfare of their members. Such a policy would be decentralist and emphatically not statist. This view is still criticized by state-orientated socialists (see Plant in Le Grand and Estrin eds 1989, 71).

Finally, there was a vigorous attempt in the 1980s and 1990s (eventuating in the New Labour administrations) to make socialists rethink the notion of the market. In Britain this idea was prefigured in the work of Hugh Gaitskell and Evan Durban. It also embodied many of the ideas of the social market economy promulgated in German post-war politics. In Britain some in the Fabian Society and Socialist Philosophers Group in the 1990s advocated market socialism as a response to the advances of the New Right ideology. The basic idea was that market socialism was committed neither to full-blooded capitalism nor to state centralization. It was, though, interested in a society 'where power is more widely distributed ... where the interests of owners of capital, of workers, and of consumers, are all taken into account with none taking automatic priority' (Le Grand and Estrin eds 1989, 23). The market, decoupled from capitalism, could be retained as a useful allocator of goods and services. All citizens ought to be enabled to enter the market on as fair terms as possible. The equal *worth* of liberty, for all citizens, was as important as the principle of equal liberty. To take advantage of the market, to use our liberty and shape our lives, we needed to be *enabled* to do so. Adequate health-care and educa-tion could thus form the basis and means for adequate choice. In this context a socialist market economy could flourish, allowing for the maximum compatibility of equality and liberty. Planning would still exist, but it would very be far less interven-tionary. An accommodation to the market has even been evident since the 1990s in the remaining *apparently* Marxist regimes, in Vietnam, Cuba and China, which have adapted themselves (virtually totally in the case of China) to market behaviour.[28]

In sum, the usual charge made against socialism of being attached to state-run com-mand economies, wholesale nationalization and opposed to markets (caricatured particularly in the East European post-1945 experience) is simply false. Socialism, like most ideologies, embodies deep, subtle and often contradictory views.

Conclusion

The future of one form of socialism now seems to be at an end. Subsequently many have raised the question as to whether socialism has any future (see Geoghegan 1996). It is certainly true that one of most dominant elements of the socialist tradition in the late nineteenth and twentieth centuries (institutionalized Marxist-Leninism) received some fatal body-blows in the 1980s and 1990s, particularly with the collapse of the old USSR and the Eastern European bloc. Although this was fatal for a stultified association of Marxist socialism with command economies, it was by no means fatal to the broad socialist tradition (which still incorporates Marxism in a different format), which has not necessarily looked to overthrow markets. It is worth noting, though, that Marxism itelf has mutated and developed in various unexpected ways in the last few decades, particularly in writers such as Michael Hardt and Antonio Negri, and predominantly in the critical context of the globalization of capitalist markets.[29] Although it is hazardous to make any predictions in the ideological realm, it is clear that some radical changes are beginning to take place in left-inclining politics, and Marxism is but one facet of this. Some aspects of the anti-globalization and anti-capitalist movements could well be developing and showing a new dimension of ideological politics, particularly on the Left. There are, though, overlaps here with anarchism, ecology and, to a lesser extent, feminism and poststructuctural theory, which at this stage are difficult to interpret.

Reformist state socialism has come in for less severe criticism in the last few decades, though its attachment to certain types of nationalization policy and public ownership has been perceived to be a failure. However, given that such nationalization policies have also been supported by certain schools of both conservatism and liberalism, this is hardly a fault to be laid at the door of reformist socialism. The more ethical, reformist state and market socialist perspectives have been well able to adapt to more positive conceptions of the market order. Elements of the anti-capitalism perspective have certainly not disappeared from the ideological scene. On the contrary, they have reappeared or been transmuted (with a less certain ideological character) into more populist anti-capitalist and anti-globalization theories which may well develop much further in the next few decades.

The notions of market socialism and the social market economy have been explored by a number of socialist theorists over the last few decades. In fact because of the overlap between these traditions and social democratic and social liberal traditions, for many they have appeared to provide one of the more feasible alternatives to both conservative and classical liberal ideological visions. Socialism, despite the manifest dangers in some of its formats, its tendency towards communal nostalgia and its occasional attachment to a mechanistic statism and elitism, is still a fruitful and immensely adaptable ideological tradition which reflects an important mode of human self-understanding and moral aspiration and will continue to develop new ideas into the twenty-first century.

5

Anarchism

The discussion of socialism leads fairly naturally on to anarchism, with which it shares a number of ideological affinities. In point of fact, some of the ideas and schools of anarchy have been categorized as forms of socialism, although equally it should not be forgotten that some have been classified as liberal. Indeed, anarchy clearly overlaps with both ideologies.

The word 'anarchy' is a compound of two Greek words, *an* and *arkhê*, which means, literally, the absence of government or rulers. More commonly the term 'the state' (in place of government or rulers) is used through the nineteenth and twentieth centuries. An ambiguity creeps in here which can be destructive of a clearer understanding of the ideology. The idea of being 'without a state and government' can slip into the notion of being 'without authority or rules', which can in turn become, by verbal slippage, an equivalent to disorder, chaos or confusion. We can recognize these two senses in ordinary speech, namely, where anarchy can refer to a way of life without the state, or where it can denote complete mayhem. The latter is sometimes personified and parodied in the cartoon caricature of the anarchist about to throw a smoking bomb.[1]

Anarchists rightly object to such confusions in speech. Yet, they have not always discouraged the idea that anarchy might involve terror, destruction and mayhem. There has been an ironic wit and pleasure in the confusing implications of the idea of anarchy, a confusion emphasized by proponents and critics alike (see Ward 2004). The Russian anarchist Mikhail Bakunin's famous, if ambiguous, comment that 'the destructive urge is a creative urge' catches something of the flavour of this playful duplicity (see Dolgoff 1972; Kelly 1982; Leier 2006). Certainly late nineteenth- and early-twentieth century literature which portrayed anarchists, such as Joseph Conrad's *The Secret Agent* (1907) or Émile Zola's *Germinal* (1885), plays upon this ambiguity.

Yet anarchy itself, as an ideological movement, is, as most commentators agree, difficult to pin down with precision. Like other ideologies it incorporates a wide spectrum of opinions.[2] It should therefore not be over-simplified.[3] This complexity is due not only to the multiplicity of anarchy's exponents, but also to the problematic questions at the very centre of the ideology. For example, does the notion of 'doing without the state' automatically imply 'doing without government'? Do anarchists reject all authority or do they distinguish between types of authority? Is there a distinction to be drawn between authoritarian domination and moral authority? If the state, and possibly government, are absent, does any form of collective identity, such as society, remain? Is society simply an aggregation of contracting individuals or an organic unity?

As in the ideologies previously discussed, the word 'anarchy' is of comparatively recent origin. It entered into political currency fairly late in the nineteenth century. The first use of the term to denote a political position is to be found in Pierre-Joseph Proudhon's work *What is Property? An Inquiry into the Principle of Right and Government* (1840). This work not only coined the notoriously equivocal remark 'all property is theft', but also contained a clear assertion of, and commitment to, anarchy. As Proudhon stated: 'As man seeks justice in equality, so society seeks order in anarchy. Anarchy – the form of government to which we are every day approximating.' Proudhon defined anarchy as the 'absence of a master, of a sovereign' (Proudhon 1970b, 88–9; see also Woodcock 1972b). This and other similar statements in the book gave rise to the appellation 'father of anarchy', in respect of Proudhon, though the man has remained a profoundly confusing figure.

Before Proudhon, anarchy was used more as an abusive term, implying disorder. It retained connotations of abuse even up to the First International (1864). Thus Bakunin initially did not utilize the term as a means of self-description. From the late 1860s he preferred the term 'collectivist', partly indeed to dissociate himself from the followers of Proudhon.[4] In addition, collectivists were not necessarily anti-statist, a point which has continued to make some anarchists uncomfortable with Bakunin. Marx, on the other hand, did employ the word 'anarchist' as an insult, indicating not only utopian impracticality, but also those individuals who, in his view, wanted to destroy the International. His target was most often Bakunin, who, in consequence, initially tried to distance himself from the term. The nomenclature 'anarchy' subsequently followed a tortured and circuitous history in the congresses and heated debates of the International through the 1870s. It was not until the 1880s that it began to be used more widely in Europe and America to denote a comprehensive movement and a distinct ideological position (see Cahm 1989, 36–43).

The Origins of Anarchist Thought

Debates about the origins of anarchism can be broken down into three main types. The first of these need not detain us long. There are those who claim that anarchism is essentially an all-pervasive universal and ahistorical libertarian disposition. It is argued that from the Ancient Greek writers onward we can find anarchist sentiments expressed. In the same vein it is also asserted that anarchist themes are to be found within ancient Chinese texts such as the *Tao te Ching*. The American anarchist writer John Clark describes this Taoist work as 'one of the great anarchist classics' (Clark 1986, 163; see also Marshall 1993, ch. 4; Sheehan 2003).[5] General libertarian-inclined movements and thinkers, from the time of Socrates, are all in imminent danger of being incorporated into this 'catch-all' perspective. Sophists, ranters, anabaptists and counter-culture movements from the 1960s become part of the same libertarian disposition. There is an intellectual weak-mindedness here that ignores historical and sociological factors. A similarly shallow view can be found, at some point, in the explanation of most ideologies. There is a strong demand for an 'ancient lineage' in all ideologies which often overwhelms intellectual caution.

The second perspective enjoys a more substantial credibility. It is rooted in the anthropological investigation that began in earnest in the nineteenth century with writers such as Lewis Morgan. Here, the basic claim is that anarchism either has strong parallels with, or (more forcefully) that anarchism can be found in embryo in, primitive acephalous forms of society throughout the world. The early example of the stronger thesis is to be found in Peter Kropotkin's work *Mutual Aid* (1902). A modern form of the claim, with different intellectual roots, is represented by Michael Taylor's *Community, Anarchy and Liberty* (1982). As Taylor argues: 'During almost all the time since *Homo Sapiens* emerged, he has lived in stateless "primitive" communities' (Taylor 1982, 33). Many of these societies can be described as primitive anarchies. Taylor distinguishes between certain types of primitive societies, finding that 'acephalous' societies approach 'much more closely to the pure anarchy'.[6] Defending his thesis, Taylor remarks: 'I do not see how anyone interested in anarchy or in community can or ought to avoid examining these communities, for they constitute the chief, almost the only historical examples of anarchy and quasi-anarchy and they are important examples of community on almost any account of the concept' (Taylor 1982, 33).

This view of the origins of anarchy presents a number of problems. There is still a facet of the 'ancient lineage' perspective here, although less pronounced, which lays it open to the charge of sociological and historical anachronism. A false conceptual universalism pervades this view, even though it is premised on the more respectable concepts of nineteenth-century anthropological positivism. There is also a certain ingenuousness concerning the types of organization. Because something is stateless, or headless, does not necessarily mean that it has to be placed under a very particular nineteenth-century rubric of anarchy. Why not conceive of it as another form of social organization? Why the desire to incorporate such phenomena into the categories of contemporary ideologies? Furthermore, the religious and social views of such primitive societies appear very different to the world of nineteenth- and twentieth-century anarchy. Again there is an element of almost romantic parochialism in the attempt to assimilate such different worlds. Rousseau's noble savage appears to lurk behind the neat public-good arguments. The forms of belief and the forms of control in such primitive societies might in fact now be considered considerably worse than state control.[7] Many of these primitive societies, despite not having over-arching authority, were immersed in sorcery, magic, cruelty, threat, mutual hostility, and certainly do not look like exemplars of mutual respect or liberty. As one investigation of such primitive groups argued:

> The absence of the State as a method of social organization does not *necessarily* involve
> the absence of those other undesirable features of western society that we would like to

see abolished: competition, class division, status seeking, authoritarianism, restrictions on individual freedom, and so on. The acceptance of this myth is partly a result of the nine-teenth-century tendency to seek universal monocausal explanations. (Pilgrim 1965, 367)

The third view of the origins of anarchism locates it as a comparatively late off-spring of the Enlightenment and the French Revolutionary era (Thomas 1980, 7–8; Cahm 1989, 7; Marshall 1993, x–xi). Apart from William Godwin (1756–1836) – who certainly expressed much of the sense of the concept of anarchy, feeding into one of the diverse currents of the French Revolution – anarchy itself was a product of the later nineteenth century (see Clark 1977; Marshall 1993, 191ff). Its forceful appearance in the 1880s was not fortuitous. Anarchy can be seen as a confluence of, or an interstice between, liberalism and socialism. As the German anarchist Rudolf Rocker aptly put it, anarchism is 'the confluence of the two great currents which during and since the French Revolution have found such characteristic expression in the intellectual life of Europe: Socialism and Liberalism' (Rocker 1989, 21).[8] This does not mean that there is nothing distinctive about anarchy, yet it does signify considerable overlaps between it and other ideologies.

The period of the anarchist movement can be dated from approximately the 1880s until the 1930s. The Spanish Civil War saw the last vigorous attempts to set up anar-chistic communes, unless, that is, one includes the counter-culture movement of the 1960s (see Brenan 1969; Smith 2007; Graham 2008). Anarchists were essentially involved on the edge of two major revolutions: in Russia and in Spain. In both cases they were fairly quickly eliminated. In the example of the Ukrainian anarchists led by Nestor Makhno after the Russian Revolution, their success was prolonged through war conditions. Whether Makhno's movement was genuinely anarchist, given the extreme conditions of the war, is debatable (see Avrich 1967, 209–22; Guérin 1970, 98–101; Arshinov 1974).

Some writers have contended, as suggested, that a return to anarchist themes can be seen in the counter-culture movements of the 1960s, as well as in the anti-capitalist, anti-globalization and new social movements of the 1990s, to the present day (see Marshall 1993; Sheehan 2003; Tormey 2004; Day 2005; Franks 2006; Mayer 2008). The only difficulty which occurs here is that many of these latter movements, although clearly ideological and influential in certain sectors, are as yet difficult to read. The movements, to date, appear to contain elements of a more negative local-ized resistance to global forces, combined with positive forms of anarchism, ecology, feminism and socialism. The ideas of Michael Hardt and Antonio Negri on the dif-fuse, leaderless and unstructured character of *multitude* encapsulates some of this sense of deep internal complexity; although these particular authors see this multi-tude category as signalling a new and potentially emancipatory politics (see Hardt and Negri 2006). Issues such as growing industrialization, globalized capitalism, nuclear power, pollution, the threat of global ecological crisis, the escalation of state power and warfare, have clearly radicalized a new generation with, what might appear at times to be, anarchistic ideas (Marshall 1993; Purchase 1995; Day 2005). Anarchist writers from the 1950s (or in some cases from the 1930s), such as Paul Goodman, Herbert Read, Alex Comfort, Colin Ward, Noam Chomsky and Murray

Bookchin, all addressed similar themes from within a methodical anarchist perspective (see Ward 1973, 2004; Bookchin 1982, 1986a, 1986b, 1992; Marshall 1993, 539ff; Chomsky 2004).[9] A new generation of journals, such as *Black Rose*, *Harbinger*, *Telos* and *The Raven*, have continued to promote the anarchist critique. In addition, the Freedom Press, Black Rose and AKPress continue to publish large amounts of anarchist-related literature.

The question as to why anarchism developed from the 1860s and 1870s is complex, the answer often being specific to particular societies. For example, the reasons for the development of Russian anarchism might be very different to the reasons for the development of the American, Spanish or French variants. To some extent there is also an intellectual dimension to the origin of different forms of anarchy, a point that will be discussed in the next section. Thus the origin of individualist anarchism has closer intellectual affinities to classical liberalism, whereas communist and collectivist anarchism were forged in the heated intellectual debates with Blanquism and Marxism in the International. From the 1880s onwards, anarchisms appeared in all European societies, as well as in India, South America, Japan and the USA (see Marshall 1993, 496ff).

It is not really possible to uncover a transparent rationale underlying the development of anarchism. A rough guide would include the following points. In the nineteenth century we see certain crucial historical developments. Most important was the growth and increasing centralization of nation states, something which a number of ideologies, including liberalism, have found profoundly worrying. In addition, there was the marked expansion of industrial capitalism and the tremendous social, economic and political upheavals and distress attendant upon it. One consequence of this, particularly in more rural societies, was a clash between industrial and agricultural ways of life. It was not by accident that anarchism had, until the 1930s, its most vigorous support in the more rural, peasant-based societies of India, Russia, Spain and Italy.

The above social development coincided with a powerful European revolutionary tradition. Certain dates in this tradition became part of the iconography of socialism and anarchism, each with its accompanying hagiograhy and provoking violent disagreement as to its true meaning. The European revolutions of 1789, 1830, 1848, 1871, 1917 and 1930 were seen as a developmental sequence imbued with a sacred teleology of liberation. This iconography was given its imprimatur and propagandized in the great debates of the First, Second and Third Internationals from the 1860s onwards. The anarchists saw themselves as part of this process of liberation. In many cases their opposition to the state and to wide-scale industrialism took its cue from an opposition to Marxism, which it saw as betraying the task of liberation and selling out to a form of state capitalism.

The Nature of Anarchism

Anarchism, like socialism, is subject to a great deal of critical contestation. Most commentators, and many anarchists themselves, recognize a diversity of view. This is to be expected in one sense, given the strong belief in liberty of opinion implicit within much anarchist argument. Also, like most ideologies, there are a number of ways in which the movement can be categorized. We can either classify anarchisms according to the particular ideas and goals promulgated, or by the particular tactics employed, that is, pacifist or violent (see Friedrich 1972). This particular fraught debate has carried through into recent debates on anti-capitalist and anti-globalization strategies in the the 2000s (Day 2005).

There is, in addition, considerable disagreement as to the number of schools of anarchy. My own preference is to distinguish between individualist, collectivist, communist, mutualist and anarcho-syndicalist versions. These might be described as classical forms of anarchy (see Crowder 1991).[10] The typology adopted here includes some subvariants. For example, one of the more popular versions of individualist anarchist thinking in the USA, in the last two decades of the twentieth century, was associated with the name of Murray Rothbard and acquired the nomenclature 'anarcho-capitalism' (Rothbard 1978). There are other possible variants on this scheme. There has, for example, been some minority interest in developing a concept of postmodern anarchy (see May 1994). This identifies the idea with the subtle critique of the pervasiveness of power in modern society that has been mounted by postmodern writers such as Michel Foucault, Gilles Deleuze and Jean-François Lyotard. This critique is seen to have roots in anarchist thinking.[11] Whether one can make a strong link between classical anarchy and poststructuralism remains an open question.[12] Further, anti-capitalism, anti-globalization and aspects of new social movements have also been considered by some as a unique development of anarchism (see Day 2005; Franks 2006). Some of the earlier more extreme 'propaganda of the deed' anarchists in the 1880s and 1890s verged upon nihilist anarchy.[13] In the late twentieth century, the American anarchist Murray Bookchin described himself as an 'eco-anarchist'. Others have also spoken of 'feminist anarchism'. I have chosen to follow a more established typology. Thus, postmodern anarchy, nihilist anarchism, eco-anarchism, anti-capitalist anarchism and feminist anarchism will not be considered as separate categories of anarchy. While there is a much stronger case to be made for Bookchin, the present account will treat him as a unique exponent of communist anarchism (with a strong interest in eco-anarchism) (see Bookchin 1986b, 92 and Bookchin 1992).

Individualist anarchy can be clearly observed in American writers such as Josiah Warren, Benjamin Tucker, Albert Jay Nock and Murray Rothbard. Rothbard does not fit so easily within this category on account of his particular obsession with capitalism. Although individualists differ markedly on many issues, the common thread that holds them in an uneasy alliance is their rigorous commitment to the sovereign individual, and, in many cases, their affirmation of the central importance of individual liberty. In the American tradition there is also an assertion of the value of private property. However, their firmest commitment is to a pristine individualism.[14] Beyond this, disparities arise. Apart from the central importance of the individual, the ideas of Max Stirner do not fit very easily with other individualist anarchists (see Leopold introduction to Stirner 2000). The same point holds for William Godwin and Leo Tolstoy, who, despite their focus on the individual, do not cohere with the American conception of individualism.

Collectivist anarchism was primarily associated with the ideas of Mikhail Bakunin (Kelly 1982; Leier 2006). Apart from his idiosyncratic pan-Slavist ideas and anti-German sentiments, Bakunin was celebrated for his belief in revolutionary spontaneity, his theoretical solemnization of the destructive urge, his virulent anti-Marxism and his conception of revolutionary anarchist dictatorship. In organizational terms Bakunin believed in the collectivization of the means of production, where distribution would be determined by the criteria of work. Peter Kropotkin thus argued that collectivist anarchists had a very different conception of justice to the communist anarchists, who thought in terms of need (Kropotkin 1914, 217ff).

Communist anarchism is one of the strongest components of anarchist thought to the present day. Kropotkin is the best-known early exponent of this variant. Others included Errico Malatesta, Alexander Berkman, Emma Goldman, Colin Ward and Murray Bookchin (see Ward 2004; Fellner 2005; Guérin ed. 2005; Goldman 2006). Communist anarchism is committed to the common ownership principle, in terms of property, production and housing. In the case of Kropotkin, distribution is premised on need. Such a commitment overlaps with some aspects of reformist socialism and social liberalism. Communist anarchists also assert the necessity of social solidarity and cooperative dispositions. Such notions are seen to be implicit in human nature. This tendency is repeated by Bookchin in his writings and linked with themes of ecological balance and harmony (see Bookchin 1982, 1986b, 1992).[15] The first communist anarchist work to present this case was Kropotkin's *Mutual Aid*. Freedom remains a slightly ambivalent issue in communist anarchy. It is usually related to the moral growth and self-development of the individual within a community, which might be better understood as a positive concept of liberty, yet there are exceptions to this within some communist anarchist writings. Finally, like collectivist anarchism, communist anarchy disapproves of market activity and the private production of goods.

Mutualist anarchy was associated with the 'father of anarchy', Pierre-Joseph Proudhon. Proudhon's views changed during his lifetime. He later even balked at the title 'anarchist'. His early views on anarchy can be summarized by the term 'mutualism'. He surmised that political organization premised on the state would be replaced by economic organization. Governments and states would disappear and individuals would relate to one another through mutual economic contracts. Mutualism, sometimes also called 'guaranteeism', was a form of contractarian anarchy. The only organization which would not be contractual was the family, which remained unradicalized, hierarchical and patriarchal. Women were, by and large, excluded from the benefits of anarchy. Men would possess private property (so long as they were not exploiting or abusing others), and work for themselves. They could start businesses by borrowing credit, without interest, from a 'mutual credit bank'. Their products could also be exchanged for credit notes guaranteed by the bank. Distribution would be unpatterned and dependent upon work and productivity. Despite this, there was still a background of substantive egalitarianism and liberty. Contracts could not be made under economic duress or under conditions of unequal liberty. A just society would be one in which equality and freedom of contract were upheld. Proudhon called his contractarian notion of justice 'commutative justice'.

The final strain of anarchism is anarcho-syndicalism, which grew out of the broader and slightly older movement of syndicalism (see Jennings 1990). The term 'syndicalism' has two meanings. On the one hand, it can denote simply trade unionism in a neutral sense. On the other hand, it signifies revolutionary or militant trade unionism, devoted to the overthrow of capitalism and the state. The usual mechanism of overthrow was the general strike. Syndicalism envisaged the eventual reconstruction of society according to a non-state, federalized format, premised on existing syndicalist producer groups. This movement had been growing during the 1880s and 1890s in France. In the early 1900s it spread to the USA with the famous Industrial Workers of the World (Wobblies), acquiring highly effective, if idiosyncratic, exponents in Eugene Debs and Daniel de Leon (Marshall 1993, 500–1). It also developed in Italy, Spain, Australia, Latin America and Britain among other countries. In Britain its effect was felt most intensely in the South Wales coalfields before 1914, though its precise role and effect in fomenting industrial unrest is still hotly disputed (see Morgan 1975; Holton 1976).

Because of its militant anti-political and anti-state stance, syndicalism attracted the support and interest of some anarchists, though not all. Some were drawn by its deeply anti-political organizational roots within the working class. Communes did not have to be constructed; revolutionary culture and popular decentralist structures were already in place. After a 1907 anarchist congress in Amsterdam many anarchists tried to unify with syndicalism, hence the title 'anarcho-syndicalism'. Some, such as the German anarchist Rudolf Rocker, regarded anarcho-syndicalism as the future path for anarchy to take. Others, in mainstream syndicalism, such as Victor Griffuehles, and in mainstream anarchism, such as Malatesta and Kropotkin, repudiated any relationship between anarchism and syndicalism.

Basically anarcho-syndicalism rejected all state-orientated politics – parties, parliaments, democracy, and the like. It also displayed a strong anti-intellectual tendency, rejecting bourgeois education and forms of thought. It advocated class war and the destruction of capitalism by armed violence and general strikes. Producer groups would form the nuclei of the new society. These would be democratically self-organized and self-directing federated associations of workers who would create their own social, political and economic culture and do so even before the revolution. This autonomy had been vigorously advocated in the late 1890s by Fernand Pelloutier, the leading light of early French syndicalism, as one important component of his concept of the *Bourse du Travail*. The *Bourse* was envisaged as a meeting-house within a locality for workers of all syndicates. It had many functions: as a labour exchange, meeting-place, holding a strike chest, and as an educational centre with a library. As well as serving practical and strategic functions, the *Bourse* would also enable a new workers' culture to be built.

Before moving on to discuss features of anarchist thought, one problem within this scenario of 'schools of anarchy' needs to be reviewed. Can all the above schools be described as anarchist? Within the literature there have been a number of attempts to limit the field. Apart from the communist anarchists, nearly all the schools of anarchy are subject to this attempt at restriction. For example, from the time of its inception many considered that anarcho-syndicalism was outside the main anarchist movement. Yet, even if anarcho-syndicalism is considered to be part of anarchy, writers who are popularly associated with this school, such as Georges Sorel, Edouard Berth and Hubert Lagardelle, are often dismissed as having contributed little to it. Thus Rudolf Rocker commented that none of these figures had 'any mentionable influence' on either anarchy or anarcho-syndicalism (Rocker 1989, 134). Another commentator, David Miller, remarks that syndicalism was 'always an alliance between ideologically disparate elements', and that it was 'not explicitly anarchist in character' (Miller 1984, 125, 132). Yet Rocker, amongst others, did not share this latter view. He saw anarcho-syndicalism as the vital centre of anarchy.

Another particular favourite for exclusion is Max Stirner. As John Carroll noted in his introduction to Stirner's *The Ego and His Own* (1844): 'intellectual studies of anarchism have tended to exhibit a deep hostility to the philosopher of the self' (Carroll introduction to Stirner 1971, 33; also Leopold introduction to Stirner 2000). Carroll suggests that Stirner might better be considered a nihilist than an anarchist, and he is not alone in this assessment. He continues: 'Stirner's uncompromising advocacy of self-realization sets him apart from other anarchist philosophers, especially Proudhon and Kropotkin.' Not all agree with this judgement, however. John Clark, in his study *Max Stirner's Egoism*, contends that Stirner's 'influence on individualist anarchism has continued to the present, and I strongly suspect that it is in fact growing' (Clark 1976, 89; see also Patterson 1971).

Again, Jerry Gaus and John W. Chapman have suggested that not only should 'anarcho-syndicalism' be ruled out, but also individualist 'anarcho-capitalism' (Gaus and Chapman in Pennock and Chapman eds 1978, xxv). This point is repeated in an essay later in the same volume by David Wieck, who comments that the latter movement is 'entirely outside the mainstream of anarchist theoretical writings' (Wieck in Pennock and Chapman eds 1978, 215). Those within the communist anarchist movement have been particularly keen to expunge individualist anarchists, such as Rothbard. It is obviously uncomfortable to find themselves as bedfellows with such antipathetic ideas. Rothbard himself did not appear to be worried by this critique, and clearly saw his own affinities as lying squarely within an individualist libertarian anarchism.

If one looks more closely at the anarchist movement, this process can be repeated *ad infinitum*. Most communist and collectivist anarchists expressed distaste for Proudhon's contractarian anarchism, which was seen to evince a 'shopkeeper's mentality' (Graham in Goodway ed. 1989, 163). They also felt uncomfortable with his labour theory of value, his notion of a market-based commutative justice, his patriarchal view of the family, his striving to become a parliamentary candidate, his support of the South and slavery in the American Civil War and, not least, his later belief in the role of a federal state. In the same vein, anarchist commentators, including Vernon Richards and Daniel Guérin, have seen Bakunin's collectivism as conforming more to a Marxist position than to anarchism (Richards in Malatesta 1984, 209; also Guérin in Goodway ed. 1989, 118). This process of mutual repudiation and delimitation is potentially endless and does not appear to be a very profitable path to follow.

Finally, it is worth remarking that various schools of anarchism have existed in a tense, overlapping and immensely complex relationship with both Marxism, liberalism and more recently ecology (see Thomas 1980). This point will not be dealt with separately, but will be touched upon in the course of the discussion. Having outlined the schools of anarchy, some of the elements of anarchist thought will now be examined through the lenses of the various schools.

Human Nature

There are three essential points to note in respect of the issue of human nature. First, anarchists most emphatically do not all hold to the same concept of human nature. There are marked differences evident between thinkers and schools of anarchy. Second, their notions of human nature do not always evince optimism or perfectibilism. They are often accused of holding naïvely optimistic beliefs, but as Rothbard notes: 'I confess that I do not understand the basis for this charge. … I assume with most observers that mankind is a mixture of good and evil, of cooperative and criminal tendencies' (Rothbard in Pennock and Chapman eds 1978, 193). Earlier in the twentieth century the communist anarchist Malatesta made exactly the same point with regard to the fallibility of human nature.[16] Third, anarchists do not necessarily all hold an absolute or fixed concept of human nature. In the case of writers such as Kropotkin and Elisée Reclus, human beings were still seen to be biologically evolving creatures. Both Kropotkin and Reclus were geographers and natural scientists by training. Their explanations of human behaviour were ultimately premised on the natural sciences. Other anarchists, both earlier and later, have believed that humans gradually change through the cultivation and development of reason. With the growth of literacy and the availability of books, human society must ultimately progress. Godwin articulated this from an Enlightenment perspective, whereas writers from Bakunin to Bookchin linked this theme with a more Hegelian standpoint on the growth of reason.

The idea of human nature, however, remains central to anarchist thought. What differentiates perspectives within the anarchist movement is their starting-point. These may, crudely, be seen as individual or social. One perspective locates human beings as independent autonomous agents framing their own plans of the life outside society; the other portrays humans developing within a community and achieving freedom and individuality through it. These represent broad tendencies within anarchist thought.

One of the most famous examples of the social tendency can be found in the work of Kropotkin. He rejected the dominance of the competitive notion of evolution. From his study of animal behaviour and primitive communities in Siberia, and stimulated by the work of the zoologist Karl Kessler, he came to the conclusion that animals, including human beings, only flourish in cooperative communities. As a result of his observations of many animal species he was led to remark: 'In all these scenes of animal life which passed before my eyes, I saw Mutual Aid and Mutual Support carried on to an extent which made me suspect in it a feature of the greatest importance for the maintenance of life, the preservation of each species, and its further evolution' (Kropotkin 1914, ix). Social solidarity and mutual aid come naturally to human beings. It is part of the law of nature. Kropotkin was profoundly optimistic about the cooperative, creative and altruistic qualities of human nature. Nature was the teacher of morality – a claim that Kropotkin explored in a book on ethics (Kropotkin 1924). Kropotkin did not deny the element of struggle, but suggested that it had been over-emphasized by Darwin's acolytes. Fallow deer, pelicans, bees, badgers, are all taken as corroboration of the mutual aid hypothesis. Linking this with political theory, Kropotkin noted with due seriousness: 'The ants and termites have renounced the "Hobbesian war" and they are better for it' (Kropotkin 1914, 14).[17]

The basic thesis was that the biologically fittest were the most cooperative. Nature is not red in tooth and claw. Even for primitive human communities this is obvious.[18] Kropotkin notes that primitive peoples find it as impossible to grasp our individualism as we do their cooperation. For primitives, 'self-sacrifice in the interests of the clan are of daily occurrence' (Kropotkin 1968, 112). In subsequent chapters of *Mutual Aid* Kropotkin traces this human solidarity through village communes, medieval cities and guilds. Competitive life in the state, for Kropotkin, is an historical aberration. Cooperation and mutual aid in fact still go on regardless of the existence of the state.

Kropotkin clearly had a touching and optimistic faith in the mass of human beings, an attitude that led even some fellow communist anarchists to accuse him of naïvety.[19] His faith in nature still finds an echo in the writings of the contemporary communist anarchist Murray Bookchin, who comments that: 'Ecology recognizes no hierarchy on the level of the ecosystem. There are no "kings of the beasts" and no "lowly ants". … Virtually all that lives … plays its coequal role in maintaining the balance and integrity of the whole' (Bookchin 1986b, 59–60). Nature is thus intrinsically anarchic to Bookchin. This belief in 'natural' anarchy has some parallel with the remark of Alexander Berkman that all children 'show an instinctive tendency to individuality and independence, to non-conformity manifested in open and secret defiance', and thus may be considered to be naturally anarchistic (Berkman 1977, 27; see also Fellner 2005).

Not all socially orientated anarchists shared this faith in nature. Bakunin, for one, disliked the idea of set rational patterns of progress towards anarchy. In his view, nature, like history, was to a large extent irrational and unsystematic, and characterized by sudden unexpected explosions of instinctual and spontaneous activity.[20] In the same vein, Bakunin spoke of the 'revolt of life against science'. Preordained laws or rules were to be rejected in favour of anti-intellectualism and instinct. The instincts of the uneducated peasant were more reliable than the intellectual systems of the educated. Revolution was instinctively present in the masses. As he commented, 'The most renowned geniuses have done nothing, or very little, specifically for the people. … Popular life, popular development, popular progress belong exclusively to the people themselves' (Bakunin 1990, 205).[21]

Leaving aside the question as to whether Georges Sorel was, or was not, a spokesman for anarcho-syndicalism, this reliance on instinct was also characteristic of Sorel's general position in *Reflections on Violence* (1908). In the case of Sorel it was not the peasants who experienced this instinctual response; rather, it was the industrial proletariat. The instinct was to be channelled through myths like the general strike. The instinctual psychology which dominated Sorel's thinking had deeper theoretical roots than it had for Bakunin, namely, in the work of Gustave Le Bon, Eduard von Hartmann, Friedrich Nietzsche and Henri Bergson (Sorel 1975; see also Jennings 1985).[22] Furthermore, the epic state of mind of such proletarians was clearly at odds with anything that Bakunin would have comprehended.[23]

On the individualist reading of human nature further disparities arise. William Godwin was noted for his individualistic stance. He believed the nature of human beings to be determined by their environment. In other words, human beings were ductile. They were also possessed of the capacity to reason. The particular moral theory he embraced was utilitarianism. True happiness lies in the development of our individuality. The individual alone can be a judge of his or her utility. This led Godwin to suggest that all forms of cooperative activity should be regarded with suspicion. As he put it: 'Everything that is usually understood by the term coopera-tion is in some degree evil' (Godwin 1976, 758). Anything which prevents people from thinking for themselves – communal labour, communal meals, marriage, even theatrical or musical performances – could be seen to be an invasion of individuality. Humans ought to be able to stand without one another. As Godwin stated: 'He is the most perfect man to whom society is not a necessity of life but a luxury' (Godwin 1976, 761; see Marshall 1993, 191ff; also Crowder 1991).

The above position bears some similarities to the twentieth-century individualist Murray Rothbard, except that Rothbard repudiates utilitarianism in favour of a natural rights theory. For Rothbard, human beings have a definite specifiable nature. We are self-interested acquisitive beings, who are capable of rationality. We feel, think, and act as individuals and should be allowed the liberty to learn and to develop our faculties. We fundamentally 'own' ourselves. We can cooperate with others, but this is an individual choice that we make. Rothbard calls this the 'self-ownership principle'. Individuals recognize the self-ownership principle, acknowl-edge the right of property embodied in it, and thus relate to each other through the free market.

Another individualist, Max Stirner, certainly accepted the self-ownership princi-ple, but his notion of *Eigenheit* implied a great deal more (see Stirner 1971). Stirner argued so rigorously for individualism that even the recognition of others' rights to private property, the contractual basis of interaction, and the important role of the market were regarded as mere fabrications placed over the individual. The 'ownness' of the solitary ego even comes before liberty. Stirner's human being is totally self-enclosed, constructing its own world and values. This is anarchistic individualism taken to its ultimate degree. Even pure altruism is seen to be profoundly egoistic. This doctrine has been called 'psychological egoism'. Its roots lie in a very different intellectual debate within the peripheries of Hegelianism, more precisely in Stirner's critique of some his fellow young Hegelians (see Leopold introduction to Stirner 2000 and Leopold 2007). Each individual ego is the only arbiter of reality. In this scenario nothing is important except the ontological supremacy of each ego.

It can be seen from the above examples drawn from anarchy that there is no one clear reading of human nature. In fact, anarchy appears to be more subject than other ideologies to enormous diversity on this issue. This makes the discussion of anarchist politics that much more complicated.

Critique of the State

If there is one theme which recurs in discussions on anarchism it is the critique, and rejection, of the 'state', and also sometimes 'government' and 'authority'. There are a number of problems with such a rejection. First, there is a lack of clarification in anarchist writings as to what these terms mean. Consequently it is difficult, on occasion, to ascertain *what* is being rejected. Second, anarchists often differ markedly as to whether concepts such as government, authority and the state should be considered to be synonymous or separate. In other words, can authority be maintained under anarchy without a state or government? Third, the normative grounds on which anarchists attack the state and justify alternatives to it are premised on amazingly diverse moral sources. Lockian natural rights theory, radical utilitarianism, psychological egoism, neo-Kantianism, Hegelianism, evolutionary theory and Christian principles are just the better-known among the normative resources.[24] This diversity of moral justification alone makes the arguments difficult to discuss coherently. I will briefly examine the meanings of these terms and then turn to the question of why the state is rejected.

Oddly, there is remarkably little written by anarchists on what is meant by the state. Usually they have in mind the institutional structures of legislative, executive, judicial and bureaucratic administration, also occasionally the police, armed forces and, for some, religion and education. Some concentrate on the structure of coercion; others on a psychological statist disposition (see Landauer 1978). None of these assessments is particularly sensitive to the nuances of the state tradition. In addition, some of Proudhon's writings appear to treat government, state, sovereignty, law and authority as virtually synonymous. Proudhon speaks of the abolition of the state as the abolition of both government and authority (Proudhon 1989, 292).[25] On the other hand, the American anarchist Albert Jay Nock in *Our Enemy the State* (1946) distinguished sharply between government and state. Government was concerned with intervention to secure natural rights to life, liberty and property (see Nock 1946). A state is always an oppressive structure; in fact it is a criminal organization. Rothbard follows the same line of argument, interpreting taxation as a more sophisticated form of robbery (Rothbard in Pennock and Chapman eds 1978, 195).

What, therefore, is wrong with the state and government? Again anarchist responses vary. Generally the state is seen to be an artificial and alien institution which, in its worst aspect, is a brigand or criminal organization writ large. As Alexander Herzen put it vividly, the state is 'Genghis Khan with the telegraph', although today a computer and CCTV camera might be more apt. Such a view stretches across the schools of anarchy. A state denotes the centralization of coercion and violence. Historically, states are usually built on the back of military dominance. Their resources are always legalized plunder. The existence of the state thus implies the total denial of liberty.[26] As Bakunin commented: 'States can find no other grounds for joint action than the concerted enslavement of the masses who constitute the overall basis and purpose of their existence' (Bakunin 1990, 3). Furthermore, because states involve hierarchy and domination, they also necessarily entail the denial of human equality. Most anarchists contend that the state structure is defended by a caste of academics, priests and intellectuals. This judgement goes some way towards accounting for the anti-intellectualism redolent of certain anarchists.[27]

Individualist anarchists focus primarily on the state's denial of individual rights and freedoms, particularly the freedoms of the market and property. This is especially true for many of the American individualists. Individualist anarchists, in concert, tend to mistrust any talk of collective, corporate or communal entities, the state being the most heinous of such collectivities. For Godwin, Stirner and Rothbard, as we have seen, cooperation or collective action are intrinsically mistrusted. For Stirner, given the ontological primacy of the ego, society is inevitably viewed as another mental 'spook'.[28] Godwin rejected cooperation on the grounds of his individualistic utilitarianism (Godwin 1976; Clark 1977). Rothbard, from a natural rights base, similarly denies the very existence of society, commenting that, 'There is no existing entity called "society"; there are only interacting individuals' (Rothbard 1978, 35). Humans are intrinsically egoistic. Society can only be a convenient label for interacting individuals.

The collectivist, mutualist and communist anarchists also have their own idiosyncratic views on this issue. Proudhon and Bakunin tend to see the state as a brutal but passing phase in the development of society. For Bakunin, the Germans were the only really committed statists in Europe. He made direct links in this context, not without some passing amusement, between Marx and Bismarck. He also looked with interest and sympathy on American federalism and considered that the British did not really have a state tradition at all (Bakunin 1990, 14 and 26).

Kropotkin's work (and, in the late twentieth century, Bookchin's) is more wide-ranging and optimistic than that of Bakunin. For Kropotkin the state does not undermine and destroy individuals *per se*, but rather the natural, harmonious, organic communities in which individuals develop. Bookchin calls such natural communities 'affinity groups'. Kropotkin sees a pattern in the development of societies, remarking that 'whenever mankind made a new start in civilization, in Greece, Rome, or middle Europe, it passed through the same stages – the tribe, the village, community, the free city, the state – each one naturally evolving out of the preceding stage' (Kropotkin 1914, 165). The state exists to destroy all natural forms of federated union. For Kropotkin this destruction was the policy of popes, Continental monarchs, parliaments, and even the revolutionary convention of France. Kropotkin believed, though, that beneath this stifling state control, mutual aid still lived in an 'infinity of associations' (Kropotkin 1914, 294). The task of anarchy was to encourage the full re-emergence of these natural associations.

It is important to realize that for the majority of anarchists *nothing* redeems the state. However, Proudhon and Bakunin are exceptions to this point.[29] The liberal constitutional tradition, the Jacobin state, liberal parliamentary democracy and more especially the socialist state are seen as illusions by virtually all the schools of anarchy. Thus Bakunin used to refer to the Marxist state as the 'great lie of the century – red bureaucracy'.[30] And Kropotkin declared with equal disdain: 'The modern radical is a centralizer, a State partisan, a Jacobin to the core, and the Socialist walks in his footsteps' (Kropotkin 1903, 41).

Liberty and Equality

For many anarchists the reason why the state is to be abhorred is that it is the root of all compulsion. As Berkman argued: 'A life without compulsion means liberty'. The anarchist commitment to the value of liberty necessarily entailed a rejection of the state (Berkman 1977, 9). Liberty was not, on this reading, an abstract philosophical 'end' to aim for, but, as Rocker maintained, 'the vital concrete possibility for every human being' (Rocker 1989, 31).

It might be assumed from this that all anarchists were committed to the value of liberty. Two problems arise here, one more complex than the other. To take the simpler one first: it is not clear that all anarchists have valued liberty or autonomy above all else. Stirner, for one, explicitly elevates 'ownness', or *Eigenheit*, above liberty. Liberty is, in other words, always subordinate to the value of the ego. Similarly, for Stirner, much of the supposed value and content of liberty was nothing more than a series of unauthentic illusions and mental 'spooks' of the bourgeois mind. As Stirner put it in his stark prose: '"Freedom" awakens your *rage* against everything that is not you; "egoism" calls you to *joy* over yourselves, to self-enjoyment; "freedom" is and remains a *longing*, a romantic plaint, a Christian hope … "ownness" is a reality' (Stirner 1971, 118). Even when Stirner discusses freedom, it is far from clear whether he accepts either the negative or positive notions. The American anarchist writer John Clark, following Stirner's insight, comments that 'Anarchism is the one major political theory which has attempted to synthesize the values of negative and positive freedom into a single, more comprehensive view of human liberty' (Clark 1976, 61ff).

Yet this desire for synthesis is certainly not shared by the majority of anarchists. This leads to the second problem, namely, that, similar to the case of liberalism, there are major differences of interpretation regarding the meaning of liberty. As with liberalism, these distinct senses of liberty carry differing social and economic implications. The most orthodox view of anarchists is that they share a conception of negative liberty, virtually the same as that of many of the classical liberals (see Fowler 1972). Liberty is read in this context as a paucity of intentional physical coercion or compulsion. This view is particularly characteristic of American anarchism. Rothbard quite clearly defines coercion as 'aggressive physical violence against person and property' (Rothbard in Pennock and Chapman eds 1978, 193). Thus, like Berkman (a communist anarchist), he contends that the abolition of the state will mean the abolition of the main source of coercion, and hence the enhancement of liberty. Rothbard's argument links up with his self-ownership principle and non-aggression axiom: that if individuals have absolute rights of ownership over their bodies, then no one should coerce them. Thus everyone has 'the absolute right to be "free" from aggression' (Rothbard 1978, 23).

On the other hand, some communist anarchists appear to be arguing more in the vein of positive liberty (see Crowder 1991, 10). This particular notion of positive liberty has not facilitated a more benign attitude to the role or function of the state, however, as it did with the social liberalism of T. H. Green. Anarchists who have entertained a more positive understanding of liberty are as vociferous as the individualists in their rejection of the state. There are several elements present in this positive conception of liberty. First, liberty was not just about lack of compulsion, although it is clear that compulsion was still accepted as an important factor in examining liberty. In this sense liberty was freedom from compulsion in order to pursue a positive goal. Positive liberty involved self-government, legislating to oneself, choosing one's own goals autonomously. One particular neo-Kantian variant of this argument, R. P. Wolff's *In Defense of Anarchism* (1970), has attained particular publicity in some academic circles. In spite of showing very little grasp of the diversity of anarchist thought, Wolff offers a powerful philosophical argument aimed at showing that the recognition of authority is inconsistent with our overriding obligation to act as autonomous self-directing agents. Any duty to obey authority *de jure* implies an abdication of autonomy. Wolff's argument has generated a minority taste of philosophical literature in the last four decades. But, despite its intrinsic interest, it is peripheral to the mainstream of anarchist thought and practice.[31]

Second, liberty is concerned with choosing goals which, minimally, do not abuse, exploit or demean others. In other words, the goals must have a moral dimension. This moral dimension is part of the constitutive meaning of liberty.[32] Third, liberty is concerned with the self-development of human beings, or, as Rocker put it, bringing 'to full development all the powers, capacities, and talents with which nature has endowed him' (Rocker 1989, 32). Finally, the constitutive moral goals must be embedded in a community. In fact, the goals and purpose themselves are derived from a community or from the natural communal instincts of our natures. This is a fundamental premise of communist anarchism.[33]

In respect of equality, anarchist beliefs vary according to their conceptions of human nature and the character of value. The starkest view of equality – that of Stirnerite egoism – sees everything over and above the ego as illusory. Egos may thus be taken as formally or procedurally equal. All claims to hierarchy or superiority should be treated as bogus by the egoist. In the case of other individualist anarchists the nature of equality becomes more explicit. With Godwin's position, every human is equally possessed of the capacity to reason and judge his or her own interests and happiness. No hierarchy is acceptable; each individual should be approached as equally capable of reason. In the American anarchist tradition, equality stems from the isolated ego demanding the natural right to property in his or her own body and not to suffer aggression, and also to have equal access to the market. In the case of Leo Tolstoy, equality was based on the Judaeo-Christian principle of equality of souls. For Tolstoy, the kingdom of God was within each of us and implied mutual religious respect for each person (see Tolstoy 1974).

The more formal reading of equality in individualism can be contrasted with the more substantive vision of equality to be found in the communist anarchists. For communist and collectivist anarchists, political, legal or economic equality was not viewed as adequate. Equality was something more far-reaching. In the case of Kropotkin, equality was premised on need. Each person had certain fundamental physical, mental, and cultural needs which ought to be met equally within society. These needs constituted the well-being of the human individual. In the case of the communist anarchists, specifically, equality in a substantive social sense tied in closely with the achievement of genuine positive liberty. In the case of individualists, the more formal procedural reading of equality linked up with negative liberty – in the form of an equal right to equal liberty. The attempt to establish individual substantive needs, and satisfy them through a community, would have struck most individualists as a denial of liberty.

Justice, Property and the Economy

Another of the values widely appealed to by anarchists was justice. Justice was usually considered independently from law. The concept of law was linked with the practices of government, state and authority.[34] Thus, if there were any relation between the two it would be that justice acted as an evaluative yardstick to set against legislative practices. Hence the notion of the morally just society is central to anarchist thought, but the question remains – what is justice? There are two distinct senses in which the notion of justice is deployed in anarchist thought. As with the concept of equality, one is linked to a more procedural understanding and the other to a more substantive and distributive model.

The above points are also revealing about the nature of anarchist views on the economy. Generally it can be said that all anarchist schools oppose the notion of state capitalism and the state-based command economy. Apart from this more negative judgement, it becomes difficult to identify a common ground. There is certainly some vague attachment to a decentralized economy. With the American individualists – the anarcho-capitalists in particular – the totally unregulated market becomes the model.[35] Production becomes a very different question to distribution. In communist anarchy, production and distribution are both completely linked and communalized. Proudhon's contractarian market model and social individualism hang midway between these ideas. His theory is more or less equivalent to an anarchist form of market socialism.

The first self-conscious anarchist to deploy the concept of justice robustly in his discussion of society was Proudhon. However, it should be mentioned that, despite any *prima facie* radical reputation, his understanding is economistic and comparable to some forms of classical liberalism. Proudhon, paralleling something of Sir Henry Maine's 'status to contract' argument and Spencer's 'militant to industrial society' idea, argued that societies as they developed towards anarchy moved from government to contract. This was not a contract *with* any government. Proudhon was deeply critical of 'contract of government' theorists such as Locke and Rousseau. For Proudhon, contract replaced government. Contract, he maintained, is opposed to authority and denotes mutuality (Proudhon 1989, 206–7). People would take the responsibility for their own lives and interact via contract and exchange. The contract is a totally self-assumed obligation. For Proudhon, therefore, it is an ideal vehicle for anarchy. The only exception to this contractarian vision was the *family*, which Proudhon still conceived of, inexplicably, in hierarchical and wholly patriarchal terms. In general, Proudhon was adamant that there must be substantive equality of contract, and it is this substantive equality that differentiates him from later individualist anarchists.

Contract served two functions: first, it entailed the guarantee of equivalent economic exchange; second, it guaranteed liberty, since relations were purely voluntary and free from coercion. Contract was to characterize the new form of society, something that Proudhon also called a 'guaranteeist society'. Proudhon came to speak of this society in almost mystical and religious terms.[36] What is unsurprising, and yet puzzling, is the notion of justice that he deployed. Justice is concerned with equal contracts. Proudhon calls this 'commutative justice'. In the present era we are more used to Hayek and his acolytes deploying this idea, which only reinforces Proudhon's more market-orientated appearance. Proudhon notes: '*Commutative justice*, the *reign of contract*, the *industrial* or *economic system*, such are the different synonyms for the idea.' Of significance here is the fact that in arguing for this procedural and commutative idea, Proudhon poured scorn on the distributive senses of justice, which we might now tend to associate with reformist socialism and social liberalism. Distributive justice, he argued, relates to authority, law and government. It implied that someone was planning and patterning. Like Herbert Spencer, Proudhon saw distributive justice as feudal in character. It is important, however, to grasp that despite his dislike of communism and distributive justice, he had no love for the idea of an unregulated market (see Proudhon 1989, 112).

Later individualist writers, especially in the American tradition, recall some of Proudhon's ideas. Certainly there is a clear opposition to distributive justice. In the case of writers such as Rothbard, the natural right to one's body, property and liberty are of supreme importance. This entails a far more formal understanding of procedural justice. Rothbard is not concerned with the substantive equality of parties to contracts, only that individuals should not be prohibited from contracting. Property rights in one's body, and capital, should not be interfered with and one should not be subject to harm or aggression. Justice is concerned with sustaining a voluntary 'libertarian law code', focused on formal individual rights (Wieck in Pennock and Chapman eds 1978, 217). Rothbard ignores all large accumulations of property and social handicaps which might affect the ability to contract. Neither Proudhon, Stirner nor Godwin would have accepted this latter argument, especially the sacred quality that Rothbard confers upon property rights. Each would have rejected the argument for very different reasons. Proudhon, in particular, rejected the absolute right to property as encouraging its abuse. This is what lay behind his elusive statement 'all property is theft.'

The American individualists thus endorse a very much more rigid application of a free market. The difference between individualist anarchists and minimalist classical liberals is slight on this point, namely, that many classical liberals believe that human beings are egoistic and self-interested and cannot be trusted in a completely unregulated forum. In addition, given that each ego recognizes this, it is rational that individuals would agree on a minimal state apparatus to perform certain public functions. Certainly this was the direction of liberal writers such as Robert Nozick and James Buchanan. On the other hand, individualist anarcho-capitalists suggest either that humans will adapt to a purely unregulated condition or that individuals will hire out services (previously performed by governments) on the free market, including policing and judicial work.

For communist and collectivist anarchists, justice was seen almost exclusively in distributive terms. For Kropotkin, this was tied to an evolutionary development. As he stated: 'Feelings of justice develop, more or less, with all gregarious animals. ... Sociability thus puts a limit to physical struggle, and leaves room for the development of better moral feelings' (Kropotkin 1914, 58–9). There were differences in the respective criteria for distribution. Bakunin's belief in distribution was premised upon the performance of work or labour in a commune. Kropotkin regarded such a process as faulty since it contained the seeds of unequal treatment (see Avrich 1967, 29). Desert, or work, were replaced in Kropotkin by 'need' as the key distributive principle. In fact, distribution is a misleading word since no one would be *doing* the distribution; rather there would be a change in the character of production and in the way people consumed.

Kropotkin's analysis was premised on the argument that no production was individual. It is the human race which creates wealth. This wealth is seized illegitimately by a few. Private property is therefore at odds with the nature of production and wealth creation. For human beings to develop fully, wealth must be reappropriated for humanity. The principle, as Kropotkin put it, should be: 'All is for all! ... What we proclaim is THE RIGHT TO WELL-BEING: WELL-BEING FOR ALL!' (Kropotkin 1968, 15). Everyone has the right to live. To live is to have needs, and such needs are met when wealth is reappropriated and redistributed according to needs. Needs are both physical in respect of food, clothing and housing, and cultural in respect of education. In this context, the communist anarchist view of the economy becomes markedly distinct from that of the individualist anarchist. Production and distribution are envisaged as integrated communal enterprises, in which goods are produced to meet the needs of all. Kropotkin defines the science of political economy as 'The study of the needs of mankind, and the means of satisfying them with the least possible waste of human energy', or as he renames it: 'the Physiology of Society' (Kropotkin 1968, 238, 241).

The Problem of Political Organization

One of the major problems for anarchy in formulating any account of political organization is the accusation that anarchy is a distinctly unrealistic, naïve and utopian doctrine that is unlikely to work. Anarchy has been replete with models of the ideal society. Some anarchist writers have undoubtedly been wild and impractical in their proposals, whilst others have been more balanced, pragmatic and piecemeal in their approach. Those who have worked through the medium of education on anarchist themes have obviously had a longer-term view. The Summerhill school of A. S. Neill is one example.[37]

There are some common beliefs within anarchism concerning the organizational base of society. Most anarchists hold that any future society would be non-hierarchial, non-coercive and libertarian. Furthermore, the nation state is quite definitely seen as passing from the historical scene, with its bureaucracies, judiciary, police and army. If some elemental government were to remain it would be minimized and premised upon consent. It would be, as one writer has put it, 'government without politics' (see MacIntosh in Pennock and Chapman eds 1978, 268). There might be, in some cases, loose non-compulsory federations, but 'decentralization' would be the watchword. Beyond this minimal agreement a number of different views arise.

With the American individualists, and in particular the anarcho-capitalists, much previous government or state activity could be carried out by individuals in a free market. As the American anarchist Benjamin Tucker put it, 'genuine anarchism is consistent Manchesterism' (quoted in Clark in Pennock and Chapman eds 1978, 19). Anarchy exists where there is 'no possibility for coercive aggression against the person or property of any individual' (Rothbard in Pennock and Chapman eds 1978, 191–2). To be opposed to the state, for Rothbard, is not necessarily to be opposed to the services it performs. Rothbard envisages a situation of complete voluntaristic individualism. Even the word 'society' is seen as a collective fiction. As long as individuals voluntarily agree to arbitration, they would be able to hire out even judicial courts and police. Rothbard contends that people could be invited to attend a court and be judged under a libertarian code of law. Of course, in the final analysis, there is nothing that could compel individual compliance except a feeling that a libertarian consensus *ought* to develop if all individuals achnowledged natural rights (which, of course, they do not). Moreover, it is difficult to see what could be done in the individualist perspective about a mass murderer, the physically handicapped or the insane. Also, as many have noted, the empirical evidence that exists on private security and policing firms does not inspire great confidence. There is nothing to stop criminals themselves setting up as private police or security firms. In the end, punishment becomes a matter of retaliation. If no agreement can be reached, then violence is the only resort. In this situation the market would encourage not order but lethal disorder. Rothbard comforts his audience here with the bland observation that there would nevertheless be no state-led equivalent to Hiroshima or Dresden in such localized conflict.

Max Stirner at least was not so sanguine about consensual libertarian agreement. He appears more directly honest and hard-headed about individualism than does Rothbard. Stirner believed that punishment would be replaced by retaliation between egos. Since all the mental 'spooks' of the bourgeois mind – including natural rights, property and markets – would be ruled out, the most that could be hoped for would be a vague 'union of egoists', where each would be seeking to satisfy his or her own interest.[38] Society simply would not exist. It would be replaced by nothing but the solipsistic ego. As Stirner commented, 'Every people, every State, is unjust towards the egoist' (Stirner 1971, 142). On this reading of social life, as Stirner was prepared to admit, crime was as valid an enterprise as punishment or retaliation.

In the case of the communist anarchists a much stronger moral claim is made for communal values and organization. This in turn makes it more problematic to account for individual liberty or autonomy. In responding to the individualist case, communist anarchists contended that individualism was anachronistic and flawed, too reliant on the vagaries of markets to achieve liberty or substantive equality, and ultimately set for collapse into state capitalism. The communists and collectivists envisaged humans living in small-scale decentralized, federated, non-hierarchical communes linking up with age-old village community traditions. As we have seen, Bookchin calls them 'affinity groups' (Bookchin 1986b, 47–9). Communes would be voluntary. Yet most anarchists of this persuasion believed that people would flourish, develop and desire to live in this context. Kropotkin gave this claim a strong biological gloss with his theory of mutual aid. Interestingly, Kropotkin was also inspired in some of his writings by the voluntary efforts of the Red Cross and the British Lifeboat Association, as well as his better-known admiration for medieval guilds and cities (Kropotkin 1968, 179–84). Such communes would be spontaneous, solidaristic and altruistic. They would be small-scale in terms of membership, functionally specific, and would produce for local needs (see Kropotkin 1974). Technology would be scaled down to meet these. Bookchin therefore, in his work, calls for a 'peoples' technology' (Bookchin 1986b, 68–9).[39] Physical and mental labour would be integrated and production performed on a human scale in self-governing workshops. Most communist anarchists have been particularly keen to overcome the separation between hand and brain, mental and physical labour. Many looked to the reform of the family and marriage. Kropotkin was adamant that communist anarchy would lead to the true emancipation of women from both patriarchal and domestic drudgery. One of his suggestions was that labour-saving machinery in the home would help to achieve this (see Kropotkin 1968, 161).[40]

In the case of Proudhon we encounter a different vision, one which incorporates elements from individualism, communism and liberalism. Thus Proudhon has been described as a 'liberal in proletarian clothes' (Graham in Goodway ed. 1989, 157). His opinions altered during his lifetime, but he is usually identified with a form of contractual federation peopled by social individualists. Society would be constituted primarily through contracts between individuals and groups which would replace the need for government and politics. Federated groups would also make agreements for national defence and the arbitration of disputes. Proudhon's view later shifted back to the support of a federal state, something that he had espoused in his early years. Most notably, his conception of a mutual credit bank would play a crucial role in any future federal society. This would issue labour notes and interest-free credit to enable individuals to set up in business. What Proudhon really objected to was not private property and private business as such but 'the earning of income from the labour of others through such means as rent, interest and wage labour' (Graham introduction to Proudhon 1989, ix).

Revolutionary syndicalism and anarcho-syndicalism were both anti-political and anti-statist movements that concentrated 'on the revolutionary potential of working-class economic organization, notably the trade union or industrial union' (Holton 1976, 17; see also Brown ed. 1974). Syndicalism, in general, had no faith in representative democracy. It rejected all forms of state organization, whether capitalist or socialist. In Britain the Independent Labour Party, official unionism and social democratic liberalism were treated with equal disdain (see Mann in Brown ed. 1974; Morgan 1975). The market economy was as objectionable as the centralized command economy and nationalized industries. The British syndicalists were deeply antagonistic to the new liberal welfare reforms in the period 1906–14. As one writer has commented, the syndicalists saw the first elements of the welfare state as simply 'designed to promote industrial efficiency and social discipline' (Holton 1976, 35).

The principal economic actors for syndicalism and anarcho-syndicalism were the working-class producer groups, not the consumers. Both the state and capitalism had to be destroyed by the revolutionary 'direct action' of such producers. Violence was fully legitimated in such action. Georges Sorel, in his *Reflections on Violence*, made much of this particular theme. Unions were not only conceived of as the means to revolutionary direct action, but also as the nuclei for a future decentralized federal society. Workers in a locality would be members of a union. Unions would then link together in a central cartel or *Bourse*. This would propagandize, educate and prepare workers to take control of their lives. Labour cartels would unite or federate in a region and eventually form a national federation. Such great industrial alliances would form the basis not only for revolt but also for a future society. Although they tended to despise abstract theory and bourgeois intellectualism, syndicalists none the less placed considerable emphasis on working-class self-education. This is something that can be seen in Pelloutier's *Bourse du Travail* in France, in the Plebs League, the Industrial Syndicalist Education League and the Central Labour College in Britain (see Brown ed. 1974, 5ff; also Joll 1964, 197–200; Marshall 1993, 491).

There is a problem in anarchist theory of reconciling authoritative organization with the liberty or autonomy of the individual. If political authority entails the right to rule, and those subject to it do not have the choice of whether or not to obey (otherwise it would not *be* an authority), then liberty appears to be negated. This is a particular dilemma for communist and collectivist anarchists confronted with the issue of the need and desire for some form of community and authority. The individualist does not face this problem so directly, but simply sidesteps it by denying its relevance.

One way of tackling this difficulty is to utilize the notion of democracy. Democracy mediates and carries the individual's autonomous decision into the public sphere. Authority therefore derives from the will of the people. There are, however, problems with this argument too. First, as one commentator has recently noted: 'The relationship between anarchism and democratic theory has always been ambiguous' (Graham in Goodway ed. 1989, 171). Despite a more overt sympathy for the participatory model of democracy, all anarchist schools have been profoundly critical of democracy *in toto*, for a number of reasons. Primarily majoritarianism appears dangerous even to communist anarchists. Majorities can make grossly immoral decisions. Potentially, they can crush individual liberty. Furthermore, democratic parties are both manipulative and intolerant, voters being at the mercy of unscrupulous party machinations. It is the liberty of the individual, or of the minority, that is at particular risk in democracy. For the American individualists, democracy can even undermine and destroy private property. As Proudhon remarked, in a different context, there is little to choose between the tyranny of an absolute monarch and the tyranny of popular sovereignty. Both can rule the individual in a despotic manner (Proudhon 1989, 146, 244).

Representative democracy came in for particular criticism. Electoral change and universal suffrage make no difference, according to Proudhon. They simply place a veil over state coercion. Universal suffrage, as Proudhon noted, meant universal despotism. Representation is always viewed as false by anarchists. Bakunin therefore criticized the 'pseudo-sovereignty of a sham popular will, supposedly expressed by pseudo-representatives of the people in sham popular assemblies' (Bakunin 1990, 13). Ultimately, for many anarchists, representative democracy linked up with party politics and statism. Direct participatory democracy fared somewhat better than the representative model, especially as it was seen in the Paris Commune. Nevertheless, even this was viewed with suspicion (Ritter in Pennock and Chapman 1978, 131). The premise once again was that individual liberty was of primary importance and that it could easily be swamped by majorities, even in fully participating assemblies. For this reason, democracy does not necessarily allow anarchists the means to bypass the problem of authority and liberty.

One final problem in anarchist theory concerns the method of achieving the new form of political organization. Virtually all anarchists wanted to bring this about through revolution, whether peaceful or not. The nature of the revolution was usually perceived in terms of social change. Political or economic revolution was not enough. There had to be a change in social attitudes and dispositions. Proudhon and Rothbard argued that anarchism could be achieved by reformist means, working through existing state structures. For Bakunin, this was anathema; the destruction of state structures was the essential preliminary for all change. Godwin, on the other hand, believed in the power of reasoned persuasion. This idea has by no means disappeared. In fact, persuading others through education and the printed word appears to be the most favoured route for anarchists today. The idea of setting an example or sponsoring alternative communities has also had perennial appeal. This is somewhat reminiscent of the clearly pacifist anarchist methods of Tolstoy and his admirer Gandhi.

On the other hand, as is well known from the various caricatures of nineteenth-century anarchists, the path of violence has also had immense appeal. The forms of direct violent action proposed have varied. At one extreme was the so-called 'propaganda of the deed' movement, which engaged, usually on an individual basis, in random acts of bomb-throwing or assassination. Parallel to this was the advocacy of criminality and brigandage as anarchy. The most extreme exponent of the latter tendency was the short-lived companion of Bakunin, Sergei Nechaev. Nechaev (with or without Bakunin's help) constructed the notorious *Revolutionary Catechism* pamphlet, which advocated total criminal terrorism as the way forward (see Avrich 1974). Others favoured more organized armed insurrection, but this presented problems owing to the fact that anarchists are, almost by definition, not good organizers. Anarchists have also looked to various forms of strike activity. Although they have used the sympathy strike, the form favoured by most syndicalists and anarcho-syndicalists was the general strike. This entailed a total stoppage of work and, ultimately, the collapse of the political and economic system. Within the workplace, anarchists and anarcho-syndicalists also advocated boycotts and sabotage as ways of undermining regimes.

In anarchist literature, violence was often distinguished, in a vague manner, from force. Force was exercised illegitimately by states and police. Violence was legitimated in terms of its objectives. This left Kropotkin feeling distinctly uncomfortable with such a position. In one sense, violence, certainly in the manner in which anarcho-syndicalists and Bakunin spoke of it, was conceived of as cathartic or therapeutic; it was a way of cleansing the Augean stables of bourgeois society. However, such a cleansing could be dangerous in terms of unleashing unnecessary destruction and loss of innocent life.[41]

Conclusion

More than other ideologies, anarchy suffers from a profound divergence of views and tactics. Yet it still has a perennial appeal. The reasons for this are apparent. Not only does it contain a continual plea for the liberty of the individual against all forms of regimentation and coercion, something which has struck a deep note in European thought since the Reformation and the Enlightenment, but it also represents a continual questioning and challenge to group life, particularly the associated life of the state. This very logic has trapped anarchism in a number of insoluble dilemmas. On the one hand, anarchism is committed to the importance of individualism. Yet the strict logic of individualism carries it to the boundaries of absurdity. Stirner's psychological egoism is the most hard-headed reading of this logic. If the individual is the supreme value and the sole arbiter of value, then anything over and above the individual is of necessity suspect. Other anarchists, such as Rothbard, Godwin or Tolstoy, never carry the underlying logic of individualism to its conclusion. They always seek some consensual terminus, whether it be reason, natural rights, markets or the Sermon on the Mount. These provide bulwarks against facing the full implications of radical individualism head on.

On the other hand, those communal anarchists who find such radical atomized individualism intolerable face a different problem. Potentially, communal values and objectives stand as a barrier to individual freedoms. Once a community is organized it seems that immediate limitations are placed by it upon individuals. In such circumstances liberty is almost inevitably curtailed. There are, of course, ways round this. Kropotkin suggested that human nature evolved naturally to embrace this communal condition; in other words, free will does not enter into the argument. Individual behaviour would be biologically determinate. Others suggested that true freedom was experienced within a community and its values. Kropotkin's biology now appears very shaky and the positive freedom argument places communal anarchists in close proximity to ardent statists who see the state embodying such freedom. The particular difficulty of the freedom of the individual within a community, for anarchists, can be seen in their attempts to deal with crime, punishment, laziness and social deviance. The answers to these issues verge on the naïve. Some anarchists argued that crime and social deviance were overrated. They were the offspring of statism, capitalism and social hierarchies. Individuals could be persuaded and educated, or, if all else fails, socially ignored or excluded from a community. As much as some of these suggested solutions may appear reasonable, it is difficult to believe that they would really meet the problems of criminality and deviance. It is also hard to reconcile such anarchist practices with the value of liberty. They do not appear to be very different conditions to living under a formal rule of law; in fact, they might be far worse.

When anarchists do speak of their hoped-for communities, unless there is an anachronistic and anthropologically weak-minded appeal to past primitive village communities, the whole position appears as charming, but unrealistic and deeply nostalgic. Apart from some of the more rigid and strange absurdities of individualist anarchists, the communist, collectivist and mutualist anarchists express a millennial vision of what we would really like to be in our better moments, but which we know is relatively hopeless.

6

Fascism

The word 'fascism' was a product of the twentieth century.* One noted scholar of fascism remarked that even in 1920 'the word "fascism" was known to very few people in Europe, and even Mussolini placed it between quotation marks as being a neologism' (Nolte 1969, 17). Its late emergence on the political scene is viewed by some political sociologists as profoundly significant for the somewhat heterogeneous character of the movement (Linz in Laquer ed. 1979, 14).

The word 'fascism' derives etymologically from the Latin *fasces*, bundles of rods bound together symbolizing strength in unity, which were traditionally carried before consuls in the Roman Republic, indicating their authority. It is not certain that the word was chosen for its association with ancient Rome, although this was later emphasized by the fascists in the 1920s (see Mussolini in Oakeshott ed. 1953; Payne 1995, 89ff, 168; Passmore 2002, 10; Eatwell 2003, 17ff). It had initially sentimental, more socialist connotations in revolutionary Sicilian groups who referred to themselves as *fasci* in 1892. The term retained this socialist connotation up to 1914, when *fascio* groups called for intervention in the First World War and declared themselves against neutralism. The national defence groups organized after the Italian defeat at Caporetto in 1917 also called themselves *fasci*. The word thus had strong socialist origins and later came to imply extra-parliamentary and non-party nationalist activity. The young socialist Mussolini became involved in, and then led, the Milan *fascio* in 1915. After the war, in 1919 Mussolini reconstituted the Milan *fascio* under the title Fasci di Combattimento. Even Mussolini did not initially publicize the term 'fascism'. It was only after the somewhat mythical March on Rome that fascism moved self-consciously, and with startling rapidity, into European political debates. This was especially the case after the consolidation of the fascist regime in Italy post-1925.

---

* In this chapter, unless indicated otherwise, I will use the word 'fascism' as a generic which includes 'national socialism', although this should not be taken to mean that I regard them as identical, or that Italian fascism was *the* model. In the course of the chapter, the differences between Italian fascism and German national socialism are examined.

There are a number of problems in examining fascism. Of all the ideologies that we have dealt with, fascism, virtually alone, has given ideology a bad press. Despite its innocuous image to all but the communists in Europe in 1920, it now still conjures up, justifiably, visions of horrifying pogrom and unprecedented European destruction. From the 1950s this negativity has contributed to its somewhat hackneyed use as a term of political abuse.

Another problem concerns the relationship between 'fascism' and 'national socialism' (see Griffin 1983). Although there are marked differences between the movements, there are also enough affinities to treat them as part of the same generic compound – or as Roger Griffin argues, 'there is common denominator between all forms of fascism' (Griffin ed. 1995, 3). An additional key problem, which recurs throughout the assessment of fascism and national socialism, is the fact that the ideology is tied so strongly to particular nationalisms. This national particularity, from one standpoint, has the effect of limiting its universal applicability. The problem was very acute (although not insurmountable) for those who conceived of a Fascist International in 1935 (see Passmore 2002, 26; Griffin ed. 1995, 8). It is still a serious problem in the post-1945 era for those who see fascism as a legitimate descriptive term to use in contemporary political science or historical work. If fascism is so tied to the ends of particular nations, it is difficult to see how it can have universal appeal or application, except insofar as it asserts, formally, universally conflicting nationalisms. The main counter-argument to this claim is made forcefully in Griffin's prolific writings on fascism over the last three decades. In this case there is, what he calls, a common core of 'palingenetic ultra-nationalism' at the heart of fascism (Griffin ed. 1998, 163).[1] I am not persuaded, though, that this surmounts the internal deep tensions within the various fascist arguments. The stress on ultranationalism could not really be a *unifying* theme, except in a very abstract sense.

There is an additional problem concerning the relations between fascism as an ideology, the political movements which espoused it, and the actual activity of fascists whilst in power. This problem appears in other ideologies, yet in fascism it is particularly perplexing. The ideology is at times self-consciously anti-ideological, disparaging the whole effort to engage in rational discourse. The movements which espoused it, and the governments who claimed to be fascist, do not therefore appear to be easily explicable in rationalist terms. As one commentator remarked on fascism: 'Some observers were reminded of the magic mirror in which everyone, whether militaristic, reactionary or extreme pacifist on the left, could see his heart's desire' (Mack Smith 1983, 47). Fascism often occupies a middle ground somewhere between rational political ideology, on the one hand, and opportunistic adventurism, on the other. Stated purposes do not always tell us much, although they can sometimes be very revealing. There is some truth, though, to the point that fascism was initially more of a technique or method of acquiring power, and that the ideological doctrine was *ex post facto* elaboration. Yet even if it was *ex post facto*, this still should not lead us to underrate or totally ignore it.[2] There has been, though, a protracted debate, since the 1990s, amongst scholars of fascism over the question of what is called 'the fascist minimum', namely, whether or not there are core generic components of fascist thinking which can be identified. This argument would allow leeway to extend the term to the present day (see Eatwell 1996 or Payne 1995, ch. 13).

A number of difficulties must be faced in trying to characterize the ideology. Fascism is profoundly eclectic and occasionally bizarre. Many of its statements appear as simple-minded, vague rhetoric and propaganda. Yet should we always expect consistency and high levels of analysis from ideology? In other words, is there always such a clear, hard-and-fast distinction to be drawn between ideology and propaganda? Ideology can appear in many guises, from the simple to the most complex. We should not disregard something *because* it is bizarre, simplistic, eclectic or propagandist in intent.

Another difficulty concerns the relation of fascism to other ideologies. This is a complex area which can only be touched upon. On the one hand there were clearly puzzling relations between socialism, conservatism, syndicalism and fascism. The appellation 'national socialism' was certainly not accidental. Early fascists in Italy also called themselves 'national syndicalists'. It should not be forgotten that many fascists, such as Mussolini in Italy or Oswald Mosley in Britain, had early socialist affiliations. There were also strong affinities with forms of conservatism. Overall, as Mosley's biographer has commented, 'To the historian fascism is Janus-faced. One face looks forward, in the spirit of the Enlightenment, to the rational control and direction of human life; the other face looks backwards to a much simpler, more primitive, life when men struggled to live' (Skidelsky 1975, 299).[3] Ideologically, fascism was neither clearly socialist nor conservative in character. This vagueness and ambiguity, especially in its early years, contributed to its initial positive reception.

The Origins of Fascist and National Socialist Thought

There are two main issues dealt with in this section. The first is concerned with the origin and history of fascism and national socialism. The second considers the diversity of scholarly approaches to the ideology and the movement. The two issues are not unrelated, partly because many of the attempts to explain the nature of fascism incorporate diverse perspectives on its origin and history. To try to keep this discussion within manageable proportions, the origin and history will only be reviewed in outline.[4] The key focus will be on the second main issue: the diversity of scholarly approaches.

There are roughly four points of origin to which fascism is traced. The first sees fascism as an instinctual state of mind found in all forms of social organization from the beginning of civilization. This was articulated, from a more positive standpoint within fascism itself, by those German commentators who linked national socialism with the 'folk consciousness' and history of the Nordic race, or the Italian fascists who related their vision to the history of the Roman Empire. In addition, some psychological explanations in the twentieth century merged fascism with a certain type of universal personality structure, a structure which is implicit potentially in all humans. The second point of origin, which appears particularly in Italian fascism, sees it emerging from European cultural movements such as the Renaissance or the

Enlightenment. The Italian fascist Alfredo Rocco saw, for example, Machiavelli as the founding father of fascism. Rocco maintained that 'Fascism learns from him not only its doctrines but its actions as well' (Rocco n.d., 42–4). Rocco also discusses Vico and Mazzini in a similarly anachronistic vein.

The third, more viable point of origin regards fascism and national socialism as tardy aspects of the complex negative reaction to the French Revolution in European thought. The critical and fatalistic response by many European thinkers and regimes to the growth of liberalism, egalitarianism, democracy, rationalism, industrialization and later socialism, over the course of the nineteenth century, forms a backdrop to fascism. As one commentator has noted: 'The growth of fascism ... cannot be understood, or fully explained, unless it is seen in the intellectual, moral, and cultural context which prevailed in Europe at the end of the nineteenth century' (Sternhell in Laquer ed. 1979, 333; see also Weiss 1967; Sternhell et al. 1995; Sternhell 1996; Eatwell 2003, part 1). In this context, the intellectual movements of German romanticism, *völkisch* thought, social Darwinism, elite theory, syndicalism, corporatism, vitalism, and the like, are often discussed as components of such a response. Works such as Mussolini's 'Doctrine of Fascism' (1932) or Hitler's *Mein Kampf* (1925) can, in this sense, be seen as the simplistic, shallow top-dressing to a much older intellectual tradition. A large amount of scholarly interpretation congregates in this area.[5] The final point of origin is the 1920s. As F. L. Carsten remarked: 'There was no "Fascism" anywhere in Europe before the end of the First World War' (Carsten 1980, 63; also Payne 1995, ch. 2). Ernst Nolte, in his *Three Faces of Fascism* (1969), more or less accepted this view. One of its best-known expositors is Hugh Trevor-Roper, who commented that 'The public appearance of fascism as a dominant force in Europe is the phenomenon of a few years only. It can be precisely dated. It began in 1922–3 with the emergence of the Italian fascist party. ... It came of age in the 1930s. ... It ended in 1945 with the defeat of the two dictators' (Trevor-Roper in Woolf ed. 1968, 18). Trevor-Roper does not deny that there were precursors to fascism. Yet, in terms of the public history of fascism, they were not significant. Fascism was 'inseparable from the special experience of one generation' (Trevor-Roper in Woolf ed. 1968, 18). In this reading, fascism was a recent and short-lived ideology which had little or no relevance outside of the inter-war years. The experiences and legacies of the First World War, the effects of the Versailles Treaty, the great world depression and the collapse of the Weimar Republic were a unique concatenation of events. This account of fascism would of course deny its relevance as a category in post-1945 politics. Thus any debates about fascist movements in the 1990s or 2000s would be seen as a category mistake.

Moving now to the second main issue of this section, concerned with the diversity of scholarly explanations of fascism, many of these explanations show little or no interest in political ideas. In fact, it would be appropriate to note here that by far the most popular accounts of fascism have been non-ideological. It is these non-ideological views which will now be examined. In some cases the concern for non-ideological explanation is quite self-consciously pursued, ideology being regarded as offering very little help in grasping the nature of fascism. The ideology is viewed as either too fragmented, eclectic, bizarre or confused to be of any use whatsoever.

Some explanations assume this to be the case without further discussion. Although it is necessary to cover these differing non-ideological accounts, in order to give a comprehensive coverage of fascism, the bulk of the discussion in this chapter is none the less given over to the ideology itself. Although I am persuaded that there are economic, political and even pathological dimensions to fascism, I still believe that it is necessary to analyse its ideas and values. They should not be simply dismissed as absurd, partly because they often overlap and have close affinities with other ideologies. The non-ideological explanations can be dealt with under five main categories: Marxist, psychological, religious and moral, historical and sociological, and, finally, political. Many of these theories, it should be noted, would see fascism as a more generic category.

By far the most popular explanation of the fascist era of the 1930s was Marxist, although it still has its later twentieth-century proponents (see Poulantzas 1974 or Beetham 1983). There was no single, consistent account within Marxism, however. Fascism was basically explicable through the underlying economic laws or logic of capitalism. In general terms it was part of the crisis of monopoly capitalism.[6] As Herbert Marcuse argued, 'The roots of fascism are traceable to the antagonisms between growing industrial monopolization and the democratic system' (Marcuse 1973, 410). The argument, in sum, was that in order to allow monopoly capitalism to survive, the democratic and working-class opposition had to be neutralized. Accordingly, existing democratic institutions could no longer serve as a vessel for capitalism; in fact, increasing democratization was threatening capitalism. Interestingly, this latter view is still shared by classical liberals such as Friedrich Hayek. Thus, for production to continue and profits to be maintained, totalitarian terror had to be instituted. Fascism was a tool of monopoly capitalism at a particular stage of its development. It was used to repress the working class in the interests of big business, banks and financial concerns. Fascism was therefore causally related to the development of capitalist economies.

Some argued that fascism was the particular agent of finance capitalism alone and not necessarily of industrial or agrarian capital. This early view on fascism was encapsulated in the 1933 Comintern definition of fascism as 'the openly terroristic dictatorship of the most reactionary, most chauvinistic and most imperialist elements of finance capital' (quoted in Turner ed. 1975, 119). Others saw fascists as the anti-communist and anti-trade union shock troops for industrial manufacturing capital. Some Marxists also adapted Marx's argument from the *Eighteenth Brumaire* and saw fascism as a form of Bonapartism or Caesarism, whereby an extra-parliamentary group exploited the difference of interests between finance and industrial capital and ran the state autonomously (Poulantzas 1974). Fascists, in this sense, were not the pawns of any class.

Antonio Gramsci, despite his association with the Caesarist view, was the first Marxist writer to note that the ideology of fascism was a material force. It appeared to meet many of the ideals and aspirations of the masses. Thus the ideological hegemony of fascism could not simply be ignored. For Gramsci it had to be combated as a body of ideas as well as a political and economic practice. It was too simple to dismiss fascism as absurd. It was not by accident that Gramsci's *Prison*

Notebooks should have scrutinized in such detail the mechanism for the production and maintenance of hegemony. Gramsci's friend and a founding member of the Italian Communist Party (PCI), Palmiro Togliatti, also noted the power of fascism to successfully coalesce and mobilize the masses. In fact, it was acknowledged that fascism was far better at such mobilization in times of crisis than either liberalism or socialism. Togliatti was probably one of the first to realize the significance of Gramsci's notion of hegemony. However, the mainstream of Marxism in the 1930s could not accommodate the idea of an extreme right-wing political movement enjoying a significant influence on public consciousness.

There are numerous problems with the Marxist position. Apart from the disagreements on interpretation within Marxism, there is the unanswered question as to why there was such a body of anti-capitalist argument within fascism. In addition, many of the practices pursued under fascism, as in the racial extermination programmes under national socialism, cannot be easily accounted for using capitalist criteria. Furthermore, how could fascism appear in non-capitalist (or at least very low-level capitalist) societies such as Italy or Hungary, and dominate in some highly industrialized societies such as Germany but not in others like Britain? If there was a transparent deterministic relation between capitalism and fascism, how did it fit into the above scenario? Also it is not clear that manufacturing, industrial and financial interests consistently supported fascism politically or financially (Mosse 1978a, 49; see also Mommsen in Laquer ed. 1979, 157). Moreover, as certain Marxist writers have noted, there appears to be no explicit one-to-one relation between fascism and particular social classes (Forjacs ed. 1986, 43). There is often a blind spot for certain Marxists on the instrumental relation of classes and political power.

A second non-ideological explanation of fascism concentrates on the psychology of fascists. This is an argument which has largely dropped out of usage in the last few decades. The basic thesis of the psychological explanation, with many subtle variations, is that fascism needs to be explained in terms of certain forms of personality types and/or disorders. The ideology or historical determinants of fascism are of secondary significance to the basic personality traits. Like the Marxist argument, there are many possible variations. Some approach fascism purely from within the structures of Freudian, Jungian or other schools of psychoanalysis. The particular use of this approach in historical work has given rise to the epithet 'psychohistory'. Others focus on the psychological character of certain classes, or generational factors, particularly the lower middle class and socially deprived adolescents after the First World War. Finally, some of the Frankfurt school of Marxists, such as Erich Fromm, Theodor Adorno and Wilhelm Reich, tried to bridge the economic and psychological explanation, linking Marx with Freud.

Psychohistory tends to look at the childhood of fascists to reveal the deep structure of their later beliefs. Certain forms of isolation, displacement, sublimation and projection, often relating back to childhood, are seen to be characteristics of fascist personalities. The repression of early sexuality in authoritarian families (genital repression), denial of creativity, the Oedipus complex and fear of castration in males can lead to a sense of frustration, guilt and powerlessness. This in turn can give rise to aggression and sado-masochism, which can express itself politically in the bizarre male fantasies of fascism. The psychologist Erik Erikson remarked of Hitler's childhood that 'Now and again, history does seem to permit a man the joint fulfilment of national fantasies and of his own provincial and personal daydreams' (Erikson 1958, 104; also Binion 1973). Richard Koenigsberg, in *Hitler's Ideology: A Study in Psychoanalytic Sociology*, also notes that Hitler's ideology offered 'a means whereby his fantasies might be expressed and discharged at the level of social reality' (Koenigsberg 1975, 85).

Wilhelm Reich, in *The Mass Psychology of Fascism* (1975), also saw fascism growing out of the suppression of infantile and adolescent sexuality. In this sense, all humans were potentially fascists. Fascism was the political expression of the average human character when exposed to certain conditions. It had nothing to do with race, nations or parties. Whereas Marx had called for a social and economic revolution for liberation, Reich called for a sexual revolution. At this point his thoughts drifted into the virtues of sexual freedom to avoid the fascist mentality. Another German compatriot of Reich was Theodor Adorno, who postulated the idea of the authoritarian personality (Adorno 1950). The lower middle class, suffering alienation, self-hatred and loss of security after the First World War, developed sadistic and masochistic traits of character, which constituted the authoritarian personality. Noël O'Sullivan sums up this authoritarian personality as follows: 'a wretched creature, overwhelmed inwardly by sexual deprivation and afflicted outwardly by the ruthless economic order of capitalism, constantly liable to panic under the burden of a freedom for which he really has no use. ... In a desperate endeavour to escape from his misery, he welcomes political extremism' (O'Sullivan 1983, 25).

The weaknesses of the psychological approach stem from the dearth of evidence on the childhoods of major fascists such as Hitler. Too much reliance is placed on sketchy personal testimonies. There are also doubts concerning the 'scientific' status of the psychoanalytic approach. Furthermore, it is difficult to see how such studies can be used for explaining mass electoral support or mass membership of fascist groups. Finally, if the psychological perspective is true, then we might as well all train to be psychologists, since it would explain the whole of history and politics, which is not a particularly convincing hypothesis.

The third non-ideological explanation was again characteristic of the late 1930s, although it can even now be found in some discussions. The basic idea was that fascism was an aspect or symptom of a moral and religious crisis or malaise in Western civilization.[7] This perspective was more ready to consider the ideological content of fascism, although there was still a tendency to see the practice of fascism as the result of a deeper religious or moral cause. In the 1920s and 1930s, philosophers such as Benedetto Croce and R. G. Collingwood saw fascism as a negative challenge and a denial of human liberty. For Croce, fascism was a corruption of the Italian tradition of liberty. He argued that 'authoritarian governments endure only among decadent peoples' (quoted in Ruggiero 1927, 343). In Britain, Collingwood also viewed fascism as a new form of barbarism and a sign of a loss of faith in liberty and liberalism. Liberty for Collingwood had been 'distilled from the body of Christian practice'. The barbarism and paganism of fascism and national socialism challenged the whole Christian tradition (Collingwood 1940, 170ff).[8] In more recent years another, more positive perspective has developed on the issue of religion; this in essence identifies fascism through the category of *civic religion*. Fascism is thus taken to represent a politicization of the sacred and embodies much that would expect from a religion, minus a deity. This idea has been explored by a number of scholars, with fascism taking pride of place (see Gentile 1996 and 2006; Burleigh 2001 and 2006; see also Griffin ed. 1995, 5–6).[9]

Other writers worried by the moral and cultural status of fascism refocused on the issue of nihilism and moral collapse. One of the first critical German commentators saw national socialism specifically as a form of profound cultural and moral nihilism (see Rauschning 1939). Fascism has also been seen as an aspect of the 'death of God' movement in European thought, dating from the work of Friedrich Nietzsche, and the overall loss of religious belief and transcendent values. Catholic writers such as Jacques Maritain, following this line, saw it as a form of pagan 'demonic pantheism' (Maritain quoted in O'Sullivan 1983, 24). Later scholars, such as Robert Pois, have argued a similar point. Pois comments that 'Nazism was most definitely a rebellion against the Judaeo-Christian tradition', and that it 'was singular in its efforts to consciously supplant Judaeo-Christian forms' (Pois 1986, 28). Other writers, such as G. L. Mosse, Fritz Stern and P. J. Pulzer, have seen fascism, and more particularly national socialism, as a deeply rooted cultural malaise (see Pulzer 1964; Mosse 1966; Stern 1974).[10]

Some commentators dismiss this view, finding little hard evidence for the latter point, just a series of generalized assertions about moral decline or cultural despair (e.g. Gregor 1974, 45). Such a judgement seems, though, unnecessarily severe. There is a great deal more scholarship backing some of these explanations than in fact can be found in many of the Marxist or psychological accounts.

The fourth, now rather dated, explanation concentrated on the historical and sociological context of fascism. The basic claim was that fascism was the result of rapid development and modernization, or sometimes the particular manner of industrialization, in certain societies. The aim of such studies was to gain more empirically respectable economic and statistical indices for the occurrence of fascism. A. F. Organski, and later Barrington Moore, Jr, were initially associated with this line of thought.[11] All traditional societies, over the nineteenth and twentieth centuries, were subject to transformation, comprising rapid industrialization, urbanization, secularization and rationalization. Various paths were taken to modernization, and fascism was one possible route. However, compared to Germany, industrialization and modernization came late to Italy. This raises an immediate problem. If Germany was highly industrialized by the 1920s, but Italy was not, then in terms of the socio-economic modernizing criteria, as one writer puts it, 'Italian fascism and Nazism do not belong in the same category' (Sauer in Turner ed. 1975, 132). If fascism is linked closely with rapid modernization and industrialization, then it does not appear to explain what happened in Italy and Germany. Thus it remains a deeply unsatisfactory account (see Bracher in Laquer ed. 1979, 205).

A final broad band of explanations is 'political' in character. The term 'political' is used rather loosely here.[12] To some extent this explanation is set against the background of a crisis of parliamentary democracy. It was one of the key fascist arguments that parliamentary democracy had failed. The most traditional political explanation of fascism sees it as old-fashioned tyranny and personal aggrandizement by figures such as Hitler. The task is therefore to unpack, at the micro level, the biographical features, actions and thoughts of tyrants. Alan Bullock's *Hitler: A Study in Tyranny* (1962), Ian Kershaw's *Hitler* (1998–2000), Dennis Mack Smith's *Mussolini* (1983) or R. J. B. Bosworth's *Mussolini* (2003) broadly follow this line. It is also to some extent present in the writings of Hugh Trevor-Roper and Ernst Nolte. Discussing contrasting attitudes among the national socialists, Bullock remarks that 'To Strasser National Socialism was a real political movement, not, as it was to Hitler, the instrument of his ambition. He took its programme seriously, as Hitler never had' (Bullock 1962, 237).[13] Some would argue that over-concentration on tyrannical personalities gives the wrong impression of fascist movements. Not only does it appear to absolve many others from responsibility, making the fascist parties totally monolithic and focused on their leaders; it also ignores the deep inner confusion, bitter infighting and power struggles which took place in all fascist groups (see Carr in Laquer ed. 1979, 122ff).

Another popular line of political explanation was to incorporate fascism, with communism and Stalinism, under the general rubric of 'totalitarianism', or alternatively under the rubric of mass politics (see Eatwell 2003, 74ff; Passmore 2002, 18ff). These views, particularly the former, were developed in the Cold War period of the 1950s. Initially, totalitarianism was explored in a more philosophical manner in works such as Hannah Arendt's *The Origins of Totalitarianism* (1951) and Karl Popper's *The Open Society* (1945). However, it soon became part of the conventional language of academic political science, as expressed in J. L. Talmon's *Origins of Totalitarian Democracy* (1952) and C. J. Friedrich and Z. K. Brzezinski's *Totalitarian Dictatorship and Autocracy* (1966), amongst many others. Fascism, as totalitarianism, was characterized by a monolithic single party, no separation between state and society, complete control of the state structure and the economy, total mobilization of the masses, and domination of mass communication. The masses in this context become rootless, isolated and atomized (see Gregor 1974, 118ff).

The weakness of the totalitarian approach is that it plays down the deep chaos, general incompetence and internal feuding which in fact characterized fascism. In other words, it overrates the totalitarian capacities of, particularly, Germany and Italy. It is doubtful whether any of the features associated with totalitarianism were actually instantiated completely in either country. The approach also underplays the role of authoritarian conservatism within fascism. Further, it ignores the differences between communism and fascism, by lumping them under the same category. In addition, within national socialism, it is far from clear that either Hitler or many of the key protagonists actually wanted totalitarian statism.

Finally, despite the fact that many scholars associate fascism with the lower middle class, others argue that fascism was a latecomer to the political scene, cross-cutting existing structural, political and social allegiances (see Carsten in Laquer ed. 1979, 460). It was thus a 'conjunctural phenomenon' combining heterogeneous social class and generational support. As Juan B. Linz suggests, this accounts 'for the often quite different social composition of the initial nucleus'. For Linz, the vagaries of war and foreign aid helped fascism fortuitously to play a political role, but as a pragmatic and ideological mix. Fascist parties, in fact, prefigure the post-1945 development of ideologically mixed political parties in Western Europe. Linz adds that, 'The more fluid social structure, the exhaustion of ideological passion, the needs of national reconstruction in post-fascist Europe made programmatically eclectic heterogeneous parties possible and successful.' Linz insists, however, that any full study of fascism has to take into account the unique sociological, political and historical context of each society. Thus he notes that the only kind of viable empirical generalization is that 'Fascism was that novel response to the crisis … of the pre-war social structure and party system' (Linz in Laquer ed. 1979, 16–18). Linz's view is in fact characteristic of much political sociology in recent decades.

The Nature of Fascism

In examining the nature of fascism there is an immediate problem of which writers to include and which to exclude. Some scholars include French writers such as Maurice Barrès and Charles Maurras, with particular reference to French organizations such as Action Française (see Soucy 1972, 1979 and 1986). Others see these as pre-fascist, reactionary or authoritarian Right groups as distinct from fascism (see Weber 1964). Spain before 1933 and the Falange, despite having a rightist anti-parliamentary Movimento Nacional, still did not have an overt fascist grouping (Payne in Turner ed. 1979, 151). In Germany, whereas the more traditional Right had little of a worked-out programme, the national socialist group quite clearly did (Wood in Eatwell and O'Sullivan eds 1989, 141–3).[14]

Related to this whole debate is the question as to how broadly fascism can be extended. Were Jean Degrelles Rexists in Belgium, the Romanian Legion of the Archangel Michael, Portugal under Salazar, Argentina under Peron or the later Junta, Hungary under General Gombüs, Japan during the Second World War, or France under de Gaulle – to name but a few of the suggestions – all fascist (see Cassels in Turner ed. 1975; see Payne 1995, ch. 10)? Despite the concentration on Italy and Germany in this chapter, it should not be assumed that all the above movements were automatically non-fascist or pre-fascist. This is a vast and unresolved scholarly debate which can only be mentioned in passing. Germany and Italy have been dealt with on grounds of space and as being the most obvious cases.

Most commentators on fascism agree that it incorporated many groups and tendencies. On the most general level, there are ideological differences between German national socialism and other European fascisms in Italy, France, Spain and Britain. For some, these differences are so great that they baulk at including national socialism in the same genus as Italian or Spanish fascism.[15] The most profound difference is the centrality of the issue of race. There is also an absence of a strong *Volk* tradition in other variants, whereas it is central to the German case. This Germanic *Volk* factor alone alienated French fascists such as Brasillach and Drieu de Rochelle, Spanish fascists such as Primo de Rivera, and even Italians such as Mussolini. Mussolini used to refer to Germany in the 1930s as a 'racialist lunatic asylum'.[16] Certainly in many of the ideological tracts from Italy, Spain, France and Britain over the 1920s and 1930s, there is no mention either of the race question or of the virtual cosmic significance of anti-Semitism which obsessed so many national socialists. Italian and other such fascist groups only gradually assumed a more anti-Semitic stance in the late 1930s. Even then, they never reached the intense and vitriolic levels that prevailed in Germany (see Burleigh and Wipperman 1993). The intensity of controlled violence and terror is another distinguishing mark of Germany as distinct, certainly, from Italy.[17] In addition, little attention is given outside Germany to the *Lebensraum* issue. This question was of particular concern to Hitler and lay behind his obsessive foreign policy (quite clearly articulated in the closing chapters of *Mein Kampf*) for the eastward expansion of Germany into Russia and the decimation of the Slavic peoples. In Italy, expansion was usually conceived of in terms of traditional European aggressive imperialism. In Germany it was again tied obsessively to the issue of race.

Finally, whereas fascism in Italy was premised, with some qualification, on a more traditional Western rationalism, German national socialism was more self-consciously committed to an irrationalist and vitalist position, where every human artefact, the arts, sciences, societies and history, were judged from one salient perspective – race. In Italy there was often a definite impetus, in some though not all sectors of the fascist movement, towards rational modernization, where the state would play a dominant creative role (see Griffin 2007). In Germany, the race question overshadowed all such endeavour, at least in the ideological output. The German state in fact was irrevocably subservient to the *Volk* and to racial issues.

Within the various national groupings of fascism, including the German, there were again quite marked subdivisions. There are a number of ways of conceptualizing these subdivisions. Nolte speaks of early, normal and radical fascism (as well as his category of pre-fascism). Alexander de Grand, in his study of Italian fascism, speaks of conservative, national, technocratic, *Squadrismo* ruralist and national syndicalist fascism (Nolte 1969, 574; Grand 1989, ch. 10). A somewhat simpler basic ideological subdivision occurred between more socialist- and more capitalist-inclined wings. Some were prepared, within a disciplined societal order, to give capitalism a full head; others wanted seriously to curtail it. In Italy, Mussolini was initially, in the early 1920s, and at the end of his life in the Republic of Salò, associated with the socialist stance. During the late 1920s he tried to sit astride both tendencies.[18] The national syndicalist and corporatist Catholic input into fascism ensured the continuance of the socialist line of thought. One Italian writer, Angelo Olivetti, placed Left fascism firmly in the tradition of Proudhonian socialism (Roberts 1979, 318)![19]

A similar division of opinion occurred among the national socialists in Germany. Party activists such as Gottfried Feder and Gregor Strasser were much more inclined towards socialist methods. Feder, for example, called for wide-scale nationalization; a centralized state-controlled banking system; state management of public utilities, transport, credit; and control of prices and wages with state confiscation of excessive profits. The well-known Twenty-Five Points of the NSDAP programme of 1920–3, the Agricultural Programme 1930 and the Full Employment Programme of 1932 incorporated a great deal of anti-capitalist material.[20] Alfred Rosenberg, Hitler and Goebbels did not appear to be as enthused by this line. This does not mean, however, that they wished to pursue a more overtly capitalist policy. In the case of Rosenberg, the racial line was far more significant.

In the context of the common fascist denigration of intellectualism, it is often difficult to pick out important fascist themes, programmes and ideologists. Italian fascism had some clever apologists, such as Giovanni Gentile, who constructed (so it subsequently appears) much of the 'Doctrine of Fascism' article for Mussolini, as well as writing a sophisticated political treatise, *The Genesis and Structure of Society* (1946) (see also Gentile 2004). Critics are none the less divided on how representative Gentile is of fascism (see Bellamy 1987a, ch. 6; see especially Gregor 2001). The national socialists did not have anyone so distinguished as Gentile. Hitler's *Mein Kampf*, which Mussolini described as 'a boring tome that I have never been able to read', does not really serve as a foundational text, although there are undoubtedly influential ideas present within it (Mack Smith 1983, 200).[21] Rosenberg contributed his own rather disjointed rambling on the Nordic race. There were also writings on national socialist themes by Gregor Strasser, Gottfried Feder and Joseph Goebbels. More sceptical academic figures on the sidelines, such as Carl Schmitt or Martin Heidegger, added some element of respectability to the literature.[22]

Given the above points, it is difficult to find common ground for a discussion of fascism(s). One starting-point is the negative ideological 'anti's' of fascism. As Linz suggests, 'The various "anti's" of fascism served to define its identity' (Linz in Laqueur ed. 1979, 15). The majority of fascists were anti-liberal, anti-Marxist, anti-parliamentary, anti-individualist and anti-bourgeois (see Griffin ed. 1995, 4ff). They felt that the bourgeois age was spiritually empty, hypocritical and materialistic, estranged from the actual world, and lacking any sense of community. These were undoubtedly common themes, but they do not tell us a great deal. More light can perhaps be shed by a consideration of fascist views on human nature, to which we now turn.

Human Nature

The intellectual background to the fascist understanding of human nature is an odd mixture. The ideas promulgated were a peculiar concoction of social Darwinism, nineteenth-century racial theory, intuitivist and vitalist philosophies, syndicalism, elite theory, romanticism, crowd psychology and the psychology of the unconscious. Out of this unholy brew a number of recurring, more formal, themes on the character of human beings can be discerned.

First, human nature was characterized by the primacy of will and activism. Humans were first and foremost creatures of volition and action. Thought was something which appeared almost *ex post facto*. Abstract thought distorted or diverted us from action. In exercising our will and acting in the world we express our true natures. It was argued that we should act on the basis of instinct and intuition rather than on the basis of reasoned argument. The philosophical roots to this line of thinking lie in a number of sources, but more particularly in Henri Bergson's and Friedrich Nietzsche's distinct vitalism, William James's pragmatism and aspects of German *Lebensphilosophie*.

It is important to grasp the context of such activism and vitalism and the manner in which it was manipulated and distorted by fascists. A large percentage of recruits to early fascist groups had fought in the First World War (this included Hitler, Mussolini and Mosley). In the case of Italy, France and Germany, many of the Squadristi, Camelot du Roi, Freikorps, Brownshirts and SS were initially ex-servicemen. The post-1918 generation was brutalized and militarized, both acclimatized and accustomed to death and extreme levels of violence. In peacetime many still thrived on an atmosphere of intimidation, which they fomented. In this sense, the violence and activism of fascists appeared as self-justifying, especially since the same tactic was also adopted by their communist opponents. Pre-war liberal tolerance was seen as a cause both of the war and of post-war social distress. It was also utterly inappropriate to the new world. Beating up communists, Jews, trade unionists or political opponents was the fascist stock-in-trade. Violence was normalized, in Germany, by Hitler's murder of Ernst Röhm and the Brownshirts and the launching of *Kristallnacht*, and, in Italy, by Mussolini's murder of his political opponent Giacomo Matteotti, the beating-up of the communist deputy Francesco Misiano in parliament, and the regular street battles. Fascist instinctivism and activism were contrasted with ineffectual flabby parliamentary liberal rationalism. The mythology and symbolism of fascist movements were expressed in terms of active battles, marches and *Putsche*.

Such politically orchestrated violence was given the intellectual gloss of social poetry. Violence had almost an aesthetic appeal. Writers such as Georges Sorel, in *Reflections on Violence* (1908), were influential here in linking philosophical vitalism with political violence. In fact, given its instinctual and emotive base, vitalism could be allied, by almost imperceptible shifts of logic, to all artistic creative experience, via the all-inclusiveness of concepts like intuition and instinct. In the same way that it is difficult to unpack the emotional experience of artistic creation into abstract theory, so equally with heroic, crusading political violence. Violence becomes alchemically transmuted into an aesthetic mystery.

In one sense this link between art and violence was consciously pursued in some of the writings of Italian futurists as a kind of *fin-de-siècle* aestheticism. Many talented artists were drawn to fascism, particularly in the initial stages before the murder of Matteotti. Mussolini's mistress, Margherita Sarfatti, was especially enthusiastic about patronizing the arts, although she personally favoured the link between fascism and a form of neo-classicism, rather than futurism. Futurism itself came out of the same cultural matrix as fascism, emphasizing direct action, life, instinct and creativity over reason and system. The author of *The Futurist Manifesto* (1909), Filippo Marinetti, saw futurism as the art of fascism, but it is not so certain that Mussolini shared this view. Marinetti declared, in the opening sections of the *Manifesto*, some of the main elements of his credo:

1 We want to sing the love of danger, the habit of energy and rashness.
2 The essential elements of our poetry will be courage, audacity and revolt.
3 Literature has up to now magnified pensive immobility. ... We want to exalt movements of aggression, feverish sleeplessness, the double march, the perilous leap, the slap and the blow with the fist.

4 We declare the splendour of the world has been enriched by a new beauty, the beauty of speed. A racing automobile with its bonnet adorned with great tubes like serpents with explosive breath ... a roaring motor car which seems to run on machine-gun fire. (Marinetti, 'Futurist Manifesto' in Lyttelton ed. 1973, 211)

Younger fascists were thus encouraged to think of violence in romantic, crusading, almost chivalrous terms. When Sorel linked violence with Bergson's *élan vital* (a spontaneous evolving creative 'life force' which lifted the whole human species to higher levels of development), and others linked it with the achievement of the historic mission of racial purity, violence took on cosmic significance. Such violence was not the same as the force exercised by liberal states. Violence was instinctual, linking the individual with unconscious spiritual depths. It encouraged the epic state of mind of the hero, or *Übermensch*. It was a cathartic, character-changing experience. As the Italian fascist Giovanni Papini noted: 'While the democratic mob raise outcry against war ... we look on it as the greatest possible tonic to restore flagging energy, as a swift and heroic means to attain power' (Pappini in Lyttelton ed. 1973, 106).[23] We might recognize here a mundane but, in this case, glossy platitude, namely, that human nature can be transformed in situations of dire hardship and danger. This is often stated by those who have never experienced dire hardship.

Within such a scenario, fascist writers frequently referred to the ideology as not so much a programme as a state of mind or a way of being. Primo de Rivera, the leading light of the Spanish Falange, commented: 'Our movement will not be understood if it is thought to be merely a way of thinking; it is not a way of thinking, it is a way of being' (Primo de Rivera 1972, 56). Papini also noted: 'We are not putting forward programmes but a passionate attitude of mind to make an end to words and turn programmes into action' (Papini in Lyttelton ed. 1973, 100; see also Gentile 1928, 292; Mussolini in Oakeshott ed. 1953, 170–1). It was in a similar vein that Nazis often proclaimed that one should think 'with the blood'.

It is not surprising in this context that fascism should be seen as an anti-intellectual doctrine. The philosophical premise incorporates an implicit assumption that it is the unconscious depths – will, creative emotion, instinct, intuition, *élan*, blood, and so on – which really characterize human nature. This is contrasted to the superficial 'intellectual' surface. This attitude constituted part of the very attraction of fascism for many artists, writers and intellectuals, particularly the two former groups. Gentile's response (as a Hegelian and thus an anti-intuitivist) to the question of whether human beings were motivated by rationality or irrational/volitional drives was to argue that we should not conclude that fascism was 'a blind praxis or purely instinctive method'. Fascism, for Gentile, was the heart of reality, 'living thought', in other words, concrete as opposed to abstract thought (Gentile 1928, 301; see also Gentile 2004). Fascism is only anti-intellectual if, as Gentile notes, one divorces 'knowledge from life, ... brain from heart, ... theory from practice' (Gentile 1928, 300–1).[24] Fascism is thus seen to be immanent in reality itself.

Another aspect of this vitalism was that the masses were often viewed as instinctual and herd-like. Their instincts could be manipulated by the superior few. Crude forms of social Darwinism, combined with the doctrine of the *Herrenvolk*, suggested that the less fit or corrupt specimens of humanity could be removed in the same way that we would engage in the selective breeding of any domestic animal. Humans could thus be regarded *en masse* with benevolent contempt. Mussolini indeed appears to have had an abysmal view of human beings. He generally assumed that everyone was utterly selfish and untrustworthy. This parallels Bullock's summary of Hitler, where 'Distrust was matched by contempt. Men [for Hitler] were moved by fear, greed, lust for power, envy, often by mean and petty motives. Politics ... is the art of knowing how to use these weaknesses for one's own ends' (Bullock 1962, 37; see also Kershaw 1998–2000). Mussolini's major criticism of Machiavelli's credentials for being a founding fascist was that he did not have enough contempt for the masses. Overall Mussolini regarded the masses as easy to deceive and dominate. Essentially they were like children who had to be scolded and rewarded in turn. As Mack Smith comments, Mussolini 'was glad to find that the herd – this was the word he liked to use – would gratefully accept inequality and discipline' (Mack Smith 1983, 145; see also Bullock 1962, 37).

Most fascists considered that humans were social or communal creatures by nature. No fascists denied this thesis, although they had different understandings of it. One common critical target, which appears in the work of nearly every fascist writer at some point, is classical liberal individualism. Thus Alfredo Rocco argued that, contrary to liberal individualism, 'A human being outside the pale of society is an inconceivable thing – a non-man. Humankind in its entirety lives in social groups.' For Rocco, fascism 'replaces therefore the old atomistic and mechanical state theory which was at the basis of the liberal and democratic doctrines' (Rocco n.d., 33; see also Mussolini in Oakeshott ed. 1953, 166).[25] There was, as indicated, a marked difference of understanding of this social nature, particularly between the Italian and German writers. In the writings of Gentile, Rocco and Mussolini, the 'social' dimension was understood more conventionally through the concept of the nation state. Gentile, in his article 'The Philosophic Basis of Fascism' (1928), argued that 'Since the State is a principle, the individual becomes a consequence' (Gentile 1928, 301; see also Gentile 2004). In his last systematic treatise he expressed it thus: 'At the root of the "I" there is the "we". The community to which an individual belongs is the basis of his spiritual existence' (Gentile 1960, 82). The gist of Gentile's point was that for European peoples – from the satisfaction of the most basic needs to the realization of freedom and morality – the development of the individual is integral to the existence of the state. In fact, the state and the individual are of the same substance. As Gentile noted: 'The State is the universal aspect of the individual ... it is not a presupposition of his existence ...but the concrete actuality of his will' (Gentile 1960, 131; also Mussolini in Oakeshott ed. 1953, 167–8; Gentile in Lyttelton ed. 1973, 307).

The national socialist interpretation of the term 'social' was distinct from that of the Italian fascists. National socialists tended to focus their attention on the racial and *völkisch* dimension rather than on the state. An individual was constituted through the community. This community was constituted in terms of a racial or folk soul (*Volkseele*). A romanticized conception of nature lay behind this claim. Nature was not understood as a lifeless, orderly mechanism which could be coldly observed;

on the contrary, it was understood as a 'life force' which animated and gave purpose and meaning to both humans and their *Volk* (Mosse 1966, 15; Sternhell in Laqueur ed. 1979, 337). The instinctive, emotive life of human beings linked them not only with their *Volk* but also with the inner 'life force' of nature. Human beings could be glorified, therefore, according to their oneness with nature, not through their dominance of it. Unlike the Italian fascists, national socialists celebrated, in a bogus, mystical sense, nature, pastoral landscape and rural peasant life. The soul of a people was supposedly present in their landscape. It should not be forgotten that the national socialists were the first in Europe to set up nature reserves and pursue deciduous woodland reforestation schemes, for nationalistic ecological reasons.[26]

A further point here was that unconditional inequality was biologically determined and irremovable. All Nazis accepted an inequality of races and folk souls. The Aryan, at one with the landscape and people, was superior in all respects to Jews, Slavs or Negroes. Hitler described Aryans as the 'genius race'. The unconditional inequality of peoples did not alter inequalities within the Aryans themselves. There were some – for example, the genius or hero-figure – who were born superior. Great things could only be accomplished by peoples through the efforts of great individuals. As Hitler put it: 'The progress and culture of humanity are not a product of the majority, but rest exclusively on the genius and energy of the personality' (Hitler 1969, 313).

A related point about genius or leader figures was made in Italian fascism. In this latter case it was not premised on hazy accounts of racial or biological genius, but on an interpretation of the sociological writings on elitism of Vilfredo Pareto, Gaetano Mosca and Robert Michels. Elite writers not only contributed to the theories of leadership, but also helped to generate suspicions concerning parliamentary democracy, suspicions which were rife among fascists. It should be noted that only Michels became an open supporter of fascism. Admittedly, this more intellectual side of Italian fascism was not always evident. The element of self-deluding pomposity and neurosis was also a strong feature of Mussolini's, and Hitler's, visions of their own role.[27]

All fascists suggested that because of the corruption of human nature brought about in liberal democratic societies some change had to be contemplated. In the case of national socialism this campaign had to produce, as Ernst Krieck put it, a '*Volk*-bound German man' (quoted in Pois 1986, 70). For Mussolini, the fascist Italian was to be created on a par with the Renaissance Italian. The attempt to bring about the fascist man had its absurdly amusing side, as in the campaign against pasta as an anti-fascist food, spaghetti not being the right 'food for fighters'.[28] Mussolini anticipated that the new Italian man would be more heroic, optimistic, less critical and individualistic, more serious, hard-working, courageous, less talkative, abjuring comfort and spending less money on pleasurable food or wine, sleeping less and being physically fit (Mack Smith 1983, 174).

The major difference between the German and Italian visions of a reform of human nature was that for Mussolini the new man was already present, but had to be disencumbered. For some Nazis, such as Rosenberg, the blond Aryan also existed (Tacitus had, after all, noted him lurking in Teutonic forests) but had to be protected against racial admixture. For Himmler and the Waffen-SS, the new man had to be eugenically and selectively bred for the future and other 'race units' had to be eliminated.

Nature, Race and *Volk*

Fascist thinking on human nature is further elucidated if we consider the issues of nationalism, race and *Volk* in a little more depth. In fascist terms, human beings, as should be obvious by now, are first and foremost creatures of a nation, race or *Volk*. There is therefore no human *per se*, only a German, Frenchman, Italian, and so on. This idea runs directly counter to Enlightenment and later liberal and socialist internationalism and cosmopolitanism.

Fascist nationalism was distinct from nineteenth-century liberal nationalism (see Griffin ed. 1995, 2–3). When Gottfried Herder examined the linguistic character of nations he did not suggest the notion of either superiority, conquest or mutual national hatred. In many ways the more insular, xenophobic and aggressive use of nationalism was already integral to more authoritarian conservative groups at the close of the nineteenth century; fascists simply adopted it.

The common features of fascist nationalism were, first, the older conservative contrast to liberal or socialist internationalism. As Papini noted, socialism is 'an international, that is to say anti-national party', and 'in order to love something deeply you need to hate something else' (an idea which has strong parallels to the work of Carl Schmitt on politics), thus the true nationalist cannot possibly be internationalist (Papini in Lyttelton ed. 1973, 101–3; Grand 1989, xii). Second, fascist nationalism was orientated to a communitarian ideal. True identity was found in the community of the nation, and the nation was prior to the individual. As the Italian fascist Charter of Labour stated: 'The Italian nation is an organic whole having life, purposes and means of action superior in power and duration to those of individuals ... of which it is composed' (Charter of Labour, 21 April 1927). Third, nationalism was used as a counterbalance to class struggle. The nation transcended such division. As Primo de Rivera put it: 'The class struggle disregards the unity of the fatherland because it destroys the integrity of the concept of *national production*' (Primo de Rivera 1972, 60). In addition, nationalism was opposed to the liberal bourgeois conception of life. Nationalism prepared the nation for heroism, self-sacrifice, conflict and, ultimately, war. The bourgeoisie undermined such ambitions and wasted time on materialistic longings and parliamentary politics. Before the First World War, Enrico Corradini summarized this contempt as follows:

> Every sign of decrepitude, sentimentalism, doctrinairism, outmoded respect for transient human life, outmoded pity for the weak and humble, utility and mediocrity seen as wisdom, neglect of the higher potentialities of mankind, the ridiculing of heroism, every foul sign of loathsome decrepitude of degenerate people can be found in the contemplative life of our ruling and governing class, the Italian bourgeoisie. (Corradini in Lyttelton ed. 1973, 139)[29]

Finally, nationalism was used as a device to bestow legitimacy on certain senses of democracy and socialism. These were often referred to in fascist writings as the 'nobler democracy' and 'nobler socialism'. Socialism and democracy, when devoted to the primacy of the nation, were seen as superior to, on the one hand, bourgeois representative democracy and, on the other, internationalist socialism. The worst of all worlds was the mutual contamination of socialism and democracy. In this case the best aspects of socialism and democracy – their collective devotion to nation – were lost in the mists of internationalism and the false equality between peoples.

The major difference between the German and Italian variants of nationalism again rests on the race issue. With Italian fascism, nationalism was a more traditional form of xenophobic imperialism and patriotism. In national socialism, the German nation expressed the *Volk* spirit and was underpinned by a biological doctrine of racial purity. To be German was to be of a particular biological racial stock. More significantly, in Italian fascism, as Mussolini put it, 'It is not the nation that generates the State. ... Rather the nation is created by the State' (Papini in Lyttelton ed. 1973, 104). Yet conversely, in Nazism, as Hitler put it, 'The *state* in itself does not create a specific cultural level; it can only preserve the race which conditions this level.' He continued, 'We, as Aryans, can conceive of the state only as the living organism of this nationality' (Hitler 1969, 357–8). Clearly, there was a complete reversal of ideological priorities between Nazism and Italian fascism. Finally, there was a clear difference of emphasis in terms of the significance accorded to the nation. Whereas in German national socialism it was shrouded in a quasi-religious aura, this was not present in Italian fascism.

One explanation for these differences is the idiosyncratic intellectual heritage of Nazism. The most important elements of this were the racial theories of Arthur de Gobineau and the British aristocrat and Germanophile Houston Stewart Chamberlain and the German romantic *Volk* tradition, as focused initially in the writings of figures such as Paul de Lagarde, Julius Langbehn and Moeller van den Bruck (see Stern 1974). As Marx and Engels had seen the motor of history in class struggle, Gobineau and Chamberlain saw the motor in racial struggle. Gobineau's *Essay on the Inequality of the Human Races* (1853–5) was an attack upon nineteenth-century liberalism and socialism – in sum, on the radical legacy of the French Revolution. False moralistic notions of human equality came up against the apparently immovable scientific fact of unequal racial origin. For Gobineau, there were three basic racial units arranged in a hierarchy, each with specific characteristics: the white, the yellow and the black. The lowest was the black and the highest was the white. Within the white there was a group – the Aryans – a form of super-elite who had to be kept free from admixture. Gobineau's message was not just one of racial typology. A great tragedy had befallen the human race, namely, the inevitable mixture or miscegenation of races. This spelt decay and entropy in civilization.

Little note was taken of Gobineau until the end of his life, when he was befriended by the composer Richard Wagner in 1876. In 1894, twelve years after both men's deaths, Wagner's widow Cosima, with Ludwig Schemann, set up the Gobineau Society, with its own racial archive. A noted member of this group was the above-mentioned Houston Stewart Chamberlain, whose *Foundation of the Nineteenth Century* (1899) carried on the theme of racial speculation. Drawing upon Gobineau, he noted the immense significance of race. Unlike Gobineau, however, anti-Semitism appears as a dominant motif, combined with the superiority of the Teutonic Aryan. Again unlike Gobineau, Chamberlain looked more optimistically to the role of the Germans in maintaining purity and preventing miscegenation or *Volk*-chaos in Europe. Chamberlain joined the Nazi Party shortly before his death in 1927. Hitler and the Nazi ideologist Alfred Rosenberg remained profound admirers of his work.

The above pseudo-scientific racial ideas were linked by Nazi writers with the much older romantic *Volk* traditions of the early 1800s. Romanticism had gloried in the importance of intuition, emotion and feeling. This was subtly integrated into the nationalist perspective. As Pois comments: 'What Fichte seemed to be establishing philosophically … the poets Arndt and Körner and the somewhat cruder patriot, Father Jahn, established on an intellectual level: the heroic, self-sacrificing individuality of *Volk*' (Pois introduction to Rosenberg 1971, 19). By the early 1900s this heady concoction had combined with long-standing traditions of European anti-Semitism, philosophical vitalism and crude social Darwinist speculation about the fittest races. These formed a back-cloth to national socialist speculations of the 1920s.

Given the above context, it was hardly surprising that national socialism developed an idiosyncratic vision of nationalism. The components of this vision can be summarized as follows: first, nationalism was *Volk*-orientated. The notion of the *Volk*, as Mosse noted, 'signified the union of a group of people with a transcendental "essence". This "essence" might be called "nature" or "cosmos" or "mythos", but in each instance it was fused to man's innermost nature' (Mosse 1966, 4). Mosse and other commentators have charted the immense influence of *Volk* ideas across German culture. The *Volk* culture was contrasted to bourgeois culture. Alfred Rosenberg, particularly, focused on the centrality of the *Volk*, as expressed through Nordic peoples, in *The Myth of the Twentieth Century* (1930). The task, as laid down by Rosenberg, was clear: 'defence against the infiltrating hordes of Africa; closing frontiers on the basis of anthropological characteristics; and the establishment of a Nordic European coalition in order to cleanse the European motherland of the ever-expanding disease-centres of Africa and Syria' (Rosenberg 1971, 80). Suspect history, classical studies, anthropology, phrenology, philology, the religious mysticism of Meister Eckhart and even the mythology of the Nibelungen and *Edda* were all summarily roped in to support the case of the Nordic *Herrenvolk* (master race). The same bogus racial history was used by Hitler to justify his *Lebensraum* doctrine. The preservation of the Aryan entailed the growth of both numbers and soil to meet this expansion. Thus, as Hitler commented, 'Only an adequately large space on this earth assures a nation freedom of existence' (Hitler 1969, 587). As might be expected, this Nordic perspective was imbued with an occult pagan religious significance, often used as a contrast to Christianity. Hitler, and many of his compatriots such as Rosenberg and Himmler, were deeply attracted by the occult.

The necessity of racial cleanliness encouraged positive support for eugenics programmes. National socialism, early on, set its face against mixed marriage and later legally prohibited Aryan marriage to Jews. Medical science, for Hitler, had to be devoted to such racial goals (Hitler 1969, 365–7). One of the systematic Nazi writers on this theme was a trained agronomist. Richard Walter Darré, in works such as *The Peasantry as the Life-Source of the Nordic Race* (1928) and *A New Aristocracy out of the Blood and Soil* (1930), proposed a comprehensive eugenics programme in Germany comparable to animal husbandry, one of his actual specialisms.[30]

Because of its rural naturalism and worship of landscape, the Nordic *Volk* perspective tended to idolize the peasantry and farming community. Urban life was seen to be dominated by the bourgeoisie and Jews.[31] The true *Volk* was in the countryside. Darré saw the peasantry as the ideal eugenic breeding stock for sustaining the Nordic *Volk* (see Bramwell 1985). This led to preferential and positive policies being adopted towards the farming communities by the national socialists, providing tax incentives and subsidies. How successful such policies were in encouraging people to stay on the land and reproduce is highly questionable.

The other major aspect of this Germanic nationalism was its anti-Semitism. In fact, some would see it as the defining feature. Anti-Semitism, as stated, had not only been part of a European tradition, but was also integral to most of the German *Volk* writers throughout the nineteenth century. It had different manifestations in the Nazi Party. Some saw Jewishness as a spiritual or cultural problem; others saw it as a racial one. Jewishness was also associated with Bolshevism and urban and bourgeois life. Undoubtedly, though, under Hitler's obsessive and manic racial tutelage, the Jews became a central focus of nationalistic hatred and radical depersonalization. Their fate in the death camps in the Second World War is too well-known to dwell upon and well illustrates the terrifying power and immense responsibility that can become attached to ideas. Yet it should still be noted that such awful events virtually surpass our comprehension. The Nazi death camps stand like appalling monoliths before our moral and spiritual understanding. Given some of the recent attempts to dismiss the holocaust, it is worth reminding ourselves continually of the horrors which so many innocent human beings suffered.[32]

States and Leaders

The question of nationalism leads to a consideration of the question of the state in fascism. There was a common negative background to fascist views of the state. These expressed contempt for the liberal democratic state and particularly for the notion of multi-party systems. Parties signified compromise and coalition-making, which stultified the national interest. As Primo de Rivera noted: 'It is essential to put a stop to political parties. Political parties are the result of a wrong political system, the parliamentary system. ... What need have the people of these political intermediaries?' (Primo de Rivera 1972, 61–2; see also Mussolini in Oakeshott ed. 1953, 166; Hitler 1969, 416).

One German academic theorist, Carl Schmitt, who later joined the national socialists, encapsulated some of the initial anti-parliamentarianism in his book *The Crisis of Parliamentary Democracy* (1923), although such ideas had already been explored by the Italian theorist Pareto in the 1890s. The problem, for Schmitt, was that parliamentary government was premised on openness and discussion. These were the two essential principles of constitutional thought. Yet the reality of parliamentary life was far removed from this. The crisis of parliamentary government was that it was a façade. For Schmitt, 'small and exclusive committees of parties or of party coalition make their decisions behind closed doors', usually in cahoots with large business interests (Schmitt 1985, 50). Political parties were simply power-brokers attempting to manoeuvre themselves into influential positions through numerical majorities.

Mass democracy was subject to a different, but mutually aggravating, crisis. Public discussion (which Schmitt defined as 'an exchange of opinion that is governed by the purpose of persuading one's opponent through argument') was an empty formality. The masses were won by propaganda, not by discussion. The people had no say and yet, paradoxically, liberal democracy assumed that there was some kind of unity of interests of governors and governed. Once liberal parties gained power they jettisoned democracy and pursued their own interests. As Schmitt remarked: 'Against the will of the people especially an institution based on discussion by independent representatives has no autonomous justification for its existence, even less so because the belief in discussion is not democratic but originally liberal' (Schmitt 1985, 5 and 15). Liberal parliamentary parties asserted this very autonomy. Mass democracy was therefore a façade.

There was also a view shared by fascists that liberal parliamentary states had not only fostered the social and economic crises of the 1920s out of greed and self-interest, but were unwilling to solve the problems. Some, such as Oswald Mosley, after the 1914–18 war, were aware of just what could be done by states in times of crisis. States could act decisively and collectivize in war whereas, in peacetime, liberal democracy lacked the will, though not the means, to do something positive (Skidelsky 1975, 72).[33]

The fascist conception of the state had a number of features which are highly inconsistent. Many fascists, such as Mussolini, Gentile and Primo de Rivera, happily admitted that their vision of the state was 'totalitarian', although the meaning of the term, even in the 1920s and 1930s, was far from clear.[34] Gentile's explanation of totalitarianism was, in essence, that there was no separation between the individual and the state. Those who separate the individual from the state have not moved beyond abstract thinking. Concrete thought demonstrates that 'There is nothing really private … and there are no limits to State action.' The state 'comes to birth in the transcendental rhythm of self-consciousness' (Gentile 1960, 179, 183). Since the state is the only foundation of the individual's rights and freedoms, it therefore 'limits him and determines his manner of existence' (Gentile 1928, 301).[35]

The fascist state was often linked with the notion of force. 'Force' was opposed to 'right', and 'organicism' to 'mechanism'. Crude social Darwinist ideas lay behind these concepts. Thus, the state was the result of a 'struggle for existence'. As Alfredo Rocco wrote: 'The stronger and more powerful a state, the higher and richer the life of its inhabitants.' It is in fact the state's duty to be strong. Rocco continued, in a somewhat piqued tone, 'This idea of the state as a force (which as a result of the current general state of ignorance is seen as a German Prussian idea) is plainly a Latin and Italian one. It is directly linked with the intellectual tradition of Rome and was refurbished by Machiavelli's political philosophy' (Rocco in Lyttelton ed. 1973, 262).

The fascist understanding of freedom should be noted here. Freedom for most fascists coincided with the purposes of some wider entity such as the nation, state or *Volk*. Freedom was never a purely individualistic notion. It had a definite social dimension. Freedom could never conflict with the state or nation. The stronger the state or nation, the richer the freedom of its citizens. This inner notion was contrasted with the external liberal freedom, defined as 'an unlimited natural right of the individual' (Rocco in Lyttelton ed. 1973, 260).[36] As Rosenberg noted, this selfish liberal individualist dogma of liberty should be 'excluded from serious consideration' (Rosenberg 1971, 93). Freedom was seen as a spiritual idea, contrasted to the 'grubby materialism' of liberal freedom. The bearing of this argument upon economic freedom should also be noted. Economic freedom was tolerated only so long as it coalesced with the national interest. True freedom was therefore an inner condition of the individual, willing a higher national purpose.

There were, once again, different perceptions of the notion of 'inner'. In Italian fascism, as Mussolini argued, 'the only liberty which can be a real thing [is] the liberty of the State and of the individual within the State. Therefore, for the Fascist, everything is in the State, and nothing human or spiritual exists ... outside the State' (Mussolini in Oakeshott ed. 1953, 166).[37] Freedom is for the individual to will the ends of the state, an idea which was further elaborated in the concept of the 'ethical state'. For national socialists, such as Rosenberg, the case was different. The essence of the individual was the *Volkstum*. Thus, as Rosenberg commented, 'Freedom in the German sense consists of an inner independence. ... Today, everybody indiscriminately speaks of an external "freedom", one which can only deliver us to race chaos. Freedom means fellowship of race' (Rosenberg 1971, 98). Freedom was therefore identified with the objectives of the race unit.

Despite sharing similar ideas on rights, organicism and force, the Italian fascist, often more Hegelian, vision of the *Totaler Staat* was rejected by national socialists. First, Hegel was repudiated as being too closely associated with the liberal *Rechtsstaat* tradition. Second, as previously emphasized, the state emphatically was not primary for national socialists. The nation and the *Volk* took absolute priority. As Rosenberg argued: 'The National Socialist movement is ... moulded for the security of the collective German *Volk* and of its blood and character. The state, as a most powerful and virile instrument, is placed at the disposal of the movement. ... Only in this connection does the National Socialist state-concept become truly alive' (Rosenberg 1971, 192).[38] It followed from this, for Rosenberg, that 'it behoves National Socialists not to speak any more of the total state, but of the National Socialist *Weltanschauung*, of the NSDAP as the embodiment of the *Weltanschauung*' (Rosenberg 1971, 192).[39] Finally, following the establishment of the priority of the *Führerprinzep*, the state could not be primary or total for the Nazis. The *Führer* embodied the sovereign authority of the *Reich*. State authority was really *Führer* authority (see Kershaw 1985). Minimally, this might be called a Caesarist or Bonapartist notion. The idea of an independent state authority in this context was meaningless. As the notion of the *Duce* developed in the 1930s, an obvious but subtle contradiction began to emerge within Italian fascism over the importance of the state. How could both the *Duce* and the national state be supreme?

It is worth remarking here on the supposed organizational efficiency and coherence of the Nazi state. As suggested earlier, there is now a widely accepted view that the Nazi state was internally chaotic. In reality there was no clear top-down governance. The Nazis worked *with* an existing state bureaucracy, many of whom, despite pressure, had not joined the Nazi Party even by 1939. The Nazi-based SS, and other militarized elements, worked in tandem with the state police and army, not always communicating. Most of the concentration camps functioned on the edge of the official state framework. The power of the *Führer* jostled with shifting alliances within the confused structure of the national socialist party, a career civil service, a powerful military and large-scale industrialists. Martin Broszat has thus described the Nazi regime as an 'organizational jungle', where 'to suggest that the development of National Socialist policy consisted in steering towards and carrying out pre-fabricated long-term ideological aims in small doses is an over-simplification' (Broszat 1981, 358).

The above points throw some light on the notion of the leader – *Führer* or *Duce* – within fascism. There were a number of theoretical and historical precedents for the idea of the leader. Solon, Pericles, Alexander, Caesar and Bonaparte appeared as role models for some fascists. As Gentile put it, 'It is always the few who represent the self-consciousness and the will of an epoch' (Gentile 1928, 291). Mosley once defined fascism as 'collective Caesarism' (Skidelsky 1975, 313).[40] The notion was also given a vague theoretical warrant in the political philosophies of Hegel and Rousseau, amongst others. In Italy and Germany, at the close of the nineteenth century, it received a sociological *imprimatur* in the elite theories of Mosca, Pareto and Michels, in the crowd psychology of Gustave Le Bon and in the notion of charismatic authority developed by Max Weber. The dynamism, realism and focus of effective decision-making by the leader were contrasted with the time-wasting of parliamentary coalition politics. The leader became the locus of the national interest. There was no need for elaborate democracy.

There are many problems with the leader concept. It did not appear to be essential for all the ideologists of national socialism in the early 1920s (see Griffin ed. 1995, 5). In Italy it was comparatively late in developing. Elite theory, although accepted by many fascists, was often interpreted to mean collective leadership. Hitler and Mussolini, in the early 1920s, were not always revered. They were regarded as key figures in collective groupings but the realities of leadership were different from the theories. As Hans Mommsen has noted, in both Germany and Italy traditional entrenched institutional interests and shifting alliances within the fascist parties forced repeated concessions and circumscribed both Hitler's and Mussolini's rule (see Mommsen and Bracher essays in Laquer ed. 1979). Over-concentration on the leaders gives a false impression of the order and coherence of the regimes and implies that responsibility rested primarily with these men. It also neglects the empty theatricality, delusions of grandeur and burlesque quality of Mussolini's leadership in particular.

Finally, the fascist state vision had an odd, immensely complex and tangled relationship with the ideas of 'syndicalism' and 'corporatism'. Both doctrines were far more characteristic of Italian fascism than of German national socialism. In the main, especially after 1933, the national socialists showed little concern for corporatism, either in theory or in practice. Hitler himself was only temporarily interested in the ideas, and then simply as a propaganda device. This does not mean that corporatist theory did not appear in Germany. National socialists such as Gottfried Feder, Gregor Strasser, Walther Darré and to some extent Rosenberg were overwhelmingly in favour of some form of corporate organization. The emphasis of the Nazi writers, however, was far more towards a neo-medievalist reading of corporations.[41] Corporations were part of the ancient *Volk*. This tradition went back to more romantic conservative theorists such as Moeller van den Bruck and, later, Otto Gierke. The Italian fascists, on the other hand, explicitly repudiated the neo-medievalist reading of corporatism. They took a more rationalist and modernist approach to corporations, seeing them as a 'new way' forward which superseded both liberal and socialist conceptions of social organization, rather than as a means of recovery from the past.[42]

In Italian fascism, the corporatist idea related closely to the syndicalist tradition, which was not the case with national socialism. In addition, it is worth pointing out that the Catholic tradition in Italy has always had strong organicist and corporatist leanings. It therefore provided a receptive intellectual climate for corporatism. Syndicalism emerged in Italy in the early 1900s, at roughly the same time as in France, Spain and Britain. It was as much a reaction to Marxism and reformist socialism as to liberalism and capitalism. Gentile noted particularly the influence of Sorel on Italian syndicalism (Gentile 1928, 296).[43] Most of the Italian fascists were qualified admirers of syndicalism for its anti-parliamentary and anti-democratic rhetoric, its highly moralistic tone on violence and its repudiation of compromise or collaboration with the bourgeoisie (see Lanzillo in Lyttelton ed. 1973, 202–3). For Italian fascists, syndicalism represented a natural and important phenomenon of social development. It had played an important role in resisting liberalism, capitalism and individualism. Yet, as Alfredo Rocco argued, the time had come for the state to nationalize the syndicates. He contended that 'They must be placed firmly beneath the control of the state, which must lay down their precise functions' (Rocco in Lyttelton ed. 1973, 280). State-controlled national syndicalism incorporated associations within the body politic. The state directed the associations for the ends of the nation. Syndicates would then provide expertise to the state, as well as professional training and public assistance, and they would arbitrate disputes and prevent strikes and lockouts. As Rocco commented: 'Through these reconstituted syndicates the state would at last possess the technical bodies to enable it properly to fulfil the various functions in the economy which necessity forced upon it' (Rocco in Lyttelton ed. 1973, 281).

It is at this point that we can see the direct connection between syndicalism and corporatism. The state was the association of associations, or the corporation of corporations. As Gentile put it:

Fascism has ... taken over from syndicalism the idea of syndicates as an educative moral force, but since the antithesis between state and syndicate must be overcome, it has endeavoured to develop a system whereby this function should be attributed to syndicates grouped together into corporations subject to state discipline and indeed reflecting within themselves the same organization as the state. (Gentile in Lyttelton ed. 1973, 312)[44]

In fascism we see the corporation of syndicates governed for the national interest. If any form of parliamentary structure remained it would be an economic or social parliament of economic producers without the encumbrance of time-wasting parties. Employers' and workers' syndicates or associations would be linked together in the same corporate association. They would then change from being aggressive and defensive bodies into collaborative groups. There were attempts to establish such a structure in Italy, particularly between 1929 and 1932 under Giuseppe Bottai. The results, though, were profoundly flawed. In March 1930, a National Council of Corporations was set up with three levels, incorporating employers' and workers' organizations, a representative assembly of economic and social associations and the state bureaucracy, and, finally, the Central Corporative Committee, comprising government ministers, presidents of workers' and employers' confederations and top civil servants. All of these were under the watchful direction of Mussolini (see Lyttelton 1987, ch. 9).

Nothing of comparable interest developed in Germany. Furthermore, not all fascists were as enthusiastic about corporatism. Primo de Rivera, in a speech to Spanish fascists in April 1935, remarked: 'This stuff about the corporative state is another piece of windbaggery', although in his writings he was not always so unsympathetic to aspects of corporatism (Primo de Rivera 1972, 172). The other important issue concerning corporatism was its illusory aspect. Most scholars, on Italy particularly, admit that corporatism was a façade and never really succeeded in practice. As one writer commented, corporatism was 'a cloak for ruthless exploitation of labour and a reservoir of jobs for party hacks' (Cassels in Turner ed. 1975, 70; see Grand 1989, 88, 163). It served an excellent propaganda function and also helped to integrate and emasculate intellectuals.

The Economy

In the fascist understanding of the economy we encounter many of the themes already discussed. There are four points to emphasize: first, politics took priority over economics; second, the focus of politics was on the nation and *Volk*, therefore economics was essentially determined by national objectives; third, the economic practices which were adopted were a mixture of socialist and liberal policies; and, finally, there was, as in other areas of fascist ideology, a tension between prescription and reality in fascist economics.

In typically Hegelian fashion, Gentile wrote: 'The State is concrete universal will, whereas economics is concerned with the subhuman life of man – the corporeal. ... It follows that there is an economic element in the will, and hence in the State; but it has been transcended, transfigured by the light of freedom' (Gentile 1960, 147). In essence, for Gentile, politics was the realm of will and freedom and was a higher form of life than the mechanism of economics. It therefore followed that politics, as expressed in the nation state, was spiritually and morally superior to economics. In the case of national socialism, race and the *Volk* occupied this position.

Corporatism and autarky were typical of this priority of politics over economics. The former has already been touched upon. The corporate state integrated employers and employees. Each association regulated its membership and the nature of production. Industrial strife would be minimized in the interests of the nation. This was the 'third way' between capitalism and socialism. Organic and economic representation in a producers' parliament, guided by national ends, would replace geographical demo-cratic political representation. As Alfredo Rocco argued: 'a Fascist economy is not an economy of association nor merely directed or controlled economy, it is above all an organized one. It is organized by the efforts of the producers themselves, with the state to direct and control them from above' (Rocco in Lyttelton ed. 1973, 295). Some of the most significant ideas utilized by fascism appear in this area. Mosley, pursuing these corporative notions in Britain, was the first politician who seriously attempted to understand and apply the ideas of Keynesian economics in his book *Greater Britain* (1932).[45]

In the case of autarky, which was officially inaugurated by Mussolini on 23 March 1936, and was largely being pursued in Germany from the same period, the idea was for a self-sufficient economy to marshal its economic resources for national ends. The idea had been present in the writings of J. G. Fichte and Friedrich List.[46] In the case of both Germany and Italy it was tied to the war-footing of these countries in the later 1930s. In Germany, from 1936 onwards, the aim was economic self-sufficiency in preparation for international conflict (Bullock 1962, 358–9).

The puzzling question concerning fascist economics is its precise orientation. Given the early Marxist critique of fascism as the tool of monopoly capitalism, it is strange to find such vigorous anti-capitalist rhetoric throughout the whole corpus of fascist writings. If one looks at the work of Nazis such as Gottfried Feder, Dietrich Eckhart and Gregor Strasser particularly, the NSDAP Twenty-Five Points, Primo de Rivera's *Guidelines of the Falange*, Mosley's *Greater Britain*, Drieu de Rochelle's writings or the various national syndicalist and corporatist proposals of some Italian fascists, the overwhelming impression is one of anti-capitalist argument.

Primo de Rivera stated in his 1935 *Guidelines*, 'We reject the capitalist system, which disregards the needs of the people, dehumanizes private property and trans-forms the workers into shapeless masses prone to misery and despair' (Primo de Rivera 1972, 134). Equally the Nazi writer Gregor Strasser argued in his 'Thoughts about the Tasks of the Future': '*We are Socialists*, are enemies, mortal enemies of the present capitalist economic system with its exploitation of the economically weak, with its injustices in wages, with its immoral evaluation of individuals according to wealth and money ... and we are determined under all circumstances to abolish this system!' Strasser goes on to advocate an economy premised upon human 'need' as against 'profit'. The definition of 'humanity', however, was crucial. Strasser saw human beings as members of a nation or *Volk* and not of a class. Therefore it was the needs of the national, and not class, members which were really primary. Thus Strasser referred to fascist economics as 'national economies'. He noted that 'We have to learn that the ideas "world trade" – "balance of trade" – "export surplus" are ideas of a declining epoch ... and were *born out of speculation, not out of necessity,* not out of the soil!' (Strasser in Miller Lane and Rupp eds 1978, 89). The programmes of these fascist groups and individuals encompassed wide-ranging economic and welfare proposals for altering the whole character of the economic system in line with national purposes, including employment programmes, nationalization, profit-sharing, expropriation of excessive profits, abolition of unearned income, and interference in loan capital and interest.

The socialist conception of economics, which was not tied to national ends, fared no better in the fascist framework. Marxist and bourgeois socialism were declared spiritually bankrupt, rooted in the same form of thinking as capitalism itself, that is, not rising above the material categories of money and profit, as ends in themselves, and therefore unable to fulfil the higher spiritual objectives of the nation. However, not all fascists supported this argument. It was claimed by many that as long as personal self-interest, private property and capital accumulation did not undermine or interfere with national ends, then liberal capital economics was to be tolerated. In fact, it was to be encouraged (Rocco in Lyttelton ed. 1973, 294). As Hitler declared:

> We must ... not dismiss a business man if he is a good business man, even if he is not yet a National Socialist; and especially not if the National Socialist who is to take his place knows nothing about business. In business, ability must be the only authoritative standard. ... In the long run our political power will be all the more secure, the more we succeed in underpinning it economically. (Hitler quoted in Bullock 1962, 281–2)

Overall, the central ambiguity of both the German and Italian fascist regimes was that they employed 'a battery of economic controls to which left-wing governments, outside the Soviet Union, could still only aspire to'. Yet the beneficiaries of these proposals were groups which usually 'supported more right-wing parties' (Milward in Laqueur ed. 1979, 409).

The final issue for discussion concerns the illusion and reality of fascist economics. We have already noted the well-established view of the illusion of the corporate state. Equally, the notion of autarky was very much a pipe-dream, particularly in Italy. It is difficult to make clear comparisons between Germany and Italy on the question of economics, since they were at very different stages of economic development in the earlier part of the twentieth century. In the early 1920s Italy had 21 per cent of its economically active population employed in industry; in Germany the percentage was 42.2. In addition, the proportional levels of GNP achieved by the industrial sector in Italy in 1920 had already been reached by Germany in 1870 (Milward in Laqueur ed. 1979, 411). Further, despite the propaganda, it is questionable as to how far national socialists and Italian fascists consciously achieved any improvement in their economies. Massive rearmament, economic luck in terms of an upturn after the depression of the 1920s, punitive and disciplinary state work-programmes, wide-scale statistical juggling and massive propaganda created the impression of an economic miracle. Many have argued that, in fact, in neither economy did fascism have any really distinctive effect. Certainly Hitler and Mussolini appeared to have little interest in, or commitment to, economic theories, as long as their nationalist and imperialist ambitions could be financially underpinned. As Mosse noted on national socialism: 'It nationalized when it wanted to nationalize. ... It allied itself with big business when it wanted such an alliance.' Overall, it lacked a specific economic commitment (Mosse 1978a, 48).

Conclusion

As already indicated, there are major difficulties in dealing with fascism. Because of the experiences of the Second World War there is considerable and justifiable moral censure attached to the ideology. Fascism has also had an ambiguous relation to the concept of ideology itself. Not only did fascists cultivate an irrationalist and anti-ideological stance, which makes it difficult to deal with the doctrine on the same level as other ideologies, but it is also questionable as to how far the ideology actually informed the conduct of fascists in power. In addition, the ideology includes some quite strange, crude and bizarre components. A charitable view might regard these as the eclectic, slightly mad and over-extended fragments of recognizable European traditions of thought about race, the state or human nature. A less charitable view would dismiss them as pathological ravings. The difficulty that scholars have had with the ideology has led many to seek alternative non-ideological accounts of the character of the movement within the disciplines of psychology, economics and sociology, which were outlined in the earlier part of this chapter.

This latter tendency is one way of ignoring the uncomfortable fact that a closer look at some of the ideas of fascism and national socialism reveal affinities and overlaps with more acceptable ideologies, such as liberalism, conservatism, syndicalism and socialism. It also avoids the point that Roger Griffin has argued, namely, that there are some quite recognizable value components which enable us to identify fascist ideology – a specific form of ultranationalism being one such core notion. Griffin's point would allow us to extend the analysis of fascism, or fascist-like movements, to the present day and thus well beyond the period covered in this chapter. In this sense, there might be a case for arguing that, what might be seen presently as extreme Right groups, in, say, Europe, are in fact fascist in all but name. This point relates closely to debates concerning the fascist minimum, that is, what allows us to identify a core concern for all fascists to the present day (see Eatwell 1996). This particular issue remains an open, fraught and unresolved concern both within and outside fascist scholarship.[47]

Further, notions of an interventionist welfare-orientated state; corporatism and a more social-market economy; a social parliament of economic producers; a preoccupation with the effects of modernity; strong ecological concerns about the destruction of nature; a belief in the importance of European civilization; the problem of the unconscious, emotive and violent sides of human nature; and a concern over the sense of alienation, decadence and spiritual emptiness of modern bourgeois liberal civilization are not exactly alien ideas to other ideological traditions. This affinity should alert us to possible misinterpretation. The above ideas were often combined with highly emotive, xenophobic and occasionally vicious and bellicose nationalism; fuzzy pseudo-scientific biological racism; unstructured, messy and unexplained uses of academic theories such as elitism, vitalism, pragmatism and social Darwinism; and the bizarre and over-optimistic claims of elites and leaders.

In fact, in fascism we see many contradictory strands. There is a fundamental dichotomy between the particular and insular character of the ultra-nationalism it promotes and the claims it makes for universal appeal. There are deep unresolved tensions between the notions of race, nation and state in both fascism and national socialism. There is also a paradox concerning their mixture of enthusiastic populism, on the one hand, looking to a new fascist individual, and their extreme reclusive elitism and vitriolic contempt for the masses, on the other. Fascism, as such, is not a particularly convincing ideology, in intellectual terms, but this does not mean that we should dismiss its ideological content out of hand. Many of its basic nostrums still permeate the ideological discourse of extreme Right groups to the present day. However, its intellectual confusions, lack of coherence and horrific conduct whilst in power need to be continually highlighted.

7

Feminism

Unlike certain other ideologies – for example, conservatism or liberalism – the word 'feminism' causes few etymological problems since its *prima facie* meaning is comparatively transparent. At its simplest, the word denotes the investigation and understanding of the discrimination against and oppression of women and the subsequent attempt to abolish such domination and thus to promote the role and emancipation of women in all spheres. Even this core idea might still cause considerable debate and criticism, partly because of its progressive emancipatory message. However, a different set of problems attach themselves to feminism – tied to the self-conscious identity of the movement. These problems, which will be touched upon in the following pages, may in part be due to the fact that feminism has moved through a complex range of overlapping debates with other ideologies, such as Marxism and liberalism. Further, many of these debates have changed markedly over the last four decades. We now have the even more puzzling phenomenon of postfeminism, which has been coined for a range of reasons. For some, for example, the notion of gender or sexuality has become so mainstream in policy debates that there is little need any longer for a strong feminist ideology – an idea that would have been unthinkable even in the mid-1990s. In addition, many who in the 1980s and 1990s partook in women studies programmes are now in key positions of influence and power in public agencies and governmental departments. This is not to say that gender issues have been solved – far from it – but rather the nature of the debate has changed in character. For example, it would be difficult now in a US or European context to carry on a successful policy debate about citizenship, employment, equality, and so forth, where gender was not incorporated as an essential dimension.

The study of feminism is still, though, subject to intense deliberation, but the debates now have changed somewhat in focus since the 1980s and 1990s.[1] Feminism remains a profoundly active/practical-orientated movement. This active/practical aspect is at one level still relatively unique, since its challenge is not only at the academic or political level, but is also directed at certain deeply held beliefs about the very character of our society, our thought patterns, our bodies and our personal and most intimate relations. In the case of significant recent feminists such as Judith Butler, this challenge remains fundamental (Butler 1997 and 2004). This immanent critique has permeated every field: all dimensions of artistic creation, the social sciences, humanities and natural sciences. In fact, some would still claim that it destabilizes the foundations of Western culture. In other ways, though, feminism has none the less been a remarkably successful ideology and its achievements for women in the policy field should be both recognized and in some cases justly celebrated.

In terms of the history of feminism over the past four decades there has been, occasionally, a somewhat insular character to some of the theoretical contributions. Many feminist writers, journals, presses and academic courses seemed, during the 1980s and early 1990s, to be solely addressing other feminists or just women in general. There was, though, a perfectly consistent logic at work within this apparent insularity. In the ideological parlance of the time, if men were the *problem*, and it was in their interest to suppress women, why address anything to men or pay anything but hostile attention to their writings? Men, in this argument, would either not understand or they would try to subvert women, consciously or unconsciously. If language (including the technical languages of the various academic disciplines) embodied subtle forms of sexual power and domination, how could men actually be addressed? If the feminist tried to express her point of view in such language, she would already have subscribed to her own subordination and would have lost the argument from the first syllable (see Spender 1980). This view had parallels with the position of many anarcho-syndicalists, anarchists and Gramscian organic intellectuals on the question of language, thought and oppression. The more general argument from these latter groups was that workers or peasants needed to develop their own educational programmes and forms of thought. As soon as regular patterns of bourgeois thought were adopted, the argument and revolution were near to being lost. Rather, as Gramsci argued, proletarians must look for hegemonic power within even the canons of language and common sense. Analogously, women resisted the hegemonic patriarchal phallic themes within language and common sense. There were also grounds here for developing a new form of feminine discourse, a point that will be returned to. A related issue here for some 1980s feminists was the fact that many of the problems, traumas and difficulties experienced by women, such as childbirth or menstruation, remained issues for women. They could not be fully grasped by men and had, indeed, often been made taboos by them. Such issues were part of the unique experience of women and could only be experienced *by* other women. However, behind these arguments was a contention that women were both unique and possessed an essential and universal nature. Other feminist writers contested this point, pointing to differences *between* women as well as the constructed character of both difference and identity.

Another difficulty with the essentialist claim concerning women (particularly of radical feminists in the 1970s) was that it often seemed that the world had been simply waiting for radical feminism, and the future 'truth' of history lay in its domain. Radical feminism was by no means alone in this teleological essentialism: most radical ideologies have experienced an initial sense of their messianic purpose. Also, given that men, until comparatively recently, had tended to write the bulk of history and philosophy, such work was often regarded by radical feminists as intrinsically suspect. Although it was quite easy to see the reasoning behind this position, it none the less sounded rather like the vulgar Marxist claims from the Second International period that all non-Marxist thought was bourgeois ideology and 'false consciousness' and could be largely ignored. This kind of radical judgement has tended to fade in the same way as the vulgar Marxist view.

Beyond the rather generalized description of 1980s and 1990s feminism offered above – roughly a concern for the investigation of oppression and an understanding and promotion of women – it becomes immediately very difficult to suggest a more substantive definition of the term. It should be pointed out here that certain feminists have questioned the search for any such definition, specifically those who have interrogated the very character of language, whether from a poststructuralist or constructionist viewpoint, or alternatively, because other dimensions of knowledge more closely represent the female pattern of thought than rational concept formation. Many postmodernist-inspired feminists have argued that even the binary opposition of terms such as 'feminine' and 'masculine' are questionable, insofar as they offer a grand narrative of supposedly universal notions, which are in reality highly specific cultural and linguistic constructs. Following Foucault's attack on the categories of Enlightenment thought, as one writer has put it: 'Feminist analysis tends to regard the Western antinomies of subject and object, mind and body, reason and emotion ... all in their gendered meaning and suspicious correspondence with the hierarchical division of Male and Female ... these are the instrumentalities of power' (Aladjem 1991, 278; see also Coole in Freeden ed. 2001; Butler 1990 and 2004; Lloyd 2007).[2]

If we put this issue to one side for the moment, it is still clear that if the history of feminism as a movement is examined over the last forty years, then feminism has clearly stood for many different and, at times, totally opposed ideas. Forms of feminism have been linked with both the promotion of chastity and the opening-up of free sexual relations, supported by freely available contraception. Some feminisms have stood for more open and freer heterosexual relations and others for political lesbianism. Some have celebrated the difference of women and their uniqueness, while others have gone so far as to advocate androgyny (almost an evolutionary hermaphroditism). Given the accounts that have been offered of other ideologies so far, this internal diversity should come as no great surprise to the reader. Feminism has partaken of the same overlap and ambivalence on its substantive values as most ideologies.

This uncertainty is reflected in all the attempted definitions. The broadest notion would be that feminism is pursued by 'any group that have tried to *change* the position of women or ideas about women' (Banks 1981, 3). This draws the net far too wide for some, since it could also include anti-feminists. Others have spoken of the essence of feminism being concerned to attain 'equal worth with men in respect to their common nature as a free person' (Charvet 1982, 1). This definition is close to the idea that feminism is ultimately about sexual justice. Feminism exists, in this reading, to rectify the systematic injustices that women experience because of their sex (Radcliffe-Richards 1982, 13–14; Nussbaum 1999a and 2001). Some would see this as narrowing the focus too much to a formal legalistic notion. Feminism is, for

others, 'a general critique of social relationships of sexual domination and subordination' (Bouchier 1983, 2) or an 'opposition to any form of social, personal or
economic discrimination which women suffer because of their sex' (Randall 1991,
514). These definitions would widen the terms of the critique. For many feminists,
much of the most insidious exploitation and domination of women takes place in
areas underneath the surface of formal political and economic relationships in society.
More recent poststructuralist feminists, however, would resist this whole effort of
definition as another flawed attempt at metanarrative, namely, trying to fix and
close a system of thought (Coole in Freeden ed. 2001, 160ff).[3] There are no absolutes
or solid grounds for definition.

Many of the above definitions in fact represent quite distinct strands of the overall
feminist movement during the 1980s and 1990s. Despite the fact that there is a more
general impetus behind feminism, concerned to improve the condition of women
and resist oppression, there are diverse schools of feminist thought which give very
different analyses of this process.

Origins of Feminist Thought

Debates over the origins of feminism tie in with the substantive debates about the
ideology itself, although it is worth noting that many of these debates of the 1980s and
1990s have now diminished somewhat in significance.[4] There was initially significant
sensitivity over the question of the historical origins of the movement. Because men
had tended to dominate historical writing, there was considerable criticism of the
marginalization of women's history. It was contended, in this context, that women had
been written about by men, and men tended to be, consciously or not, systematically
gender-biased. Therefore the history of women had to be rediscovered by women for
women. This sensitivity to historical origins, coupled with the fact that the discipline of
history itself could be viewed as part of a patriarchal male order, made women writers
initially much more sensitive to accounts of the feminist movement.[5] In many ways
the situation has now changed markedly: feminist history has, since the early 2000s,
become mainstream, with a well-established scholarly base in the history discipline.

Another difficulty which occurred in the last decades of the twentieth century was
the question as to whether a concern with women's issues was the same as feminist
ideology. This might seem a small point, but it was regarded as significant. There
were thus many women and men who were concerned about the treatment of women
in the family, education and at work, who supported full equality in these spheres,
yet who would have found it odd to be called feminists. Further, there were a number
of women who had advocated changes in attitudes to women and argued for practical reforms: for example, later nineteenth- and early twentieth-century British reformers such as Mrs Humphrey Ward, Octavia Hill or Beatrice Webb. However, it would
be anachronistic to simply label them as feminist. The latter two were, for example,
even antagonistic to female suffrage.

Broadly, the debate concerning the origins of feminist thought and practice breaks
down into four categories. The first three assume that the concept precedes the word.

The first argued, in effect, that feminism dated from the dawn of human consciousness. The 'woman question' had always been with us. The female psyche was unique, unchanging and wholly different to the male. In fact some feminists suggested that it was superior to the male in its innate ecological capacities and that the history of the human species had gone disastrously astray due to the dominance of males. Susan Griffin contended, from an eco-feminist standpoint, that women were closer to nature than men. She identified the key voices of her book, *Women and Nature*, as 'the great chorus of woman and nature, which will swell with time' (Griffin 1978, xvii).[6] This more ahistorical notion, which derived from the realms of biological conjecture, psychoanalysis, religious speculation and Jungian archetypes, need not detain us (see also Daly 1984, ch. 2).

Despite the fact that some have looked back to Plato's feminism, the more usual second point of origin is the early 1400s. The figure of Christina de Pizan is usually focused on here. We might, though, take note of Dale Spender's caution that 'virtually any woman chosen as a "beginning" would have predecessors' (Spender 1983, 33). Christina de Pizan produced a work, *Book of the City of the Ladies* (1405), on which a great deal has been written by feminist scholars. There is an unresolved debate here as to whether de Pizan was concerned with something that could genuinely be called feminism. In other words, is it anachronistic to try to impose our present configuration of thought on the past (see Hawkesworth 1988, 452–3; Brown-Grant 2003)? A similar question could also be asked about the figure most frequently cited from the 1600s as the third point of origin – Aphra Behn (1640–80). She was a dynamic personality by all accounts, whose comparatively short life spanned some spectacular experiences. She was involved in a rebellion in the West Indies, spied for the Court of Charles II against the Dutch and was a prolific author, writing seventeen plays and thirteen novels. She also appears to have actively promoted the idea of equality for women.[7]

Finally, the most popular – and probably correct – starting-point for considering a more self-conscious feminism is the late 1700s, particularly the immediate aftermath of the French Revolution. Western feminism, like most other ideologies, finds its origins here, although certain strands of thought predate the revolution. The actual political movement is of course a much later product. The most significant event for the history of feminist thought in the revolution phase was the publication, in 1792, of Mary Wollstonecraft's *A Vindication of the Rights of Woman*. Miriam Kramnick has observed that 'Mary Wollstonecraft was the first major feminist, and *A Vindication of the Rights of Woman* ... is the feminist declaration of independence' (Kramnick introduction to Wollstonecraft 1985, 7; also Bryson 1992, 19ff; Tomalin 1992). This primacy of Mary Wollstonecraft – providing the first systematic statement of a feminist perspective – was widely recognized in late twentieth-century feminist thought.

If we focus our attention on this last period, which saw the most prolific output in feminist writing, political agitation and self-consciousness, then a number of subdivisions must be noted. The most conventional division is between two waves: the first wave spanning the period 1830–1920 and the second wave from 1960 to the present. This periodization usually contends that the interval 1920–60 was one of relative stagnation. Not all feminist writers follow this periodization precisely. The second wave has been subdivided again into two, and up to five, phases. Some writers have contended that postmodernist feminism is a third wave (see Dietz 1985, 19; Coole in Freeden ed. 2001, 163ff).[8]

If we follow the more conventional two-waves account, the background for the first wave lies in the classical liberal rights perspective and the widespread utilization of Lockian language in the early nineteenth century. This perspective had its most immediate impact in America. Its more general format was the vigorous push for female enfranchisement and the extension of the normal civil and political rights to women. In the USA the background for such programmes lay in powerful, often middle-class, non-conformist religious movements, which encouraged women to become socially active in campaigns on such issues as temperance and the control of prostitution. Such women inevitably developed their own positive intellectual contributions to certain social debates. At the same time the growth of industrialization and modernization were already bringing more women into the workforce. This alone gave some women greater independence.

Most important in the American setting was the involvement of women in the anti-slavery and suffrage movements of the nineteenth century. The discourse of such movements argued against the 'rights-based' constitutional background of the American Declaration of Independence. The language of such criticism was readily available in the American constitutional documents. This debate was first raised in a public setting in the famous American Seneca Falls Convention of 1848, organized by Elizabeth Cady Stanton and Lucretia Mott. They issued an alternative Declaration of Independence paraphrasing the first Declaration line by line, but incorporating women into the document. The upshot was a series of demands for equalization of property, educational opportunities and an opening-up of the professions, all expressed through the language of natural rights (see Banks 1981, 29). After the conflagration of the American Civil War, black males gained suffrage rights in 1866. It struck many women activists who had worked against slavery and for black suffrage before, during and after the Civil War as utterly incongruous that they should have struggled for the basic political rights of black men, which were apparently then denied to women. The contradiction was starkly obvious to many. From 1878 onwards, the Nineteenth 'Anthony Amendment' was introduced into the US Congress every year until its acceptance in 1920.[9] The process of achieving enfranchisement was aided by organizations such as the National American Women's Suffrage Association, formed in 1890 to campaign for the vote on a federal level.

In Britain and France, from the 1830s, utopian socialists in the Saint-Simonian and Owenite schools raised the question of female equality. The idea had, of course, already been argued by Mary Wollstonecraft. Further, Harriet Taylor and J. S. Mill also raised the issue in liberal public debate. There had been women's involvement in movements such as the Anti-Corn Law League, agitation for the reform of property law, and campaigns for professional, educational and employment opportunities. There was also, as in America, a strong involvement in charity, social work and moral reform movements over the nineteenth century. The first politically effective pursuit of suffrage reform was in Mrs Pankhurst's Women's Social and Political Union, set up in 1903.

Yet with the achievement of the vote for women in the 1920s, many writers on feminism see a period of relative stagnation, apart from campaigns on pacifism. The Great Depression and the war periods absorbed much of women's attention and energy. The issues that were fought over in this period were practical and immediate welfare concerns, namely, to uphold and support the family unit. Ideas on family endowments, adequate health-care, school meals and maternity benefits were pursued vigorously over the 1930s and eventually became part of regular public policy in post-1945 Britain, at least until the 1980s. The post-war era, particularly the 1950s, also saw a relatively fast growth in the economies of Britain and America. Large proportions of the populations of both countries experienced an increase in affluence. Convergence politics, consensus on the values of a pragmatic liberalism, the 'end of ideology' debate and political apathy were characteristic of the 1950s. Women's issues were thus submerged for a time in a range of welfare concerns and material aspirations.

The second wave, in most estimates, began in the 1960s. A number of reasons have been offered for this rise of interest in feminism. There had been a widespread growth in women's education across Europe and America, particularly from the 1940s. Women were increasingly gaining the qualifications to enter into the various professions previously dominated by men – although this was a long and still continuing process. In addition, a number of social and legal changes in the 1960s – legislation on abortion, equal pay and civil rights, the introduction of widely available birth control, particularly the contraceptive pill – facilitated women's greater freedom of choice in both public and private spheres.

Literature focusing on women's issues was slowly beginning to expand during this period. Simone de Beauvoir's *The Second Sex* (originally published in 1952, this became a popular paperback in 1961) and Betty Friedan's *The Feminine Mystique* (1965) were only the inauguration of this process. In Britain the work of Germaine Greer and Juliet Mitchell (particularly the former) made feminism a household term (Greer 1971).[10] In addition, there were changing social attitudes to marriage, divorce and work. Women were now becoming gradually more independent, financially, socially and morally, of institutions such as the family. Finally, a number of women's groups began to capitalize on these developments. In America particularly, apart from the better-known and more institutional associations such as the National Organization for Women, there was a veritable explosion of women's groups in the late 1960s and early 1970s.

Apart from the more usual liberal-rights-orientated claims, the early 1970s had other important components. In parallel with the radical anti-slavery experience of women in the nineteenth century, a number of women who had worked in civil rights campaigns, anti-Vietnam and peace movements in the 1960s began to shift their interests, for a variety of reasons, into feminist agitation. The primary reason for this change of focus was a disenchantment with the 'sexism' implicit in 1960s radical groups. Women often felt demeaned by the males in these groups and relegated to supportive roles. Consequently they took their Marxist-socialist and left-libertarian beliefs into feminism. In America, the left-libertarian element adopted a much more exuberant form. In Europe, the socialist component had a much higher profile.

In the last three decades of the twentieth century the feminist movement grew significantly in Europe and North America. The literature also swelled exponentially and a number of specialist journals and women's presses came into being.[11] Despite considerable intellectual and practical consolidation, the 1980s was still a tricky time for feminism. The literature in all fields went on growing, courses in women's studies began to flourish in higher education, and consciousness-raising on women's issues continued. Yet the 1980s also saw the predominance in Europe and America of the New Right, the reassertion of the importance of the traditional patriarchal family, attacks on abortion legislation and civil rights, plus the increasing stresses introduced by the ideological assaults on the welfare state. In addition, unemployment grew during the decade. The New Right was not sympathetic to the feminist movement. There was the potential for some marginal sympathy in the classical liberal and libertarian market-orientated wing of the New Right, but this was rejected by the more predominantly socialist and left-libertarian tendencies of the feminist movement at the time. Finally, the very late 1980s and early 1990s, ironically, saw a shift of intellectual interests in the feminist movement away from direct political and economic issues and towards identity politics and cultural, psychological and linguistic preoccupations. This latter theorizing burgeoned in the later 1990s, particularly with the preliminary surge of interest in French feminist writing, Foucauldian poststructuralism and deconstruction theory. However, this large amount of postmodern theorizing coincided with a nagging awareness of the social and economic plight of women both in the developing world and within minority and ethnic groups in developed societies, creating further internal ideological fissures within feminist thinking (Nussbaum and Glover 1995; Nussbaum 2001).[12]

The Nature of Feminism

Feminism, like all of the ideologies we have been considering, has been influenced by certain historical traditions and has interacted and overlapped with a number of other ideologies. The Enlightenment emphasis on the language of reason, attacking superstitions, taboos and prejudices, has been one influential theme. The experience of the French Revolution and the powerful discourse on democratic rights was also crucial for the early stages of feminist argument. The impact of a more evangelical Protestantism was important for encouraging many women into active social work and involvement in social and political issues. The unitarians were especially noted for their belief in the role of women. The impact of the early utopian socialists was also significant, particularly the disciples of Saint-Simon, Charles Fourier and Robert Owen, all of whom, in their various ways, attacked the institution of marriage and the bourgeois nuclear family, promoted female equality and advocated much freer sexual relations and communal child-care arrangements.

In terms of the movement of feminism, it is difficult to identify a consistent body of concerns, except in a very formal manner. Many of the equivocal and often contradictory principles we can observe in ideologies such as socialism can also be seen in feminism. Feminism has fragmented into a number of different schools of thought, which quite often reflect very different emphases and doctrines. Some feminists have expressed discontent with this fragmentation, although it is a forlorn protest. Rosalind Delmar, for example, commented that it 'signals a sclerosis of the movement' (Delmar in Mitchell and Oakley eds 1986, 3). Such sclerosis, if indeed it is sclerosis, is part of every nineteenth- and twentieth-century ideology.

By the early 1990s, the main schools within feminism had acquired a conventional status in the literature. Liberal feminism, Marxist-socialist feminism and radical feminism were the three main substantive schools most often cited. It is now, though, fairly customary to include (in any historical overview) the views of postmodernist feminists as a separate category, partly because these initially generated such intense interest in the mid- to later 1990s (see Nicholson 1989; Flax 1990). This latter movement, although influencing some important feminist writers into the 2000s, such as Judith Butler, Moira Gatens, Diana Coole and Iris Marion Young, has unexpectedly tended to fade somewhat in overall significance. This loss of interest is, though, shared particularly with radical and Marxist feminism in the 2000s.

Despite the predominance of these schools over the last two decades of the twentieth century, it was argued, on the peripheries of the feminist movement, that there should be a recognition of other elements. Black feminists claimed a critical independence, arguing in effect that other feminists were 'race-blind'. Anarchist feminists also maintained their unique difference, premised upon recognizable anti-authoritarian arguments. A closely related element to anarchism was eco-feminism, particularly in America in the work of writers such as Carolyn Merchant and Dolores LaChapelle (see Devall and Sessions 1985, 229–31 and 247–50). Patriarchy was linked with themes of global environmental destruction and pollution, while women were associated with a concern for nature and the earth. Finally, there were some debates on 'maternal thinking' and the 'ethic of care' which are difficult to categorize. There were also those who contrasted 'civic feminism' with 'maternal feminism'. Some aspects of maternal feminism acquired the surprising title 'conservative pro-family feminism'. These latter debates will be examined briefly at the end of this section.

The discussion now turns to the various schools in more detail. Liberal feminism is the most practically effective and (on the surface) most reasonably argued form of feminism, although one immediate criticism here is that there has not been enough attention to the internal diversity within liberal thought. There is often assumed to be a consensus of beliefs around liberalism, which is far from true.

The language of liberalism has a perennial attraction for some feminists, particularly the language of contract and rights, which is a potent weapon to use against patriarchal traditions.[13] Liberals adhere formally to the values of rationalism, procedural equality, freedom, individualism – including certain robust beliefs on the value of individual property ownership – the power of education, representative democracy and the possibility of rational legal reform. Also, if one takes another belief central to much classical liberal thought, the free economy, it is clear that *all* (regardless of sex) should have equal access to compete in the market. Monopolies, whether private, public or gendered, are intrinsically suspect. Unjustified male monopoly, like any economic cartel, is implicitly frowned upon by the logic of market theory.

Free markets imply free individuals, including women, who can compete on equal terms. The theme of overt feminist capitalism, however, has not ever really been developed within the ideology, certainly not to the same extent as that of conservative capitalism, market socialism or green capitalism. This was partly due to the fact that many feminists associated the market qualities of competition, individualism and self-interest with patriarchalism and masculinity.

Socialist and radical feminist writers were less sanguine about the future of liberal feminism and complained that liberalism had been, in fact, so deeply assimilated into our culture that it had virtually become invisible. Liberalism was seen, by such writers, as a 'specific ideology seeking to protect and reinforce the relations of patriarchal and capitalist society' (Eisenstein 1981, 5).

The liberal tradition, depending on when you date its inception, provides a number of openings for feminist criticism and argument, particularly in its social contract format (see Elshtain ed. 1982; Pateman 1988; Nash 1997). The social contract tradition in Hobbes, for example, begins by stripping humans down to their basic motivations, in order to build a picture of the commonwealth. The image of deconstructed humans is intrinsically genderless (in appearance). The later inclusion by Hobbes of families, fatherly authority and male rulers is for some feminist commentators an unjustified addition to the argument. Social contract argument, unless customs are incorporated within it, provides a medium for talking about human equality. Social contract writers, such as Locke, also attacked divine right and traditional patriarchal theory. There is, potentially, a logical extension from criticizing patriarchalism in political sovereignty to criticizing it within the family (see Okin 1979, 200). This step was never taken by Locke, although it is an implication of his argument. The arguments for social contract turn on the idea of separate free and equal individuals, *not* males or females. Finally, the politics of contract theory is built upon the foundations of reason, not of custom or tradition. Again this represents a potential challenge to the supposed 'natural order' of patriarchy. With some exceptions, however, most liberal theorists did not initially take these potentialities very seriously (Figes 1970).[14]

Dale Spender, in *Women of Ideas* (1983), cites a number of female writers who were exploring the liberal terrain in the nineteenth century, if not so systematically as Mary Wollstonecraft.[15] Among those who stand out as liberal feminists are Harriet Taylor, J. S. Mill, Margaret Fuller, Harriet Martineau – plus a large American contingent with activists such as Lucretia Mott and Elizabeth Cady Stanton. In the post-1945 decades one of the books to have generated most interest in the liberal standpoint, during the early stage of the second wave, was Betty Friedan's *The Feminine Mystique* (1965). Since the 1990s some of the more prominent and luminous exponents of liberal feminism have been Susan Moller Okin and Martha Nussbaum.

Before moving on to the other schools of feminism it is important to draw attention to the fact that there have been significant variations within liberal argumentation. The most important of these for early liberal feminism was that between the natural rights and utility-based arguments, which are virtually irreconcilable in some formats. This separates out the liberal arguments of J. S. Mill and Mary Wollstonecraft.

In addition, the relation of feminism to subsequent developments of liberalism into the twentieth century, as examined in chapter 2, has not as yet been systematically explored by feminist writers. The more Rawlsian-inspired social liberalism that we find in liberal feminists such as Janet Radcliffe Richards, Susan Moller Okin or Martha Nussbaum is as much at odds with both the natural rights and utilitarian liberalism of Wollstonecraft and J. S. Mill as it is with the classical liberalism of Hayek.[16]

The second major school is socialist feminism. Despite the separation sometimes made in the literature between socialist and Marxist feminism, Marxism will be regarded as a species within the genus socialism. As argued in chapter 4, Marxism is emphatically *not* the summation of socialism. There are strong feminist themes running through many of the early socialist writers: for example, Fourier, the Saint-Simonians (rather than Saint-Simon directly), Robert Owen, William Thompson and Ann Wheeler. In the later nineteenth and early twentieth century some of the more important theoretical contributions came from Friedrich Engels, August Bebel, Alexandra Kollontai and Clara Zetkin.

Both Fourier and the Saint-Simonians premised the achievement of socialism on the equality and freedom of women. Progress was measured by the improvement in the condition of women. In the case of the Saint-Simonians it was also linked with their cult of the Great Mother, who was seen as a messianic saviour for humanity (Markham introduction to Saint-Simon 1964, xxxvii–xxxix). In Fourier, women were to have as full and equally fulfilling lives in the *Phalansterie* as men. Both Fourier and the Saint-Simonians also regarded marriage as outmoded. In Fourier, specifically, free love, bisexuality, lesbianism and polygamy were to be encouraged in the utopian community. He also advocated communal kitchens, housework and shared child-rearing.

Although not interested in the amorous experimentation of Fourier, Owen, in the course of his critique of property relations and religion in *New Moral World* (1842), called for the abolition of marriage. For Owen, marriage was an artificial restraint on natural feeling and a cause of vice and misery, creating social inequalities and poverty. In fact, all three misfortunes were linked in his mind. *Religion* sustains *marriage* and this, in turn, encourages a *competitive economy* which generates poverty. Owen, in fact, believed in the natural superiority of women to men in terms of their capacities for sympathy and compassion. He also believed, like Fourier, in communal education, production, eating and child-care within the utopian society.

An admirer of Owen, William Thompson (1785–1835), was stimulated to write directly on the question of women after reading one paragraph of James Mill's *Essay on Government*. In discussing the franchise, Mill had incorporated women's interests into those of men. Thompson tried to show in works such as *An Appeal of One Half of the Human Race, Women, against the Pretensions of the Other Half, Men* (1825) that women should have equality of rights with men. All humans were equally capable of happiness in a future cooperative socialist society. He also challenged the monogamous family and existing divisions of labour. Similar themes were developed in Ann Wheeler's writings, although she was more directly influenced by the Saint-Simonians (see Taylor 1983, 22).

Marx and Engels, in their early years, said very little on the question of women. Marx seemed to assume that women would be liberated under socialism. The human emancipation he anticipated in his essay 'On the Jewish Question' (1843) incorporates the liberation of women. Many of Marx's and Engels's ideas on women were in fact derived from the utopians. In Engels, particularly, there is the added dimension of the materialist conception of history, and the placing of the human essence into labour. Engels also suggests that the family as a social unit, domestic labour and the position of women were not essentially part of nature but were rather due to mutable, historical and material circumstances, labour and the nature of property. The central contention was that the oppression of women was rooted in the impersonal logic of capitalism and private property, although Engels still made the fatal assumption, for many later feminists, of assuming some natural division of labour. Engels, unlike Marx, developed these ideas in his well-known work *The Origin of the Family, Private Property and the State* (1884).

August Bebel (1840–1913), a leading figure and co-founder of the German SPD, followed roughly the same track as Engels, but his work *Women under Socialism* was, at the time of its publication in 1878, more overtly popular.[17] Bebel, despite some sympathy with J. S. Mill and Mary Wollstonecraft, argued that bourgeois liberal reform was in the end ineffective (see Coole 1988, 208ff). Bebel tried to show the economic factors underpinning social and legal inequality. In bourgeois marriage, private property is fundamental. For Bebel, women needed liberation from both bourgeois property and its concomitant, domestic slavery. Moreover, to gain true liberation, they needed to join the historic struggle of the proletariat as a whole. As a number of commentators have noted, the end product of Bebel's reflections is more imaginative than Engels's work. In Bebel we have Fourier without the eroticism. He was deeply impressed by the 1892 Chicago Exhibition, specifically the time-saving electrical gadgets for the kitchen and household. His vision was of an administered society, with a great deal of leisure, art and science, low-cost food, air travel and masses of electrical devices. Children would become a public responsibility. Monogamous relationships, however, if freely chosen on the basis of love, would still be present.

Alexandra Kollontai, Clara Zetkin and Charlotte Perkins Gillman extended the Marxian framework into the twentieth century, particularly Kollontai in the context of the Russian Revolution. By and large, most orthodox socialist interpretations of the role of women, from 1920 until the late 1950s, were embodied within a utopian or Marx–Engels format. The late 1960s and early 1970s saw some qualified rejection of this older framework, particularly of Engels, and an attempt to forge a new socialist feminism. The older Marx and Engels position was seen to be 'sex-blind'. This movement, however, did not move very far from the stage of negative appraisal of traditional Marxism. Alison Jaggar commented on this in the 1980s: 'Socialist feminism is a very recent political tendency and it is still undeveloped, both practically and theoretically. For this reason, one cannot turn to an existing body of systematic theory. ... Instead, one must attempt to extrapolate a systematic theory from the existing fragments' (Jaggar 1983, 304; see also Eisenstein ed. 1979, 1; Tong 1989). This debate over Marxism and feminism still carries on in some quarters to the present day (see Bryson 2004).

The school of radical feminism was undoubtedly more than anything an American development. It made few inroads into European feminism, although some tried to identify it as the major component of the 'second wave'. Radical feminism began in the late 1960s and early 1970s. The term itself had a shifting meaning. Some saw it as the great hope of feminism; others, such as Betty Friedan, viewed it as the Achilles' heel. The apparent extremes of radicalism were seen by some as a reaction to the rightward move of politics in the 1980s, although the roots of radicalism in fact pre-date the emergence of the phenomenon of the New Right.

Radical feminism was a somewhat elitist movement. It developed, as Alison Jaggar remarked, from 'the special experiences of a relatively small group of predominantly white, middle-class, college-educated American women' (Jaggar 1983, 83). This elitism and occasional intellectual strangeness had an alienating effect on many women. Initially, radicalism derived from an acerbic critical relation to Marxism in the late 1960s. In one sense it represented a rejection of the New Left. Radicals argued, far more vigorously than the socialist feminists of the 1970s, that Marxism was 'sex-blind'. Yet their own arguments utilized both radicalized Freudian psychoanalysis and forms of social theory that bear the clear imprint of certain early critical theory writers, such as Wilhelm Reich and Herbert Marcuse (see Firestone 1971; Greer 1971; Millett 1970).

It is difficult to say whether there was an explicit theory at work within the radical perspective. Jaggar commented that radical feminists 'are not identified by adherence to an explicit and systematic political theory' (Jaggar 1983, 84). Readers of the radical literature could encounter anything from Zen Buddhism to astrology. In this context it was difficult to find consistency in the ideas. There were two reasons for this. Rational consistency itself was subject to critical debate within radical feminist thinking. It was, for example, contended that Cartesian rationality was potentially another aspect of male domination.[18] Further, with hindsight it was doubtful whether there were any core values within radical feminism; there were rather a jumble of incommensurable views and intellectual influences.

Despite this ambiguity, certain characteristics do stand out for both observers and critics of radical feminism alike. Unlike the Marxist feminists, many radicals formulated their ideas in an ahistorical manner. This was partly due to the fact that many of their ideas were rooted in an emphasis on either biologism or psychologism. They often contended, for example, that there were 'essential' universal characteristics to all women. Further, radicals did not suffer any of the anguish of socialist feminists over issues of sex and class. This was virtually absent from their writings. Despite the comparatively small size of the radical group, because of their outspoken commitment to certain ideas, they acquired initially more of a reputation than other feminist schools. Certain over-arching, often clashing ideas characterized the movement: for example, a concern to attack all forms of patriarchy and sexism, a belief in both androgyny and difference, an anxious focus on the sex and gender debate, political lesbianism, mothering, radical studies on the character of rape and on the future of the family.

One minor issue which briefly characterized debates in the late 1970s and early 1980s was the relation between socialist and radical feminism. There were claims that a new self-critical socialist feminism (distinct from the older Marxist forms) had the possibility of forming a single systematic theory *with* radicalism. Others saw (what was called at the time) a 'dual system' developing between the two. Yet others vigorously denied that there could be any relation at all between radicalism and socialism (see Bryson 2004).

The late 1980s and 1990s saw a steady growth of feminist interest in poststructuralism, deconstruction theory and postmodernism, initially from the areas of literary and cultural criticism. Derrida, Lyotard, Lacan and Foucault were the key intellectual influences, with Foucault taking pride of place. One of the first to develop this form of theorizing was the French-based strand of poststructuralist psychoanalytic feminism, particularly the writings of Julia Kristeva, Hélène Cixous and Luce Irigaray (see Moi ed. 1987). There was also some North American support in the 1990s for some of these writers.

The central issue was that language embodied our sense of reality. This idea derived initially from the work of Ferdinand Saussure. Speech as a collection of signs was underpinned by language, which was understood as a formal system of underlying conventions. The laws of language formed a deep structure to speech, and such structures could be studied scientifically. This structuralist idea influenced a number of theorists such as Claude Lévi-Strauss and Roland Barthes. The common theme was that these deep underlying structures of meaning were constituted by certain basic binary oppositions, such as raw/cooked or man/woman. Signs did not work on their own but rather in the context of a network of contrasts, oppositions or differences, which constituted a language. The idea that we were constituted by the underlying structures of language was also developed by the French psychoanalytic theorist Jacques Lacan. The parallel between, on the one hand, the surface of speech and the underlying deep structure of conventions and, on the other hand, the psychoanalytic notion of conscious and unconscious is fundamental to Lacan's thinking. For Lacan, the unconscious structures constitute our identity. The uncovering of language through language is the nub of Lacanian psychotherapy. This is one of the keys to unlocking the French feminist theories.

Foucault's poststructuralism and Derrida's deconstruction challenged the basic foundational binary oppositions uncovered by structuralists. Primarily Foucault genealogically exposed the 'power' underlying all our knowledge and language.[19] All the key intellectual assumptions of Western thought were divested of their epistemic privilege, and that included notions of rationality and human agency. As indicated, Foucault uses the Nietzschean notion of genealogy to unpack these oppositions. Genealogy exposes the often random motives, pressures and complex power underlying our purported rationality (see Squires 2000, 35ff). All the sciences and disciplines (what Foucault calls our 'discursive formations') are shown to be congealed sets of preconceptual, unrationalized elements which constitute a society's regime of truth.

As suggested by the title of his work, *Margins of Philosophy* (1972), Derrida's deconstruction idea worked in a less overtly political manner. He was not concerned to 'show' the power underlying knowledge or discursive formations. Rather he tried, with an immensely close reading of texts, to examine the basic, often unconscious, conventions, beliefs and oppositions within texts, in order to exhibit their arbitrariness or ambiguity. For Derrida it was the casual metaphors, footnotes or margins of the text which were the most revealing aspect of even works in philosophy. As one writer observes: 'Deconstruction, at its simplest, consists of reading a text so closely that the conceptual distinctions, on which the text relies, are shown to fail on account of the inconsistent and paradoxial employment of these very concepts within the text as a whole. Thus the text is seen to fall by its own criteria' (Lawson 1985, 93). Meaning, for Derrida, therefore became immensely difficult to establish. It was never simply present in any text. Meaning was deferred and remained impossible to pin down, playing endlessly within the complex web of linguistic signs. There was thus no pure meaning marking something objective in the world. There was also nothing outside 'the sign' and no definitive singular meaning to a sign. This was the substance to Derrida's neologism *différance*. The meaning of a sign was seen to be dispersed throughout a body of signifiers. Thus, any final meaning was withheld. Deconstruction thus represented a permanent withholding operation. We remained permanently suspended between alternatives. The attempt to fix upon a specific meaning, which Derrida termed 'logocentrism', was doomed to failure.[20]

In social and political theory, postmodernists contend that there are no privileged authorities. Lyotard, for example, famously speaks of the postmodern condition as 'incredulity to metanarrative' (Lyotard 1984, xxiv). All we have are multiple socially constructed fictional discourses. Postmodern theorists thus play and ironize amongst these fictions, refusing to reify any of them. They therefore oppose all closure and erasure of difference. They do not believe in any ultimate truth, rationality, knowledge or coherent epistemology. The human self is simply a series of surface signifiers with no depth. Contradiction and difference are embraced. Therefore the task of the postmodernist is to destabilize all attempts at certainty or theoretical closure. There is no certainty but uncertainty.

The French feminists adopted some of these elements, reading Lacan's psychoanalytic work through poststructuralist eyes. They contended that there was nothing outside language – no *hors texte*. As Cixous stated, 'Everything is word, everything is only word ... we must grab culture by the word, as it seizes us in its words, in its language' (quoted in Stanton in Eisenstein and Jardine eds 1990, 73). The world was a text, or series of texts, embodying symbolic systems based upon certain basic binary oppositions of subject and object, reason and emotion, truth and falsity. Using, but altering, the more Foucauldian poststructuralism, the French feminists tried to show the *male* power underlying these oppositions in language. As Mary Hawkesworth noted: 'the locus of the individual's acquisition of language and the origin of all culture and social life, is characterized as unidimensional, structured in accordance with "l'hom(m)o sexualité". ... Because it is language that structures sexuality around the male terms within systems of consciousness, the problematic of language and the problematic of sexuality become coterminous for women' (Hawkesworth 1988, 449). Following Derrida's description of closure as 'logocentrism', Luce Irigaray suggested that this underlying *male closure* in language was 'phallocentrism', which represented a form of deep linguistic patriarchy. This was a form of oppression not previously perceived. What we thought we perceived as the real was in fact a symbolic order constructed by men.

There were a number of strategies that could be adopted here. First, Irigaray advocated disrupting or deconstructing male discourse, to resist all male attempts at systematization and to 'interrogate *the conditions under which systematicity is possible*' and consequently to concentrate on the metaphors, margins and codes of male discourse (Irigaray 1985, 74). Like Lacan's linguistically orientated psychotherapy, the French feminists saw language as an area for therapeutic renewal. In this context, a second strategy was suggested, namely, to construct a woman's language and writing. Women would thus write and speak themselves into existence. Thus Irigaray coined the term *le parler femme* (women's speech) and Cixous *écriture feminine* (women's writing). This process would allow women to express their unique character or 'sex-embodiedness', which would in turn liberate them from linguistic phallocentric patriarchy.

The above ideas do not totally correspond to postmodernism, although there are clearly many overlaps. Many who regarded themselves as postmodern feminists were in fact followers of the French theorists. Full-blown postmodernism resists *all* closure. Having let deconstruction genii out of the bottle, every discourse is disrupted, not just male discourse. Namely, reason is completely disordered and all certainty or privilege, including *écriture feminine*, is lost in the fictional play of language. Those, such as Jane Flax or Christine Sylvester, who viewed themselves as postmodern feminists created more problems than they solved. Feminism itself, in this context, becomes another suspect certainty which needs disrupting.[21]

It was not surprising that the French feminists (with one eye on deconstruction) were suspicious of the title 'feminist', because of its more overtly 'grand narrative' implications. There were, though, problems with the arguments of French feminism which will be touched upon later, not least in many feminist eyes because once again it drew attention to women's difference, potentially essentializing womanhood. It was also profoundly elitist and tended to theorize about language at the expense of social, economic and political concerns. The notion of feminist postmodernism consequently still remains unclear. Some feminist critics have even regarded it as a frivolous nihilism, an opiate for intellectuals. These, and other points, make the notion of postmodern feminism difficult to handle to the present day.

A number of other debates in feminism in the 1980s and 1990s circled around the question of maternal thinking and caring. The psychoanalytic work of Nancy Chodorow and Carol Gilligan on the distinctive qualities of the female personality gave rise to the supposition that because women were brought up in a society structured by gender (where women care for children), in consequence they had a different moral view on the world. For Gilligan, especially, women have a 'caring' approach: they are more altruistic, nurturing and self-sacrificing. Gilligan linked this disposition with an 'ethic of care', which she contrasted to a more male-orientated 'ethic of justice' (see Chodorow 1978; Gilligan 1982; see also Mackay 2001). Morality for women was therefore concerned more with a caring disposition, attending to responsibilities and relationships, than with finding the right or best principle, following rules and focusing on rights and fairness, which were viewed as characteristic of the ethic of justice. Other writers, such as Sara Ruddick and J. B. Elshtain, also argued that women were primarily involved in nurturing and preserving the lives of children; unlike Gilligan, however, they thought that such an idea would have an immense impact on restructuring the public sphere. Ruddick and Elshtain in particular thought that 'maternal thinkers who make responsibility to children and families their central commitment could radically reform public values, could even create an "ethical polity" devoted to a politics of compassion' (Boling 1991, 608). They thus believed that this view could have a dramatic impact on politics.

This particular debate gave rise to two further developments. First, the 'maternal thinking' argument was vigorously contested from a 'civic feminist' perspective. Mary Dietz's work was probably the most systematic. She adopted a more traditional, virtually liberal feminist stance, arguing that women and men, as citizens, 'can collectively and inclusively relate to one another … as equals who render judgements on matters of shared importance, deliberate over issues of common concern, and act in concert with one another' (Dietz 1985, 28). Dietz put forward a reinvigorated social liberal feminist case for equality and consequently denied the relevance of male and female difference. The second development was the maternal thinking position taken by Elshtain and Ruddick (although not necessarily Gilligan), which has been called 'conservative pro-family feminism' (see Elshtain 1981 and 1985; Ruddick 1980).[22] This latter faction was not well received by other sections of the feminist movement. It was regarded as a move backwards into the older stereotyping of women's difference into gender roles (see Flax 1986; Boling 1991, 608ff).[23]

Given the diversity of feminist thought it is difficult to identify clear motifs within the feminist movement. However, it is possible to discern certain broad formal themes which have been the common core of much feminist reflection. The response to these themes is in itself quite diverse. Those that will be dealt with in the remainder of this chapter are: sex and gender, the nature of oppression and subordination, the issue of equality and difference, and the personal as the political.

Sex and Gender

This section touches upon the more traditional subject of human nature. In the case of feminism, human nature is tied to one of the key issues of ideological discussion and therefore must be approached in a rather oblique manner. It is sometimes contended that feminism 'does not entail any particular view of human nature' (Levitas in Forbes and Smith eds 1983, 116). Despite this point, accounts of human nature are given by some feminist writers, accounts which overlap with other ideologies such as liberalism. Others are more concerned to question the relation of sexuality and gender to human nature. In this context the issue of human nature is not absent but is slightly more complex and difficult to articulate.

The problem of sex and gender has parallels with the debates on nature and nurture. The central issue here is whether the nature of women is biologically determined or socially constructed. The usual response to this is to argue that gender is a socially constructed artifice, whereas sex is biological. Women have been slotted into certain roles 'as if' they were natural or biologically determined for them. Such roles in fact have nothing natural about them. The psychology of women has been defined by men. The task of feminism is therefore to make women aware of this fact.

This particular argument can be found in a different format in the early liberal feminists such as Mary Wollstonecraft. One of her primary claims was that women should not be identified as sexual beings, but rather as human beings. The terminology here is slightly different to the sex and gender debate, but close enough for some comparisons. Wollstonecraft was using the notion of 'sex' as virtually equivalent to gender, although she was also contending that even the biological aspect of women was not really an important point of difference. As she argued: 'The first object of laudable ambitions is to obtain a character as a human being, regardless of the distinction of sex' (Wollstonecraft 1985, 82). The important point was that the distinguishing mark of humans, as opposed to 'brute creation', was human reason. Sexuality, as such, was not very significant. Reason was understood as 'the simple power of improvement; or, more properly speaking, of discerning truth' (Wollstonecraft 1985, 142). As Wollstonecraft argued: 'The perfection of our nature and capability of happiness must be estimated by the degree of reason' (Wollstonecraft 1985, 91). A woman's first duty was therefore to reason. In fact, any duty she might be required to perform required reason, for 'how can a woman be expected to cooperate unless she knows why she ought to be virtuous?' (Wollstonecraft 1985, 86, 156). The target for much of Wollstonecraft's argument was in fact Rousseau. She returned to him frequently during the course of the text. Rousseau, in works such as *Émile*, had emphasized the sexual nature of women. He dwelt upon their submissiveness, dependence, voluptuousness and amusement for males. Furthermore, Rousseau had contrasted civic equality with the natural order of the family, predicated on the difference of the sexes. Women, because of their nature, appeared unsuited to the public, autonomous role of citizens. For Wollstonecraft, this idea of sexual difference in Rousseau was a destructive and dangerous artifice.

Wollstonecraft also uses arguments based upon the existence of a rational God to support her thesis concerning human nature. In short, she contends that a rational God would not create one half of the human race virtually mindless. Her religious mentor, Richard Price, had argued that all humans were equal and responsible before God. How, therefore, could women be excluded? As Wollstonecraft argued: 'Why should the gracious fountain of life give us passions, the power of reflecting, only to embitter our days and inspire us with mistaken notions of dignity?' (Wollstonecraft 1985, 94).

Apart from the theological theme, this argument is echoed in a different context by J. S. Mill. Women's sexual nature is again seen to be a socialized artifice. 'I deny', says Mill, 'that anyone knows, or can know, the nature of the two sexes. … What is now called the nature of woman is an eminently artificial thing – the result of forced repression' (Mill 1989, 138).[24] For Mill, we are clearly ignorant of the conditions in which character is formed; in fact, the majority of men appear to be plainly ignorant about women; however, Mill did look to the possibility of a future science of character. He called it ethology. According to Mill, it cannot be said that women accept their servitude as natural. They campaign for suffrage, education, and the like.

Most often it is unreasoning male habits which keep women in such servitude. If women can develop and grow, then there are no grounds for seeing them as inferior. The liberation of women, for Mill, is thus only a matter of time. In the same way as slaves, vassals and black people have been liberated, so also will women. As he put it: 'The social subordination of women thus stands out as an isolated fact in modern social institutions' (Mill 1989, 137).

In the early Marxist accounts, the natures of women and men are formed by historical and economic circumstances, although those specific circumstances can dictate markedly different roles for the sexes. As Marx and Engels stated in *The German Ideology* (1845), 'The first division of labour is that between man and woman for child breeding' (Marx and Engels 1968, 503). This thesis was developed by Engels in later writings. Women and the family are rooted, at least by Engels, in the economic conditions of life. Monogamous marriage leaves most women in the position of domestic slaves. Man earns the family wage (at least in propertied classes) and his wife works at home. As Engels remarked: 'In the family, he is the bourgeois; the wife represents the proletariat' (Engels in Marx and Engels 1968, 510).

The difficulty of speaking about human nature in Marxism is its mutability. It would be hard to make out a clear case for the universality or unchangeable qualities of human nature within this argument. The apparent nature of humans is not fixed, but changes through historical circumstances. Thus the Marxist feminist finds some firm theoretical backing for the claim that much of the sexual/gendered nature of women is a product of particular historical and economic conditions of life. This lends more credence to the claim that artifice is at work. In the final analysis, this might lead to the conclusion that there are no significant differences between men and women. Nearly every role can be performed by both sexes.

Despite the above theoretical conclusion, many early male Marxist writers still appeared to accept the more domestic role of women. This latter tendency was criticized by socialist feminists from the late 1960s. They then pushed their critical analysis of the division of labour into the realm of the family. They also accepted certain aspects of the radicals' analysis, namely, that in addition to historical and economic conditions there were also biological and psychic aspects to the exploitation of women. As Alison Jaggar has argued, traditional Marxism has come to be viewed as a halfway house where 'unspecified biological differences between men and women would mean that there could never be a complete abolition of the sexual division of labour' (Jaggar 1983, 69).

The future of human nature in this form of socialist feminism was more or less genderless and sexless. This would in fact appear to be the logical implication of the original Marxist argument. The ideal of many of the socialist feminists was therefore 'that woman (and man) will disappear as socially constituted categories' (Jaggar 1983, 132). This process would be advanced if technologies developed to such a point where women could be relieved from both pregnancy and childbirth.

Many of the diverse elements of radicalism, which used the sex/gender argument most robustly, were none the less deeply critical of both the socialist-Marxist and liberal perspectives. As one initial radical writer, Catherine MacKinnon, commented, radicalism stands to marxism as marxism does to classical political economy: its final conclusion and its ultimate critique. Compared with marxism, the place of thought and things in method and reality are reversed in a seizure of power that penetrates subject and object and theory with practice. In dual motion, feminism turns marxism inside out and on its head. (MacKinnon in Keohane et al. eds 1982, 30)

Marxist socialism, in this interpretation, always denoted a certain type of method, which MacKinnon identified as dialectical materialism. Genuine feminism (by which MacKinnon means radical feminism) was alternatively concerned with the very different method of consciousness-raising, which she described as 'the collective critical reconstitution of the meaning of woman's social experience' (MacKinnon in Keohane et al. eds 1982, 29). Thus, she contended that the two methods were fundamentally irreconcilable.

For all the confidence of the radicals' analysis there was little consistency on the question of human nature and the sex/gender issue. The earliest statements on the question arose in Simone de Beauvoir's writings (Beauvoir 1954). She rejected many of the biological and historical materialist accounts. For Beauvoir, women had essentially the same nature as man, but they had been hampered and enslaved by one important fact – their bodies. The body did not determine the true nature of women, but it did explain much about their history. Despite some lack of intellectual sympathy with the feminist movement, she did envisage the future of women in fairly optimistic terms. With the greater availability of abortion, effective birth control and the redundancy of monogamy, women might finally begin to gain control of their bodies and join men in their cultural projects. Maternity would cease to rule the destiny of women. As Beauvoir put it: 'The fact that we are human beings is infinitely more important than all the peculiarities that distinguish human beings from one another' (Beauvoir 1954, 684). Some radicals found Beauvoir's analysis lacking in awareness of the depth of patriarchy and the nature of women's oppression.

Beauvoir's position, which has parallels with some of the early liberal arguments (although set in a totally different philosophical framework, namely, her commitment to Sartrean existential philosophy), is worth comparison with another of the early radicals, Shulamith Firestone. Firestone's work *The Dialectic of Sex*, like Beauvoir's, argued that men and women were not really very different. For Firestone, as with Beauvoir but stated in much stronger terminology, it was the biology of women which determined their 'sex class' (a novel term introduced by Firestone to integrate Marxism into the analysis) (Firestone 1971).[25] The sex class was embedded in the family, where women and children were at the mercy of men. Biologically reproductive differences led to sexual divisions of labour. Firestone looked to new technologies for liberation. These technologies were far more extensive than anything anticipated by Beauvoir. Artificial insemination, test-tube babies and domestic cybernetics would emancipate women (and children) from their biology. Firestone contended that with advances in medical science there was even the possibility of males carrying the foetus in implanted wombs and possibly eventually lactating. Gender and sex would thus become redundant in an androgynous or unisex future.[26]

These early phases were superseded by other theories within radicalism. An androgynous aim may be a valuable ideal to strive for, but gender was the source of many problems which had to be addressed, particularly the problem of male patri-archal exploitation. In addition, there were aspects of the masculine nature which radicals found abhorrent: for example, sexism, aggression and the potentiality for rape. Rape was, in fact, seen by some radicals as the defining aspect of masculinity and patriarchy.[27] As Robin Morgan put it, 'The violation of an individual woman is the *metaphor* for man's forcing himself on whole nations' (quoted in Jaggar 1983, 264). Women, it was argued, would not want to combine with any such masculine features in an androgynous future.

Radical feminists thus moved away from androgyny towards criticism of the 'male nature' and the way in which men tried to define femininity. This criticism had both a negative and a positive side. The negative side involved a critique of the masculine nature as the source of most social, political and international problems. For Andrea Dworkin, masculinity *per se* represented death, violence and destructiveness (Dworkin 1981, 52–3). Women, in this reading, were always the victims. Widely publicized infor-mation about rape, the nature and effects of pornography, and the abuse of women in marriage increased the profile of this point, although later this kind of approach was criticized by other feminists for 'essentializing' the nature of women (Randall 1991, 522). On the positive side, the nature and qualities of the female were held to be morally and spiritually superior and consequently led to 'woman-centred analysis'.

Woman-centred analysis took different forms. Some writers praised aspects of the feminine which were previously perceived as taboos or obstacles to women's lives, such as menstruation, motherhood and maternal thinking. 'Maternal thinking' thus took on a high profile in the writings of J. B. Elshtain, Sara Ruddick and Carol Gilligan, although the latter theorist did not emphasize the impact of maternal think-ing on the public realm. Ruddick's and Elshtain's views were, though, accused of promoting a conservative pro-family perspective which was driving women back into the home. In this latter debate the argument on maternal thinking, as a way of criticizing the male mode of thought, lost some of its sting. Women's thought was accorded crucial importance, but not as a direct replacement for male thought. Elshtain claimed, though, that these nurturing qualities should be manifest in the public sphere, as well as in the family.

Other writers used this latter approach as a radical cultural device. As Jane Alpert comments:

> Feminine culture is based on what is best and strongest in women, and as we begin to define ourselves as women, the qualities coming to the fore are the same ones as a mother projects in the best kind of nurturing relationship to a child: empathy, intuitive-ness, adaptability, awareness of growth as a process rather than as goal-ended, inven-tiveness, protective feeling towards others, and a capacity to respond emotionally as well as rationally. (quoted in Jaggar 1983, 97)

In Mary Daly, this cultural radical feminism emphasized that women and their culture were both different and culturally superior to males. Such difference was expressed through the whole lifestyle and thought of women. Postmodernist feminists and poststructuralists tended, however, to oppose the binary opposition of linguistic terms such as masculine or feminine. The qualities associated with such terms could in fact be adopted by either sex. Thus this whole debate could be seen as a rhetorical fiction.

Other radicals, ignoring the postmodernists, confidently suggested that 'feminine thinking' might be extended into a new form of superior epistemology and natural science. This aspect of radicalism was occasionally singled out as a distinctive school called 'standpoint feminism' (Randall 1991, 521; see also Harding 2003). Standpoint theory, like postmodernism or poststructuralism, attacked notions of objectivity in science, rationality and logic in Western thought. This formed the basis to the question of whether 'the whole process of rational and scientific discourse might not be somehow inherently masculine' (Coole 1988, 266; see also Macmillan 1982; Lloyd 1984). Masculine thought was seen to work in certain ways: for example, conceptually separating mind and matter, self and other, reason and emotion. Writers such as Adrienne Rich, Catherine MacKinnon and Evelyn Fox Keller consequently argued that the very notion of objectivity and rationality implied distance and separation which coincided with the male desire for autonomy – with all the problems accruing to such an attitude (see Rich 1976 and Keller 1985). However, unlike postmodernism and poststructuralism, standpoint theory rejected relativism and presented epistemology in the name of an unspecified, but none the less superior objective feminine epistemology. In fact, some argued that Western culture was in desperate need of such a new way of thinking (Eisenstein 1984, 66).[28]

The Nature of Oppression and Subordination

The analysis of oppression follows the same contours of argument as in the previous section of this chapter. The liberal feminist perspective concentrated on justice, equality and rights. For Mary Wollstonecraft, the source of oppression was clear. As she commented:

> Women are everywhere in ... [a] deplorable state; for in order to preserve their innocence ... truth is hidden from them, and they are made to assume an artificial character before their faculties have acquired any strength. Taught from their early infancy that beauty is woman's sceptre, the mind shapes itself to the body, and roaming round its gilt cage only seeks to adore its prison. (Wollstonecraft 1985, 131)

Women were denied the means to develop their reason. The gender and character of women were the result of their education. Men expected women to bring up children, act virtuously and manage a household, but this could not be done except by cultivating reason. Men, Wollstonecraft complained, acted quite absurdly in this sphere. They wanted women to be noble beings, but tried to deny them the right to rational development. Men argued that women were naturally incapable of benefiting from education and also tried to deny it to them. Women in such an uneducated situation were equivalent to soldiers in a standing army where blind ignorance and obedience were the sole requirements. Such a mentality could only appeal to a despot (Wollstonecraft 1985, 124–5). Thus the source of oppression of women was the irrational denial of rights, particularly to education and the cultivation of reason. Ultimately such cultivation would lead some women to participate in employment and commerce. The purpose of Wollstonecraft's book was therefore to persuade men by reason to acknowledge and uphold the rights of women.

For J. S. Mill, the roots of oppression lay in a number of disreputable male motives. Like Bentham, Mill repudiated the natural rights perspective, although not the idea of legal rights for women. Men, in complete ignorance, claimed that women were naturally inferior. Yet, like Wollstonecraft, Mill contended that 'what women by nature cannot do, it is quite superfluous to forbid them doing' (Mill 1989, 143). Men appeal to custom to uphold their oppression, but absolute monarchy and black slavery have appealed to the same idea. We should therefore be sceptical of such notions. Women could be educated and develop their own plans of life. Again Mill looked to the repudiation of certain legal and educational limitations on women for the sake of human progress. As he commented:

> the principle which regulates the existing social relations between the sexes – the legal subordination of one sex to the other – is wrong in itself, and now one of the chief hindrances to human improvement; and that it ought to be replaced by a principle of perfect equality, admitting no power or privilege on the one side, nor disability on the other. (Mill 1989, 119)

In one of his earliest essays, 'On the Jewish Question', Marx, like Mill, scorned the natural rights perspective. Marx, however, saw it as a cover for bourgeois property interests. Oppression was premised on the class and economic relations within capitalism. Women's oppression was rooted in the impersonal logic of capitalist expropriation. The family, private property, division of labour, domestic labour and the position of women were due to mutable historical and economic circumstances which underpin the legal and political injustices. As Engels remarked on the origin of monogamous marriage: 'It was the first form of the family based not in natural but in economic condition, namely, in the victory of private property over original, naturally developed, common ownership' (Engels in Marx and Engels 1968, 502). For Engels, the first forms of exploitation can be observed in the family, namely, that the well-being of the man is maintained on the basis of the repression of the woman. The majority of women do not stay with men for love, but for economic support. It is thus that we have Engels's famous description of bourgeois marriage as legalized prostitution (Engels in Marx and Engels 1968, 504).

The key to understanding oppression, in the view of many radical and socialist feminists, was encapsulated in the term 'patriarchy'. Patriarchy was 'a political structure which favours man' (Eistenstein 1981, 8). The essence of this view was not to locate the oppression of women in legal and social rights or economic determinism, but rather in the deep psychic roots of masculine psychology, thought and language. Patriarchy lay in the masculine demeanour. The tendency was thus psychological, linguistic and biological. This masculine demeanour could be wholly identified with the male sex; alternatively it could be identified with certain qualities which might be manifest in either sex.

Socialist feminists found themselves in an uncomfortable situation here. In interpreting patriarchy they tried to uphold, on the one hand, the historically mutable economic dimension and, on the other hand, the radicals' universalistic biological, linguistic, psychological and essentialist claims. For socialists, 'male supremacy and capitalism are defined as the core relations determining the oppression of women today' (Eisentstein ed. 1979, 5). Traditional Marxism was seen to be 'sex-blind', but the opposite error was committed by radicals, who were accused of being 'history-blind', namely, ignoring the historical and material base to patriarchy.[29] Traditional Marxism failed to recognize the other forms of oppression suffered by women. This was the oppression which pre-dated and would post-date capitalism, and which resulted from reproduction and domesticity. By concentrating on large-scale industry, traditional Marxists failed to analyse women as workers in domestic settings (since the proletariat were viewed *within* industry). They also failed to note who benefits from such domestic labour (Hartman in Sargent ed. 1986, 9).

Socialist feminists were therefore attempting to widen our understanding of the division of labour and the oppression of women, to focus our attention on crucial links between reproduction and production, and thus on the role of the family within capitalism. In this sense, the understanding of women's alienation and oppression was deepened. Patriarchy was a combination of economic and sexual factors. Capitalism functioned *with* patriarchy. The oppression of women was thus more deeply entrenched than suspected by traditional Marxism. Patriarchy had a material base.

The reaction of many radicals to this analysis was predictable. The oppression of women had its roots in male biology and psychology. Some saw this oppression in the very notion of masculinity, which was rooted in violence and aggression. For others, this violence and dominance was rooted in male language, thought and behaviour. French feminism had concentrated its attention on this latter area of language embodying 'phallocentric' concerns. The more psychoanalytic approach, in writers such as Kate Millett, suggested that gender roles were socialized into children through the family and often reinforced by religion, myth and education. This at least provided some hope that males could be socialized into more acceptable attitudes in future. In the case of Irigaray, Cixous and Kristeva, therapy was premised upon women developing their own forms of language and writing.

Equality and Difference

The idea of equality again highlights some of the central tensions within the feminist movement as a whole. Despite the fact that equality has taken a very high profile within the liberal feminist perspective, it was regarded by Marxist feminists as suspect.[30] Some radicals were suspicions about equality as a way of assimilating females into male norms. It was, of course, possible to be different but still equal. Yet in some cases feminists argued that they simply do not want equality with men, since females were by nature superior, something the American liberal feminist Betty Friedan called 'female chauvinism'. The central problem of the equality-and-difference argument was therefore focused on the question: should the aim of feminism be civil, political and social equality or, alternatively, should women repudiate equality and celebrate their difference? A number of problems arose here concerning the ambiguity of the notion of 'difference' and whether there was any 'essential' masculine or feminine gender. This latter issue tied in with the postmodernist refusal to reify any categories (such as gender).

The equality argument has had its most vigorous support in the more liberal wing of feminism. Equality was measured by Wollstonecraft in terms of legal rights to basic civil freedoms. Wollstonecraft's target was as much aristocratic as male privileges, namely, the Burkean heritage which denied such equal rights and insisted on legal and political hierarchies. She was thinking here primarily of rights to life, liberty, economic independence, education and access to the professions.[31] For Wollstonecraft, God 'impressed' such rights equally on all human souls. Apart from overt physical strength there is, according to Wollstonecraft, very little difference between men and women. In fact, women in the future should be able to strengthen both their bodies and their minds.

In the later nineteenth century, liberal equality arguments focused on the demand for the extension of political rights of suffrage. Mill, in his writings, contended that liberty was the great want of human nature. Without the chance to form one's own plan of life the individual remained stunted.[32] Maximizing liberty entailed maximizing utility. Liberty, for Mill, necessarily led to a presumption in favour of equality. For Mill, contracts, marriage law, property law, education and suffrage should all be equalized (see Coole 1988, 144).

In the twentieth century, liberal feminists initially concentrated their attention on acquiring equality across a range of social welfare rights. In some cases the demand was for increasing support and benefits for families and children; in others, for equal opportunities in terms of education, employment, pay, marriage, property, political participation and citizenship. Such demands had some marked successes in Britain and America during the 1960s and 1970s. As indicated earlier in this chapter, many of these concerns (with citizenship, equality, and so forth) have, though, changed in character in the early twenty-first century. By and large, even if they have not been fully realized, liberal feminist aims have now become mainstream in public policy debates. Feminism – as an accepted public concern in Europe, North America and elsewhere to address the oppression of women – is an ideological battle which *in public terms* has been largely won, even if in practice there are still multiple abuses to be empirically addressed. This is one reading of the term 'postfeminism' (see Mascia-Lees and Sharpe 2000). Feminist debates in the last decade have, though (from the more sustainable liberal or social liberal feminist perspective), moved away from broad feverish theoretical debates and concerns about the status of feminism itself and mutated much more decisively towards critically addressing and finessing specific issues, such as citizenship, equality, liberty, culture, justice, rape, migration, immigration, postcolonialism and multiculturalism.[33] In this sense a form of liberal and social liberal feminism has now become very much part of the contemporary political lingua franca.

One aspect worth noting here is that the liberal and social liberal feminist perspective – apart from its fuller integration into the public vernacular – has also become profoundly academicized in the last decade. These feminist-inspired writings are largely embedded in sophisticated academic texts of history, philosophy and social and political theory. In one sense this presents an unexpected scenario, compared with the 1980s and 1990s. On the one hand there is an institutionalized and normalized feminist perspective in the vernaculars of public institutions which no one really seriously questions. On the other hand, there is an immensely scholarly body of regularized academicized feminist literature, which is regarded as a normal and respected dimension of the academy. However, if one then asks where is the political movement and active ideology of feminism, the answer is not so clear. If anything it has oddly faded. Perhaps the fact of its normality in academic and public activity has squeezed out the urgency of the ideological movement which was so voluble and articulate during the last decades of the twentieth century.

Despite the fact that egalitarian themes punctuated the history of socialism during the nineteenth and twentieth centuries, equality was often viewed as just another bourgeois illusion, particularly when classical Marxism dominated the debate. Like justice and rights, equality was regarded as part of the liberal capitalist ethos. For Marxists, inequalities undoubtedly existed and would be rectified by communism. Inequality *per se* was not, though, an evil; rather it was the symptom of a deeper malaise. Inequality was a feature of a society riven by class conflict. The position of women under capitalism was not due to their unequal treatment; unequal treatment was a consequence of capitalism itself. Legal, political or social reforms could only be placebos; they would solve no problems. As such, the theme of equality did not make much headway within traditional Marxism or later socialist feminism.

In the case of the radicals, the theme of equality and difference was pivotal. Initially, there were some egalitarian themes within radical feminism. For example, the early arguments for androgyny were based on a form of egalitarianism. It was a somewhat strange egalitarianism, in some cases premised on technological advances in biology. The later rejection of androgyny, as previously mentioned, led to a critical attitude towards equality both as a value and as a political goal. This was the phase which celebrated women's difference from men. The divide between males and females became known in radical literature as the 'gender gap' (Hawkesworth 1988, 464 n. 16).

The arguments surrounding difference theory are quite diverse and the history of its development since the 1960s has been immensely tangled and still remains as such in the 2000s (see Young 1990, 1997 and 2000; Benhabib 2002; Squires 2007). The earliest ideas on difference go back to theorists such as Kate Millett who saw the masculine/feminine distinction as part of patriarchal exploitation. To a large extent the differences were viewed as social artifacts, constructed to keep women within certain roles. Difference was then attacked by writers such as Shulamith Firestone. In arguing for androgynous equality she wanted to destroy the political uses of difference. In the 1970s, however, difference began to reappear as a virtue. Initially, in the radical cultural feminists, it encompassed notions of female supremacism, the moral superiority of women, the value of sisterhood, political lesbianism, and separatism from men. It was also contended that women had very different attitudes to their bodies from men. The physical capacity to bear children gives the female a highly positive life-affirming attitude, whereas the male is more easily caught up in negative life-denying aggression, ambition and destructiveness. This particular theme was taken up again by the eco-feminists, who often located the environmental crisis in negative male values and attitudes to nature.

In the later 1980s the tendency to cultural separatism gave way to a number of new developments. First, because of the importance of women's different culture and experience, the academic study of women's distinctive knowledge developed, acquiring the title 'woman-centred analysis'. The differences of women constituted a distinct way of life and thought. This led to the massive growth of women's studies courses. Most social science and humanities disciplines gradually (particularly over the 1990s) began to incorporate feminist studies components as crucial for the curricula. Second, the experience rather than the patriarchal institution of motherhood was again taken seriously, particularly in the writings of, for example, Adrienne Rich. Third, the different but unique values of maternal thinking were highlighted. Women's distinct personalities and psyches were explored in the writings of Nancy Chodorow. Others argued that women, unlike men, embodied values of truthfulness, sensitivity to emotion, altruism, cooperation, nurturance and pacifism. Carol Gilligan, as we have seen, developed her ideas on a women's 'ethic of care', as against the masculinist 'ethic of justice'. However, other feminists have identified more unpredictable aspects to this ethic of care (see Mackay 2001). Ruddick and Elshtain, also mentioned earlier, suggested that such maternal value and thought could be of immense benefit if brought into the public realm.

The late 1980s also saw the impact of French feminism, which celebrated women's difference. It was, though, suspicious of notions of equality and even of the term 'feminism' as an assimilation into bourgeois reformism. Although influenced by deconstruction themes and suspicious of the biological conceptions of difference, French feminists none the less repudiated the masculine 'phallocentric' domination of language and called for a linguistic recoding. In this argument, difference largely settled upon language. This latter issue overlapped with 'radical standpoint theory', which also argued for a new and discrete feminine epistemology and science (Harding 2003).

French feminism and difference theory in general were criticized from three perspectives. First, more rigorous feminist postmodernist and poststructuralist critics drew attention to the binary opposition of gender (male and female) which essentialized womanhood and established closure (Nicholson 1989; Flax 1990; Gatens 1996). In other words, difference arguments relied on certain basic oppositions which themselves required deconstruction. The meaning of 'male' and 'female' must be deferred. Simple-minded essentialism of the female obscured a multiplicity of possible constructs and interpretations. In writers such as Judith Butler a much more nuanced cultural understanding of gender and sexuality has been developed. This emphasizes the 'sexed body' as a complex and culturally constructed difference embedded in (Foucauldian) regulative disciplinary discourses. This culturally constructed body is subject to performativity, that is, repetition of stylized bodily acts which gives the 'sexed body' a natural ontological status (see Butler 1990 and 2004; also McNay 1999; Lloyd 2007).

Second, a related but more practical criticism of difference theory contended that the danger of essentializing women was that they would once again be forced into a 'natural' place in the family. In this sense, difference, the 'gender gap' and essentialism can be viewed as devices in the patriarchal toolkit. Third, the supposed difference between men and women ignores the differences between women themselves, in terms of age, race, class, culture, ethnicity, nationality, sexual preference and marital status. These differences can, in fact, be far broader than any supposed and fictive gender difference. To try to crush all women into one category and all men into another is a form of totalizing and repressive discourse. In this context, it is also suggested that there are *no* universal or essential features to women. Gender essences are reified social constructs. In fact, purportedly natural qualities, which we associate with masculinity and femininity, can be practised by both sexes.

The Personal as the Political

The heading for this section became the key slogan of the feminist movement certainly up to the early 2000s. The idea is fairly simple, although the ramifications are multiple. The contention was that what have been previously regarded as the discrete realms of the private and public were in fact deeply ideological and manipulative devices, reflecting male patriarchal interests. Thus the time-honoured distinction of 'public' and 'private' was in reality flawed and obscured some highly political issues.

The origins of the 'personal as the political' critique lay in the liberal feminist position. Liberals had traditionally identified the personal life of individuals, the family and the economy as private. It was particularly towards the former two areas that liberal feminists addressed their criticism. In the case of the early liberal feminists, such as Wollstonecraft, the idea that women had their natural place in, and primary duty to, the home was an illusion. Women's first duty was to reason. In fact, this reasoning was a necessary logical preliminary to the performance of any duty, even within the family. As Wollstonecraft argued: 'The mind naturally weakened by depending on authority, never exerts its own powers, and thus the obedient wife is rendered a weak indolent mother' (Wollstonecraft 1985, 166). The idea of woman's sexual nature being a natural and private realm, or the notion of the family as a private realm, were seen as absurd propositions to Wollstonecraft. Her own favoured ideal was a civic republican model of the family, as a training ground for the public-spirited citizen and not as a realm of private passions. Marriage should be companionate and friendly in character rather than passionate.[34] Passion disturbed the minds of individuals and undermined the fabric of society.

Mill, and many of the liberal feminist tradition, have shared most of the above sentiments. In the 1960s this issue came to the fore in Betty Friedan's work *The Feminine Mystique*. She coined the phrase 'the problem which has no name' to describe the fact that many women found themselves in a family context which was private and personal and also supposed to satisfy them, and yet experienced deep frustration and discontent, something they could not quite put a name to. Friedan's contention, in essence, was that all women shared a fundamental problem of inequality – in status, rights and opportunities – with men. The private family structure obscured the patriarchal interests of men in maintaining this inequality. Overall, the liberal critique of the personal/political issue was to identify certain rights which were being denied to women. These rights could, in the main, be rectified by legal, social, political and educational reform. Such rectification would not destroy the family. In fact, liberals still envisaged women playing an active role in family life, although men would be expected to take an equal part in domestic work and the rearing of children. The family therefore still had an important traditional role to play, as Wollstonecraft also believed. To some extent this more egalitarian conception of the family was endorsed in large part by the proponents of 'maternal thinking', the 'ethic of care' and pro-family feminists. The novel idea of the pro-family feminists was their suggestion that such maternal thinking (from either sex), which had previously been consigned to the family, should in future enter into the public realm (see also Mackay 2001). This broke up the older continuities of the public/private division in an original manner.

Marxist and socialist feminists addressed the problem of the 'personal and political' in the economic sphere, although Marxism was predisposed to reject any separation of public and private from the outset. The distinction was regarded as an obscurantist device of liberal ideology, where the notion 'private' focused largely on 'private property'. In Engels, the family was seen to be an historically changing institution. Previous societies had manifested different marital arrangements, such as polygamy, according to different modes of production and ownership. The modern patriarchal monogamous family had nothing to do with loving relations; rather 'It was the first form of the family based not on natural but on economic conditions, namely, on the victory of private property over original, naturally developed, common ownership.' The first class antagonisms arose within the family since it was always a situation where 'the well-being and development of the one group are attained by the misery and repression of the other' (Engels in Marx and Engels 1968, 502–3). The permanent addenda to bourgeois marriage, for Engels, were prostitution and cuckoldry.

Although Engels looked forward to emancipation, easily dissoluble marriages, the destruction of men's dominance and equal employment for women, he still appeared to envisage both the continuance of monogamous marriage and the possibility that it was more natural for women to be involved in the bringing-up of children. Thus a Marxist blessing was put upon a sexual division of labour in the family. Alexandra Kollontai, in the early decades of the twentieth century, did not share this idea (Kollontai 1977). Marxism was also criticized by later socialist feminists. Such critics contended that classical Marxism did not explain why it was more natural for women to adopt this role (Jaggar 1983, 67–9; also Hartmann in Sargent ed. 1986). Furthermore, it ignored the deeper roots of patriarchal dominance. There were forms of oppression other than private property and class. Such oppression pre-dates and post-dates capitalism. Marxism therefore needed to become involved in an analysis of women's labour in the family. It needed to ask who benefits from domestic labour. Patriarchal dominance was thus seen to have much deeper, if still material and historical, roots than previously anticipated. Women, within this sexual division of labour, serviced both men and capitalism. The subordination of women in the family was part of the economic foundation of society. In this reading, the private and public overlapped and interpenetrated. The 'personal as the political' was seen to be a deep-rooted biological, psychological, historical and fundamentally economic fact (see Petchesky in Eisenstein ed. 1979, 376–7). This focus on the family led to a number of debates spilling over into New Left circles on the question of the Marxist interpretation of such things as housework and domestic labour (see Barrett and MacIntosh essays in Lovell ed. 1990).

In the case of the radicals, the tendency was to extend the critique of patriarchy within personal life to include biological, psychological and linguistic perspectives. Radical feminists made most use of this 'personal as the political' critique. They tried to tackle the problem of patriarchy head on. They tended to relocate the whole issue of power in the personal realm and totally denied the private/public divide. For some radicals, male power in the personal realm was identified universally and ahistorically across cultures in practices such as suttee, foot-binding, rape, pornography, genital mutilation, witch-burning and even male-dominated gynaecology. Mary Daly, for example, saw these as universal male sado-masochistic rituals designed to discipline and subdue women (see Daly 1979). For some radicals the culture of Western, and other, societies embodied a form of 'sexual fascism'. The personal and political in this case radically intersected. Radical standpoint theorists also argued that even male language, rationality, science and philosophy embodied subtle, deep-rooted forms of patriarchal domination. Thus, if a woman believed that she was free from political manipulation when she was thinking in a private manner, she was fundamentally mistaken. Male patriarchal epistemology could colonize and dominate even her most personal thoughts. The standpoint argument overlaps again with the French feminists and Foucauldian feminists, who have contended that masculinist themes (especially binary oppositions such as public and private) often dominate and discipline both discourses and the construction of the body and the self (see Nicholson 1989; Butler 1990; Gatens 1996; Coole in Freeden ed. 2001).

Such beliefs on the 'personal as the political' led some radical feminists to suggest policies such as separatism (separate living from men) and to the formulation of distinct feminine modes of thought. This in turn led to some damning indictments of the family and, in other cases, to a recommendation for its abandonment and suggestions for new forms of communal living.

Conclusion

The primary objective of liberal feminists is to bring women into the full rights of democratic autonomous citizenship. They envisage a future where legal, political, social and economic rights and freedoms will have been achieved for all women. They will be on an equal footing with men in all spheres. This will be brought about by reason, persuasion and constitutional reform. The reformed family will remain, but men will have an equal role in domestic duties, and women's careers and lives will in no way be artificially hampered by the rearing of children. The institution of the family is thus seen to have a continuing and important role but it will be supported financially and socially in order to prevent inequalities occurring. Heterosexuality in established relationships is still seen as the social norm. Liberal-minded feminism, in sum, anticipates a future of sexual justice and, in fact, in some cases a justice which extends well beyond women to all forms of unequal treatement (see Nussbaum 2001 and 2006).

Classical Marxism envisaged women entering more fully into the workforce in large-scale industry. As Engels argued, 'The emancipation of women becomes possible when women are enabled to take part in production on a large, social scale, and when domestic duties require their attention only to a minor degree' (Engels in Marx and Engels 1968, 579). Engels also favoured more easily dissoluble marriages, as well as economic independence. Kollontai, during the early stages of the Russian Revolution, was responsible for the introduction of a number of proposals and laws on women's issues, later stifled by Stalin. She managed, for example, to arrange for centralized domestic cleaning services, nurseries and child-care, and public kitchens, and worked towards the possibility of communal households in the future, mass free education and abortion on demand. She also believed (like Wollstonecraft) that intense monogamous relations should be discouraged since these made women vulnerable to men, and (unlike Wollstonecraft) that frequent changes of partner were far healthier. This gave rise to a remark, which is often quoted out of context, that sex is like thirst and needs simply to be satisfied. In Kollontai's view, sex should not be taken so seriously; in fact, she suggested that jealousy and sexual possessiveness should be discouraged by the state as the last vestiges of an outworn private property mentality (see Kollontai 1977).

Socialist feminists in the 1980s, in widening their vision of exploitation, like Kollontai, suggested the expansion of free birth control, abortion, health-care for women, child-care centres and state recognition of domestic labour. There was, though, an ambivalence about the role of the family in this setting. Men would obviously play a significant part in child-rearing, although there was some suggestion (a point that showed the influence of the radicals) that heterosexuality would not necessarily be the norm. For socialist feminists, therefore, 'Normative heterosexuality must be replaced by a situation in which the sex of one's lover is a matter of social indifference' (Jaggar 1983, 132).

Radical feminism embodied a diversity of proposals. Beauvoir argued for freely available birth control, abortion and less significance accorded to monogamy in order to facilitate the entrance of women into the cultural world with men. In Firestone, we enter a world of cybernetic communism, peopled by androgynes, where all humans participate in child-bearing and child-rearing. With the rejection of this androgynous future, other radicals identified the main problems as patriarchal culture. If males were the major problem, what strategy could be adopted? At its most extreme and most rare, a male pogrom was suggested. At a less extreme level, lesbianism or separatism were advocated. Mary Daly proposed a totally different and separate women's utopian culture. The use of the term 'lesbianism' has parallels here. Lesbian usually denotes 'one who has withdrawn herself from the conventional definitions of femininity' (Eisenstein 1984, 51). Although some advocated sexual lesbianism, most radicals attracted to this strategy envisaged it as more political. If women consciously focused on their own culture and experience, then they could begin to achieve some autonomy from patriarchy. This point was expanded by the radical standpoint theory into a conception of a feminist epistemology. It was also contended by some radicals that only women allow each other a sense of self. Women, apparently, did not try to define each other. The suggestion of political lesbianism and separatism led, for a period, to the practice of 'sisterhood communities', where only women were allowed to live. Radicals did not resist heterosexual relationships or the idea of the family, but heterosexuality was no longer seen as the norm. Further, any notion of the family would have to be totally transformed so that women would not carry the burden of child-rearing or domestic work.

Postmodern and poststructuralist feminism concentrates on language, culture and identity. The key concern is primarily to deconstruct or genealogically analyse existing discourses. Language is seen to be a potent weapon to undercut and expose patriarchy across the whole domain of culture. In addition, French feminism was concerned to emphasize the unique manner in which women have contributed, and can in future contribute, to literary and imaginative culture. The most optimistic of such commentators would contend that if language can be decoded to expose the basic oppositions and unargued assumptions, then eventually our cultural symbols can be subtly recoded, thus effectively transforming, via language, our perceptual and cognitive worlds. The less optimistic have denied the essential character of femininity and masculinity, viewing them as social constructions which require deconstruction. It is difficult to know whether feminism means anything substantive any more in this latter context.

The bulk of informed criticism of feminism has arisen from *within* the feminist movement itself. The liberal feminists, for example, were attacked by both socialist and radical schools. Liberals, it was argued, appeared content with the existing family structure and accepted a weak and ineffective policy of equality, rights and justice. In so doing they neglected both the material and deep-rooted inequalities of capitalism and patriarchy and most of the deeper needs of women. Marxist feminists, on the other hand, were accused of sex-blindness, even by the socialist feminists, and condemned for continuing to adhere to an uncritical view of the natural place of women and the family. Even the socialist feminists were accused by their radical critics of being sex-blind and caught in an unnecessary historical and materialist framework. Liberals took the more conventional tack against the Marxists, criticizing their dogmatic materialism and abandonment of important values such as individual liberty, justice and rights. This latter intellectual struggle has not been solved in the 2000s; it has simply dropped off the key critical agenda. Many feminist who are still attracted by Marxism have usually tried to blend it with an eclectic mix of poststructuralism and critical theory (see, for example, Young 1990; Fraser 1997; Zerelli 2005).

In the case of the radicals, the most distinctive criticism was of their outlandish proposals. Liberals contended that feminism would not be taken seriously whilst radicals were advocating political lesbianism, androgyny and separatism. Further, the more extreme measures suggested by the radicals were seen to entail quite drastic assaults on individual freedoms, which many liberals found completely unacceptable.

In fact radical feminists now, in the 2000s, have largely dropped out of public sight, partly because of the incoherence and oddity of many of their ideas. Marxist and socialist critics of radicalism also accused them of ignoring the historical, economic and material basis to patriarchy and thus becoming trapped in an ahistorical and suspect biologism or psychologism.

Postmodern critics focused on the deconstruction of language and discourse – a practice which is still carried through with commitment and vigour to the present day (see Coole 2000; Butler 2004). Liberal, socialist and radical feminists alike are all subject to the same genealogical or deconstructive assaults. Postmodernists deny the idea of any privileged narrative position. Words and things have become unstuck in this analysis. However, the French feminists, in particular, did not appear to have grasped the logic of their own position. There was, as such, no reason to stop any critique at phallocentrism; 'feminocentrism' might also needs deconstructing. As one critic sourly remarked, 'Although [feminists] support postmodernism's practice of universalizing suspicion, they don't seem to regard *their* cause as suspect. They know *their* credentials to be intact' (Kariel 1990, 255). What we are left with is another series of fictions. As another critic observed, what can, at most, be hoped for from postmodern feminism is another moderately successful 'metafiction, or at least a fiction that will buy us time' (O'Neill in Silverman ed. 1990, 78–9). A number of feminist writers have sensed that the postmodernist and poststructuralist roads will ultimately destroy any case for feminism itself.[35] Nussbaum, for example, sees the need for clear substantive universal account of justice, rights and equality to make the case for an effective feminism (Nussbaum 1999a).[36] In Nussbaum's reading, therefore, the postmodernist path is simply a dead-end.

In examining the feminist movement, one central problem strikes the observer. Many of the arguments of feminism revolve around the question of sameness and equality or difference. Those who reject the argument for difference between male and female, rather like those who rejected payment for housework, argue that in effect such moves can stereotype women or fix them into certain roles. But the claim that all difference is socially or linguistically constructed can also lead to the proposition that there is no real difference between men and women. This latter proposition is deeply puzzling to ordinary men and women. It is even more puzzling when one considers the feminist point that there are as many differences *between* women (and also between men, for that matter). To complicate matters even further is the assertion that many of these differences are not natural but culturally constructed. In fact, many have suggested that there is no essence to either men or women in either biological or psychological terms. However, if the notion of difference *is* defended it becomes difficult, other than by denigrating men or masculinity, not to see some difference in roles for both men and women – not necessarily unequal roles, but unquestionably different. The emphasis placed by some feminists on childbirth, mothering and nurturing reflects this point. It is hard to know how these various views, which characterize the feminist ideology, can ever be reconciled.

8

Ecologism

It would be no exaggeration to say that ecology is now a crucial part of global debate. This has happened largely in the last forty years. Despite this more contemporary dimension to ecology, like all the ideologies examined, it has its claimants for ancient lineage. There are some serious debates concerning the origins of the movement which have repercussions on how we view it at the present moment. However, these debates will be considered in the next section.

There are immediate problems, though, with the word 'ecologism', which can have implications for the identity of the ecology movement. First, the word 'ecologism' can be daunting, carrying the specialized character of its initial and continuing usage in the mainstream sciences. Further, the more scientific aspect of the term can limit its ability to convey the deeply personal and political connotations for those working in the movement. In consequence, many of those who write on the ideology will refer to it, with some justification, as 'green thought' or 'environmental thought'. Even the term 'green' is not without its own internal difficulties. This particular debate was reflected in the change in name of the British Green Party (previously Ecology Party). Despite my sympathy for the titles 'green' and 'enviromentalism', I have not adopted them for the basic reason that they do not necessarily incorporate all that I wish to discuss under the rubric 'ecologism'.[1] The title 'green', for example, can be strongly linked in some discussions with a specific (often more left-leaning) political stance; this does not serve my immediate purpose.[2] The ecology movement in fact overlaps with and often embodies ideas which might be described as conservative or authoritarian. In this sense the present chapter might be said to be taking a slightly unorthodox view of the movement.

The ecology movement developed in the public domain from the 1970s. The movement appears in this sense to be historically very specific to the last decades of the twentieth century. The human race has, of course, been intervening in nature for a long time. However, the growth of industrialization in the last two hundred years accelerated this process of human intervention to worrying levels. The post-1945 era of industrial growth has been particularly staggering. As one of the environmental reports of the 1970s commented, 'In the last twenty-five [years], the power, extent and depth of man's interventions in the natural order seem to presage the most revolutionary [change] which the mind can conceive' (Ward and Dubos 1972, 37). It is the very scale and speed of growth in the fifty years which many have found alarming. For many it is the industrial growth of states such as India and China since the late 1990s – and in fact the industrial development model is still being widely adopted by countries across the globe – that is now causing immense anxiety. This has particularly been the case since the publicity surrounding the 1997 UN Kyoto conference on climate control and the mounting evidence on climate change.

Ecology as a scientific perspective has drawn attention to one very simple but important point from which a great deal follows, namely, that the ecosphere is an interrelated system. This in itself is an ontological point, but it is none the less a very significant ontology. What we call the environment is 'a system which includes all living things and the air, water and soil which is their habitat' (Goldsmith 1972, 69). In other words, the human species is part of an immensely complex, variegated and interrelated structure. What we sow in terms of industrial pollution, we will reap from the instability of the ecosphere. Climate change, with any reservations we may have here on the evidence, seems to be one crop that we are about to reap.[3] We cannot divorce ourselves from the ecosystem. This point constitutes the unique potency of ecologism. Before moving on from this it is worth noting immediately that the basic impetus, significance and public awareness which have been accorded to ecology have derived from its scientific support and evidence, not primarily from its moral or political stance (see Yearley 1991, 45; also Lomborg 2001; Bluhdorn 2008). On the other hand, ecology claims have had a uniquely personal dimension, not always shared by other ideologies (apart from aspects of feminism). Many ecologists have linked what they do in their personal or localized lives – in terms of anything from purchasing toilet paper, recycling, to using public transport – to a global or universal crisis that has ramifications minimally for the next few generations.[4] This complex global/local/individual perspective is, in one sense, quite unique among ideologies.

The word 'ecology' is a compound of the Greek terms *oikos* (meaning household or habitat) and *logos* (meaning the argument or science of something). In this sense there is a close and early relation to the term 'economy', which, in its original use, going back to Aristotle, meant management of the household. Ecology was initially designed as a science dealing with the systematic relation between plants and animals and their habitat or environment.[5] It has retained, to the present day, its character as a distinct systematic scientific discipline, which has been of interest not only to biologists but also to physiologists, zoologists, biologically inclined mathematicians, physical scientists, geographers, economists and town planners. From its beginnings as a science it has had powerful and fruitful cross-disciplinary connotations. From its inception, ecologism has been characterized by a strong and traditional scientific empiricism. The more normative usage of the word, in terms of morality, politics and economics, is a slightly later and subtle modulation. Even in the 2000s there is still a tangled and uneasy relationship between those who perceive ecology as an established science and those who mesh the scientific findings with strong doses of normative theory.

The Origins of Ecological Thought

As mentioned in the first section, the debate about the origins of ecologism is pertinent to the character of the movement in the present. This point is not always immediately apparent from the literature on ecologism. There are some skeletons in the ecological cupboard which many prefer to ignore or pass over. Most of these skeletons, some of which are comparatively harmless, relate to the longer-term origins of ecological ideas. It is contended in this chapter that we should not pass over these longer-term roots in silence, since they reveal the ideological complexity and diversity within the ecological perspective, a complexity which cannot be shunned by simply renaming one's perspective 'green'.

There is little contention concerning the first usage of the word 'ecology'. It was employed by the German zoologist and philosopher Ernst Haeckel in the late 1860s.[6] Haeckel's use of the term in works such as *General Morphology* (1866) denoted 'the science of relations between organisms and their environment' (quoted in Bramwell 1989, 40). There is, however, some argument about the importance of Haeckel's ideas, which will be dealt with shortly. To be brief, there are three basic positions (largely internal to the ecology movement) taken on the question of origins. There is also some recent growth in social scientific explanations of ecology movements which will be mentioned later in the chapter.

The first account of origins will not detain us long, since it is common to most ideologies. This is the attempt to trace ecological sentiments back to the dawn of the human species, at least to the Palaeolithic or Neolithic periods. Various groups, such as the Celts, became *idées fixes* for ecological writers. The basic point that was often made in the 1980s and 1990s, and is still repeated in contemporary debates concerning 'primal' or 'tribal' peoples, is that they were, or are, 'naturally' more ecologically aware than us. Early humans (some would go so far as to say 'before industrialization') had a much more responsive and caring view of the world around them. The impression is that pre-industrial or primal peoples implicitly respected nature and only took from it what they needed; whether they were hunter-gatherers or market gardeners, their more animistic perspective led them to care for nature. Some would place a heavy emphasis here on the pre-Christian, rather than pre-industrial, peoples.[7] Primal peoples are thus often accorded a kind of natural ancient wisdom which we would do well to rediscover. Hence, ecological literature has often been peppered with quotations from shamans, mystics, tribal elders and gurus of various types.

There is something misty-eyed and vague about this kind of thinking. Every ideology stakes a claim here, but the ecology movement, in its search for holistic roots, has referred to it more intensely than others. The claim is of course unverifiable, at least in Neolithic terms. In the present day there is a danger that we will look with unseemly ardour (like some anarchists) for those very sentiments that we want to find in primal peoples, translating their mythologies into our social or environmental anxieties. We also ignore, at our cost, the fact that the 'slash and burn' mentality and the disregard for pollution and habitat destruction were as characteristic of early Neolithic human beings as of those who are now destroying the Brazilian rainforest.

Such practices are often tied initially to survival economics. The landscape of Europe, for example, has not simply been shaped by industrialization. In earlier periods, humans were limited by population numbers, technology and their social and economic environment. However, if certain Neolithic humans had invented a smooth-stone chain-saw, they would doubtless have used it freely.[8]

The second account of origins, which is by far the most popular and widely utilized, dates the ecology movement from the 1960s and 1970s. Many see this process of ecological awareness beginning in the 1960s.[9] Some focus on certain seminal writings from the same decade. The earliest of these was Rachel Carson's *Silent Spring* (1962). Nearer the end of the decade Paul Ehrlich's *The Population Bomb* (1968) and Garrett Hardin's 'The Tragedy of the Commons' (1968) raised the spectre not only of environmental collapse but also of its relation to overpopulation (see Meadows 1972; Worster 1977; Pepper 1984). Others find the early 1970s a more convincing period, particularly in view of the widespread public reaction to events such as the oil crisis and deeply resonant reports such as the unofficial UN report *Only One Earth* (1972); the Club of Rome's *The Limits to Growth* (1972); the *Ecologist* journal volume *Blueprint for Survival* (1972); the US Carter administration's *Global 2000 Report* (1982); and the Brundtland Report *Our Common Future* (1987) (see Spretnak and Capra 1986, 157ff; Weston ed. 1986, 15ff; Eckersley 2004, 72). A vigorous case was made in these reports for our concerns to be focused on the wholesale depletion of the environment. The later 1970s also saw the newly developed green parties contending at times successfully for political office, most notably the West German Greens from 1979 (see Hülsberg 1988). It is undoubtedly true that there has been both a vast growth of ecologically sensitive literature and a multiplication of politicized green organizations since the 1970s.

There is a great deal to be said for the second perspective, in that the ecology movement has unquestionably moved into the forefront of politics and economics in the 2000s. It should, though, be allied to a third perspective. There are positive and negative aspects to this third view, which identifies the roots of ecological ideas in the nineteenth century, although there is still some debate as to precisely when. One point – which is acknowledged by many writers, even those who favour the 1970s account – is that ecologism, to some degree, incorporates a critical reaction to the European Enlightenment tradition (Dobson 1990, 8–9). Ecologism does occasionally look with mistrust on the supreme value of reason. It does also deny at points the central place of human beings and further that nature is without value and can simply be manipulated by humans for their own interests. In this reading, ecologism has been associated with part of the romantic movement's reaction to the Enlightenment in the early nineteenth century. The weakness in this account is the crucial role that rationality and empirical science play in the presentation of large areas of the ecology movement. In addition, the beliefs concerning global or universal equality of humans and species, which are also present in ecology, do not square with the traditionalist, localized and often more hierarchically orientated character of romanticism. This also raises (not necessarily insuperable) problems with categories such as conservative or nationalist ecology (see essays by Scruton and Avner de-Shalit in Dobson and Eckersley eds 2006).

If we move later into the nineteenth century, and consider the impact of both Malthusianism and Darwinism, we find something very different. Philosophies developed which tried to integrate a strongly materialist and scientific perspective with an immanent and naturalistic understanding of religion and morality. In other words, nature and evolution were imbued with a spiritual significance. On the one hand, such a philosophy accepted the developments of evolutionary science and the decline of more orthodox religion. On the other hand, it looked with an extremely sceptical eye on philosophies of consciousness such as idealism. Humans were subject to the evolutionary laws of nature. Into this scenario, an underlying significance, or pattern, to evolution and nature was imported. We can see this attempt clearly in many writers, some already encountered in this book, such as Peter Kropotkin, L. T. Hobhouse, J. A. Hobson and Herbert Spencer. With the loss of God or gods, 'nature' and its underlying ontological significance became of supreme importance. Sciences could uncover these underlying patterns and structures, which, whether consciously or not, took on a sanctified aura. Evolution was spiritualized. One of the most overt, one might almost say caricatured, examples of this in the twentieth century was the work of Teilhard de Chardin, which influenced sections of the ecology movement (see Russell 1982).

What is significant here is that the first writer to use the neologism 'ecology' was overwhelmingly part of the above perspective. Ernst Haeckel was an influential figure whose ideas affected not only the scientific, but also the literary and religious establishments before the First World War. He was the product of a wave of evolutionary materialism in Germany, influenced by Darwinism, in the last decades of the nineteenth century. He felt that Darwin had put evolution on a firm scientific base. In serious academic works and more popular texts, such as *The Riddle of the Universe* (1899), Haeckel tried to develop a philosophical monism (premised on vitalist, as opposed to mechanistic, biology) which would ultimately act as a valid substitute for religion. Like Herbert Spencer (whom he deeply admired) and later Henri Bergson, Haeckel posited an evolving force or substance within the material world of nature, governed by a basic law – what he called the 'law of substance' (Haeckel 1929, 224, 310). Also like Spencer, he did not see evolving nature as lifeless. Denying atheism, he referred to his view as 'pantheism'. God, for Haeckel, was completely immanent in nature, or as he put it, 'God, as an *intramundane* being, is everywhere identical with nature itself' (Haeckel 1929, 236).[10] With the death of the old gods, Haeckel proclaimed optimistically that 'the new sun of our realistic monism ... reveals to us the wonderful temple of nature in all its beauty'. A nature religion thus replaced 'the anthropistic ideals of "God, freedom, and immortality"' (Haeckel 1929, 311).[11] Haeckel saw nature as a unified, balanced organism of which humans were a part, an organism which had religious significance. This monistic, natural and harmonious organism had lessons to teach us in terms of the organization of society as well as our relations with nature.

From its beginnings in the 1870s, ecologism has embodied scientific and evolutionary ideas. These were often meshed into a subtle pantheistic, holistic spiritualism. Nature itself was seen to have worth and moral standing and was tied integrally to our destiny as animals. Nature embodied a dynamic teleology which we ignored at our cost. Those now studying ecology who try to maintain the purity of the scientific motif, unsullied by religious input, need to pause for a few moments to study the history of their discipline. From Haeckel onwards, ecology has had moral and religious import for humanity. The manner in which we organized our societies, economies and personal lives had bearing on the same naturalistic logic and teleology of nature. Such a vision was also markedly not focused primarily on humans; it was, rather, non-anthropocentric. In addition, 'nature' and the 'natural' became the ultimate commendation. Living a natural life was therefore the best life. This has had (and will continue having) colossal implications into the twenty-first century, stretching across our attitudes to the countryside, naturism, folk tradition, folk music, wholefood, organic vegetable growing, nature reserves, natural energy, wind, wave and solar power, alternative and homeopathic medicine, and so forth – a vast litany of beliefs which cannot be examined here, but all of which existed well before the First World War, and all of which are still informed by a deep underlying ontology.

The disturbing aspect of the above claim for many in the ecology movement is twofold. First, it is clear that from its inception the ecological perspective incorporated, occasionally, some much unexpectedly conservative (aesthetics-in-nature) and nationalist components, particularly via the 'folkish' movements across Europe in the 1920s and 1930s (see Bramwell 1985 and 1989; Biehl and Staudenmaier 1995). It is just fortuitous that dissatisfied socialists and anarchists formed the initial core membership of the ecology movement from the 1970s. Their powerful conjunction of pacifist, socialist, often anti-statist attitudes has obscured this more diverse ancestry. A related problem here is that many of those who have written widely on political ecology since the 1970s have been the believers in some form of either anarchist or socialist-inclined ecology (Pepper 1993; Kovel 2007).[12]

A second worry is the manner in which some of these ecological ideas developed, particularly the strong ecological perspectives of many fascist and Nazi movements in the 1920s and 1930s. The Third Reich was keenly exploring wind technology, methane gas, bio-mass and other sources of alternative soft-energy. The National Socialists were the first to set up nature reserves in Europe and to plant deciduous woodlands in expansive planned programmes of reforestation. In addition, they were experimenting broadly on bio-dynamic and organic farming methods. Many, such as Hitler, were keen vegetarians and Himmler, the head of the SS, was an ardent anti-vivisectionist (see Bramwell 1985, 1989 and 1994; also Biehl and Staudenmaier 1995). This detail is a subtext underlying the heated debates within ecologism over potential authoritarianism and eco-fascism in some areas of the movement. It also raises serious issues as to whether ecology has any intrinsic or conceptual ties with democratic or social justice-based movements (see Smith 2003).

Outside of the above views there have been attempts in sociological and economic literature to deal with the history of the ecology movement, some of which link with a longer-term nineteenth-century perspective. Philip Lowe and Jane Goyder, for example, in their study of environmental groups in politics, identified 'waves' of concern with ecological problems: the 1880s up to 1900; 1918 to 1939; and the 1950s and 1970s (Lowe and Goyder eds 1983, 15ff).[13] The authors argued that 'It is perhaps no coincidence that each of the periods of sudden growth of new environmental groups in the 1890s, the late 1920s, and the late 1950s and early 1970, occurred as similar phases in the world business cycle – towards the end of periods of sustained expansion' (Lowe and Goyder eds 1983, 25). Once material needs have been satisfied for a certain sector of society, through economic prosperity, people begin to express concern about the 'costs' of prosperity, and also about the 'natural' surroundings which they now have the leisure and time to enjoy. They have the time, education and financial security to be able to be alarmed about the environment (see also Martinez-Alier 2003).[14]

Other social investigators have contended that those who express ecological anxieties are often members of social classes on the periphery of industrialization, usually in the professional service sector of the community (academics, teachers, artists, actors, clergy, social workers, and so on) (Lowe and Goyder eds 1983, 26–7). Advanced industrial economies show a marked growth of such service-sector occupations. Thus value-shifts towards ecology are tied to the changing occupational patterns of advanced industrial economies. The central ironic paradox here, of course, is that economic growth, with its consequent environmental effects (which are deplored by ecologists), has facilitated the expansion of an affluent, educated service sector which has in turn developed the capacity to enjoy the environment which is being disrupted by such growth. Interesting as these sociological and economic views are, however, they express little concern for the ideology *per se*. From the sociological and economic perspective, value-shifts and ideology tell us very little in themselves; it is the economic, class and occupational changes in advanced industrialization which reveal the real nature of ecology.

In conclusion, it has been contended that the attitudes we associate with ecology are not new. They did not suddenly spring upon us in the 1970s with pure radical credentials. Rather, they relate to a subtle and immensely potent conjunction of attitudes to nature which have been present in European thought minimally since the late nineteenth century. Despite their widespread promotion by many different and politically diverse groups throughout the twentieth century, it is the accidental conjunction of circumstances, individuals and events in the 1970s (to the present day) which provided a dynamic refocus for the ecological vocabulary. This act of refocusing has led to some attempts to rule out earlier proponents. Despite the fact that this chapter will deal mainly with the 1970s phenomenon, the net of ecology is purposely widened to incorporate a broader array of political attitudes. Ecology may be a new form of ideological awareness, but it is also a complex form which incorporates, like all ideologies, a variety of often contradictory tendencies.

The Nature of Ecology

There are a number of problems in dealing with ecology as a political ideology which are tied to the comparative newness of the movement (comparative to ideologies such as liberalism or socialism which formed in the immediate post-French Revolution era). First, there is the problem that some in the movement believe that ecology is not an ideology. Ecology is seen to transcend ideology. Second, there is the troublesome relationship between contemporary eco-philosophy and the political ideology and practical movement of ecology. Finally, there is the issue of diversity within the movement, which raises the issue of classifying ecological schools of thought. This section will look at these three problems and then offer a working classification of schools of ecology.

One of the oft-cited slogans of the British and German Greens was 'Neither left nor right, but forwards'. What is really implied by this comment is not a new ideology, but something which goes beyond ideologies altogether. For many, ideologies are part of a package of ideas and values which characterize an age or epoch. As one writer put it: 'Politics as we know it can no longer deal with these [environmental] issues because it shares the very mentality out of which they arose' (Ash 1987, 15–16) – a view which is still shared by many in the movement.[15] Ideologies of all persuasions are simply 'abstract systems, sets of logically consistent ideals ... governing our conduct, pronouncing truth about society'. As such, the writer continues, 'They are more lethal than any physical danger the world holds, because their logic would enslave us' (Ash 1987, 27–8). Thus the task is to go beyond ideology altogether towards an ecological consciousness.

The above view obviously has inspired some in the movement. However, the same idea can be seen in all ideologies – that is, each ideology is often non-ideological for its proponents. It is an obviously convenient lever to establish truthfulness – namely, 'I speak from the realm of objective ecological truth, you are an ideologist.' Without rehearsing the arguments again, contrary to this latter view, much of what we expect to find in an ideology is clearly present in ecology. There are deep accounts of the nature of reality, human nature and the role of humans in the world, evaluations and assessments of the constituents of the best political, economic and social life, and recommendations and persuasive arguments concerning what ought to be done in these spheres. In fact, most of ecology's component parts have been with us in various guises for more than a century. Thus, as will be obvious from its inclusion in this book, ecology *is* an ideology.

Another awkward problem concerns the relation of eco-philosophy to the ideology and political practice of ecology. Andrew Dobson focused on this point, noting that 'The politics of ecology does not follow the same ground rules as its philosophy' (Dobson 1990, 69). If one examines the ecology literature over the last four decades there appear to be several discrete sets of activity going on, which often seem to be only vaguely aware of each other. This is unusual in terms of the previous ideologies that we have examined, where there is a much closer 'fit' between the more sophisticated philosophical thought and the ideological and practical sentiments. There is, on the one hand, an ever-growing amount of eco-philosophy, with sophisticated journals and many books on environmental epistemology, political philosophy and ethics, and, on the other hand, a conglomeration of ideological, economic, New Age, practical pamphlets, books, communities, public policy-makers, green consumers and businesses, and forms of ecological experimentation. Neither tendency appears to show much interest in the other. With the philosophers, this is due to a combination of professional rigour and academic compartmentalization; with the other tendency, it stems from a mixture of motives, most likely focusing on general sentiments like 'fine words don't butter parsnips' – namely, that the philosophers are little concerned with the practice of ecology. This lack of contact is none the less perplexing.[16] An additional problem with the more practice-orientated ecology is a contradiction in itself. On the one hand, there is a tendency in some recent 'practical' literature to identify explicitly (on a fairly superficial level) with one of the rather more controversial wings of eco-philosophy, for example, deep ecology (see Bunyard and Morgan-Grenville eds 1987, 281; Schwarz and Schwarz 1987, 126–7; Tokar 1987, ch. 1). On the other hand, in the same literature, and in actual practice, the key arguments deployed are often 'human prudential' arguments, which pay scant attention to, in fact blatantly contradict, the thrust of deep ecology and even milder forms of eco-philosophy. Ecology, in other words, occasionally justifies itself simply on grounds of human survival. This point will be returned to later.

The third problem is diversity. Whereas many ecologists have recognized the value of diversity in the ecosphere, they are not so happy about its appearance within the ideology itself. There is a powerful desire in the movement for ideological purity and newness, unsullied by contact with other worn-out schemes. Yet it is clear that 'just as there are many socialisms and many liberalisms, so there are many ecologisms' (Dobson 1990, 11). In addition, these ecologisms derive from, and overlap with, many other established schemes of thought. The most tempting strategy is to simplify what is to count as ecology and to rule out stipulatively certain categories. My own categorization will incorporate much that has been ruled out by other commentators.[17]

The ecology movement, both politically and philosophically, has two broad tendencies with a large intermediate component. Let us take the philosophical typology first: at one end of the spectrum we can identify what might be called a 'light anthropocentrist' wing where the main body of arguments stresses that human beings are the sole criterion both of what is valuable and of what can value.[18] The value of nature in this component is usually instrumental in character, namely, that the natural world (including animals) functions or has value only *for* humans or insofar as humans give it value. Nature can still have considerable value here: it can be an early-warning system for us in terms of impending ecological disaster; it supports and nourishes us; we can do valuable experiments on it; we can exercise in it; and we can admire, relax in, be psychologically refreshed and aesthetically moved by its beauty. All of these assets, however, are anthropocentric and instrumentally orientated. It would be no exaggeration to say that much of the political theory on ecology in the last few decades has tended to appear in this dimension (see, for example, Goodin 1992; Baxter 2004; Dryzek 1987 and 2005; Barry 1999 and 2006). Nature without humans is thus largely valueless, although it is worth noting that there are a number of subtle variations of this argument within such theories.[19]

The other end of the philosophical spectrum is the deep ecology wing. This wing is closest to what is sometimes called the 'holistic' perspective. The primary locus of value is not the human individual but the ecosphere as a whole. It is therefore ecocentric as opposed to anthropocentric. Value here is intrinsic usually to the whole ecosphere; it is not given to it by humans and therefore the ecosphere cannot be used instrumentally for human ends. This is the most controversial eco-philosophy wing, whose inspiration came initially from the North American writer Aldo Leopold's

A Sand County Almanac (1968) and later from the philosopher Arne Naess (see Naess 1973 and 1989; Drengson and Inoue 1995; Sessions 1995). This position already contains a number of tendencies: there is J. R. Rodman's emphasis on ecological sensibility; those following the early Naess writings who concentrate on intrinsic value and deep questioning; those who see profound religious (usually Buddhist) implications in deep ecology; and finally those – most notably Warwick Fox – who try to offer a profound new metaphysical philosophy focusing on the need for a fundamental change in human ecological consciousness and self-realization (see Rodman in Scherer and Attig eds 1983).[20] However, in all these tendencies, humans are viewed as just one aspect of the ecosphere.

In between these two components is a broad intermediate category which can be usefully subdivided into two further tendencies. The basic position of the intermediate view is not to accept either pure anthropocentrism or ecocentrism. As indicated, the bulk of contemporary ethical and political eco-philosophy subsists in this category. The two subtendencies of the intermediate position can be called 'moral extensionism' and 'reluctant holism'.[21] A rough-and-ready distinction between these subtendencies is that the former is more inclined towards anthropocentrism, whereas the latter is far less so.

Under the 'moral extensionist' category, the best examples are the various animal liberation and rights arguments of figures such as Peter Singer or Tom Regan – often called 'ethical sentientism'. Singer argues that 'sentience' is the locus of value. Animals are sentient, therefore animals are of value (see Singer 1983, 123; also Regan 1983). It follows that non-sentient life does not possess value. We extend value to creatures because we can reasonably see that they possess the faculty of sentience. Thus plants, rocks or rivers are ruled out. As Singer puts it: 'There is a genuine difficulty in understanding how chopping down a tree can matter *to the tree* if the tree can feel nothing' (Singer 1983, 123).

The 'reluctant holism' wing extends arguments concerning value beyond sentience to a variety of notions: the intrinsic value of nature or the value of the total biosphere including plants. Most reluctant holists are, in other words, prepared to go much further than the moral extensionists in locating value well beyond humans and animals. This is the defining aspect of reluctant holism. Some would also contend that 'wholes' such as the biotic community have value (see Taylor 1986).[22] Yet such wholes do not usually include mountains or rivers. Many of the arguments within reluctant holism employ some form of intrinsic value claim, but most writers here, including J. Baird Callicott, Holmes Rolston III and Paul Taylor, would still want to keep a critical distance from the more absolute holism of deep ecology thinkers such as Arne Naess and Warwick Fox (see Callicott in Scherer and Attig eds 1983; see also Callicott 1984; Rolston 1988).

One final point of clarification, before moving to the political typology, concerns the notion of intrinsic value. It has been implied in some studies that what marks out deep ecology from other types of eco-philosophy is the former's commitment to intrinsic value. Intrinsic value can be formally defined as belonging to something which is valuable in itself, rather than belonging instrumentally (see Attfield 1987, ch. 2). There are two points to be made here in passing. First, there is no one single straightforward intrinsic value argument or claim. There are in fact mutually hostile intrinsic value claims. There are philosophers who see intrinsic value in objects in the world (see Rolston 1988). Others identify intrinsic value with the states and activities of objects, particularly those 'states of affairs' which contribute towards the flourishing of something.[23] Second, intrinsic value arguments are used across the eco-philosophical spectrum; they do not just inhabit the realm of deep ecology. In fact, deep ecologist philosophers, such as Warwick Fox, appear to rest little reliance upon them (Fox 1986 and 1990). On the other hand, intrinsic value theory can be used within anthropocentric ethics to speak of the intrinsic value of human persons as distinct from nature. Its most prevalent use is in the various elements of the intermediate eco-philosophical position, in very different formats, in the work of philosophers such as Holmes Rolston III and Robin Attfield, amongst others.

The question of the classificatory relation between the above philosophical views and the spectrum of political opinions must now be briefly explored. The same broad groupings can be identified as in the philosophical typology. One point that should be mentioned is that the political format in which these groups appear veers across pressure groups to political parties. There is no precise one-to-one correlation between any of these philosophical categories and political forms. Deep ecologists are therefore just as likely to be in parties or pressure groups. Thus, on the one hand, there is a 'light', more reformist wing within ecology. This wing is often divorced from the ecology perspective altogether (see Bookchin 1986b, 27). Within this category we find some of the most traditional environmental groups: for example, conservation groups, preservation, single-issue and recreation groups. In fact, the large bulk of politically successful environmental groups tend to function in this category. Their major appeal is most usually premised on the importance of valuing and retaining some aspect of the environment for the benefit or survival of human beings. In other words, what underpins their appeal is the human prudential anthropocentric arguments. The reformist wing essentially works within existing institutional frameworks and political processes, although its members might resort to some form of public demonstration to make a point.

At the other extreme is the deep ecology wing. Its appeal is to the Arcadian mentality, as Donald Worster calls it (Worster 1977). Deep ecologists usually want a total value-change in society – where the whole perception of the world and nature changes. In this sense there are a number of what have been called 'ecotopias' lurking in the wings. As argued in the philosophical typology above, there are a variety of tendencies here. There are those who believe in setting up alternative communities based on religious or secular principles and utilizing alternative techologies. They have a very distinctive social philosophy premised on concepts such as 'bioregionalism', which we will come to. This area has also attracted support from a small group of eco-feminists who see the deep ecology society as the most likely to realize non-patriarchy.[24] More controversially there is a somewhat forgotten nationalist and *völkisch* component which attracted enthusiasts earlier in the century. Haeckel's philosophical monism (and those who utilized variants of it) conforms most closely to the deep model. The arguments of fascism and national socialism concerning the attachment of humans to land and place, examined in chapter 6, resonate within this perspective.[25]

Finally, and most controversially, we can clearly identify a violent and extremist wing within the deep ecologists. The Earth First! movement, originating in the USA, but also having affiliates in many other countries, takes some of the deep arguments to their logical but absurd conclusions. Nature becomes more important than human beings. Wilderness becomes an ultimate value. Industrialization is viewed as a foul corruption of the planet. Many Earth First! followers consequently looked with benign tolerance on the mass spread of AIDS, famine and the possible reintroduction of a reinvigorated smallpox virus as the ecosphere reasserting a natural balance on the planet. Others have advocated policies of compulsory mass human sterilization. Some Earth First! followers have also engaged in direct action (what has become known colloquially as 'ecotage'): for example, spiking selected trees with long nails so as to mutilate loggers with chain saws and thus to deter future logging. Critics of this tendency, even within the ecology movement, have labelled it (and deep ecology) as eco-brutalism (see Bookchin 1992).

The intermediate position again attracts a diversity of political views. However, the gap between the light reformist anthropocentric wing and the intermediate is very narrow. Another point to note here is that the intermediate position is differentiated from the reformist wing not so much by strategy as by a stronger overt ideological commitment to moderate non-anthropocentrism. Furthermore, there is no precise 'fit' between the intermediate ideological/political views and the intermediate philosophical views, whereas there is a fairly close correlation between deep philosophers and deep practitioners.

The breakdown between views on the political dimension has led to the reappearance of some well-established ideological beliefs. There is, for example, a growing interest in what has become known as 'eco-capitalism'. This sees the market as the best device to control environmental problems (see Anderson and Leal 2001). In addition, following the work of Rudolf Bahro, there have been vigorous discussions of eco-socialism. The eco-socialists have two main views on ecology which parallel socialist attitudes to liberalism. On the one hand, eco-socialism comes to destroy bourgeois ecology (understood as a reformist middle-class and hopelessly utopian phenomenon).[26] The other view is that eco-socialism comes to fulfil, or bring to fruition, the radical materialist destiny of ecology. Eco-socialism also divides over the future of society, whether it moves towards an enlightened eco-socialist state or towards a non-state pluralist/commune socialism (see Pepper 1993; Eckersley 2004, ch. 3).

Another 'intermediate political position' is social ecologism, focusing on the work of the communist anarchist Murray Bookchin. As argued in chapter 5, this position tries to ally ecological concerns with traditional communist anarchism – a tradition which boasts Peter Kropotkin as an illustrious forebear. The ideal structure or 'affinity group' (for Bookchin) settles predictably upon the traditional democratic commune idea.

The social ecologist position appears to solve rather nicely many of the problems of 'actual' life and organization present within ecological thought, by feeding into a well-established tradition of thought. Thus it often provides the focus for discussions of what ecology actually implies in political terms. Ironically and puzzlingly, despite

Bookchin's open and viciously expressed contempt for deep ecology (which he calls either eco-fascism or mystical 'eco-la-la'), the anarchistic democratic commune nestling within a bioregion appears also to form a model of organization within the deep category. In a slightly more authoritarian format (which was not unknown to anarchy) the commune is ironically a model for some more nationalistic ecologists (Goldsmith 1972).

There are certain themes affirmed by philosophical and political ecologists of all types. Most assert, in some shape or form, the systematic interdependence of species and the environment. Although many have a very particular focus, they usually think in terms of the whole ecosystem. There is also a much less damaging and more positive attitude to nature than is found in all other ideologies. In addition there is a tendency to be, minimally, sceptical about the supreme position of human beings on the planet. Further, there is a shared general anxiety about what humans, via industrial civilization, are actually doing to the planet. As in previous chapters I will discuss many of these themes through the categories of human nature, politics and economics, trying to bring out the varying responses from the ecological schools.

Nature and Human Nature

The concept of human nature in ecologism cannot be easily discussed apart from the notion of nature in general, partly because of the philosophical centrality of the debate over anthropocentrism and non-anthropocentrism. The notion of nature in Western thought has oscillated between hero and villain. The idea of the villain is one which many ecologists see characterizing pure anthropocentric thought. Nature in this reading is regarded as valueless, but still a potentially unruly and threatening entity, something which must be conquered, colonized, manipulated and exploited for human ends. Eco-feminists associated this attitude with patriarchical views of nature (see Plumwood 1993). This adversarial view of nature is one that most political ecologists see as the 'world-view' of the natural sciences up to this century. Bacon, Hobbes, Descartes and the Enlightenment make frequent appearances in ecological writings as the perpetrators of this attitude.

The hero, or at least the benign, view of nature, which derives from the later nineteenth century, has two dimensions, extrinsic and intrinsic. The 'extrinsic view' would contend that nature is valuable for us, but that it is we who include nature in our moral constituency. Nature can be a valuable resource, but it is we who value it as such. It can even be judged to be intrinsically valuable, but only in relation to human beings. Thus nature becomes a hero because we value our survival and flourishing. In this reading, nature becomes valuable because of the value of human nature. This view is characteristic of many reformist and environmentalist groups.

The second or 'intrinsic view' (which can be found in the political intermediate and deep ecology wings) is that nature has an inner importance. For many political ecologists this intrinsic argument is indissolubly linked with the claim that humanity is tied to the totality of nature. Human nature is thus understood within the context of the totality of nature. Humans must therefore learn to subsist by way of nature and not against it. The most popular idea which encapsulates this linkage, for some political ecologists, is James Lovelock's Gaia hypothesis (Lovelock 1979).[27] Lovelock, as a working scientist, put forward the hypothesis that the earth might be considered as a single self-regulating superorganism. For Lovelock, the existence of the atmosphere did not create living things; rather, living things, from bacteria onwards, created the atmosphere of the earth, merely by living. The fertility of the soil, the temperature of the atmosphere, the amount of oxygen we breathe, all are related to the complex interaction of organisms. Despite considerable scientific doubts concerning the hypothesis – in fact it might simply be interpreted, minimally, as a thesis concerning the demonstrable importance of diverse organisms for the balanced ecosystems of the planet – it has none the less become, for a time, a virtual talisman for sections of the political ecology movement. This has declined now in the 2000s, especially since Lovelock has presented a much darker and gloomier thesis on the 'revenge of Gaia' (Lovelock 2007).

However, Gaia for a time, in the 1980s and 1990s, much to Lovelock's deep consternation, was spiritualized. Not only was the hypothesis seen to demonstrate our interdependence with the ecosphere (again this could still be read in anthropocentric and instrumentalist terms), but it shifted humans from the centre-stage, and affirmed an ecological equality with the totality of organisms. In more mundane terms, as one writer commented: 'The pragmatic strength of the Gaia hypothesis is that it offers to combine environmental science with morality. It thus seems to provide the kind of authority which … a more routine dependence on science fails to deliver' (Yearley 1991, 146).

One reading of the latter intrinsic view sees certain values within nature itself. If humans are simply part of nature, then they are equal to other species. This doctrine takes on the garb of a central principle in deep ecology, namely, 'biospherical or biocentric egalitarianism' (see Fox 1990, 118; and Devall and Sessions 1985, 67). An additional confirmation of this point for some writers is that, apart from humans, nature embodies no authority hierarchies or stratification. A stable ecosphere tolerates and in fact fosters biological equality and diversity of species. This stable sustainable harmony, equality and tolerance of diversity of species are often viewed as a natural morality by some ecological writers. In other words, the qualities of harmony and tolerance are deciphered as natural values for the human species to cultivate. Some interpret primal societies as cultivating such a natural morality.[28]

There are a number of complex problems with the intrinsic view and its linkage with the Gaia idea. Many eco-socialists have complained that the notions of nature, the environment and human nature are unduly narrow. As Michael Redclift comments: 'When we refer to "the environment" … we are referring to something which has been produced by history through struggles and exploitation' (Redclift in Weston ed. 1986, 86; Pepper 1993). Much of our environment and nature (including human nature) is causally related to poverty, ill-health, alienating work and simply the need to survive under an oppressive system (see Martinez-Alier 2003; Kovel 2007). Certain ecologists are therefore seen, in this latter context, to be in danger of romanticizing nature and relating all our problems to personal values. We are part of nature, but nature reflects the depredations of our social and economic arrangements.

Environmental problems are therefore, as much as anything, political and economic problems spawned by capitalism.

Another problem relates to Lovelock's description of Gaia as a self-regulating organism. If humans pollute the atmosphere and poison themselves, then Gaia will adapt over millennia. It does not matter whether humans massively pollute the planet, die out as a species or shepherd resources and survive, the superorganism is indifferent. In this sense the argument is serviceable neither for ecology to use against polluters nor for the importance of the survival of the human species. There is therefore no necessary ethical significance here; the Gaia theory is simply an observation of a natural process.

Most seriously of all, it is difficult to see what notion of human nature is derived from the intrinsic view and its linkage with the Gaia theory. If humans are simply part of nature, in the more 'indifferent' position of Gaia, then presumably we are free, like all other animals, to utilize the world around us. If it is in our nature to exploit and if we therefore destroy ourselves, the universe will not even blink. Yet not many political ecologists would accept this view. Usually a moral component is imported, most significantly our survival as a species, but more often the message is that as a species we can, via our self-consciousness, stand back and moderate our activities. As a species we are partially removed from the normal functioning of biological evolution.[29] We might be asked at this point in time to act in more ecologically caring ways and not to despoil our environment. The assumption behind this latter position is that qualitatively we are *not* quite part of nature. As a species we are uniquely distinct, although the Gaia view would still appear to want to deny this. Unless we imbue Gaia with a spiritual purpose and ontology, we appear caught in its indifference. If we step back from it, we either affirm directly the value of the survival of our own species, or we look for ways in which we can ensure an ethical response to nature. Both positions appear to assume that the human species is qualitatively distinct from nature. One of the many implications of this discussion is that there are potentially a number of different accounts of both nature and human nature present in ecology, the debates between which remain unresolved.

The Political Dimension of Ecologism

One central difficulty of ecologism is the variety of political visions present in the movement. Again it is tempting to delimit the study and identify one particular tendency as the key: for example, the social ecologists' commune. There is also the problem of the public and private faces of ecology, namely, the private affirmation of beliefs and the coincidental public actions which appear to contradict them. Ecology is not alone in this; most ideologies manifest this internal tension.

One of the problems which has affected the judgement of the political dimension of ecologism since the 1970s has been its close affiliation predominantly with socialism and, less significantly, with anarchism. This affiliation with both tendencies has muddied the waters concerning political beliefs. The problem is intensified by the fact that, particularly with socialism, we face a number of different schools, often with contradictory beliefs. In one of the socialist interpretations, for example, Bahro contended that Western industrialized, state-based societies were part of the environmental problem. Humanity, he insisted, had reached the point where it had to 'find a new stable life-form'; he went on to describe this as the '"reconstruction of God" – in other words, the kind of regulation which can only come from the recreation of spiritual equilibrium, within those levels of nature neglected by Marx'. Later in the text he noted that 'a solution to problems is best found in small groups', and mentioned the model of the Benedictine order of monks (Bahro 1984, 221–2). Other eco-socialists predictably have found this an unsatisfactory and utopian notion. Thus, Martin Ryle drew a vigorous distinction between the decentralist anti-statism of 'Greens', as distinct from the enlightened statism of eco-socialists. To deal adequately with multinational companies, penalize polluters, and the like, ecology *needed* an 'ecologically progressive "strong State" ... to challenge the often remote and autocratic centres of power which now determine the economic fate of entire communities' (Ryle 1988, 69). The debate about an eco-state has clearly been a continuing and important theme for ecological writers to the present day (see also Dryzek et al. 2003; Eckersley 2004; Hurrell in Dobson and Eckersley eds 2006).[30]

As mentioned already, Bookchin's nostrums rely heavily upon the traditions of communist anarchism. In *The Ecology of Freedom* (1982), Bookchin, like his intellectual forebear Kropotkin, finds his eco-anarchist promptings from within a more benign conception of nature. Nature is seen to be egalitarian and non-hierarchical. Bookchin links these ideas directly with the communist anarchist perspective, which has close affinities with the pluralist/commune socialism of figures such as Bahro – although he would have no doubt given Bahro's Benedictine theme short shrift.

The upshot of these eco-socialist and eco-anarchist reflections is simply to add to the perplexity of what ecologism presents as a political perspective. The picture is further clouded by mutual recriminations. Social ecologists attack the deep ecologists for engaging in mystical claptrap. Deep ecologists, amongst others, attack the eco-socialists as still at root being tied to industrial growth, therefore being part of the problem. Reformist environmentalists attack the social ecologists as re-dreaming the hopelessly nostalgic utopias of nineteenth-century anarchy. Before moving on to a more systematic presentation of the political visions within ecology, it is worth mentioning that there are still some formal common political concerns within the ecology movement, though responses to these differ markedly.

There is a strong sense in which many ecologists are probably as concerned about individual values and activities as they are with politics in general. Individuals are viewed as possessing varying levels of responsibility, but individual values are still seen to count in many significant ways. The stress on individual values and autonomy tends to make political ecology less likely to accept materialist accounts, although biology and evolutionary materialism do still have a firm foothold in ecology (usually underpinned by some implicit moral pattern). The ecology perspective also tends to combine, uniquely, both respect for local autonomy in communities and a global message. In addition, all ecological schools are concerned to raise questions about the limits of economic growth in industrialized societies. This in turn leads to critical reflections on consumption patterns, production in industry and agriculture, energy use and the nature of technology, the concept of work and, finally, demographic patterns and population growth. These concerns are common to all ecologists. They all focus on the central theme of a *sustainable society*, one which will not damage, but will exist harmoniously with, the ecosystem. The responses to this theme vary widely.

It is difficult at this historical phase of the ecology movement to produce a definitive typology, yet there appear at present to be three distinct political visions at work within the ideology. Adopting the terminology of William Ophuls, these can be called the maximum-sustainable society, the frugal-sustainable society and the eco-anarchist commune (Ophuls in Pirages ed. 1977; also Ophuls 1977). The last vision is associated primarily with the work of Bookchin and communist anarchism. This will not be discussed since it would be duplicating what has been examined in chapter 5; also, many of the decentralist ideas of social ecologism appear within the second vision. The focus of the discussion will therefore be on the first two.

The maximum-sustainable vision for Ophuls denotes 'a society that aims to exist in equilibrium with its environment, but that is still based on such fundamental "modern" values as the dominance of man over nature, the primacy of material and other hedonistic wants and so on' (Ophuls in Pirages ed. 1977, 162–3). My own use of this term differs from that of Ophuls insofar as the ideas of dominance over nature and hedonistic wants do not figure as either central or necessary elements. What I take this idea to cover is the conglomerate of ecological and environmental groups who subscribe to the belief that the present nation state and its legal structure, modified to a greater or lesser degree by ecological consciousness, is adequate and in fact necessary to the task of meeting the requirements of ecological ideology. This is the most notable and most successful face of ecology. It is characterized by a strong dose of realism and tends to soft-pedal on most issues, partly out of the need to gain agreement from electorates or institutions, and, in fact, in many cases it has been successful electorally.

One of the more hopeful signs here is a realization that ecological concerns are linked with political and constitutional questions and indeed questions of human rights for certain theorists (see Hayward 2005). In fact ecological reform might well be dependent, more so than many have realized, on constitutional ecological change within contemporary states, a change involving not only the extension of accountability on limitations and the exercise of executive authority, but also much closer and regularized scrutiny of the links between governments and industry.

This vision encompasses both pressure groups and political parties. It also includes, somewhat paradoxically, the various political and philosophical dimensions of the ideology. It can, in other words, be found in weak anthropocentrism and strong non-anthropocentrism. One would not expect to find it among the social ecologists (eco-anarchists), although it is clearly an important motif within eco-reformist arguments and for some eco-socialists. It also forms a background to eco-capitalism. It has, in other words, a fairly wide appeal. Jonathan Porritt, though in some writings adhering (in appearance) to a deep ecological value position, criticizes the eco-anarchists for their 'chronically unrealistic escapism'. He maintains that the visions of such people 'have often been rather elitist and their reluctance to dirty their hands in the muck and grime of contemporary politics is regrettable' (Porritt in Goldsmith and Hildyard eds 1986, 345). Despite still adhering to the deep ecological notion of a sea-change in values, he contends that it is necessary to work within the political system as it stands. Porritt, like many others, remains clearly committed to established electoral and pressure group politics and a reformist agenda.[31]

To dream of immediate small-scale non-state societies is thus to live in a private comfortable dream world. Other writers, particularly some of the eco-socialists, appear more confident than Porritt about a progressive and strong eco-state. A state is needed not only to deal with the massive problems of poverty and redistribution (which are intimately related to the whole ecological problem for most eco-socialists), but also to take on the vast powerful structures of multinational corporations (Eckersley 2004; Hayward 2005). It is also worth noting here that the more statist and reformist dimension of the ecology movement have become much more focused on specific issues in the last decade. Many of these imply the need for a strong constitutional ecological-state. In many ways the debate about the eco-state has divided between reformist socialist and social liberal factions of the ecology movement. If anything the social liberal dimension has been the most successful dimension in the 2000s. For historical reasons, socialism (and thus eco-socialism) has declined as a viable ideological option since the late 1990s. This has, in consequence, led to a spate of writings focusing on the relation between ecology and conventional social liberal concerns: for example, social justice, civil and human rights, active citizenship and deliberative conceptions of democracy. All these issues have been under intense discussion over the last decade, primarily as integral to a social liberal vision of a constitutional ecological state (see, for example, Gillroy 2002; Minteer and Taylor eds 2002; Baxter 2004; Bullard 2005; Dryzek 2005; Dobson 1998, 1999 and 2006; Schlosberg 2007). It is worth noting, though, that there are still many unresolved difficulties with the extension of terms like justice, citizenship, rights or democracy to the environment.[32]

One final, much smaller group are the eco-capitalists (Elkington and Hailes 1988; Elkington and Burke 1989; Anderson and Leal 2001). Again, this perspective sees the state forming a minimalist rule-of-law background to the basic procedures of the market and consumer choice to protect the environment. By definition this perspective views the state as having an important but strictly limited role. Eco-capitalism, in effect, utilizes the more classical liberal and right-wing libertarian vision of the minimal state, as discussed in chapter 2. It also places a tremendous weight upon role of the free market as the way of resolving economic, political and environmental issues. It should be noted that many critics, including more social liberal environmentalists, see this conception of classical liberalism and capitalist free markets as undermining ecology.[33]

The second political vision – of the frugal-sustainable society – is most characteristic of the deep ecologists. It is a society devoted to what Erich Fromm called a 'being' as opposed to a 'having' society (see Fromm 1979). Those who propound this 'being' vision claim that it is based on a total value-shift, a new renaissance or paradigm change in the whole of humanity (see Robertson 1985, 76–9; also Spretnak and Capra 1986, xvi, 29). Ophuls describes this as a relatively low-energy throughput society. It would be a more labour-intensive society, with little emphasis on material consumption, and encouragement of personal self-sufficiency and voluntary personal frugality. This vision most importantly places a heavy emphasis on the virtue or personal moral responsibilities of the individual. Ophuls observes that it represents a return to a classical type of politics. He remarks that 'The picture of the frugal society that emerges resembles something like a return to the city-state form of civilization, but on a much higher and more sophisticated technological base.'[34] The difference from the classical *polis* is that Ophuls admits that a macroauthority would be needed to prevent conflict. Thus 'local politics would have to exist within a regional or global empire of some kind' (Ophuls in Pirages ed. 1977, 168). It is certain that deep ecologists would not agree with the notion of an eco-empire. In fact, this clearly separates Ophuls's rather stark semi-authoritarian vision from deep ecology. Some of the deep ecologists appear more enamoured of the idea of re-establishing fragmented tribal cultures. Thus one writer, deploying the concept of bioregionalism, identified one of its positive attributes as leading to the '"breakdown of nations" into self-sustaining, cooperatively-relating, ecologically-scaled entities' (Tokar 1987, 31).

The notions of frugality, self-reliance and voluntary simplicity carry a number of implications. In economics the call comes for Schumacher's vision of the Buddhist system, premised on meeting human need and caring for the environment (see Schumacher 1973, ch. 4). This would be a society where energy would come from renewable sources such as the sun and wind, and all non-renewable energy would be conserved and recycled. Technologies would be appropriate and not harmful. For many, this frugal society implies a strong spiritual dimension, usually of either a Buddhistic or a pantheistic form, which requires respect for the ecosphere. Again the principle of non-violence often figures as an adjunct to the Buddhist perspective (Henning 2002). It also implies a massive personal reassessment of our everyday activities; as two supporters comments: 'Living simply is not just a question of keeping paper bags and making compost; it implies an awareness of what products we are using, what food we are eating, how it was produced and who was helped or exploited by our use' (Schwarz and Schwarz 1987, 207).[35] There is also an altered concept of work, moving towards what James Robertson referred to as an 'ownwork' society (Robertson 1985).

There are a number of stipulations on size and geographical location laid down in this vision by writers such as Edward Goldsmith and Kirkpatrick Sale. To use the vocabulary: a society needs to respect 'ecological carrying capacity', people need to 'dwell in place' and it needs to be 'human scale'. As Goldsmith argued: 'It is probable that only in the small community can a man or woman be an individual. In today's large agglomerations he is merely an isolate.' Goldsmith suggested neighbourhoods of no more than five hundred individuals, within communities of approximately five thousand and regions of five hundred thousand. Kirkpatrick Sale suggested communities of five hundred to a thousand and larger units of five thousand to ten thousand (Goldsmith 1972, 51, 53; Sale 1985, 62–4).

On the question of geographical location, the most significant concept developed is that of the *bioregion*. Bioregions are not national, ethnic, administrative or overtly political units, but rather ecologically and biologically sustainable units. A bioregion can be defined as 'an area of land defined, not by political boundaries ... but by the natural, biological and geological features that cast the real identity of a place'. Mountain ranges, rivers, vegetation, weather patterns, soil, plants and fauna characterize a bioregion and replace political/state boundaries. Within such a bioregion there is a sustainable ecosystem where humans can 'live in place' without damaging their environment, as long as they 'strive to create self-supporting ways of life that fully complement the flows and cycles of nature that already exist there' (Tokar 1987, 27). Not only do bioregional ideas benefit the environment by linking our social, economic and political life with a natural self-sustaining entity; they also link the human being intimately with nature. Some writers make further subdivisions between local watersheds and mountain ranges. Kirkpatrick Sale offers a more complex division, again comprised of ecoregions, georegions and morphoregions (see Sale 1985). Such communities would, according to their proponents, encourage cultural diversity and autonomy.

A number of implications are seen to follow from the above idea. There is a strong suggestion that such small-scale communities would be characterized by grass-roots participatory, as opposed to representative, democracy (Spretnak and Capra 1986, 35; Bahro 1986, 222; Bookchin 1986b, 216; Tokar 1987, 98). The idea of decentralized public participatory assemblies meeting within bioregions to decide on policy appears as the central motif.

Outside of this participatory democratic vision there are other, somewhat darker aspects. One of the suggestions of bioregionalists is for economic autarky and regional self-sufficiency. This obviates the need for any trade except on absolute necessities. Trade encourages the satisfaction of unnecessary 'wants' or luxuries as opposed to needs, invites dependence on others outside one's bioregion, and is profoundly wasteful of time and fuel resources. On the question of wasted resources, some, such as Bahro and Ophuls, suggest that we travel too much anyway, often for frivolous purposes. The bioregional society, for some exponents, is one which will not tolerate scarce resources being frittered away on pleasurable travel. Passenger aircraft use vast amounts of non-renewable fuels to transport people often for no other purpose than personal hedonism.[36] The frugal society will thus be a limited-mobility society, where people will spend their lives in one place, cultivating their own bioregional community loyalties. This latter idea also has strong communitarian, nationalist and conservative ecological resonances (see essays by Scruton, Eckersley and de-Shalit in Dobson and Eckersley eds 2006).

One implication of the above argument (much discussed in the 1970s and 1980s) was that the human population must be kept under strict control for the bioregional idea to work, and this gave rise to the term 'neo-Malthusianism'. As Goldsmith remarked, 'Clearly we must go all out for the "unlikely event" of achieving the replacement-sized family (on average about two children per couple) *throughout the world by the end of the century*' (Goldsmith 1972, 48). He suggested there could be massive publicity and advertising campaigns concerning population levels, in relation to food and quality of life. This could be supplemented by free contraception, sterilization and abortion. Finally, research should be funded in all areas of demography and population control (Goldsmith 1972, 49). Others made suggestions concerning the legal restriction on couples having more than the prescribed number of children, in the form of 'baby licences', and tax incentives for having fewer children.[37] Finally, there were also suggestions for much tougher immigration control.

The above vision of the frugal society has a number of possible implications. One impression often given is that it is a democratic and egalitarian vision. This is where the strong affinity to communist anarchism can be observed. However, it is far from clear that all its proponents favour democracy and freedom. Goldsmith's ideas may be legitimately described as fostering an authoritarian, not a democratic, vision. The long transition to a genuine commune life will require the curtailment of many freedoms. Goldsmith notes that 'Legislation and the operation of police forces and the courts will be necessary to reinforce this restraint' (Goldsmith 1972, 50). In addition, the suggestions for controlling population from the neo-Malthusian wing would certainly be hard to reconcile with autonomy and equality. Goldsmith perhaps unwittingly fed into a more traditional nationalistic or conservative ecology with roots earlier in the twentieth century (see Bramwell 1989).

Even within the more egalitarian perspective, the fostering of diversity would certainly not tolerate bioregions which opted, for example, for slavery or infanticide. In other words, despite the overt commitment to tolerant diversity, there still appears to be a lurking demand for consensus underneath. There is therefore no necessary correlation between bioregionalism and decentralized communes, on the one hand, or democracy and equality, on the other hand. It is perfectly ecologically feasible to have authoritarian as well as more egalitarian communes.

One major unresolved difficulty of the frugal society which appears in all its formats is the question of an over-arching authority, such as the state, to resolve potential conflict. Ophuls, as mentioned earlier, envisages some form of eco-empire. Others express deep disquiet at any over-arching structure. One writer thus comments that 'the direction of Green politics is local life – together, conversely, with the end of the Nation State as we know it'; he continues: 'The Nation State is the political expression of a dualistic cast of mind, and all its disjunctions are inimical to ecology' (Ash 1987, 53–4). For Goldsmith, self-conscious individualism *per se* and central-ized statism went hand in hand. Both undermined the ecological small-scale com-munity. This point was also emphasized from an eco-socialist perspective in the writings of Bahro, and from a more radical deep egalitarian perspective in those of Tokar, Spretnak, Capra, Robertson and Sessions. However, it is clear from other aspects of the eco-socialist and social liberal wings that some would conversely like to tie certain facets of a more frugal vision to an ecologically sensitive state.

This unresolved question of the state in ecological thought raises difficult ques-tions concerning political and moral values. How is a socially responsible policy of egalitarianism, social justice and freedom to be guaranteed in a non-state situation? The concepts of freedom, citizenship, democracy and justice in ecological thought remain conceptually problematic in virtually all spheres of ecological thought. Bioregional anti-statist ecologists appear to run into the same series of problems as many anarchists, namely, how to guarantee important values without resorting to violence or threat. Some stress appears to be laid on changes in human nature or, alternatively, on persuasive reasoning. Surely, though, it might legitimately be argued that many necessary ecologically beneficial functions would be far better performed by a sensitive rule-of-law state, than haggled over by fragmented bio-regional assemblies?

A New Economics?

One of the key economic themes of many in the ecology movement is the insistence that the major economic problem we face is neither capitalism nor the command economy but industrialism. As Porritt comments:

> By 'industrialism', I mean adherence to the belief that human needs can only be met through *permanent* expansion of the process of production and consumption – regardless of the damage done to the planet, to the rights of future generations. … The often unspoken values of industrialism are premised on the notion that material gain is quite simply more important to more people than anything else. (see Porritt in Goldsmith and Hildyard eds 1986, 344–5)

The battle against industrialism is therefore one that is against a 'super-ideology', which subsumes all the other major ideologies. For Porritt, and many like him, the struggle against this super-ideology takes place as much in the realm of values as in technical questions concerning economics. This form of analysis is severely qualified by eco-socialists, however, who deny, either from Bahro's commune position or from Ryle's statist position, that socialism is automatically committed to industrialism. Further, writers such as Weston and Pepper argue that the real problem is capitalism, not industrialism, and that the talk about values is more or less irrelevant (see Pepper 1984, 5; also Pepper 1993; Kovel 2007).

Most ecological writers would be in moderate agreement that industrialism and capitalism are committed to the idea of economic growth. Growth is the panacea for social and economic problems. Yet for ecologists, growth is the root of the problems of destruction in the environment, loss of community and social alienation. Over the nineteenth century, in the industrializing economies, growth was possible and produced a cornucopia of rewards for certain societies. However, because growth produced some worthwhile goods for an historically short period, this does not mean that more growth is always desirable (Spretnak and Capra 1986, 78). In the main, the systematic expression of 'economic growth' and the related ignorance concerning ecological problems can be found in most orthodox classical economic theories.

Industrialism and classical economic theories for many ecologists (although not all) are committed to a false and narrow conception of human beings – rational economic man – where money, the maximization of the satisfaction of interests, and profits are the measures of all things. Cost and benefit in classical economic theory appear to have taken no account, until recently, of the benefits of clear water, a stable atmosphere, a predictable climate. These are accorded no economic value. In the words of Edward Goldsmith and Nicholas Hildyard: 'It does not appear to have occurred to economists that if our activities interfere too radically with the workings of Nature, then Nature might no longer be capable of providing the benefits we now take for granted and upon which our survival depends' (Goldsmith and Hildyard eds 1986, 25). The authors describe this as a 'cock-eyed view of the world'. Conversely, the 'New Economics', as it is often referred to in the ecology literature, is 'based upon a different perception of reality itself, it embodies a change in outlook as fundamental as, say, the Copernican revolution in astronomy' (Ekins ed. 1986, xviii; see also Daly and Cobb 1990).

One of the central arguments of this new economics is that classical economic theories assume that growth can go on infinitely. But in a world where resources, such as non-renewable fuels, are finite, how *can* growth be infinite? Fossil fuels are ephemeral and will probably quite quickly be exhausted. As Dennis Pirages suggests, 'Most seem to agree that petroleum and natural gas will become scarce shortly after the year 2010' (Pirages ed. 1977, 3). He contends that the majority of the industrialized world faces the ending of cheap non-renewable fuel. Yet, for Pirages, the modernization of all societies, especially the Third World countries, is still measured in terms of the faulty logic of economic growth. Instead of feeding their populations, these countries race, with International Monetary Fund encouragement, to expand exports. Local needs, a clean environment, healthy citizens, are simply ignored in the economic equation. These are not included as indicators of economic success.

In summary, growth-orientated economies cannot go on using finite resources. Technological innovations cannot solve the problems indefinitely, although appropriate small-scale technologies are seen as one aspect of the solution. Technological advances can only postpone the problems. Governments and their bureaucracies are often seen in this context to be hand-in-glove with industry, effectively controlling information on environmental collapse through the multiple techniques of secrecy, scientific whitewashing and public relations campaigns. For many ecologists, a radical change is needed to our whole conception of the economic world. This is the root of the ongoing TOES (The Other Economic Summit), devoted to promulgating an alternative economic strategy. In sum, a sustainable economic order must replace a growth-orientated economic order.

The visions of what constitutes a sustainable order vary (see Sagoff 1988). These play upon two variations of a post-industrial society. They also cross-cut the various component elements of ecologism. One vision poses a decentralized, commune, agrarian and non-state order as the ideal. The other envisions a technologically sophisticated, affluent ecological state order.

The eco-socialist answer, as argued, varies according to the socialist affiliation. Bahro put his faith in frugal decentralized commune life where needs and wants were reduced to the bare minimum. Martin Ryle, on the other hand, despite questioning growth in a fairly conventional manner, contends that the new economics of the TOES group does not go far enough in its attitude to large corporations. As Ryle notes, if we reject the ideas of the older economics, 'we must be prepared to confront the institutions which embody and enforce them' (Ryle 1988, 46). Ryle's views rely largely on an eco-state to perform this task. Variations on this view also appears in writers such as Weston, Pepper, Eckersley, Dobson and John Barry, amongst others.

Pepper and Weston, though, are far more vitriolic in their criticism of mainstream deep Greens, accusing them of putting up a 'smokescreen' around market-based capitalism (Weston introduction to 1986; Pepper 1984 and 1993).

There are, in fact, mainstream converts to the view that capitalism has got the answers. Elkington and Burke, particularly, contended that although market capitalism may have been part of the problem, with the help of green capitalists it could be part of the solution (Elkington and Burke 1989, 23: also Pearce et al. 1989). The authors predicted that the 1990s would be the green decade, when consumers would demand products that were environmentally friendly. The environment would thus become 'a major new competitive area for business' (Elkington and Burke 1989, 239). The authors argued that, instead of engaging in Luddite sentimentalism towards industry, we should carefully distinguish not between a sustainable economy and an industrial growth economy, but rather between sustainable and unsustainable growth. The former is one which, via the market, adjusts to recycling, cleaner technologies, infrastructural investment and alternative energy – all generated by the demands of the green consumer. The Body Shop and supermarket chains such as Tesco and Sainsburys are held up as typical of this new trend. The authors invoked this as a 'new age capitalism' (Elkington and Burke 1989, 252). To some extent, some of these predictions in the 2000s have actually come about, although it is highly questionable that these have been solely driven by consumers. Acknowledgement of ecological risk and profound anxiety over climate change have actually pushed many states, after Kyoto particularly, into legislative ecological action and public investment in greener technologies, a trend which will no doubt accelerate over the next few decades.[38]

The other side of the post-industrial and economic vision is that of the decentralized commune – the more frugal society. James Robertson describes this as a SHE economy (Sane, Humane, Ecological) as opposed to a HE economy (Hyper-Expansionist) (Robertson 1985, 5). This SHE vision has a number of component elements. It tries to redefine most of the major economic concepts such as demand, supply, production, consumption and economies of scale in ecological terms. Thus, whereas in much classical economic theory humans are regarded as consumers or producers, the new economics puts humans and their total physical, moral and spiritual welfare first (Ekins ed. 1986, 44ff). Taking their cue from Schumacher's and Fromm's work, the new economists regard morality as integral to economics. The qualitative goals of a satisfying and meaningful life are seen as more important than quantitative values. Instead of economic growth, human development and the satisfaction of physical, social, economic and cultural needs are regarded as more significant. Needs are seen as being 'of absolutely central significance to the New Economics' (Ekins ed. 1986, 55). Needs extend beyond those of physical survival and include cultural well-being.

Formal contractual relations are replaced by mutual ethical concerns between people. Intuitive sympathetic concern would supplant intellectual and rational distance. Highly specialized occupations would be displaced by the all-round competence and self-reliance of citizens. Large-scale and destructive technologies would be replaced by human-scale and relatively harmless ones.

The concept of work changes radically in this vision. New concepts of employment are fostered. Writers such as James Robertson and Guy Dauncey suggested the development of informal 'ownwork' to replace the concept of formal employment, something that most exponents see as applicable as much to Third World as to industrialized societies (Robertson 1983 and 1985; Dauncey 1981 and 1983). We should not confuse, according to this argument, *work* with a *job*. Work needs to be rethought, localized and linked with many other occupations, including housework, growing your own vegetables, sharing a job or doing DIY. As Robertson comments: 'Ownwork means activity which is purposeful and important and which people organize and control for themselves. It may be either paid or unpaid' (Robertson 1985, x). The vision here is of a total radical shake-up of the way our whole society views work. It is also a vision of self-reliance, self-help and decentralization, labour-intensive, localized and small-scale in terms of technology (Robertson 1985, xii; Ekins ed. 1986, 169). For most writers on this theme it means the extension of workers' cooperatives.

One other strategy which pervades most of the formulations of the frugal vision is the replacement of welfare benefits with what is generally called a 'Basic Income Scheme', or at least some form of minimum income scheme. The idea in fact goes back to the 1920s and Major C. H. Douglas, although Henry George's theories also appear to be inspirational for some writers (Robertson 1985, 175). In the post-war era it has been considered by social policy analysts outside the ecology movement (see van Parijs 1995). Basic Income ideas suggest a national wage to replace welfare benefits – financed from administrative savings and higher taxation, particularly (for ecologists) from those who pollute or use non-renewable resources – to be paid to all citizens over a certain age, regardless of work. The Basic Income would create a sense of independence for the majority of citizens. Work would be 'socially' expected from citizens; however, with changes in the concept of work, this could be performed in any number of contexts. This point is also tied, in some writings, to schemes for localized banking (and occasionally currencies) and marked changes in taxation, usually entailing much greater redistribution of wealth.

Wealth in this theory is measured not just by monetary values or capital interests but also by the health and well-being of people. As Robertson comments:

> The idea that the development of healthier people, and the creation of a social and physical environment which enables people to be healthy, might be treated as productive investment in a society's capital assets, as the development of its most important resources (its people), is alien to conventional economics. The New Economics, in contrast, redefines the creation of wealth to include the creation of health. (Robertson in Ekins ed. 1986, 114)[39]

Thus health and need replace monetary wealth and growth. In addition, new economic indicators are suggested. The old indicators are seen as 'inadequate and inappropriate' (Ekins ed. 1986, 128). Ekins, and many like him in the TOES group, suggest that new indicators would include social justice; satisfaction of the whole range of human needs; achievement of aspirations by citizens; more equitable distribution of income and work; greater self-reliance and self-esteem; greater conservation and ecological enhancement and sustainability; and more efficient use of resources. All this entails the replacement of gross national product (GNP) with the adjusted national product (ANP). ANP, unlike GNP, takes full account of social and environmental costs. It incorporates health and social indicators and the informal economy with its new working patterns (Ekins ed. 1986, 139–65).

The most systematic expression of this more frugal vision is the steady-state economy, which is closely associated with the work of Herman Daly (Daly ed. 1973; also Daly in Pirages ed. 1977). The idea can be found stated in J. S. Mill's economic writings in the nineteenth century. The basic point for Daly is that industrial economies must change in the next few decades. He suggests, in a neo-Malthusian vein, that populations must be stabilized. As indicated in the previous section, this could be achieved by many different means. Wealth would be more evenly distributed. Further, the amount of stock produced should be stabilized to minimize throughput. Ideally, all raw materials would be recycled to slow down depletion of finite resources. As Daly states, in a now recognizable argument which he links to the law of entropy: 'in a finite world nothing physical can grow forever' (Daly in Pirages ed. 1977, 107).[40] Growth could still take place in such an economy, but it would be tied to knowledge and less harmful technology. Yet it would not be the aim of economic activity. Economies which simply maximize throughput and do not try to conserve energy deplete the finite stock of our planet's energy and create pollution. This, in turn, requires more energy to cope with waste. Such wasteful economies measure GNP by a growing throughput, which contains a suicidal logic for Steady Staters.

Daly suggests an economy based on slowed-down throughput, stable population, energy conservation, use of renewable resources such as solar power, insulation, wider use of public transport and bicycles. Daly believes not only that this is necessary on an economic and scientific base, but also that there is a strong moral case for such changes. He claims that we need to develop the idea of stewardship and also greater humility towards our planet and its resources.

There are several ambiguities with the above schemes. Apart from the worries expressed by many concerning the population controls of the neo-Malthusians (discussed in the previous section), it is also not particularly clear as to the intended role of public authorities and the state. There are a series of stipulations against social injustice and excessive inequalities of wealth and a strong dislike of commercial advertising. There are also suggestions for taxation changes, Basic Income Schemes, a denial of the necessity of trade and the promotion of protectionism and autarky in the economy. Yet these are all linked with an encouragement of local autonomy and a denial of the relevance of the state. It is difficult to see how any of these reforms could be achieved without some form of central authority.

Each of the above proposals has its own body of criticism. The Basic Income Scheme, for example, has come in for close and critical scrutiny. Would the scheme offer enough to provide a decent standard of living? Surely it would not tackle the question of wide-scale disparities in income; in fact, it could risk stigmatizing a new underclass. Further, what if people did not work at all? How could their behaviour be dealt with? Unless a steady-state frugal society was achieved quickly, the Basic

Income would have to keep up with inflation, and this would entail more economic growth, which would appear to contradict the general thrust of the frugal argument.

Conclusion

There have been shifts in perspective within the ideology of ecology since the 1990s. Ecology does, though, continue to draw attention to our global responsibilities and indicates, in a very successful way, that we are interrelated with the ecosphere. Further, many of the key themes of the ideology have now gone truly global. Green parties and movements have appeared in a large number of societies across the world, although such movements in developing societies often have a very different agenda to those in developed industrial societies. In addition, partly due to the massive publicity concerning climate change, post-Kyoto ecological movements are often being brought much closer to decision-making structures of certain governments and corporations.

However, it is still worth pointing out a number of endemic problems within the ideology. There still seems to be little consciousness of the gulf which separates the philosophy from the political practice of ecologism. On one side, philosophers carry on meandering through the well-worn byways of environmental philosophy, recommending utilitarianism, forms of anthropocentrism or ecocentrism, while, on the other side, the green practitioners appear drawn to rather uncomplicated generalizations, the consequences of which they do not appear very certain about. In addition, the debate concerning anthropocentrism and non-anthropocentrism, which is so central to philosophical discussions, appears to have little bearing on the way environmental policies are now being justified in practice.

Another odd disjunction in the movement is the attitude to the natural sciences and to the scientific discipline of ecology. As suggested at the beginning of this chapter, the strength of the political ecology movement derives to a large degree from the scientific standing of its analyses. However, this strength is combined with a continual moral and philosophical critique of the character of natural science and its fatal link with industrialism. Although some writers have insisted on the distinction between the outdated 'mechanistic' and the new 'systems' conception of natural science, the scientific community themselves do not appear to have taken the distinction seriously and express, at times, hostility or indifference to the political ecologists.

The ideology of ecology has suffered, since its appearance in the political limelight, from the tension between two streams of thought. The 1970s saw the upsurge of both environmental interests and the beginnings of disillusionment with socialism in many quarters, something that accelerated again in the 1990s. The ecology movement provided an ideal haven for disillusioned socialists and anarchists. Yet it was also at this stage in the 1970s and 1980s that attempts began to be made to popularize and systematize the ideas of the movement. In consequence, late nineteenth- and early twentieth-century socialist and anarchist vocabulary, with all its baggage of diverse and often contradictory meanings, was fully employed in strategies of justification. Although this has faded somewhat in the 2000s, there is still, for example, a lurking anarchistic utopianism in certain sectors of the movement.

In the same period socialist and anarchistic affiliates found themselves ecological bedfellows with another vocabulary, which concentrated on the terminology of deeply held values, spiritual reverence for nature, Spinozist metaphysical world-views, frugality, simplicity, the wisdom of ancient primal peoples, living in harmony with the land and its folk memories. Socialist and anarchist writers, quite understandably, reacted with hostility to this form of vocabulary, accusing it of mysticism, racism, simple-minded religiosity, genuflecting to capitalism, and affluent middle-class utopianism with no grasp of political and economic realities.

This socialist/anarchist anxiety is understandable since the roots of ecology are in fact as faithfully reflected by the deep ecology, frugal and spiritual movement. The ancestry of such views can be found in the changing philosophical and ontological beliefs concerning nature and social existence in the latter half of the nineteenth century. Such beliefs were expressed in terms that are still recognizable today within dimensions of the ecology movement. Many of these ideas were utilized by political movements, such as folkish nationalism, conservatism and national socialism in the early twentieth century. Many in the green movement regard such ideas with disquiet. However, it is worth pointing out that such a vocabulary is not the exclusive property of 'right-leaning' ecology movements. There is no reason why it should not be re-explored in a sensitive and open manner by others. Yet the ancestry of this vocabulary is still often denied or airbrushed out. There are two reasons for this. First, ecologists wish to distance themselves, understandably, from any association with eco-fascism and eco-authoritarianism. Second, there is a rather bland belief for some that we have reached, or are about to reach, a new paradigm where such ideologies will appear antiquated. This latter millennialist belief is simply misguided. Ecology is just another internally complex ideology constitutive of an understanding of reality; it is not an objective truth.

At the present moment the ideology of ecology has begun to find more of a temporary equilibrium of sorts in a form of eco-social liberalism. How long this will last is open to debate. This latter interpretation of ecology relies heavily on a transformed understanding of the role of the constitutional ecological state as a key device for achieving green aims. This tendency has led to a number of recent works focused on themes of environmental justice, citizenship, rights, law and democracy. This seems, for the moment, to be a fruitful path to follow. The only potential difficulty would be that the central impetus of the ecological perspective is to draw attention to our deep interrelation with nature; however, social liberal themes such as justice, rights and citizenship are profoundly linked (conceptually and historically) with a more anthropocentric position. The firm link that many wish to establish between citizenship, justice, human rights or democracy and ecological concern is still very tenuous and hard to maintain, and many in the more traditional ecology movement will retain an understandably deeply sceptical stance towards this intellectual tendency.

9

Nationalism

The word 'nation' derives from the Latin terms *nasci* (to be born) and *natio* (belonging together by birth or place of birth). Immediate English cognates would be words such as natal or nature, some of which figure obliquely in nationalist discourse. The initial commonplace sense of *natio* is thus concerned with people related by birth or birthplace. One important connotation is that such a birthplace provides the basis for a 'natural' form of human association. *Prima facie* one can begin to appreciate immediately the difficulties of categorizing nations (as etymologically related to nature or natural) as human artefacts. The critic who asserts that nations are artefacts is fighting on a number of fronts, not least semantics. The word 'nation', as a noun, appeared in English and French in approximately the fourteenth century. However, as most commentators point out, the term had, initially, no immediate political connotations. The words 'nation' and 'nationalism' – denoting something more directly political – crept into European vocabularies in the late eighteenth and early nineteenth centuries.[1]

There have been a number of attempts at defining nationalism.[2] However, this does not seem to be a very profitable path to follow. As many commentaries observe, it is difficult to provide any clear over-arching sense to the diverse claims of nationalism.[3] My strategy will be to follow the general pattern of the other chapters in this book and to consider the various schools of nationalism and then to look at the very broad themes which the schools address.

Most scholars writing on nationalism are faced with a number of primary cognate words to nationalism, which are tied etymologically to the same root. Words such as *nation*, *national self-determination*, *nationality*, *national character* and *national interest* proliferate and occasionally directly overlap. These need to be initially kept distinct, although there is no hard-and-fast way of doing so, partly because there are no accepted over-arching definitions of any of the terms involved. However, there does seem to be some point in trying to keep these moderately separate, partly because they serve at times distinct functions. In addition, in later twentieth-century discussion this vocabulary grew and often became fixed into institutions. We thus have a United Nations, transnational, multinational corporations and national defence forces and nationalized industries. Each of the above primary cognates will be briefly elucidated.

The term *nation* usually denotes a group of people who have some common ancestry, history, culture and language, which figure as a focus of symbolic loyalty and affection. This sense might also be taken as a definition of ethnicity; however, whereas a nation can imply ethnicity, it does not necessarily have to do so. For example, where the nation is seen to formally coincide with a state, there may be a variety of distinct ethnic groups who nonetheless subscribe allegiance to an official nation state, as distinct from their own ethnic fidelity. *National self-determination* is linked closely to sovereignty and state theory, implying independence (through secession or unification) from the control of other states and consequently the capacity of a people to formulate law and exercise jurisdiction within a given territory. *Nationality*, in legal parlance, denotes juridical citizenship of a particular state – as in nationality laws – although this still does not account for the determinants of nationality such as residence, place of birth or family.[4] An extended use of nationality denotes a social group who wish to be respected as an independent community, but do not aspire to statehood.[5] *National character* is a slightly more archaic term which resonates more with the Enlightenment social scientific (and later romantic) concerns to identify the characteristic behaviour of 'national types'. Although it has largely faded from serious discussion, it still figures subliminally in contemporary popular discourse.[6] *National interest* is a term which has more direct diplomatic and foreign policy implications and is virtually equivalent to the 'will of the prince' or 'reason of state', in relation to the external activities of states. In other words, it relates closely to the history and evolution of the state and its spheres of interest.[7]

Nationalism is often seen as an ideology (or a form of behaviour) which makes national self-consciousness, ethnic or linguistic identity into central planks of a doctrine which seeks political expression. My focus in this chapter is primarily on this latter notion of nationalism. However, this by no means delimits my account, since many of the above primary cognates are none the less relevant to the discussion.

One other small but significant point to note about these primary cognate terms is that they often give rise to different academic concerns. Some scholars are interested in the growth of nations and ethnic groups, but have little interest in the late eighteenth- and nineteenth-century 'ideology' of nationalism. Similarly, studies can be made of the national interest and nationality laws, which will have little or no connection with nations or nationalism. Slightly more perversely, but with sound reasons, scholars can be interested in the historical, economic or sociological rise of nationalism, but have little interest in the political ideology. Some of these ideas will be examined in this chapter.

There are also a number of *secondary* cognates, which do not derive from the same etymological root as nation or nationalism, yet are often, with varying degrees of precision, associated closely with nationalism. The key concepts here are patriotism, ethnicity and racism. The relation between these terms and nationalism remains deeply contested and unresolved. Thus, in some of the literature, patriotism has been conceived to be the more affable and older aspect of nationalism. It has been the conventional wisdom to see patriotism as concerned with loyalty, pride and love of one's country. This use of the term 'patriotism' is usually dated to the advent of Roman republicanism. In fact, in this context, patriotism is often considered a more acceptable form of allegiance than nationalism (Viroli 1995). Other commentators are less sanguine and see the two terms (patriotism and nationalism) as permanently fused, for better or worse.[8]

The term 'ethnic' designates a more focused phenomenon than patriotism. Ethnicity usually refers to inborn factors such as kinship, which are understood mostly in biological or genetic terms. Ethnic groups are usually considered to be smaller, more pervasive, exclusive in their membership, and older than nations. The connections with nationalism are immensely complex. Some see ethnic nationalism as either the very essence of nationalism or, conversely, an important category *within* nationalism. Anthony Smith, in his various writings, has made a particular issue out of the ethnic origins of nations, as well as the ethno-symbolic character of nationalism (see Smith 1986 and 2001; see also Hastings 1997; Spencer and Wollman 2002, 101ff).

After the powerful impact of national socialism in the mid-twentieth century, 'race' has had an awkward relationship with nationalism. Race has often been understood, in terms of its history in the European vocabulary over the nineteenth and twentieth centuries, as a biological or genetic category (see Mosse 1978; Hannaford 1996). Nationalism, with its occasional naturalistic forays, can be read through the lens of race, and undoubtedly has been by the national socialists, amongst others, with their cumbersome racial legal codes and beliefs. Many scholars of nationalist thought contend, however, that national socialism is an aberration and should not be taken as the norm of nationalist thought. However, nationalist discourse does slip with remarkable ease into racism, as has been shown time and again in the nineteenth and twentieth centuries.[9] This latter notion is not a detail to be put aside lightly.

Nationalism presents a number of problems for the prospective student. Firstly, there are a number of paradoxes running through the bulk of nationalist discussion. Historically, nationalism, as a political ideology and movement, is a comparatively recent phenomenon in European discussion, which only appeared with the advent of democracy, industrialization and popular sovereignty theory. Conversely, however, one of its central claims is its very antiquity. Indeed, nationalists often identify the roots of nationalism as within nature. As stated earlier, this arises out of the semantics of the term 'nation'. Yet it is clear from even the most cursory study of the subject that a great deal of the ideology of nationalism is a modern human construction. In addition, as noted in the opening comments of chapter 6, 'Fascism', nationalism is in the peculiar position of claiming a formal universality for its ideas, yet the ideology only makes sense in terms of its particularity and localism. The practical difficulties of this latter point are revealed by the problems experienced in the 1930s in forming a fascist international. Yet it is also clear that certain strands of nationalist thought, particularly liberal nationalism, have not seen themselves in the context solely of particularism or localism, but have envisaged their views as compatible with cosmopolitanism and universalism. They have thus found it far easier to accommodate the idea of other nations. Finally, and most significantly, there is the disabling problem of, on the one hand, the immense power of nationalism, coupled with, on the other hand, nationalism's theoretical naïvety and philosophical incoherence. Paradoxically, nationalism has probably been more deeply successful *because* it has no coherent substantive doctrines.

One final problem is the direct overlap between nationalism and other ideologies. Nationalism has clearly, in its tortured history, eaten its fill from most ideological banquets. There have been, and still are, liberal, socialist, conservative, fascist and even some anarchistic nationalisms. There are no hard-and-fast lines to draw between these ideologies, and it is not surprising that we should encounter such ideological hybrids. There are, rather, direct and clear overlaps between ideologies, even more so in the case of nationalism, which is an intellectual vacuum desperate to be filled with something of substance. In relation to the above point, it is also clear that there are marked and predictable differences within nationalism itself corresponding to distinct ideological affiliations. There is no one nationalist doctrine – there are, rather, nationalisms.

The Origins of Nationalist Thought

There are close parallels between fascism and nationalism simply in terms of the manner in which the literature has dealt with these ideologies. Many discussions of nationalism, as of fascism, focus on the explanatory preconditions of nationalism – why it comes about and why it has had such an effect. Yet such accounts are often loath to pay much attention to the ideas of nationalists. This is explicable given the evident intellectual thinness of the ideas compared with the immense and demonstrable power of the movement in historical and sociological practice. Thus a great deal has been written on nationalism by historians, political scientists and political sociologists, but comparatively little by political theorists until the mid-1990s. Although they have subsequently made up for lost time.[10] The fact that nationalism formed such a key plank in fascist and national socialist discussion only adds more weight to this explanatory supposition and tendency. For many commentators both doctrines are ideologically inchoate movements which require some form of descriptive causal explanation. Thus, as in chapter 6, 'Fascism', this section will be divided into two parts.[11] The first will review the origins and history of nationalism and the second will examine some of the differing scholarly approaches to nationalism.

As with all the ideologies that we have dealt with, the origins of nationalism are deeply contested. The first account of nationalism associates it with ancient ethnic groups or tribes. The nation is thus seen as a concept of great antiquity, virtually identifiable with a genetically based social instinct in human beings. Sociobiologically influenced writers are inclined to this form of interpretation, viewing nationalism as a biological rather than a normative category (see Kellas 1991). Nationalism is consequently understood as a distinctively premodern idea, expressive of either a form of ethnicity or a straightforward normative commitment to a common birthright.[12] Much depends in this kind of discussion on whether an explanation is being given of either premodern nation-building or pre-national forms of allegiance. The former sees nationalism as a premodern idea; the latter identifies nationalism with modernity, but contends that there have been pre-national forms of allegiance, such as tribal loyalty, which should not be confused with the modern concept of nationalism. Anthony Smith's work takes a middle position, between premodernist and modernist claims, asserting, in short, that ethnicity is subtly transformed into modern nationalism. Smith argues that ethnicity is an essential preliminary to full-blown modern nationalism. He notes that 'modern nations simply extend, strengthen and stream-line the ways in which members of *ethnie* associated and communicated'. Unlike Ernest Gellner's and Benedict Anderson's stress on the novelty or modernity of nationalism, Smith emphasizes its continuity with the past, although he recognizes that certain changes transform *ethnie* into nationalisms. Yet he still contends that nation states do more effectively what 'premodern ethnicists tried to do, that is, keep out foreigners and diffuse to their kinsmen the traditions and myths of their ances-tors, using the modern education system' (Smith 1986, 215–16; also Smith 2001, ch. 3).

More specific views of the origins of nationalism have focused on medieval Europe, although usually only in terms of the etymology of the word 'nation'.[13] The contem-porary legal philosopher Neil MacCormick envisages evidence for some conception of national identity in the sixteenth century in Britain and, more particularly, Scotland. MacCormick remarks that 'The distinctiveness of nations was, long before 1789, advanced as a reason why they ought to live under their own kings subject to their own laws.' Thus it is 'quite irrelevant that the term "nationalism" as a term of art in political theory comes into general usage only in the nineteenth century' (MacCormick 1982, 256 and 260). Leah Greenfeld and Adrian Hastings focus, largely, on nationalist origins in sixteenth-century England (Greenfeld 1992; and Hastings 1997). Hans Kohn, the doyen of post-1945 commentators on nationalism, also focused on the late 1600s as the seedbed of nationalist ideas, although he saw this as a more unconscious form of national awareness (Kohn 1945, 4). Hasting's work, however, presents a more robust and resolute argument for this latter position (Hasting 1997). Lord Acton favoured the 1772 partition of Poland as the ground-work for both Polish and European nationalism (Acton 1907). The Enlightenment and more particularly the eighteenth century is also another favoured point of deri-vation for nationalism (see Walicki 1989). Yet other scholars, such as Elie Kedourie, are quite explicit in tracing nationalism to the revolutions in eighteenth-century German philosophy, particularly in the work of thinkers such as Kant, Fichte, Schlegel, Schleiermacher and Arndt. However, the most favoured point of origin is the period leading up to and immediately after the French Revolution.[14]

Finally, some scholars have argued that nationalism is a product of the early nine-teenth century. Hobsbawm, for example, claims that the modern usage of the term 'nationalism', as distinct from 'ethnicity', is in fact comparatively recent (Hobsbawm 1992). The modern idea probably only dates from the 1830s, although some aspects of its populist meaning were traceable to the American and French Revolutions. This latter point more or less coincides with the thrust of Gellner's work, which also presents nationalism as a modern term corresponding to the growth and moderniza-tion of states in the nineteenth century (Gellner 1983). My own sympathies lie with those scholars who see nationalism as a distinctly modern movement emanating from the French Revolutionary era. This does not deny that there were earlier forms of group loyalty and allegiance. However, they were not nationalist in the context of nineteenth- and twentieth-century understandings.

Many of the above accounts identify phases of nationalist development. One of the more popular theories, which is widely quoted in the recent literature, is by Miroslav Hroch. He sees three distinct phases. First, nationalism is embodied in nineteenth-century folklore, custom, and the like. This is essentially a cultural idea, fostered by the middle and upper classes, with little or no political implication. Second, nationalism is pursued as a political campaign. It is usually connected with and fostered by political parties. Finally, nationalism becomes translated into mass support and mass movements. Each of these phases is linked by Hroch to economic and cultural changes (Hroch 1985). Hobsbawm also identifies three phases or periods: initially 1830–80, which is dominated by liberal nationalism; then 1880–1914, which sees a sharp movement to the conservative right in nationalist thinking; and, finally, the apogee of nationalism is identified with the period 1918–50 (see Hobsbawm 1992). Although some scholars have envisaged nationalism as on the wane in the period 1950–80, there clearly was a resurgence of its impact in the 1990s in Eastern Europe and elsewhere.

Moving now to the second part of this section dealing with the forms of explanation of nationalism: the initial writings on nationalism in the nineteenth century, by writers such as J. S. Mill, Lord Acton, Guiseppe Mazzini or Ernest Renan, tended to be ethical or philosophical in character. The only exceptions to this were the writings of Marx and Engels and the tradition which derived from them. The Marxist interest in nationalism was primarily driven by concerns in political economy. Nationalism was a phenomenon of a stage of economic development. However, there were oddities within the Marxist interpretation which inhibited its grasp of nationalism. These will be examined later. In the period 1920 to 1950, work on nationalism was less ethically orientated and more distanced and historical in character, while still retaining a marked interest in the doctrinal content of nationalism. Writers such as Hans Kohn, Hugh Seton Watson, Carlton Hayes, Alfred Cobban and Louis Snyder dominate this period. From the late 1950s, American political science eclipsed previous work, and the central theme of its research was premised on a strong commitment to empirical investigation, seeking to understand the causal patterns underpinning nationalism. The key methods of investigation were modernization theory, functionalism and development theories. With some rare exceptions, variants of modernization theory have informed the bulk of research until recently. The key writers through the 1960s and early 1970s were academics such as David Apter, Karl Deutsch, Lucien Pye and Clifford Geertz. This form of more empirically-orientated research focusing on the effects of modernization – whether viewed critically or not – also informed the work of writers in the 1980s and 1990s such as Ernest Gellner, Anthony Smith, Peter Alter, Leah Greenfeld and Adrian Hastings, amongst others.

Modernization theory is immensely pervasive in the literature on nationalism. It deals with the economic and social preconditions for the existence of nation states. Its crucial early components are functionalism and development theories. Functionalism deals with functional roles of nation states in the modernizing process. Nation states are viewed as specialized agencies associated with the division of labour in advanced industrial societies. The function of the nation state is to mediate and reduce conflict and tension between sectors of society. States only come into being when they possess enough resources to be able to dominate the peripheries of society. Development theory sees definite stages in the growth of nation states. The growth is assumed to be progressive, rational, continuous, uniform and endogenous. The nation state is conceived as arising at a particular stage of the economic development of society. The key to modernization, in relation to nationalism, is that 'To survive painful dislocation, societies must institutionalize new modes of fulfilling the principles and performing the functions with which earlier structures can no longer cope. ... Mechanisms of reintegration and stabilization can ease and facilitate the transition'; crucial among such mechanisms is nationalism (Smith 1971, 50).

Modernization thus involves a society's capacity for self-sustaining growth and the absorption of the changes it generates through a mechanism of reintegration. The failure to modernize produces imbalances and the maladaptation of groups and sectors within society. Rapid industrialization and modernization require a flexible political system and an ideology such as nationalism which integrates the individual with the state, in order to maintain communal solidarity. Nationalism thus helps to bridge the gap between more traditional communities (*Gemeinschaft*) and modern associations (*Gesellschaft*). As Anthony Smith remarks: 'To maintain communal solidarity and the regime's legitimacy, a new mythology is erected around the rebirth of the purified nation bent on restoring a golden age' (Smith 1971, 49). Nationalism is seen as the *sine qua non* of economic development, industrialization and thus modernization. Modernization theory, in general terms, is consequently interested in the larger historical, sociological and economic forces which give rise to nationalism, rather than the ideology of nationalism itself. It concentrates on processes such as industrialization and urbanization in order to explain its role and function.

There are a number of variations of modernization theory in relation to nationalism. For Karl Deutsch, for example, nationalism facilitates a common culture and 'community of communication'. Communication theory is a variant of modernization emphasizing once again the functional aspect of nationalism. Deutsch sees the nation as a pattern of functional communication transactions, modernization being measured by the efficiency of such transactions. What is needed for adequate modernization is therefore the presence of sufficient and effective modes of communication. Thus, a nation becomes an amalgam of individuals, linked to regions and groups by channels of social and economic communication. Deutsch sought to quantify and measure elements of nationality, via these communication processes (Deutsch 1953). For Ernest Gellner, however, nationalism exists at the 'point of intersection of politics, technology and social transformation'. He prefers the idea of 'modernization from above', arguing that nationalism 'is essentially, the general imposition of a high culture on society, where previously low cultures have taken up the lives of the majority' (Gellner 1983, 57; see Hobsbawm 1992, 10). He also stresses the role of material conditions in shaping national thought, proposing economic grounds for nationalism and self-consciously avoiding the question of ideology. For Gellner, particular forms of polity and civil society are required for industrial growth. Industrialization requires flexible change. There is thus a need for more social homogeneity – which explains the demand for uniformity of language and national education systems. For Gellner, the vanguard of modernization is the intelligentsia, who are closely linked to education and communication processes. He argues that the precondition to full effective citizenship is literacy. National principles tend to override all other forms of allegiance or loyalty. As Gellner notes, the nationalist-orientated society is premised upon 'a school-mediated, academy supervised idiom, codified for the requirements of reasonably precise bureaucratic and technological communication' (Gellner 1983, 57).

The modernization thesis in general offers a thin and attenuated understanding of the ideology of nationalism, which, in the main, it tends either to ignore or sideline. Because it overemphasizes the economic and sociological factors giving rise to nationalism, it also fails to explain the intensity of the emotional appeal of national-ist ideas. Gellner, for example, appears simply to assume the existence of something called the nation, which is imbricated in the modernizing process, and consequently he precludes any adequate conceptual account of the ideology of nationalism. In addition, Gellner's thesis particularly offers a rather monoglot vision of political and civil culture. He leaves very little room for phenomena such as multiculturalism or multinationalism within states. Some degree of cultural homogeneity appears crucial for his conception of the nation state, which, in terms of present historical develop-ments in many states, is a problem.

Historically, Marxism has been deeply uneasy with nationalism. Tom Nairn describes it as Marxism's 'historical failure' (Nairn 1977, 329). Nationalism was seen generally as a bourgeois distraction, despite the fact that many twentieth-century Marxist-inspired revolutionary movements have also been nationalist in character, particularly the anti-colonial movements in, for example, Vietnam or Algeria.[15] For Marx and Engels, nationalism could play an instrumental and tempo-rary role in serving the historical interests of the proletariat; nationalist concerns were of no lasting or profound significance – they were phenomena that would wither and fade. Secessionist nationalism and self-determination ideas were toler-ated, even by Lenin, but only again if they assisted the optimal development of capitalism within bourgeois states, thus contributing to capitalism's ultimate demise. In a phrase, class conflict was primary and national conflict came a poor second.

Most early Marxist accounts were limited by the internal parameters of their own arguments. First, there was an implicit assumption within Marxism of a natural universal law of development towards the classless society. The particularity or local-ism of nationalism was seen to conflict with this universal historical goal. Second, there was a strong tendency towards economic reductionism within orthodox Marxism. Nationalism was explained through the economic logic of capitalism. Third, Marxism claimed a universal theoretical status, such as to explain national phenomena wherever they occurred. However, the distinct and separate realities of nationalisms resisted such monocausal explanation. In addition, both Marx and Engels were largely Europe-focused and supported, at points, the 'civilizing mission' of European state colonialism.[16] They also contended that national groups that were not capable of forming viable states should be allowed to vanish or be assimilated into larger states. For example, Marx considered that both Croatia and Bohemia should be absorbed by larger political units.

For Marx and Engels, the modern nation state was the outcome of a process whereby capitalist production had succeeded feudalism. The transition to the market economy impelled states to develop cohesive languages, to develop centralized institutions and to suppress local differences. National languages were the idioms for traders and the conditions for successful market economies. In Marx and Engels's work this standardization of languages and the concomitant political centralization were modelled on the French Revolutionary events and particularly the ideas of the Jacobins. However, such a nation was only a stage in the evolution of societies. Nationalism related to the manner in which the economy was developing. It was a necessary moment of economic evolution. However, emancipation and revolution would see the overcoming not only of classes and capitalism, but also of nationalism. This was the common view taken during the first and second Internationals.

The only alleviations to the above views were the ideas of Antonio Gramsci, and, more particularly, the Austrian Marxists Otto Bauer and Karl Renner, who, virtually alone in the Marxist tradition, appeared to appreciate the complex heterogeneity and significance of nationalist movements.[17] Bauer's work entailed a partial break with and critique of more traditional Marxist economism and reductionism. He contended, in fact, that nations would not wither with the disappearance of class. He argued instead that the expansion of socialism would entail the differentiation of national communities, remarking that 'Integration of the whole people in their national cultural community, full achievement of self-determination of nations, growing spiritual (*geistig*) differentiation of nations – this is the meaning of socialism' (quoted in Nimni 1991, 142). Bauer thought, in fact, that national character was not something to be frowned upon by socialists. Yet he did not, in the end, totally break with Marxist economism, and as one commentator remarks, 'It seems that in Bauer's work there is an almost unsustainable tension between the imaginative analysis of the nation as a community of fate, and the narrow one-sidedness of the ... class reductionist perspective' (Nimni 1991, 193).

The Nature of Nationalism

There are a large number of typologies within the literature on nationalism. In considering such typologies a great deal depends upon the particular approach adopted. Anthony Smith, for example, suggests in one of his earliest books that nationalism is 'most fruitfully conceptualized as a single category containing subvarieties, genus and species' (Smith 1971, 193). What this adds to our knowledge of nationalism is debatable. Alternatively, a typology premised upon nationalist strategies and aims could be constructed. In this context one might distinguish unificatory from secessionist nationalisms, although the ideological complexion of, say, two secessionist nationalisms might be diametrically opposed. Or one could focus on historical phases in the growth of nationalism or the specific ideas, however inchoate, within the various proponents. The focus of this chapter will be more particularly on the ideas. Even here, though, there are many forms. Typologies range from twofold up to fivefold classifications of nationalism.[18]

The typologies of nationalism are in many ways much less settled than other ideologies which are dealt with in this book. Thus, selecting a particular typology is a hazardous affair. The typology adopted in this chapter reflects the way in which nationalism crosses over the territory of other ideologies. The first type or school is 'liberal *Risorgimento* nationalism'.[19] The manner in which some recent reformist and market socialists have adopted nationalist language also reflects another dimension of liberal nationalism (see Miller in Brown ed. 1994). Second, there is a more traditionalist conservative nationalism. Third, there is integral nationalism, which is the form most closely associated with fascism and national socialism (and has been largely dealt with in chapter 6, 'Fascism').[20] There are other possible variants, such as socialist nationalism and anti-colonial nationalism. Romantic nationalism strays across all these forms. However, all of these variants either overlap or form sub-aspects within the major categories outlined above.

Liberal *Risorgimento* nationalism asserts most of the core liberal values. Its roots lie largely in the Enlightenment. Writers who adhere to some form of liberal nationalism do not see it as in any way incompatible with either cosmopolitanism or pacifism. In many ways President Wilson's Fourteen Points, promulgated after the First World War, represent, if only symbolically, the high point of liberal nationalism insofar as they stressed 'the absolute sovereignty of the national state, but sought to limit the implications of this principle by stressing individual liberties – political, economic, and religious – within each national state' (Hayes 1949, 135). Formally, for the Fourteen Points, each nationality should have its own state, but it must be one embodying constitutional government, democracy and the rights and freedoms of the individual. The most well-known early promulgator of these general ideas was Guiseppe Mazzini (1805–72). Although one would hesitate to class him as a systematic theorist, he was a major influence on liberal nationalist thought. In works of glowing, somewhat rhetorical prose, such as the *Essays on the Duties of Man* (1860), Mazzini put forward a doctrine of the ultimate compatibility of nationhood with humanity at large. Mazzini was clearly a humanitarian internationalist. His 'Young Italy' movement sparked a wave of enthusiastic imitations across Europe culminating in Young Europe (La Giovane Europa), with Italian, Polish and German branches. This led in turn to a number of similarly motivated associations, such as the Democratic Friends of All Nations (1844), The Fraternal Democrats (1845) and the People's International League (1847).

Mazzini's ideal in the 1850s was for a Europe of, at most, eleven nations. He felt that size was a limitation, denying, for example, that the Irish were large enough to form a nation state. The obstacles to nationalism perceived by Mazzini were large multinational groups and imperial multinational states, such as the Habsburg Empire. Liberal nationalism basically assumed that each nationality (large enough to survive) should be independent, but with constitutional democratic government. The general excitement in Europe over the Greek struggles against the Ottoman Empire and the Polish struggle against the Tsarist Empire in the 1830s attracted the enthusiasm of liberal nationalists. Thus the heyday of this original form of *Risorgimento* liberal nationalism was largely from the Congress of Vienna (1814–15) up to the Treaty of Versailles and Wilson's Fourteen Points. The key background theme was the right of self-determination by nations. The major problem with this form of nationalism was that, once having promulgated the idea of the self-determining nation, it was difficult to know where to halt. As President Wilson quickly saw, how could one prevent every moderately sized community perceiving itself as a nation, and thus a state? In addition, how was one to resolve conflicts between liberal nation states and, more problematically, secessionist movements within liberal nation states?[21]

It is worth noting that there has been some resurgence of interest in liberal nationalism since the 1990s. For example, John Plamenatz's work, utilizing Kohn's earlier ideas, distinguished between an acceptable moderate Western nationalism – essentially liberal nationalism – and a more bellicose East European cultural nationalism. This distinction was taken up again by some theorists (echoing the same Mazzinian liberal sentiments, although without the uplifting moral rhetoric), who tried to reconcile sensible moderate national sentiment with some form of moderated cosmopolitan liberalism (see Vincent 2002, ch. 4). The conception of moderate liberal nationalism confronts another argument in the post-1945 era which asserts that liberalism is utterly incompatible with nationalism. Liberalism, in this sense, is equated with full-blown cosmopolitanism and universalism, and denies the relevance of nationalism. However, in recent years there has been some contention over this question. As one liberal nationalist notes, 'Underlying nationalism is a range of perceptive understandings of the human situation, of what makes human life meaningful and creative. ... Liberals are challenged to accommodate those worthy elements' (Tamir 1993, 6). [22]

The second type or school is 'traditionalist conservative nationalism', which also achieved a very powerful rendering in elements of romantic cultural nationalism. As suggested earlier, romantic nationalism affected both liberal and integral variants; thus, it is by no means exclusively traditionalist. In terms of the schemes of Kohn, Plamenatz and Friedrich Meinecke, traditionalist nationalism also has close affinities with the Eastern and cultural conceptions of nationalism. Traditional nationalism derived its initial impetus from the reaction to the French Revolution. Historical continuity and tradition were set against reason and revolution. The nation stood for the continuity and unique destiny of a traditional organic community, expressed in legal, political and social life. In the work of writers such as Edmund Burke and Joseph de Maistre the nation was seen as ordered hierarchy of an organic community, instead of a body of equal citizens. In other words, nationalism was transformed into the prose of traditionalist conservatism.

In some of the German variants of the above thesis, romanticism came to the fore, particularly in writers such as Friedrich Schlegel, Adam Müller and Friedrich Novalis, many of whose ideas were derived from a particular interpretation of Herder and Fichte. Schlegel and Novalis particularly identified the nation with purity of language, folk mythology and culture. They desired the restoration of what they perceived to be ancient communal traditions. Nations were founded primarily on a common culture, with a unique spirit, will or soul, expressed in language, myths, laws, customs and history. Thus, there was a clear acceptance of the spiritual necessity of cultural diversity. Languages took on a particularly strong significance in this reading (something that will be examined in more detail later). The interest in folk art, poetry and music in the mid- to late nineteenth century had its root in the same themes. Such themes also entered deeply into the educational curricula, festivals and even the architecture and monuments of certain nineteenth-century states (see Eade ed. 1983). The initial impetus, in common with much traditionalist conservative thought, was an anti-Enlightenment stress. Enlightenment thought was seen to be both materialistic and mechanistic. Yet the nation was viewed as a spiritual organism, occasionally personified, shaped by history, prior to any individuals and possessing its own uniqueness. Many scholars of the time, committed to these latter ideas, devoted themselves to the task of uncovering the antiquity of this spiritual organism within its language and folklore. The philosophies of language developed by Herder, Grimm, Fichte, Schlegel and Humboldt formed much of the initial intellectual back-drop to this interest.

At the time, many of the above theorists were also reacting to French political and cultural hegemony within German states. Fichte's *Addresses to the German Nation* (1806) was the best known of such reactions (see Engelbrecht 1933). The political form of this movement was well expressed in Friedrich Meinecke's idea of the *Kulturnation*. Culture, uniquely identifying a particular people, preceded and was expressed in the 'aesthetic state'. The state took on a more sacred role for these romantics, who extended and modified ideas from Rousseau and Hegel. The personified cultural nation, in the vocabulary of the time, demanded both the right to self-determination and *Bildung* – aesthetic self-realization. In Fichte, other themes came to the fore, particularly the idea of superiority and inferiority in national types. Yet this hierarchical idea did not neces-sarily follow from the romantic perspective. Hierarchy was, however, a possible infer-ence from a particular treatment of language. Yet for most early romantics there was a strong belief in the ultimate harmony of nations. For example, in Novalis this was pre-mised upon the idea of a restoration, via Catholicism, of a revivified medieval Europe – a renewed *Respublica Christiana*. The romantics also had a peculiar and somewhat tortured relationship with democracy. Self-determination could be equally at home in traditional, integral or liberal nationalisms, although *prima facie* it appears to be closer to liberal nationalism. Despite appearances, even some of Fichte's arguments can be read as exemplars of the value and significance of democratic self-determination. It is often forgotten that Fichte was, and, according to some, remained, a stalwart admirer of Jacobin popular democracy. Romanticism therefore had both traditionalist conservative and liberal faces. It could both fulsomely support modernizing demo-cratic tendencies and also stand as a traditional bulwark against such changes.

It is worth briefly noting at this point that writers such as Lord Acton, and in the late twentieth century Elie Kedourie, have seen romantic nationalism as virtually the core of nationalism *per se*. For these writers, nationalism, in general, was a perni-cious doctrine which was the bane of humanity in the twentieth century. For Kedourie, it derived its force and original impetus from German philosophy, particu-larly Fichte and the offshoots of Kantian ideas of freedom (Kedourie 1974). Most other scholars have seen a much broader framework to nationalism.

The third school or type is 'integral nationalism', which has already been encoun-tered in chapter 6, 'Fascism'. In the case of national socialism in Germany, the racial theme came prominently to the fore, although much of the content of such nationalist discussion was also premised on the *Volk* tradition, social Darwinism, philosophical vitalism and an assortment of other sources. In the case of Italian fascism the focus was more exclusively statist, in a more totalitarian vein. However, both Italian fascism and German national socialism promulgated an aggressive, xenophobic, irrationalist conception of nationalism which was deeply hostile to claims of both internationalism and liberal nationalism. Some commentators see Jacobinism as having produced a foretaste of integral nationalism (Alter 1989, 40). Paradoxically, there are some connections between integral nationalism and the other nationalist variants. Liberal *Risorgimento*, traditionalist and integral nationalisms all focused, for slightly different reasons, on the self-determining nation state. Without the existence of such independent states, nationalism would have been impossible.[23] In other words, the success of liberal nationalism in the nineteenth century both prepared the ground for integral nationalism, giving force and resonance to its claims for self-determination, and also provided much of the formal substance for the integral arguments on self-determination. However, integral nationalism, unlike liberal nationalism, was self-consciously imperialistic, illiberal, irrationalist and militaristic and was often premised on the superiority of particular peoples or nations. In other words, integral nationalism was premised upon a hierarchical understanding of nations.

As in most ideologies, certain formal *regulative* ideas can be identified within nationalism. Various schools of nationalism interpret these ideas differently. Formally, nationalism asserts that the world is divided into distinct nations, each with its own historical continuity, language, beliefs, symbols and destiny (see Smith 2001, 9ff). The nation is seen to be deeply rooted in the past. It is the source of political and social power and can only be fulfilled when embodied in a state. Nationhood is also commonly identified with a territory with identifiable boundaries. Each nation purports to have its own distinctive customs, traditions, folklore and symbols which structure the basis of its solidarity. Religion can be a force within nationalism – Poland, the USA or Iran, for example, would be difficult to understand without religious categories entering somewhere into the national equation – but this is by no means always the case.[24] The nation also becomes the political and moral sovereign, and thus the ultimate ground of legitimacy and loyalty. Loyalty to the nation tends to override other allegiances, although this varies with the type of nationalism. Human beings must identify with their nation if they wish to be free and realize themselves. The idea of nationalism can give rise to the ideas of equality and fraternity among nationals, although these ideas are more immediately prevalent in liberal nationalism. Finally, nations must be free, independent and secure from external threat if peace and justice are to prevail in the international order.

The organizing themes of the remainder of this chapter will be human nature, language, the nation state and the national economy. These themes will encompass most of the above *regulative* ideas.

Human Nature

It is sometimes contended that nationalism does not have a theory of human nature (Tamir 1993, 14). There appear to be five main reasons for this. First, exponents of nationalism have not written much about human nature. It has not, therefore, been a subject of theoretical or practical concern. Second, where nationalists have addressed the issue, they have done so within the varying nationalist perspectives or schools outlined above. Thus, in Burke, Maurras, Barrès or Treitschke there is a more distinctive and recognizably traditionalist conservative perspective, whereas in Mazzini or J. S. Mill more obviously liberal themes arise (see Rosen 1997). A more distinctive and singular reading of human nature can be found within integral nationalism, particularly in national socialism, where the theme of race becomes crucial in interpreting the real nature of human beings. However, such a racial interpretation only represents an aspect of nationalist concern. Third, there is a potentially inhibiting factor implicit within nationalist argument. If humans *are* creatures of their nation, then it follows that there can be no *common* identifying nature, since human identity would be formed within the diverse national units. This is not a total restraint on the argument. Herder, for example, although adhering strongly to the national diversity of human beings, none the less contended that there is a common humanity (*Humanität*) which is not affected by national difference. Fourth, because of the strong historical emphasis of certain nationalists, there is a sense in which human nature is in continual flux. If it is in continual flux then how can it be adequately described? There is no settled core or identifiable continuity. Fifthly, the romantic stress within certain nationalist theories on self-creation and self-formation (*Bildung*) reinforces the sense of mutability and flux in human nature. If nationalism denotes self-determination or self-formation, then to some extent nationalists make their own natures through imagination, culture and language. These natures are continually being remade or recast. Thus, there is no fixed essence which can be identified in human nature.

Despite the force of the above points, there are certain readily identifiable aspects to human nature which can be found in most nationalist writers. To have a concept of human nature is not to claim that all humans are identical. What nationalism appears to be asserting is that, structurally, humans are social beings. These social beings find their idiosyncratic roles, values and thoughts from within nations, which are the most fundamental social units. The outcomes of such agency might be very diverse, since different national units will give rise to different value systems, but the *conditions* within which humans establish their differences are none the less common to the species. Thus, for nationalists, all human beings possess the capacity for self-determination; in addition, the human self is socially rooted; finally, humans discover and realize themselves *through* their national communities (since the self contains the filaments of nation). This latter proposition gives rise to the claim, by moral argument and metaphorical language, that the nation can determine itself within international society, that is to say, the nation is given a metaphorical 'self' or 'personality'.

Not all nationalists would rest content with the above characterization of human nature. Some would feel constrained by the argument that distinct national units can determine their own values and plans of life. Liberal nationalists, for example, could argue that non-interference and tolerance between nations are premised upon some mutuality of non-interference and non-harm. If one nation harms another, or even, possibly, harms its own nationals in some unacceptable manner, then there are grounds for intervention and the imposition of a correct conception of human behaviour. Some liberals would go beyond this, as most liberal nationalists in fact do, to assert universal cosmopolitan theses about all human beings, with the important rider that harmless idiosyncratic cultural traits are both tolerable and enriching for humanity. Thus, for liberal nationalists, regardless of the idiosyncrasies of nationhood, there are still core moral factors common to all humans which should be accorded respect.

The most elusive argument arising from the above is that if certain liberal values are embedded in the political and moral fabric, then national members can determine or form themselves through such liberal beliefs without raising the question of nationalism. We might call this a communitarian or embedded liberalism. In this latter view, which implicitly asserts the universality of liberal ideas, liberals appear to be implicitly proposing the content or substance of what individuals should want or desire. They also maintain implicitly that we should realize such content through the institutional processes of an 'embedded' liberal polity. There is some truth to the argument, at this point, that liberals, even where they express a strong antipathy to nationalism, none the less assume the background of national unity on primary goods such as justice, liberty and individual rights. Therefore, they simply do not have to address the question of nationalism *because* liberal values are so embedded within the community.

The argument which partially rebuts the 'embeddedness' claim *also* figures as another central prop of nationalist argumentation. Thus, the genealogy of human beings, their psychological propensities and their moral and political conceptions shift markedly between groups and communities with their distinctive histories. Even more stringently, if the nature of humans is reduced to distinct cultural histories, and particularly to distinct languages, then human nature becomes simply an aspect of the distinct languages. In other words, human nature is articulated through a series of separate linguistic narratives, which figure in the distinct nations. Human nature is 'constituted' within different languages. We could, therefore, have no access whatsoever to any objective factors or psychology of human beings outside of the constitutive national discourses. Liberal nationalism in this reading would thus have no purchase beyond a particular localized liberal narrative. The embedded sense of liberal beliefs is therefore taken with full seriousness.

Yet in laying too much stress upon the theme of embeddedness, we appear to lose any over-arching sense of human nature. There is rather a complex series of nationalist narratives, each of which constitutes a conception of human nature. The concept itself is constituted through the multiple narratives. There is no referent for the concept of human nature, only the various national discourses. Of course, as already observed, not all thinkers associated with nationalism have actually accepted the above argument. Herder and Mazzini contended that there was a common humanity over and above particular nations. However, apart from that claim, it is still feasible to ask why we should go on referring *to* something called 'human nature' when there is nothing 'out there' to which it refers. What is the relevance of 'to' in the previous sentence, or is it just a syntactic nicety? One way of partially resolving this conundrum is to suggest that what nationalisms do in their various accounts of human nature is to describe surface differences. Underlying these differences are deeper human traits which form the underlying substrate of all peoples. National descriptions therefore form the surface of a group of people; underlying it there are still common human activities – being born, being educated, making love, dying – which are subject to more immediate common knowledge. Life in any society is often about the surfaces; it is the realm in which we carry on most of our everyday existence. Yet, in saying that, we can still claim that there is something of a common humanity underlying the surface. It is this common demeanour which responds to basal facts of births, deaths, and the like. Thus, the fact that we might see the world nationalistically does not mean that such theoretically informed seeing should edge out the elemental facets or demeanours of a common humanity.

However, it is unlikely the keen-eyed exponents of nationalism would be impressed by the above arguments. Copulation, birth and death are quite clearly interpreted differently by the various cultures and nations. However, the contrast between either 'having a common human nature' or 'finding human nature constructed within various nations' may be too sharp. My suggestion would be that there is a *via media*. Nationalism does accept, as suggested above, certain formal theses about human beings: we are self-determining and culture-producing creatures; the human self is socially or communally situated; and humans discover and realize themselves *through* their national communities. These theses could be said to form a regulative conception of human nature. Yet the manner in which they are read or interpreted by nationalisms will vary considerably.

The first thesis concerns self-determination. Nationalism commonly utilizes this liberal argument for self-rule. Admittedly, not all nationalists see all human individuals as possessing this capacity, although clearly liberal nationalists do.[25] In the case of liberal nationalists, self-determination by individuals is still compatible with the liberal nation being self-determining. However, one caveat should be added to this latter point, namely, that liberal nationalists do not resolve the enigma of the relationship between individual self-determination and national self-determination.[26] Liberal nationalists do not argue that individuals can stand outside their nation with a 'view from nowhere'. Rather, individuals exercise freedom with the cultural tools to hand (Tamir 1993, 33). Other nationalists, particularly integral and some traditionalist variants, see individuals as more the direct product of national and/or racial communities and virtually imprisoned in their cultures or *Volkstum*. This is particularly the case with some romantic interpretations. However, it is still a fundamental point in these latter claims that nations are or ought to be self-determining and independent. What we have here is an ambiguous transposition of the argument of self-determination from the individual to the collective level. The nation becomes the self-determining higher-order individual or self. Yet in all these variants self-determination remains crucial.

The second and third theses on human nature can be briefly expanded by making a direct comparison with the contemporary communitarian movement, the main intellectual components of which resonate with the nationalist mentality.[27] A central thesis of both nationalism and communitarianism is the belief that political and moral goods cannot be determined by abstract universal reasoning; they arise, rather, out of particular historical or national communities. There is no neutral premise or idea on which to structure a theory. Second, the community or nation forms the basis of practical reason, value and political judgement. The particularity of historical communities is thus often set, by communitarians and nationalists, against the claims of liberal universality. Third, the self or person is constituted through the community or nation. There are no 'unencumbered selves', to use Michael Sandel's phrase (Sandel ed. 1984, 5–6). Fourth, there are no external universal rational or moral foundations to draw upon outside of nations and historical communities. In addition, we do not need theoretical foundations for a practical communal or national life; rather, we draw upon the interpretations of an already existing tradition or form of life. Praxis in a community is distinct from the arguments of philosophy.[28] This formal communal root of human beings is not really an area of contention between the various schools of nationalism, although the manner in which it is read is open to debate. Liberal nationalists tend to opt for a slighter, more plural notion of the community, which is not incompatible with individual freedoms. Traditional and integral nationalisms argue for a stronger understanding of community which firmly embeds individuals within national or racial norms. Integral nationalists would also add the dimension of superior and inferior nations.

The major differences between nationalists and communitarians are that the latter only deal with community on an abstracted theoretical level, whereas nationalists have been overly concerned to provide an enriched practical content (see Vincent 1997). There are countless millions of people across the world who self-identify with a nationality, and who are directly motivated by such identification. This cannot be said of communitarians, who subsist in a more rarefied realm. Further, nationalists try to identify nations directly with states. Communitarians, to date, have been oddly indifferent to this issue, and, with rare exceptions, have certainly not tried to link their communal conceptions with the juridical state. Communitarians are faced, though, by the additional problem that many communities and associations (like churches, tribes or business corporations) transcend states, which puts the state/community relation into a major difficulty. However, this particular difficulty is not unknown to nationalism and ethnicity. Finally, communitarianism, in much of its output, has not so much been a critique of liberalism as partial salvation from historical critics. What we see in communitarianism is, oddly, 'liberal nationalism' in another format. Michael Sandel's notion of the self is constituted within a liberal community. Charles Taylor is essentially trying to save true moralized liberal individualism or a modern identity from misrepresentation. Michael Walzer's defence of spheres of good (and his injunctions to not invade each other's good and self-understanding) is a more complex argument for a pluralist left liberal society.[29]

One final comment on human nature and its connection with nationalism: a central theme that one finds in romantic thought is self-creation, which can be viewed as a more aesthetic rendering of the self-determination argument. In the German philosophical tradition it has affinities with the idea of *Bildung*.[30] For romantic thought, self-creation and imaginative invention took priority over discovery or representation. The idea of *Bildung* has a subtle place in the nationalist lexicon which is not often fully appreciated – although it is not exclusively tied to nationalism.

In nationalism and much *Bildung* theory, the aim is harmony and freedom within oneself. Freedom is essentially self-determination and the process of learning and forming oneself. If, as many nationalist writers claim, the self is formed out of the filaments of the nation, then it follows that self-formation is simultaneously nation-formation. This claim can be particularly well observed in the arguments over language. For Herder, language is the 'organ of the powers of the soul as the means of our innermost *Bildung* and education' (quoted in Vandung in Eade ed. 1983, 141). Language is seen by Herder as not just an instrumental or representational device, but an active spiritual power which constitutes reality. Each language has a different soul for Herder and is the source of the *Bildung* of each nation and the individuals within it. This point leads to the centrality of language for nationalism.

Languages and Nations

Anyone coming upon the thesis that states are primarily single linguistic entities might be excused some initial scepticism. It is quite clear, if one examines the majority of states today, that different linguistic groups are present, even though in many states certain languages might be more commonly spoken. In some nation states, however, there are no dominant languages; for example, the Swiss have four languages. In addition, even though many highly educated Swiss speak German, it is unlikely that residents of the Ruhr or Bavaria would always clearly understand their dialect. Norway and Denmark have a very similar language and ethnic origin, but regard themselves as different nations. In fact, print-based Norwegian was roughly the same language as Danish till the early twentieth century. Ibsen can be easily read by any educated Dane. Print-based Norwegian, as a separate entity, is a nationalist invention of the twentieth century. In summary, there are often multiple languages within nation states and similar or identical languages spoken across different nation states. There can also be different national units within one state, for example, the Scottish and Welsh in Britain: who commonly (although not exclusively) speak the same language. Finally, the same language can be almost incomprehensible between regional dialects.[31] The crucial point concerning language is, though, can it be used or ought it to be used to separate nations? The answer would appear to be no. Language does not appear to be a clear or precise identification of nationhood. Despite this point, language has figured very predominantly in nationalist discussion. The reasons for this can be divided into two broad areas: historical/empirical grounds and normative grounds.

On the historical/empirical grounds, it is difficult to reject totally the centrality of language to nations. As Hobsbawm remarks, 'One can hardly deny that people speaking mutually incomprehensible languages who live side by side will identify themselves as speakers of one' (Hobsbawm 1992, 51). As many proponents of modernization theory have noted, language, and particularly language homogeneity, are crucial factors in the development of states, and are usually fostered through state education policies. Language conformity also becomes crucial in most states in terms of entry into literary, administrative and political elites, as well as an essential device to facilitate communication and domestic economic markets. Most centralizing and developing states in the late eighteenth and nineteenth centuries, even liberal regimes, were fairly brutal about pursuing such linguistic homogeneity. An early example of such conscious state activity was the Jacobin policy after 1789.[32] The Jacobins imposed the French language coercively and rigorously. There was no room for multiethnicity or tolerance.

One point to note about the above is the fact that even if language does have an important modernizing role to play, it is still often the result of artifice, whether for the purposes of state centralization or secession from a state. Much of the impetus of the nationalist claim for language is premised on its naturalness and antiquity. Yet, as already noted, print-based Norwegian was an invention of the early twentieth century. Before that it was simply Danish. The early 1800s Slovak poet Jan Kollár believed (under the influence of Herder) that there was a pure Czechoslovak language. Although Czech at the time was only a *lingua rustica*, Kollár willed it by literary means to be recognized as one of the Slav literary languages (with Russian, Polish and Serbo-Croat). Many Slovaks were not impressed. Similar literary efforts were made by others to establish Serbo-Croat as the key dialect of the Southern Slavs. Serbo-Croat also developed initially as a literary and folk language from the 1830s. The languages of Galician, Catalan, Basque (Eskuara) and Gaelic were all brought out, dusted down by nationalist philologists and reintroduced in nationalist literature, mostly during the nineteenth century (see Schenk 1966, 16–17).

One of the central arguments in the recent literature which emphasizes the historical importance of language to nationalism, and also takes full cognizance of its artificiality, is contained in Benedict Anderson's work. For Anderson, nations are 'imagined communities' *in toto*, cultural artefacts created near the end of the eighteenth century in terms of local vernaculars. He suggests that nations are, in fact, better understood as equivalent to older cultural systems like religion, rather than nineteenth-century self-conscious ideologies. Anderson interprets the development of vernacular languages in Europe in terms of 'print capitalism'. He remarks that: 'Nothing served to "assemble" related vernaculars more than capitalism, which, within the limits imposed by grammars and syntaxes, created mechanically-reproduced print-languages, capable of dissemination through the market' (see Anderson 1983, 47; also Synder 1954, 21). The Reformation, particularly, saw an immense expansion of publishing in the local vernaculars. Vernacular languages were also increasingly used as part of the administrative machinery of absolute monarchs and state institutions. Printed language, in effect, laid the basis for national consciousness by providing the ideal medium for the imagined community. One decisive invention here was the newspaper, which refracted the totality of world events into the vernaculars of the imagined national communities.

With the intense focus and spread of vernaculars, intellectual interest in philology, lexicography, etymology, grammar and bilingual dictionaries also developed. Immense intellectual energies were expended on these various enterprises.[33] Nineteenth-century Greek, Russian and Serbo-Croat nationalisms were all inspired by language studies, detailed philology and literary inventiveness. 'Everywhere,' says

Anderson, 'as literacy increased, it became easier to arouse popular support, with the masses discovering a new glory in the print elevation of languages.' He continues, 'by the second decade of the nineteenth century ... a "model" of "the" independent national state was available for pirating'. The lexicographic revolution of the nineteenth century established the belief that languages were the personal property of certain groups, imagined as nations. In the later nineteenth century, Anderson envisages the merger of dynastic regimes such as Russia with nationalism as constituting in effect an 'official nationalism' – although he adds 'a certain inventive legerdemain was required to permit the [Russian] empire to appear attractive in national drag' (quotes from Anderson 1983, 77, 78 and 83). Official nationalism was essentially the conservative or traditionalist adaptation of more popular liberal nationalism. The last big wave of nationalism to appear was colonial, in Asia and Africa, and arose partly in response to imperialism. It was again due, to a great extent, to the spread of printed vernaculars, particularly the availability of literature on European nationalism. The latter provided the basis for the invention of new imagined communities.[34] Colonial nationalisms were thus largely modelled on the European experience, although they constructed such nationalisms within their own vernaculars.

Thus, in sum, there are sound empirical and historical reasons for seeing language, particularly in the context of printed language, as crucial to the understanding of nationalism. However, within nationalist literature there is also a great deal of normative argument for the significance of language. The key figure – who is usually given pride of place in such discussions – is Herder. Herder is often placed in the ranks of the anti-Enlightenment, romantic nationalists. This perception is ill founded. Herder was a keen admirer of much in the Enlightenment. He had only limited concerns in common with romantics such as Schlegel or Novalis. He shared nothing of the romantics' yearning for the Middle Ages, revivified Catholicism, cultivation of the isolated feeling ego, nature mysticism and sentimentalism, nor their fascination with metaphysical intoxication.[35] Despite his profound association with the importance of national diversity, a central concept of his whole philosophy was the very Enlightenment notion of *Humanität*, which implied a common essence to humanity. In spite of national differences, which for Herder enriched human existence, all humans were essentially of the same species. Ultimately, all human beings aimed for the highest and most harmonious development (*Bildung*). *Humanität* took on a religious aura for Herder. He noted that 'human essence – *Humanität* – is not readymade, yet it is potentially realizable. And this is true of a New Zealand cannibal no less than of ... Newton, for all are creatures of one and the same species' (Herder, *Idea for a Philosophy of History*, in Herder 1969, 266).[36] Herder's politics were far from conventional. In fact he repudiated the conception of a statist society, preferring instead something equivalent to pluralist anarchy. Isaiah Berlin, for example, compares him to Proudhon, Thoreau and Kropotkin (Berlin 1976, 181). Herder also had no interest in what might now be termed political nationalism. His focus was on cultural nationalism. Although totally enthused by the restoration of Germanic culture and language, its folklore, folk poetry and songs, he none the less denounced simple-minded patriotic favouritism and felt that there was no sense in which one could discuss the superiority or inferiority of nations or races.

Despite the above qualifications, Herder did quite clearly present a theory of language which was immensely prescient of the conjunction between language and nationalism. Herder's theory arose almost fortuitously from an abstruse debate concerning the origin and nature of language. Herder was critical of a particular theory of language which he associated with Condillac, Rousseau and Süssmilch, although exactly how different he was from them and how innovative is open to question. The theory he opposed saw language as an instrument of information storage and communication. Words were taken to designate things in the world and thoughts in the mind. Herder adopted a more expressive or constitutive approach to language. Words, for Herder, were 'companions of the dawn of life'. As one Herder scholar remarks, 'the essence of language formation is not the creation of *external* sounds, but the *internal* genesis of word symbols' (Barnard introduction to Herder 1969, 20). Language was integral to the conscious activity and development of human beings. It was essentially, therefore, a form of action. It did not just record or designate external objects, but conversely had a constitutive and active role. Humans both make and were made within language. Humans perceived nature through the medium of speech and reflection. Natural languages, in the form of primitive cries, are distinct from developed human speech (see Aarsleff 1982, 151). Language, as developed human speech, is the essential medium of freedom and consciousness, reflecting the totality of human energies. The human capacity for self-awareness is also formed in language. For Herder all our conscious states are formed in language. Language is thus integral to thought. The human being develops through thoughtful self-creation, in which language is an integral part.

For Herder, language not only describes, but it also expresses the feelings, emotions, thoughts and will of the person, considered as a totality. He frequently warned against considering reason alone as the dominant faculty of human beings, which was his basic criticism of Kant's conception of human nature. For Herder, language is built out of sense impressions. Since sense impressions of one's locality form the basis of language, it follows that local conditions (geography, climate and traditions of the community) will stimulate differing responses. As languages develop, so do societies and cultures. Language forms the essential historical continuity of a society and its traditions – traditions not being viewed as static phenomena, but rather as processes in continual flux. Culture is the spiritual bearer of this process. All humans using language in this context will therefore form, through dialogue and conversation, distinctive cultures, mythologies and modes of expression. In other words, each *Volk* (people or nation) forms a distinct language community. Each people has a distinctive national spirit, which is not biological or racial, but rather 'a historical and cultural continuum'.[37] For Herder, it is part of the immense richness of the world that we find such different language communities and cultures, each being unique and unrepeatable. It follows, therefore, that knowledge of the way humans have used language 'yields the story of changing uses and meanings' (Berlin 1976, 169). Herder was immensely keen on the idea of extending empirical studies of this richly diverse anthropological material.

We can see clearly the normative importance of language to nationalism for Herder. Later thinkers were to make much of this and supplemented it with other more problematic considerations. After Herder, one of the most notable German writers to focus on language was Fichte, particularly in his *Addresses to the German Nation*. One of the most worrying aspects of Fichte, which is worth considering, is that he accepts the centrality of language to nationality, with the important rider that he is definitely concerned with political nationalism and that certain languages (and thus nations) are superior to others. These points are not found in Herder's theory.

Fichte contended that language characterizes humans, stating that 'men are formed by language far more than language is formed by men'. It constitutes the real human essence. Fichte, however, drew a distinction between natural and compound languages. The German or Teutonic language is a natural *Urvolk* language. As he put it, the German language 'has been alive ever since it first issued from the force of nature'. French and English are compound neo-Latinate languages which show the effect of admixtures. As Fichte comments, 'in neo-Latin languages … incomprehensibility is of their very nature and origin'. Such languages only move 'on the surface', but are 'dead at the root'. The problem he sees for German culture and politics is the import of foreign elements into the language. He gives the example of words such as humanity (*Humanität*), popularity (*popularität*) and liberality (*liberalität*), commenting: 'When these words are used in speaking to a German who has learnt no language but his own they are to him nothing but a meaningless noise.' Fichte continues, 'Now if, instead of the word humanity (*Humanität*), we had said to a German the word *Menschlichkeit*, which is its literal translation, he would have understood.' The introduction of neo-Latinate foreign words, to Fichte, is leading to a lowering of ethical standards. According to Fichte, those racial Teutons, such as the French and English, who have introduced such neo-Latinisms have degenerated ethically and nationally. Thus, he asserts that 'The German, if only he makes use of all his advantages, can always be superior to the foreigner and understand him fully, even better than the foreigner understands himself.' To Fichte, whereas the Germans unite their living language and their mental culture, other degenerate cultures separate out their culture from their language. Mental culture becomes an 'ingenious game'. Only the Germans, as a whole people, can be totally earnest and diligent concerning their mental culture. Thus, for Fichte, the philosophy of other nations always remains thin. To think philosophically or poetically in German is to be transfigured and liberated, since one is in immediate contact with one's nature. Foreigners speaking compound languages are cut off from their natures 'because their life deviated from nature originally and in a matter of the first importance' (all quotations from Fichte 1979, 4th Address, 55–84).

Two crucial conclusions from the above are drawn out in a later address. First, all peoples who speak an original language are or must form a nation and, ultimately, a state. As Fichte notes, 'wherever a separate language is found, there a separate nation exists, which has the right to take independent charge of its affairs and to govern itself' (Fichte 1979, 215–16). If a people has ceased to govern itself, then Fichte maintains that 'it is equally bound to give up its language'. Second, all nations must speak an original language.[38] The frontiers of such a nation state would be internal to language speakers. As Fichte notes: 'the first, original, and … natural boundaries of States are beyond doubt internal boundaries. Those who speak the same language are joined to each other by a multitude of invisible bonds by nature herself' (Fichte 1979, 224). External boundaries of states are the outcome of internal boundaries. Geographical factors are, for Fichte, of little consequence compared to language. If such geographical factors coincide with linguistic boundaries, as in England, then it is fortuitous. Fichte adds here an ominous note, saying that when the territory of a natural people has become too narrow or it wishes to exchange a barren for a fruitful region, it can 'enlarge it by conquest of the neighbouring soil in order to gain more room, and then it will drive out the former inhabitants' (Fichte 1979, 226).

It is anachronistic to try to foist the twentieth-century experience of nationalism onto these earlier thinkers; however, they do bring out very precisely the significance of language for nationalism. Language forms one of the core elements for most nationalist movements up to the present moment. It constitutes a particular focus for secessionist movements such as the Welsh, Quebecois, Flemish and Basque. This particular theme was a key factor in even the liberal *Risorgimento* unificatory form of nationalism during the nineteenth century. *Risorgimento* means 'resurgence', and many such resurgent liberal movements of the nineteenth century were linked closely and often preceded by intense philological research, rediscovery of ancient myths, folk song, poetry and customs. The enormous study undertaken in Germany under the auspices of Baron von Stein – the *Monumenta Germaniae Historica* (1819) – collated vast amounts of historical and philological material relating to German history. In consequence of this work, as Peter Alter remarks, 'past political orders were reinterpreted as the forerunners of nation-states to come' (Alter 1989, 63). This process was repeated throughout Europe. Thus liberal nationalism was not exempt from this linguistic ardour, although at first sight it all looked fairly innocuous. Traditionalist nationalism moved closer to the exclusivism and away from the universalism of liberal nationalism, in some cases moving onto the Fichtean ground of the superiority of particular nationalisms. Language figured slightly less predominantly in integral nationalism in the twentieth century, but its place was taken, especially in the case of national socialism, by racial and biological factors.

Nation States

The nation state was the most popular form of political organization in the nineteenth and twentieth centuries and developed with great rapidity over that period.[39] The older multinational states of the nineteenth century were seen, at the time, increasingly as anachronisms – 'prisons of peoples'. This was the fate of the Habsburg, Tsarist Russian and Ottoman Empires. The nation state was seen, over the nineteenth century, not only to be the precondition to genuine freedom, but also as the ground for modernization and economic development. Some scholars have seen a pattern to this evolution: the first nation states growing from the original West European absolutist and semi-absolutists states, such as France and England, followed by cultural nation states in central and Southern Europe, and particularly unificatory nation states, such as Germany and Italy. Finally, secession nation states expanded in number, and led to the consequent disintegration of multinational states.[40]

In considering the nation state there are a number of conceptual and empirical problems which need to be examined. There is first the problem of the term 'state'. This is one of the more complex ideas in the European political vocabulary. It is a deeply contested term which has been a focus for reflection over the last three to four hundred years. Simply put, the state can denote a people who are organized politically in some manner (depending on how one considers the term 'people'); or the institutions of government (or particular institutions within government – such as the executive or legislative branches); and, finally, it can mean a legal or constitutional structure of rules or even the legal personality of the ruler(s), offices or institutions (see Vincent 1987 or 2002, ch. 2). It is not clear how any of these are related to the nation, except possibly via an interpretation of the people 'being' the state, although such 'popular sovereignty' discourse predates and does not immediately overlap with nationalism. Further, given that there are absolutist, constitutional, ethical, communist, pluralist, federalist and legalistic conceptions of the state, it is not clear whether any or all of them link in with nationalism. In other words, the nation state does not necessarily imply any particular type or form of state. It is void as a theory. Extreme totalitarianism is as likely to conform with nationalism as liberal constitutionalism. Given, therefore, the linguistic commonplace 'nation state' and its renown, it remains perennially puzzling that this total lack of clarity persists on both the nature of the state and its precise relation to the nation.

Second, as implied above, there is a profound ambiguity on the character of the nation itself. There are clearly conceptions of the 'nation state' within the different schools of nationalist thought. Thus, the substance of the nation state will adjust to the particular typology. In terms of the general typology adopted in this chapter, there are liberal, traditionalist and integral conceptions of the nation state. The first of these developed in the nineteenth century and largely corresponds to the classical (and later new or social liberal) view of the state, tempered by moderate nationalist claims. Liberal nationalists have usually upheld forms of parliamentary government, representative democracy, individual rights and freedoms, a flourishing civil society, market economy and the rule of law. In fact, despite the nationalist reputation for emphasizing particularity and localism, liberal nationalists have usually advocated the liberal nation as the universal type. This was certainly the aim of the Mazzinian-inspired 'Young Italy' group and is still advocated by liberal nationalists such as David Miller and Yael Tamir. Equally important is the emphasis laid by all nationalist schools on self-determination. Despite its cryptic history in the twentieth century, self-determination is usually identified as a strong liberal motif. The self-determining individual and the self-determining nation are parallel in some liberal minds.[41] One small additional qualification is necessary here in relation to the theme of liberalism. The 1990s upsurge of interest in moderate nationalism in writers such as David Miller uses nationalism to underpin the distributive justice of 'market socialism' (see Miller 1990 and 1995; Miller in Brown ed. 1994). This could give rise to the idea that there is a socialist nationalism. My own view is that socialist nationalism has usually (especially in much recent discussion) drawn upon liberal forms of argument and is thus more easily considered within the liberal nationalist category.[42] Traditionalist conservative nationalism and integral nationalism developed their own distinctive conceptions of the state. In the case of the conservative traditionalist writers this varied considerably; some elements in Britain being wholly at home in the *Rechtsstaat* tradition, others in France and Germany looking to more corporatist, organicist and hierarchical models. In the case of integral nationalists (as in fascist Italy) it was a vision of an ethical totalitarian state.

Apart from the above ambiguities of the state, the nation and their relation to each other, there is a further problem concerning which came first – state or nation. The reason for seeking an answer to this question is simple: many nationalist writers have wished to prioritize the nation as a natural entity, or at least something possessing great antiquity, and thus suggest that nations create states in their own image. However, in spite of Anthony Smith's elusive arguments on the ethnic origins of nations, the evidence tends to point the other way, especially if one considers 'nations' rather than 'ethnie'.[43] Dynastic, absolutist states precede the existence of nations by centuries. Undoubtedly the common membership, legal structures and traditions of stable absolutist states provided the ideal locations for 'proto-nationalisms'. But the vocabulary of nationalism is not present till much later. Even if nationalism now figures more predominantly, it is also important to grasp that there can be other forms of loyalty, allegiance and legitimacy within states and that nationalism is only one which has arisen in the last two centuries. Thus states pre-exist nations by several hundred years in Europe and, despite nineteenth- and twentieth-century nationalist mythology, do not appear to require nationalism to survive or maintain continuity of rule.

A further related, and already intimated, problem concerning the precise relation between nations and states follows on from the above. The central question here is alarmingly simple: did nations and states in the nineteenth and twentieth centuries – the heyday of nationalist argument – coincide in such a way as to make sense of the compound term 'nation state'? There are a number of ways of examining this question. First, it is arguable that a state is more governable if, pragmatically speaking, a nation coincides with it. This, however, could mean two things. It could be a simple observation that it is empirically the case, or, alternatively, that nationalists deliberately foster the idea to govern more easily. The initial observation is linked to the classic treatment of this question in some more traditional writers, such as Herder or Fichte, where the state and nation are seen to be more or less coterminous on an empirical or naturalistic level. As Herder commented: 'The most natural state is *one* nationality with one national character' (quoted in Ergang 1931, 243–4). The second observation implies that nations are mere artificial constructs which states engineer to govern more easily. This corresponds to those, such as Anderson or Gellner, who see the nation as an imagined artifice. Another way of conceiving the nation/state relation is that a nation is more stable if self-governed through a state. The state forms the protective shell for the nation. This can also relate to the first point, since it can be observed that a state is more governable when it coincides with a nation, but it can also be argued that the nation only flourishes within a state structure.

Despite the above issues there are a number of major difficulties. States are quite clearly more impersonal legal structures where membership is defined by law. Conversely, nations are a different type of social entity, more personal, culturally orientated, emotive and generally defined by other types of criteria (Smith 1991, 14–15). As indicated, the state also precedes historically the nation by many centuries and clearly has subsisted without it. These issues are relatively innocuous. However, they become more problematic when linked with other issues, namely, that there are clearly multiple nationalities and ethnic groups within the large majority of states (see Alter 1989, 111–12; Hobsbawm 1992, 17; Kymlicka 1995a and 1995b). This multiethnicity and multinationalism has intensified over the last fifty years with the decline of Western empires, increased communication, international travel and large migrations of peoples. It is also fostered to some degree by the growing interest in decentralization, regionalism and federalism within states. The phenomenon of multi-culturalism particularly (which might simply be reconfigured as multinationalism or micro-nationalisms) has become, since the 1980s, a more regular feature of Western-orientated states such as Canada, New Zealand and Australia, and is becoming an increasingly widespread phenomenon in many other states, including Britain, Germany, France and the USA; although, admittedly, states such as Japan, amongst others, still appear to frown upon multicultural policy (see Vincent 2002, ch. 7).

Thus, whereas the old multinational states, in the nineteenth century, used to be generally derided by nationalists, it would appear to be the case that the reverse is now true for many states. It is largely a fallacy to think of all states coinciding with nations. The real anachronism and prison of humanity is possibly the conception of the exclusive nation state. Further, nations, ethnic groups and languages move across and transcend state borders. There are, in addition, a large number of transnational groups; multinational companies; global corporations with resources larger than many states; international associations; global trade and communications; and supranational institutions. None appear to be confined to the nation state. Many problematic aspects of life – pollution, environmental control, nuclear technologies and modern warfare – are neither simply national nor state-based problems. The state obviously still has immensely important functions, but its role has been in part diminished and these functions could perfectly well be performed without nationalism. It is still, though, difficult at the present moment to even conceive of a stateless world.

One of the major problems in dealing with the nation/state relation is that it has become firmly enmeshed with other terminology. For example, there is a strong link between nationalism and sovereignty theory. Sovereignty terminology is compara-tively old, in terms of the European political vocabulary, and there are a number of senses in which it has been used which predate nationalism by centuries. One crucial sense of sovereignty, which arose in the seventeenth century, is the sovereignty of the people or popular sovereignty. This becomes particularly significant in the vocabu-lary of the French revolutionary era. Sovereignty is no longer conceived in terms of the law, the monarch or ruler, but rather in terms of the people (or *Volk*), and in many discussions, the term 'people' becomes coterminous with the 'nation'. A people *or* nation is considered sovereign when it is supreme in terms of law-making and self-governance within its own state. States intensified this synonymity of the people and nation by consciously homogenizing populations through language and state-based education policies.

Nationalists always address themselves to the whole collectivity of the people (with the occasional exception of immigrants or foreign workers). They also focus political legitimacy within that whole. Once the legitimacy and political significance of the whole people are established, it is then a short step to another crucial concept – democracy – which is the apparent expression of the will of the nation (Kohn 1945, 191–2). Such national democracies can be liberal, revolutionary or strongly conservative. Popular or national consciousness is an unwieldy vessel and it often veers, under the leadership of certain ruling elites, into mass chauvinism and xenophobia. Democracy is not an intrinsic value; it is more of an instrumental device. It solves certain problems of legitimation, but where it becomes identical with the national ends of states, then it becomes wholly unpredictable.[44] The linkage between democracy and nationalism was also reinforced in the writings of figures such as Ernest Renan and J. S. Mill. Renan had famously described the nation as a 'daily plebiscite' and for Mill the national will was just another expression of the principle of representative democratic government (see Birch 1989, 39). However, there are other senses of democracy, such as participatory democracy or democratic centralism. Democracy is not necessarily linked to liberal democracy alone. The democratic national sovereignty of the people can potentially ride roughshod over the rights of individuals. This can be observed within exponents of the 'nobler democracy' of fascist nationalism.

The most crucial concept of the nationalist canon, which again links closely with democracy and sovereignty, is self-determination. This is the principle that a nation has the right to constitute itself as an independent state and determine its own government and laws. It is a concept which figured particularly strongly in twentieth-century discussions, although its lineage goes back into the early nineteenth century. Its time of greatest early prominence appeared with President Wilson's promulgation of the Fourteen Points after the First World War. As one commentator observed, 'self-determination was to Wilson almost another word for popular sovereignty' (Cobban 1944, 20; see also Moore ed. 1998, 2ff). *Vox populi* was in effect *vox dei*. Wilson himself was deeply surprised by the sheer number who wished for self-determination.[45] Like Mazzini in the nineteenth century, Wilson conceived of only a limited number of nations. Both thought that size and viability would place limitations on the number of nation states.[46] After the Second World War, self-determination was one of the key elements of the vocabulary of decolonizing states (see Bhalla in Twining ed. 1991, 91–2).[47] With the development of the United Nations, self-determination became a central, if still deeply ambiguous, term of late twentieth-century political discourse.[48]

As remarked earlier, there is a subtle transposition in the argument on self-determination of a more conventional liberal argument concerning the freedom of the individual. The free individual is self-determining, thus the free nation is also apparently self-determining. The nation becomes a synonym for the governed. Apart from the difficulty of speaking about the 'self' of a nation, the crucial problem here is the fact that national self-determination does not necessarily correspond to individual self-determination.[49] Liberal nationalists assume some form of automatic 'carry-over' from one to the other. All self-determining nations would somehow be liberal nations.[50] Representative democracy would therefore be embodied in the substantive institutions. Self-determination at the individual level would mean that the government would be determined freely by the voters. Yet, self-determination, in other contexts, implies the right of a state or community to its own independent and distinctive existence. The right of the German *Volk* under the national socialists, or any other such autocratic regime, also becomes legitimized by self-determination. In this latter context, individuals participate or identify their selves with the national policies. In other words, there is little place in this latter perspective for orthodox individual liberty or representative democracy, in the liberal or social democratic mode. In fact it is very difficult to see how pure individual self-determination could be reconciled with national self-determination. The two appear to be potentially at odds, depending upon exactly how one interprets the relation of the individual with the nation. Formally, nationalism as self-determination is as compatible with fascism as with liberalism. Thus self-determination is as elusive as both democracy and sovereignty.

The National Economy

Economic nationalism has provided one of the more dynamic, if still equivocal, practical challenges to more orthodox liberal political economy. Basically, economic nationalism is a doctrine designed to make the nation relatively self-sufficient in times of war and prosperous in times of peace. It holds that nations will try primarily to provide acceptable standards of living for their own members by giving preferential treatment to their own industries and encouragement to consumers to purchase domestically produced goods, in order to underpin a balance of trade and national standards. National well-being is therefore envisaged as intimately related to economic well-being. At its most basic level it contends that economic processes are determined primarily within the boundaries of nation states and not by international trade. Such economic nationalism can be pursued aggressively – where it will often mutate into imperialism – or defensively – in order to protect infant industries against the predations of other states.

A number of distinct ideas are often associated with economic nationalism. It is important initially to differentiate them. Economic nationalism is, though, often seen as equivalent to two specific earlier European movements – cameralism and mercantilism. Thus, for example, economic nationalism often appears in the literature described as 'neo-mercantilism'. It is also associated with economic autarky, tariffs and protectionism. All of these elements can express different forms and degrees of economic nationalism.

Cameralism developed from the sixteenth century within certain German states. It was promulgated by a number of civil servants and agents of the political rulers.[51] Their main interest was in the overall welfare of the particular states. The key to such welfare was the revenue to supply the needs of the states. Cameralism thus developed as a civic technology for administering and ruling. Economics, particularly fiscal revenues, was not regarded as an independent realm from politics, but rather as an important integral aspect which contributed to the general well-being of the state. In other words, economics was subordinate to the political welfare of the state. Many German states at the time, even up to the early 1800s, were small in population and territory, largely agricultural and peasant-based. Some were minor absolutist states ruled by a single prince. Individuals were seen as subordinate to the state – the state being envisaged as an enlarged family unified in the prince.

The cameralists have often been compared with mercantilists, although the comparison has limitations. In the heyday of cameralism, political economy was not a separate science distinct from the state. Mercantilism was however a self-conscious conception of political economy, although still tied to the ambitions of centralizing dynastic states. Mercantilism was concerned with the support of domestic industries by means of tariffs, subsidies, and the regulation of manufacturing. Even the acquisition of colonies was viewed in the same light as providing the raw materials for domestic industry and manufacture. It also saw the deliberate management of the balance of payments as crucial for a successful economy. It advocated the promotion of domestic employment via subsidized exports and a positive discouragement to imports. Mercantilism was a powerful, and, in some cases, dominant doctrine, in England and Continental Europe, of political economy up to the eighteenth century. By some proponents of the time it was also viewed as a process of acquiring gold and silver, by means of a favourable balance of trade. Mercantilists always aimed at a predominance of exports over imports in order to increase the inflow of precious metals. The mercantilist conception of wealth was thus associated with the possession of such precious metals. None of the mercantilists believed in a self-sufficient economy. Some trade was always needed; but mutual benefit in trade was a chimera.

The history of the idea of the self-sufficient state dates back to some of the early forms of political community in the Ancient Greek world (see Finley 1973, 125). However, one of the fullest expositions of the idea can be found in Fichte's book *The Closed Commercial State* (1800), which derived, according to some commentators, from his close observation and admiration for the Jacobins' efforts at state control of the economy after the French Revolution. At the time, in Prussia, mercantilism was under pressure and was eventually abolished in 1786, which led in turn to an economic crisis. Fichte favoured neither mercantilism nor free trade. He argued for a more extensive state controlling the lives, work and security of all citizens. He felt that work should not be a daily burden for citizens, but a joy. Such joy would be secured initially by contracts, enforced by the state, for workers to establish their total security of livelihood in work. Everyone would be free from want throughout their lives. People would be looked after by the state, thus no one would have any further need to hoard money or save extensively. In fact the whole structure of the state was envisaged as a complex series of such contracts between licensed groups of producers, artisans and merchants.[52] The uncontrolled economy, for Fichte, led to a mad scramble for money, which culminated in anarchy and war. The only tax levied would be to pay for officials of the state, teachers and the army, all of whom would have equal pay with the other groups. The state would in turn establish, by diktat, all prices and values. Values would be premised upon use and exchange. The basic value would be a bushel of grain. Thus all values in exchange would be measured by 'grain money'. Fichte argued for the replacement of coinage with a special *Landgeld*, as distinct from exchangeable *Weltgeld* (which should be removed from circulation and totally controlled by the state). A bushel of grain would be equivalent to one note of *Landgeld* – Fichte suggests it could be a piece of leather.[53] Finally, the frontiers would be closed, by gradual steps, to all foreign commerce and the state would become economically self-sufficient. Fichte felt that, 'In a rational state the private citizens simply cannot be allowed to trade directly with a citizen of a foreign country' (Fichte quoted in Heilperin 1960, 86). Any partial closure of frontiers would only cause resentment. It therefore had to be as total as possible. Machines, raw materials and seasonal produce would be brought in by the state, but otherwise borders were sealed. The only people allowed to travel would be the scholars, who would bring back information concerning new discoveries and techniques.[54] They would be expected to work closely with home industries to introduce new techniques and discoveries. In Fichte's opinion, such a state could become idyllic. It would have total security for all its members and no poverty, it would be prosperous, taxation would be light, and little crime would be committed. It is worth recalling that Fichte combined the above autarky with a strong belief in national identity premised on language, a theme developed in his *Addresses*. A state could only effectively close commercially once it had reached its 'natural boundaries'; these boundaries could, however, be sought by war and conquest if necessary (see Fichte in Heilperin 1960, 19; see also Mayall 1990, 80).

Fichte's book moved into obscurity in the nineteenth century, although there were those, such as Ferdinand Lassalle, who remained deeply interested in the work. Many of Fichte's themes also appear in other contexts – some seeing his ideas as implicit in the heyday of Soviet planning, although this seems slightly far-fetched (see Heilperin 1960, 63). However, some economic interest in Fichte's work in Germany was rekindled by the allied blockade of Germany in the First World War, and again after 1933 under the Nazi economic minister Hjalmar Schacht, one of the prime architects of German programmes for autarkic self-sufficiency. Fichte's ideas were generally viewed, at the time, in the context of a war economy, which was in many ways alien to Fichte's conception. Fichte's theories do, though, have some definite resonance with integral and traditionalist nationalism, rather than liberal nationalism. Yet it is fairly certain that Fichte himself would have been distinctly uncomfortable with such an association.

The name most closely associated with economic nationalism and protectionism in the nineteenth century is the German economist Friedrich List, particularly in his work *The National System of Political Economy* (1841). The background to List's work lay primarily in his hostility towards English free trade policies and the incursions of English manufactures into German markets. He strongly advocated a customs union for certain German states (*Zollverein*), which would protect them against the predations of English industry.[55] For List, the history of English commercial treaties involved the attempt to extend English manufactured goods into new markets and 'to ruining the native manufacturing power of those countries' (List 1966, 66–7). List saw England's commercial policies as one of the roots of the American Revolution (List 1966, 95). He was particularly irked by the history of the English Navigation Acts and the conflict between England and the Hanseatic League. England had initially risen from agricultural barbarism through commercial intercourse with the

Hanseatic traders. It then moved into manufacturing and commercial supremacy by protective policies, such as the Navigation Acts, which effectively inhibited foreign trade in British ports. Thus the Methuen Treaty (1703) hindered Dutch and German trade within English ports. List saw this as leading to restraint on the trade of the Hanseatic League, German states and Dutch, and also to the immigration of skilled workers from Europe into England. England actually encouraged this process to enhance its own industries. The same principle was adopted in coal and fisheries. England then effectively policed its trade areas with an extensive navy (List 1966, 47). In fact, it was prepared to go to war to maintain such policies, as in the Anglo-Dutch naval conflict. Having once achieved this commercial supremacy, by ruthlessly protectionist means, England then transformed itself into the pure apostle of free trade, which, in reality, was another means to maintain its economic stranglehold on markets. List's aim was, therefore, to free Germany, and other nations, from England's free trade policies.

List felt that Adam Smith, for one, appeared to have selective amnesia concerning the details of Britain's commercial history.[56] List attacked free trade, *laissez-faire* and cosmopolitanism, but placed his arguments carefully within an historical framework. He contended that all nations move through stages: pastoral; agricultural; manufacturing combined with agriculture; and, finally, the climax of economic evolution, commercial and manufacturing combined with agriculture (List 1966, 177). The latter stage was most favourable to national independence, so long as the nation had a large enough territory, population, adequate natural resources and raw materials. For List, a nation was identified by language, literature, history, customs, laws, territory and institutions and there were often marked differences between them. A nation without an adequate territory or separate language was, he considered, doomed. Like many of his contemporaries he thought that nations differed by climate – the more successful nations residing in temperate zones.[57] Free trade was appropriate to certain stages, like the agricultural stage; however, when manufacturing was in its infancy, in the third stage, it should be protected by tariffs to allow full development. International freedom of trade, at this third stage, meant national servitude. List's 'infant industry argument', which is applied to this third stage, is traceable to Alexander Hamilton's *Report on the Subject of Manufactures* (1791), where Hamilton advocated governmental measures for the encouragement and protection of domestic industries. This argument was expanded by List, who saw the German states and industries of his time at stage three. Free trade might again become appropriate at the fourth stage, once the nation was strong enough to meet competition. Yet the policy of free trade had to be treated with care in order to avoid economic retrogression (see List 1966, 131).

List drew a distinction between what he called cosmopolitical and national economy. Only at stage four could cosmopolitical economy, and thus free trade, function. Before that, the national economy was necessary in order to take full account of the survival and flourishing of the indigenous industries of the nation. List associated cosmopolitical economy with both the physiocratic school and Adam Smith (List 1966, 347). He denied that national economy was thereby advocating a full-scale return to mercantilism. Conversely, he claimed that he had only borrowed certain valuable elements from mercantilism (List 1966, xxx). He had no ultimate objections to cosmopolitical economy. In fact, he was clear that a healthy economic system must, in the final analysis, aim at free trade. He also insisted that a healthy economic system must be premised on liberal institutions and values such as those in Britain or the USA. A rich commercial existence only flourished with some degree of domestic individual freedoms (List 1966, 172). List was therefore quite open in his admiration and commitment to liberal values and professed to be a liberal in politics. However, he was also convinced that most orthodox liberal economists did not know how to deal with the nationalist underpinnings of their own arguments.

List considered it necessary to be aware of certain important aspects about liberalism. First, liberal nations, such as England, which had been strongest in upholding free trade had only attained their pre-eminence by having denied free trade in the past and seeking to protect their own national industries. Second, for those who came late to the industrial race, the advantages of free trade looked less immediately apparent. In fact, in the eyes of the developing nation, free trade looked more like the expansionist and imperialistic nationalism of more powerful nations, in another guise. Third, liberal free trade and liberal values worked for internal domestic markets, but they were not always appropriate for external trade. The free trade argument was a logical extension of the argument attacking government restraint in the domestic sphere. However, such an extension was not always warranted. List notes that '"free trade" has become popular without drawing the necessary distinction between freedom of trade within the State and freedom of trade between nations' (List 1966, 11). This very basic point was, he contended, ignored by Adam Smith. Fourth, cosmopolitical liberalism simply did not take full account of the existence of nations. It overlooked their powerful political and cultural effects and opted instead for an asocial individualism. In liberal economy the conception of the universal consumer took precedence over the national citizen. Fifth, cosmopolitan liberalism failed to grasp the point that real wealth was measured not by money, but by powers of production. Contrary to Adam Smith's views, the powers of production were not facilitated by the division of labour so much as by the union of labour in common production. As List commented: 'As in the pin manufactory, so also in the nation does the productiveness of every individual – of every separate branch of production – and finally of the whole nation depend on the exertions of all individuals standing in proper relation to one another' (List 1966, 160). The unity of the nation underpinned both production and prosperity. Sixth, cosmopolitical liberalism, as a consequence of its blindness to commercial history, neglected the fact that it rested upon the pre-existence of the nation. There was always a residual suppressed statism and nationalism implicit in all liberal thought. States and nations formed the essential backdrop to successful liberal markets. The framework of national law, national defence, national well-being, national aims and the national state was the secure, virtually unconscious background for the market. For List, it was thus not without significance that Adam Smith's key book was entitled *The Wealth of Nations* (1776). Smith's position was typical of a liberal economics which refused to recognize the importance of nationalism to the economy. List advocated making national ends explicit within a liberal framework. Government manipulation of the national market by protectionism was making explicit what was already implicit in liberal theory. It should be clear here that List was advocating not xenophobic, traditionalist or integral nationalism, but a form of qualified and sophisticated liberal nationalism.

Conclusion

Of all the ideologies that have been dealt with in this book, nationalism presents some of the most intractable problems. Even the most casual observer of political events over the last few decades can hardly deny that nationalism is an immensely powerful force in world politics. In spite of the enormous surge of nationalisms in post-war Asia, Africa and the Middle East, some have, none the less, considered that nationalism is still *passé*, its real heyday having been in the nineteenth and early twentieth centuries and coinciding with the growth of the state. It is undoubtedly true that the post-1945 world was an inhibiting element on some nationalist aspirations. The historical association of nationalism with fascism and national socialism initially dampened some potential enthusiasts up to the 1980s, particularly in Europe. In addition, the immediate post-1945 impact of both liberal democracy and communism (via the Cold War) presented an unholy alliance in the face of nationalism. In common parlance, neither ideology has been overly sympathetic to nationalist thinking, partly because both have cosmopolitan or universalist aspirations. In addition, the Cold War military and political confrontation between the USA and the USSR curtailed many overly disturbing nationalist sentiments within the spheres of influence of both powers.[58] Liberal democracies also, in appearance, have tended to slow the effects of nationalism partly through their emphasis on tolerance, pluralism and diversity within civil societies. Finally, the comparative material and economic prosperity of many liberal democratic regimes in the post-1945 era limited the appeal of nationalism as a vehicle of protest.

The concept and practice of nationalism are, though, in an unusual position at the present moment. As stated above, many felt that nationalism, in the post-1945 era, was on the wane. The main exception to this process was the wide array of anti-colonial nationalisms in Africa and Asia. Defenders of the 'waning thesis' have interpreted such anti-colonial nationalism as facets of nation-building, which would weaken fairly quickly once the states established themselves. Indeed, it is partially true that the unity of liberationist and nationalist movements gradually fragments as states are established and develop. However, the events of the post-1989 world have not exactly borne out the hopes of those who looked to the demise of nationalism, particularly in Europe. Many of the older nineteenth- and early twentieth-century fears, criticisms and doubts about nationalism suddenly appear to be relevant again. Nationalism looks, in many contexts, like a rediscovered tribalism, which raises once again the spectres of racism, pogrom and military adventurism. In fact, nationalism appears to share some intellectual territory with the current spate of fundamentalisms in the 2000s. As Hobsbawm comments, 'It seems probable that the visiting extraterrestrial would see exclusiveness and conflict, xenophobia and fundamentalism, as aspects of the same phenomenon' (Hobsbawm 1992, 175). A key difference between religious fundamentalism and nationalism is that nationalism has the flexibility of being vaguer and less programmatic. Anything can fill the vacuum of nationalism and generate wild enthusiasm. This is, in fact, a primary criticism that can be raised against it. Unlike all the other ideologies that we have dealt with in this book, nationalism is the most lacking in substantive doctrine. It tends to absorb the ethos around it and thus reflects what its proponents would most like to see. It is the ideological Janus *par excellence*. This makes it both a deeply frustrating doctrine to deal with and also profoundly elusive.

In reflecting on the occasional xenophobia of countries such as Britain during the Falklands war, or Eastern Europe in the 1990s, it is difficult not to have some sympathy again with Acton's essay on nationalism, published in 1862. He argued that nationalism represents a retrograde step in politics – both for the protection of individual liberty and for the development and cohesion of civilization. Loyalty and obligations to a state are usually directed to a more impersonal body of institutions and rules. In the case of nationalism, loyalty is to some form of ethnic group or body of unrationalized cultural symbols, and in consequence can lead to the oppression or repudiation of other groups. In this sense, it is clear that groups, even ethnic groups, attain far more tolerance and acceptance within the confines of a larger plural constitutional state which is not ethnically or nationally orientated. A self-consciously multinational constitutional state, in this context, would help far more effectively to promote human liberty and civilized behaviour. States, as such, have rarely coincided with nations.

The role of nationalism in contemporary world politics remains problematic. In terms of recent events, it is highly unlikely that nationalism *caused* any changes in Russia, Eastern Europe or Germany. Rather, nationalism was the beneficiary of stark economically orientated decisions made in Moscow and elsewhere. Economic difficulties in the old USSR entailed initially military and economic withdrawal. The events of the 1990s also bear upon unfinished business from peace treaties earlier in the twentieth century. More recent nationalism in other industrialized and developing countries appears to be more a result of factors such as a sense of displacement in the face of rapid global socio-economic change or population movements. In other words, nationalism is either a facet of nation-building and modernization or (in more developed economies) a reactive attitude which expresses feelings of unease with disruptive novelty or sudden economic, political or demographic change.

Furthermore, national economies and nation states have experienced both internal and external pressures. Although Friedrich List's arguments on the 'infant industries' of developing states still have some purchase, none the less in larger established industrialized states (with important exceptions such as Japan) the national economy vision has been subtly modified. The rapid post-war growth of international trade and international trade treaties (such as GATT), international financial organizations (such as the IMF or World Bank), international legal, political and military organizations (such as the UN, the International Criminal Court, and NATO), international travel and migration, and intergovernmental and non-governmental agencies reduced some of the functions of the nation state. In Europe, particularly, the growth of central European institutions, legal and trade processes, and the increasing emphasis on regionalism again have constrained the original role of the nation state.

The more intelligent responses to the growth of nationalism have been threefold. The first has been to reject nationalism as a dated, inchoate and haggard ideology in favour of a renewed emphasis on cosmopolitanism and universalism. This is represented by the various movements of cosmopolitanism, human rights argument and universal justice across boundaries. The central weakness in this claim is that it sounds, occasionally, dangerously like 'whistling in the wind'. It is unlikely that nationalist demands will vanish or that the nation state will not be the fundamental unit of international society for the foreseeable future. The popularity of the 'nation state' has certainly not diminished to the present day. The second response argues that nationalism is a desirable mode of human association and loyalty; however, an important distinction is drawn between bellicose and moderate expressions of nationalism. It is the moderate nationalism which is most acceptable. This response harks back to the distinction drawn originally by Kohn, and then imitated by Plamenatz, between Western and Eastern nationalism. This second response is one taken in a number of recent writings and reflects the emphasis of liberal nationalists (see Tamir 1993, 167). The major drawback with this claim is that nationalism is not an ideology which has any clear substantive doctrines. Once having been fulsomely invited in, it remains unpredictable and is as likely (in fact more than likely) to produce irrationalist blood and soil claims as liberal respect for persons. There is a strong sense that nationalist beliefs drift towards the lowest and most irrationalist common denominator. The third response is to try to separate out the claims of nations and states and to insist that their identification has always been bogus, which is not difficult to do. The task is then to encourage states to embrace both internal regional and ethnic diversity and external linkages with larger bodies such as the European Union. This external linkage would also include subscription to, and full endorsement of, international economic, political, legal, environmental and educational ties. Although this path would not eliminate nationalism, it would certainly contribute towards its constraint and ultimate diminution.

One problem with writing about nationalism, in general, is not only that it encourages prolixity, but also, where predictions are concerned, that events have the propensity to quickly overtake even the most knowledgeable writers.[59] It is, therefore, unsafe to make any firm predictions. It is undoubtedly the case, as stated, that ethnic and nationalist claims will not diminish for the time being. Nationalism will remain a facet of global politics for the best part of the twenty-first century. However, its long-term effects can be overrated. Many of the canonical vague elements of nationalist doctrine, such as the identification of the state with a nation and people, look increasingly odd now. The major difficulty for the foreseeable future will be how to constrain and limit the effects of nationalism.

10

Fundamentalism

The words 'fundamentalism' and 'fundamentalist' are products of the late nineteenth and early twentieth centuries. The first well-established usage is not disputed. Every commentator who writes on fundamentalism concurs that these words were first used in North America, in fact in California, in the first two decades of the twentieth century.[1] The more specific history of its usage will be dealt with in the next section, concerning the origins of fundamentalism. On one level the term 'fundamentalism' itself is relatively unproblematic. Like other ideological concepts it can have an ordinary (often derogatory) as against a descriptive (or more technical) connotation. Thus fundamentalism can ordinarily imply fanaticism, dogmatism, intolerance, anti-intellectualism, terror or extremism. This sense can and does apply to many who would be described as religious, but it can extend well beyond any overt religious connotation. Anyone can be excessively narrow-minded and dogmatic. One could thus be a fundamentalist Marxist or a fundamentalist free-market liberal. This extension of usage beyond religion has indeed been given credence in certain writings. However, religion, particularly in the last decade has tended to take the limelight – contributing to what Mark Juergensmeyer calls a more general 'fundaphobia' (Juergensmeyer in Marty and Appleby eds 1995, 354).

The more ordinary usage – although remaining an inevitable subtext in all discussions – is not the key concern of this chapter. The broader descriptive account is also not dealt with here. The primary focus is on the religious connotation of fundamentalism. This latter usage, certainly since the 1980s, has been explored predominantly in historical, sociological and comparative religion studies, and primarily within the sociology of religion. My own emphasis in this chapter will be to scrutinize the ideological use of the term.

The origin of the descriptive sense of the word 'fundamentalism' is Latinate. The Latin term *fundus* means ground or base; a *fundamen* or *fundamentum* is a foundation; a *fundator* is a founder. In this sense the term 'fundamentalism' implies a return to, revival, or basing oneself upon an established ground or foundation. As one writer has commented, fundamentalism can be characterized as 'the reaffirmation of foundational principles and the efforts to reshape society in terms of those reaffirmed fundamentals' (Voll in Marty and Appleby eds 1991, 347). Apart from this descriptive understanding there is little over-arching consensus within the literature on its distinctive features (Kuikman in Schick et al. eds 2004, 51).

One semantic complication arises with regards to the more universal deployment of the word 'fundamentalism'. Does it correspond to all religions, cultures and more particularly languages? This would chiefly be important in the case of contemporary radical Islamism – which conventionally many commentators identify as an archetypal example of modern fundamentalism. Thus is there an equivalent word or phrase in, say, Arabic or Farsi for the term 'fundamental' or 'fundamentalism'? In Arabic the word *usul* (or *usuli*) – denoting roots – is one possible candidate. The Arabic term *usuliya* can also refer to fundamental aspects of Islamic jurisprudence. There is little solid agreement here. Thus the jury remains out on this comparative semantics question. Exposito, for example, thinks that 'it tells everything, at the same time, nothing' (Exposito 1983, 7). The same semantic point holds for both Farsi and Hebrew. There are Hebrew terms that Israelis employ to describe the more extreme religious Right (*yamina dati*): for example, groups such as the Gush Emunim (Bloc of the Faithful) and the Haredim. However, there is no indigenous Hebrew word precisely equivalent to 'fundamentalist'. The same holds for the languages which encompass, for example, Hinduism, Sikhism and Buddhism. Despite this latter point, the term 'fundamentalism' has still been frequently applied in both the pejorative and descriptive senses to aspects of all the world religions. This broad application is in large part due to certain conceptual characteristics of fundamentalism which possess what a recent commentator has called 'family resemblances' (Ruthven 2004, 4). Further, for others, no other coordinating term 'was found to be as intelligible or serviceable' for social scientific inquiry (see Marty and Appleby eds 1991b, viii and ix).

The semantic status of fundamentalism relates closely to another question. Does fundamentalism actually qualify as a political ideology? This is a troubling issue. One fact that is difficult to avoid is that the term is currently used very widely *as if* it were a political ideology. In fact many have seen it as the most significantly worrying political ideology of the early twenty-first century. Some see it as inheriting the mantle of the ideological extreme Left (or indeed extreme Right), entering the political vacuum in the later 1990s with relish and energy and initiating a new version of the Cold War – in this case focused on terror. Pushing this more speculative issue to the side, the only point to note here is that if is considered to be an ideology, it is an *untypical* one for some commentators, certainly in comparison to the others analysed in this book. In the course of this chapter I do make the assumption that fundamentalism can be dealt with as an ideology; however, it is none the less important to register and canvass some of the difficulties with this claim.

For the sceptical critic, fundamentalism could be considered untypical, for a number of reasons: first it does not appear, *prima facie*, to have any core conceptual beliefs which mark out an idiosyncratic political stance. If anything, for the critic, there are a wide range of often incommensurable religious beliefs. In this sense it might be simply mistaken to refer to 'it' (fundamentalism) in this singular sense. It gives the verbal impression of a largely bogus unity; not that any ideologies considered in this book necessarily embody a totally definitive conceptual consensus. Therefore in terms of fundamentalism, at most one might say there are contingent fundamental beliefs – Christian, Islamic, Jewish, and so forth. Second, for the critic there seems to be little which marks out a unique or distinctive view of human beings, community, the economy or the state – as one might find in, say, liberalism or conservatism. In fact, if anything, there are marked differences on these issues which can be located in distinct religious structures. There are therefore miscellaneous religious beliefs about the nature of the economy or state, but nothing that appears necessarily to unify them. Once more, this point is *not* wholly decisive in terms of more conventional secular ideologies considered in this text – all embody internal diversity. Third, where does fundamentalism begin and end? There is an unexpectedly odd, more eclectic usage of the word 'fundamentalist' in contemporary discourse – although further reflection will indicate that it is not so odd. Thus, one could theoretically be a fundamentalist liberal, agnostic, atheist or secularist. This would certainly be the case if one felt that there were basic fundamental truths which characterized these domains, which had to be held to dogmatically at all costs. In other words, there could be no viable compromise on these fundamental truths.

Finally, an issue which is not often canvassed in the fundamentalist related-literature: if one compares fundamentalism with other ideological structures of thought, there is something slightly unsettling about the terminology 'fundamentalist'. Virtually all ideologists (and ideologies) are wholly content to accept the title of their chosen doctrine. Thus, self-conscious liberals, feminists or even fascists are usually quite content, if not eager, to accept the ideological label. There may be contestation about the precise accuracy of a label, and most ideological labels can, of course, be used pejoratively. One could also refine the label, for example, and insist that one is a classical liberal and not a social liberal. This is all fairly predictable. It thus often follows that a liberal called a fascist or a fascist called a liberal might both take exception to the description.[2] However, the standard response would usually be to correct the description. Yet, this is manifestly not the case with the large majority of fundamentalists. Within the diverse literature, only a tiny minority of those who are designated as fundamentalist accept the label, whereas, in terms of contemporary usage, the large majority of those identified as fundamentalist tend to reject the designation as a mis-description. Despite these critical points this chapter will take seriously the proposition that fundamentalism can be considered to be an ideology, and will try to show certain core conceptual features which enable us to identify it.

The Origins of Fundamentalism

Before we can move any further in the discussion it is important to get some historical purchase on the term 'fundamentalism'. Where did it derive from? This section will therefore review some of the key accounts concerning the historical origins of the concept. As mentioned earlier, there is no contention about the *original* uses of the term 'fundamentalism'. However if one were to try to encompass the wider fundamentalist movement, then things do become messier. As Marty and Appleby comment, 'One could continue almost indefinitely with examples of fundamentalist or fundamentalist-like movements simply by scanning any days' headlines ... [regarding] dozens of ... flash points around the world where religion forms at least an ideological basis, and often the cultural and social contexts, for complex and highly sophisticated movements' (Marty and Appleby eds 1991, 814). However, sticking to the precise origin of the terminology of fundamentalism is initially more straightforward. Two devout US oil-based businessmen brothers, Milton and Lyman Stewart, embarked on a programme of sponsoring Protestant Christian pamphlets devoted to fighting against the entrapments of humanism, liberal theology and religious progressivism. They funded the free distribution of pamphlets to pastors across America. The pamphlet series was focused on what was termed the 'Fundamental of the Faith'. The series title was *Fundamentals: A Testimony of Truth* (1910–15) (see Schick et al. eds 2004, 7).[3] The final set of pamphlet writings amount to approximately twelve volumes. The term 'fundamental' implied that it was necessary to go back to the basics of what it was to be a Christian. These were largely a belief that the Bible was the inerrant word of God, that the world was created *ex nihilo* by God, that miracles were authentic works of God, that Jesus Christ was the result of a virgin birth, and that he was crucified and resurrected. The doctrine of substitutionary atonement (that is, he died for our sins and he would return in the context of the Last Judgment) was also a central tenet.

There were additional beliefs to note, as well as some internal divisions. Because both the Stewarts believed in – what are often referred to as – 'end-time' prophecies in the biblical narratives of Ezekiel, Daniel and particularly the Revelation of Saint John, they held to an idea which still characterizes many US fundamentalists to the present day – namely 'Rapture'. Rapture denotes that on a specific day (a day which many have tried actually to designate) the faithful or righteous will be, in a moment, lifted up to God. Some have even speculated on the demographic effect of this![4] Furthermore, a large section of US fundamentalists also believe in the Second Coming or dispensation of Christ, that is, when Christ comes to initiate his thousand-year reign. Dispensationalism was a term coined by the nineteenth-century religious writer John Nelson Darby (1800–82) to describe Christ's Second Coming. Subsequently there have been many debates on the nature and number of such dispensations. In fact the Second Coming doctrine forms a core to three other big religious movements in the US: the Mormons, the Seventh Day Adventists and the Jehovah's Witnesses. The concern with the Second Coming has generated an enormous interest amongst fundamentalist groups, and continues to do so. A number of authors who focus on the Rapture and speculation on post-Rapture experience, such as Hal Lindsay, Salem Kirban, Tim LaHaye and Jerry B. Jenkins, have been immensely successful writers. Lindsay's works, for example, have sold somewhere in the region of twenty-eight million copies. There are some slight differences, particularly between what are called premillennial and postmillennial dispensationalists. Premillennialists believe that Christ's coming will trigger the millennium; up to that moment they anticipate a worsening of conditions, particularly under the rule of the Anti-Christ and with the onset of the Apocalypse. Postmillennialists believe in a state of perfection before Christ's coming – they are, though, far less common in fundamentalist ranks.

The 'ist' dimension of 'fundamentalist' was first used by a Baptist, Curtis Lee Laws, in the 1920s as part of a positive self-description. Returning to a point made earlier, it is clear that at this stage there were those who were more than happy to be described as fundamentalist, although it is worth noting that their political pro- gramme was virtually non-existent. This is the only time when the word was embraced, by a significant grouping, as a positive self-description. It should also be noted here (which circumscribes this whole debate) that they were exclusively a group of North America Protestants. As A. L. Mencken quipped, this was a time when if travelling across America by train and heaving an egg out of the window anywhere, one was more than likely to hit a fundamentalist. The turning-point for this terminology, to the present day in the USA, even for those who had previously embraced it in the 1920s, was the famous, or infamous, 'Monkey' trial in Dayton, Tennessee in 1925. Without going into the minutiae of the trial (which was premised on a biology teacher John Scopes and the teaching of evolutionary biology in school), it created a media frenzy and the American Civil Liberties Association used it as a device to pillory Tennessee State Law on such contentious issues. The cross- examination by Clarence Dow of various witnesses defending the biblical version of creation against evolution, which was widely publicized across the USA, was, to put it mildly, profoundly humiliating. Although Scopes was convicted – a conviction quashed on appeal – the upshot of the trial was a strong sense of the ignorance, shal- lowness and stupidity of the fundamentalist position, as used against Scopes. The result of this was, as most scholars acknowledge, a massive loss of confidence and a partial withdrawal from public debates among such believers and significantly a hesitance and deep unease with the terminology 'fundamentalist' being generally applied to them. Even in the period of fundamentalist recovery from the 1970s to the present day (when the category has been picked up by the academy), there is still a tangible reluctance to accept the overt description 'fundamentalist'. This may well be because it still denotes in many contexts dogmatic intolerance and simple-minded ignorance.

As pointed out in the previous section, the issue becomes semantically and his- torically awkward when we move into other religious forums. No other religions – for example, Islam, Judaism, Buddhism or Hinduism – have ever had any historical moment or 'word usage' precisely equivalent to the origin of US fundamentalism, that is, where the term 'fundamentalism' was accepted by a whole group as a posi- tive self-description. The scholar of fundamentalism Bruce Lawrence suggests the word was used as an external description of Islamic movements by H. A. R. Gibb in his book *Mohammedanism* (1953) (later titled *Islam*) with reference to the pan- Islamic reformer Jamal al-Din al-Afghani (Lawrence 1989, 272 n. 10). It was also used – again as an external description – of the activist Abd al-Aziz Ibn Saud in the 1930s by the then British chief minister in Jeddah, Sir Reader Bullard. These Islamic activists all shared certain anxieties over colonial rule and the unpredictable advances of modernization, a dislike of the impact of Western culture and, probably most importantly, the conviction that Muslims needed to return to their basic beliefs. It has also subsequently, with hindsight, been applied broadly to groups such as the Muslim Brotherhood (founded in Egypt in 1928), the Jamaati-Islami in Pakistan and the Refah Party in Turkey, as well as to particular theoreticians, such as Hasan al-Banna, Sayyid Qutb, Abdul Ala Mawdudi and Youssef M. Choueiri. In the case of Islam this has often led to a distinction between Islam and Islamism, Islamism (or radical Islam) being equivalent to fundamentalist Islam.[5] This in turn has led to continuing arguments as to where true Islam lies. A similar argument appears in most religions.

Many modern Islamic fundamentalists, like fundamentalists of most religions, do, though, see some continuity with their own religious past. The fundamentals that have to be recovered or revived are often seen to be in some earlier period. Thus there is a frequent citing of a golden age of Islam (or Christianity or Judaism), as well as a sense of linkage with eighteenth- and nineteenth-century traditions (Voll in Marty and Appleby eds 1991, 348). There are subtly distinct accounts of Islamic history amongst different elements of Muslim culture.[6] In this sense there are often dissimilar perceptions of the past between, for example, the Islamic fundamentalists and the more traditional or conservative elements of Islamic culture. All generally claim to represent the truth of Islam. A lot also depends on whether one is a Sunni, Shi'ite, Wahabbi or indeed a Sufi. Further, as Abdullah A. An-Na'im argues, each Islamic response needs to be historically contextualized in terms of particular circumstances and crises (An-Na'im in Juergensmeyer ed. 2005, 29). However, outside of these complex internal genealogical debates, most scholars do trace the origin of Islamic fundamentalism very specifically to Egypt in the period 1902 to 1928. The 1928 founding of the Sunni Muslim Brotherhood is usually cited as the key event (see Voll in Marty and Appleby eds 1991, 354 and 366). The central message of this latter movement was a recall to the religious fundamentals of faith and the concomitant social and moral reconstruction of society on this revived basis.

Many were reacting to specific events. For some early twentieth-century Muslim intellectuals the advent of the First World War did puncture the idea of a rationally motivated West. Many still carried on with themes of nationalism, liberalism and democracy. Marxism also had an impact up to the late 1960s. However, all these ideas began to mutate slowly within fundamentalists movements from the 1920s. There was a conscious sense of resistance to Western legal, political and moral concepts. Such concepts were linked with the Western colonial and imperial legacy. The French and British colonial impact upon Egypt, Syria, Palestine and Iraq, and later, and more significantly, the recognition of the state of Israel in 1948 by the United Nations, caused profound disquiet in the Islamic world. Radical Islamism, like most fundamentalisms, posed an alternative to the secular and ex-colonial Western ideologies of liberalism, nationalism, socialism and Marxism.

Fundamentalism has often made its public mark by attempting to set the social and political agenda and by defining what should carry weight in public discourse. It has done this by claiming to represent true Islam (or alternatively true Judaism or true Christianity). This notion of true Islam (or true Judaism or 'born again' Christianity) is sometimes set against a conception of traditional Islam (or Judaism or Christianity), which has either become too accommodating and accepting of secular ideologies, or has simply lost the fundamentals of the faith. The gradual Islamicization of public debates in countries such as Pakistan, Egypt and even Turkey over the mid to late twentieth century testifies to the partial success of this strategy. The US Christian fundamentalists also had some limited success with the Republican Party over the 1980s, although it was constrained by the broader democratic and constitutional factors of American society.

In terms of fundamentalism in different religious contexts, Catholicism has tended to place a more immediate authority in the hierarchy of the church itself, rather than scriptural or text-based sources. This fact alone has tended to put it at one remove from fundamentalist urges. However, with the advent of Catholic '*intégrisme*' – particularly with the various polemical critiques of the liberalizing aspects of the Second Vatican Council (1962–5), by the likes of Archbishop Lefebvre, Father Gommar De Pauw and Father Francis Fenton in the 1970s and 1980s – something approximating to fundamentalism appeared within Catholicism (see Dinges in Marty and Appleby eds 1991, 81ff). There has been a definite shared sense (with Protestant fundamentalism) of a religiosity marked by objective, legalistic, unchanging fundamentals.[7] Practices such as the Latin-based Tridentine mass, particularly, took on an objectivist fundamental character. Catholicism was thus seen to have an activist core determined to fight a spiritual war against the subversions of modern liberalism, secularism and humanism. Some have even suggested that organizations such as Opus Dei have a definite fundamentalist character.

In Judaism the key two groups associated with fundamentalism have been Gush Emunim – who although comparatively small have none the less made their mark, particularly over the settlement policies of the Israeli government – and the Haredim. Again with both these latter groups we are largely speaking of developments since the 1970s. Gush Emunim have been helped by links with the Likud Party. It thus represents, in part, what one writer has called a 'crystallization of fundamentalism', a stance which has been closely linked 'to the stance of the revisionist extreme right' (Aran in Marty and Appleby eds 1991, 288–9). Some critics have indeed called it 'Israeli Khomeinism'. In the Jewish case there seems to be a much closer link between nationalism and fundamentalism.[8] A similar comparatively recent pattern of fundamentalist politicization has also occurred within Hinduism, Sikhism and Buddhism. Elements of these religions have all attracted the terminology of fundamentalism.[9] All such elements developed in this manner gradually from the 1970s and 1980s.

In summary the word 'fundamentalist', used as a positive self-description, originated with a specific group of North American Protestants in the 1920s, who later repudiated and indeed often continue to repudiate its use. The decisive change of perspective took place following the Scopes trial in Tennessee. After a hiatus and period of withdrawal, fundamentalism in the USA came back with a vengeance in the 1970s and 1980s. A similar temporal trajectory holds for Islamic fundamentalism, deriving from the 1920s, becoming swamped for a time by nationalism, Marxism and liberal debates, and then re-emerging in a religiously orientated format in the two decades up to the 1990s. Subsequently, particularly in the 2000s, the term 'fundamentalism' has been much more widely applied and there has consequently been a search for similar words in other languages and religious traditions. Some of these uses of fundamentalism do, at points, seem, however, strained, especially in religions such as Buddhism.

The Nature of Fundamentalism

Having reviewed certain theories about the origins of fundamentalism, this section is primarily focused on an overview of some of the key theoretical explanations and interpretations of fundamentalism that figure in the literature. This will, however, still entail some brief historical reference. This section will conclude with a brief clarification of what fundamentalism should not be associated with, primarily as a way of preparing the ground for the conceptual discussion in the following sections.

In the same period (the 1970s and 1980s) that North American fundamentalists were recovering their confidence and expanding their political programmes, the more vehemently many of them denied the description 'fundamentalist' – a description they would have been largely content with in the 1920s. However, this later period of denial also saw ironically the sudden development in academic discussion of fundamentalist studies, a discussion which moved way beyond the North American exemplar. Between 1988 and 1993 this academic awareness culminated in the large fundamentalism research project, directed by Martin E. Marty and R. Scott Appleby, who organized ten conferences with over one hundred scholars and ultimately published five very substantial volumes of case studies, via the University of Chicago Press, between 1991 and 1995. This project utilized the term 'fundamentalism' on a multi-faith level. We can see in these volumes a range of sophisticated interpretative and explanatory accounts being employed to explain the phenomenon. However, the dominant academic motif tended to be sociological in character

It is only comparatively recently that fundamentalism has made an appearance in political studies – sometimes tangentially via the focus on terrorism. However, it is still a minority preoccupation and, to date, it has been sociologists who have made the running on research. One key reason for this sociological interest in fundamentalism is pertinent. The general presentiment of the whole discipline of sociology, up to probably the 1980s, in terms of what would be regarded the assumptions of its founding figures – Saint-Simon, Comte, Marx, Spencer, Weber and Durkheim – was that social evolution was a movement away from a religion-centred conception of social life towards a more secular, scientific and rationalized conception. Sociology itself was, in a sense, part of this increasing scientization and rationalization process of society. Comte is one of the better known initial expositors of this view in his conception of the development of positivist science. In Durkheim's sociology the movement is neatly caught in the distinction between mechanical and organic societies, that is, the distinction between ritual or mythically imposed structures of meaning, as against self-generated social structures. Durkheim's conception of 'collective conscience' did function in a similar way to a religion, although 'function' is the key word. Durkheim saw religion as a means by which society accomplished integration, by linking itself with beliefs and values that internally make sense to that collectivity (see Durkheim 1995). This conception of religion gives a vital functional role to the experience of sociality, rather than to any notion of a deity. Weber also linked the Protestant religion with the process of secularization itself, particularly in terms of its subtle relation with capitalism, leading ultimately to spiritual disenchantment as a concomitant of modernity.

In summary, from its inauguration as a discipline, sociology has been steadfast in seeing religion in the current world as a meagre survival from archaic times, and fated to evaporate with the development of science and enlightenment. Something similar holds for the whole gamut of social scientific understandings of religion. Religion is a curiosity to be studied, not to be taken seriously as a substantive form of understanding. In the light of the centrality of presuppositions such as secularization, modernization, rationalization, and so forth, to the discipline of sociology, it is understandable that the recent rise of fundamentalism has caused some flurries of concern in the sociological fraternity. Given the character and development of the sociology discipline, why is religion making such a come-back in all types of society? In the work of some more recent sociologically inclined writers, such as Robert Bellah's *Beyond Belief* (1991), Phillip Hammond's *The Sacred in a Secular Age* (1985) or Harvey Cox's *Religion in the Secular City* (1985), the contention is that religion has not so much collapsed or disappeared with the advent of secularization and modernization as subtly adapted to modern circumstances.

There is one further point which could explain the interest of sociology in fundamentalism. Fundamentalism shares something noteworthy with ideologies such as fascism. Because of the oddity, bizarre or just random quality of national socialist or fascist beliefs, there has often been a view in twentieth-century literature on fascism that the important thing is to focus on non-ideological explanation. Fascism is thus sometimes considered as more of a pathology. Psychological, historical, sociological or economic approaches might be more revealing. Thus, a great deal more insight can be gained (so the arguments goes) into fascism by bypassing ideas and beliefs and refocusing instead on the economic conditions, psychological or biographical profiles and social functions of fascist organizations. In fact this type of explanation would be the preferred account of fascism in much sociological or historical commentary. The same point could also be applied with some ease to fundamentalism. Fundamentalism might thus be better *explained* as a social pathology rather than an ideology. In this sense the social, economic or psychological causes behind fundamentalism become really significant. One can see the attraction of this approach, since it allows the observer to ignore the doctrinal claims of fundamentalists and shifts attention to causal social explanations and general pathologies. It allows a more unified field of explanation.

However, as suggested in the fascism chapter, there are none the less certain intellectual themes, concepts and values which can be disentangled in fascism, even if they do not necessarily look that overtly reasonable. The same broad point holds for fundamentalism. Further, on another count, fundamentalism does share some unexpected formal and, at points, some substantive ideological affinities with fascism. Indeed some key fundamentalist writers, such as the Pakistani writer Sayyid Abdul-A'la Mawdudi, did express an open admiration for aspects of European fascism.

However, the question still remains: what are the core themes of the ideology? Before moving to a discussion of these intellectual themes in the next section, I want to focus briefly on the issue as to what fundamentalism should not be associated with. This is intended to prepare the ground for a more substantive ideological account.

Primarily fundamentalism is not synonymous with all and every form of extremism. Most movements of any complexion – even bird-watching or stamp collecting – can have extremists, that is, those who are deeply reluctant to exhibit any compromise with their sincerely held values and will do virtually anything to prevent such a compromise. Undoubtedly many religious fundamentalists are or have been extremists, but whether this is a genetic tag for all fundamentalists is open to question. Because certain Islamic fundamentalists attacked the World Trade Center does not entail that all fundamentalists entertain the same extremist approach. In fact this strategy would be repudiated by a majority of US Christian fundamentalists.

Further, there is a frequent denial in the literature that fundamentalists are simply religious conservatives or traditionalists. In fact, in practice, in religions such as Islam, Christianity and Judaism it is often the case that fundamentalist factions are in conflict with conservative or traditional institutional forces. This has certainly happened in Islam, where fundamentalist activists have come into conflict with the more traditional scholars of the *ulama*.[10] There are still, though, undoubtedly overlaps between the two dimensions. Thus, the early Protestant fundamentalists in the 1920s were probably more conservative and traditionalist by instinct. In addition all fundamentalists – in all religions – to the present day, usually make some form of appeal to a purer or more primal traditional past, as a way of setting boundaries and attracting loyalties. In this sense religious fundamentalism does encode an understanding of tradition, which is then treated as, in some manner, inviolate. No commentators would deny this. However, the fundamentalist past is different. It is often a mythic or manipulated past, used more for symbolism and rhetorical flourish in the present. Most of the current fundamentalists are far from overtly traditional; they are frequently younger, more educated, often highly adaptable to modern conditions and technologies. The use of an invented tradition is more to focus on current social prescription for either national or cultural rejuvenation. In this sense fundamentalists are more concerned to adapt traditions as a way of challenging, criticizing and modifying modernity. Defence of the old or traditional, because it is old, is not what fundamentalists are about. Their *modus operandi*, if anything, is to use tradition instrumentally as part of a wider programme of current public action.

Finally it would also be wrong to think of fundamentalism as just a cult. The cult reliance on the authority of charismatic leaders (such a David Koresh of Branch Davidian or Jim Jones in Guyana) is not so prominent within fundamentalism, although again there are still undoubtedly important charismatic leaders within fundamentalist groups, such as Al-Qaeda's Osama Bin Laden or Hezbollah's leading figure, Sheik Muhammad Hussein Fadlallah. Such figures unquestionably have an authoritative status. However, more generally, they would tend to derive their authority not so much from being charismatic figures, as from an authoritative reading of scriptures, such as the Qur'an, Bible or Torah. Thus, even the leaders themselves wish to be seen as acting in concord with established tradition and textual authorities. In cults there is usually a break with tradition and extra-heavy reliance upon leaders. The death of a cult leader usually leads to the demise of the cult. This is not the case with fundamentalist groups.

In summary, it is a mistake to try to think of fundamentalism as simply a form of political or religious extremism. It would also be an error to try to locate fundamentalists either as simply religious conservatives or traditionalists, or as a modern form of a cult. The picture is more complex.

Politics and Religion

These next few sections now turn to the ideological components of fundamentalism. As in all the ideologies studied in this book, there is no pristine monolithic fundamentalist ideology, in the same way as there is no monolithic liberalism or anarchism. There are, rather, a series of formal core conceptual commitments which embody both deep internal complexity and contestedness as well as overt family resemblances. However, for fundamentalists themselves – like most ideological protagonists – the majority of these conceptual commitments are seen as essentialist, that is, having a secure uncontested meaning. Many of these commitments will be examined in the next few sections

What are the core ideas which enable us to identify the ideology of fundamentalism? It is worth reminding ourselves here that this would have to cover a diverse range of phenomena and groups, many of which eschew the terminology. The really distinctive idiosyncrasy of fundamentalism is connected to religion. However, the relation with religion is complex and multi-faceted. One should not rush to any simple-minded conclusion on the issue. A critical point arises here which needs to be immediately addressed: is fundamentalism really about religion? This question has a number of dimensions to it which stretch way beyond the discussion of this chapter. Let me approach the easiest of these. The basic gist of the point is that many of the features that we might *prima facie* associate with fundamentalist religious groups – say a central body of truths accompanied by authoritative text or texts, a demand for unconditional obedience to this truth, and so forth – can all be associated with what might loosely be called secular bodies of ideas. Thus, the argument is that fundamentalism is something far broader than religion. As one commentator has remarked, 'fundamentalism has replaced communism as the spectre haunting the Western consciousness: a spectre that looms ever larger in the aftermath of 9/11'. He continues that 'it's not too fanciful to suggest that when you step outside the door in the morning, you step into a fundamentalist world, a new dark age of dogma' (Sim 2004, 4 and 7). In this context many apparently secular ideologies come under the rubric of fundamentalism, not least free-market liberalism, nationalism, environmentalism, feminism and even, for the above author, the pervasive performance management culture that currently governs Britain's public services.[11]

In this context it is difficult not to think that most ideologies and thought structures, of many and various types, have their fundamentalist components. As Malise Ruthven puts it: 'Virtually every movement, from animal rights to feminism, will embrace a spectrum ranging from uncompromising radicalism or "extremism" to pragmatic accommodationism' (Ruthven 2004, 32). In all such movements there are those who are unwilling to negotiate their fundamental principles. However, whereas some see fundamentalism as something which characterizes our age (religion being but one potential fundamentalist offender), other commentators are much less certain. In my own reading I contend that fundamentalism is something that – at the present moment – is more predominantly associated with religion. This is the general line of scholarly reasoning which developed from the Fundamentalism Project of the 1990s, with which I concur. To draw it beyond religion is to make the category too broad.

Thus, my response to this more comprehensive use of fundamentalism is to suggest that it has more purchase, as an ideological concept, if we think of it in the context of religion. However, and this is where things begins to get messy, if we are addressing fundamentalism as an ideology, then we have to think of religion and politics in tandem in some manner. What does this relation imply in practice? Second, an even more awkward question which has been blithely neglected to date, what do we mean by religion? Third, one of the critical issues mentioned by most commentators on religious fundamentalism – including the bulk of the sociological commentary – is that it tends to be a reaction or challenge to a crisis of secularization and modernization. What, then, is meant by secularization and modernization in this context?

This first question is important in terms of delineating the precise area for analysis of fundamentalism. Crudely put, there are a number of ways in which the relation of politics and religion can be configured. On one count, religion can be completely separated from politics. This can be done for religious or political motives. Thus Augustine's two cities idea is one well-established form of the religious argument. Politics in this latter context is a hopeless realm of irremediable imperfection and a mere staging post to a more perfect existence in the heavenly city. It can also be argued, from the politics side, by those who see, for example, religious civil war as something to leave well behind, that religion and the secular state should be completely separated. However, one other dimension here is the possible fusion or subtle linkage of politics with religion. This can again be initiated from the religious or political side. Put at its simplest, in one reading religion colonizes or subjugates politics and in the other reading politics colonizes or subjugates religion.

If one were to delve further into this rough typology: on the religious or political sides there could be a highly individualized perspective. In fact the individualist idea – that religion is a matter of private judgement by the individual which politics should be kept apart from – is highly characteristic of liberal and constitutionally based politics, although it can exist in other contexts.[12] Such individualist notions thrive on the idea of the neutrality of politics towards religion. Another dimension of this advocacy could be a religion which maintains itself self-consciously apart from politics, as in the Amish sect in the USA. On the political side, sects could be regarded with either hostility or complete indifference. This implies, though, a conscious distancing from politics by a religious sect. However, there are religious groups and churches which self-consciously accept and identify the utility of separating religion and politics and agree that constitutional limits need to be laid upon all religions.

Finally, there are religions which consciously try to add their weight to the legitimacy of politics, that is, they offer support and try to sacralize the political order, often becoming wholly identified with nationalism. Shintoism in Japan and aspects of Jewish Zionism would be examples. To complete this picture there are religions which desire ultimately to bend politics to their will and judgements and match all religious expectation with political and legal forms. In the final analysis this can imply the complete merger of politics with religion (from the religious side), in other words theocracy, that is, governance by religious elites and scriptural authority, as in modern Iran.

The opposite dimension of this typology is the subjugation of religion by politics. What I have in mind here is what some recent commentators have called 'political religion', or, alternatively, what some writers yearn for in 'civil religion'. In this sense politics colonizes religious vocabulary. In fact politics can quite simply become a self-suffing religion. In recent studies of this phenomenon, fascism and national socialism have formed the key area of scholarly interest. In writers such as Michael Burleigh, in his *Sacred Causes* (2006), Emilio Gentile, in his *Politics as Religion* (2006), or John Gray, in works such as *Black Mass* (2007), what might look like secular political ideological movements fulfil virtually everything one would expect of the sacred, including an account of human nature, the fall, perdition and redemption. As Gentile puts it,

> a political movement confers a sacred status on an earthly entity (the nation, the country, the state, humanity, society, race, proletariat, history ...) and renders it an absolute principle of collective existence, considers it the main source of values for individual and mass behaviour, and exalts it as the supreme ethical precept of public life. It thus becomes an object for veneration and dedication, even to the point of self-sacrifice. (Gentile 2006, 18–19)[13]

In many ways this point picks up a theme already touched upon in Eric Voegelin's *The Political Religion* (1938), Jacob Talmon's *The Origins of Totalitarian Democracy* (1952) and Norman Cohn's *The Pursuit of the Millennium* (1970), namely, that political ideologies reinscribe religious vernaculars (see Shorten 2007).

In sum, if one were seeking to place fundamentalism into this typology of the sacralization of the political or the politicization of the sacred, then my surmise would be that it would appear as a dimension of the sacralization of the political. In fact it would fit most neatly in the category of religions which try to bend politics to their religious sentiments and judgements. In this sense, the ideal (if it could be achieved) would be full-blown theocracy. Muslims, and some Jews, are more open and explicit about this than fundamentalist Christians, certainly in terms of the last thirty years.

The next question is: what is religion? This is a risky question, not least because of the deeply contested character of the term; however, it is still necessary to ask insofar as religion is the central aspect of fundamentalist thinking. As William James commented on religion in 1902, 'the very fact that there are so many and so different from one another is enough to prove that the word "religion" cannot stand for any single principle or essence, but is rather a collective name' (James 1971, 46).

The term 'religion' derives from the Latin *religare*, meaning to 'bind fast', 'tie' or, by extension, 'to place an obligation upon'. In itself this has no necessary connection with any sense of spirituality or God(s). Religion, even in the spiritual dimension, can be theistic, polytheistic or have no overt sense of any deity, as in Buddhism. J. S. Mill indeed saw the possibility of a 'religion of humanity' as perfectly entitling the term 'religion' (Mill 1874, 110ff).

However, in more conventional usage, religion tends to denote a number of characteristics. The visible world is largely seen as part of something more significant – some form of unseen spiritual world which adds meaning, lustre and purpose. There is strong sense in most religions of the mysterious, majestic, numinous and ultimately unrationalizable quality of this unseen. The theologian Rudolf Otto, writing in 1917, called this a sense of the holy, that is, 'something of whose special character we can feel, without being able to give it clear conceptual expression' (Otto 1972, 30 and 109). For Otto, if we neglect this numinous aspect we impoverish our whole grasp of religion. Further, the aim of religion is in some manner to establish a relation between the invisible and the visible worlds. The manner in which this is established is usually via diverse forms of ritual, prayer, meditation, good actions or worship. Religions also contain bodies of doctrine which aim to tabulate the rules and imperatives concerning this spiritual dimension. Such beliefs are regarded as both true and having an impact on the totality of life, and indeed may effect the 'salvation', 'well-being' and even mortality of the believer. Many of these doctrines are contained in mythical narratives and stories. Core doctrines also frequently give rise to bodies of ethical principles. Religions usually also have a social and communal dimension to them, that is to say, they have institutional and organizational aspects. Further, religion will often place a strong emphasis on an experiential dimension, that is to say, some notion of the (frequently highly emotive) experience of the spiritual, although this is often reliant upon personal testimony.[14] The above points are all ideal type generalities and need to be fleshed out. There are also considerable substantive variations on these themes within distinct faith traditions.

What is distinctive about the fundamentalist view of religion? There is a tangle of conceptual issues here. On the surface, fundamentalist attitudes to religion can look quite ordinary and predictable. The devil is largely in the detail. The first of these concerns the fact that certain commentators contend that Abrahamic monotheisms are more prone to fundamentalism than polytheisms. Thus, in speaking about fundamentalism we are in fact addressing, by and large, Jews, Muslims and Christians, rather than Hindus or Buddhists. The reasons for this claim are fairly obvious on one level. If there is one God it is far easier to think of one unique will and one authoritative set of imperatives. This is also helped with a single authoritative text, such as the Bible or Qur'an. In polytheistic religions or religions which do not actually have any firm notion of deity, it is harder to gain any distinctive consensual authority. The same point holds for core texts. What, for example, is the core authoritative text in Hinduism or Buddhism? There are many texts which are revered, but no single documents. Thus, as the argument goes, degrees of tolerance and pluralism are built in by default into these latter religions.

The counter-argument to this usually involves an appeal to empirical and historical detail, namely, that if we look at, say, the Buddhists in Sri Lanka and their cultivation of nationalist beliefs, the doctrine and attitudes of the Hindu BJP (Bharatiya Janata Party) and, more particularly, the Hindutva movement (which has, in fact, developed the notion of a singular God now – Rama), they all have a fundamentalist demeanour, despite being intrinsically polytheistic. That is to say, they are anti-secular, sceptical about modernity, absolutist in their beliefs, exclusionary and often violent. A similar point is often made about the Sikhs who defended the Golden Temple in Amritsar and assassinated Mrs Gandhi for violating it. These points seem to confirm the contention that there are fundamentalist factions within polytheisms as well as monotheisms.

A second issue concerns literalism and inerrancy (indicating freedom from any error). It is important to realize here that I do acknowledge a distinction between literalism and inerrancy. They are not necessarily reconcilable and yet both ideas do appear in fundamentalist writings. Fundamentalists themselves are not always aware of the potential incoherence here. Basically, fundamentalist literalism claims not to be interpreting scripture. Rather the argument is that scripture is the literal word of God.[15] In point of fact such fundamentalists do not avoid all taint of interpretation; rather they give a narrow and unimaginative interpretation and then call it God's word. They can also be quite selective in their reading. For example, the premillennial dispensationalists in the US base their core views not so much on scripture as on an interpretation of certain scriptures by one or two nineteenth-century writers.[16] Similarly the Gush Emunim movement in Israel are heavily dependent on the interpretations of the Torah in the writings of Rabbi Zvi Yehuda Kook. In such narrow interpretations words are taken to mean exactly what they appear to say; thus if the Bible says that creation took six days, that is exactly what it means. Of course, in practice, many fundamentalists hedge on this and other texts: that is to say, do we have the same *conception* of day and night as God (that is, in our understanding six days)? However, there is still a shared sentiment for many, despite some problems in our understanding, that the religious text stands as the literal word of God.

Literalism is not always an issue for fundamentalists; inerrancy is more significant. Muslim commentators such as Sayyid Qutb did not seem so worried about the idea of literal truth, although he did still believe that the Qur'an embodied the inerrant word of God (see Nettler 1996). The issue of consistent literal narrative is not such an immediate problem in the Qur'an, which is organized in a quite different manner to the Christian Bible. Qutb's interpretations of the Qur'an are quite open, poetic and fluid. Further, the notion of higher theological criticism which developed systematically in nineteenth- and twentieth-century Christianity has, to date, made little headway in Islam.[17] However, there are still real problems with literalism insofar as it can bring disturbing factual contradictions to light in the authoritative texts. Close readers of the Christian Bible will know this only too well. Literalism thus needs to be supplemented by another doctrine of inerrancy. Inerrancy implies that texts such as the Bible or Qur'an should be regarded as internally divinely perfect. If there are textual problems, they are ours, the imperfect readers, not those of the text. The text remains inerrant as the word of God. The word of God, although inerrant, still needs to be drawn out from the text. Thus, whereas pure literalism can lead to textual problems, inerrancy creates a harmonious text. Inerrancy, in this sense, is sometimes seen as the safer path for fundamentalists.

A third related issue concerns the quite distinctive way the central texts are often read by fundamentalists – whether it is a literalist reading or a drawing out of the inerrant word of God. This has been noted by a number of writers on fundamentalism. Texts are not seen as subtle or complex human documents with manifold possibilities for human error and misunderstanding. They are not read as either historically contingent or symbolic narratives. There is no room for doctrinal nuance. Even if something is inerrant or the word of God, one might still be prepared to admit that it has complex symbolic aspects. On the contrary, and this if anything is really distinctive about the fundamentalist mentality with regard to religion, the texts are read as blueprints or technical operational manuals for action. They contain therefore not subtle human ambiguity but prosaic factual instruction. They are the spiritual equivalent of technical manuals. Thus in the famous sword verse in the Qur'an, this is frequently taken factually.[18] The same type of reading is given to the term 'Jihad'.[19] Equally when US Christian fundamentalists 'end-timers' read about the Jewish Temple needing to be rebuilt on Temple Mount in Jerusalem (presumably over the ruin of the Al-Aqsa Mosque), this is again taken as a simple 'technical' instruction, which is a necessary preliminary to Armageddon and the Second Coming of Christ. Thus, part of the ceremony for this rebuilding requires a pure red heifer to be sacrificed, and, indeed, there are Christian fundamentalists now in the US who are financing an expensive selective breeding programme to produce the purist red heifer for this purpose.

Karen Armstrong has given this type of reading a slightly more grandiose interpretation. The gist of her argument is that two sources of human knowledge and understanding have been confused in this type of fundamentalist reading: *mythos* and *logos*. The *mythos* mentality (more predominantly a premodern conception) takes religious narratives as mythical and symbolic stories which have to be interpreted and read carefully. The *logos* mentality has developed largely with the natural sciences. It is concerned with a more directly rationalized and secularized understanding. Indeed as commentators on fundamentalism have noted, many of those who currently advocate or actively support fundamentalist ideas come from a natural or applied science background.[20] In this factualist reading of texts, *mythos*, in effect, becomes *logos*. Myths become actual history. The material actions of fundamentalists then become God's actions. Their will and judgement – as based on the inerrant technical manual – become God's actions in history. As Ruthven comments, when fundamentalists translate myth into empirical fact, they release the potential violence of the text. Thus fundamentalism, in an odd way, 'is religion materialized, the word made flesh, … with the flesh rendered, all too often, into shattered body parts by the forces of holy rage' (Ruthven 2004, 191).

One other related dimension of this way of reading authoritative texts is what might be called a Manichean mentality. The world is divided up for fundamentalists into actual warring presences of light and dark, good and evil, God and Satan, or the orthodox and heterodox. There are no shades of grey, no subtle ambiguities.

Consequently there is a clear and identifiable enemy who has to be struggled with. Spiritual and physical warfare with the dark, evil, ignorant, infidel, unbeliever, heterodox becomes a religious imperative. Religious thought in this context can never be exploratory, investigative, historical or interpretative. It is always expository and apologetic of the objective truth, set against the lies of the unbeliever.

A fourth distinctive aspect of fundamentalist religion is that it is not an individualist, private or subjective practice. If anything these would be frowned upon by fundamentalist of all stripes. Religion should conversely be a public and communal activity. It is not about a private subjective relation with a deity or some process of spiritual self-cultivation. It is rather something which demands public action, obedience, communal involvement, moral and social regeneration and, certainly in the last thirty years for many, political mobilization. There are undoubtedly more passive aspects to fundamentalists, namely, those who have advocated withdrawal from and rejection of the world. This happened to US Protestant fundamentalism between the 1930s and 1970s. But the current tendency of Christian, Jewish, Islamic and other such fundamentalists is to become directly involved in the political world and try to elicit legal and political change, if not revolution (as in Iran). In Northern Ireland, also, during the 1980s, the Democratic Unionist Party under Ian Paisley presented a potentially revolutionary form of Protestant fundamentalism – although this latter case is more historically complex. After all, if the Bible, Torah or Qur'an is the inerrant word of God, which only needs to be read like an instruction manual, with clear defined rules, then it would seem strange in the extreme if the authority of scripture simply stopped at the political or legal door. These latter realms need to be colonized and bent to the sovereign will of God.

Human Nature and Modernity

One of the key aspects of thinking about fundamentalism concerns its relation with modernity and the implications this has for an understanding of human nature. There is a substantial debate about when the term 'modern' and 'modernity' first appear. Some have tracked the term (*modernus*) to the fifth century AD, as a way of distinguishing Christians from the older Roman pagans. Others focus more usually on the Renaissance or the seventeenth-century Enlightenment. The latter is of particular significance for some scholars insofar as it introduced ideas of the authority of human reason over all other forms of understanding (see Habermas in Rabinow and Sullivan eds 1987, 142–3). As Jürgen Habermas notes, modernity in this context 'consisted in … efforts to develop objective science, universal morality and law', implying 'the rational organization of everyday social life' (Habermas in Rabinow and Sullivan eds 1987, 149).[21] Part of the initial dynamic development of the natural sciences grew from this recognition of the authority of reason. Modern, in this conventional sense, denotes that ideas, religious or otherwise, are not self-sufficient in terms of explanatory power; they have to maintain themselves via the critical authority of reason. In this sense the idea of the 'modern' hangs over all religious claims. This is not to say that modernity, reason and indeed many modern ideologies do not contain trappings of a politicized religion.[22] However, for those who wish to sacralize the political, modernity does raise certain problems.[23] Some of these problems simply relate to the way in which natural scientific reasoning seeks more technical and material causes for events, and, further, that truths can and do change according to adequate corroborated material or empirical evidence. Accurate empirical explanation also allows more secure prediction, which in turn gives more power and control to human beings over the world. The inner logic of such argumentation does not, in itself, refute religion, but it rather begins to constrict the role of religion in terms of providing genuinely satisfactory explanations.

The advent of modernity also has slightly looser links with values such as equality. This is, to a degree, an unintended or contingent consequence of certain religions such as Protestantism, that is, of seeing individuals as equal in the eyes of God. For some scholars, such as Max Weber, this was an important precursor to both industrialization and modern capitalism.[24] But it also had the consequence of undermining notions of hierarchy and traditional authority patterns and thus indirectly facilitating the growth of ideas such as individualism and even human autonomy (see Bruce 1995, 27). I want to pause for a moment on this conception of individualism and autonomy. This is a theme which has appeared already in a number of ideologies, although liberalism (and certain forms of anarchism) has been very closely associated with it. For many fundamentalists, particularly those in the USA, this idea of the autonomous reasoning individual links closely with the concept of 'humanism'. Humanism, for fundamentalists, denotes that individual human agency is self-sufficient and contains all necessary reasonable moral and epistemological resources within itself. There is therefore no need for any resort to religious argument to account for human existence. One leading fundamentalist US writer, Tim LaHaye, has consequently described individualistic humanism as 'anti-God, anti-moral, anti-self-restraint, and anti-American' and part of a more general anti-religious conspiracy (quoted in Armstrong 2004, 272).[25] In fact US fundamentalists have tried through various legal means to designate humanism as a rival secularist religion.[26]

In the midst of this more hysterical reaction there is a comprehensible motif, namely, that certain ideas are embedded in Enlightenment humanism and individualism which are problematic for many fundamentalists. Humanism – as a product of modernity – represents not only the loss of a spiritual dimension, but also a sense that it has reversed the basic priorities of human existence. As indicated above, humanistic reason is seen as a self-sufficient source of authority. As the Young Hegelian philosopher Ludwig Feuerbach succinctly remarked in the mid-nineteenth century, for we moderns all theology is at root anthropology. Human nature is identified wholly within non-religious parameters. It is humanity who have articulated God(s) in their own image. In this sense, humanism (and modern individualism) represents something quite elemental for all fundamentalists, namely, a cosmic reversal of the order of the world. Humans are prior to any idea of God; human nature is identified by wholly non-spiritual components. For the majority of fundamentalists in all religious faiths the reverse is true: it is God or the spiritual dimension which is the source of all value, knowledge and morality. God (particularly for the dominant Abrahamic religions) is the sole architect of human nature and human value and nothing should impede this absolute truth. In attacking humanism, fundamentalists would claim therefore to be restoring the correct priorities of human existence and consequently re-enchanting the world with spirituality.

At it simplest the response of fundamentalism to modernity is predictable. Modernization represents (at a deep level) a risk to religion, not just to its claims to truths about God, and so forth, but also to its conception of certain basic issues concerning the family, gender roles, education and work. For fundamentalists, humanism and secular individualism can pervade all of these spheres and corrupt them. This does not mean that any of these particular practices have necessary features for fundamentalists. Thus the family or gender roles could take a number of possible shapes for fundamentalists. Gender roles, for example, may be equal or unequal. However (and this is the key issue), if God, or some form of spirituality, is not acknowledged as the prior ground for such practices, then they will inevitably be corrupted. Fundamentalism is, of course, not the only ideology to respond critically to modernity. Indeed, in terms of its critique, it shares or overlaps with the ideological traditions of the counter-enlightenment and conservatism – although it is worth noting here that there are also some significant differences particularly to conservative ideology. Thus, fundamentalism does not share the scepticism inherent in traditionalist conservatism, it is not reactionary *per se*, and its interests in clerical leadership, populism, moral and psychological regeneration and ultimately theocracy draw it apart from traditional conservatism.

Despite the above remarks, the reaction of fundamentalism to modernity is not at all straightforward. One dimension of the fundamentalist response has been clearly reactive and anti-modernist. Modernity denotes corruption and a god-less existence. The solution for this is a spiritual re-enchantment, which in many situations can be both harsh and unforgiving on every level of society, from the family up to the state. Many fundamentalists (although not always verbalizing it) would clearly like to see the totality of life re-engaged and governed by religious values and laws. The everyday political and legal role of divine Shari'a law within radical Islamism is an example of this idea.[27] However, unexpectedly, it has been noted by a number of commentators that fundamentalism is none the less still committed to aspects of modernity. As the authors of a recent study comment, 'In spite of the surety of its dogma, fundamentalism is tied to the modernist project of the late nineteenth and twentieth centuries, even as it rejects modernism' (see Schick et al. eds 2004, 13).[28] It is important to realize, though, that modernity is not a singular idea; it embodies many streams of possible interpretation. Many of these streams are indeed contradictory.

A more accurate view of the relation between fundamentalism and modernity would be one of syncretism.[29] This works on a number of levels: it has been observed frequently that many of the active membership of fundamentalist groups are relatively well educated, often in one of the natural or applied sciences, rather than with any developed understanding of theology. In fact the theology of fundamentalism is focused on dogmatics and apologetics rather than anything truly critical or interpretative. Fundamentalists also show a comfortable familiarity with modern technologies, specifically in areas such as communications, media, computing, international banking and in some cases modern armaments.[30] In fact their manipulation of modern media and technology is fairly sophisticated. Further, on a more substantive level, fundamentalism does address and to a large degree actively parasitizes upon the sense of anomie, dislocation and alienation that can accompany rapidly modernizing societies, the movement from rural to urbanized life and the subsequent cultural and economic sense of rupture. Fundamentalism offers a very immediate sense of identity, deep reassurance and a fixed sense of purpose to a potentially deracinated group (Ruthven 2004, 202). Although often appealing rhetorically to an ancient past, which needs to be recovered as part of that identity, in point, most fundamentalists have very little actual interest or real sense of that past. Their focus is very much on the modern present.

One final point that needs to be mentioned here, in relation to modernity, concerns the concept of secularization.[31] Given that a crucial dimension of modernization entails secularization and given that fundamentalism exists in a complex and, at points, quite awkward relation with modernization, it follows that secularization equally comes under suspicion. This issue has already been touched upon earlier in terms of the development of disciplines in the social sciences such as sociology.[32] When religion appeared in writers such as Durkheim it was socialized into a form of organic social solidarity.[33] However, does secularity necessitate the total rejection of religion? It does entail that religion is subject to the forces of modernity and has a more limited place in certain domains of modern life, such as the public realm of politics and the state. Yet, the idea of secularism itself is context-sensitive and dependent on the type of religion, the place and the circumstances. Thus, in a plural society, or a society such as India with multiple religions, one could argue that secularism 'is necessary for freedom of religion, rather than antagonistic to religion' (An-Na'im in Juergensmeyer ed. 2005, 32). In other religions, such as Islam, there seems to much less overt concern about or even interest in secularism. In many ways Islam has been remarkably resistant to aspects of secularism, which in itself requires additional research. Christian fundamentalism has probably been most exercised by secularization, although, as suggested, the secular is not necessarily something which is always antagonistic to religion. In fact, if we considered the notion, articulated earlier, of political religion, namely, where ideologies such as fascism politicize the sacred, then the notion of secularity looks increasingly difficult to pin down as a concept.[34]

The Politics of Fundamentalism

There is a profound relationship between the language of politics and that of religion which has continued to the present day, although it is not always fully appreciated. This idea was alluded to by a number of writers in the twentieth century.[35] The gist is that there is an antique relationship between political and religious concepts – well before the advent of modern fundamentalism. Religion has always had an intimate connection with politics in terms of language. However, it is a two-way dialectical relation. Thus if one thinks of God as king, ruler, powerful, with dominion, sovereign, having majesty, or as a judge and lawgiver, and so forth, all of these are ideas derived quite directly from conceptions of political rule. John Donne, in speaking about heaven, described angels as God's ambassadors and ministers. Devils could be political informers or agent provocateurs. Donne is one of multiple historical examples. God, described as an authoritative father, had an immediate, quite direct impact, for example, on the seventeenth-century Christian doctrine of patriarchalism. Kings as fathers of the people were seen to have derived their authority from the fatherhood of Adam and the ultimate fatherhood of God. The issue has been complicated by the fact that that there has also been church government, in addition to ordinary political government (that is, *sacerdotium* and *regnum*) – which in the case of the papacy was and always has been a political as well as a religious role (see Nicholls 1994, 8 and 14).

Alternatively, there is sense in which politics itself borrowed conceptions from religious language to express political ideas. Notions of majesty and sovereignty have particularly subtle resonances here. Images of God have markedly affected political behaviour, as well as political preferences affecting religious conceptions. Sometimes images of God can strengthen a polity; sometimes they can undermine it. There is no precision here. One result, for example, of the idea of the perfection of God's polity was the notion of self-sufficiency and autarky. The autarkic image of God carried over into the autarkic sovereignty of the sovereign state. Overall, this is not a causal relation, but a symbiotic dialectical one which involves complex and imaginative uses of metaphor, analogy, simile and, at points, stark literalism. This whole politico-religious link is neither just about theology nor socio-political theory; on the contrary, it is a multi-faceted and interwoven relation. Indeed, the depth and subtlety of this relation are hard to unpack in a short compass.

The heavenly or divine government can therefore be a literal model for the earthly form; alternatively, at other points the earthly is seen as an analogue for the divine. It is important, though, to note that neither God nor the Hobbesian 'mortal God', as a sovereign entity, has any necessary link with absolutism and tyranny. The God of Locke, or the Independents in the English Civil War, was a covenanting, deliberative, contracting and constitutional God. The God of the US Republic in 1776 was a federal God. By the late nineteenth and early twentieth century there was even a welfare state God, as well as a God who was a free-market capitalist. God can indeed be a democrat as well as a celestial tyrant. Probably it is easier for absolute notions of kingship or sovereignty to be configured with Abrahamic monotheisms, whereas a democratic God might find an easier home in polytheism or possibly at least Trinitarianism, although this is not always the case. Strict monotheism, depending on the understanding of God, can also be an egalitarian comrade to the oppressed, as in Catholic liberation theology. In fact, in the late nineteenth century, we can see God being adapted to movements at the epicentre of purported secularism, such as the *bête noire* of much Christian fundamentalism, Darwinism. God can, then, be seen to be 'evolving' as opposed to being in a state of static perfection.[36]

In the above context we should not be surprised to find modern fundamentalism utilizing religious language in politics and referring, for example, to the sovereignty of God over politics and the need to re-colonize law and the state. Despite purported secularization, the ground for this kind of fundamentalist yearning had been well prepared. Religion and politics already had a long and tangled historical genealogy.

What fundamentalism brings, however, is a very narrow or thin focus on this interwoven language, narrow both in terms of politics and in terms of conceptions of God and religion.

What might be taken, therefore, as the core political sensibilities and values of fundamentalism? One core theme is a particular understanding of religion (as outlined earlier). To summarize again very briefly: it is a conception which appears much more at ease in monotheisms (although not exclusively by any means). It reads authoritative texts as direct instructional manuals for politics and morality. Interpretation, symbolism and historical critique are dismissed. Finally, it tends to think of religion as very much a public activity. Private spiritual cultivation is frowned upon. One additional aspect of this conception of public life is the view that politics needs to be bent to or integrated with the imperatives of religion. This might then well require firm religious guidance by a hierocratic spiritual elite. Eligibility for such political leadership would thus depend upon religious qualifications. This has actually developed quite fully in contemporary Iran.

A second feature is a strong sense that religious rule – theocracy – will in the final analysis provide the key to resolve the problems of modern politics. In most fundamentalisms, power is a significant asset, and the most significant power to have is that of the modern state. This has certainly been a very direct concern in countries such as Iran, Pakistan, Sudan and Afghanistan (under the Taliban), amongst others. Iran has been the most successful example here.[37] The dominance of the state has also been an aspirational theme for other groups such as the Muslim Brotherhood, Hezbollah and Hamas. In writers such as Ayatollah Ruhollah Khomeini, the theocratic is explicitly argued for: for example, his *Hokomat-e eslami* (*Islamic Government: Governance of Jurisprudent*, 1971) elaborated a specifically Shi'ite doctrine of clerical rule, something which has subsequently developed (imperfectly) in Iran. For Khomeini (as for Qutb or Mawdudi), 'once faith comes, everything follows' (quoted in Armstrong 2004, 257).[38]

For the large majority of fundamentalists, politics and law needs to be turned to the sovereign will of God and the technical imperatives of the authoritative scriptural texts. There is, in other words, a true and right political and legal order, one governed by divine precept. Thus, the ultimate answer for politics lies in theocracy – or some form of religious dictatorship.[39] The exact form of this theocracy is difficult to generalize on, although we do have actual and quite clear exemplars in Iran. Whether Shia theocracy would look exactly the same as Sunni or Christian is open to question. Further, theocracy does represent a deep challenge to the Westphalian model of the state, that is, as a model which tried to distance the public realm of the state from any overt affirmation of religion.[40] Theocracy is essentially premised on the strong sacralization of the political. The only theoretical issue which inhibits this process is that Abrahamic religions often claim a world sovereignty. God cannot therefore be limited to the political state. Consequently, there is a sense that theocracy is often perceived as but a staging post to world-wide dominion. Certainly this theme appeared forcibly in certain key radical Islamist writers such as Qutb. No state and no world order will function unless divine law rules as sovereign (via a world-wide caliphate). For Qutb, while the world, as a whole, does not recognize the sovereignty of God, it remains in pagan ignorance (*jahiliyya*).[41] In an odd way this debate over the role of the nation state in fundamentalism has a peculiar resonance with the debate between Trotsky and Stalin in the 1920s over whether Marxism could be achieved in one state or whether it required world revolution.

The exception to this theocratic urge is fundamentalists within established liberal democratic societies. In the USA, for example, the logic of the religious argument does still lead fundamentalists quite naturally to theocracy. Thus for premillennial dispensationalists the expected thousand-year reign of Christ is undoubtedly the pure doctrine of theocracy (that is, absolute sovereign government by Christ with no need for democracy); none the less there is still a sense that for these US fundamentalists there is an underlying unease that part of their identity, as patriotic American citizens, is tied up with the constitutional necessity of keeping religion and the state separate.[42] This issue thus remains fuzzy and unresolved in Christian fundamentalism, although not so much in radical Islamism. This may well be because of a different historical trajectory within Islam.[43] Further, the character of civil society and social membership in many Muslim societies is often markedly different in terms of the role of the family, clans and tribal networks. Politics in Islam has historically often been much more closely tied to other factors such as family or group patronage. One only has to consider the Gulf Sheikdoms to see this in practice on an everyday basis. Further, the idea of a separate church and state does not exist in Muslim culture, where the formal notion of an institutional church does not really make that much sense.

In relation to this general conception of the theocratic state, fundamentalism does have an ambiguous unresolved relation with nationalism. Some commentators on fundamentalism have seen a clear relation between the terms; both categories are indeed modern and both imagine a cohesive community. Others commentators see the terms as polar opposites.[44] A lot depends here on how nationalism itself is regarded and where precisely one sees its origin. The fundamentalist reaction to nationalism often derives from the specific historical experiences of a group. It is clear that some fundamentalists find no difficulties with nationalism. In the USA and Israel, fundamentalist ideas are barely distinguishable at points from nationalism. In India, the BJP Hindu party (which shows some of the trapping of fundamentalism) certainly identifies religious motifs in its nationalist identifications.[45] In Palestine's Hamas or Lebanon's Hezbollah there is a clear blending of radical Islamism with nationalistic yearnings.[46] There can undoubtedly be underlying tensions, but the blending of these elements evidently works for some fundamentalists. Nationalism does indeed conform closely to the notion of a civil or political religion. However, outside of political religion, nationalism, unlike Marxism, does not have to be linked to the profane. Some fundamentalists, for example, have seen an overt religious destiny in their nation. In Islamic regimes in the twentieth century fundamentalists thus frequently took a lead on nationalist ideas. Consequently failure of the nationalist project can be taken as a sign of a loss in religious faith. Indeed in states such as Iran under Khomeini, or Pakistan under General Zia-ul-Haq, there has was a conscious attempt to forge a more fundamentalist understanding of religion within the national project.

Yet, at other points, particularly in certain Islamic contexts, nationalism has been seen as opposed to fundamentalism. For example, Nasser's Arab nationalism in

Egypt or the Baathist regime in Iraq were taken by fundamentalist writers such as Qutb and movements like the Muslim Brotherhood as a definite hangover of Western colonial categorization (see Ruthven 2004, 150). Nationalism denoted secularism, modernism and colonialism, an antagonistic spirit to religious faith. Fundamentalism was seen to be self-sufficient and having no need of any nationalist inspiration. Fundamentalism could indeed cater to many of the implicit demands of nationalism. As Ernest Gellner astutely observed, 'Islam fulfils some of the very functions which nationalism performs elsewhere – the transition to a modern society where, for the first time in history, high culture has become the general culture of the total society. This phenomenon, which elsewhere expresses itself as nationalism, expresses itself in the Muslim world as religious revivalism, as fundamentalism' (Gellner in Marty and Appleby eds 1995, 285–6; see also Green in Schick et al. eds 2004). One internal difficulty, though, that most fundamentalists do encounter with nationalism, particularly within the Abrahamic monotheistic faiths, is the very basic idea that nationalism implies particularity and localism. The sovereignty of God is over the world, indeed the universe. To try to limit this cosmic purpose to a singular nation, as against the world-wide *Umma* (world-wide Islamic community) or Christian community of believers, and so forth, seems to many fundamentalists as a possible blasphemy, unless of course one believes that one's own nation is simply the chosen people of God.

A third dimensions concerns the fundamentalist desire to revive a golden age of theocratic rule. In this context there is definite element of utopianism present in many fundamentalist writings. In some Christian, Jewish and Islamic writings there is clearly an interest in spelling out the detail of a future state where all human needs will be fulfilled. There is thus a vision of some form of arcadia or utopia – sometimes in the past – where life was or will be in tune with God's sovereignty. Thus, for some Muslim fundamentalists there is a vision of what Mecca was like (as guided by Muhammad and his successors, the 'rightly guided' Caliphs), or alternatively a vision of what a future earthly paradise might be like. Equally for Christian fundamentalists there is a dream of life in simpler New England communities of the past, or alternatively a concern with the life 'post-Rapture'. In fact this latter interest has generated a very popular fundamentalist literary genre (Armstrong 2004, 82–3). In sum, embedded within all fundamentalisms are utopian sentiments; however, they are not obsessed with this utopianism to the exclusion of all else.

A fourth dimension, which derives from the interest in theocracy, is an anxious and unresolved relation with democratic practices (see Wickham in Juergensmeyer ed. 2005). In states such as Iran this whole issue remains extremely sensitive and fluid, namely, can one retain religious coherence and absolute truths in the midst of a genuinely democratic culture? The answer of many fundamentalists towards democracy tends toward the negative presentiment. Democracy implies a potential risk for religious certainties. One additional related issue here – explaining in part why democracy is undesirable – derives from a particular conception of humanity. Apart from the fact that many prospective democratic voters might well be secular-ists, unbelievers or atheists, human nature in itself, for many fundamentalists, is intrinsically corrupt and imperfect, especially if has been affected radically by modernization and secularization. Human nature needs salvation or renewal through recognition of God's sovereignty. This might require correct religious guidance, discipline and possible dictatorship in the first instance. Any political system which premises itself on the authority of this corrupt nature is bound to be equally corrupt. A corrupt sinful human nature therefore leads to a venal democracy. For democracy to work there must be prior religious concordance. In this latter sense it is still possible to think positively about representative, participatory or even deliberative democracy from a fundamentalist standpoint. However, it would be a radically different sense of the term 'democracy' – although familiar to the early American Puritans. Democracy would have to be religious in the sense that there would have to be a prior acceptance (or fore-structure) of sovereign spiritual values (see Hadji Haidar 2006).[47] Such a spiritual agreement would acknowledge the sovereignty of God over all human affairs; only then would democracy be correctly aligned and function properly.

A fifth feature follows a similar logic to the previous point, namely, that fundamentalist politics cannot immediately entertain, without qualification, doctrines such as liberalism or open societal pluralism. If there are absolute truths which are embedded in law (such as purportedly divine Shari'a law or Christian natural law), then there is no room for liberal neutrality or liberal tolerance and there is no space for radical pluralism. However, as noted above, if the pluralism or liberalism is rooted in a preceding perfectionist religious premise, it would still be possible to think of pluralism as compatible with fundamentalism. In the same way it is possible to conceive of an acceptable religious democracy. This is not to say, therefore, that some notion of civil pluralism is not pragmatically possible; undoubtedly this type of civil pluralism does exist in, for example, Iran. However, it is still an uneasy and constrained pluralism where there is always a lurking suspicion from religious authorities that not all accept the prior premises. The core theme is thus that there is a conception of a strong perfectionist monistic religious good for the whole of society which has to be reflected in institutional and legal processes, whether these are democratically pluralist or not.

A sixth feature which is developed by most contemporary fundamentalists concerns gender roles and the significance of the family in political order. Issues relating to gender roles, sexuality, parenting and, more particularly, the traditional patriarchal conception of the family have a regular profile in current fundamentalist writing. Male and female roles are seen to be determined by scriptural imperatives. Scriptural authorities, such as St Paul for Christians or the Hadiths for Muslims, are usually employed to establish the authoritative case for gender inequality. Of course this whole notion can become quite excessive. The most extreme example was the Taliban in Afghanistan during the 1990s, who decreed that women should have no public role whatsoever, should remain uneducated, were the literal property of their husbands and should not work outside the home. In effect, women, and indeed women's sexuality in general, are seen frequently to need control. Indeed a great deal of the fundamentalist output appears almost obsessively focused on a sense of unease with women and their precise role. Fundamentalist writing appears to give inordinate attention to controlling women. The tendency is to see the role of women as largely reproductive, providing a mothering and domestic service for men. Fundamentalism thus provides an archetypal current case of patriarchy for modern feminists. It is not certain, though, whether this position of women, in current fundamentalist thinking, is merely a contingent doctrine, or something more permanent. It seems perfectly logical to argue that gender equality and family reform could be fully consonant with a prior acceptance of God's sovereignty.[48] One would have to interpret the inerrant word of God slightly differently from certain current theological views, but that is par for the course. Thus there seems nothing illogical in suggesting that one could be a devout fundamentalist Muslim, Christian or Jew and still accept gender equality and the necessity for the reform of the patriarchal family. Currently, though, this appears to be a minority argument.

Seventh, there is a propensity in some, although not all, fundamentalists for using violence or extremes of militancy as a legitimate purifying tactic – whether this entails attacking abortion clinics or blowing up civilians. As mentioned, this is a characteristic tendency of all fundamentalists, at least as a potential strategy. Many see militancy and martyrdom as justifiable tactics to achieve religio-political ends. Some violence, as in Islamic suicide bombers, the assassination of leaders such as Anwar Sadat in Egypt or the violence contemplated by both Christian and Jewish fundamentalist in relation to the destruction of the Mosque on the Dome Rock and the rebuilding of the temple in Jerusalem (as the predicted preliminary to Armageddon) takes on an excess of religious symbolism. In the USA the violence has been more muted, but it is worth bearing in mind that attacks on abortion clinics by fundamentalists over the 1980s and 1990s led to many thousands of arrests, particularly of members of Operation Rescue. By 1985, for example, 92 per cent of US abortion clinics reported some form of attack by fundamentalist sympathizers. The only reason why fundamentalists in Europe and the USA are more muted on violence and militancy is that they sense that many of their aims can be achieved potentially through conventional political means.[49]

Finally, there is an apparent rejection of aspects of political modernity (as argued earlier) in most fundamentalist movements. This usually is connected to the strong sense of moral and spiritual decay in modern secular societies. The malaise of contemporary sexual ethics comes in for particularly strong attention. The imposition of traditional laws, such as Shari'a, or some form of theocracy are seen to be the only solution to this spiritual decay. What is paradoxical about this whole conception of the corruption of modernity is that, as most commentators have noted, there is nothing really genuinely old or traditional about fundamentalism itself. On the contrary it is largely a modern phenomenon. Most of its central themes – for example, the application of Shari'a in Islam, or the notion of premillennial dispensationalism in Christianity – are all comparatively modern artifice.[50] Thus one of the key tactics of certain Islamic fundamentalists is terror, on a global scale, something which would never have been available to them in any premodern setting. The fact that terror is the chosen instrument suggests to John Gray that if we wish to understand them, then we have to grasp that their nearest equivalents are embedded in a darker side of Western modernity. For Gray, these early precursors 'are the revolutionary anarchists of late nineteenth-century Europe' (Gray 2004, 2). In fact, Gray compares

Osama Bin Laden with the Russian nihilist anarchist exponent of the 'propaganda of the deed', Sergei Nechaev, discussed in chapter 5.[51]

Modernity, as many have noted, is not one thing. The totalitarian experiments of the twentieth century were all aspects of modernity. Revolutionary terror as a way of carrying though a programme and remaking humans is a well-trodden path in the modern West. Such terror uses all the powers of modern technology (and the state if it can gain control of it) to achieve its radical transformatory end. Thus, for Gray, 'Like communism and Nazism, radical Islam is modern.' He continues that although 'it claims to be anti-Western, it is shaped as much by western ideology' (Gray 2004, 3). Fundamentalism can thus be seen as another facet of a polyvocal modernist project, dedicated to remaking humans on a global scale. To achieve this end what is needed is another form of totalitarian rule, in this case a form of theocracy. Fundamentalism is thus, despite the paradox, both modern and Western in its political and terroristic aspirations.

Fundamentalism and Economics

Most fundamentalist movements do have an economic agenda; however, whether one could actually call such agendas distinctively fundamentalist is doubtful. Each fundamentalist movement tends to draw on different traditions of social and economic understanding. Thus, whereas radical Islamism has been associated with the complete abandonment of interest, this practice has not impacted in the slightest on Hindu or Buddhist economics (Kuran in Marty and Appleby eds 1993b, 289ff). In certain respects, though, the economic agenda of fundamentalists has been driven by the parallel issues of modernization and globalization. These forces have been disruptive in certain contexts. Fundamentalism embodies one possible reaction and answer to such disruption.

Firstly there is a consistent core belief shared by all fundamentalist factions on the question of the economy, which directly parallels theocratic politics: that is, 'the wellspring of economic legitimacy is … the divine will' (Kuran in Marty and Appleby eds 1993b, 292). In other words we need to acknowledge the sovereignty of God or the spiritual within economics. Consequently, as Timur Kuran notes, 'what renders Islamic, Christian, Hindu, and Buddhist economics fundamentalist is their commitment to the idea of unchanging fundamentals on which a just economy must rest' (Kuran in Marty and Appleby eds 1993b, 292–3). The sovereignty of God or Allah rules over this sphere as over all else. Second, the source of authority over economics is scriptural, for example the Bible, Qur'an or Torah. Thirdly, morality comes prior to economics. However, what precise conception of morality and how it pans out can be crucially quite different in the various fundamentalisms. Yet there is still a core belief that only those who think and act morally (and thus religiously) can comprehend economic processes. Outside of these fundamentals, economic responses have tended to vary considerably, and what some fundamentalists perceive to be deeply problematic other fundamentalists welcome. Starkly put, God can be a rampant free-market capitalist or a paternalistic-inspired Keynesian; he can be a free trader or a protectionist; he can believe in high interest or no interest. Whereas one fundamentalist group will cherish market freedoms. others will want to severely curtail them (see Kuran in Marty and Appleby eds 1993b, 298).

These positions do break down in predictable ways, although we should not rush to hasty generalization. The advocacy of a recognizably classical liberal and indeed libertarian conception of the free-market capitalist economy can be found most frequently in forms of Christian Protestant fundamentalism. One crucial point in the Christian fundamentalist perspective on capitalism is that there can be no amoral consumerism. Moral reform of the individual and his or her consumption pattern is as much required as a deregulated economy (see Kuran in Marty and Appleby eds 1993b, 296). There is thus an unexpected sense that consumer choices have to be morally circumscribed and re-educated even within capitalism. Indeed frugality of choice is admired in some fundamentalists. This point alone would alarm most secular classical liberal economists.

Yet North American Protestant fundamentalism does not present a wholly consistent picture. If it does not sound too far-fetched, there are in fact more extreme libertarian and more social democratic dimensions even within the US scenario (see Iannaccone in Marty and Appleby eds 1993b, 342). Unquestionably a large number of Christian Protestant fundamentalists in the USA are committed to a rigorous defence of the free-market capitalist economy. Their continued support for the Republican Party indicates their general preference (see Iannaccone in Marty and Appleby eds 1993b, 360). Yet it would also be true that the bulk of the 'Moral Majority' – and, particularly, key figures such as Jerry Falwell – have never tried to innovate or extend the standard market arguments that one finds in Milton Friedman, Friedrich Hayek or Ludwig von Mises. They also have a predictable negativity to all socialist or social democratic economic argumentation. Oddly, most of the fundamentalist-inspired educational university institutions, such as the Bob Jones University or the Liberty University, have little or no interest in economics. Falwell's Liberty University has an economics section, but it is remarkably small and embedded in business (Iannoccone in Marty and Appleby eds 1993b, 346). However, Liberty University was involved in setting up CEBA (Contemporary Economics and Business Association) (1987), although, again, its precise relation with fundamentalism remains uncertain. CEBA is a think tank and ginger organization for free-market capitalist economics. It is also linked to a journal, *Christian Perspectives: A Journal of Free Enterprise*, which does point towards a Christian defence of the market order; again, whether one could describe this as overtly fundamentalist remains open. However, undoubtedly CEBA and the journal are committed to the idea that private enterprise and respect for private property rights are crucial to the whole biblical ethos (Iannoccone in Marty and Appleby eds 1993b, 347). This same theme has also been argued for in the Christian Reconstructionists writings of Rousas Rushdoony and Gary North. In these writers biblical justification falls neatly in line with Hayekian market economics. God, it appears, is adamant that flat poll taxes are the only legitimate forms of taxation and that all collective economic planning is un-biblical. Further, the biblical commandment 'thou shalt not steal' embodies an outright denial of any theories of social justice or redistribution. Social justice is thus defined as institutionalized theft – a mantra of even secular libertarians. The Reconstructionists are in point devout postmillenialists, arguing in effect that Christ will return as the efforts of Christians bear fruit in the world, including the spreading of free-market thinking.[52]

It is worth noting that the above picture is not wholly accurate. There are some Christian fundamentalists in the US (admittedly a much smaller number) who believe that God is concerned with poverty, social justice and inequality. In this context a handful of US fundamentalists have flatly rejected the idea of free-market capitalism in favour of some form of social justice and redistribution. An emphasis is placed on the fact that the early church had no sense of private property and thus held goods in common (as in monasticism). This is an idea familiar to older Protestants sects in the USA such as the Amish, Hutterites and Mennonites. In sum, it is difficult to conclude that there is 'a' biblical view of economics. Most economic tendencies can identify justificatory passages in the Bible, if they look long and hard enough.[53] In fact many will use the same passage to justify wholly different economic policies.

In the case of radical Islam the situation is different again, although appearances can be deceptive. In 1979 the Islamic-inspired government of Pakistan ordered its banks to offer an interest-free alternative to conventional banking practice. They were required to abandon interest within five years. This interest-free idea has won support within Islam in general (outside of fundamentalist sects). Another economic theme, commonly referred to as *zakat*, entails the compulsory giving of a percentage of a Muslim's wealth to charity. *Zakat* is regarded as a mode of worship and self-purification. It is not primarily about charity. It comes from a recognition that everything derives from God and that we only possess goods on a temporary finite basis. This was certainly the prevalent theme in the writings of key fundamentalist Islamists such as Sayyid Qutb (in Egypt) and Sayyid Abdul-A'la Mawdudi (in Pakistan). As in the realms of politics and law, the crucial issue is the sovereignty of God over all aspects of existence. The logic of the point is fairly straightforward in these writers. Islam is understood as a complete way of life, thus economic behaviour, like all other behaviour, must also be ruled by Islamic precepts.

Islamic interest-free banking and the idea of *zakat* have now spread widely in a number of Muslim countries, including Malaysia, Saudi Arabia and Sudan. There are also banks with an explicit Islamic motif in North Africa and South Asia (and indeed in New Zealand and California). The idea of Islamic economics has also generated research centres dedicated to its study and implementation, as in the International Centre for Research in Islamic Economics at King Abdulaziz University in Jeddah and the International Association for Islamic Economics in Leicester (UK). It also has an academic *Journal of Islamic Banking and Finance* dedicated to its promulgation. A number of academics working in this context explicitly see themselves as Islamic economists.

Exactly how Islamic economics pans out after the recognition of *zakat* and interest-free banking remains unclear. Most Islamic economics embodies fairly predictable policy debates on issues such as economic growth, employment and efficiency. Such debates have a recognizable character; thus the Pakistani fundamentalist Mawdudi in his writings appeared sympathetic to a more free market of goods and services, whereas Qutb looked more favourably on state involvement to rectify inequalities. There have also been ongoing debates, even within the domain of interest-free loans, as to what precisely interest-free really means in accounting practice. Thus it has been questioned whether loans should be indexed to the rate of inflation in order to protect purchasing power, and so forth. It must be difficult to get scriptural answers to such technical economic questions. For some commentators, 'Islamic economics is hardly as comprehensive as its exponents apparently believe' (Kuran in Marty and Appleby eds 1993b, 330–1). So far it appears that the advent of Islamic or Christian economics has largely been cosmetic.[54]

Conclusion

Fundamentalism is a tricky phenomenon to get a theoretical handle on for reasons that have been canvassed in this chapter. There is a case for considering it as an ideology; however, it is untypical in comparison to many of the standard ideologies that have been encountered to date. One reason why fundamentalism has been written about most succinctly and broadly by sociologists is that, in an unexpected way, it seems to raise a quite deep-rooted challenge to the discipline itself. Be that as it may, one further reason why many of us with interests in political ideology might feel unsettled by taking fundamentalism on board as a potential ideology has a direct resonance with the sociology issue. Ideological study is rooted in a comparatively recent history, one which dates from about the last two hundred years (from 1800s). Ideologies themselves are part of a movement, with roots in the Enlightenment, which had begun to slowly and ambiguously to assimilate important aspects of modernity and secularization. This genealogy of ideology and ideologies means that, in part, we (who study ideologies) share some of sociology's anxiety. Ideologies in large part have little overt space for serious religious theory, for the basic reason that ideologies are so intimately tied to secularization and the modernist mentality. The one key proviso here is the equivocal category of political religion.

As suggested, there are profound ambiguities in the concepts of religion, secularity and modernity; however, the key conceptual issue that all fundamentalist adhere to, in fact it is the lynch-pin of their whole position, concerns the sovereignty of the spiritual or God over all human affairs. In the final analysis, as argued earlier, the core conceptual claim concerning God and the spiritual leads to a strong notion of theocracy. This contention is unsettling for the contemporary ideological mentality. The theocratic contention potentially goes well beyond any polite sense of tolerance that might be accorded religion as part of a liberal pluralist society. In the fundamentalist case it is potentially a modern full-blown attempt to sacralize the political. In this sense, even within modernity, it starts as a polar opposite to liberalism. Fundamentalism has, as indicated earlier, assimilated aspects of modernity. It thus, ironically, co-subsists with liberalism within modernity. It is not a throwback to a premodern past.

Ironically, fundamentalism often has more in common with the totalitarian experiments of the twentieth century to remake human nature, or at least to uncover the deep springs of human nature covered up by (in its own terms) the secular excrescence of modern liberal culture. In fact, where national socialism has been envisaged by certain scholars as a 'politicized religion', fundamentalism can also be seen as a 'sacralized politics' (that is, a potential totalizing theocracy). In this format, fundamentalism has much in common with national socialism (or Marxism-Leninism) as a totalized political project. The extremities of 'politicizing the sacred' and 'sacralizing the political' join force in an epiphany of trying to *remake* modern human beings. In the twentieth century we experienced politicized religion to the full in the various totalitarian experiments of national socialism and Marxism-Leninism. However, the perceived failure in modernity of the politicized religion (in terms of the collapse of totalitarian societies) has not dulled the deep urge of the modernist enterprise to remake humanity on a global scale. Fundamentalism – as an attempt to sacralize the political – is in some ways (in potential) yet another modernist totalizing experiment, viewed from a very different angle. The sacralization of the political (theocracy) is a mirror image of the politicization of the sacred (national socialism or Marxism-Leninism). We could thus once again potentially experience year zero, in this case from within a modern fundamentalist theocracy.

11

Icons and Iconoclasm

What has been achieved in this book? Certain facets of ideologies have been examined. First, ideologies are more complex internally than we are often aware of. This problem is usually dealt with within ideologies by denunciation or silence. The book has been premised on this internal complexity. We are faced by ideologies which look, *prima facie*, moderately coherent. Yet, closer analysis often reveals profound internal disagreement within each body of arguments. Second, each ideology has certain core questions, values and ideas. However, these elements are purely formal and can only be considered as general signposts. They gain substance in the various schools within each particular ideology. Sometimes these core themes will alter between schools *within* an ideology and will also mutate in different political circumstances. Consequently what is a core belief for one school (within an ideology) might be more peripheral for another. This is where major internal differences of interpretation arise. Third, ideologies are not just internally complex; they also overlap with each other and frequently use common modes of argument. In fact there are, on occasions, more affinities between schools of differing ideologies than there are similarities between schools within an ideology. This has given rise to the many compounds such as liberal conservatism, social liberalism, eco-anarchism or communist anarchism. This might be called the external complexity, although 'internal' and 'external' begin to look rather insignificant in such a context. We are, rather, confronted by a vast web of interlinking concepts. Fourth, ideologies function at various levels, from the more sophisticated abstract theory, through to realms of public intellectual debate, policy-making, political activism and ordinary discourse. However, much of the written articulation of ideology takes place in the sphere of public intellectual debate; certainly this is where many (although not all) of the durable texts of many ideologies are constructed. These ideas then become mobilized in groups and utilized in political activism, policy-making and ordinary discourse as a way of navigating the political world.

Each and every skein of ideological concepts and values has its own iconography. Most skeins with ambitions to explain or understand usually claim that their iconography is not just another 'ism', but rather is the actual ontological nature of reality.

The end of history has been posited by a number of different ideologies in the last few centuries, without any apparent success, leaving successive generations of iconographers and hagiographers with the additional problem of explaining not only the icon, but also why it has not yet instantiated itself successfully in reality. Some icons just fade; others have second and third comings, rising miraculously, but always appearing frayed at the edges after comparatively short historical periods.

In this book I have taken as my task the unpacking of a collection of icons which have markedly affected human life over the last two centuries. The fact that I have unpacked them in this manner might be regarded as a form of iconoclasm. Others may regard my analysis as trivial, in that ideologies do plainly contain diverse overlapping components. In this sense it is a flawed iconoclasm. Even if this is true, there is a residual therapeutic function in such analysis. Others still may regard my argument as an attempt at being 'positionless' or to step beyond ideological beliefs and deny the reality of all icons. What, after all, it might be said, is *my* ideology or my iconography? Are not all iconoclasts secret iconographers? This has been a prevailing aspect of much ideological work. The mitigating circumstances are that I have tried to comprehend the arguments and further that there is a clear difference, in my mind, between the critical study of ideologies and the active promotion of an ideology.

Each of the ideologies examined could potentially perform a running commentary on all the others. In fact the book, in its totality, could have been written from each distinct ideological perspective. I have tried, however, to avoid this particular path. Rather I have unpacked and examined the passion of the arguments from within each perspective, concentrating on their internal complexity. Each and every ideology usually thinks of its own position as *the* ontology or the real presence of politics. There is nothing intrinsically wrong with this situation. This appears to me to be the human condition. We often believe in systems and real presences, and have doubts, occasionally quite paralysing reflexive doubts. But we cannot live by reflexive doubt. That is both a burden and a blessing of the negative side of our reasoning capacity.

This book might best be considered as a rather complex critical dialogue about conceptions of the real in politics, which many wish to live by, even though accompanied by the inevitable doubts. The reader will also have gathered that I consider certain ideologies as pragmatically much easier to live by than others. However, if the study of ideology is considered as a critical dialogue, then that does imply listening. It also implies doubt, self-doubt, mutual respect, a sense of one's fallibility, and some humility in dialogic understanding. This could have the effect of undermining, partially, the absolutes of particular ideologies, which would be no bad thing.

Notes

Chapter 1   The Nature of Ideology

1   As one writer remarked, 'According to Tracy, Newton was the great theoretical systematizer of previous empirical research, the man who was able to demonstrate that all facts now and in the future, followed the patterns specified by a few simple laws' (Head 1985, 28).

2   Kuhn, *Structure of Scientific Revolutions* (1970); Feyerabend, *Against Method* (1975); Lakatos and Musgrave, *Criticism and the Growth of Knowledge* (1970); Hesse, *Revolutions and Reconstructions* (1980).

3   Thus, David Raphael – in a popular textbook of 1976 – noted that ideology is simply 'a prescriptive doctrine that is not supported by argument' (Raphael 1976, 17); for similar judgements: Hacker 1961, 6; Gewirth 1965, 2; Germino 1967, 42ff; Quinton 1967, 1; Kateb 1968, 8; Copleston in Parel ed. 1983, 23; Gaus 2000, 36–42. This might be described as the conventional liturgy of conceptual introductions to political theory throughout the second half of the twentieth century. In the majority of these introductory works, despite the ritualized claims to analytical rigour, the judgement of ideology is usually always asserted and never argued.

4   '[T]he path from the empirical observability for us of an ensemble to its historical accept-ability, to the very epoch when it is effectively observable, passes through an analysis of the knowledge-power nexus that supports it, grasps it from the act that it is accepted, in the direction of what it acceptable not, of course, in general, but solely where it is accepted' (Foucault in Schmidt ed. 1996, 394–5).

5   Freeden was much inspired by Clifford Geertz's subtle cultural anthropology writings. Geertz developed a careful and systematic understanding of ideology as a form of complex cultural symbolism representing reality and ordering social spaces (see Geertz 1993).

6   It is defined as 'those systems of political thinking, loose or rigid, deliberate or unintended, through which individuals and groups construct an understanding of the political world' (Freeden 1996, 3 and 125).

7   There are also some resonances here with the writings of Pierre Bourdieu, particularly his *Outline of a Theory of Practice* (1977). Bourdieu did not employ the notion of ideology; if anything he expressed impatience with it. But his understanding and deployment of the con-cept of *habitus* does have parallels with the more expressive sense of ideology as a form

of social unconscious. Habitus denoted a set of robust dispositions which engender particular practices. Habitus also implied an open-ended system which facilitates individuals in handling unanticipated situations and thus coping with and navigating the political world.

8   Yet, as he adds, 'the decline of the status of "truth" in the social sciences has combined with the realization that the older abstracts and model-building of political theory cannot satisfy the critical exploration of concrete idea-phenomena. The more political philosophers attempt to engage in their perfectionist enterprise, the more remote from the sphere of politics ... do their findings become' (Freeden 1996, 131).

9   This theory forms the basis for Habermas's understanding of both discourse ethics and ultimately deliberative democracy.

10 Whereas Gadamer, for example, is accused of seeing language as an unfettered pristine system of exchange; Habermas suggests that language can be, as much, a system of power, deception and domination, and consequently it needs a deeper ideological critique (see Vincent 2004, ch. 10).

11 Žižek uses the term 'Real' as capitalized.

12 As Žižek notes, 'The fundamental level of ideology ... is that of ... phantasy structuring our social reality' (Žižek 1989, 33).

13 As an empty space, for Žižek, demarcated from the symbolic, the Real is still a negative space. It has no substance. This is an idea which is difficult to get a precise handle on.

14 Žižek's account is fascinating, but he raises more problems than he solves. I remain ultimately puzzled by his use of the Real and how one could deploy it in language (psychoanalytic language in this case) as distinct from the phantasy of ideology. Is Lacan's or Žižek's psychoanalytic language just another symbolic phantasy? Is the notion of an unstructured 'lack' part of this phantasy? For a critique of Žižek, see McNay 2003.

15 As Freeden has argued, there are clearly core, adjacent and peripheral concepts which characterize each ideological schema or indeed schools within ideologies. I would want to stress here though that the core themes can occasionally mutate quite markedly between schools *within* an ideology. Thus, I am probably slightly more sceptical than Freeden about what a core denotes for an ideology, although I would not deny that each ideological argument tries to 'decontest' the core.

16 There is nothing wrong with this latter approach, but it would be difficult (in a short manageable compass) to present it satisfactorily in a general text on ideologies. The micro-analysis of policy output or the general sentiments of ideological activists would require a different type of very fine-grained and immensely detailed approach.

17 There are inevitable limits in the production of a textbook.

18 Thus, as Seliger remarks, 'Compromises cause ideology to bifurcate into the purer, and hence more dogmatic, fundamental dimensions of argumentation and the more diluted, and hence more pragmatic, operative dimension. In the latter, morally based prescriptions are often attenuated ... by technical prescriptions' (Seliger 1976, 120).

19 Not all ideological positions are so burdened, but given time the syndrome will develop. Some of the most perplexing are those who claim to be writing *about* the concept of ideology itself in an academic manner. They offer the reader something which claims to be an impartial judgement on ideology, but is in fact subtly part of another ideological perspective. There is a danger of this tendency in all writing on ideology, though some writers seem less aware of it or less prepared to admit it than others.

20 For Ricoeur, 'the capacity for distanciation is always a part of theory' (Ricoeur 1986, 233).

21 One additional problem here, which I will not canvass, is: what to include as the key ideologies? The present text does not claim to be a complete rendition of all ideologies, only the key ones. One other possible candidate (although it remains a contestable claim) is that globalism constitutes another distinct modern ideology (see, for example, Steger 2008).

Chapter 2   Liberalism

1 In fact, the situation in France was far more complex than this. The more constitution-ally orientated liberals were also divided over various issues.

2 For the positive view of Spencer, see Greenleaf 1983, 48, and Gray, 1986a, 31. The 'maverick' interpretation can be found in Eccleshall 1986, 31. The debate over Spencer continues to the present day – see Taylor 1992, Spencer 1994 and Offer 2006.

3 If one reviews the literature on liberalism, a number of attempts have been made to identify such schools. For example: integral as against formal liberalism (Hallowell 1946, 20); rationalist Gallican liberalism as against British sceptical liberalism (Hayek 1960, 55–6); minimum function *laissez-faire* liberalism as against pluralist interventionary liberalism (McCloskey 1965–6, 250ff); rationalist transcendental liberalism as against mechanistic reductive liberalism (Dunn 1979, 34); collectivist as against libertarian liberalism (Greenleaf 1983); classical versus modern liberalism (Gaus 1983); classical versus revisionary liberalism (Gray 1986a); Kantian versus utilitarian liberalism (Sandel ed. 1984); autonomy versus tolerance-based liberalisms (Kymlicka 1991); Enlightenment versus Reformation liberalisms (Galston 1991); comprehensive versus political liberalisms (Rawls in Strong ed. 1992); procedural versus non-procedural liberalisms (Taylor in Gutman ed. 1994); and autonomist versus integrationist liberalisms (Walzer 1987). Some have seen endemic tensions within the whole liberal tradition between individualism and collectivism, constructivism and anti-constructivism, and rationalism and scepticism (see Gaus in Freeden ed. 2001). Another version of an endemic tension in liberalism is John Gray's later work (that is, after his early dalliance with Hayek and the New Right). Gray sees a deep conflict between the more universalizing tendencies of liberalism, set against a *modus vivendi* liberalism simply trying to render peaceful co-existence between different ways of life possible (see Gray 2000). Other commentators see liberalism as a complex series of traditions with a symbolic unity around certain political strategies (see Manning 1976 or Eccleshall 1986). Most serious commentators on liberalism now, though, identify liberalism as a complex multi-voiced creature (for a recent overview and discussion see Freeden 2005). James Kloppenberg (2000) also provides a rich scholarly overview of the diverse currents within American liberalism. There are, though, stalwart, if slightly weird, exceptions to this judgement, namely, those who still see some form of pristine philosophical unity to the whole liberal tradition, often encapsulated in the writings of comparatively recent contributors (see Kelly 2004).

4 As Pocock remarks: 'Though Locke supplied a theoretical background to the constitution, he did not write or think within the changing framework of commonly accepted ideas about the constitution, and it is arguable that in the eighteenth century he was a writer largely for those who were situated somewhat outside the established order' (Pocock 1973, 144).

5 As Eccleshall remarked: 'Both liberals and socialists ... have dipped into a shared stream of radical beliefs which flowed from the civil war of the seventeenth century' (Eccleshall 1986, 44).

6 Some had the temerity to call this a 'New Enlightenment' in the 1980s (see Graham and Clarke 1986). However, the dominant mode of Anglo-American political philosophy from the late 1970s to the present day has largely been focused on various forms of liberalism and conventionally the theme of liberal justice (see, for example, Freeden 2005, 32–7 or Vincent 2004, ch. 4).

7 In many ways the New Labour administrations of the 1990s and 2000s in Britain have embodied an uncomfortable adaptation of neo-liberal ideology and its grafting onto aspects of the socialist tradition.

8 Working on the proofs of this book in October 2008, during the wholesale collapse of the banking system and stock markets across the world, it is tempting to speculate that the ideological domination of neo-liberalism may finally be reaching its end.

9 This applies mainly in Britain and to some degree in Germany before the First World War. However, the new liberal ideas also developed slightly later in other European countries, for example in Italy, in the writings of Guido de Ruggiero (1927) and Benedetto Croce (1946) (see Bellamy 1987b).

10 In the sense that it could be argued, via a traditional contractarian liberalism (Locke), that individuals are actually prior to society and possess fundamental rights. However, this could be interpreted as not so much indicating any actual or natural priority as a hypothetical moral priority of the individual to society. The hypothetical dimension is largely Kant's position on contract. It also characterizes the Rawlsian liberalism of the 1980s.

11 See Parekh in an essay in Berki and Parekh eds 1972, 81.

12 Rand calls this 'objectivist ethics'. As she states: 'The Objectivist ethics proudly advocates and upholds *rational selfishness* – which means: the values required for man's survival *qua* man – which means: the values required for *human* survival. ... The Objectivist ethics holds that *human* good does not require human sacrifices and cannot be achieved by the sacrifice of anyone to anyone' (Rand 1964, 31).

13 Kant's liberalism was, in certain ways, close to Humboldt's. However, Kant was primarily interested in moral and philosophical argumentation concerning the moral respect for individuals as ends-in-themselves. The upshot of Kant's apparent liberalism is far from clear in political practice; in fact it might be better to describe him as a form of republican. See discussion in Williams 1983, 128.

14 See, for example, Spencer 1940, essay 4; Nozick 1974, 32–3; Arblaster 1984, 350–2.

15 John Gray follows Hayek in scolding Mill. In an early essay he remarks that 'The dominant Millian paradigm of contemporary liberalism is radically defective and ought to be abandoned. We are wise, I believe, if we return to the classical liberals' (Gray in Haakonssen ed. 1988, 137).

16 See Green 1883, section 234ff. For an outline of Green's overall contribution, see Vincent and Plant 1984, Vincent ed. 1986, Carter 2003, Leighton 2004 and Wempe 2004.

17 See, for example, Berlin's essay in Sandel ed. 1984; also MacCallum 1967.

18 As Hayek put it, 'Law, liberty and property are an inseparable trinity' (Hayek 1982, 107).

19 For Nozick there are certain areas where freedom can be restricted: for example, if the genuine entitlement to property is interfered with or where the Lockian provisos are infringed (see Nozick 1974, 85, 178–82).

20 Macpherson redefined negative liberty as 'counter-extractive liberty', which implied 'immunity from the extractive power of others'. For Macpherson, this 'moves away from the mechanical image of negative liberty as a "field (ideally) without obstacles"'. It also implied restraining market activity (see Macpherson 1973, 118).

21 J. A. Hobson also commented that 'Free land, free travel, free power, free credit, security, justice and education, no man is "free" for the full purposes of civilized life today unless he has all these liberties' (Hobson 1909, 113).

22 This debate over freedom and poverty can be found in the writings of Thomas Pogge, Amartya Sen and Martha Nussbaum (see, for example, the discussion in Pogge 2002 and Vizard 2005).

23 Each of the two major branches of justice theory – proceduralism and distributive justice – can be subdivided again. Thus under the rubric of classical liberalism Friedrich Hayek's commutative account of justice embodies a different argumentative base to Nozick's entitlement theory account of justice. Robert Nozick describes his own theory as distributive, but it is an 'unpatterned' distribution with no direct or intentional human intervention. Under the rubric of distributive or social justice, there is, though, a great deal more complexity. Twentieth-century discussion of distributive (or social) justice was concerned largely with the slightly more abstract distributive principle(s) 'to each according to his or her due', or, more simply, the fair allocation of burdens and benefits in society. The fine-tuning of this idea arose with the interpretation of what is the more substantive principle which determines due.

24 Hayek also drew a distinction between teleocratic and catallactic political and economic orders. The teleocratic order is directed at a specific purpose, whereas a catallactic order (which for Hayek corresponds to a free liberal society) is a spontaneous order which arises from the diverse activities of individuals.

25 As Gaus has observed: 'All modern liberals – Rawls and Mill included – argue that we ought to accord others equal opportunities for development' (Gaus 1983, 43).

26 The liberal debates on justice from the 1970s tended to focus largely on contractarian argument. Such arguments subdivided between what Brian Barry has usefully typologized as 'justice as mutual advantage' and 'justice as impartiality' arguments (see Barry 1989). In the former theory, liberal justice is seen as the outcome of a mutual bargaining process among individuals in an initial position (Buchanan and Gauthier). Essentially, this theory is a form of rational choice argument which has much closer affiliations with classical liberal accounts of justice. In the latter, justice is seen to be the outcome of a rational agreement between discrete individuals in a hypothetical situation or original position where constraints are placed upon the context and character of reasoning that can be used (Rawls and Barry). This theory provides a sophisticated reading of the social liberal position on distributive justice. The contract device, in Rawls particularly, aims to represent a choice situation and show why individuals have good reasons to adopt justice as fairness. For Rawls, 'All social primary goods – liberty and opportunity, income and wealth, and the bases of self-respect – are to be distributed equally unless an unequal distribution of any or all of these goods is to the advantage of the least favoured' (Rawls 1971, 303). Rawls's theory of justice is a uniquely brilliant argument given that he utilizes devices from classical liberalism, such as contractualism and rational asocial individualism, to establish a social liberal position on distributive justice. In Rawls's account, rational self-interest ultimately achieves the same ends as benevolence and altruism.

27 As Rawls notes, 'My aim is to present a conception of justice which generalizes and carries to a higher level of abstraction the familiar theory of the social contract as found, say, in Locke, Rousseau, and Kant. In order to do this we are not to think of the original contract as one to enter a particular society or to set up a particular form of government. Rather, the guiding idea is that the principles of justice for the basic structure of society are the object of the original agreement' (Rawls 1971, 11).

28   As Rawls comments: 'A correct account of moral capacities will ... involve principles and theoretical constructions which go much beyond the norms and standards cited in every-day life' (Rawls 1971, 47).

29   Liberal theorists such as John Rawls and Ronald Dworkin also embody this Kantian approach, but they interpret the notion of a 'fair' or 'right' order in a much more gener-ous way than does Hayek or Nozick.

30   For a brief exposition of this point in relation to idealism, see Sullivan essay in Douglass et al. eds 1990, 149.

31   Classical liberals (as argued) tended to regard democracy with some unease. When they did accommodate democracy, it was viewed as simply an aggregation of private prefer-ences, registered through a vote. Individuals' interests, in the classical liberal model, tend to remain forever private. However, deliberative theory in, for example, the later writings of Rawls on political liberalism (and Joshua Cohen's work) identifies public deliberation and reason as at the heart of a well-ordered liberal democratic polity (see Rawls 1993; Cohen in Benhabib ed. 1996; and more general discussion in Dryzek 2002).

32   Adam Smith had been committed to state education; Cobden wanted state regulation of railways and education; Mill always saw conspicuous exceptions to *laissez-faire* – chil-dren and the insane, for example, must be looked after paternalistically; Sidgwick was also clear that defence and care of children, postal networks, regulation of canals and seaways, weights and measures, etc., must be looked after by the state.

33   In fact movements such as liberal feminism, liberal environmentalism, liberal national-ism, and so forth, during the late twentieth century continued to change the complexion and character of the movement. See other chapters in this book.

34   Neo-liberalism, in its present format, although seemingly at the moment impregnable, will mutate and ultimately subside in the longer term.

35   The political writings of Anthony Giddens (discussed in ch. 4) come into this category.

36   The political liberal, for Rawls, is aware that any substantive moral beliefs she or he may have will not be carried into the public sphere, and thus seeking minimal conditions for cooperation. Like Judith Shklar, Rawls also envisions his own version of liberalism as one arising out of a conception of 'fear', not offering any moral end, but rather maintain-ing conditions for living peacefully together (see Shklar 1984).

Chapter 3   Conservatism

1   For some critical commentary on this argument see Aughey's essay in Eatwell and O'Sullivan eds 1989, 102.

2   There is another subtle variant here worth considering, and that is Albert Hirshman's thesis that conservatism employs a 'rhetoric of reaction', involving a *perversity thesis*, which claims that any purposive action in politics exacerbates problems; a *futility thesis*, which argues that any attempt to change the world will never succeed; and, finally, *a jeopardy thesis*, which asserts that the costs of any change will always be too high and endanger what we have, see Hirschman 1991.

3   Pocock notes a peculiarity here, that 'If conservatism is the defence of the existing order, the conservatism of the eighteenth century was the defence of a revolution' (Pocock 1985, 158).

4   Honderich tries to redeem Hume from the clutches of conservatism for the sake of his philosophical reputation as 'no doubt the greatest of British philosophers' (Honderich

1991, 47). Quinton, however, does see a conservatism implicit in Hume's philosophy (see Quinton 1978, 45ff; see also Muller 1997).

5 On the inception of conservative thought at the time of the French Revolution, see Eatwell in Eatwell and O'Sullivan eds 1989, 63.

6 The sceptical attack on perfectibility in politics is still being made in the name of conservatism (see, for example, Kekes 1998 and Sullivan 2006).

7 In the 1980s and 1990s, American writers such as Nathan Glazer, Irving Kristol and Daniel Bell were often described 'neo-conservatives'. In the early 2000s these neo-conservatives had a powerful impact on American policy, particularly foreign policy. They certainly showed a willingness to use one facet of the state (its military aspect) to broad effect. Although bewailing the existence of 'big government', the growth of welfare budgets and the weakening of individual self-reliance, the neo-conservatives were not concerned to defend the economic interests of unregulated capitalism (see Kristol 1970). Rather, unregulated markets were seen to undermine the political values of American society. (Kristol, 'When Virtue Loses All Her Loveliness', quoted in O'Sullivan, 1976, 145; see also selection in Stelzer 2004; and for a more philosophical treatement of aspects of US and British conservatism in relation to the work of Strauss and Oakeshott, see Devigne 1994. For a highly sympathetic and traditionalist appraisal of Oakeshott, see Sullivan 2006, 196ff.)

8 See Norton and Aughey 1981; also Roger Eatwell's discussion of 'styles of thought' in the Right, namely, the reactionary, moderate, radical, extreme and new Rights (Eatwell in Eatwell and O'Sullivan eds 1989, 63ff).

9 O'Sullivan criticizes Scruton on this count. He contends that 'Scruton … has in fact committed the greatest of political errors'; he has 'asked too much of politics. Ironically, the result is that he threatens to submerge civil in social philosophy' (O'Sullivan in Eatwell and O'Sullivan eds 1989, 180).

10 See, for example, Bosanquet 1983; Hall and Jacques eds 1983; Levitas ed. 1986; Barry 1987; King 1987; Hoover and Plant 1989; Harvey 2005; Turner 2008.

11 Honderich still thinks Burke is deeply religious (see Honderich 1991, 159).

12 Liberal conservatives such as Hayek, however, utilize the 'imperfection argument' in terms of the limited stock of knowledge of those who work in government, especially in relation to regulation of market orders.

13 See Coleridge's explanation of the 'Idea' in the opening sections of his *On the Constitution of the Church and State*, which expounds this theme (Coleridge 1976, 12–13; for discussion of this, see Muirhead 1954, 65ff; also Calleo 1966, 63ff and Morrow 1990).

14 For selection of Novalis's and Müller's writings see Reiss ed. 1955.

15 Nisbet asserts confidently that 'Conservatism is unique among major political ideologies in its emphasis upon … the Judaeo-Christian morality' (Nisbet 1986, 68; see also Cecil 1912, 75; Rossiter 1982, 44; Hogg 1947, ch. 2).

16 For commentary upon this see Quinton 1978, 90; Scruton 1980, 171; Allison 1984, 18; Tännsjö 1990, 30; Tseng 2003, 131–3.

17 Mallock indicates that his use of the word 'aristocracy' refers to 'the exceptionally gifted and efficient minority, no matter what position in which its members may have been born'; he later notes that 'the civilization of the entire community depends alike for its advance and for its maintenance on a struggle which is confined within the limits of an exceptional class' (Mallock 1901, v and 151).

18 Some argue that the elites of conservatism in Britain have changed markedly since 1688. They shifted from aristocratic landed groups, to commercial and industrial groups, and finally to the middle classes in the twentieth century (see Eccleshall 1977).

19   Quintin Hogg remarks that the 'basis of the justification for the right to own private property is ultimately the belief in the infinite value of human personality, but this value can only be seen in its true light in a world assumed to be theocentric – God-centred' (Hogg 1947, 98–9).

20   Despite the fact that liberal conservatives were keen to maximize market freedom, they felt definite qualms concerning how far such freedoms should extend. When social and moral issues of, for example, sexual, family and private morality arose, then many liberal conservatives appeared far less keen to extend freedom. However, there were libertarian aspects of the New Right spectrum which did wish to extend freedoms. The anarcho-capitalist dimension of this latter movement will be explored in chapter 5 under the rubric of anarchy.

21   This would certainly still be true of American neo-conservatism (see note 7).

22   Discussing parsons, stock-jobbers, naval and military officers, Cobbett in his *Rural Rides* notes: 'Here are thousands upon thousands of pairs of this Dead Weight, all busily engaged in breeding gentlemen and ladies; and all, while Malthus is wanting to put a check upon the breeding of the labouring classes; all receiving a *premium for breeding*! Where is Malthus? Where is the check-population parson?' (Cobbett 1985, 161).

23   For an explanation of Sorelian syndicalism, see chapter 5.

Chapter 4   Socialism

1   This notion of contract is used predominantly within the liberal contractarian tradition (from Locke to Rawls), to explain the character of our obligations and the nature of authority. However, it has also been utilized by some anarchists, particularly Pierre-Joseph Proudhon, who favoured it as a device to oppose the state. Proudhon's view will be explored in chapter 5.

2   Marx's interpretation has admittedly a lot more to it. He also saw 1789 and 1848 as necessary political events in the historical movement towards a social revolution of the proletariat.

3   See p. 90ff.

4   'The inner organization of this primitive Communistic society was laid bare, in its typical form, by Morgan's crowning discovery of the true nature of the *gens* and its relation to the *tribe*' (Marx and Engels 1967, 79).

5   In the preface to the 1888 English edition, Engels writes of the *Manifesto* as 'the most international production of all Socialist literature' (Marx and Engels 1967, 61).

6   The early utopian communist Étienne Cabet was also an admirer of More (see Newman 2005, 7–8).

7   The socialist revisionist writer Eduard Bernstein also wrote his first Marxist-inspired work on the English Civil War. Other contemporaries to Winstanley, such as James Harrington, are sometimes also singled out. A number of scholars have explored the dynamics of the claim that the various individuals and groups during the English Civil War, such as the Diggers or Levellers, were precursors of modern socialism. One of the first was C. B. Macpherson's *The Political Theory of Possessive Individualism* (1962). It is worth noting briefly, though, that George Woodcock saw Winstanley as an original libertarian anarchist. He comments that 'the effort of Winstanley and his friends to follow out its principles on St George's Hill stands at the beginning of the anarchist tradition of direct action' (Woodcock 1975, 46).

8   In some ways the recent decline of socialism from the 1990s to the present day has not been so much a decline of ideas or an acceptance of capitalism as the transformation of many previously socialist arguments into less structured new social movements and more particularly anti-capitalist movements (see discussions in Giddens 1994; Mattson 2002; Callinicos 2003).

9   On the unique development of Swedish social democracy, see Tilton 1991.

10 Named after the British Labour minister and socialist theorist Anthony Crosland (1918–77).

11 For Proudhon see chapter 5.

12 It is worth noting here that the idea of a 'third way' has a considerably broader provenance than socialism. There are certainly strong parallels here with President Clinton's policy of triangulation. For discussion of the broader provenance see Bastow et al. eds 2002 and Bastow and Martin 2003.

13 The equality implied here was a 'starting-gate' equality, rather than an 'end-state' equality. Starting-gate equality provides an enriched reading of equality of opportunity, establishing 'thickened' equal conditions for citizens to compete.

14 As George Orwell put it, the genealogy of belief in an attainable 'earthly paradise' could be traced 'leading back through Utopian dreamers like William Morris and mystical democrats like Walt Whitman, through Rousseau, through the English Diggers and Levellers, through the peasant revolts of the Middle Ages, and back to the early Christians and the slave revolts of antiquity. ... Underneath it lies the belief that human nature is fairly decent to start with, and is capable of indefinite development. This belief has been the main driving force of the Socialist movement' (quoted in Crick 1982, 507).

15 'Finely graded passions had to be correctly combined in groups and series so they could obtain free expressions and satisfaction' (Riasanovsky 1969, 42). Fourier believed that there were twelve basic human passions, subject to 810 subtle nuances. If one allowed a doubling of these nuances, in order to accommodate mutual passions between individuals, then one could calculate the ideal population size for a *Phalansterie*, which was approximately 1620. See also Fourier 1996.

16 Lenin's own position was not wholly consistent. He blended, paradoxically, a voluntaristic stance with a rigid materialism. It is not easy to reconcile the activism of his work *What Is to Be Done?* (1902) with the crude determinism of his philosophical work *Materialism and Empirio-Criticism* (1909). Indeed, it is difficult not to see Lenin as something of a revolutionary opportunist.

17 Beatrice Webb, for example, admired Herbert Spencer, whom she knew personally, noting that 'he taught me to look on all social institutions exactly as if they were plants or animals – things that could be observed, classified and explained, and the actions of which could to some extent be foretold if one knew enough about them' (Webb 1926, 38).

18 Fourier remarked that 'Truth and commerce are as incompatible as Jesus and Satan'; merchants were considered as no better than highway robbers (see Riasanovsky 1969, 161–2).

19 Beatrice Webb also speaks of the development over the nineteenth century of a 'class consciousness of sin among men of intellect and men of property' (Webb 1926, 179–80).

20 I am taking these as more or less equivalent in this case, although with the advent of feminist criticism of socialism, it is wise to be very cautious about the value of 'fraternity'. The majority of nineteenth-century socialists, trade unions and the like were literally talking in terms of brotherhood. Many contemporary socialists would *not* relish this gender-biased description and would find it a very limited understanding of

community, which undoubtedly must include all women as equal citizens. For discussion of this point, see Anne Phillips' essay 'Fraternity' in Pimlott ed. 1984.

21　This is not so apparent in market socialism or indeed in the third way socialism of recent years which shows much of the overlap and influx of ideas drawn from the New Right and classical liberalism.

22　For example, are needs absolute or relative to particular circumstances? If needs are absolute, what is to be included under such rubric? What is the relation between needs and wants? Can there be a clear hard-and-fast distinction between such notions? These and many other questions plague the discussion of need.

23　As Beatrice Webb commented, 'We do not have faith in the "average sensual man", we do not believe that he can do much more than describe his grievances, we do not think that he can prescribe the remedies. ... We wish to introduce the professional expert' (Webb 1948, 120). On Fabian elitism, see Callaghan 1990, 34–5.

24　On the Kantian rational will argument, see Bernstein 1961. Mill's later reflections, 'Chapters on Socialism', figure in the utilitarian guise (see Mill 1989).

25　Beatrice Webb described the rank and file socialists as 'unusually silly folk (for the most part feather-headed failures) and heaped together in one hall ... they approached raving imbecility' (Webb 1948, 134).

26　Two fairly dynamic economies such as Japan and Germany have generally had very sensitive and diverse forms of state activity within their economic policies. Indeed, it is worth noting that even some European Communist Parties have, since the 1990s, advocated very diverse policies sensitive to the logic of markets, and consequently repudiated the older centralist and nationalization methods.

27　It has developed in a different context in the anti-capitalist movements of the late 1990s and early 2000s. If we are to believe the work of Michael Hardt and Antonio Negri, a new form of radical politics has developed in this period, which has integrated, transformed and transcended many of the central categories of nineteenth- and twentieth-century socialism into a new global era of 'Empire' and 'multitude' (see Hardt and Negri 2000 and 2006; also see further discussion in note 29 below).

28　It would be probably be a misnomer to describe present-day China as in any way Marxist. A better description might be authoritarian capitalist.

29　In works such as *Empire* (2001) and *Multitude* (2006), Hardt and Negri have developed their own quite unique theories which abandon the idea of the Marxist revolutionary proletariat. The authors suggest that in fact we have gone beyond the tenets of classical Marxism and even beyond the age of nation states. In this sense the Left is seen to be in a process of rapid transformation. At the present moment, for the authors, the nation state system is largely unravelling in the face of global capitalism. New forms of sovereignty are being created by, for example, international corporations. However, this process of economic globalization does not necessarily mean the triumph of capitalist markets; on the contrary the global society is a world full of new insurrectionary vigour. A novel form of fragmented, non-state-based, largely leaderless, diffuse structure has begun to open up in a global network, which the authors see embodied in a new conception of 'Empire'. Empire is constituted by a 'multitude', which Hardt and Negri think of as a fragmented biopolitical grouping. In replacement of the industrial proletariat, the disjointed multitude constitutes a new form of potentially radical politics which, in turn, is gradually undermining global capitalism; in fact the authors think that capitalism is exceptionally vulnerable to this new diffuse and wholly unpredictable entity. The counterculture and anti-capitalist movements of the 1990s and 2000s are seen as signatures of this new global insurrectionary politics premised on multitude. This new form of insurrectionary potential has been accelerated by the actual character of the 'intellectual labour' in the global economy (on which global capitalism is highly dependent); this, in turn, makes capitalism potentially that much more vulnerable, not just to anti-capitalist riot or protest, but also to internal subversion. The multitude is also a field for radical new democratic developments within a global commons, which moves beyond the older representative democratic models of the nation states. The ideas being developed here are fascinating, although it is probably too early to ascertain how accurate they are and how far the older Left will take up these ideas.

Chapter 5   Anarchism

1   The notion of doing without the state or government, in a more positive sense, can be taken in two senses. Either it can imply a harmless, antiquated, but unworkable utopianism, something to be grown out of, or it can betoken a contemporary, workable alternative to the state. The capacity to live in such a stateless society stands in precise ratio to personal and political maturity.

2   As one writer comments, 'Anarchism, encompassing as it does such a broad spectrum of ideas, cannot be as precisely defined in ideological terms as Marxism' (see Cahm 1989, ix; see also discussion in Gaus and Chapman in Pennock and Chapman eds 1978, xvii; Perlin ed. 1979; Ritter 1980; Miller 1984, 2; Walter 2002; Sheehan 2003; Ward 2004).

3   For some commentators it is pretty hopeless and meaningless as an ideology (see Hobsbawm 1977b).

4   Marx's criticisms of Proudhon in *The Poverty of Philosophy* were regarded favourably by Bakunin.

5   James Joll speaks of Zeno and the Stoics as anarchist (see Joll 1964, 13; also Marshall 1993, 70).

6   Taylor contends that peasant communities, village communities, Kibbutzim and utopian communes within developed states have an anarchist character (Taylor 1982, 35–7).

7   To be fair, Taylor partially recognizes this latter claim, although he still tends to treat it in a somewhat sanitized, ahistorical conceptual manner.

8   David Apter also put the same point quite neatly, namely, that anarchism combines a socialist critique of capitalism with a liberal critique of socialism (see 'The Old Anarchism and the New', in Apter and Joll eds 1971, 1–2; see also, for roughly the same idea, Miller 1984, 3).

9   There was a small but active group of anarchist writers in Britain during the period of the 1940s up to the 1970s (see, for example: Read 1938; Comfort 1946; Woodcock 1972a; Stoehr ed. 1977; Goodway ed. 1994).

10   Crowder's classical anarchists include Godwin, Proudhon, Bakunin and Krotoptkin (see Crowder 1991). My list is more extensive.

11   Some might also include the situationists as anarchist (see Marshall 1993, 549ff or Knabb 2007).

12   A large element of the communist and individualist anarchist tradition had very strong optimistic enlightenment beliefs in human nature and objective reason in human affairs; this perspective is hard to link with a poststructural position.

13   There might be interesting parallels between aspects of the 'propaganda of the deed', in the 1890s, and some anti-capitalist activists in the early 2000s, although the earlier movement was probably more intrinsically violent in tactics.

14   This individualist tradition in the USA is not the only tradition. There are traditions of both syndicalism and communist anarchy. The latter particularly is associated with writings of Alexander Berkman and Emma Goldman (see Fellner 2005; Avrich 2006; Goldman 2006).

15   As well as a deep distrust of elements of the ecology movement, such as deep ecology.

16   He remarked: 'We do not believe in the infallibility nor even the general goodness of the masses' (in Malatesta 1984, 109).

17   Hobbes's individualism is linked by Kropotkin with the views of T. H. Huxley and competitive evolution. In fact Huxley, in his essay 'The Struggle for Existence in Human Society', which stimulated Kropotkin to draft *Mutual Aid*, uses Hobbes to elucidate his notion of competitive evolution. Huxley's essay appeared in journal *The Nineteenth Century* in February 1888.

18   As Kropotkin notes: 'Sociability and need of mutual aid and support are inherent parts of human nature that at no time of history can we discover men living in small isolated families, fighting each other for the means of subsistence' (Kropotkin 1914, 153).

19   On Kropotkin's faith in the 'good sense' of the masses, see Kropotkin 1968, 109. On the judgement of Kropotkin's naïvety, see Malatesta 1980, 34–5.

20   The instinctive, destructive and unsystematic image of Bakunin's ideas, which he liked to foster, can be overdone. For a correction to this view, see the study by Kelly 1982. On Bakunin's legacy, see Avrich 1970.

21   For a discussion of Bakunin's disapproval of Kropotkin's conception of evolution and progress, see Thomas 1980, 286–8; Avrich 1967, 92ff; and Avrich introduction to Bakunin 1970, vi.

22   On Bergson's general influence on Sorel, see Scott 1919 or Pilkington 1976.

23   Sorel spoke of an epic state of mind in the vein of Homeric heroes or Nietzschean supermen – a new age of chivalry and chasteness (see Sorel 1975, 230ff). As T. E. Hulme, his translator, commented: 'It is difficult … to understand a revolutionary who is anti-democratic, an absolutist in ethics, rejecting all rationalism and relativism, who values the mystical element in religion … who speaks contemptuously of modernism and *progress*, and uses a concept like *honour* with no sense of unreality' (Hulme 1965, 250).

24   The best-known Christian defence of anarchy is by Leo Tolstoy, though it could hardly be called an orthodox interpretation of Christian belief (see Tolstoy 1974).

25   It is clear, though, that Proudhon did not use the notion of the state, sovereignty or law in a very consistent fashion (see Vernon 1986, 82ff).

26   For today's anti-capitalist anarchists the enemy has mutated to both globalized capitalism and globalized corporations. The state, though, is still seen as oppressive and largely at the mercy of these global forces.

27   This theme of anti-intellectualism (or at least a scepticism with academic approaches) has, in a different format, reappeared in some of the anti-capitalist strategies of the 1990s and 2000s.

28   The term 'spook' is Stirner's.

29   There are some ambiguities here: for example, Bakunin's and Proudhon's interest in American federalism, or Proudhon's dalliance with parliamentary politics and later interest in the state. As one commentator notes, Proudhon 'uses the term "state" without embarrassment and, what is more to the point, ascribes to the state enormous importance; it is "prime mover and general director". … On the question of jurisdiction, however, what Proudhon proposes, fairly abstractly viewed, is more like a federal state than a confederation' (Vernon 1986, 82–3).

30   Bookchin puts the point in a similar way, suggesting that 'Marxism may well be the ideology of capitalism *par excellence* precisely because the essentials of its critique have

focused on capitalist production without challenging the underlying cultural sensibilities that sustain it' (Bookchin 1986b, 29).

31   On the issue of self-government, see Bakunin 1970, 30; Proudhon, 1970b, 94; Clark 1986, 225; also see Wolff 1970 and Carter 1971. For some of the ripostes to Wolff, see essays by R. T. De George, G. Wall and P. Riley in Pennock and Chapman eds 1978.

32   Leo Tolstoy argued that true liberty corresponded to the ethical code of the Sermon on the Mount (see Tolstoy 1974; see also Malatesta on freedom necessarily being tied to moral goals, Malatesta 1980, 24).

33   Bookchin makes a very strong point on this in his various writings (see discussion in Clark 1986, 224ff). In some writers it involves assertions that rationality, authenticity and self-expression are also involved in liberty. Michael Taylor, in a discussion of this issue, argues that he could share such a view of self-expression and autonomy 'if it could be shown that the critical choosing activity central to this conception of autonomy does not itself have causal determinants'; however, he contends that this is unlikely to be done. Taylor also points to a problematic element on the linkage of positive liberty (autonomy) with community, namely, that 'it is precisely those things which limit autonomy which also limit the degree to which these [anarchistic] utopias are truly communities' (Taylor 1982, 150 and 164).

34   There were exceptions to this. Rothbard for one tried to construct, in his various works, an anarcho-capitalist law code, redeemed from government or the state, and premised essentially on rights to self-ownership, non-aggression and homesteading. Other anarchists also try to redeem government from the state.

35   Ironically this is precisely the core argument that anti-capitalists anarchists object to.

36   Proudhon comments: 'The Social Contract is the supreme act by which each citizen pledges to society his love, his intelligence, his labour, his services, his products and his goods in return for the affection, ideas, works, products, services and goods of his fellow citizens' (Proudhon 1989, 114).

37   A school which, despite government and inspectorate ambivalence in Britain, still exists today.

38   As Clark comments: 'The union of egoists is an association in which people work together, not for the common welfare, or greatest happiness, but because of each individual's desire that he or she should own as much as is possible' (Clark 1976, 79).

39   This point finds echoes in both Gandhi's and Schumacher's idea.

40   Kropotkin shared this view with a number of others at the time: for example, the Marxist writer August Bebel (see Bebel 1971). By the 1980s it was subject to a critique from within feminist ideology (see ch. 7).

41   These intense early anarchist debates about violence have reappeared, to a degree, in the anti-capitalism and anti-globalization movements of the late 1990s and 2000s, particularly after the anti-capitalist confrontations in Seattle in November 1999, Davos in January 2000 and Washington in April 2000. Some anti-capitalists have argued, though, that new forms of resistance need to be found other than direct violent confrontation. In this context notions such as carnival and clowning have been suggested. I am not certain, though, whether this is being articulated, at the present moment, as a distinctively anarchist strategy.

Chapter 6   Fascism

1   This is defined by Griffin in terms of a 'mythic core that forms the basis of my ideal type of generic fascism', that is, 'the vision of the (perceived) crisis of the nation as betokening

the birth-pangs of a new order. It crystallizes in the image of the national community, once purged and rejuvenated, rising phoenix-like from the ashes of a morally bankrupt state system and the decadent culture associated with it' (Griffin 1995, 3). It is worth noting here that if Griffin's argument is correct, then it would allow the extension of the term 'fascism', as a descriptive ideological term, to the present moment.

2   For the counter-claim to this, which sees a number of core ideological components, see Griffin 1991, ed. 1995, ed. 1998 and 2007.

3   On the complex relation of fascism to the Right, see essays in Eatwell and O'Sullivan 1989; Passmore 2002, 72ff; Sternhell 1996.

4   Since completing the second edition of this book in 1995 there has been an unexpectedly rich and diverse surge of work on fascism and nationalism socialism, which it is virtually impossible to summarize with brevity. A selection of these would include: Payne 1995; Sternhell et al. 1995; Gentile 1996; Kershaw 1998–2000; Neocleous 1997; Blinkhorn 2000; Burleigh 2001; Morgan 2002; Passmore 2002; Eatwell 2003; Griffin ed. 1995, ed. 1998 and 2007; Paxton 2005; Robson 2006.

5   It should be noted, though, that there are a number of subtly distinct views expressed by scholars. For example, nineteenth-century intellectual themes could be viewed as an innocuous backdrop, with a number of potentialities for later development. Alternatively, there could be said to be quite definite continuities of ideas. Nineteenth-century thinkers were thus fascist in all but name. Again there could be some formal intellectual continuities, but the fascists totally distorted the ideas for their own nefarious ends. Finally, the continuity of ideas existed but these would not have developed in the way they did without the catalyst of war, depression and social unrest.

6   One of the older, if still fairly sophisticated, accounts utilizing this general determinist line of argument was Franz L. Neumann's *Behemoth* (1942). See also Martin Kitchen's *Fascism* (1976).

7   An aspect of this religious crisis was expressed by the psychoanalyst Carl Jung. He argued that Christian myths have died. In our present civilization 'myth has become mute, and gives no answers'; thus, 'We stand perplexed and stupefied before the phenomenon of Nazism. ... We stand face to face with the terrible question of evil and do not even know what is before us' (Jung 1967, 363–4). In one sense the work of Gentile (1996 and 2006) provides one answer here; how effective the answer is remains open to debate.

8   This essay has been reprinted in Collingwood 1989. Boucher discusses the essay in the introduction to this latter volume and in his larger study of Collingwood (see Boucher 1989).

9   This idea is touched upon in chapter 10, on fundamentalism.

10   Although, again, recent scholars such as Roger Griffin disagree with this idea of cultural malaise, seeing fascism rather as an ideology closely to tied to modernity and the promulgation of certain positive, if utopian and ideal-type, values. Fascism can thus be 'be treated as a man-made, explicable phenomenon which falls just as much within the remit of the human sciences as any other historical phenomenon'. We should not therefore, for Griffin, rush to demonize it (see Griffin ed. 1998, 325; also Griffin 2007).

11   Barrington Moore, Jr, in *Social Origins of Dictatorship and Democracy* (1967), uses the term 'conservative modernization' to describe the Italian fascist development. See also Apter 1965; Black 1967; and Organski 1969.

12   There are other notable and interesting views which could be reviewed, given space. For example, O'Sullivan, in his work on fascism, speaks of fascism as a new 'activist style' of politics contrasted to 'limited' politics. This activist style is identified by certain features

like a new theory of freedom, an exaggerated belief in the potency of the human will, a theory of popular sovereignty and a new theory of evil (see O'Sullivan 1983, ch. 1).

13   See also Trevor-Roper 1947; Nolte 1969; Mack Smith 1983. Also for some discussion of this interpretation, see Pois 1986, 15ff.

14   Primo de Rivera, the leading light of the Spanish Falange, also attempted to differentiate fascism from the Right, although he claimed (in a characteristic move by fascists) that they were neither left nor right (see 'Foundation of the Spanish Falange' in Primo de Rivera 1972, 53–4). It should also be pointed out again here that fascism has an equally problematic relation to socialism, often being seen in Italy during the 1920s, for example, as the organic, natural successor to socialism (see Lyttelton in Laqueur ed. 1979, 83).

15   Zev Sternhell remarks that 'Nazism cannot ... be treated as a mere variant of fascism: its emphasis on biological determinism rules out all efforts to deal with it as such' (Sternhell in Laqueur ed. 1979, 328).

16   For the general response of European fascists to Germany, see Mosse 1966, 314ff. On Mussolini's quite ripe remarks, see Mack Smith 1983, 216. Mussolini noted to his colleagues that when Hitler spoke on these issues he was like a 'gramophone with just seven tunes and once he had finished playing them he started all over again'. Admittedly, Hitler had also stated in conversations with Mussolini that Italians, presumably because of their darker complexion, might have traces of Negroid blood and therefore were inferior to the Aryans, which certainly would not have endeared him to Mussolini (see Mack Smith 1983, 214–15; see also Bosworth 2003).

17   On the issue of violence, see Epstein in Turner ed. 1979, 17.

18   See, for example, Mussolini's article 'Which Way is the World Going?' from the party journal *Gerarchia*, February 1922; also Lyttelton ed. 1987.

19   Roberts continues that 'The problems that bothered ... non-Marxist critics of liberalism, from Proudhon and Mazzini to Durkheim and Duguit, were very much involved in the crisis of liberal Italy. ... Had it implemented the corporativist revolution, left fascism would have brought to fruition a major strand in the tradition of anti-Marxist criticism of liberalism and capitalism' (Roberts 1979, 319–20).

20   The Twenty-Five Points can be found in Miller Lane and Rupp eds 1978 and Oakeshott ed. 1953. The programme was committed to: full employment (7); the abolition of unearned income and the emancipation from interest charges (11); confiscation of all war profits (12); nationalization of all business combines (13); profit-sharing in industry (14); communalization of department stores and aid to small traders (16); confiscation of land without compensation for communal purposes (17); the death penalty for usury and profiteering (18); nationalized education (20); abolition of child labour, etc.

21   Interestingly, this squares with Bullock's assessment of Hitler's early ideas as wholly unoriginal: 'They were the clichés of radical and Pan-German gutter politics' (Bullock 1962, 44).

22   Schmitt's contribution tends rather to substantiate some of the more negative criticisms employed by national socialism (see Schmitt, *The Crisis of Parliamentary Democracy* (1985); see also McCormick 1999). Heidegger's role is more ambiguous. Although initially fairly enthusiastic about national socialism, he appears to have become disenchanted (see Ott 1994 or Wolin 2001).

23   Papini also noted: 'Mourning over the dead, wasting one's time in sentimentality, humanitarian moaning, drawing back in the face of all the platitudes on the sacredness of human life, would be to deny the force of life that is throbbing and growing and glowing all around us. And life is not worth living unless it is full and intense: sacrificing the

heroic intensity of such a life in favour of life that is merely ephemeral would deprive the world of its greatest value' (Papini in Lyttelton ed. 1973, 107). For similar views on the spiritual necessity of war, see Gentile 1928, 290.

24 I have only given a very thin summary of Gentile's answer here. Gentile in fact situates the argument on intellectualism in his doctrine of immanent idealism. Whether or not immanent idealism really ties into the fascist case, Gentile's account is probably the most sophisticated response from any fascist to this issue (see Gentile 1960). For a systematic attempt to link Gentile's thinking with fascism, see Gregor 2001, also Gregor's edition of Gentile 2004.

25 Sternhell comments on this that 'Fascist ideology was born of a political tradition that considered the individual as a function of group life' (Sternhell in Laqueur ed. 1979, 364).

26 As Robert Pois comments: 'The wish to live in close harmony with nature (to live authentically) and revulsion against the admittedly often alienating life-patterns of urban existence – these are phenomena extant throughout a Western World increasingly uncomfortable with the problems attendant upon first mechanized, and now automated, societies. Taken but slightly out of context, many of the statements of Nazis ... would be applauded by the average, somewhat unreflective, environmentalist' (Pois 1986, 122). Hitler's well-known love of animals and enthusiastic vegetarianism are not unrelated to this perspective. For some broader commentary upon the idea of nature in Nazism, see Bramwell 1985 and Dominick 1987.

27 One scholar notes that Mussolini 'liked to think of himself as man excluded from communion with others as if by some divine law'; however, much of the time Mussolini appeared to feel simply socially inadequate and ill at ease. It is contended that one of the reasons for his introduction of the Roman salute instead of the handshake was his personal revulsion against physical contact (see Mack Smith 1983, 127).

28 See also for wonderful accounts of Marinetti's "Fascist cookbook", O'Sullivan 1983, 143.

29 See also Goebbels, 'National Socialism or Bolshevism', and Rosenberg, 'The Folkish Idea of the State', in Miller Lane and Rupp eds 1978, 70, 78. Goebbels, in the above, argues that national socialism is anti-capitalist, anti-Semitic and anti-bourgeois.

30 Darré comments thus: 'He who leaves the plants in a garden to themselves will soon find to his surprise that the garden is overgrown by weeds and that even the basic character of the plants has changed. If therefore the garden is to remain the breeding ground for the plants, if, in other words, it is to lift above the harsh rule of natural forces, then the forming will of a gardener is necessary. ... Exactly thus, speaking now of the folk, was the old German legal order intended, whose weeding and tending (which no doubt arose out of the blood consciousness of the Germanic peoples, based on an ideological foundation) created the conditions of existence needed for life and growth' (quoted in Miller Lane and Rupp eds 1978, 115). For a detailed study of Darré see Bramwell 1985.

31 The human soul was closely linked to landscape in this tradition. Late nineteenth-century German writers such as Friedrich Ratzel and Wilhelm Heinrich Riehl were concerned to elucidate this point in their writings. As Mosse comments, Riehl 'analysed the various population groupings of Germany in terms of the landscape they inhabited' (see Mosse 1966, 19ff).

32 See the essay by Eatwell, 'The Holocaust Denial: A Study in Propaganda Technique', in Cheles et al. eds 1991.

33 Gentile also defines fascism in one passage as 'a conception of the state, with the purpose of solving the political problems that had reached exasperation as a result of the unbridled passions of the uninformed masses after the war' (Gentile in Lyttelton ed. 1973, 306).

34   See Mack Smith 1983, 173; Gentile in Lyttelton ed. 1973, 301; Primo de Rivera, 'Guidelines of the Falange: The Twenty-Six Points', November 1934, Point VI, in Primo de Rivera 1972. For the various senses of totalitarianism, see Forjacs ed. 1986, 2–3.

35   Mussolini, who expressed little interest in individual liberty, described it as a 'decomposing corpse' (quoted in Mack Smith 1983, 162).

36   Gentile commented on this theme that 'The absurdities inherent in the liberal concept of freedom were apparent to liberals themselves early in the nineteenth century. It is no merit of fascism to have again indicated them' (Gentile 1928, 304). The context of the Germanic understanding of freedom has been well documented; see discussion in Stern 1974, xxix.

37   See also Papini, Rocco and Gentile in Lyttelton ed. 1973, 110, 260, 313–14; Gentile 1928, 303; and for the concept of freedom developed in the most systematic manner, see Gentile 1960, 122–3.

38   Hitler makes exactly the same point when he remarks, 'We, as Aryans, can conceive of the state only as the living organism of a nationality which not only assures the preservation of this nationality, but … leads it to the highest freedom' (Hitler 1969, 358).

39   Pois remarks that the Nazis 'generally did not accept the notion of the total or "totalitarian state"' (Pois 1986, 67).

40   Mussolini appeared to admire Lenin for his dynamic leadership. He also liked to encourage the comparison of his achievements with great figures of the past. The monthly fascist periodical *Gerarchia* likened Mussolini to Socrates, Plato, Machiavelli and Napoleon (see Mack Smith 1983, 194).

41   Gottfried Feder provides a typical example of the national socialist attempt to outline a corporate state idea. He called for a new type of state to replace the liberal Weimar Republic: 'It must especially break with parliamentary parties and parliamentary cliques, and above all, it must not mix political and economic types of popular representation in a *single* parliament … The *House of the People* (as the first chamber) represents the political interests of the whole people, while the *Central Council* must represent the *economic* interests of the working population' (see 'The Social State', reprinted in Miller Lane and Rupp eds 1978, 34).

42   On Moeller van den Bruck, see Mosse 1966, 283. On the repudiation of medieval corporatism, see Rocco in Lyttelton ed. 1973, 296; also Cassel's essay in Turner ed. 1975, 75.

43   On the odd relation of Sorel to Mussolini, see Jennings 1985, 159–60. For a detailed study of syndicalism in relation to Italian fascism, see Roberts 1979.

44   Rocco also speaks of 'syndicalism or corporativism'; presumably the two ideas had been perceived as one and the same (see Rocco in Lyttelton ed. 1973, 276).

45   Skidelsky remarks that 'In terms of economic understanding, the programme expounded by Mosley in *Greater Britain* was far in advance of anything produced by continental fascism' (Skidelsky 1975, 302).

46   See chapter 9 for discussion of these writers.

47   The chapter has tended to focus predominantly upon the historical fascism of the 1920–45 period. However, there are various arguments, such as Griffin's, which suggest that there are movements – for example, the German Deutsche Volksunion and Die Republikaner groups, the Belgian Vlaams Blok, the Dutch Centrumdemocraten, the French Front Nationale, the Italian Movimento Sociale Italiano or the British National Party, to name but a few – which could be described as political heirs of fascism. Some might now characterize these as 'extreme Right' or 'post-fascist' movements. Many of the actual protagonists of these movements would also repudiate the title 'fascist' (mainly

because of its historical associations); however, they clearly share some of the core beliefs of the earlier fascist movements (for example a stress of extreme ultranationalism, a consequent focus on the problems of immigration, and sometimes a distinct unease with democracy) and could be considered as part of the lineage of the earlier movements. For discussion of this point see Eatwell and O'Sullivan eds 1989; Cheles et al. eds 1991; Mudde 2002; Ignazi 2006. This particular discussion is immensely complex and takes me beyond the historical focus of this chapter. However, its pertinence to future ideological study is unquestionably important.

Chapter 7   Feminism

1   My own chapter here now has more of an historical or genealogical feel to it than it did in 1995. However, most of the basic parameters of feminist ideology still remain intact, if some of the key emphases have changed (and others have been considerably downplayed).

2   Writing in 2000, Diana Coole argues that feminists now are 'more likely, under the influence of Foucault, in particular, to integrate everything into the discursive on the grounds that it is within discursive fields that structures of power are constituted and that there is no prediscursive reality that acts as an independent referent. In this sense, the validity of postmodernism's representations of more heterogeneous spaces cannot be established simply by appealing to a reality whose truth they might more or less accurately convey' (Coole 2000, 351).

3   One definite aspect of poststructuralism is, in Toril Moi's words, that it 'sees all metanarratives, including feminism, as repressive enactments of metaphysical authority' (see Moi in Lovell ed. 1990, 368).

4   In some ways much of the discussion about feminisms, at the close of the twentieth century, appears at points like snapshots of a moving object.

5   Dale Spender, commenting on the exclusion of certain important females from more general historical writing, remarked that this 'constitutes an example of almost every technique men have used to abuse, devolve and erase women' (Spender 1983, 34).

6   Griffin also stated that: 'The fact that man does not consider himself a part of nature, but indeed considers himself superior to matter, seemed to me to gain significance when placed against man's attitude that woman is both inferior to him and closer to nature' (Griffin 1978, xv). The work of Mary Daly is also linked with this perspective – see Daly, *Gyn-Ecology* (1979) and *Pure Lust* (1984).

7   Virginia Woolf discusses her impact in Woolf 1929.

8   Hestor Eisenstein (1984) asserts that there are four waves or phases. On postmodernist feminism being a 'third wave', see discussion of Sylvester in Zalewski 1991, 33.

9   Named after Susan B. Anthony, a veteran campaigner who introduced the proposition.

10 Mitchell moved more decisively towards psychoanalytic interests in *Psychoanalysis and Feminism* (1974).

11 As in the prestigious Virago Press, established in 1973.

12 It also led in writers such as Martha Nussbaum to a deeply critical (continuing) impatience with feminist poststructural theory (for example, see Nussbaum 1999b).

13 Although it is worth pointing out immediately that one of the classic ground-breaking feminist texts of the late twentieth century – Carole Pateman's *The Sexual Contract* (1988) – involved a vigorous scholarly critique of the deeply patriarchal roots of liberal contract theory (see also Pateman 1989).

14 For the exceptions – Condorcet, Helvetius, Von Hippel and Wollstonecraft, see the excellent and detailed essay on these and other theorists by Ursula Vogel in Evans et al. eds 1986.

15 Aphra Behn, Mary Astell, Catherine Macauley and Olympe de Gouges (see Spender 1983, 44–50).

16 Okin comments that all feminists 'acknowledge the vast debts of feminism to liberalism. They know that without the liberal tradition, feminism would have had a much more difficult time emerging' (Okin 1989, 61). However, Okin, Radcliffe-Richards and Nussbaum want Rawlsian liberalism and theories of justice to be extended fully to the family and women (and indeed beyond). Child-rearing, domestic work, and the like, must be included in any discussion of justice. Okin regards this as a logical progression of Rawlsian arguments. One of the more controversial aspects of the Rawlsian feminist liberalism has involved its spirited criticisms of multiculturalism and identity politics (see particularly Okin et al. 1999).

17 Bebel's *Women under Socialism* was indeed an immensely popular work, a fact which appeared to irritate Engels. It was subsequently revised in 1883 and 1891. The fiftieth German edition appeared in 1910.

18 Women-centred theory 'demands the dethroning of logic and reason, and an acceptance of the postulate of woman's especial ties to nature; of those who do not share it, it requires a Kuhnian-style non-rational conversion to a new paradigm' (J. Evans, 'Overview of the Problem for Feminist Political Theorists', in Evans et al. eds 1986, 4).

19 'The kind of historical inquiry Foucault summons here is accordingly both genealogical and archaeological. The genealogist would not think of women's history as a continuous narrative or project, but as a matrix of many interventions – threads and plaits, power and resistance – which may be quite heterogeneous' (Coole in Freeden ed. 2001, 162).

20 Postmodernism remains immensely difficult to pin down. Its initial influence was in areas such as architecture and fine art. In the art world it usually denotes a mixing of traditional styles and a celebration and play on their differences. In this sense, some see it as a reaction to the confining style of modernism (although it is interpreted by others as an extension of modernism). Literature is harder to articulate in postmodern terms. For example, are James Joyce's *Ulysses*, T. S. Eliot's *The Waste Land* or Ezra Pound's *Cantos* modernist or postmodern? They have been seen as the crowning achievement of modernism, although they also embody multiple traditional styles and 'rhetorics' in the characteristic postmodern vein.

21 Thus Toril Moi asks: 'Is "postmodern feminism" simply another oxymoron, a new quagmire of contradictions for feminists to sink in?' (Moi in Lovell ed. 1990, 368).

22 For critical discussion and further bibliography on this, see Dietz 1985; see also Stacey essay in Mitchell and Oakley eds 1986.

23 It is worth noting that there was group in the later 1990s who called themselves 'third way feminism' (see Heywood and Drake eds 1997; Baumgardner and Richards 2000; Mascia-Lees and Sharpe 2000). This approach does not appear to have come to much. It seems to have been largely a challenge to younger women, in 2000, to re-engage with the feminist movement and to fulfil the goals of second-wave feminism.

24 In Mill, and Engels, there are still clearly quite strong residual beliefs about the 'natural' place of women. On Mill see Stafford 2004.

25 Jaggar sees Firestone's work as the first 'sustained and systematic work by a contemporary radical feminist' (Jaggar 1983, 85).

26 Kate Millett preferred the term 'unisex' to 'androgynous'.

27 Speaking of the German extermination camps of the Second World War, the 1980s feminist writer Andrea Dworkin claimed that 'in creating a female degraded beyond human

recognition, the Nazis set a new standard of masculinity, honoured especially in the benumbed conscience that does not even notice sadism against women because that sadism is so ordinary' (Dworkin 1981, 145). The various writings of Dworkin pursued similar themes; see Dworkin's *Women Hating* (1974) or *Intercourse* (1987).

28 Vicky Randall contends that standpoint theory is over-ambitious (see Randall 1991, 523).

29 As Heidi Hartmann put it: 'While Marxist analysis provides essential insight into the laws of historical development, and those of capital in particular, the categories of Marxism are sex-blind. Only a specifically feminist analysis reveals the systematic character of relations betwen men and women. Yet feminist analysis by itself is inadequate because it has been blind to history and insufficiently materialist. Both Marxist analysis, particularly its historical and materialist method, and feminist analysis, especially the identification of patriarchy as a social and historical structure, must be drawn upon if we are to understand the development of Western capitalist societies and the predicament of women within them' (Hartmann in Sargent ed. 1986, 2–3; see also Rowbotham 1972; Kuhn and Wolpe eds 1978; and Eisenstein ed. 1979 for more detail and bibliography on these debates).

30 The equality issue still figures importantly in feminist debate (see Phillips 1995 and 1999; also Squires 2007).

31 Wollstonecraft mentions, very tentatively, at the end of her book, the equal rights of suffrage, but it is only a passing remark (see Wollstonecraft 1985, 260).

32 As Mill argued: 'The principle which regulates the existing social relations between the sexes – the legal subordination of one sex to the other – is wrong in itself, and now one of the chief hindrances to human improvement; and that it ought to be replaced by a principle of perfect equality' (Mill 1989, 119).

33 The literature here is now very extensive, certainly over the last decade. A brief update would include: Brown 1995; Fraser 1997; Okin et al. 1999; Phillips 1995 and 1999; Young 1997 and 2000; Mackay 2001; Nussbaum 1999a and 2001; Benhabib 2002; Dietz 2002; Hirschman 2002; Fraser and Honneth 2003; Mohany 2003; McNay 2000 and 2007; Squires 2000 and 2007.

34 As she observed: 'A master and mistress of a family ought not to continue to love each other with passion' (Wollstonecraft 1985, 113).

35 Martha Nussbaum, for example, thus launched a vigorous attack on Judith Butler's work, describing her as the 'Professor of Parody' (see Nussbaum 1999b).

36 As another critic remarked, 'Feminist postmodernism might be described as an oxymoron – two completely incompatible terms' (Zalewski 1991, 34; see also Moi in Lovell ed. 1990, 368; Aladjem 1991, 279–80).

Chapter 8   Ecologism

1 The division of views on how to name the movement is reflected in the titles for introductory texts: thus there is Andy Dobson's *Green Political Thought* (1990; 4th edition 2007); Robyn Eckersley's *Environmentalism and Political Theory* (1992); John Barry's *Rethinking Green Politics* (1999); Neil Carter's *The Politics of the Environment* (2007); James Connelly and Graham Smith's *The Politics of the Environment* (2002); Mark Smith's *Ecologism* (1998); and Andrew Dobson and Robyn Eckersley's collection *Political Theory and the Ecological Challenge* (2006).

2   As Meadowcroft notes 'most observers (and many greens) now agree that the centre of gravity of contemporary green politics is actually towards the left' (Meadowcroft in Freeden ed. 2001, 181; also on the implicit green critique of capitalism see Kovel 2007).

3   There has been an enormous amount of debate on this issue over the last decade. Part of this was sparked by the Bush administration's unwillingness to take the scientific evidence on global warming very seriously and thus to view the UN Kyoto conference with some suspicion. However, texts such as Lomborg's *The Skeptical Environmentalist* (2001), which argued that much of the apparent evidence on global warming and climate change was an over-exaggerated statistical artefact, have certainly made the debate that much more confusing, emotionally charged and problematic.

4   Green politics starts with the recognition 'that we find ourselves in a multi-faceted, global crisis that touches every aspect of our lives' (Spretnak and Capra, 1986, xv). This also touches upon the very current theme of environmental citizenship (see Smith 1998; Minteer and Taylor eds 2002; Dobson in Skinner and Stråth eds 2003; Dobson 2006).

5   According to Anna Bramwell, the early use of 'ecology' had strong etymological relations to other terms such as 'ethology' (Bramwell 1989, 14–15; one might also add here 'ethnology' [the study of races]).

6   Haeckel was Professor of Zoology for many years at the University of Jena.

7   The significance of Christianity here is that some have traced the ecological crisis back to the very character of Christianity. The classic article to first introduce this idea was White in Barr ed. 1971. However, it is disputed by a number of writers. Much of the debate turns on the interpretation of the concept of 'Christian stewardship'. See Robin Attfield's discussion, *The Ethics of Environmental Concern* (1983). For a different perspective on this issue see Fox 1983.

8   Max Oelschlaeger's *The Idea of the Wilderness* (1991) argued, in fact, that things began to go wrong in the Neolithic period; before this time hunter-gatherers had not unduly affected the environment.

9   As Brian Tokar notes: 'The real origin of the Green movement is in the great social and political upheavals that swept the United States and the entire Western world during the 1960s' (Tokar 1987, 34).

10   Haeckel's views have strong parallels with Spinoza's monistic philosophy. It is therefore not completely fortuitous that more recent eco-philosophers such as Naess, Devall, Sessions and Warwick Fox have been clearly fascinated with Spinoza's philosophy.

11   The peculiar term 'anthropistic' appears to be Haeckel's, or his translator's, neologism. There is a close term 'anthropic' (meaning 'of or belonging to a human') which the *Oxford English Dictionary* records as 'rare' and dating from 1859.

12   As Scruton comments: conservatives should stop trying to pretend 'that the environment is an exclusively left-wing concern, and one that has no place in conservative thinking'; the best defence of the environment for Scruton is the conservative belief in local loyalties and limited territorial affections. In this sense nationalism would also be a defence of nature. See Scruton essay in Dobson and Eckersley eds 2006, 19.

13   Tim O'Riordan has also spoken of three waves: the first dating back to the early romantic period, approximately 150 years ago, incorporating figures such as Wordsworth, Emerson and Thoreau; the second phase between 1900 to 1920, incorporating the age of the environmental technocrat and thus programmes of reforestation, soil conservation, and so on; and the third phase, from the mid-1960s, when environmental concerns became part of vigorous public debate, well-informed pressure groups were formed and

environmental regulations were developed and institutionalized (discussed in Porritt and Winner 1988, 20).

14   Another way of approaching this is in terms of Anthony Downs' idea of 'issue attention cycles', where the public become alarmed about a particular issue (like environmental pollution); enthused about trying to solve it; then become entrapped in spiralling costs and cynicism; and finally abandon it in favour of another 'issue' which alarms them. Possibly, however, this appears too cynical a view (see Downs 1972).

15   Porritt, in 1984, contended that, 'Having written the last two general election manifestoes for the Ecology Party, I would be hard put even to say what our ideology is. Our politics seems to be a fairly simple mixture of pragmatism and idealism, common sense and vision. If that's an ideology, it's of a rather different sort from those that dominate our lives today'; however, he goes on later to attack both socialism and conservatism, contending that 'there must be something with which we can replace [them]; not another super-ideology (for ideologies are themselves part of the problem) *but a different world view*' (Porritt 1984, 43–4; see also Porritt and Winner 1988, 11; and Schwarz and Schwarz 1987, ch. 1).

16   There are attempts to bridge this gap. Dobson drew attention to the problem (see Dobson 1989 and 1990). In a response to Dobson, Robin Attfield claimed that his own work with Katherine Dell, *Values, Conflict and the Environment* (Attfield and Dobb eds 1989), 'is the most developed attempt to carry through Dobson's project of relating ecophilosophy to social practice' (Attfield 1990, 65). They deployed a sophisticated form of cost–benefit analysis premised on 'an analysis of the value-impacts of actions and policies', which in turn allowed some judgements to be made concerning decisions on the environment. Given the massive problems that public policy analysis has had with cost–benefit analysis on issues such as airport or railway location over the last three decades, omens do not bode well for this approach.

17   I should point out here that in my own categorization in the text, I will be simplifying and also avoiding the philosophical problems of the particular components, so as not to unduly complicate matters. However, the typology that I utilize is still more complicated than usual. A more extensive enriched typology is outlined in Vincent 1993. For related debates see Stavrakis 1997; Wissenburg 1997; Talshir 1998. The usual typology to be found in the literature (which I am *not* deploying and do *not* endorse) is to draw a distinction between 'shallow' and 'deep' ecologists, usually along the following lines:

Deep	*Shallow*
Ontological monism	Ontological divisions
Ethics derived from metaphysics	Ethics separate from metaphysics
Intrinsic value	Instrumental value
Voluntarist	Determinist
Systems science	Mechanistic science
Biosphere or ecosphere of value	Humans of primary value
Radical	Reformist
Advocates sustainable future	Endorses industrialism

18   Richard Sylvan called this form of argument the 'Sole Value Assumption'; see his 'Critique of Deep Ecology' (1984/5). A form of this argument can be found in an article by

W. H. Murdy, 'Anthropocentrism: A Modern Version'. Murdy argues that: 'To be anthropocentric is to affirm that mankind is to be valued more highly than other things in nature – by man. ... It is proper for man to be anthropocentric'; he later contends that our ecological problems do not stem from anthropocentrism *per se*, but rather from conceiving anthropocentrism too narrowly (see Murdy in Scherer and Attig eds 1983, 13, 20).

19   One can clearly be human-centred without being human instrumental. There is thus a difference between strong and weak anthropocentrism. Nature is not necessarily simply grist to the mill of human self-interest. Further, naturalness, itself, can be a source of value; nature's independence might be said to be crucial to its meaning and value. John Barry calls his own version of this argument a form of 'critical anthropocentrism' (Barry 1999, 35).

20   The second tendency is best seen in the work of Arne Naess and also exemplified in Devall and Sessions 1985; for the Buddhist interpretation, see Gary Snyder's essay 'Buddhism and the Possibilities of a Planetary Culture', appendix G in Devall and Sessions 1985 or Henning 2002; Warwick Fox's work is best exemplified in the detailed reply to Sylvan's critique of deep ecology (see Sylvan 1984/5; Fox 1984) and in a comprehensive study by Fox, *Toward a Transpersonal Ecology* (1986). A summary of eco-philosophy literature describes Fox's 1986 piece as 'The best explanation and defence of the deep ecology position' (see Katz 1989); on the deep ecology perspective see also Drengson and Inoue 1995; Sessions 1995; Humphrey 2000.

21   The terminology here roughly corresponds to that of J. R. Rodman and Robin Attfield.

22   Taylor distinguishes vigorously between 'human-centred' axiology and 'life-centred' axiology, identifying himself with the latter. On the biocentric life-centred view, see Taylor 1986, 99–100.

23   'The kind of things which can be of intrinsic value are not objects, people or other creatures, but experiences, activities and the development of capacities ... talk about the intrinsic value of people, when it is not another way of talking about their standing or their rights, should be taken to concern the intrinsic value of their living a worthwhile life' (Attfield 1987, 31).

24   For a more recent critical eco-feminist approach which contests the links made by earlier feminists between mothering, womens' natures and nurturance of nature, see MacGregor 2007. See also Collard and Contrucci 1988; Plumwood 1993; also Plumwood's essay in Dobson and Eckersley eds 2006.

25   'The green analysis of environmental and social issues is within the broad framework of right-wing ideology and philosophy. The belief in "natural" limits to human achievement, the denial of class divisions and the Romantic view of "nature" all have their roots in the conservative and liberal political traditions' (Weston ed. 1986, 24).

26   As Weston remarks: 'To think that whooping cranes are important (possibly more so) than people one has to be free of the more pressing human problems like that of poverty' (Weston ed. 1986, 3). See also Martinez-Alier 2003 on poverty and ecology and Kovel 2007 on capitalism and ecology.

27   The word 'Gaia' in its original use was the 'earth goddess'. It should be noted, though, that the idea of the earth as a self-regulating organism – 'living earth' – had already been discussed by a number of scientists and philosophers at the end of the nineteenth century (see Bramwell 1989, 61ff).

28   As Brian Tokar noted: 'Modern civilizations have abandoned the life-affirming qualities of primitive cultures and created a way of life that is increasingly mobilized for death' (Tokar 1987, 9–10).

29 One way out of this impasse is to argue that our self-consciousness has evolved natu-
    rally and is therefore part of nature. Yet there is always something puzzling and unre-
    solved in such an argument. The theory of evolution is premised on our *being*
    self-conscious. The theory of evolution is a product of self-consciousness. Therefore
    self-consciousness is the premise upon which the theory of evolution develops. Yet the
    above argument, in asserting that self-consciousness has evolved naturally, implies that
    natural evolution is the premise to self-consciousness. This appears to conflict with the
    second argument. My own view of this is that self-consciousness implies some difference
    from the normal functioning of evolution, although I am not quite sure of the nature of
    that difference.

30 Ryle capitalizes the 'state'. On the other hand, he does admit that such a state would still
    owe more of its values to William Morris's vision of socialism than to Marxism (see Ryle
    1988, 69–70).

31 'I'm not an anarchic green or a fourth worlder; that approach to life is ludicrously nos-
    talgic. It refers back to golden ages or ideas about human communities that have little
    relevance and are singularly unhelpful in terms of getting across to people the utterly
    unrealistic alternatives that we've got. I'm increasingly critical of what I call the manic
    minusculists. ... I would see the state as exercising its present functions but in a more
    sensitive way: in terms of basic services like education, health, and income distribution. ...
    I would always uphold the need for some distributive mechanism to ensure basic fairness
    across regions' (Porritt 1984, 10–11).

32 Can we be just or unjust to the environment? Is it really feasible to think of concepts such
    as rights, justice or democracy in relation to the environment? The most straightforward
    answer to this question is that the environment is *not* something that one can be unjust
    or unjust to. It cannot possess rights. The reason for this is that one can only be just or
    unjust to entities worthy of moral consideration – that is, moral agents. The only occa-
    sion on which extending moral consideration beyond human agents is feasible is where
    it directly affects human agency. Justice is a concept applying to the states of affairs of
    human persons. It is linked to the security of human life, liberty and property. If a clean
    or protected environment is, though, linked with human security, then it can be included
    within justice via the moral agency of human beings. For a critical discussion of some of
    these issues, see Vincent in Boucher and Kelly eds 1998.

33 For Wissenburg, 'classical liberalism cannot meet the ecological challenge, however that
    challenge is defined' (Wissenburg in Dobson and Eckersley eds 2006, 31). Also see
    Dobson 1998; Wissenburg's book-length study of ecology and liberalism, Wissenburg
    1998; Vincent 1998b; and Hailwood 2003.

34 I am not suggesting that Ophuls is a deep ecologist; rather the vision he outlines here
    contains much that is attractive to the deep ecologists. Interestingly Bookchin, in discuss-
    ing his vision of a social ecological commune, also focuses, in the steps of Kropotkin, on
    a reinvigorated understanding of the *polis* (see Bookchin 1986b, 104).

35 Oddly this perspective can clearly be integrated with an eco-statist concept. The ideas
    outlined in this quoted sentence are now (in the 2000s) pretty much becoming main-
    stream in public policy and the personal lives of citizens in many European countries,
    Australia, North America and elsewhere.

36 With the rising cost of fuel and the empirical correlation between pollution, CO_2 and
    aircraft fuels in recent years, there is unexpectedly some drift of policy in this direction.

37 The Earth First! group had their own bizarre solutions to these problems, as already
    mentioned.

38   The response to such classical liberal views from the eco-socialists has been predictably critical. But the eco-capitalist conviction also brought a stinging dismissal from Porritt and Winner: they argued that 'all that has happened is that some … companies are making a lot of money causing pollution – and then making even more by cleaning up some of the mess' (Porritt and Winner 1988, 151). Eco-capitalism is thus seen as a classic case of double standards, offering no answers to the massive destruction of the environment by industry.

39   This Ruskinian notion of 'health as wealth' is in fact one of the main points of Robertson's earlier book, *The Sane Alternative* (1983).

40   Daly notes that in mining concentrated ores we convert usable energy into unusable energy. Entropy, as distinct from the conservation of energy, implies that in rearranging matter we continually reduce energy in the whole system. Usable energy is a finite resource (see Pirages ed. 1977, 107–10).

Chapter 9   Nationalism

1   On the word origin, see Synder 1954, 7ff; Shafer 1972, 13–14. In French the term *nationalisme*; German *Nationalismus* (although the term *Volk* was historically initially more significant); in Italian *nazionalismo*; and Spanish *naçionalismo*. Anthony Smith notes that the term entered the wider European lexicon from the early 1700s: in Hubner's *Staats-Lexicon* in 1704; in Herder and Abbé Bernal in 1798; and in broader English usage from the 1830s (see Smith 1971, 167).

2   'Nationalism is a state of mind, permeating the large majority of a people and claiming to permeate all its members; it recognised the nation state, as the ideal form of political organisation and the nationality as the source of all creative cultural energy and economic well-being' (Kohn 1945, 16); 'Nationalism … [is] a condition of mind, feeling or sentiment of a group living in a well-defined geographical area, speaking a common language, possessing a literature in which the aspirations of the nation have been expressed, attached to a common tradition, possessing traditional heroes, and, in some cases, having a common religion' (Snyder 1969, i); nationalism 'describes a group (of some size) of people united, usually, by (1) residence in a common land, … (2) a common heritage and culture, (3) common interests in the present and common hopes to live together in the future, and (4) a common desire to live and maintain their own state' (Shafer 1972, 15); nationalism 'means the recognition of a people and its need for status, perhaps including the state' (Kellas 1991, 33); 'a named population sharing an historic territory, common myths and historical memories, a mass, public culture, a common economy and common legal rights and duties for all members' (Smith 1991, 14). For more recent work on definitional issues, see Canovan 1996, 50ff; Smith 2001, 9ff; Spencer and Wollman 1998 and 2002, 26ff; Grosby 2005; Hearn 2006.

3   'We have as many definitions of nationalism as we have scholars who write about it' (Peter F. Sugar in Palumbo and Shanahan eds 1981, 67).

4   It can be argued here that the juridical idea of citizenship should be kept distinct from the idea of nationality since it implies that citizenship is always premised upon something like family or kinship relations. However, nationality can simply be a shorthand for legal citizenship. The problem here is the connotations which haunt the term 'nationality' through its common linguistic root to nationalism.

5 An example here might be the various ethnic nationalities under the Habsburg Empire who did not aspire to statehood (and in some eyes therefore nationhood) until the late nineteenth century (see Alter 1989, 18).

6 Interest in national character has some parallels with the eighteenth-century fascination with phrenology, physiognomy and early anthropology. A number of key figures in the late eighteenth century were interested in the idea of national character: for example, Immanuel Kant, *Anthropology* (1974), Part 2, 'Anthropological Characterisations', or David Hume, 'Of National Characters', in *Essays* (1994). However, the term 'national character' was deployed at the time as a more descriptive and empirical idea, almost on the level of a social scientific observation. The term has more or less dropped out of academic usage since the latter part of the twentieth century (unless one included the term 'political culture' as a contemporary replacement for 'national character'), although it still figures in febrile popular discussion of what to 'expect' from an Englishman or German.

7 '"National interests" is the most comprehensive description of the whole value complex of foreign policy' (Frankel 1970, 26). For systematic study of nationalism in terms of the practice of the state, see Breuilly 1993.

8 Carlton Hayes seems relatively unworried by the fusion (see Hayes 1926, 6). Others are deeply concerned by the blurring effect of the fusion of the terms and suggests political theorists should do all that they can to prise them apart (see Mary Dietz in Ball et al. eds 1989, 191–2). Others apparently see little hope, describing nationalism as 'patriotism's bloody brother' (see Schaar 1981, 285). Others again just express *Realpolitik* cynicism for all this word-play (see Keens-Soper 1989, 700). For more general discussion on patriotism and its relation with nationalism, see Vincent 2002, ch. 5. Also see Primoratz ed. 2002 and Primoratz and Pavković eds 2007.

9 'Racial hatreds seem to be at the core of the most hideous expression of violent collective emotion' (Berlin 1990, 252).

10 Since the early 1990s the literature by political theorists has massively accelerated. See, for example: Tamir 1993; Miller 1995; Guibernau 1995; Archard in O'Sullivan ed. 2000; Canovan 1996; Cohen ed. 1996; McKim and McMahan eds 1997; Gilbert 1998; Beiner 1999; Vincent 2002; Day and Thompson 2004; Spencer and Wollman 2005. The list gives just a brief snapshot of a massive literature over the last few decades.

11 I am not suggesting here that nationalism and fascism are directly parallel, but rather that scholars have been attracted to similar types of treatment of both ideologies.

12 Some of these accounts are dependent upon the terminology used. Anthony Smith's work is typical of this: he initially portrays ethnic communities (*ethnie*) as distinct from nationalism, with the major qualification that *ethnie* are still embodied in and carry over into nationalism. Thus, although nationalism, as a movement and an ideology, might legitimately be regarded as a fairly modern idea and practice, *ethnie* are ancient units, which are as old as human cooperation (see Smith 1986 or 2001).

13 The Faculty of Arts of many medieval universities was divided administratively into 'nations' for voting purposes, according to place of birth (see Snyder 1954, 29; Shafer 1972, 14; see also Reynolds 1984).

14 See Kohn 1945, 3, although Kohn does see strong elements of what he calls an 'unconscious nationalism' predating the French Revolution; Snyder 1954, 29; Kedourie 1974, 12; Smith 1979, 1. Kedourie also places a strong emphasis on the French Revolution in conjunction with certain crucial philosophical ideas. See also Birch 1989, 4; Mayall 1990, 43; Kamenka introduction 1976, 4; Berlin 1990, 244.

15   'Since World War II every successful revolution has defined itself in *national* terms – the People's Republic of China, the Socialist republic of Vietnam, and so forth – and, in so doing, has grounded itself firmly in a territorial and social space inherited from the pre-revolutionary past' (Anderson 1983, 12).

16   As Engels put it: 'In my opinion the colonies proper, i.e., the countries occupied by a European population – Canada, the Cape, Australia – will become independent: on the other hand, the countries inhabited by a native population, which are simply subjugated – India, Algeria, the Dutch, Portuguese and Spanish possessions – must be taken over for the time being [following the revolution] by the proletariat and led as rapidly as possible towards independence' (Friedrich Engels to Karl Kautsky, 12 September 1882, in Marx and Engels 1974, 342; see also Davis 1978 and Nimni 1991).

17   Bauer's key book was *Die Nationalitätenfrage und die Sozialdemokratie* (1907). See translation as Bauer 2000.

18   The earliest and most influential twofold classification was Hans Kohn's Western and Eastern nationalisms (see Kohn 1945); Plamenatz follows roughly in the same path in 'Two Types of Nationalism', in Kamenka ed. 1976. Friedrich Meinecke distinguished *Staatsnation* and *Kulturnation* (see Meinecke 1970; and see also Minogue 1967, 13). In many of the twofold classifications there is usually a fierce desire to keep Western, more liberal-minded nationalism distinct from the nationalism associated with fascism and national socialism (see Kohn 1945, 351; Smith 1971, 7 and 1979, 83–5; Tamir 1993, 90). There are threefold typologies in Kellas, who distinguishes ethnic, social and official nationalism (Kellas 1991, 52); also Peter Alter's *Risorgimento*, integral and reform nationalisms (in Alter 1989). There are fourfold classifications via historical phases – for example: 1815–71, integrative nationalism; 1871–1900, disruptive nationalism; 1900–45, aggressive nationalism; and, finally, 1945 to the present, the world-wide diffusion of nationalism (see Snyder 1954, ch. 5). Carlton Hayes uses a fivefold classification: Jacobin; liberal; traditionalist; economic protectionist; and integral totalitarian (see Hayes 1926 and 1949). For an overview of some of these diverse classifications, see Spencer and Wollman 2002.

19   *Risorgimento* meaning 'resurgence' or 'awakening'. The idea was used during the nineteenth-century Italian wars of independence.

20   The term 'integral nationalism' is attributed to French writer Charles Maurras. Some writers have seen Jacobin nationalism, at the time of the French Revolution, as a forerunner to integral nationalism.

21   'International *Risorgimento* nationalism had no blue-print to hand for avoiding the growing number of situations in which the competing aims of different nationalisms were hopelessly at loggerheads' (Alter 1989, 33).

22   The contention of the book cited here, by Yael Tamir, is that 'the liberal tradition, with its respect for personal autonomy, reflection and choice, and the national tradition, with its emphasis on belonging, loyalty and solidarity … can indeed accommodate one another' (Tamir 1993, 10). She later comments that 'this book takes liberal theory as its starting point, it attempts to "translate" nationalist argument into liberal language' (Tamir 1993, 14). The antecedents to this idea lie in Kohn's work and the central distinction between Western and Eastern nationalism, Plamenatz's adoption of the same idea, and also Isaiah Berlin in his various writings. As one commentator remarks on Berlin, 'It is important to stress that Berlin's sympathy with nationalism is sympathy with the nationalism of the Risorgimento and with the European revolutionaries of 1848; it is sympathy with the nationalism of Verdi and Clemenceau, not with the nationalism of Treitschke and Barrès' (Hampshire in Margalit and Margalit eds 1991, 132). Subsequently

the same broad notion, consciously or not, has been adopted by some of Plamenatz's pupils and admirers: David Miller, Brian Barry, Neil MacCormick. For example, see Brian Barry, 'Self-Government Revisited', in Miller and Seidentop eds 1983.

23   Alter sees earlier variants of integral nationalism in Wilhelmine Imperial Germany in the 1880s. The work of Heinrich von Treitschke and the Pan German League, founded in 1891 (surviving until 1939), saw national unification in Germany as nothing but a stepping stone for Germany to develop as a world power (see Alter 1989, 41–2).

24   Unless, of course, one interpreted nationalism itself as just a form of religion, see G. L. Mosse, for example, who defines nationalism as a 'new style of politics … based upon a secularized theology and its liturgy; democracy meant participation in the drama which grew from these foundations. Such a theology determined the self-representation of the nation, the way in which the people objectified their general will' (Mosse, 'Mass Politics and the Political Liturgy of Nationalism', in Kamenka ed., 1976, 39). The more recent work of Michael Burleigh (2006), Emilio Gentile (2006) and John Gray (2007) is highly relevant to this issue.

25   Integral fascist nationalists disapproved of the idea of liberal individual self-determination. They had no objection, though, to the nation being self-determined. For a more recent moderately enthusiastic collection of articles on liberal self-determination, see Moore ed. 1998.

26   In fact, in my reading they do not solve a further conundrum of how the nation self-determines, namely, given that the bulk of liberal epistemology and ontology is rooted in individualism (of various sorts), it is not immediately apparent how this could be used explain or account for group selves (nations). Liberalism has historically and philosophically been uneasy with collective personality or methodological holism.

27   A quick overview of communitarianism can be found in Kymlicka 1991 and 2001; Fraser and Lacey 1993; Mulhall and Swift 1996; or Vincent 2002, ch. 6.

28   It is important to grasp that there are different forms of this communitarianism. There are anti-individualistically inclined communitarians, liberal communitarians and rationalist communitarians. The anti-individualist stance is possibly best identified with Alasdair MacIntyre's works *After Virtue* (1981), *Whose Justice? Which Rationality?* (1988) and *Three Rival Versions of Moral Enquiry* (1990). The liberal communitarian stance I would identify with Michael Walzer's *Spheres of Justice* (1983) and *Interpretation and Social Criticism* (1987), Michael Sandel's *Liberalism and the Limits of Justice* (1982) and, to some degree, Charles Taylor's *Ethics of Authenticity* (1991). The rationalist communitarian (also liberal) stance is Joseph Raz, *The Morality of Freedom* (1986). See Vincent 2002.

29   MacIntyre is a slight fly in the ointment; however, his appeal is based upon nostalgia for ancient groups and a yearning for small group solidarity in the present, premised upon Pope Leo XIII's *Aeterni Patris*, which is not exactly a work with widespread appeal (MacIntyre 1990, 25).

30   *Bildung* was initially concerned with the formation of the person, particularly the inward development of human personality. In German mystical thought the inward journey also involved the discovery of God. *Bildung* became enshrined in the *Bildungsroman* novel tradition, relating to the inward growth and development of the person, as in Goethe's *Wilhelm Meister's Lehrjahre*. In writers such as Fichte, the central relation of the ego to the nonego was a *Bildung* relation. The self grew and developed by assimilating the not-self. In Hegel this same idea was given a strong historical dimension. The historical process of *Geist* for Hegel was one of *Bildung*.

31 In this sense it is fortunate that print-based mandarin is understood by all Chinese, otherwise the multiplicity of dialects in the diverse Chinese regions would have caused immense problems for understanding.

32 According to Hobsbawm, in the 1790s approximately 50 per cent of the population spoke the French language and only around 12 to 13 per cent spoke it correctly (see Hobsbawm 1992, 60).

33 Anderson notes Hobsbawm's point that 'the progress of schools and universities measures that of nationalism, just as schools and especially universities become its most conscious champions' (quoted from Hobsbawm 1977a, 166, in Anderson 1983, 70).

34 On the myth-building aspect of nationalism, one writer has remarked: 'The Kikuyu … whose coherence is now so important to understanding Kenyatta and nationalism in Kenya, had no certain identity before the imposition of British rule and the alienation of land to the settlers: distinctive groups like the Sikhs in India, Ibo in Nigeria, and Malays in Malaysia were barely conscious of their "sameness" one hundred years ago' (Greenberg 1980, 14–15).

35 These form central themes in Schenk's discussion of romantic thought (see Schenk 1966; see also Barnard introduction to Herder 1969, 55–8).

36 As Herder also noted: 'I wish I could include in this word *Humanität* everything that I have said so far about the noble constitution of man for reason and freedom, finer sense and impulses, the most delicate and most robust health, the realisation of the purposes of the world. … For man has no nobler word for his destiny than that which expresses the essence of himself as a human being, and which thus reflect the image of the Creator on earth' (Herder, *Idea for a Philosophy of History*, in Herder 1969, 266–7). The term 'humanity' in Herder still, however, remains deeply obscure (see Ergang 1931, 83).

37 Barnard introduction to Herder 1969, 31; Ergang 1931, 85–6. As Ergang notes: 'Having a body and a soul … the group becomes a single being, an individuality, a personality. This being expresses itself in all the phenomena of its history, in language, in literature, in religion, in custom, in art, in science … and the sum of these expressions is the culture of a nationality' (Ergang 1931, 87).

38 'Fichte and his fellow nationalists strove to prove … that the fact of speaking one language was sufficient reason for upsetting all political arrangements, and for bringing about a new one. … If language becomes the criterion of statehood, the clarity essential to such a notion is dissolved in a mist of literary and academic speculation' (Kedourie 1974, 69 and 70).

39 Among the nations created were: 1830 Greece; 1831 Belgium; 1861 Italy; 1871 Germany; 1878 Romania, Serbia and Montenegro; 1905 Norway; 1908 Bulgaria; 1913 Albania; 1917 Finland; 1918 Poland, Czechoslovakia, Estonia, Latvia, Lithuania; 1922 Ireland. The League of Nations founded in 1920 had forty-two members, the United Nations, founded in 1945, had fifty-one, by 1969 eighty-two, by 1973 135, by 1988 159, and in 2008 192.

40 'The entire band of states stretching from Finland in the North, via the Baltic states to Poland and Czechoslovakia, and on to Albania, Romania and Greece in the South are the products of political secession'; secession also occurred elsewhere, as in Belgium breaking from the United Netherlands (1831), Norway from Sweden (1814); Southern Ireland from Britain (1922); Iceland from Denmark (1944) (see Alter 1989, 99). This pattern would need to be extended to include the large number of post-1945 post-colonial nationalisms in Africa and Asia.

41 'National self-determination and individual self-determination were declared part of the historical self-deliverance of mankind from ignorance and tyranny' (Keens-Soper 1989, 702).

42   I have no strong feelings about considering a separate category of socialist nationalism. Most twentieth-century regimes establishing themselves under the rubric of Marxism or communism were usually nationalist in orientation. However, as pointed out in the earlier section on 'The Nature of Nationalism', Marxists (with rare exceptions) have never been able to cope very easily (on a theoretical level) with the phenomenon of nationalism. In fact, they have theoretically never really resolved the problem, with rare exceptions such as the Austrian Marxists Otto Bauer and Karl Renner. Reformist and liberal socialists have partially resolved the problem in the same manner as liberal nationalists, namely, by embedding universalist moderate liberal values within national communities (and possibly even fostering them through self-conscious education policies).

43   'Nations do not make states ... but the other way round' (Hobsbawm 1992, 10; see also Sugar in Palumbo and Shanahan eds 1981, 81).

44   As Hobsbawm remarks on the development of such democracies by the end of the nineteenth century, 'Its tragic paradox was that ... it helped to plunge them willingly into the mutual massacre of world war one' (Hobsbawm 1992, 89).

45   As Wilson confessed to a Senate Committee of Foreign Relations, 'When I gave utterance to those words ("that all nations had a right to self-determination"), I said them without the knowledge that nationalities existed, which are coming to us day after day. ... You do not know and cannot appreciate the anxieties that I have experienced as a result of many millions of people having their hopes raised by what I have said' (quoted in Cobban 1944, 21).

46   Many have assumed that nations must be of a certain size in order to be a both a nation and a state. Mazzini thought that there could only be maximally eleven viable nation states in Europe. He considered the Irish, for example, to be far too small to be a nation state and advised them to stay with Britain (see Hobsbawm 1992, 31). President Wilson was faced by an Irish delegation at the 1919 Peace Conference insisting upon an Irish state. Like Mazzini, he also appeared to consider them too small to be viable. One commentator notes that 'Wilson consistently refused to take any notice of the many petitions from subject nationalities of the Allies which he received' (Cobban 1944, 22). It is worth noting that Marx and Engels also had similar views about the size and viability of nation states (see references in Nimni 1991, 31–3). The term *Kleinstaaterie* (mini-states) became a term of abuse similar to 'Balkanization' in the later nineteenth century. The same note was even reflected in Adolf Hitler's speech on the Austrian question in March 1938 when he remarked, 'What can words like "independence" or "sovereignty" mean for a state of only six millions?' (quoted in Cobban 1944, 2). Hitler obviously had other things in mind here.

47   Alter remarks that Wilson's Fourteen Points 'gave only vague contours to a process that was really to take off after the Second World War, a conflict that also affected Asia and Africa' (Alter 1989, 117).

48   The doctrine of self-determination is embodied in international law, though what it includes precisely remains indeterminate (see Sieghart 1986). In the first article of the two International Covenants on Human Rights (1966) adopted by the UN General Assembly, it is declared that 'All peoples have the rights of self-determination. By virtue of that right they freely determine their political status.'

49   Some critics find the idea of 'self' totally mythical in this sense (see Richard T. DeGeorge in Twining ed. 1991, 1–4). Other theorists appear quite unfussed by the moral rights of nation states to be self-determining entities (see Walzer 1983; and Walzer in Beitz et al. eds 1985).

50   Certainly this was Mazzini's supposition. More recent liberal nationalists are more circumspect and usually hedge the concept of self-determination around with moral and legal restraints.

51   The term 'Cameralism' (developed from the Latin *camera* or, in German, *Kammer*) was originally derived from the apartment where the counsellors charged with administering the revenues of states assembled. *Cameralia* or *Cameral-Wissenschaften* were theories upon which the administration of revenues was based. It later came to denote the science of the administration of the state in general. A Cameralist was one who understood the science of the administration of the state theoretically or practically. Cameralism was the routine of the bureau (initially fiscal) in which the administrative employees of the government performed their work (see Small 1909).

52   Fichte envisaged that workers would register themselves with the government. Controls would be exercised on each trade and profession, since 'If he [the worker] registers for a branch of activity where the largest number of employees allowed by law is already engaged, the authorisation will be refused and he will be suggested other lines of work' (Fichte, *Der Geschlossene Handelsstaat*, quoted in Heilperin 1960, 85).

53   Fichte had a different concept of wealth than mercantilists, who measured it in terms of precious metal. He saw wealth in terms of raw materials and food.

54   Although, while the experiment was being set up, Fichte felt that people should be allowed to emigrate. He also noted that if foreign visitors came to admire the new state (which he thought would happen), then their *Weltgeld* would be taken by the state and replaced with *Landgeld* whilst the visit took place.

55   He even suggested that it might have been English agents who encouraged certain German manufacturers to support free trade and oppose protectionism.

56   List notes that Smith appears unwilling to deal with the role of the Navigation Acts and that 'Power is more important than wealth ... simply because national power is a dynamic force by which new productive resources are opened out, and because the forces of production are the tree on which wealth grows. ... Power is of more importance than wealth because a nation, by means of power, is enabled not only to open up new productive sources, but to maintain itself in possession of former and of recently acquired wealth' (List 1966, 46).

57   'Countries with a temperate climate are (almost without exception) adapted for ... manufacturing industry. The moderate temperature of the air promotes the development and exertion of power far more than a hot temperature' (List 1966, 212ff). This was an idea also developed in the geographical writings of Friedrich Ratzel (1844–1904). Ratzel's basic premise was that nature and humanity are ontologically linked. Geography was the science for studying this ontology. For Ratzel, humans live naturally in national groups, and each national group needs a physical space which it will naturally try to exploit and then, through demographic pressures, expand. Ratzel coined the term *Lebensraum* to cover this idea. This argument goes way beyond List.

58   There were obvious exceptions to this, as in post-1945 Yugoslavia, which struggled with the nationality question under communist rule.

59   Just two examples of many: Peter Alter, in his 1989 book, observed: 'Under present circumstances ... it is highly unlikely that an all-German national state could be recreated by non-violent means, as the constitutional imperative demands, and the chances of it happening seem to be constantly diminishing. A reunited Germany with a population of 80 million would run against the interests of both the Soviet and east European peoples, and the Western powers' (Alter 1989, 131); or Anthony Smith in his 1991 book: 'if the

nation need not be culturally homogeneous, can there be such a thing as a nation that subsumes several incorporated nations? ... Here the Yugoslav model springs to mind ... the separate histories of Slovenes, Croats, Serbs, Macedonians and Montenegrins, as well as religious differences, have suggested the possibility of Yugoslavia providing a model of the "transcended nation" in the form of a federation of nations, which could be replicated on a larger scale elsewhere' (Smith 1991, 146–7).

Chapter 10   Fundamentalism

1   The *Oxford English Dictionary* dates it as 1923.
2   The exception to this might now be a fascist who would (for historical reasons) prefer to be called an exponent of the extreme Right or an ultra-nationalist; however, given what he or she believes a more accurate description might be fascist.
3   See also Marsden in Cohen ed. 1990; Ammerman in Marty and Appleby eds 1991, 2ff.; Armstrong 2004, 167ff.
4   In the sense that it is anticipated, by such 'Rapture' commentators, that countless millions of 'born again' believers would simply disappear in a single moment.
5   Such radical Islamists have tended to be urban, from small local communities, younger, employed or trained in modern clerical or professional jobs, have higher status than their parents, tend to have had some form of higher education (often in the natural or applied sciences) and are often impatient with traditional Islam (see Greifenhagen in Schick et al. eds 2004, 72).
6   Sunnis accept the Umayyad dynasty that succeeded the Prophet. The Shi'ites see Ali, Hassan and the martyr Hussayn as significant figures. A major Shi'ite idea is that of the twelve Imams. The last Imam, Muhammad al-Madhi, it is said, did not die in AD 874, but rather went into supernatural hiding and will return again. Ayatollah Khomeini played on this idea when he returned to Iran after the fall of the Shah (see Bruce 2000, 42).
7   In Northern Ireland the Unionists and particularly the Democratic Unionist Party under Ian Paisley presented (in the 1970s and 1980s) another strong form of Protestant fundamentalism, often marked out by its extreme anti-Catholicism.
8   'Jewish fundamentalism was born of the dashed hopes of religious Zionism ... religion usurps nationalism and presents nationalism as its own manifestation' (Aran in Marty and Appleby eds 1991, 297).
9   See, for example, the essays by Gold (Hinduism), Madan (Sikhism) and Swearer (Buddhism) in Marty and Appleby eds 1991.
10 The same point would hold in Christianity, where, for example, in the Anglican, Methodist or Baptist communions religious conservatives and evangelicals are often keen to keep a definite distance from fundamentalism.
11 The term 'market fundamentalism', which many associate with the policies of the World Bank and IMF, was in fact first coined by George Soros.
12 My surmise here would be that this state of affairs obtained in Andalucia under the Moorish Caliphate between the eighth and twelfth centuries, when Jews, Christians and Muslims seemed to be able to co-exist with a large degree of tolerance.
13 As John Gray comments, 'The Enlightenment ideologies of the past centuries were very largely spilt theology. The history of the past century is not a tale of secular advance, as *bien-pensants* of Right and Left like to think. The Bolshevik and Nazi seizures of power were faith-based upheavals just as much as the Ayatollah Khomeini's theocratic

insurrection in Iran. The very idea of revolution as a transforming event in history is owed to religion. Modern revolutionary movements are a continuation of religion by other means' (Gray 2007, 2).

14 There are exceptions to this, namely, where it is not so much personal testimony as a collective or communal affirmation of belief which is crucial.

15 A Gallup survey in the 1980s found 40 per cent of the American public believed that the Bible was the literal word of God (see Ruthven 2004, 59).

16 In fact the whole Rapture industry seems to be based upon *one* random remark by Saint Paul about believers being 'taken up into the clouds'.

17 However, Turkish Muslim scholars have recently (2008) made a systematic study of the Hadith, the second most sacred book in Islam, on the basis of restructuring and editing out the 'cultural' from the genuine theological and doctrinal components.

18 The Sura reads: 'slay the idolators wherever you find them, and take them (captive), and besiege them, and prepare for them each ambush' (Qur'an, Sura 9:5, 146).

19 This is particularly characteristic of Qutb's and his radical Islamist admirers' reading of the Qur'an (see Qutb n.d.).

20 This would include people such as Qutb, Osama Bin Laden and all of those who attacked the World Trade Center. One of the things which is also notable about certain modern fundamentalists is their easy facility with modern technologies, which they use to great strategic effect.

21 The term 'modernization' in this context denotes, in more sociological terms, increasing fragmentation of social life, greater division of labour and more specialized units of production. The public sphere becomes more instrumental and rational and the private world is seen as expressive and more emotive (see Bruce 2000, 18).

22 For John Gray, for example, enlightenment positivism can be viewed as a theory of redemption in the guise of theory of history. 'The conflict between Al Qaeda and the West is a war of religion. The Enlightenment idea of universal civilization, which the West upholds against radical Islam, is an offspring of Christianity. Al Qaeda's peculiar hybrid of theocracy and anarchy is a by-product of western radical thought. Each of the protagonists in the current conflict are driven by beliefs that are opaque to it' (Gray 2004, 105 and 117).

23 Because modernity and its accompanying constellation of values and beliefs has become a global phenomenon, it is not surprising that fundamentalism has also become internationalized.

24 In turn this underpinned conceptions of pluralism, differentiation and diversity within societies and a concomitant recognition of diversity of belief and ultimately conceptions of toleration. Modernity, for certain religions such as Islam, did, though, represent something else, namely, the legacy of colonialism and empire. This was not just because the ex-colonial powers had promulgated many of the values and aspirations of modernity, but also because indigenous ruling post-colonial elites in such societies in the 1950s and 1960s had adopted many of those same modernist nostrums for the sake of economic and political benefit (see Greifenhagen in Schick et al. eds 2004, 66).

25 Armstrong also comments that 'Just as Sayyid Qutb's description of a modern *jahili* city was difficult for liberal Muslims to recognize, the vision of America that Protestant fundamentalists were evolving was radically different from that of the liberal mainstream. Fundamentalists were convinced that the United States was God's own country, but did not seem share the values that were so prized and lauded by other Americans.' Thus the American fundamentalist figurehead Pat Robertson saw the American Revolution as

inspired by Calvinists (and was thus wholly different to the French Revolution). For Robertson this Calvinist idea was not democratically focused. In many ways there is as much suspicion of democracy in some Christian fundamentalists as one finds in Muslim and Jewish circles (see Armstrong 2004, 273).

26 The teaching of Darwinism in schools is seen to be one of the key interventions of humanism.

27 Shari'a refers largely to the whole body of Islamic law. Etymologically it implies a 'way' or 'well-trodden way'. For some, all aspects of a Muslim's public and private life should be directed by Shari'a. This includes business, banking, marriage, family, as well as public life. It derives from a blend of sources including the Qur'an, the Hadith (sayings and conduct of the Prophet Muhammad) and fatwas – the rulings of Islamic scholars. It is primarily a religious law with a divine origin and created for the benefit of humanity. It is seen as the ground for a morally and spiritually upright life.

28 As Ira Lapidus notes 'fundamentalism is profoundly critical of as well as constituted by assumptions regarding the requirements of modernity and modern politics' (quoted in Euben 1999, 18). Eisenstadt also views fundamentalism as 'a thoroughly modern phe- nomenon' (see Eisenstadt in Marty and Appleby eds 1995, 259). See also Sami Zubaida, who interprets Islamic fundamentalism as a distinctly modern idea best associated with the terminology around the modern nation state. Indeed he sees Leninist ideology as probably the clearest analogy to Islamic fundamentalism (see Zubaida 1993, 18, 33, 155). Ayubi also argues that the very belief 'that Islam is by its nature a "political reli- gion" is of recent origin' (Ayubi 1991, 3–5). A similar idea is explored also in Burleigh (2006), Gentile (2006) and Gray (2007).

29 That is the attempt to reconcile disparate or contradictory beliefs.

30 This sense of the modernity of fundamentalists can be overdone at one level. The fact that they turn the technologies and weapons of the West upon the West is not necessarily evi- dence of being acclimatized to modernity. It is, rather, a logical strategy of using the best means possible to defeat the perceived enemy. However, despite this point, we should not underrate their assimilation and understanding of these modern ideas and technologies. The desirable society of the future for most fundamentalists would not be without modern technologies. Nevertheless, the overall situation here remains unclear and unpredictable.

31 The word 'secular' derives from the Latin *saeculum*, meaning 'world age'.

32 All the significant initiators, for example, of the discipline of sociology, that is, Comte, Marx, Durkheim and Weber, maintained that there had been a development from a religion-centred social existence to one premised on secular human, scientifically based self-regulation. In anthropology the same idea appears in nineteenth-century writers such as James Frazer and Edward Tylor, in the idea of a movement from magic and supersti- tion towards science, rationality and secularism.

33 Religion was viewed largely as a means by which society seeks and achieves some form of integration by bringing together the moral understandings that make internal sense of the social collectivity. It is, in itself, the experience of sociality which is the crucial utility of religion, not any notion of God. Durkheim defines religion as a 'a unified systems of beliefs and practices relative to sacred things, that is to say, things set apart and forbidden – beliefs and practices which unite into one single moral community called a Church, all those who adhere to them' (Durkheim 1995, 44). Durkheim based his ideas for moral re-integration on a state-centred political religion to celebrate the 'cult of the sacred individual'.

34 Secularization can be a doctrine of keeping religion out public or political life. This seems closer to the idea of laicism. The concept of secularization can be seen as something

milder than laicism; as indicated, it can simply be a doctrine about government which implies that for religions to exist in modern societies there need to be wide-ranging tolerance. Some secularisms are indeed open to religion and indeed in some cases necessary for their existence. Secularism can, though, mean something fiercer, namely, a conscious militant rejection of anything to do with religion, or alternatively the utter irrelevance of religion to understanding the modern world. The notion of 'political religion', however, raises a new range of problems. Thus, if what many regard as secular belief structures, such as Marxism or fascism, are political religions, then it becomes difficult to keep a firm grip on the concept of the secular (see Burleigh 2006 or Gentile 2006).

35   For example, in Carl Schmitt's famous remark that 'All the pregnant concepts of the modern theory of the state are secularized theological concepts' (quoted in Nicholls 1994, 13).

36   As in 'process theology', implied in the works of twentieth-century philosophers such as A. N. Whitehead and Charles Hartshorne, or, probably more succinctly, in the writings of Teilhard de Chardin.

37   'It is in Iran that the fundamentalists have enjoyed their greatest success. Islamicization has gone far enough there that it is destined to have a long-term impact. The government itself has been reconstituted, and the constitution rewritten to institutionalize clerical authority and the supremacy of Islamic law (however it might be interpreted). In the 1980s and early 1990s fundamentalist clerics were firmly ensconced in powerful positions and dominated the country's legal system. Laws were enacted that embodied the fundamentalists' policies of combating the erosion of the traditional social structure and value system. ... Pre-revolution advances in women's status were rolled back, the 1967 Family Protection Act repealed, and women relegated to subservient roles caring for husbands and children' (Mayer in Marty and Appleby eds 1993, 120; see also Arjomand in Marty and Appleby eds 1993b).

38   Khomeini maintained that government should be subject to expert clerical rule in order to protect the sovereignty of God. A *faqih* – clerical specialist on Islamic law – will ensure that Shari'a is correctly implemented. This is, though, a contentious argument even within Shia religious debates (see Armstrong 2004, 256–7; see also Khomeini 1979).

39   Islamic fundamentalism does often look like 'an expression of a religiously legitimized dictatorship'. The author continues, though, that 'this is also true for all other varieties of fundamentalism' (Tibi in Hawkesworth and Kogan eds 1994, 194).

40   It is not obvious, though, that there is an unequivocal Qur'anic justification for this idea. It is also questionable whether Shari'a law is such an ancient idea in terms of its public uses. Some scholars have suggested that it is quite a late, if not quite modern, invention, certainly as applying to a political order. Muslim rule in general between the eighth and thirteenth centuries, under Umayyad and Abbassid variants of Islam, recognized a distinction between religious and civil authority (see Tibi in Hawkesworth and Kogan eds 2004, 193).

41   Thus 'jihad' (understood in this sense as external physical struggle, as distinct from an inner moral struggle within the individual) has a universal political purpose.

42   '[W]hat in the end restrains the religious right is the implicit recognition by many Americans, found as much among the common people as among the justices of the Supreme Court, that the separation of church and state and the location of religion in the private sphere are not historical accidents. They are functional prerequisites for a modern democratic society that happens to be culturally heterogeneous and that places great stress on individualism' (Bruce 2000, 89–90).

43 For Bernard Lewis, 'For Muslims, the state was God's state, the army God's army, and, of course, the enemy was God's enemy. Of more practical importance, the law was God's law, and in principle there could be no other. The question of separating Church and state did not arise, since there was no Church, as an autonomous institution, to be separated. Church and state were one and the same. ... For the same reason, though Islamic society very soon developed a large and active class of professional men of religion, these were never a priesthood in the Christian sense, and could only loosely be described even as a clergy. ... it is only in Ottoman times, almost certainly under the influence of Christian example, that an organization of Muslim religious dignitaries was developed, with a hierarchy of ranks and with territorial jurisdictions. The ayatollahs of Iran are an even more recent innovation, and might not unjustly be described as another step in the Christianization of Islamic institutions, though by no means of Islamic teachings. ... It was not only the theoretical and historical basis for separation that was lacking in Islam; it was also the practical need. The level of willingness to tolerate and live peaceably with those who believe otherwise and worship otherwise was, at times and in most places, high enough for tolerable coexistence to be possible, and Muslims did not therefore feel the imperative need felt by Christians to seek an escape from the horrors of state-sponsored and state-enforced doctrine' (Lewis 1992, 50).

44 For Eisenstadt, fundamentalists appropriate the 'central aspects of the political program of modernity', including its 'participatory, totalistic and egalitarian orientations'. It is seen, though, at the same time, to resist other dimensions of Enlightenment thinking concerned, for example, with the perfectibility of humanity (Eisenstadt 2000, 91).

45 For Marty and Appleby, 'Both the nation and the fundamentalist community are conceived of as deep horizontal comradeships, "sacred" fraternities for which people will die or kill other people. Like nationalisms, fundamentalisms possess hegemonic political ambitions and demand colossal sacrifices from their devotees.' Both often inspire heroism and self-sacrifice (Marty and Appleby 1993b, 622–6).

46 In fact the conflict between Hamas and Fatah in Palestine is a complex manifestation of the deep tensions between religion and nationalism.

47 Some might argue that this appears to be a contradiction in terms, although even secular liberal democracy does require a consensus about certain values necessary for democracy to function.

48 Mary Wollstonecraft, after all, used theological claims, in part, to make her case for gender equality (see ch, 7).

49 The activity of the 'Moral Majority' in trying to influence the Republican Party policy through legitimate lobbying during the 1980s limited any tendency to militancy.

50 Gray comments that it is one of the most 'stupefying clichés to think of fundamentalist groups, such as Al Qaeda, as throwback to a pre-modern time. Conversely they are a product of modernity' (Gray 2004, 1).

51 For a broader and more comprehensive attempt to analyse Bin Laden's ideology, see McAuley 2005.

52 Consequently they reject the views of the premillennialists, who argue that we have to just wait for the coming of Christ.

53 'Observers are always surprised to see how quickly the so-called antiscientific fundamentalists embrace new technology and how readily they adapt it to their own purposes.' Thus, 'Fundamentalists appear to appropriate economic concepts in much the same way: picking and choosing, paying little attention to an item's original source and above all

using everything they can as an instrument to further their religious (and perhaps ultimately social) agenda' (Iannaccone in Marty and Appleby eds 1993b, 360–1).

54 Although Kuran does conclude with a more upbeat comment that 'just as the rise of European capitalism coincided with the emergence of new social philosophies, so, too, political and economic liberalization in the Islamic world could be accompanied by a far-reaching transformation of Islamic economics' (Kuran in Marty and Appleby eds 1993b, 332).

Glossary

Acephalous society: a society without any identifiable head, government or authority structure

Affinity groups: natural harmonious anarchist communities, associated with the work of Murray Bookchin

Anarcho-capitalism: a right-wing anarchy: highly individualistic, anti-statist, committed to a purer form of negative liberty, natural rights and focused intensely on the free unregulated market as the *only* allocator of resources

Anarcho-syndicalism: developed from the broader syndicalist movement in the early 1900s; it denoted a form of militant trade unionism which blended with aspects of communist anarchy. It was anti-statist, committed to the idea of a general strike as a means of political revolution, and saw unions of workers as the organizational base for a future society

Androgyny: in feminism denoting a form of sexlessness, that is, a combination of both sexes in one individual

Anthropocentrism: The idea that human beings and their interests and needs are the sole criterion of value and thus prior to nature. The value of nature is considered instrumentally rather than intrinsically

Autarky: applied in terms of economic self-reliance and avoiding international trade; indicates a self-sufficient economy marshalling its resources for its own national ends

Autonomy: the right or capacity for governing oneself independently

Bildung: The educational self-formation or inner development of human beings. Has subtle links with the ideas of freedom and self-determination.

Biocentric egalitarianism: the deep ecology principle that all things in nature have equal moral value

Bioregionalism: the idea of ecologically and biologically sustainable areas for a specific number of humans to reside or 'live in place' without harming the environment

Cameralism: denoted the science of the administration of the state

Capitalism: a system of socio-economic organization whereby commodity production and wealth are held largely in private hands and economic life is organized on free-market principles, that is, where good and services are bought and sold in order to make profits, without any intervention by the state

Cartesian: pertaining to the philosopher Descartes and his approach to knowledge

Civil society: at one point, prior to the nineteenth century, it referred to a type of society. After Hegel, particularly, it came to refer to an intermediate sphere between the state and the family, where individuals and groups could freely associate without interference

Classical liberalism: an older notion of liberalism, with strong intellectual links to a European-wide seventeenth- and eighteenth-century constitutionalist mentality. It focused on the negative rights, freedoms and property of the isolated individual citizen; it placed a heavy emphasis on a more minimal constitutional understanding of a rule of law state; it also laid considerable stress on the role of the capitalist market economy as the most efficient allocator of resources, compatible with human freedom and basic rights

Collectivism: late nineteenth-century concept originating in France; in political terms tends to denote the use of the state to control and regulate sectors of the economy and civil society

Communist anarchy: mainstream school of anarchy concerned with the crucial role of social solidarity, the common ownership of property and committed to the cooperative disposition in all human beings as the premise for genuine anarchy

Conceptual history: a methodological approach which argues that there are internal features to concepts which shape the ways in which we gain access to the social world. The method consequently involves a sophisticated treatment of concepts at both the analytical and historical levels

Constitutionalism: a theory concerning the necessary legal and institutional limitations on any government or state

Contractualism: the idea that the rules of justice under which society are governed must be derived from the voluntary agreement and assent of the parties or people. This is usually considered as a purely hypothetical agreement

Corporatism: conception of government whereby business, labour and political interests merge in one governmental corporate body

Cosmopolitanism: the idea derives largely from one key source – the Stoic philosophers. It is a compound derived from two Greek words, *kosmos* and *polites*, *kosmos* referring to the orderly structure of the world, *polites* to a citizen. A cosmopolitan could thus be a citizen of the world. Basically it implies that there are, or ought to be, universal legal or moral values adhered to by humanity. For example, cosmopolitan justice would be achieved if one responded to all human beings on a roughly equal basis, regardless of nationality, gender, ethnicity or location. In the context of its stress on universal equality, individualism, justice and human rights it has close links with the ideology of liberalism

Deconstruction: a way of reading and analysing texts in order to expose the underlying conceptual structures and distinctions (on which the text relies), which remain permanently unrationalized and unjustified

Deep ecology: one of the key dimensions of the ecology movement, related to a more holistic perspective. The primary locus of value is seen to be the ecosphere considered as a whole. Value is seen to be intrinsic to the whole ecosphere. It also aims at a psychological or attitudinal change in human beings towards nature and a more broad-ranging alteration in the way we organize our societies to reflect this

Determinism: A philosophical doctrine which argues that the explanation of all events can be given via antecedent causes; further that everything that happens in the world can be explained by such prior causes.

Dialectical materialism: a materialist philosophy, associated with the work of Marx and particularly Engels, which essentially identified complex, but structurally identifiable processes of mutation and change, largely in the economic and social world, determined by conflict between social classes

Dirigiste: refers to centralized state direction of, for example, an economy

Eco-anarchism: form of ecological thought which was systematically developed in the social ecology writings of Murray Bookchin; sees a direct link between the social organization and beliefs of communist anarchy and a genuine ecological disposition

Eco-capitalism: smaller aspect of the ecological thinking which identifies the free market and the green consumer as the key (via basic ordinary market pressures) to persuading governments and industries to respond to ecological demands

Ecocentrism: belief that the primary locus of moral value is the ecosphere

Eco-feminism: rarer form of feminism and ecology which identifies environmental destruction largely with male patriarchal dispositions. The female gender is also seen to be more in accord with environmental care and concern

Economic nationalism: an economic doctrine which aims to make the nation self-sufficient in times of conflict and prosperous in times of peace. Nations should favour preferentially their own industries and encourage consumers to purchase domestically produced goods; opposed to free trade

Eco-socialism: influential component of the ecology movement which identifies the economics of unregulated capitalist markets as a key source of environmental degradation. In some more dominant reformist forms of eco-socialism, it sees the idea of a strong green regulatory state as a crucial agent for solving environmental problems.

Elite theory: theory concerning the nature of political rule whereby in any form of organization in the final analysis certain elites will tend to dominate government

Empiricism: the philosophical doctrine that contends that all knowledge is ultimately based upon experience

Enlightenment: a European-wide intellectual movement, dating from the 1700s, characterized by a belief in inevitable human progress via the cultivation of reason; sees reason as the sole source of authority and consequently rejects all purportedly authoritative beliefs in religion or tradition

Epistemology: branch of philosophy concerned with the theory of knowledge

Ethical socialism: a variant of socialism, closely related to reformist state socialism, but much more focused on the idea that socialism is an ethical doctrine concerned with the correct values for humanity. R. H. Tawney was a key twentieth-century example. Capitalism therefore is not just economically inefficient, but also ethically and spiritually wrong, and thus needs detailed regulation. For ethical socialists, legal, social or economic reforms are not enough. Moral change and greater ethical responsibility from citizens are required for socialism to be achieved

Ethnicity: usually indicating where a group have a common descent or common cultural or physical characteristics

Fascism: a diffuse ideology which has taken a number of forms in different historical and political circumstances. It is focused on an extreme integral version of nationalism, that is, where the nation, and a vision of the total state, takes an absolute priority in human affairs. It is profoundly anti-liberal, anti-Marxist and disdainful of democratic and parliamentary politics. However, it has usually drawn on features of other ideologies, such as socialism and conservatism. It tends to take a somewhat bellicose view of the relation between nations. Unlike national socialism, however, fascism did *not* define the nation via racial criteria. In addition it saw itself as both a modern and revolutionary mass movement, particularly in 1920s and 1930s Italy, with broad cultural implications

Fundamentalism: at the most general level it entails a return to, revival, or basing oneself upon an established religious (or, for some, secular) foundation, from which there can be no deviation. In more specific ideological terms it implies that human existence needs to be governed by the inerrant word of God, as embodied in some form of unique text, such as the Bible or Qur'an. The crucial ideological contention is that politics should be subject to the sovereignty of God. This leads, in turn, to a strong notion of theocracy

Futurism: early twentieth-century artistic movement, largely based in Italy, which emphasized the dynamism and movement of modern life, glorifying technology, speed and violence

Gaia hypothesis: the name derives from the Greek mother goddess of the Earth. The term was coined by James Lovelock to indicate that the biosphere and ecosphere as a whole form a single related immensely complex symbiotic system which ultimately creates an environment for a habitable earth

Gender: would usually be regarded as a mutable cultural or political construct, as opposed to a biological category such as sex

Globalization: the immensely complex manner in which the world is becoming economically, politically, legally and culturally interlinked

Guild socialism: a version of pluralist socialism which focused on 'guilds' of producer groups; an anti-statist doctrine which has close parallels to syndicalist thinking

Hegemony: a concept developed by the Italian Marxist Antonio Gramsci. It represent a subtle form of cultural domination. Power is largely redefined in term of intellectual domination. The masses are co-opted and quelled by means of ideas which are internalized, ultimately in notions of common sense

Herrenvolk: the idea of the master race

Human nature: referring to certain inherent or common aspects of all human beings, indicating what is possible or feasible for human to achieve, with strong implications for the manner in which the social or political world can be organized

Individualism: an ontological and moral belief which sees the individual human person as unique and as taking priority. The individual is seen as more real and valuable than any collective entities and thus the touchstone of truth, freedom and morality

Individualist anarchy: form of anarchy which emphasizes the absolute sovereignty and autonomy of the human individual against all forms of external political or moral authority

Industrialism: for ecological writers it indicates an adherence to the belief that human needs can only be met by a process of permanent expansion of the processes of production and consumption

Inerrancy: indicating freedom from all error

Integral nationalism: doctrine closely associated with European fascism, national socialism and the authoritarian Right. Emphasized the unique, occasionally racial, qualities of a particular nation and the need to maintain and defend that uniqueness against any immigration or dilution of the purity of the nation. Often associated, in the twentieth century, with an aggressive, xenophobic and irrationalist understanding of nationalism

Intrinsic value: indicates the internal worth of something independent of how it is valued, or not, by human agents

Jacobinism: derived from the Jacobin club, formed during the French Revolution. Jacobinism denoted the views of the key leaders of French Revolutionary movement and government which dominated France from 1793 and inaugurated the Terror

Kyoto protocol: a global accord aiming to decrease international greenhouse gas emissions

Laissez-faire: a French term implying 'leaving alone'; used predominantly in relation to political economy whereby a government will leave the free market to flourish without any regulation

Lebensphilosophie: a German term for a vitalist philosophy, which contended that life cannot simply be explained by material or natural scientific principles; it requires something non-material, some non-natural force to account for it. Vitalism is associated with aspects of the German romantic movement and later philosophers such as Hans Driesch and Henri Bergson

Liberal conservatism: believes the free market and its economic demands must take priority over political imperatives. It thus tends to oppose paternalist 'one nation' conservatism. There are strong parallels between classical liberalism and liberal conservatism: that is, a commitment to individualism, a belief in negative freedom, only a lightly regulated free market, and a minimal rule of law state. In fact, many conservatives in the 1980s were revivified classical liberals in all but name. However, liberal conservatism often had a stronger social agenda than classical liberals, that is to say, it believed there were certain sectors of social life which should not be subject to market forces and, at times (in the case of the family, sexuality, health and education), these should always be regulated or minimally protected by the state

Liberal feminism: identifies the (classical or social) liberal state and legal order as the means for achieving feminist goals. The key difference to mainstream liberalism is that concepts of equality, justice, rights and freedom have to be made wholly sensitive to gender and thus broadened to fully incorporate women. This can be done through established legal and constitutional processes

Liberal nationalism: an important element of nationalist ideology which argues that liberal values can be seen to be embodied in a nationalist format. Each nationality should thus have its own self-determining state, but it must be one embodying constitutional government, democracy and the rights and freedoms of the individual. Thus to be a nationalist would also be to exhibit all that one might expect from a liberal

Libertarianism: an amalgam of doctrines which embodies elements of both anarchy and liberalism and argues largely for the supreme importance of individualism, individual freedom and rights and absolutely minimal government

Literalism: interpreting statements in a plain or literal sense

Logocentrism: largely associated with the postmodernist work of Jacques Derrida; it suggests that Western thought has been mistakenly fixated on a set of universal fixed central truths which stand outside or external to texts and needs to be discovered via some form of metaphysics. For Derrida, however, meaning remains in linguistic signs and never reaches any external object

Market socialism: an ideological doctrine which developed in the 1980s, although some see its genealogy extending back to even Marx. It proposes that free markets can be decoupled from capitalism and then used to pursue and foster (within indicative planning guidelines) socialist goals, such as equality, freedom, social justice and welfare

Marxist feminism: a variant of feminism which argued that patriarchical oppression and the male exploitation of women are largely rooted in the economic order of free-market capitalism. The end of capitalism would entail the end of patriarchy and thus the solution to the oppression of women

Materialism: a philosophical doctrine identifying reality with matter and which thereby tends to deny the non-material role of mind, human agency or any religious factors

Mercantilism: a conception of political economy concerned primarily to support domestic industry and manufacture by tariffs, subsidies and regulation of manufacturing. Developed initially in the heyday of centralizing dynastic states (*see* economic nationalism)

Metaphysics: literally what comes before physics or nature. Classically it was seen as the first science or first philosophy; generally seen to be concerned with the most fundamental concepts or assumptions we make about the world: existence, reality, substance or cause

Modernization: often equates with the social, political and economic progress of industrial societies, and with the growth of market economies and liberal democracy; also denotes an escalating fragmentation of social life, an intensifying division of labour and the development of more specialized units of production. The public sphere becomes more instrumental and rational and the private world more expressive and emotive

Moral agency: the capacity of a being to act responsibly and autonomously and to which we can impute blame or praise

Moral extensionism: the extension of moral value beyond human persons towards other organisms, particularly animals

Multiculturalism: a loose unspecific ideological term which made its first appearance in Australia, New Zealand and Canada during the 1970s, particularly with changes in immigration laws. Its critical appearance in European public policy debate occurred in the 1990s. The prefix 'multi' arises conventionally in the context of groups, not individuals. Multiculturalism views society as composed of groups, each constituted by their own culture. Culture refers loosely to the beliefs, symbols and values of the group. There are various forms of multiculturalism, but it roughly denotes that the different cultures constituting society should all be accorded basic respect, and in some case specific rights, freedoms and even laws

Mutualist anarchy: sometimes called guaranteeism: a form of anarchy premised on the idea that economic organization would eventually replace political organization. Without any state structure, individuals would relate to each other via economic contracts, underpinned and guaranteed by a mutual credit bank. Individuals would still own private property, but it could never be used for power or the exploitation of others

National socialism: a somewhat internally disjointed ideology, associated primarily with the beliefs of the national socialists or Nazi Party in Germany in the 1930s. It embodied a collection of beliefs, some of which have affinities with ideas drawn from nationalism, conservatism and socialism. Certain themes stand out: firstly, a belief in the total state which dominates all sphere of life; secondly, an overwhelmingly strong sense of the importance of the national community, as being prior to the rights and freedoms of the individual; thirdly, a sense that the national community had to be identified through biologically racial criteria; fourthly, an imperative to maintain racial purity, at all costs, from infiltration or corruption; and, finally, a scorn for democratic, parliamentary liberal politics, as a well as for Marxism

Natural rights: claims or liberties attributed to human agents; seen as intrinsic or natural in some manner. They are therefore not seen as the result of human artifice or convention; they are, rather, immemorial normative facts which both humans and states ought to acknowledge

Neo-liberalism: a revivified version of classical liberalism, sometimes called economic or neo-classical liberalism. It also has close intellectual affinities with libertarianism. The ideology has, since the 1980s to the present, permeated an enormous amount of policy debates, on a global scale. It is seen, for example, to be the dominant ideology of the IMF and World Bank. It embodies a number of internal doctrinal differences, but the basic tenet is to identify the unregulated free-market capitalist order as the crucial ground for all efficient resource allocation. It is highly individualistic, intrinsically suspicious of all collective state or trades union action, and deeply uneasy with all forms of welfare policy premised on the state

New Right: a collective noun which is both imprecise and contestable; used largely to indicate a constellation of ideological perspectives which dominated the conservative Right during, initially, the 1980s and early 1990s, in a number of developed states. Incorporated a wide range of ideological, often incommensurable components, including, for example, anarcho-capitalists and neo-traditionalists. The most well-known component of the New Right was neo-liberalism

Nihilism: derived from the Latin *nihil* – denoting nothing; in ideological terms often linked with a form of anarchistic belief which rejected all forms of social life and utilized terror and extreme violence as a key tactic

Normative: concerned with standards or norms of moral correctness or what is right

Objectivity: a complex term indicating (very broadly) that a true judgement or fact must be independent of personal or subjective appraisal

Ontology: dimension of metaphysics concerned with study of existence or being.

Pantheism: the idea that human beings and nature are manifestations of (or included within) a notion of God or some form of spiritual principle. Spinoza's philosophy is often regarded as a classic example of pantheism

Paradigm: a dominant over-arching way of conceiving the world which determines how we explain and analyse reality

Paternalism: the idea that a person or a government will assume responsibility for others (for example, citizens) and protect their interest in a fatherly manner; consequently it allows no room for autonomy or independent activity

Paternalistic conservatism: originally a nineteenth-century conception of conservatism, often linked to the 'one nation' conception of Benjamin Disraeli. It viewed political leadership and state action (in spheres such as health, education, employment or social security) much more positively and optimistically, as embodying the deep-rooted benevolent duties (of leadership groups) to ensure fairness, justice and opportunity for all citizens. Its primary emphasis was therefore on providing firm authority and leadership, for the sake of the common good of the whole nation. Although pragmatic, to a degree, politics and the unified nation still took priority over economic factors

Patriarchy: a political system which explicitly or implicitly favours men or the gender of masculinity

Philosophes: designates a group of philosophers during the French Enlightenment

Pluralism: in the most general moral or political sense it is acknowledgement of difference and diversity within societies. This diversity could be in terms of knowledge, morality, culture, ethnicities, religion, and so forth. In political terms it usually denotes a society which embodies different groups, cultures or even just opinions and lifestyles

Pluralist socialism: the key issue for pluralist socialism is that the sovereign centralized state is not the means for introducing or maintaining genuine socialism. Socialism can only come about and be sustained through self-organized associations of working people, who would take over and run all the (formerly state-run) institutions concerned with health, employment, welfare, insurance, education, and so forth. Equality cannot be achieved through a state; it rather arises from self-determining and self-organizing associations of workers. The ideology has close intellectual affiliations with syndicalism, anarcho-syndicalism, communist anarchy and, at points, social ecology

Postmodern feminism: derived from the more general theoretical impact of postmodernism and poststructuralism, with Derrida and Foucault being the key theoretical influences. It is an important, if elusive, component of feminism, which developed in the 1980s and still actively permeates sectors of the movement in the 2000s. The central focus is on language and the way in which its constitutes political realities. Oppression, patriarchy and the construction of gender are thus seen as rooted in language. The essential task of the feminist is then to deconstruct language (and texts) of contemporary society in order to expose the underlying patriarchical and oppressive themes

Postmodernism: a critical reaction to both structuralism and modernism which tries to undermine and critically dissolve the central epistemological assumptions of these latter movements. It developed initially in the early 1970s and came to fruition in writers such as Derrida (with deconstruction) and Foucault (with genealogy)

Poststructuralism: a generic term covering a range of critical reactions to structuralism in Continental philosophy. The theory overlaps with many of the concerns of postmodernism. Language is seen as crucial to reality, even to the identity of the human self. There is, though, nothing outside the context of language

Radical feminism: school of feminism which has faded since the late 1990s. The term radical covers a number of very different positions; however, its signature was initially an acerbic antagonism to Marxism and the New Left and an ideological stress on the biological and psychological factors underpinning patriarchy and the oppression of women. Its proposals tended to be quite diverse, ranging from androgyny, through female supremacism to political lesbianism

Rationalism: theory which claims to be premised on rational principles

Rechtsstaat: a state governed by law or the rule of law; in other words a constitutional state

Reformation: a collection of movements in the sixteenth century which, in short, criticized and protested against (thus *Protestant*), and ultimately broke away from, the established Catholic Church on explicit doctrinal grounds. The schism between the Catholic and Protestant churches led to massive political, philosophical and cultural changes across Europe

Reformism: a belief in slow, gradual, measured and piecemeal change

Reformist state socialism: sometimes seen as democratic socialism, revisionist socialism or even social democracy. It is also very closely allied to the social liberal tradition. The term is used to cover a range of marginally distinct doctrines. It basically identified the achievement of socialist goals, such as greater equality, social justice, efficient market regulation and social citizenship rights, with the actions of a reformist (rather than revolutionary) socialist party. This party would acquire power though representative democracy, and then use the established process of the law to achieve socialist goals. This conception of socialism, in states such as Britain or Sweden, largely constituted what has become known as the post-1945 consensus. It dominated ideological and policy discussion up to the 1970s, when it was successfully challenged by what would now be referred to as a neo-liberal ideological consensus

Relativism: a philosophical term developed in the nineteenth century, covering a wide range of theories. It tends broadly to deny notions of universal truth or reality and conversely maintains that, for example, truth is relative to certain circumstances, historical conditions, sociological or linguistic contexts

Religion: the term derives from the Latin *religare*, meaning to 'bind fast', 'tie' or, by extension, 'to place an obligation upon'. In the most general sense it implies that the visible world must be seen as part of something more significant – some form of unseen spiritual world which adds meaning and purpose to the visible. The aim of religion is in some manner to establish a relation between the invisible and the visible worlds. Religions also contain bodies of doctrine (and texts) which aim to tabulate the rules and imperatives concerning this spiritual dimension. Core doctrines also frequently give rise to bodies of ethical and indeed political principles. Religions also frequently have a social dimension to them: that is to say, they have institutional and organizational aspects

Revisionism: strictly speaking refers to the attempt to revise a previously accepted position. In ideological terms tends to refer to socialists, such as Eduard Bernstein, who tried to revise orthodox Marxism

Romantic conservatism: variant of conservative thinking which embodied a deep nostalgia for a more pastoral, quasi-feudal past; often combined with a fairly well-worked-out utopian vision of a restored rural society, which would be simpler, embodying a natural hierarchy of authority, often more religious, and saturated with communal and traditional sentiments. Their beliefs tended to be anti-industrial and suspicious of liberal political economy. Unlike traditionalists they tended to have a much more positive conception of human reason, although it was understood in a more speculative sense

Romanticism: broad-ranging eighteenth- and nineteenth-century intellectual movement in philosophy, the visual arts, literature, music, poetry and politics. In the most general terms it was suspicious of the Enlightenment ideals of rationality; it placed a strong emphasis on the expressive, intuitive, imaginative, emotive and often irrational aspects of humanity. It was often linked with a specific understanding of human creativity. In politics it had a reactionary and conservative aspect which looked back nostalgically to feudal and medieval society, emphasizing the idea of an organic or natural tradition-based community, premised on age-old customs. It also had links with early expressions of nationalism. However, other strands of political romanticism were more radical, opposing the destruction of the individual by states or nations. In this context there was also a hyper-individualistic aspect to romanticism

Secularization: generally taken to refer to the decline of religious criteria in accounting for human existence. It does not necessarily mean, though, a rejection of religion

Self-determination: the concept is fairly recent, dating from the early twentieth century. It has subsequently been embodied in human rights documentation. Politically it indicates that a nation state (or people) has a right to autonomy and to preserve its own law, political integrity, language and culture; that it has a right to make its own policy without external interference; that peoples have a right to struggle for such a state; and other states have a duty not to interfere in this process

Sentientism: premising moral value on the capacity to experience

Social Darwinism: a political and philosophical doctrine which links the evolutionary doctrine of natural selection (and the idea of the survival of the fittest in nature) with the social and political life of nations

Social ecology: a theory developed in the later twentieth century by Murray Bookchin. Essentially a powerful modern form of eco-anarchism, premised on the communist anarchism of Peter Kropotkin. It has some overlaps with deep ecology

Social liberalism: a more communitarian-orientated conception of liberalism, which developed from the 1880s; was committed to a more socialized understanding of the individual; a more active and interventionary vision of state activity; a mixed conception of the economy (embodying both free markets and regulatory action); and a more positive notion of human freedom as linked to conceptions of citizenship and the common good

Sociology of knowledge: the academic analysis of the relation between thought and the sociological context in which it arises. Originates largely with the 1920s writings of Karl Mannheim

State: a self-determining human association embodying a population of citizens, identified with a geographically specific territory, over which it holds sovereign jurisdiction, and a monopoly of power and coercion (regulated by rules)

Steady-State Economy: an economy where population would be stabilized in a neo-Malthusian sense; wealth would be more evenly distributed; there would wide-scale use of renewable energy sources and recycling. There would thus be a much slower depletion of finite natural resources. Any growth would be more carefully planned and linked to less harmful technologies

Structuralism: the key idea of structuralism (which developed in areas such as linguistics, anthropology and philosophy) is that underlying structures (in language, society or knowledge) have to be uncovered in order to reveal true meanings. It is not the surface statements of individuals themselves which are revealing, but rather what structurally underlies those statements

Subjectivity: in terms of ontology or epistemology it indicates that reality is dependent upon the individual conscious mind. In ethics it usually denotes that values are dependent upon the individual's appraisal

Substitutionary atonement: a Christian doctrine which maintains that Jesus Christ intentionally gave up his life and died to atone for the sins of humanity. This act is portrayed as an act of love, that is to say, he died as a substitute for human beings in order to ensure their salvation

Sustainable development: a genuine augmentation in human well-being that could be retained without radically affecting the environment or compromising the capacity of future generations to assure their basic needs

Syndicalism: denotes a form of anti-capitalist and revolutionary trade unionism which developed in the very early twentieth century. It was anti-statist, committed to the idea of a general strike as a means of direct action and revolutionary overthrow of the bourgeois state, and saw unions of workers as the organizational base for a future society (*see* anarcho-syndicalism)

Teleology: a theory which describes or accounts for actions, institutions or events in terms of the purposes they embody

Theory: a body of propositions which together provide an explanation of a particular subject-matter

Totalitarianism: a term employed in political science which indicates a certain type of society (for example, Soviet Russia or Nazi Germany) where the state, governed by one party, regulates every aspect of people's public and private lives

Traditionalism: the belief that customs, habits, prejudices and established practices are valuable in themselves as guides to moral and political conduct

Traditionalist conservatism: most significant component of conservatism; placed a massive emphasis on the role of tried and tested communal traditions, customs, institutions and conventions as the basis for any meaningful politics, morality or legal structures. Profoundly suspicious of all the ideologies founded on Enlightenment conceptions of human freedom and reason. Humans, in all their activities, are seen as creatures of prejudice and habit who prefer organic slow change and appreciate established time-honoured practices of authoritative rule, rather than a politics based upon reason, modernity or progress

Traditionalist conservative nationalism: stresses the immemorial continuity and unique destiny of an organic national community, as expressed through its conventional, institutional, legal, moral, religious and social life

Umma: world-wide community of Muslims

Utopia: literally means 'no-place': a worked-out vision of a possible or more perfect society

Utopian socialism: one the oldest forms of socialism which tries to sketch out a vision, in micro detail (including eating, clothing, sex, leisure, work, and so forth), of the ordering of social life, which corresponds most accurately to the true nature of humanity. Such a society could provide the conditions for ultimate human happiness and virtue. Utopian socialists contrasted this worked-out vision to what they perceived to be the deep human unhappiness of the corrupt world of liberal market capitalism and nation states

Vitalism: a philosophy concerned with the idea that life cannot be explained by material or natural scientific principles; it requires something non-material, some vital non-natural force to account for it (*see Lebensphilosophie*)

Volk: a German term indicating the whole people or nation. It conventionally implies, in nationalist writings, that there is a deep identity of history, mythology, language and culture within a people. It can indicate that a people have a moral and historical significance which is greater than the individuals who make up the whole. For national socialist writers in the 1930s it had a specific racial significance implying, for example, that Jews were not part of the racial *Volk*

Bibliography

Aarsleff, H. 1982 *From Locke to Saussure: Essays on the Study of Language and Intellectual History*. Minneapolis: University of Minnesota Press.

Acton, H. B. 1952–3 'Tradition and Some Other Forms of Order', *Proceedings of the Aristotelian Society*, LIII.

Acton, H. B. 1971 *The Morals of Markets: An Ethical Explanation*. London: Longman.

Acton, Lord 1907 *The History of Freedom and Other Essays*. London: Macmillan.

Adams, I. 1989 *The Logic of Political Belief: A Philosophical Analysis*. London and New York: Harvester Wheatsheaf.

Adorno, T. W. 1950 *The Authoritarian Personality*. New York: Harper & Row.

Aladjem, T. 1991 'The Philosopher's Prism: Foucault, Feminism, and Critique', *Political Theory*, 19, 2.

Allett, J. 1981 *The New Liberalism: The Political Economy of J. A. Hobson*. Toronto and London: University of Toronto Press.

Allison, L. 1984 *Right Principles: A Conservative Philosophy of Politics*. Oxford: Blackwell.

Alter, P. 1989 *Nationalism*. London and New York: Edward Arnold.

Althusser, L. 1969 *For Marx*. Harmondsworth: Penguin Books

Anderson, B. 1983 *Imagined Communities: Reflections on the Origin and Spread of Nationalism*. London: Verso.

Anderson, T. L. and Leal, D. R. 2001 *Free Market Environmentalism*. London: Palgrave.

Apter, D. E. 1965 *The Politics of Modernization*. Chicago: University of Chicago Press.

Apter, D. E. and Joll, J., eds 1971 *Anarchism Today*. London: Macmillan.

Arblaster, A. 1984 *The Rise and Decline of Western Liberalism*. Oxford: Blackwell.

Arendt, H. 1951 *The Origins of Totalitarianism*. London: Allen & Unwin.

Aris, R. 1965 *History of Political Thought in Germany 1789–1815*. New York: Frank Cass.

Armstrong, K. 2004 *The Battle for God: Fundamentalism in Judaism, Christianity and Islam*. London: Harper Perennial.

Arshinov, P. 1974 *The History of the Makhnovist Movement 1918–21*. Chicago: Black and Red Detroit/Solidarity.

Ash, M. 1987 *New Renaissance: Essays in Search of Wholeness*. Bideford: Green Books.

Attfield, R. 1983 *The Ethics of Environmental Concern*. Oxford: Blackwell/New York: Columbia University Press.

Attfield, R. 1987 *A Theory of Value and Obligation*. London and New York: Croom Helm.

Attfield, R. 1990 'Deep Ecology and Intrinsic Value: A Reply to Andrew Dobson', *Cogito*. 4, 1.

Attfield, R. and Dell, K., eds 1989 *Values, Conflict and the Environment*. Oxford: Ian Ramsey Centre and Cardiff Centre for Applied Ethics.

Auerbach, M. M. 1959 *The Conservative Illusion*. New York: Columbia University Press.

Austern D. M. 1984 *The Political Theories of Edmund Burke and Joseph de Maistre as Representative of Conservative Libertarianism and Conservative Authoritarianism*. Ann Arbor: University of Michigan Press.

Avrich, P. 1967 *The Russian Anarchists*. Princeton, NJ: Princeton University Press.

Avrich, P. 1970 'The Legacy of Bakunin', *The Russian Review*, 29.

Avrich, P. 1974 *Bakunin and Nechaev*. London: Freedom Press.

Avrich, P. 2006 *Anarchist Voices: An Oral History of Anarchism in America*. New York: AK Press.

Ayubi, N. 1991 *Political Islam: Religion and Politics in the Arab World*. London and New York: Routledge.

Bahro, R. 1984 *From Red to Green*. London: Verso and New Left Books.

Bahro, R. 1986 *Building the Green Movement*. London: GMP.

Bakunin, M. 1970 *God and the State*. New York: Dover.

Bakunin, M. 1990 *Statism and Anarchy*. Cambridge: Cambridge University Press.

Ball, S. 1896 'The Moral Aspect of Socialism', *International Journal of Ethics*, VI.

Ball, T. 1988 *Transforming Political Discourse: Political Theory and Critical Conceptual History*. Oxford: Blackwell.

Ball, T., Farr, J. and Hanson, R. L., eds, 1989 *Political Innovation and Conceptual Change*. Cambridge: Cambridge University Press.

Banks, O. 1981 *Faces of Feminism*. Oxford: Martin Robertson.

Barr, J., ed. 1971 *The Environment Handbook*. London: Ballantine and Friends of the Earth.

Barry, B. 1989 *Theories of Justice*. Hemel Hempstead: Harvester Wheatsheaf.

Barry, J. 1999 *Rethinking Green Politics*. London: Sage.

Barry, J. 2006 *Environment and Social Theory*. London: Routledge.

Barry, N. P. 1986 *Classical Liberalism and Libertarianism*. London: Macmillan.

Barry, N. P. 1987 *The New Right*. London: Croom Helm.

Bartelson, J. 2001 *The Critique of the State*. Cambridge: Cambridge University Press.

Bastow, S. and Martin, J. 2003 *Third Way Discourses: European Ideologies in the Twentieth Century*. Edinburgh: Edinburgh University Press.

Bastow, S., Martin, J. and Pels, D., eds 2002 'Third Way Ideologies', Special Issue, *Journal of Political Ideologies*, 7, 3.

Bauer, O. 2000 *The Question of Nationalities and Social Democracy*. Minneapolis: University of Minnesota Press.

Baumgardner, J. and Richards, A. 2000 *Manifesta*. New York: Farrar, Straus and Giroux.

Baxter, B. 2004 *The Theory of Ecological Justice*. London: Routledge.

Beauvoir, S. de 1954 *The Second Sex*. London: Jonathan Cape.

Bebel, A. 1971 *Women under Socialism*. New York: Schocken.

Beck, H. 2008 *The Fateful Alliance: German Conservatives and Nazis in 1933*. London: Berghahn Books.

Beer, M. 1984 *A History of British Socialism*. Nottingham: Spokesman.

Beetham, D. 1983 *Marxists in the Face of Fascism*. Manchester: Manchester University Press.

Beiner R., ed. 1999 *Theorizing Nationalism*. New York: State University of New York Press.

Beitz, C., Alexander, L. and Scanlon, T., eds 1985 *International Ethics*. Princeton, NJ: Princeton University Press.

Bell, D. 1965 *The End of Ideology: On the Exhaustion of Political Ideas in the 1950s*. New York: Free Press.

Bellah, R. 1991 *Beyond Belief: Essays on Religion in a Post-Traditional Society*. Berkeley: University of California Press.

Bellamy, R. 1987a *Modern Italian Social Theory*. Cambridge: Polity Press.

Bellamy, R. 1987b 'Idealism and Liberalism in an Italian "New Liberal Theorist": Guido de Ruggiero's *History of European Liberalism*', *The Historical Journal*, 30, 1.

Bellamy, R. and Mason, A., eds 2003 *Political Concepts*. Manchester: Manchester University Press.

Benhabib, S., ed. 1996 *Democracy and Difference*. Princeton: Princeton University Press.

Benhabib, S. 2002 *The Claims of Culture: Equality and Diversity in the Global Era*. Princeton NJ: Princeton University Press.

Berki, R. N. 1975 *Socialism*. London: Dent.

Berkman, A. 1977 *The ABC of Anarchism*. London: Freedom Press.

Berlin, I. 1976 *Vico and Herder: Two Studies in the History of Ideas*. London: Hogarth Press.

Berlin, I. 1990 *The Crooked Timber of Humanity*. London: John Murray.

Bernstein, E. 1961 *Evolutionary Socialism*. New York: Schocken Books.

Bernstein, G. L. 1986 *Liberalism and Liberal Politics in Edwardian England*. London: Allen & Unwin.

Bevir, M. 2005 *New Labour: A Critique*. London: Routledge.

Biagini, E. F. and Reid, A. J. 1991 *Currents of Radicalism: Popular Radicalism, Organized Labour and Party Politics in Britain 1850–1914*. Cambridge: Cambridge University Press.

Biehl, J. and Staudenmaier, P. 1995 *Ecofascism: Lessons from the German Experience*. San Francisco: AK Press.

Binion, R. 1973 'Hitler's Concept of Lebensraum: The Psychological Basis', *History of Childhood Quarterly*, 1.

Birch, A. H. 1989 *Nationalism and National Integration*. London: Unwin Hyman.

Black C. E. 1967 *The Dynamics of Modernization*. New York: Harper & Row.

Blake, R. 1985 *The Conservative Party from Peel to Thatcher*. London: Fontana, Collins.

Blinkhorn, M. 2000 *Fascism and the Right in Europe*. London: Unwin Hyman.

Bluhdorn, I. 2008 *The Politics of Unsustainability: Eco-Politics in the Post-Ecological Era*. London: Routledge.

Bobbio, N. 1987 *Which Socialism? Marxism, Socialism and Democracy*. Minneapolis: University of Minnesota Press.

Boggs, C. 1995 *The Socialist Tradition: From Crisis to Decline*. London: Routledge.

Boling, P. 1991 'The Democratic Potential of Mothering', *Political Theory*, 19, 4.

Bookchin, M. 1982 *The Ecology of Freedom*. Palo Alto, CA: Cheshire Books.

Bookchin, M. 1986a *Post-Scarcity Anarchism*. Montreal and Buffalo, NY: Black Rose Press.

Bookchin, M. 1986b *Toward an Ecological Society*. Montreal and Buffalo, NY: Black Rose Press.

Bookchin, M. 1992 *Deep Ecology and Anarchism: A Polemic*. London: Freedom Press.

Bosanquet, N. 1983 *After the New Right*. London: Heinemann.

Bosworth, R. J. B. 2003 *Mussolini*. London: Hodder Arnold.

Boucher, D. 1989 *The Social and Political Thought of R. G. Collingwood*. Cambridge: Cambridge University Press.

Boucher, D. and Kelley, P., eds 1998 *Social Justice from Hume to Walzer*. London: Routledge.

Bouchier, D. 1983 *The Feminist Challenge*. London: Macmillan.

Bourdieu, P. 1977 *Outline of a Theory of Practice*. Cambridge: Cambridge University Press.

Bramwell, A. 1985 *Blood and Soil: Walter Darré and Hitler's Green Party*. Bourne End: Kensal Press.

Bramwell, A. 1989 *Ecology in the 20th Century*. New Haven: Yale University Press.

Bramwell, A. 1994 *The Fading of the Greens: The Decline of Environmental Politics in the West*. New Haven: Yale University Press.

Brenan, G. 1969 *The Spanish Labryinth*. Cambridge: Cambridge University Press.

Breuilly, J. 1993 *Nationalism and the State*. Manchester: Manchester University Press.

Bristow, E. 1975 'The Liberty and Property Defence League and Individualism', *The Historical Journal*, 18.

Broszat, M. 1981 *The Hitler State: The Foundation and Development of the Internal Structure of the Third Reich*. London and New York: Longman.

Brown, C., ed. 1994 *Political Restructuring in Europe*. London: Routledge.

Brown. G., ed. 1974 *The Industrial Syndicalist: Documents in Social History, 3*. Nottingham: Spokesman Books.

Brown, W. 1995 *States of Injury: Power and Freedom in Late Modernity*. Princeton, NJ: Princeton University Press.

Brown-Grant, R. 2003 *Christine de Pizan and the Moral Defense of Women*. Cambridge: Cambridge University Press.

Bruce, L. 1995 *Defenders of God: The Fundamentalist Revolt against the Modern Age*, 2nd edn. Columbia: South Carolina University Press.

Bruce, S. 2000 *Fundamentalism*. Cambridge, Polity Press.

Brundtland, G. H. 1987 *Our Common Future*. Oxford: Oxford University Press.

Bryson, V. 1992 *Feminist Political Theory: An Introduction*. London: Macmillan.

Bryson, V. 2004 'Marxism and Feminism: Can the "Unhappy Marriage" Be Saved?', *Journal of Political Ideologies*, 9, 1.

Buck, P. W., ed. 1975 *How Conservatives Think*. Harmondsworth: Penguin.

Bullard, R. 2005 *The Quest for Environmental Justice: Human Rights and the Politics of Pollution*. Berkeley: University of California Press

Bullock, A. 1962 *Hitler: A Study in Tyranny*. Harmondsworth: Penguin.

Bunyard, P. and Morgan-Grenville, F., eds 1987 *The Green Alternative*. London: Methuen.

Burke, E. n.d. *Edmund Burke: Selections from His Political Writings and Speeches*. London: T. Nelson & Sons.

Burleigh, M. 2001 *The Third Reich: A New History*. London: Macmillan.

Burleigh, M. 2006 *Sacred Causes: Religion and Politics from the European Dictators to Al Qaeda*. London: HarperCollins.

Burleigh, M. and Wipperman, W. 1993 *The Racial State: Germany 1933–1945*. Cambridge: Cambridge University Press.

Butler, D. and Stokes, D. 1974 *Political Change in Britain*. London: Macmillan.

Butler, J. 1990 *Gender Trouble: Feminism and the Subversion of Identity*. London: Routledge.

Butler, J. 1997 *Excitable Speech: A Politics of the Performative*. London: Routledge.

Butler, J. 2004 *Undoing Gender*. London: Routledge.

Cahm, C. 1989 *Kropotkin and the Rise of Revolutionary Anarchism*. Cambridge: Cambridge University Press.

Callaghan, J. 1990 *Socialism in Britain*. Oxford: Blackwell.

Calleo, D. P. 1966 *Coleridge and the Idea of the Modern State*. New Haven: Yale University Press.

Callicott, J. B. 1984 'Non-Anthropocentric Value Theory and Environmental Ethics', *American Philosophical Quarterly*, 21.

Callinicos, A. 2003 *An Anti-Capitalist Manifesto*. Cambridge: Polity Press.

Canovan, M. 1996 *Nationalism and Political Theory*. London: Edward Elgar.

Carsten, F. L. 1980 *The Rise of Fascism*, 2nd edn. London: Batsford.

Carter, A. 1971 *The Political Theory of Anarchism*. London: Routledge & Kegan Paul.

Carter, M. 2003 *T. H. Green and the Development of Ethical Socialism*. Exeter: Imprint Academic.

Carter, N. 2007 *The Politics of the Environment: Ideas, Activism, Policy*. Cambridge: Cambridge University Press.

Carver, T. 1998 *The Postmodern Marx*. Manchester: Manchester University Press

Cecil, H. 1912 *Conservatism*. London: Thornton Butterworth.

Chadwick, R. ed. 1998 *Encyclopaedia of Applied Ethics*. New York: Academic Press of America.

Charvet, J. 1982 *Feminism*. London: Dent.

Cheles, L., Ferguson, R. and Vaughan M. eds 1991 *Neo-Fascism in Europe*. London and New York: Longman.

Chodorow, N. 1978 *Mothering: Psychoanalysis and the Sociology of Gender*. Berkeley: University of California Press.

Chomsky, N. 2004 *Chomsky on Anarchism*. New York: AK Press.

Chun, L. 1993 *The British New Left*. Edinburgh: Edinburgh University Press.

Claeys, G. 1989 *Citizens and Saints: Politics and Anti-Politics in Early British Socialism*. Cambridge: Cambridge University Press.

Clark, J. P. 1976 *Max Stirner's Egoism*. London: Freedom Press.

Clark J. P. 1977 *The Philosophical Anarchism of William Godwin*. Princeton, NJ: Princeton University Press.

Clark, J. P. 1986 *The Anarchist Moment: Reflections on Culture, Nature and Power*. Montreal and Buffalo, NY: Black Rose Press.

Cobban, A. 1944 *National Self-Determination*. London: Oxford University Press.

Cobban, A. 1962 *Edmund Burke and the Revolt Against the Eighteenth Century*. London: Allen & Unwin.

Cobbett, W. 1985 *Rural Rides*. Harmondsworth: Penguin.

Cohen J., ed. 1996 *For Love of Country*. Boston: Beacon Press.

Cohen, N.J., ed. 1990 *The Fundamentalist Phenomenon: A View from Within, A Response from Without*. Grand Rapids, Mich.: Wm B. Erdmans Publishing.

Cohn, N. 1970 *The Pursuit of the Millennium*. New York and Oxford: Oxford University Press.

Cole, G. D. H. 1917 *Self-Government in Industry*. London: George Bell.

Cole, G. D. H. 1953–60 *A History of Socialist Thought*, 7 vols. London: Macmillan.

Cole, G. D. H. 1980 *Guild Socialism Restated*. New Brunswick, NJ.: Transaction Books.

Cole, M. 1961 *The Story of Fabian Socialism*. London: Heinemann.

Coleridge, S. T. 1976 *On the Constitution of the Church and State*. London: Routledge & Kegan Paul.

Collard, A. and Contrucci, J. 1988 *Rape of the Wild*. London: Women's Press

Collingwood, R. G. 1940 'Fascism and Nazism', *Philosophy*, 15.

Collingwood, R. G. 1989 *Essays in Political Philosophy*, ed. David Boucher. Oxford: Clarendon Press.

Collini, S. 1979 *Liberalism and Sociology: L. T. Hobhouse and Political Argument in England 1880–1915*. Cambridge: Cambridge University Press.

Collins, I. 1957 *Liberalism in Nineteenth-Century Europe*. London: Historical Association, no. 34.

Comfort, A. 1946 *Art and Social Responsibility*. London: Falcon Press.

Connelly, J. and Smith, G. 2002 *Politics and the Environment: From Theory to Practice*. London: Routledge.

Constant, B. 1988 *Political Writings*. Cambridge: Cambridge University Press.

Coole, D. 1988 *Women in Political Theory: From Ancient Misogyny to Contemporary Feminism*. Brighton: Harvester.

Coole, D. 2000 'Cartographic Convulsions: Public and Private Reconsidered', *Political Theory*, 28, 3.

Corbett, P. 1965 *Ideologies*. London: Hutchinson.

Covell, C. 1986 *The Redefinition of Conservatism: Politics and Doctrine*. London: Macmillan.

Cowling, M. ed. 1978 *Conservative Essays*. London: Cassell.

Cox, H. 1985 *Religion in the Secular City: Towards a Postmodern Theology*. New York: Simon & Schuster.

Crick, B. 1982 *George Orwell: A Life*. Harmondsworth: Penguin.

Croce, B. 1946 *Politics and Morals*. London: Allen & Unwin.

Crosland, C. A. R. 1980 *The Future of Socialism*. London: Jonathan Cape.

Crowder, G. 1991 *Classical Anarchism: The Political Thought of Godwin, Proudhon, Bakunin, and Kropotkin*. Oxford: Clarendon Press.

Daly, H. E. ed. 1973 *Towards a Steady-State Economy*. San Francisco: Freeman.

Daly, H. E. and Cobb, J. B. 1990 *For the Common Good*. London: Green Print.

Daly M. 1979 *Gyn-Ecology: The Metaethics of Radical Feminism*. London: Women's Press.

Daly, M. 1984 *Pure Lust: Elemental Feminist Philosophy*. London: Women's Press.

Dangerfield, G. 1966 *The Strange Death of Liberal England*. London: MacGibbon & Kee.

Dauncey, G. 1981 *The Unemployment Handbook*. London: National Extension College.

Dauncey, G, 1983 *Nice Work If You Can Get It*. London: National Extension College.

Davis, H. B. 1978 *Towards a Marxist Theory of Nationalism*. New York: Monthly Review Press.

Dawson, C. 1931 *Progress and Religion: An Historical Enquiry*. London: Sheed & Ward.

Day, G. and Thompson, A. 2004 *Theorizing Nationalism*. London: Palgrave.

Day, R. J. F. 2005 *Gramsci Is Dead: Anarchist Currents in the Newest Social Movements*. London: Pluto Press.

Denham, A. and Garnett, M. 2002 'Sir Keith Joseph and the Undoing of British Conservatism', *Journal of Political Ideologies*, 7, 1.

Dennis, N. and Halsey, A. H. 1988 *English Ethical Socialism*. Oxford: Clarendon Press.

Derrida, J. 2006 *Spectres of Marx*. London: Routledge

Deutsch, K. 1953 *Nationalism and Social Communication: An Enquiry into the Foundations of Nationality*. Cambridge, Mass.: Harvard University Press.

Devall, B. and Sessions, G. 1985 *Deep Ecology: Living as if Nature Mattered*. Salt Lake City: Gibbs M. Smith Inc.

Devigne, R. 1994 *Recasting Conservatism: Oakeshott, Strauss and the Response to Postmodernism*. New Haven: Yale University Press.

Dewey, J. 1931 *Individualism: Old and New*. London: Allen & Unwin.

Dicey, A. V. 1905 *Lectures on the Relation between Law and Public Opinion in England during the Nineteenth Century*. London: Macmillan.

Dickinson, H. T. 1977 *Liberty and Property: Political Ideology in the Eighteenth Century*. London: Methuen.

Dietz, M. 1985 'Citizenship with a Feminist Face; The Problem of Maternal Thinking', *Political Theory*, 13, 1.

Dietz, M. 2002 *Turning Operations: Feminism, Arendt and Politics*. London: Routledge.

Dimova-Cookson, M. 2003 'A New Scheme of Positive and Negative Freedom: Re-constructing T.H. Green on Freedom', *Political Theory* 31, 4.

Dobson, A. 1989 'Deep Ecology', *Cogito*, 3, 1.

Dobson, A. 1990 *Green Political Thought*. London: Unwin Hyman (4th edn, 2007).

Dobson, A. 1998 *Justice and the Environment*. Oxford: Oxford University Press.

Dobson, A. 1999 *Fairness and Futurity: Essays on Environmental Sustainability and Social Justice*. Oxford: Oxford University Press.

Dobson, A. 2006 *Environmental Citizenship*. Cambridge, Mass.: MIT Press

Dobson, A. and Eckersely, R., eds 2006 *Political Theory and the Ecological Challenge*. Cambridge: Cambridge University Press.

Dolgoff, S. 1972 *Bakunin on Anarchy*. New York: Vintage Books.

Dominick, R. 1987 'The Nazis and the Nature Conservationists', *The Historian*, 49.

Douglass, R. B., Mara, G. M., and Richardson, H. S., eds 1990 *Liberalism and the Good*. London: Routledge.

Downs, A. 1972 'Up and Down with Ecology – The Issue Attention Cycle', *Public Interest*, 28.

Drengson, A. and Inoue, Y. 1995 *Deep Ecology: An Introductory Anthology*. Berkeley: North Atlantic Books.

Dryzek, J. 1987 *Rational Ecology: Environment and Political Economy*. Oxford: Blackwell.

Dryzek, J. 2002 *Deliberative Democracy and Beyond*. Oxford: Clarendon Press.

Dryzek, J. 2005 *The Politics of the Earth: Environmental Discourses*. Oxford: Oxford University Press.

Dryzek, J., Downes, D., Hunold, C., Schlosberg, D. and Hernes, H.-K. 2003 *Green States and Social Movements: Environmentalism in the United States, United Kingdom, Germany and Norway*. Oxford: Oxford University Press.

Duncan, G. 1987 'Understanding Ideology', *Political Studies*, XXXV.

Dunn, J. 1979 *Western Political Theory in the Face of the Future*. Cambridge: Cambridge University Press.

Durkheim, É. 1959 *Socialism and Saint-Simon*. London: Routledge & Kegan Paul.

Durkheim, É. 1995 *The Elementary Forms of Religious Life*. New York: Free Press.

Dworkin, A. 1974 *Women Hating*. New York: Dutton.

Dworkin, A. 1981 *Pornography: Men Possessing Women*. London: Women's Press.

Dworkin, A. 1987 *Intercourse*. London: Arrow Books.

Eade, J. C., ed. 1983 *Romantic Nationalism in Europe*. Canberra: Australian National University.

Eatwell, R. 1996 'On Defining the "Fascist Minimum": The Centrality of Ideology', *Journal of Political Ideologies*, 1.

Eatwell, R. 2003 *Fascism: A History*. London: Pimlico.

Eatwell, R. and O'Sullivan, N., eds 1989 *The Nature of the Right: European and American Politics and Political Thought since 1789*. London: Pinter.

Eccleshall, R. 1977 'English Conservatism as Ideology', *Political Studies*, XXV.

Eccleshall, R. 1986 *British Liberalism: Liberal Thought from the 1640s to the 1980s*. London: Longman.

Eccleshall, R. 1990 *English Conservatism since the Restoration*. London: Unwin Hyman.

Eccleshall, R., Geoghegan, V., Jay, R. and Wilford, R., eds 1984 *Political Ideologies*. London: Hutchinson.

Eckersley, R 1992 *Environmentalism and Political Theory: Towards an Econcentric Approach*. London: UCL Press.

Eckersley, R. 2004 *The Green State: Rethinking Democracy and Sovereignty*. Cambridge, Mass.: MIT Press.

Ehrlich, P. 1968 *The Population Bomb*. London: Ballantine.

Eisenestadt, S.N. 2000 *Fundamentalism, Sectarianism and Revolution*. Cambridge: Cambridge University Press.

Eisenstein, H. 1984 *Contemporary Feminist Thought*. London: Unwin Hyman.

Eisenstein, H. and Jardine, A., eds 1990 *The Future of Difference*. New Brunswick, NJ, and London: Rutgers University Press.

Eisenstein, Z., ed. 1979 *Capitalist Patriarchy and the Case for Socialist Feminism*. New York and London: Monthly Review Press.

Eisenstein, Z. 1981 *The Radical Future of Liberal Feminism*. New York and London: Longman.

Ekins, P., ed. 1986 *The Living Economy: A New Economics in the Making*. London: Routledge & Kegan Paul.

Eley, G. 2002 *Forging Democracy: The History of the Left in Europe*. Oxford: Oxford University Press.

Eliot, T. S. 1939 *The Idea of a Christian Society*. London: Faber & Faber.

Elkington, J. and Burke, T. 1989 *The Green Capitalists*. London: Gollancz.

Elkington, J. and Hailes, J. 1988 *The Green Consumer Guide*. London: Gollancz.

Elshtain, J. B. 1981 *Public Man, Private Woman*. Princeton, NJ: Princeton University Press.

Elshtain, J. B., ed. 1982 *The Family in Political Thought*. Brighton: Harvester.

Elshtain, J. B. 1985 'Reflections on War and Political Discourse: Realism, Just War, and Feminism in a Nuclear Age', *Political Theory*, 13, 1.

Engelbrecht, H. C. 1933 *Johann Gottlieb Fichte: A Study of His Political Writings with Special Reference to his Nationalism*. New York: Columbia University Press.

Epstein, K. 1966 *The Genesis of German Conservatism*. Princeton, NJ: Princeton University Press.

Ergang, R. R. 1931 *Herder and the Foundations of German Nationalism*. New York: Columbia University Press.

Erikson, E. H. 1958 *Young Man Luther: A Study in Psychoanalysis and History*. London: Faber & Faber.

Euben, R. L. 1999 *Enemy in the Mirror: Islamic Fundamentalism and the Limits of Modern Rationalism*. Princeton NJ: Princeton University Press.

Evans, J., Hills, J., Hunt, K. and Meehan, E., eds 1986 *Feminism and Political Theory*. London: Sage.

Exposito, J. L. 1983 *The Islamic Threat: Myth or Reality*. Oxford: Oxford University Press.

Fanon, F. 1965 *The Wretched of the Earth*. Harmondsworth: Penguin.

Fellner, G. 2005 *Life of an Anarchist: The Alexander Berkman Reader*. New York: Seven Stories Press.

Femia, J. 1981 *Gramsci's Political Thought*. Oxford: Clarendon Press.

Feuer, L. S. 1975 *Ideology and the Ideologists*. Oxford: Blackwell.

Feyerabend, P. 1975 *Against Method: Outline of an Anarchistic Theory of Knowledge*. London: New Left Books.

Fichte, J. G. 1979 *Addresses to the German Nation*. Westport, Conn.: Greenwood Press.

Figes, E. 1970 *Patriarchal Attitudes*. London: Macmillan.

Figgis, J. N. 1922 *The Divine Right of Kings*. Cambridge: Cambridge University Press.

Finley, M. I. 1973 *The Ancient Economy*. London: Chatto & Windus.

Firestone, S. 1971 *The Dialectic of Sex*. New York: Bantam Books.

Flax, J. 1986 'Gender as a Problem in and for Feminist Theory', *American Studies*, 31.

Flax, J. 1990 *Thinking Fragments*. Berkeley: University of California Press.

Forbes, I., ed. 1986 *Market Socialism: Whose Choice?* Fabian Tract 516. London: Fabian Society.

Forbes, I. and Smith, S., eds 1983 *Politics and Human Nature*. London: Pinter.

Forjacs, D., ed. 1986 *Rethinking Italian Fascism: Capitalism, Populism and Culture*. London: Lawrence & Wishart.

Fourier, C. 1996 *The Theory of the Four Movements*. Cambridge: Cambridge University Press.

Fowler, R. B. 1972 'The Anarchist Tradition of Political Thought'. *Western Political Quarterly*, 25.

Fox, M. 1983 *Original Blessing*. Santa Fe, New Mexico: Bear and Co.

Fox, W. 1984 'Deep Ecology: A New Philosophy for Our Time?', *The Ecologist*, 14.

Fox, W. 1986 *Approaching Deep Ecology: A Response to Richard Sylvan's Critique of Deep Ecology*. Hobart: University of Tasmania.

Fox, W. 1990 *Toward a Transpersonal Ecology: Developing a New Foundation for Environmentalism*. London and Boston: Shambala.

Frankel, J. 1970 *National Interest*. London: Pall Mall.

Franks, B. 2006 *Rebel Alliances*. New York: AK Press.

Fraser, N. 1997 *Justice Interruptus: Critical Reflections on the 'Postsocialist' Conception*. London: Routledge.

Fraser, N. and Honneth, A. 2003 *Redistribution or Recognition? A Political-Philosophical Exchange*. London: Verso.

Frazer, E. and Lacey, N. 1993 *The Politics of Community: A Feminist Critique of the Liberal-Comunitarian Debate*. New York: Harvester Wheatsheaf.

Freeden, M. 1978 *New Liberalism: An Ideology of Social Reform*. Oxford: Clarendon Press.

Freeden, M. 1986 *Liberalism Divided: A Study in British Political Thought 1914–1939*. Oxford: Clarendon Press.

Freeden, M. 1996 *Ideologies and Political Theory*. Oxford: Clarendon.

Freeden, M. 1998 'Stormy Relationships: Ideologies and Politics', *Journal of Political Ideologies*, 3,1.

Freeden, M. 1999 'The Ideology of New Labour' *Political Quarterly*, 70.

Freeden, M. 2003 *Ideology: A Short Introduction*. Oxford: Oxford University Press.

Freeden, M. 2005 *Liberal Languages: Ideological Imaginations and Twentieth-Century Progressive Thought*. Princeton, NJ: Princeton University Press.

Freeden, M. ed 2001 *Reassessing Political Ideologies: The Durability of Dissent*. London: Routledge.

Friedan, B. 1965 *The Feminine Mystique*. Harmondsworth: Penguin.

Friedrich C. J. 1972 'The Anarchist Controversy over Violence'. *Zeitschrift für Politik*, 19.

Friedrich, C. J. and Brzezinski, Z. K. 1966 *Totalitarian Dictatorship and Autocracy*, 2nd edn. New York: Praeger.

Fromm, E. 1979 *To Have or To Be?* London: Sphere Books.

Fukuyama, Francis 1989 'The End of History?' *National Interest*, Summer.

Galston, W. 1991 *Liberal Purposes: Goods, Virtues and Diversity in the Liberal State*. Cambridge: Cambridge University Press.

Gatens, M. 1996 *Imaginary Bodies: Ethics, Power and Corporeality*. London: Routledge.

Gaus, G. F. 1983 *The Modern Liberal Theory of Man*. London: Croom Helm.

Gaus, G. F. 2000 *Political Concepts and Political Theories*. Boulder, Colo.: Westview Press.

Gay, P. 1952 *The Dilemma of Democratic Socialism*. New York: Columbia University Press.

Geertz, C. 1993 *The Interpretation of Cultures*. London: HarperCollins.

Gellner, E. 1983 *Nations and Nationalism*. Oxford: Blackwell.

Gentile, E. 1996 *The Sacralization of Politics in Fascist Italy*. Cambridge, Mass.: Harvard University Press.

Gentile, E. 2006 *Politics as Religion*. Princeton, N.J.: Princeton University Press.

Gentile, G. 1928 'The Philosophic Basis of Fascism', *Foreign Affairs*, VI, 2.

Gentile, G. 1960 *The Genesis and Structure of Society*. Urbana and London: University of Illinois Press.

Gentile, G. 2004 *Origins and Doctrine of Fascism*. New York: Transaction Books.

Geoghegan, V. 1987 *Utopianism and Marxism*. London: Methuen.

Geoghegan, V. 1996 'Has Socialism a Future?' *Journal of Political Ideologies*, 1, 3.

Geoghegan, V. 2004 'Ideology and Utopia', *Journal of Political Ideologies*, 9, 2.

Germino, D. 1967 *Beyond Ideology: The Revival of Political Theory*. Chicago: University of Chicago Press.

Gewirth, A. 1965 *Political Philosophy*. New York and London: Macmillan Collier.

Giddens, A. 1994 *Beyond Left and Right: The Future of Radical Politics*. Cambridge: Polity Press.

Giddens, A. 1998 *The Third Way: The Renewal of Social Democracy*. Cambridge: Polity Press.

Giddens, A. 2001 *The Third Way and its Critics*. Cambridge: Polity Press.

Gilbert, P. 1998 *The Philosophy of Nationalism*. Oxford: Westview Press.

Gilligan, C. 1982 *In a Different Voice*. Cambridge, Mass.: Harvard University Press.

Gillroy, J. M. 2002 *Justice and Nature: Kantian Philosophy, Environmental Policy and the Law*. Washington: Georgetown University Press

Gilmour, I. 1977 *Inside Right: A Study of Conservatism*. London: Quartet Books.

Gilmour, I. 1983 *Britain Can Work*. Oxford: Martin Robertson.

Godwin, W. 1976 *Enquiry Concerning Political Justice*. Harmondsworth: Penguin.

Goldman, E. 2006 *Living my Life*. Harmondsworth: Penguin Classics.

Goldsmith, E. 1972 *A Blueprint for Survival*. Harmondsworth: Penguin.

Goldsmith, E. and Hildyard, N., eds 1986 *Green Britain or Industrial Wasteland*. Cambridge: Polity Press.

Goodin, R.E. 1992 *Green Political Theory*. Cambridge: Polity Press.

Goodway, D., ed. 1989 *For Anarchism: History, Theory and Practice*. London: Routledge.

Goodway, D., ed. 1994 *Herbert Read: A One-Man Manifesto and Other Writings*. London: Freedom Press.

Goodwin, B. 1978 *Social Science and Utopia*. Brighton: Harvester.

Goodwin, B and Taylor, K. 1982 *The Politics of Utopia: A Study in Theory and Practice*. London: Hutchinson.

Gorz, A. 1982 *Farewell to the Working Class: An Essay of Post-Industrial Socialism*. London: Pluto.

Graham, D. and Clarke, P. 1986 *The New Enlightenment: The Rebirth of Liberalism*. London: Macmillan.

Graham, G. 1986 *Politics in Its Place*. Oxford: Clarendon Press.

Graham, K. 2008 *Anarchism: A Documentary History of Libertarian Ideas, Vol. 2: The Anarchist Current (1939–2007)*. New York: Black Rose Press.

Gramsci, A. 1986 *Selections from the Prison Notebooks*. London: Lawrence & Wishart.

Grand, A. de 1989 *Italian Fascism: Its Origin and Development*, 2nd edn. Lincoln and London: University of Nebraska Press.

Gray, J. N. 1986a *Liberalism*. Milton Keynes: Open University Press.

Gray, J. N. 1986b *Hayek on Liberty*, 2nd edn. Oxford: Blackwell.

Gray, J. N. 2000 *The Two Faces of Liberalism*. Cambridge: Polity Press.

Gray, J. N. 2004 *Al Qaeda and What It Means to be Modern*. London: Faber & Faber.

Gray, J. N. 2007 *Black Mass: Apocalyptic Religion and the Death of Utopia*. London: Allen Lane.

Green, D. 1987 *The New Right*. Brighton: Wheatsheaf.

Green, E. H. H. 1995 *The Crisis of Conservatism: The Politics, Economics and Ideology of the British Conservative Party, 1880–1914*. London: Routledge

Green, T. H. 1883 *The Prolegomena to Ethics*, ed. A. C. Bradley. Oxford: Clarendon Press.

Green, T. H. 1888 *Works of T. H. Green*, Vol. 3. London: Longmans.

Greenberg, S. B. 1980 *Race and State in Capitalist Development: A Comparative Perspective*. New Haven: Yale University Press.

Greenfeld, L. 1992 *Nationalism: Five Roads to Modernity*. Cambridge, Mass.: Harvard University Press.

Greenleaf, W. H. 1966 *Oakeshott's Philosophical Politics*. London: Longmans.

Greenleaf, W. H. 1983 *The British Political Tradition: The Ideological Heritage*, Vol. 2. London: Methuen.

Greer, G. 1971 *The Female Eunuch*. London: Paladin.

Gregor, J. A. 1974 *Interpretations of Fascism*. Morristown, NJ: General Learning Press.

Gregor, J. A. 2001 *Giovanni Gentile: Philosopher of Fascism*. New York: Transaction Books.

Griffin, R. 1983 'Was Nazism Fascist?' *Modern Historical Review*, 5, 1

Griffin, R. 1991 *The Nature of Fascism*. London: Pinter.

Griffin, R., ed. 1995 *Fascism*. Oxford: Oxford University Press.

Griffin, R., ed. 1998 *International Fascism: Theories, Causes and the New Consensus*. London: Arnold.

Griffin, R. 2007 *Modernism and Fascism: The Sense of Beginning under Mussolini and Hitler*. London: Palgrave.

Griffin, S. 1978 *Woman and Nature: The Roaring Inside Her*. London: Women's Press.

Griffiths, R. 1978 'Anti-Capitalism and the French Extra-Parliamentary Right, 1870–1940', *Journal of Contemporary History*, 13, 4.

Grosby, S. 2005 *Nationalism: A Very Short Introduction*. Oxford: Oxford University Press.

Guérin, D. 1970 *Anarchism*. New York and London: Monthly Review Press.

Guérin, D., ed. 2005 *No Gods, No Masters: An Anthology of Anarchism*. New York: AK Press.

Guibernau, M. 1995 *Nationalism: The Nation State and Nationalism in the Twentieth Century*. Cambridge: Polity Press.

Gutman, A., ed. 1994 *Multiculturalism: Examining the Politics of Recognition*, Princeton, NJ: Princeton University Press.

Haakonssen, K., ed. 1988 *Traditions of Liberalism*. Canberra: Centre for Independent Studies.

Habermas, J. 1979 *Communication and the Evolution of Society*. London: Heinemann.

Habermas, J. 1996 *On the Logic of the Social Sciences*. Cambridge, Mass.: MIT Press.

Hacker, A. 1961 *Political Theory: Philosophy, Ideology, Science* New York: Macmillan.

Hadji Haider, H. 2006 *A Theory of Religious Democracy*. London: Islamic College for Advanced Studies Press.

Haeckel, E. 1929 *The Riddle of the Universe*. London: Watts & Co.

Hailwood, S. A. 2003 *How to be a Green Liberal*. London: Acumen Press.

Halifax, Marquess of 1969 *Complete Works*. Harmondsworth: Penguin.

Hall, J. A. 1988 *Liberalism*. London: Paladin, Grafton Books.

Hall, S. and Jacques, M., eds 1983 *The Politics of Thatcherism*. London: Lawrence & Wishart.

Hallowell, J. H. 1946 *The Decline of Liberalism as an Ideology*. London: Kegan Paul, Trench & Trubner.

Hamilton, Malcolm B. 1987 'The Elements of Ideology'. *Political Studies*. XXXV.

Hammond, P. E. 1985 *The Sacred in a Secular Age*. Berkeley: University of California Press.

Hampsher-Monk, I. 1987 *The Political Philosophy of Edmund Burke*. London: Longman.

Hannaford, I. 1996 *Race: The History of an Idea in the West*. Baltimore: Johns Hopkins Press.

Hardin, G. 1968 'The Tragedy of the Commons', *Science*, 162.

Harding, S. 2003 *The Feminist Standpoint Theory Reader: Intellectual and Political Controversies*. London: Routledge.

Hardt, M. and Negri, A. 2000 *Empire*. Cambridge, Mass.: Harvard University Press.

Hardt, M. and Negri, A. 2006 *Multitude: War and Democracy in the Age of Empire*. Harmondsworth: Penguin.

Harris, N. 1972 *Competition and the Corporate Society: British Conservatives, the State and Industry 1945–1964*. London: Methuen.

Hartz, L. 1955 *The Liberal Tradition in America*. New York: Harcourt, Brace & World.

Harvey, D. 2005 *A Brief History of Neoliberalism*. Oxford: Oxford University Press

Hastings, A. 1997 *The Construction of Nationhood: Ethnicity, Religion and Nationalism*. Cambridge: Cambridge University Press.

Hawkesworth, M. 1988 'Feminist Rhetoric', *Political Theory*, 16, 3.

Hawkesworth, M. and Kogan, M., eds, 2004 *Encyclopaedia of Government and Politics*. London: Routledge.

Hayek, F. A. 1944 *The Road to Serfdom*. London: Routledge & Sons.

Hayek, F. A. 1960 *The Constitution of Liberty*. London: Routledge & Kegan Paul.

Hayek, F. A. 1978 *New Studies on Philosophy, Politics, Economics and the History of Ideas*. London: Routledge & Kegan Paul.

Hayek, F. A. 1982 *Law, Legislation and Liberty*. London: Routledge & Kegan Paul.

Hayes, C. J. 1926 *Essays on Nationalism*. New York: Macmillan.

Hayes, C. J. 1949 *The Historical Evolution of Modern Nationalism*. New York: Macmillan.

Hayward, T. 2005 *Constitutional Environmental Politics*. Oxford: Oxford University Press.

Head, B. W. 1980 'The Origins of "Idéologue" and "Idéologie"', *Studies on Voltaire and the Eighteenth Century*, 183.

Head, B. W. 1985 *Ideology and Social Science: Destutt de Tracy and French Liberalism*. Dordrecht: Martinus Nijhoff.

Hearn, J. S. 2006 *Rethinking Nationalism: A Critical Introduction*. London: Palgrave.

Hearnshaw, F. J. C., ed. 1949 *Social and Political Ideas of Some Representative Thinkers of the Age of Reaction and Reconstruction*. Cambridge: W. Heffer.

Heilperin, M. A. 1960 *Studies in Economic Nationalism*. Geneva: Libraire E. Droz.

Henning, D. H. 2002 *Buddhism and Deep Ecology*. New York: First Books Library.

Herbert, A. 1978 *The Right and Wrong of Compulsion by the State*. Indianapolis: Liberty Classics.

Herder, J. G. 1969 *J. G. Herder on Social and Political Culture*, F. M. Barnard ed. Cambridge: Cambridge University Press.

Hesse M. 1980 *Revolutions and Reconstructions in the Philosophy of Science*. Brighton: Harvester.

Heywood, L. and Drake, J., eds 1997 *Third Wave Agenda*. Minneapolis: University of Minnesota Press.

Hindess, B., ed. 1990 *Reactions to the Right*. London: Routledge.

Hirschman A. O. 1977 *The Passions and the Interests: Political Arguments for Capitalism before Its Triumph*. Princeton, NJ: Princeton University Press.

Hirschman, A. O. 1991 *The Rhetoric of Reaction: Perversity, Futility and Jeopardy*. Cambridge, Mass.: Belknap Press.

Hirschmann, N. 2002 *The Subject of Liberty: Toward a Feminist Theory of Freedom*. Princeton, NJ: Princeton University Press.

Hirst, P. 1988 'Associational Socialism in a Pluralist State', *Journal of Law and Society*, 15, 1.

Hitler, A. 1969 *Mein Kampf*. London: Hutchinson.

Hobhouse, L. T. 1911 *Liberalism*. London: Thornton Butterworth.

Hobhouse, L. T. 1918 *The Metaphysical Theory of the State*. London: Allen & Unwin.

Hobsbawm, E. J. 1977a *The Age of Revolution: Europe 1789–1848*. London: Abacus.

Hobsbawm, E. J. 1977b 'Reflections on Anarchism', in *Revolutionaries: Contemporary Essays*. London: Quartet Books.

Hobsbawm, E. J. 1992 *Nations and Nationalism since 1780: Programme, Myth and Reality*, 2nd edn. Cambridge: Cambridge University Press.

Hobson, J. A. 1909 *The Crisis of Liberalism: New Issues of Democracy*. London: P. S. King.

Hobson, S. G. 1920 *National Guilds and the State*. London: George Bell.

Hogg Q. 1947 *The Case for Conservatism*. Harmondsworth: Penguin.

Holton, B. 1976 *British Syndicalism 1900–1914: Myths and Realities*. London: Pluto Press.

Honderich, T. 1991 *Conservatism*. Harmondsworth: Penguin.

Hoover, K. and Plant, R. 1989 *Conservative Capitalism in Britain and the United States*. London and New York: Routledge.

Hotman, F. 1972 *Francogallia* Cambridge: Cambridge University Press.

Howe, A. and Morgan, C., eds 2006 *Rethinking Nineteenth-Century Liberalism: Richard Cobden Bicentenary Essays*. Aldershot: Ashgate Press.

Hroch, M. 1985 *Social Preconditions of National Revival in Europe: A Comparative Analysis of the Social Composition of Patriotic Groups among Smaller European Nations*. Cambridge: Cambridge University Press.

Hsu, C. L. 2007 *Creating Market Socialism*. Durham, NC: Duke University Press.

Hulme, T. E. 1965 *Speculations*. London: Routledge & Kegan Paul.

Hülsberg, W. 1988 *The German Greens*. London and New York: Verso.

Humboldt, W. von 1969 *The Limits of State Action*. Cambridge: Cambridge University Press.

Hume, D. 1994 *Hume's Political Essays*, ed. Knud Haakonssen. Cambridge: Cambridge University Press.

Humphrey, M. 2000 ' "Nature" in Deep Ecology and Social Ecology: Contesting the Core', *Journal of Political Ideologies*, 5, 2.

Huntington, S. P. 1957 'Conservatism as an Ideology', *American Political Science Review*, 51.

Ignazi, P. 2006 *Extreme Right-Wing Parties in Western Europe*. Oxford: Oxford University Press.

Ionescu G., ed. 1976 *The Political Thought of Saint-Simon*. Oxford: Oxford University Press.

Irigaray, L. 1985 *This Sex Which Is Not One*. New York: Cornell University Press.

Jackson, B. 2003 'Equality or Nothing? Social Justice on the British Left, c.1911–31', *Journal of Political Ideologies*, 8, 1.

Jaggar, A. 1983 *Feminist Politics and Human Nature*. Brighton: Harvester.

James, W. 1971 *The Varieties of Religious Experience*. London: Collins.

Jay, M. 1976 *The Dialectical Imagination: A History of the Frankfurt School and the Institute of Social Research 1923–50*. London: Heinemann.

Jennings, J. R. 1985 *George Sorel: The Character and Development of his Thought*. London: Macmillan.

Jennings, J. R. 1990 *Syndicalism in France*. London: Macmillan.

Jessop, B. and Wheatley, W. eds 1999 *Karl Marx's Social and Political Thought*. London: Routledge.

Johnson, C. H. 1974 *Utopian Communism in France: Cabet and the Icarians 1839–1851*. Ithaca, NY: Cornell University Press.

Johnson, S. and Boswell, J. 1978 *A Journey to the Western Islands of Scotland and The Journal of a Tour to the Hebrides*. Oxford: Oxford University Press.

Joll, J. 1964 *The Anarchists*. Boston: Little, Brown & Co.

Joll, J. 1974 *The Second International 1889–1914*. London: Routledge & Kegan Paul.

Juergensmeyer, M., ed. 2005 *Religion in Global Civil Society*. Oxford and New York: Oxford University Press.

Jung, C. G. 1967 *Memories, Dreams, Reflections*. London: Collins.

Kamenka, E., ed. 1976 *Nationalism: The Nature and Evolution of an Idea*. London: Edward Arnold.

Kant, I. 1974 *Anthropology from a Pragmatic Point of View*. The Hague: Martinus Nijhoff.

Kariel, H. S. 1990 'The Feminist Subject Spinning in the Postmodern Project', *Political Theory*, 18, 2.

Kateb, G. 1968 *Political Theory: Its Nature and Uses*. New York: St Martin's Press.

Katz, E. 1989 'Environmental Ethics: A Selected Annotated Bibliography 1983–1987', *Research in Philosophy and Technology*, 9.

Kedourie, E. 1974 *Nationalism*, 2nd edn. London: Hutchinson University Library.

Keens-Soper, M. 1989 'The Liberal State and Nationalism in Post-War Europe', *History of European Ideas*, 10, 6.

Kekes, J. 1998 *The Case for Conservatism*. Ithaca, NY: Cornell University Press.

Kellas, J. G. 1991 *The Politics of Nationalism and Ethnicity*. New York: St Martin's Press.

Keller, E. F. 1985 *Reflections on Science and Gender*. New Haven: Yale University Press.

Kelly, A. 1982 *Mikhail Bakunin: A Study in the Psychology and Politics of Utopianism*. Oxford: Clarendon Press.

Kelly, P. 2004 *Liberalism*. Cambridge: Polity Press.

Kennedy, R. E. 1979 ' "Ideology" from Destutt de Tracy to Marx', *Journal of the History of Ideas*, 40.

Kenny, M. 1995 *The First New Left: British Intellectuals after Stalin*. London: Lawrence & Wishart.

Kenny, M. 2000 'Socialism and the Romantic "Self": The Case of Edward Thompson', *Journal of Political Ideologies*, 5, 1.

Keohane, N. O., Rosaldo, M. Z. and Gelpi, B. C., eds 1982 *Feminist Theory: A Critique of Ideology*. Brighton: Harvester.

Kershaw, I. 1985 *The Nazi Dictatorship*. London: Arnold

Kershaw, I. 1998–2000 *Hitler*, 2 vols. London: Allen Lane.

Khomeini, Ayatollah R. 1979 *Islamic Government: Governance of Jurisprudent*. Honolulu, Hawaii: University Press of the Pacific.

King, D. 1987 *The New Right*. London: Macmillan.

Kirk, R. 1967 *The Conservative Mind*. Chicago: Henry Regnery.

Kirk, R. 1982 *The Portable Conservative Reader*. Harmondsworth: Penguin.

Kitchen, M. 1976 *Fascism*. London: Macmillan.

Kitching, G. 1983 *Rethinking Socialism*. London: Methuen.

Kloppenberg, J. T. 2000 *The Virtues of Liberalism*. Oxford: Oxford University Press.

Knabb, K., ed. 2007 *Situationist International Anthology*. London: Bureau of Public Secrets.

Koenigsberg, R. A. 1975 *Hitler's Ideology: A Study in Psychoanalytic Sociology*. New York: Library of Social Services.

Kohn, H. 1945 *The Idea of Nationalism: A Study in Its Origins and Background*. New York: Macmillan.

Kolakowski 1981 *Main Currents of Marxism*, 3 vols. Oxford: Oxford University Press.

Kollontai, A. 1977 *Selected Writings*. London: Allison & Busby.

Kovel, J. 2007 *The Enemy of Nature: The End of Capitalism or the End of the World*. New York: Zed Books.

Kristol, I. 1970 'When Virtue Loses All Her Loveliness', *The Public Interest*, 21.

Kropotkin, P. 1903 *The State: Its Historic Mission*. London: Freedom Press.

Kropotkin, P. 1914 *Mutual Aid: A Factor in Evolution*. Boston: Porter Sargent.

Kropotkin, P. 1924 *Ethics: Origin and Development*. London: G. Harrap and Co. Ltd.

Kropotkin, P. 1968 *The Conquest of Bread*. New York: Benjamin Blom.

Kropotkin, P. 1974 *Fields, Factories and Workshops Tomorrow*. London: Allen & Unwin.

Kuhn, A. and Wolpe, A., eds 1978 *Feminism and Materialism*. London: Routledge & Kegan Paul.

Kuhn, T. S. 1970 *The Structure of Scientific Revolutions*, 2nd edn. Chicago: University of Chicago Press.

Kumar, K. 1991 *Utopianism*. Milton Keynes: Open University Press.

Kumar, K. 2006 'Ideology and Sociology: Reflections on Karl Mannheim's *Ideology and Utopia*', *Journal of Political Ideologies*, 11, 2.

Kymlicka, W. 1991 *Liberalism, Community and Culture*. Oxford: Clarendon Press.

Kymlicka, W. 1995a *Multicultural Citizenship: A Liberal Theory of Minority Rights*. Oxford: Clarendon Press.

Kymlicka, W. ed. 1995b *The Rights of Minority Cultures*. Oxford: Clarendon Press.

Kymlicka, W. 2001 *Contemporary Political Philosophy: An Introduction*, 2nd edn. Oxford: Clarendon Press.

Laclau, E. and Mouffe, C. 1985 *Hegemony and Socialist Strategy: Towards a Radical Democratic Politics*. London: Verso.

Laclau, E. 2006 'Ideology and Post-Marxism', *Journal of Political Ideologies*, 11, 2.

Lakatos, I. and Musgrave, A. 1970 *Criticism and the Growth of Knowledge*. Cambridge: Cambridge University Press.

Landauer, G. 1978 *For Socialism*. St Louis: Telos Press.

Laqueur, W., ed. 1979 *Fascism: A Reader's Guide*. Harmondsworth: Penguin.

Larrain, J. 1979 *The Concept of Ideology*. London: Hutchinson.

Laski, H. J. 1936 *The Rise of European Liberalism*. London: Allen & Unwin.

Lawrence, B. 1999 *Defenders of God: The Fundamentalist Revolt against the Modern Age*. San Francisco: Harper & Row.

Lawson, H. 1985 *Reflexivity*. London: Hutchinson.

Le Grand, J. and Estrin, S., eds 1989 *Market Socialism*. Oxford: Clarendon.

Lebrun, R. A. 1965 *Throne and Altar*. Ottawa: University of Ottawa Press.

Leier, M. 2006 *Bakunin: The Creative Passion*. London: Thomas Dunne Books.

Leighton, D. 2004 *The Greenian Moment*. Exeter: Imprint Academic.

Lenin, V. I. 1988 *What Is to be Done?* Harmondsworth: Penguin.

Leopold, A. 1968 *A Sand County Almanac*. New York: Oxford University Press.

Leopold, D. 2007 *The Young Karl Marx: German Philosophy, Modern Politics and Human Flourishing*. Cambridge: Cambridge University Press.

Levitas, R. ed. 1986 *The Ideology of the New Right*. Cambridge: Polity Press.

Lewis, B. 1992 'Muslims, Christians, and Jews: The Dream of Coexistence', *New York Review of Books* 39, 6.

Lichtheim, G. 1969 *The Origins of Socialism*. London: Weidenfeld & Nicolson.

Lichtheim, G. 1975 *A Short History of Socialism*. London: Fontana, Collins.

Lipset S. M. 1969 *Political Man*. London: Heinemann.

List, F. 1966 *The National System of Political Economy*. New York: Augustus M. Kelley.

Lloyd, G. 1984 *The Man of Reason*. London: Methuen.

Lloyd, M. 2007 *Judith Butler: From Norms to Politics*. Cambridge: Polity Press.

Lomberg, B. 2001 *The Skeptical Environmentalist*. Cambridge: Cambridge University Press.

Lovell, T., ed. 1990 *British Feminist Thought: A Reader*. Oxford: Blackwell.

Lovelock, J. 1979 *Gaia*. Oxford: Oxford University Press.

Lovelock, J. 2007 *The Revenge of Gaia*. Harmondsworth: Penguin.

Lowe, P. and Goyder, J., eds 1983 *Environmental Groups in Politics*. London: George Allen & Unwin.

Lukács, G. 1968 *History and Class Consciousness*. London: Merlin Press.

Lukes, S. 1985 *Marxism and Morality*. Oxford: Clarendon Press.

Lyotard, J.-F. 1984 *The Postmodern Condition*. Minneapolis: University of Minnesota Press.

Lyttelton, A. 1987 *The Seizure of Power: Fascism in Italy 1919–1929*, 2nd edn. London: Weidenfeld & Nicolson.

Lyttelton, A., ed. 1973 *Italian Fascisms: From Pareto to Gentile*. London: Jonathan Cape.

McAuley, D. 2005 'The Ideology of Osama Bin Laden: Nation, Tribe and World Economy', *Journal of Political Ideologies*, 10, 3.

McBriar, A. M. 1962 *Fabian Socialism and English Politics 1884–1918*. Cambridge: Cambridge University Press.

MacCallum, G. 1967 'Negative and Positive Freedom', *The Philosophical Review*, LXXVI.

McClelland, J. S. ed. 1971 *The French Right: From de Maistre to Maurras*. London: Jonathan Cape.

McCloskey, H. J. 1965–6 'The Problem of Liberalism', *Review of Metaphysics*, 19.

MacCormick, N. 1982 *Legal Rights and Social Democracy: Essays in Legal and Political Philosophy*. Oxford: Clarendon Press.

McCormick, J. P. 1999 *Carl Schmitt's Critique of Contemporary Liberalism*. Cambridge: Cambridge University Press.

MacGregor, S. 2007 *Mothering Earth: Ecological Citizenship and the Politics of Care*. Vancouver: University of British Columbia Press.

MacIntyre, A. 1971 *Against the Self-Images of the Age*. London: Duckworth.

MacIntyre, A. 1981 *After Virtue*. London: Duckworth.

MacIntyre, A. 1988 *Whose Justice? Which Rationality?* London: Duckworth.

MacIntyre, A. 1990 *Three Rival Versions of Moral Enquiry*. London: Duckworth.

Mack Smith, D. 1983 *Mussolini*. London: Paladin Books.

Mackay, F. 2001 *Love and Politics: Woman and Politics and the Ethics of Care*. London: Continuum Press.

McKim, R. and McMahan, J., eds 1997 *The Morality of Nationalism*. Oxford: Oxford University Press.

McLellan, D. 1977 *Engels*. London: Fontana.

McLellan, D. 1980 *Marxism after Marx*. London: Macmillan.

McLellan, D. 1986 *Ideology*. Milton Keynes: Open University Press.

Macmillan, C. 1982 *Women, Reason and Philosophy*. Oxford: Blackwell.

Macmillan, H. 1966 *The Middle Way*. London: Macmillan.

McNay, L. 1999 'Gender and Narrative Identity'. *Journal of Political Ideologies*, 4, 3.

McNay, L. 2000 *Gender and Agency: Reconfiguring the Subject in Feminist and Social Theory*. Cambridge: Polity Press.

McNay, L. 2003 'Out of the Orrery? Situating Language', *Journal of Political Ideologies*, 8, 2

McNay, L. 2007 *Against Recognition*. Cambridge: Polity Press.

Macpherson, C. B. 1962 *The Political Theory of Possessive Individualism*. Oxford: Oxford University Press.

Macpherson, C. B. 1973 *Democratic Theory: Essays in Retrieval*. Oxford: Oxford University Press.

Macpherson, C. B. 1980 *Burke*. Oxford: Oxford University Press.

Maistre, J. de 1974 *Considerations on France*. Montreal and London: McGill-Queens University Press.

Malatesta, E. 1980 *Anarchy*. London: Freedom Press.

Malatesta, E. 1984 *Malatesta: His Life and Ideas*, ed. V. Richards. London: Freedom Press.

Mallock. W. H. 1901 *Aristocracy and Evolution*. London: Macmillan.

Mannheim, K. 1960 *Ideology and Utopia*. London: Routledge & Kegan Paul.

Mannheim, K. 1986 *Conservatism: A Contribution to the Sociology of Knowledge*. London: Routledge & Kegan Paul.

Manning, D. 1976 *Liberalism*. London: Dent.

Manning, D., ed. 1980 *The Form of Ideology*. London: Allen & Unwin.

Manuel, F. E. 1956 *The New World of Henri Saint-Simon*. Cambridge, Mass.: Harvard University Press.

Manuel, F. E. 1962 *The Prophets of Paris*. Cambridge, Mass.: Harvard University Press.

Manuel, F. E. and Manuel, F. P. 1979 *Utopian Thought in the Western World*. Oxford: Blackwell.

Marcuse, H. 1973 *Reason and Revolution*, 2nd edn. London: Routledge & Kegan Paul.

Margalit, E. and Margalit, A. eds 1991 *Isaiah Berlin: A Celebration*. London: Hogarth Press.

Marshall, P. 1993 *Demanding the Impossible: A History of Anarchism*. London: Fontana.

Martinez-Alier, J. 2003 *The Environmentalism of the Poor: A Study of Ecological Conflicts and Valuation*. Cheltenham: Edward Elgar.

Marty, M. E. and Appleby, R. S., eds 1991 *Fundamentalism Observed: The Fundamentalism Project*, Vol. 1. Chicago: University of Chicago Press.

Marty, M. E. and Appleby, R. S., eds 1993a *Fundamentalisms and Society: Reclaiming the Sciences, the Family, and Education*, Vol. 2. Chicago: University of Chicago Press.

Marty, M. E. and Appleby, R. S., eds 1993b *Fundamentalisms and the State: Remaking Polities, Economies, and Militance*, Vol. 3. Chicago: University of Chicago Press.

Marty, M. E. and Appleby, R. S., eds 1994 *Accounting for Fundamentalisms: The Dynamic Character of Movements*, Vol. 4. Chicago: University of Chicago Press.

Marty, M. E. and Appleby, R. S., eds 1995 *Fundamentalisms Comprehended*, Vol. 5. Chicago: University of Chicago Press.

Marx, K. 1972 *Early Texts*. Oxford: Blackwell.

Marx, K. and Engels, F. 1967 *The Communist Manifesto*. Harmondsworth: Penguin.

Marx, K. and Engels, F., eds 1968 *Selected Writings*. London: Lawrence & Wishart.

Marx, K. and Engels, F. 1970 *The German Ideology*, ed. C. J. Arthur. London: Lawrence & Wishart.

Marx, K. and Engels, F. 1974 *Marx and Engels on Colonialism*. Moscow: Progress Publishers.

Mascia-Lees, F. and Sharpe, P. 2000 *Taking a Stand in a Postfeminist World*. New York: State University of New York Press.

Mattson, P. 2002 *Socialism in the Twenty-First Century: The Way Forward for Anti-Capitalism*. London: Socialist Books.

May, T. 1994 *The Political Philosophy of Poststructuralist Anarchism*. University Park: Pennsylvania State University Press.

Mayall, J. 1990 *Nationalism and International Society*. Cambridge: Cambridge University Press.

Mayer, M. 2008 *Anarchism for Beginners*. London: Steerforth Press.

Mazzini, G. 1924 *Essays on the Duties of Man*. London: J. M. Dent.

Meadows, D. 1972 *The Limits to Growth*. London: Earth Island.

Mendilow, J. 1996 'What is Conservatism? Some Signposts in the Wilderness', *Journal of Political Ideologies*, 1, 3.

Meinecke, F. 1970 *Cosmopolitanism and the Nation State*. Princeton, NJ: Princeton University Press.

Mill, J. S. 1962 *Utilitarianism and Other Essays*. London: Dent.

Mill, J. S. 1989 'The Subjection of Women' and 'Chapters on Socialism', in *On Liberty and Other Writings*, ed. Stefan Collini. Cambridge: Cambridge University Press.

Mill, J. S. 1874 *Three Essays on Religion*. London: Longman, Green, Reader and Dyer.

Miller, D. 1984 *Anarchism*. London: Dent.

Miller, D. 1987 'Marx, Communism and Markets', *Political Theory*, 15, 2.

Miller, D. 1990 *Market, State and Community: Theoretical Foundations to Market Socialism*. Oxford: Clarendon Press.

Miller, D. 1995 *On Nationality*. Oxford: Clarendon Press.

Miller, D. and Seidentop, L., eds 1983 *The Nature of Political Theory*. Oxford: Clarendon Press.

Miller, S. and Potthoff, H. 1986 *A History of German Social Democracy: From 1848 to the Present*. Leamington Spa and New York: Berg.

Miller Lane, B. and Rupp, L. J., eds 1978 *Nazi Ideology Before 1933: A Documentation*. Manchester: Manchester University Press.

Millett, K. 1970 *Sexual Politics*. London: Virago.

Minogue, K. 1967 *Nationalism*. London: Batsford.

Minteer, B. and Taylor, B. P., eds 2002 *Democracy and the Claims of Nature*. New York: Rowman & Littlefield.

Mises, L. von 2005 *Liberalism: The Classical Tradition*. Indianapolis: Liberty Fund Inc.

Mitchell, J. 1974 *Psychoanalysis and Feminism*. Harmondsworth: Penguin.

Mitchell, J. and Oakley, A., eds 1986 *What is Feminism?* Oxford: Blackwell.

Mohany Chandra T., 2003 *Feminism without Borders: Decolonizing Theory, Practicing Solidarity*. Durham, NC: Duke University Press.

Moi, T., ed. 1987 *French Feminist Thought: A Reader*. Oxford: Blackwell.

Moore, B., Jr 1967 *Social Origins of Dictatorship and Democracy*. London: Allen Lane.

Moore, M., ed. 1998 *National Self-Determination and Secession*. Oxford: Oxford University Press.

Morgan K. O. 1975 'Socialism and Syndicalism: The Welsh Miners Debate 1912', *Bulletin of the Society for the Study of Labour History*, 30.

Morgan, P. 2002 *Fascism in Europe 1919–1945*. London: Routledge.

Morrow, J. 1990 *Coleridge's Political Thought: Morality, Property and the Limits of Traditional Discourse*. London: Macmillan.

Morton, A. L. 1962 *The Life and Ideas of Robert Owen*. London: Lawrence & Wishart.

Mosse, G. L. 1966 *The Crisis of German Ideology: Intellectual Origins of the Third Reich*. London: Weidenfeld & Nicolson.

Mosse, G. L. 1978a *Nazism: A Historical and Comparative Analysis of National Socialism*. Oxford: Blackwell.

Mosse, G. L. 1978b *Towards the Final Solution: A History of European Racism*. New York: Howard Fertig.

Mudde, C. 2002 *The Ideology of the Extreme Right*. Manchester: Manchester University Press.

Muirhead, J. H. 1954 *Coleridge as Philosopher*. London: Allen & Unwin.

Mulhall, S. and Swift, A. 1996 *Liberals and Communitarians*, 2nd edn Oxford: Blackwell.

Muller, J. Z. 1997 *Conservatism: An Anthology of Social and Political Thought from David Hume to the Present*. Princeton, NJ: Princeton University Press.

Naess, A. 1973 'The Shallow and the Deep, Long-range Ecology Movement: A Summary', *Inquiry*, 16.

Naess, A. 1989 *Ecology, Community and Lifestyle*. Cambridge: Cambridge University Press.

Nairn, T. 1977 *The Breakup of Britain*. London: New Left Books.

Nash, K. 1997 'The Feminist Critique of Liberal Individualism as Masculinist', *Journal of Political Ideologies*, 2, 1.

Neocleous, M. 1997 *Fascism*. Milton Keynes: Open University Press.

Nettler, R. 1996 'Guidelines for the Islamic Community: Sayyid Qutb's Political Interpretation of the Qur'an', *Journal of Political Ideologies*, 1, 2.

Neumann, F. L. 1942 *Behemoth: The Structure and Practice of National Socialism*. London: Gollancz.

Newey, G. 2001 'Philosophy, Politics and Contestability', *Journal of Political Ideologies*, 6, 3.

Newman, M. 2005 *Socialism: A Very Short Introduction*. Oxford: Oxford University Press.

Newman, S. 2007 *From Bakunin to Lacan: Anti-Authoritarianism and the Dislocation of Power*. New York: Lexington Books.

Nicholls, D. 1994 *Deity and Domination: Images of God and the State in the 19th and 20th Centuries*. London and New York: Routledge.

Nicholson, L. 1989 *Feminism/Postmodernism (Thinking Gender)*. London: Routledge.

Nimni, E. 1991 *Marxism and Nationalism: Theoretical Origins and Spread of Nationalism*. London: Pluto Press.

Nisbet, R. A. 1970 *The Sociological Tradition*. London: Heinemann.

Nisbet, R. A. 1986 *Conservatism*. Milton Keynes: Open University Press.

Noble, D. 1978 'Conservatism in the USA', *Journal of Contemporary History*, 13, 4.

Nock, A. J. 1946 *Our Enemy the State*. Caldwell, Idaho: Caxton.

Nolte, E. 1969 *Three Faces of Fascism: Action Française, Italian Fascism and National Socialism*. New York: Mentor Books.

Norton, P. and Aughey, A. 1981 *Conservatives and Conservatism*. London: Temple Smith.

Nove, A. 1983 *The Economics of Feasible Socialism*. London: Allen & Unwin.

Nozick, R. 1974 *Anarchy, State and Utopia*. Oxford: Blackwell.

Nussbaum, M. 1999a *Sex and Social Justice*. Oxford: Oxford University Press.

Nussbaum, M. 1999b 'The Professor of Parody', *New Republic*, February

Nussbaum, M. 2001 *Women and Development*. Cambridge: Cambridge University Press.

Nussbaum, M. 2006 *Frontiers of Justice: Disability, Nationality, Species Membership*. Cambridge, Mass.: Harvard University Press.

Nussbaum, M. and Glover, J. 1995 *Women, Culture and Development*. Oxford: Clarendon.

Oakeshott, M., ed. 1953 *The Social and Political Doctrines of Contemporary Europe*. Cambridge: Cambridge University Press.

Oakeshott, M. 1962 *Rationalism in Politics and Other Essays*. London and New York: Methuen.

Oelschlaeger, M. 1991 *The Idea of Wilderness*. New Haven: Yale University Press.

Offer, J. 2006 *An Intellectual History of British Social Policy*. Bristol: The Policy Press.

O'Gorman, F. 1973 *Edmund Burke: His Political Philosophy*. London: Allen & Unwin.

O'Gorman, F., ed. 1986 *British Conservatism: Conservative Thought from Burke to Thatcher*. London: Longman.

Okin, S. M. 1979 *Women in Western Political Thought*. Princeton, NJ: Princeton University Press.

Okin, S. M. 1989 *Justice, Gender, and the Family*. New York: Basic Books.

Okin, S. M., Cohen, J., Howard, M. and Nussbaum, M. 1999 *Is Multiculturalism Bad for Women?* Princeton, NJ: Princeton University Press.

Ophuls, W. 1977 *Ecology and the Politics of Scarcity: Prologue to a Political Theory of the Steady State*. San Francisco: W. H. Freeman.

Organski, A. F. 1969 *The Stages of Political Development*. New York: Alfred A. Knopf.

Ortega y Gasset, J. 1972 *The Revolt of the Masses*. London: Allen & Unwin.

O'Sullivan, N. 1976 *Conservatism*. London: Dent.

O'Sullivan, N. 1983 *Fascism*. London: Dent.

O'Sullivan, N., ed. 2000 *Political Theory in Transition*. London: Routledge.

Ott, H. 1994 *Martin Heidegger: A Political Life*. London: Fontana.

Otto, R. 1972 *The Idea of the Holy*. Oxford and New York: Oxford University Press.

Owen, R. 1991 *A New View of Society*, ed. G. Claeys. Harmondsworth: Penguin

Palumbo, M. and Shanahan, W. O., eds 1981 *Nationalism: Essays in Honour of Louis L. Snyder*. Westport, Conn., and London: Greenwood Press.

Parekh, B., ed. 1975 *The Concept of Socialism*. London: Croom Helm.

Parekh, B. 1983 *Marx's Theory of Ideology*. London: Macmillan.

Parel, A., ed. 1983 *Ideology, Philosophy and Politics*. Waterloo, Ont.: Wilfrid Laurier Press.

Passmore, K. 2002 *Fascism: A Very Short Introduction*. Oxford: Oxford University Press.

Pateman, C. 1988 *The Sexual Contract*. Cambridge: Polity Press.

Pateman, C. 1989 *The Disorder of Women*. Cambridge: Polity Press.

Patterson, R. W. K. 1971 *The Nihilist Egoist: Max Stirner*. Oxford: Oxford University Press.

Paul, E. F., Miller, F. D. and Paul, J., eds 1989 *Socialism*. Oxford: Blackwell.

Paxton, R.O. 2005 *The Anatomy of Fascism*. Harmondsworth: Penguin.

Payne, S. G. 1995 *A History of Fascism 1914–1945*. Madison: University of Wisconsin Press.

Pearce, D., Markandya, A. and Barbier, E. B. 1989 *Blueprint for a Green Economy*. London: Earthscan.

Pearson, R. and Williams, G. 1984 *Political Thought and Public Policy in the Nineteenth Century*. London: Longman.

Pennock, J. R. and Chapman, J. W., eds 1978 *Anarchism: Nomos XIX*. New York: New York University Press.

Penty, A. J. 1906 *The Restoration of the Guild System*. London: Swan Sonnenschein.

Pepper, D. 1984 *The Roots of Modern Environmentalism*. London: Croom Helm.

Pepper, D. 1993 *Eco-Socialism: From Deep Ecology to Social Justice*. London: Routledge.

Pérez-Stable, M. 1999 *The Cuban Revolution*, 2nd edn. Oxford: Oxford University Press.

Perlin, T. M., ed. 1979 *Contemporary Anarchism*. New Brunswick, NJ: Transaction Books.

Phillips, A. 1995 *The Politics of Presence*. Oxford: Oxford University Press, 1995.

Phillips, A. 1999 *Which Equalities Matter?* Cambridge: Polity Press.

Pierson, C 1995 *Socialism after Communism: The New Market Socialism*. Cambridge: Polity Press.

Pierson, C. 2005 'Lost Property: What the Third Way Lacks', *Journal of Political Ideologies*, 10, 2.

Pilgrim, J. 1965 'Anarchism and Stateless Societies', *Anarchy*, 58.

Pilkington, A. E. 1976 *Bergson and His Influence: A Reassessment*. Cambridge: Cambridge University Press.

Pimlott, B., ed. 1984 *Fabian Essays in Socialist Thought*. London: Heinemann.

Pirages, D., ed. 1977 *The Sustainable Society: Implications for Limited Growth*. New York and London: Praeger.

Plamenatz, J. 1971 *Ideology*. London: Macmillan.

Plant, R. 1974 *Community and Ideology*. London: Routledge & Kegan Paul.

Plant R. 1984 *Equality, Markets and the State*, Fabian Tract 494. London: Fabian Society.

Plumwood, V. 1993 *Feminism and the Mastery of Nature*. London: Routledge.

Pocock, J. G. A. 1973 *Politics, Language and Time: Essays on Political Thought and History*. London: Methuen.

Pocock, J. G. A. 1985 *Virtue, Commerce, and History*. Cambridge: Cambridge University Press.

Pogge, T. 2002 *World Poverty and Human Rights*. Cambridge: Polity Press.

Pois R. 1986 *National Socialism and the Religion of Nature*. London: Croom Helm.

Popper, K. 1945 *The Open Society and its Enemies*. London: Routledge & Kegan Paul.

Porritt, J. 1984 *Seeing Green: The Politics of Ecology Explained*. Oxford: Blackwell.

Porritt, J. and Winner, D. 1988 *The Coming of the Greens*. London: Fontana, Collins.

Poulantzas, N. 1974 *Fascism and Dictatorship: The Third International and the Problem of Fascism*. London: New Left Books.

Primo de Rivera, J. A. 1972 *Selected Writings*, ed. Hugh Thomas. London: Jonathan Cape.

Primoratz, I., ed. 2002 *Patriotism*. New York: Humanity Books.

Primoratz, I. and Pavkovi., A. eds 2007 *Patriotism: Philosophical and Political Perspectives*. Aldershot: Ashgate.

Proudhon, P.-J. 1970a *What is Property?* New York: Dover.

Proudhon, P.-J. 1970b *Selected Writings*, ed. S. Edwards. London: Macmillan.

Proudhon, P.-J. 1989 *General Idea of Revolution in the Nineteenth Century*. London: Pluto Press.

Pugh, M. 1982 *The Making of Modern British Politics*. Oxford: Blackwell.

Puhle, H.-J. 1978 'Conservatism in Modern German History', *Journal of Contemporary History*, 13, 4.

Pulzer, P. G. J. 1964 *The Rise of Political Anti-Semitism in Germany and Austria*. New York: Wiley.

Purchase, G. 1995 *Anarchism and Ecology*. New York: Black Rose Press.

Quinton, A. 1978 *The Politics of Imperfection*. London: Faber & Faber.

Quinton, A., ed. 1967 *Political Philosophy*. Oxford: Oxford University Press.

Qur'an 1954, ed. M. M. Pickthall. New York: Mentor Books.

Qutb, Sayyid n.d. *Milestones*. Damascus: Dar Al-Ilm.

Rabinow, P. and Sullivan, W. eds, 1987 *Interpretive Social Science: A Second Look*. Berkeley: University of California Press.

Radcliffe-Richards, J. 1982 *The Sceptical Feminist: A Philosophical Enquiry*. Harmondsworth: Penguin.

Rand, A. 1964 *The Virtue of Selfishness: A New Concept of Egoism*. New York: Signet Books, New American Library.

Randall, V. 1991 'Feminism and Political Analysis', *Political Studies*, XXXIX, 3.

Raphael, D. D. 1976 *Problems of Political Philosophy*. London: Macmillan.

Rauschning, H. 1939 *The Revolution of Nihilism: A Warning to the West*. New York: Longmans Green & Co.

Rawls, J. 1971 *A Theory of Justice*. Oxford: Oxford University Press.

Rawls, J. 1993 *Political Liberalism*. New York: Columbia University Press.

Raz, J. 1986 *The Morality of Freedom*. Oxford: Clarendon Press.

Read, H. 1938 *Poetry and Anarchism*. London: Faber and Faber.

Regan, T. 1983 *The Case for Animal Rights*. London: Routledge & Kegan Paul.

Reich, W. 1975 *The Mass Psychology of Fascism*. Harmondsworth: Penguin.

Reiss, H., ed. 1955 *The Political Thought of the German Romantics*. Oxford: Blackwell.

Reynolds, S. 1984 *Kingdoms and Communities in Western Europe 900–1300*. Oxford: Clarendon Press.

Riasanovsky, N. V. 1969 *The Teaching of Charles Fourier*. Berkeley: University of California Press.

Rich, A. 1976 *Of Woman Born*. New York: W. W. Norton.

Ricoeur, P. 1981 *Hermenuetics and the Human Sciences*. Cambridge: Cambridge University Press.

Ricoeur, P. 1986 *Lectures on Ideology and Utopia*, ed. G. H. Taylor. New York: Columbia University Press.

Ritchie, D. G. 1902 *The Principles of State Interference*. London: Swan Sonnenschein.

Ritchie, D. G. 1903 *Natural Rights*. London: Swan Sonnenschein.

Ritter, Alan 1980 *Anarchism: A Theoretical Analysis*. Cambridge: Cambridge University Press.

Roberts, D. 1979 *The Syndicalist Tradition and Italian Fascism*. Manchester: Manchester University Press.

Robertson, J. 1983 *The Sane Alternative*. Cholsey: Turning Point, The Old Bakehouse, private printing.

Robertson, J. 1985 *Future Work*. Gower: Temple Smith.

Robson, M. 2006 *The Rise of Fascism 1915–45*. London: Hodder Murray.

Rocco, Alfredo n.d. 'The Political Doctrine of Fascism', in *Readings on Fascism and National Socialism*. Denver: Alan Swallow.

Rocker, R. 1989 *Anarcho-Syndicalism*. London: Pluto Press.

Rolston, H., III 1988 *Environmental Ethics: Duties to and Values in the Natural World*. Philadephia: Temple University Press.

Rorty, R. 1989 *Contingency, Irony and Solidarity*. Cambridge: Cambridge University Press.

Rosen, F. 1997 'Nationalism and Early British Liberal Thought', *Journal of Political Ideologies*, 2, 2.

Rosenberg, A. 1971 *Selected Writings*, ed. R. Pois. London: Jonathan Cape.

Rossiter, C. 1982 *Conservatism in America*. Cambridge, Mass.: Harvard University Press.

Rothbard, M. 1978 *For a New Liberty: The Libertarian Manifesto*. New York: Collier Macmillan.

Rowbotham, S. 1972 *Women, Resistance and Revolution: A History of Women and Revolution in the Modern World*. New York: Random House.

Ruddick, S. 1980 'Maternal Thinking', *Feminist Studies*, 6, 2.

Ruggiero, G. de 1927 *The History of European Liberalism*. Oxford: Oxford University Press.

Russell, P. 1982 *The Awakening Earth: The Global Brain*. London: Ark.

Rustin, M. 1985 *For a Pluralist Socialism*. London: Verso.

Ruthven, M. 2004 *Fundamentalism: The Search for Meaning*. Oxford: Oxford University Press.

Ryle, M. 1988 *Ecology and Socialism*. London: Radius.

Sagoff, M. 1988 *The Economy of the Earth*. Cambridge: Cambridge University Press.

Saint-Simon, H. de 1964 *Social Organization, The Science of Man and Other Writings*. New York and Evanston: Harper & Row.

Sale, K. 1985 *Dwellers in the Land: The Bioregional Vision*. San Francisco: Sierra Book Club.

Samuel, H. 1902 *Liberalism: An Attempt to State the Principles of Contemporary Liberalism*. London: Grant Richards.

Samuel, H. 1945 *Memoirs*. London: Cresset.

Sandel, M. 1982 *Liberalism and the Limits of Justice*. Cambridge: Cambridge University Press.

Sandel, M., ed. 1984 *Liberalism and Its Critics*. Oxford: Blackwell.

Sargent, L., ed. 1986 *The Unhappy Marriage of Marxism and Feminism: A Debate on Class and Patriarchy*. London: Pluto Press.

Sassoon, D. 1996 *One Hundred Years of Socialism*. London: Tauris.

Schaar, J. 1981 *Legitimacy and the Modern State*. New Brunswick, NJ: Transaction Books.

Schenk, H. G. 1966 *The Mind of the European Romantics*. London: Constable.

Scherer, D. and Attig, T., eds 1983 *Ethics and the Environment*. Englewood Cliffs, NJ: Prentice Hall.

Schick, C., Jaffe, J. and Watkinson, A. M., eds 2004 *Contesting Fundamentalisms*. Nova Scotia: Halifax Publishing.

Schlosberg, D. 2007 *Defining Environmental Justice: Theories, Movements and Nature*. Oxford: Oxford University Press.

Schmidt, J., ed. 1996 *What is Enlightenment?* Berkeley: University of California Press.

Schmitt, C. 1985 *The Crisis of Parliamentary Democracy*. Cambridge, Mass.: MIT Press.

Schochet, G. 1975 *Patriarchalism in Political Thought*. Oxford: Blackwell.

Schuettinger, R. L., ed. 1976 *The Conservative Tradition in European Thought: An Anthology*. New York: G. P. Putnam.

Schumacher, E. F. 1973 *Small is Beautiful*. London: Sphere Books.

Schwartz, B. 1951 *Chinese Communism and the Rise of Mao*. Cambridge, Mass.: Harvard University Press.

Schwarz, W. and Schwarz, D. 1987 *Breaking Through: The Theory and Practice of Holistic Living*. Bideford: Green Books.

Scott, J. W. 1919 *Syndicalism and Philosophical Realism*. London: A. & C. Black.

Scruton, R. 1980 *The Meaning of Conservatism*. Harmondsworth: Penguin.

Scruton, R. 2007 *Political Philosophy: Arguments for Conservatism*. London and New York: Continuum International.

Seliger, M. 1976 *Ideology and Politics*. London: Allen & Unwin.

Seliger, M. 1979 *The Marxist Conception of Ideology*. Cambridge: Cambridge University Press.

Sessions, G. 1995 *Deep Ecology for the 21st Century*. Boston: Shambhala Publications.

Shafer, B. C. 1972 *Faces of Nationalism: New Realities, Old Myths*. New York: Harcourt Brace Jovanovich.

Shaw, G. B., ed. 1931 *Fabian Essays in Socialism*. London: The Fabian Society and Allen & Unwin.

Sheehan, J. 1978 *German Liberalism in the Nineteenth Century*. London: Methuen.

Sheehan, S. 2003 *Anarchism*. New York: Reaktion Books.

Shils, E. 1955 'The End of Ideology', *Encounter*, November.

Shils, E. 1968 'The Concept and Function of Ideology', *International Encylopaedia of the Social Sciences, vol.* VII.

Shklar, J. 1984 *Ordinary Vices*. Cambridge, Mass. and London: Belknap Press of the Harvard University Press.

Shorten, R. 2007 'The Status of Ideology in the Return of Political Religion Theory', *Journal of Political Ideologies*, 12, 2.

Sidgwick, H. 1897 *The Elements of Politics*. London: Macmillan.

Sieghart, P. 1986 *The Lawful Rights of Mankind: An Introduction to the International Legal Code of Human Rights*. Oxford: Clarendon Press.

Silverman, H. J., ed. 1990 *Postmodernism: Philosophy and the Arts*. London: Routledge.

Sim, S. 2004 *Fundamentalist World: The New Dark Age of Dogma*. London: Icon Books.

Simhony, A. and Weinstein, D., eds 2001 *The New Liberalism: Reconciling Liberty and Community*. Cambridge: Cambridge University Press.

Simon, R. 1991 *Gramsci's Political Thought*, rev. edn. London: Lawrence & Wishart.

Singer, P. 1983 *The Expanding Circle: Ethics and Sociobiology*. Oxford: Oxford University Press.

Skidelsky, R. 1975 *Oswald Mosley*. London: Macmillan.

Skinner, Q. and Stråth, B., eds 2003 *States and Citizens*. Cambridge: Cambridge University Press.

Small, A. W. 1909 *The Cameralists: The Pioneers of German Social Polity Press*. New York: Burt Franklin.

Smith, A. 2007 *Anarchism, Revolution and Reaction: Catalan Labor and the Crisis of the Spanish State, 1898–1923*. London: Berghahn Books.

Smith, A. D. 1971 *Theories of Nationalism*. London and New York: Torchbook Library.

Smith, A. D. 1979 *Nationalism in the Twentieth Century*. Canberra: Australian National University.

Smith, A. D. 1981 *The Ethnic Revival*. Cambridge: Cambridge University Press.

Smith, A. D. 1986 *The Ethnic Origins of Nations*. Oxford: Blackwell.

Smith, A. D. 1991 *National Identity*. Harmondsworth: Penguin.

Smith, A. D. 2001 *Nationalism*. Cambridge: Polity Press.

Smith, G. 2003 *Deliberative Democracy and the Environment*. London: Routledge

Smith, M. J. 1998 *Ecologism: Towards Ecological Citizenship*. Milton Keynes: Open University Press.

Smith, P. 1967 *Disraelian Conservatism and Social Reform*. London: Routledge & Kegan Paul.

Smith, P. 1972 *Lord Salisbury on Politics*. Cambridge: Cambridge University Press.

Snyder, L. 1954 *The Meaning of Nationalism*. New Brunswick, NJ: Rutgers University Press.

Snyder, L. 1969 *German Nationalism: The Tragedy of a People: Extremism Contra Liberalism in Modern German History*. New York: Kennikat Press.

Sorel, G. 1975 *Reflections on Violence*. London and New York: Collier Macmillan.

Soucy, R. 1972 *Fascism in France: The Case of Maurice Barrès*. Berkeley: University of California Press.

Soucy, R. 1979 *Fascist Intellectual: Drieu de Rochelle*. Berkeley: University of California Press.

Soucy, R. 1986 *French Fascism: The First Wave (1924–1933)*. New Haven and London: Yale University Press.

Spencer, H. 1940 *The Man versus the State*. London: Watts & Co.

Spencer, H. 1994 *Herbert Spencer: Political Writings*, ed. J. Offer. Cambridge: Cambridge University Press.

Spencer, P. and Wollman, H. 1998 'Good and Bad Nationalisms: A Critique of Dualism', *Journal of Political Ideologies*, 3, 3.

Spencer, P. and Wollman, H. 2002 *Nationalism: A Critical Introduction*. London: Sage.

Spencer, P. and Wollman, H., eds 2005 *Nations and Nationalism*. Edinburgh: Edinburgh University Press.

Spender, D. 1980 *Man-Made Language*. London: Routledge.

Spender, D. 1983 *Women of Ideas and What Men Have Done to Them*. London: Routledge.

Spretnak, C. and Capra, F. 1986 *Green Politics: The Global Promise*. London: Paladin, Collins.

Squires, J. 2000 *Gender in Political Theory*. Cambridge: Polity Press.

Squires, J. 2007 *The New Politics of Gender Equality*. London: Palgrave.

Stafford, W. 2004 'Is Mill's "Liberal" Feminism "Masculinist?' *Journal of Political Ideologies*, 9, 2.

Stanlis, P. 1958 *Edmund Burke and the Natural Law*. Ann Arbor: University of Michigan Press.

Stavrakakis, Y 1997 'Green Ideology: A Discursive Reading', *Journal of Political Ideologies*, 2, 3.

Steger, M.B. 2008 *The Rise of the Global Imaginary: Political Ideologies from the French Revolution to the Global War on Terror*. Oxford: Oxford University Press.

Stelzer, I. 2004 *Neo-Conservatism*. London: Atlantic Books.

Stern, F. 1974 *The Politics of Cultural Despair: A Study in the Rise of Germanic Ideology*. Berkeley: University of California Press.

Sternhell, Z. 1996 *Neither Left nor Right: Fascist Ideology in France*. Princeton, NJ: Princeton University Press.

Sternhell, Z., Sznajder, M. and Asheri, M. 1995 *The Birth of Fascist Ideology: From Cultural Rebellion to Political Revolution*. Princeton, NJ: Princeton University Press.

Stirner, M. 1971 *The Ego and His Own*, ed. J. Carroll. London: Jonathan Cape.

Stirner, M. 2000 *The Ego and His Own*, ed. D. Leopold. Cambridge: Cambridge University Press.

Stoehr, T., ed. 1977 *Drawing the Line: The Political Essays of Paul Goodman*. New York: Free Life.

Strong, T.B., ed. 1992 *The Self and the Political Order*. Oxford, Blackwell.

Sullivan, A. 2006 *The Conservative Soul: Fundamentalism: Freedom and the Future of the Right*. New York and London: Harper Perennial.

Sumption, J. and Joseph, K. 1979 *Equality*. London: John Murray.

Sylvan, R. 1984/5 'A Critique of Deep Ecology', *Radical Philosophy*, in two parts, 40 and 41.

Talmon, J. L. 1952 *The Origins of Totalitarian Democracy*. London: Secker & Warburg.

Talshir, G. 1998 'Modular Ideology: The Implications of Green Theory for a Reconceptualization of "Ideology"', *Journal of Political Ideologies*, 3, 2.

Tamir, Y. 1993 *Liberal Nationalism*. Princeton, NJ: Princeton University Press.

Tännsjö, T. 1990 *Conservatism for our Time*. London and New York: Routledge.

Tawney, R. H. 1921 *The Acquisitive Society*. London: George Bell.

Tawney, R. H. 1964 *Equality*. London: Allen & Unwin.

Taylor, B. 1983 *Eve and the New Jerusalem: Socialism and Feminism in the Nineteenth Century*. New York: Pantheon Books.

Taylor, C. 1985 'What's Wrong with Negative Liberty?', in *Philosophical Papers: Philosophy and the Human Sciences*. Cambridge: Cambridge University Press.

Taylor, C. 1991 *The Ethics of Authenticity*. Cambridge, Mass.: Harvard University Press.

Taylor, M. 1982 *Community, Anarchy and Liberty*. Cambridge: Cambridge University Press.

Taylor, M. 1992 *Men versus the State: Herbert Spencer and Late Victorian Individualism*. Oxford: Clarendon Press.

Taylor, P. W. 1986 *Respect for Nature: A Theory of Environmental Ethics*. Princeton, NJ: Princeton University Press.

Terrill, R. 1974 *R. H. Tawney and His Times: Socialism as Fellowship*. London: André Deutsch.

Thomas, P. 1980 *Karl Marx and the Anarchists*. London: Routledge & Kegan Paul.

Thompson, J. B. 1984 *Studies in the Theory of Ideology*. Cambridge: Polity Press.

Thompson, W. 1963 *An Inquiry into the Principles of the Distribution of Wealth most Conducive to Human Happiness*. New York: Augustus M. Kelley.

Tilton, T. 1991 *The Political Theory of Swedish Social Democracy*. Oxford: Clarendon Press.

Tokar, B. 1987 *The Green Alternative: Creating an Ecological Future*. San Pedro: R. & E. Miles.

Tolstoy, L. 1974 *The Kingdom of God and Peace Essays*. Oxford: Oxford University Press.

Tomalin, C. 1992 *The Life and Death of Mary Wollstonecraft*. Harmondsworth: Penguin.

Tong, R. 1989 *Feminist Thought*. London: Unwin Hyman.

Tormey, S. 2004 *Anticapitalism: A Beginners Guide*. London: Oneworld Publications.

Trevor-Roper, Hugh 1947 *The Last Days of Hitler*. London: Macmillan.

Tseng, R. 2003 *The Sceptical Idealist: Michael Oakeshott as a Critic of the Enlightenment*. Exeter: Imprint Academic.

Tudor, H. and Tudor, J. M., eds 1988 *Marxism and Social Democracy*. Cambridge: Cambridge University Press.

Turner, C., ed. 1979 *The Case for Private Enterprise*. London: Bachman & Turner.

Turner, H. A., ed. 1975 *Reappraisals of Fascism*. New York: New Viewpoints.

Turner, R. 2007 'The "Rebirth of Liberalism": The Origins of Neo-Liberal Ideology', *Journal of Political Ideologies*, 12, 1.

Turner, R. 2008 *Neo-Liberal Ideology: History, Concepts and Policies*. Edinburgh: Edinburgh University Press.

Twining, W., ed. 1991 *Issues of Self-Determination*. Aberdeen: Aberdeen University Press.

van Parijs, P. 1995 *Real Freedom for All*. Oxford Clarendon.

Vernon, R. 1986 *Citizenship and Order: Studies in French Political Thought*. Toronto: Toronto University Press.

Viereck, P. 1950 *Conservatism Revisited: The Revolt against Revolt 1815–1949*. London: John Lehmann.

Vincent, A., ed. 1986 *The Philosophy of T. H. Green*. Aldershot: Gower.

Vincent, A. 1987 *Theories of the State*. Oxford: Blackwell.

Vincent, A. 1990a 'Classical Liberalism and Its Crisis of Identity', *History of Political Thought*, XI, 1.

Vincent, A. 1990b 'The New Liberalism in Britain 1880–1914', *Australian Journal of Politics and History*, 36, 3.

Vincent, A. 1992 'Socialism, Law and the State Tradition', in *Socialism and Law: Proceedings of the 17th Annual Conference of the Association for Legal and Social Philosophy, Archiv für Rechts- und Sozialphilosophie, Beiheft no. 49*. Wiesbaden, Stuttgart: Franz Steiner Verlag.

Vincent, A. 1993 'The Character of Ecology', *Environmental Politics*, 2, 2.

Vincent, A. 1994 'British Conservatism and the Problem of Ideology', *Political Studies*, 42, 2.

Vincent, A. 1997 'Liberal Nationalism and Communitarianism: An Ambiguous Association', *The Australian Journal of Politics and History* 3, 1.

Vincent, A. 1998a 'New Ideology for Old?', *Political Quarterly* 69, 1.

Vincent, A. 1998b 'Liberalism and Environmentalism', *Environmental Values* 7.

Vincent, A. 2002 *Nationalism and Particularity*. Cambridge: Cambridge University Press.

Vincent, A. 2004 *The Nature of Political Theory*. Oxford: Oxford University Press.

Vincent, A. and Plant, R. 1984 *Philosophy, Politics and Citizenship: The Life and Thought of the British Idealists*. Oxford: Blackwell.

Viroli, M. 1995 *For Love of Country*. Oxford: Clarendon Press.

Vizard, P. 2005 *Poverty and Human Rights*. Oxford: Oxford University Press.

Voegelin, E. 2000 *The Political Religion* in *The Collected Works of Eric Voegelin*, Vol. 5, ed. M. Henningsen. Columbia: Missouri University Press.

Waldegrave, W. 1978 *The Binding of Leviathan: Conservatism and the Future*. London: Hamish Hamilton.

Walicki, A. 1989 *The Enlightenment and the Birth of Modern Nationhood*. Notre Dame, Ind.: University of Notre Dame Press.

Walter, N. 2002 *About Anarchism*. London: Freedom Press.

Walzer, M. 1983 *Spheres of Justice*. Oxford: Martin Robertson.

Walzer, M. 1987 *Interpretation and Social Criticism*. Cambridge, Mass.: Harvard University Press.

Ward, B. and Dubos, R. 1972 *Only One Earth: The Care and Maintenance of a Small Planet*. Harmondsworth: Penguin.

Ward, C. 1973 *Anarchy in Action*. London: Allen & Unwin.

Ward, C. 2004 *Anarchism: A Very Short Introduction*. Oxford: Oxford University Press.

Waxman, C., ed. 1968 *The End of Ideology Debate*. New York: Funk & Wagnalls.

Webb, B. 1926 *My Apprenticeship*. London: Longmans.

Webb, B. 1948 *Our Partnership*. London: Longmans.

Weber, E. 1964 *Varieties of Fascism*. London: Van Nostrand.

Weiss, H. J. 1967 *The Fascist Tradition: Radical Right-Wing Extremism in Modern Europe*. New York: Harper & Row.

Wempe, B. 2004 *T. H. Green's Theory of Positive Liberty*. Exeter: Imprint Academic.

Weston, J., ed. 1986 *Red and Green: A New Politics of the Environment*. London: Pluto Press.

White, S. 2003 *The Civic Minimum*. Oxford: Clarendon Press.

White, S. 2006 *Equality*. Cambridge: Polity Press.

Williams, H. 1983 *Kant's Political Philosophy*. Oxford: Blackwell.

Williams, H. 1988 *Concepts of Ideology*. Brighton: Wheatsheaf Books.

Williams, R. 1961 *The Long Revolution*. London: Chatto & Windus.

Wiltshire, D. 1978 *The Social and Political Thought of Herbert Spencer*. Oxford: Clarendon Press.

Winstanley, G. 1973 *The Law of Freedom and Other Writings*. Harmondsworth: Penguin.

Wissenberg, M. 1997 'A Taxonomy of Green Ideas', *Journal of Political Ideologies*, 2.

Wissenburg, M. 1998 *Green Liberalism: The Free and Green Society*. London: Routledge.

Wolfe, W. 1975 *From Radicalism to Socialism*. New Haven, Conn.: Yale University Press.

Wolff, R. P. 1970 *In Defense of Anarchism*. New York: Harper & Row.

Wolin, R. 2001 *Heidegger's Children: Hannah Arendt, Karl Löwith, Hans Jonas and Herbert Marcuse*. Princeton, NJ: Princeton University Press.

Wolin, S. 1954 'Hume and Conservatism', *American Political Science Review*, 48, 4.

Wollstonecraft, M. 1985 *A Vindication of the Rights of Woman*. Harmondsworth: Penguin.

Wood, A. 1979 'Marx on Rights and Justice', *Philosophy and Public Affairs*, 8, 3.

Wood, R. 2007 *Germany's New Right as Culture and Politics*. London: Palgrave.

Woodcock, G. 1972a *Herbert Read: The Stream and the Source*. London: Faber & Faber.

Woodcock, G. 1972b *Pierre-Joseph Proudhon: His Life and Work*. New York: Schocken Books.

Woodcock, G. 1975 *Anarchism*. Harmondsworth: Penguin.

Woolf, S. J., ed. 1968 *European Fascism*. London: Weidenfeld & Nicolson.

Woolf, V. 1929 *A Room of One's Own*. London: Hogarth Press.

Worster, D. 1977 *Nature's Economy: The Roots of Ecology*. San Francisco: Sierra Book Club.

Wright, A. W. 1979 *G. D. H. Cole and Socialist Democracy*. Oxford: Clarendon Press.

Wright, A. W. 1983 *British Socialism*. London: Longman.

Wright, A. W. 1987 *Socialisms*. Oxford and New York: Oxford University Press.

Yearley, S. 1991 *The Green Case: A Sociology of Environmental Issues, Arguments and Politics*. London: HarperCollins Academic.

Young, I. M. 1990 *Justice and the Politics of Difference*. Princeton, NJ: Princeton University Press.

Young, I. M. 1997 *Intersecting Voices: Dilemmas of Gender, Political Philosophy and Policy*. Princeton, NJ: Princeton University Press.

Young, I. M. 2000 *Inclusion and Democracy*. Princeton, NJ: Princeton University Press.

Zalewski, M. 1991 'The Debauching of Feminist Theory/The Penetration of the Postmodern', *Politics*, 11, 1.

Zerelli, L. 2005 *Feminism and the Abyss of Freedom*. Chicago: University of Chicago Press.

Žižek, S. 1989 *The Sublime Object of Ideology*. London: Verso.

Žižek, S., ed. 1995 *Mapping Ideology*. London: Verso.

Zubaida, S. 1993 *Islam: The People and the State: Political Ideas and Movements in the Middle East*. London: Tauris.

Index